TEACH YOURSELF WINDOWS® 95 VISUALLY™

IDG's 3-D Visual™ Series

IDG BOOKS

From maranGraphics™

IDG Books Worldwide, Inc.
An International Data Group Company
Foster City, CA • Indianapolis • Chicago • Southlake, TX

Teach Yourself Windows® 95 VISUALLY™

Published by
IDG Books Worldwide, Inc.
An International Data Group Company
919 E. Hillsdale Blvd., Suite 400
Foster City, CA 94404
(415) 655-3000

Library of Congress Catalog Card No.: 96-076723

ISBN: 0-7645-6001-8

Printed in the United States of America

11

Distributed in the United States by IDG Books Worldwide, Inc.

Distributed by Transworld Publishers Limited in the United Kingdom; by IDG Norge Books for Norway; by IDG Sweden Books for Sweden; by Woodslane Pty. Ltd. for Australia; by Woodslane Enterprises Ltd. for New Zealand; by Longman Singapore Publishers Ltd. for Singapore, Malaysia, Thailand, and Indonesia; by Simron Pty. Ltd. for South Africa; by Toppan Company Ltd. for Japan; by Distribuidora Cuspide for Argentina; by Livraria Cultura for Brazil; by Ediciencia S.A. for Ecuador; by Addison-Wesley Publishing Company for Korea; by Ediciones ZETA S.C.R. Ltda. for Peru; by WS Computer Publishing Corporation, Inc., for the Philippines; by Unalis Corporation for Taiwan; by Contemporanea de Ediciones for Venezuela; by Computer Book & Magazine Store for Puerto Rico; by Express Computer Distributors for the Caribbean and West Indies. Authorized Sales Agent: Anthony Rudkin Associates for the Middle East and North Africa.

For corporate orders, please call maranGraphics at 800-469-6616.
For general information on IDG Books Worldwide's books in the U.S., please call our Consumer Customer Service department at 800-762-2974.
For reseller information, including discounts and premium sales, please call our Reseller Customer Service department at 800-434-3422.
For information on where to purchase IDG Books Worldwide's books outside the U.S., please contact our International Sales department at 415-655-3200 or fax 415-655-3295.
For information on foreign language translations, please contact our Foreign & Subsidiary Rights department at 415-655-3021 or fax 415-655-3281.
For sales inquiries and special prices for bulk quantities, please contact our Sales department at 415-655-3200.
For information on using IDG Books Worldwide's books in the classroom or for ordering examination copies, please contact our Educational Sales department at 800-434-2086 or fax 817-251-8174.
For press review copies, author interviews, or other publicity information, please contact our Public Relations department at 415-655-3000 or fax 415-655-3299.
For authorization to photocopy items for corporate, personal, or educational use, please contact maranGraphics at 800-469-6616.

Trademark Acknowledgments

The 3-D illustrations are the copyright of maranGraphics, Inc.

U.S. Corporate Sales
Contact maranGraphics at (800) 469-6616 or Fax (905) 890-9434.

U.S. Trade Sales
Contact IDG Books at (800) 434-3422 or (415) 655-3000.

Welcome to the world of IDG Books Worldwide.

IDG Books Worldwide, Inc., is a subsidiary of International Data Group, the world's largest publisher of computer-related information and the leading global provider of information services on information technology. IDG was founded more than 25 years ago and now employs more than 8,500 people worldwide. IDG publishes more than 270 computer publications in over 75 countries (see listing below). More than 90 million people read one or more IDG publications each month.

Launched in 1990, IDG Books Worldwide is today the #1 publisher of best-selling computer books in the United States. We are proud to have received eight awards from the Computer Press Association in recognition of editorial excellence and three from Computer Currents' First Annual Readers' Choice Awards. Our best-selling ...For Dummies® series has more than 25 million copies in print with translations in 30 languages. IDG Books Worldwide, through a joint venture with IDG's Hi-Tech Beijing, became the first U.S. publisher to publish a computer book in the People's Republic of China. In record time, IDG Books Worldwide has become the first choice for millions of readers around the world who want to learn how to better manage their businesses.

Our mission is simple: Every one of our books is designed to bring extra value and skill-building instructions to the reader. Our books are written by experts who understand and care about our readers. The knowledge base of our editorial staff comes from years of experience in publishing, education, and journalism - experience which we use to produce books for the '90s. In short, we care about books, so we attract the best people. We devote special attention to details such as audience, interior design, use of icons, and illustrations. And because we use an efficient process of authoring, editing, and desktop publishing our books electronically, we can spend more time ensuring superior content and spend less time on the technicalities of making books.

You can count on our commitment to deliver high-quality books at competitive prices on topics you want to read about. At IDG Books Worldwide, we continue in the IDG tradition of delivering quality for more than 25 years. You'll find no better book on a subject than one from IDG Books Worldwide.

John Kilcullen
President and CEO
IDG Books Worldwide, Inc.

IDG Books Worldwide, Inc., is a subsidiary of International Data Group, the world's largest publisher of computer-related information and the leading global provider of information services on information technology. International Data Group publishes over 276 computer publications in over 75 countries. Ninety million people read one or more International Data Group publications each month. International Data Group's publications include: Argentina: Annuario de Informatica, Computerworld Argentina, PC World Argentina; Australia: Australian Macworld, Client/Server Journal, Computer Living, Computerworld, Computerworld 100, Digital News, IT Casebook, Network World, On-line World Australia, PC World, Publishing Essentials, Reseller, WebMaster; Austria: Computerwelt Osterreich, Networks Austria, PC Tip; Belarus: PC World Belarus; Belgium: Data News; Brazil: Annuário de Informática, Computerworld Brazil, Connections, Super Game Power, Macworld, PC Player, PC World Brazil, Publish Brazil, Reseller News; Bulgaria: Computerworld Bulgaria, Networkworld/Bulgaria, PC & MacWorld Bulgaria; Canada: CIO Canada, Client/Server World, ComputerWorld Canada, InfoCanada, Network World Canada; Chile: Computerworld Chile, PC World Chile; Colombia: Computerworld Colombia, PC World Colombia; Costa Rica: PC World Centro America; The Czech and Slovak Republics: Computerworld Czechoslovakia, Elektronika Czechoslovakia, Macworld Czech Republic, PC World Czechoslovakia; Denmark: Communications World, Computerworld Danmark, Macworld Danmark, PC Privat Danmark, PC World Danmark, PC World Danmark Supplements, TECH World; Dominican Republic: PC World Republica Dominicana; Ecuador: PC World Ecuador; Egypt: Computerworld Middle East, PC World Middle East; El Salvador: PC World Centro America; Finland: MikroPC, Tietoverkko, Tietoviikko; France: Distributique, Golden, Hebdo-Distributique, Info PC, Le Guide du Monde Informatique, Le Monde Informatique, Reseaux & Telecoms; Germany: Computer Partner, Computerwoche, Computerwoche Extra, Computerwoche Focus, I/M Information Management, Macwelt, PC Welt; Greece: GamePro, Multimedia World; Guatemala: PC World Centro America; Honduras: PC World Centro America; Hong Kong: Computerworld Hong Kong, PCWorld Hong Kong, Publish in Asia; Hungary: ABCD CD-ROM, Computerworld Szamitastechnika, PC & Mac World Hungary, PC-X Magazine; Iceland: Tolvuheimur/PC World Island; India: Information Systems Computerworld, PC World India, Publish in Asia; Indonesia: InfoKomputer PC World, Komputek Computerworld, Publish in Asia; Ireland: ComputerScope, PC Live!; Israel: People & Computers; Italy: Computerworld Italia, Computerworld Italia Special Editions, Macworld Italia, Networking Italia, PC Shopping, PC World Italia, PC World/Walt Disney; Japan: DTP World, HP Open World Japan, Macworld Japan, Nikkei Personal Computing, Open World Japan, OS/2 World Japan, SunWorld Japan, Windows World Japan; Kenya: East African Computer News; Korea: Hi-Tech Information/Computerworld, Macworld Korea, PC World Korea; Macedonia: PC World Macedonia; Malaysia: Computerworld Malaysia, PC World Malaysia, Publish in Asia; Mexico: Computerworld Mexico, Macworld, PC World Mexico; Myanmar: PC World Myanmar; Netherlands: Computer! Totaal, LAN Magazine, LanWorld Buyers Guide, Macworld, Net Magazine, Totaal! Beurskrant; New Zealand: Absolute Beginner's Guide, Computer Buyer, Computer Industry Directory, Computerworld New Zealand, MTB, Network World, PC World New Zealand; Nicaragua: PC World Centro America; Nigeria: PC World Nigeria; Norway: Computerworld Norge, Computerworld Privat (Datamagasinet), CW Rapport Norge, IDG's KURSGUIDE, Macworld Norge, Multimediaworld, PC World Ekspress, PC World Nettverk, PC World Norge, PC World's Produktguide, Windows World Spesial; Pakistan: Computerworld Pakistan, PC World Pakistan; Panama: PC World Panama; P. R. of China: China Computer Users, China Computerworld, China Infoworld, China Telecom World Weekly, Computer & Communication, Electronic Design China, Electronics Today, Electronics Weekly, Game Camp, Game Soft, Network World China, PC World China, Popular Computer Weekly, Software Weekly, Software World, Telecom World; Peru: Computerworld Peru, PC World Profesional Peru, PC World Peru; Poland: Computerworld Poland, Computerworld Special Report, Macworld, Networld, PC World Komputer; Philippines: Computerworld Philippines, PC World Philippines, Publish in Asia; Portugal: Cerebro/PC World, Computerworld/Correio Informático, Dealer World Portugal, Mac*In/PC*In, Multimedia World Portugal; Puerto Rico: PC World Puerto Rico; Romania: Computerworld Romania, PC World Romania, Telecom Romania; Russia: Computerworld Russia, Mir PK, Sety; Singapore: Computerworld Singapore, PC World Singapore, Publish in Asia; Slovenia: MONITOR; South Africa: Computing S.A., InfoWorld S.A., Network World S.A., Software World; Spain: Computerworld Espa-a, COMUNICACIONES WORLD, Dealer World, Macworld Espa-a, PC World Espa-a; Sweden: CAP&Design, Computer Sweden, Corporate Computing, MacWorld, Maxi Data, MikroDatorn, Nätverk & Kommunikation, PC/Aktiv, PC World, Windows World; Switzerland: Computerworld Schweiz, Macworld Schweiz, PCtip; Taiwan: Computerworld Taiwan, Macworld Taiwan, PC World Taiwan, Publish Taiwan, Windows World; Thailand: Thai Computerworld, Publish in Asia; Turkey: Computerworld Turkiye, MACWORLD Turkiye, PC WORLD Turkiye; Ukraine: Computerworld Kiev, Computers & Software, Multimedia World Ukraine, PC World Ukraine; United Kingdom: Acorn User, Amiga Action, Amiga Computing, Appletalk, Computing, GamePro, Macworld, Network News, Parents and Computers, PC Advisor, PC Home, PSX Pro UK, The WEB; United States: Cable in the Classroom, CD Review, CIO Magazine, Computerworld, Computerworld Client/Server Journal, Digital Video Magazine, DOS World, Federal Computer Week, GamePro, InfoWorld, I-Way, JavaWorld, Macworld, Multimedia World, Netscape World Online, Network World, PC Entertainment, PC World, Publish, SunWorld Online, SWATPro Magazine, Video Event, WebMaster; Uruguay: PC World Uruguay; Venezuela: Computerworld Venezuela, PC World Venezuela; and Vietnam: PC World Vietnam.

Every maranGraphics book represents the extraordinary vision and commitment of a unique family: the Maran family of Toronto, Canada.

Back Row (from left to right): *Sherry Maran, Rob Maran, Richard Maran, Maxine Maran, Jill Maran.*

Front Row (from left to right): *Judy Maran, Ruth Maran.*

Richard Maran is the company founder and its inspirational leader. He developed maranGraphics' proprietary communication technology called "visual grammar." This book is built on that technology—empowering readers with the easiest and quickest way to learn about computers.

Ruth Maran is the Author and Architect—a role Richard established that now bears Ruth's distinctive touch. She creates the words and visual structure that are the basis for the books.

Judy Maran is Senior Editor. She works with Ruth, Richard, and the highly talented maranGraphics illustrators, designers, and editors to transform Ruth's material into its final form.

Rob Maran is the Technical and Production Specialist. He makes sure the state-of-the-art technology used to create these books always performs as it should.

Sherry Maran manages the Reception, Order Desk, and any number of areas that require immediate attention and a helping hand.

Jill Maran is a jack-of-all-trades and dynamo who fills in anywhere she's needed anytime she's back from university.

Maxine Maran is the Business Manager and family sage. She maintains order in the business and family—and keeps everything running smoothly.

CREDITS

Author & Architect:
Ruth Maran

Copy Editor:
Alison MacAlpine

Project Manager:
Judy Maran

Editor:
Brad Hilderley

Proofreaders:
Kelleigh Wing
Susan Beytas

Layout & Cover Design:
Christie Van Duin

Illustrators:
Tamara Poliquin
Chris K.C. Leung
Russell Marini
Andrew Trowbridge

Screen Artist:
Greg Midensky

Indexer:
Kelleigh Wing

Post Production:
Robert Maran

ACKNOWLEDGMENTS

Thanks to the dedicated staff of maranGraphics, including Susan Beytas, Francisco Ferreira, Brad Hilderley, Julie Lane, Chris K.C. Leung, Alison MacAlpine, Jill Maran, Judy Maran, Maxine Maran, Robert Maran, Sherry Maran, Russ Marini, Greg Midensky, Tamara Poliquin, Andrew Trowbridge, Christie Van Duin and Kelleigh Wing.

Finally, to Richard Maran who originated the easy-to-use graphic format of this guide. Thank you for your inspiration and guidance.

TABLE OF CONTENTS

Chapter 1: Getting Started

Introduction to Windows 2
Using the Mouse 3
Start Windows 4
The Windows 95 Screen 5
Display the Date 6
Shut Down Windows 7

Chapter 2: Windows Basics

Start a Program 10
Minimize or Maximize a Window 12
Move or Size a Window 14
Switch Between Windows 16
Cascade Windows 18
Tile Windows 19
Minimize All Windows 20
Close a Window 21
Getting Help 22
Scroll Through a Window 24
Using the MS-DOS Prompt 26

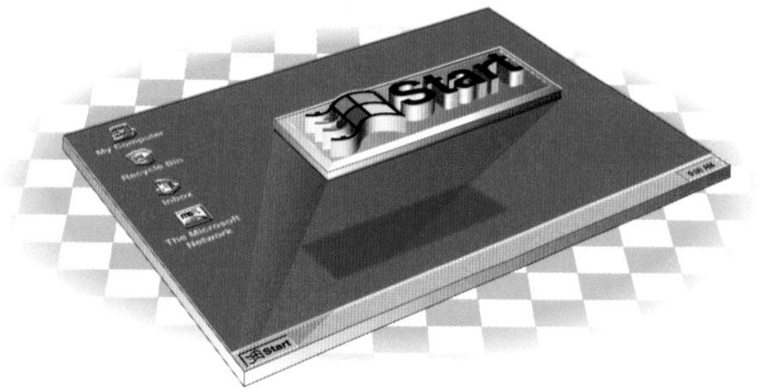

Chapter 3: Paint

Start Paint 30
Draw Shapes 32
Draw Lines 34
Erase an Area 36
Undo Last Change 37
Add Text 38
Save a Drawing 40
Exit Paint 41
Open a Drawing 42

Chapter 4: View Contents of Computer

Storage Devices 46
View Contents of Computer 48
Change Size of Items 50
Move an Item 51
Arrange Items 52
Display File Information 54
Sort Items 56

Chapter 5: Work with Files and Folders

Select Files 60
Create a New Folder 62
Move a File to a Folder 64
Copy a File to a Floppy Disk 66
Rename a File 68
Open a File 70
Open a Recently Used File 71
Preview a File 72
Print a File 74
View Files Sent to the Printer 75

Pause the Printer 76
Cancel Printing 77
Delete a File 78
Restore a Deleted File 80
Empty the Recycle Bin 82
Start Windows Explorer 84
Display or Hide Folders 86

Chapter 6: Time-Saving Features

Find a File 90
Add a Shortcut to the Desktop 92
Put Part of a Document on the Desktop 94
Add a Program to the Start Menu 96
Have a Program Start Automatically 98

Chapter 7: Personalize Windows

Change the Date and Time 102
Add Wallpaper 104
Change Screen Colors 106
Set Up a Screen Saver 108
Change Mouse Settings 110
Move the Taskbar 114
Size the Taskbar 115
Hide the Taskbar 116
Change Screen Resolution 118
Change Color Depth 120

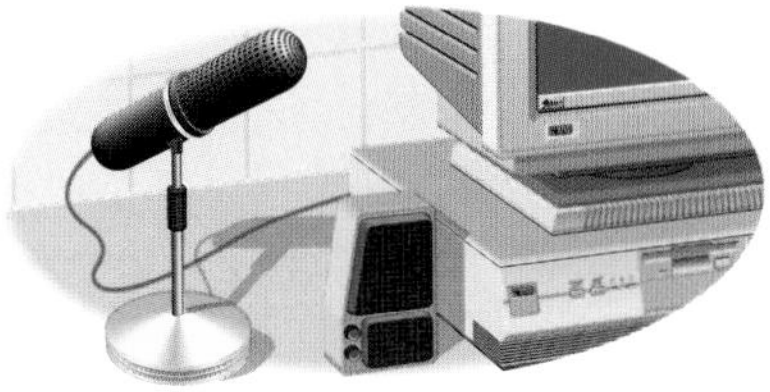

Chapter 8: Entertaining Features

Play a Music CD 124
Adjust the Volume 127
Assign Sounds to Program Events 128
Record Sounds 132
Using Media Player 136

Chapter 9: Object Linking and Embedding

Embed or Link Information 142
Edit Embedded Information 146
Edit Linked Information 148

TABLE OF CONTENTS

Chapter 10: Faxing

Start Microsoft Exchange.....152
Send a Fax.....154
Change How Modem Answers Faxes.....158
View a Fax.....160
Print a Fax.....163

Chapter 11: Electronic Mail

Add a Name to the Address Book.....166
Send a Message.....168
Insert a File in a Message.....172
Read a Message.....174
Delete a Message.....175
Reply to a Message.....176
Forward a Message.....178

Chapter 12: Add Hardware and Software

Add Fonts.....182
Add Windows Components.....186
Add a New Program.....190
Set Up New Hardware.....194

Chapter 13: Maintain Your Computer

Format a Disk.....204
Detect and Repair Disk Errors.....208
Defragment a Disk.....212
Copy a Floppy Disk.....216
Compress a Disk.....220

Chapter 14: Back Up Your Files

Introduction.....228
Start Microsoft Backup.....230
Back Up Selected Files.....232
Perform the Backup.....236
Back Up Named Files.....238
Restore Files.....240

Chapter 15: The Microsoft Network

Introduction.....246
Connect to The Microsoft Network.....248
Browse Through Categories.....250
Join a Chat Room.....252
Display Bulletin Board Messages.....254
Read Bulletin Board Messages.....256
Reply to a Bulletin Board Message.....258
Create a New Bulletin Board Message.....260
Add an Item to Favorite Places.....262
Sign Out of the MSN.....263

Chapter 16: Briefcase

Create a Briefcase 266
Work with Briefcase Files 270
Update Briefcase Files 272

Chapter 17: Networks

Introduction to Networks 278
Turn on Sharing 279
Name Your Computer 282
Share Information 284
Share a Printer 288
Set the Default Printer 290
Browse Through a Network 292
Find a Computer 294

Chapter 18: Dial-Up Networking

Introduction to Dial-Up Networking 298
Set Up Office Computer 299
Set Up Connection to Office Computer 302
Dial In to Office Computer 306

Chapter 19: Direct Cable Connection

Set Up Direct Cable Connection 310
Re-Establish Direct Cable Connection 314

INTRODUCTION TO WINDOWS

Microsoft® Windows® 95 is a program that controls the overall activity of your computer.

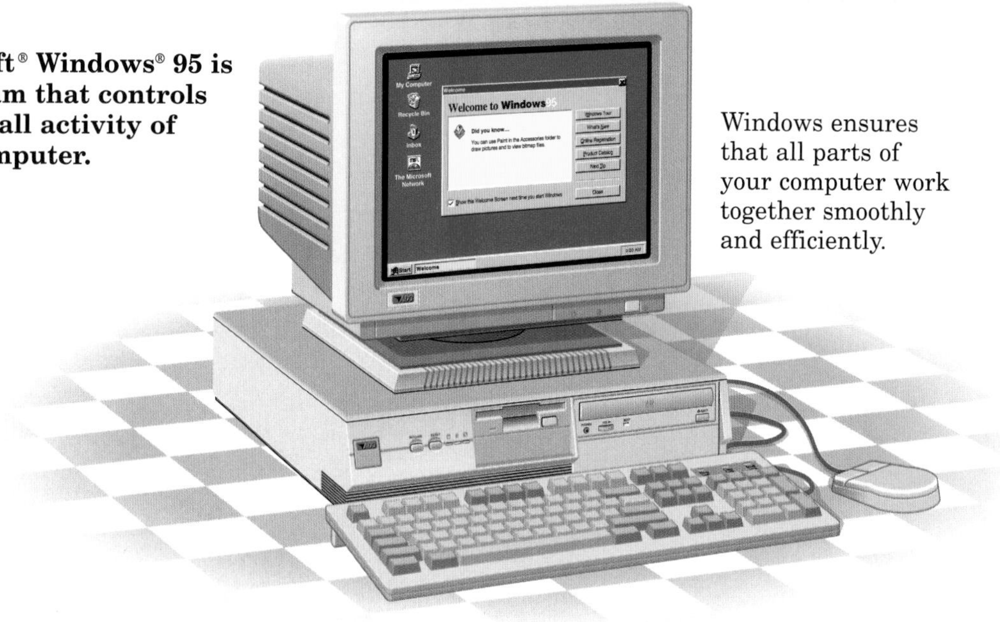

Windows ensures that all parts of your computer work together smoothly and efficiently.

CONTROLS YOUR HARDWARE

Windows controls the different parts of your computer system, such as the printer and monitor, and enables them to work together.

ORGANIZES YOUR INFORMATION

Windows provides ways to organize and manage files stored on your computer. You can use Windows to sort, copy, move, delete and view your files.

RUNS YOUR PROGRAMS

Windows starts and operates programs, such as Microsoft Word and Lotus 1-2-3. Programs let you write letters, analyze numbers, manage finances, draw pictures and even play games.

USING THE MOUSE

The mouse is a hand-held device that lets you select and move items on your screen.

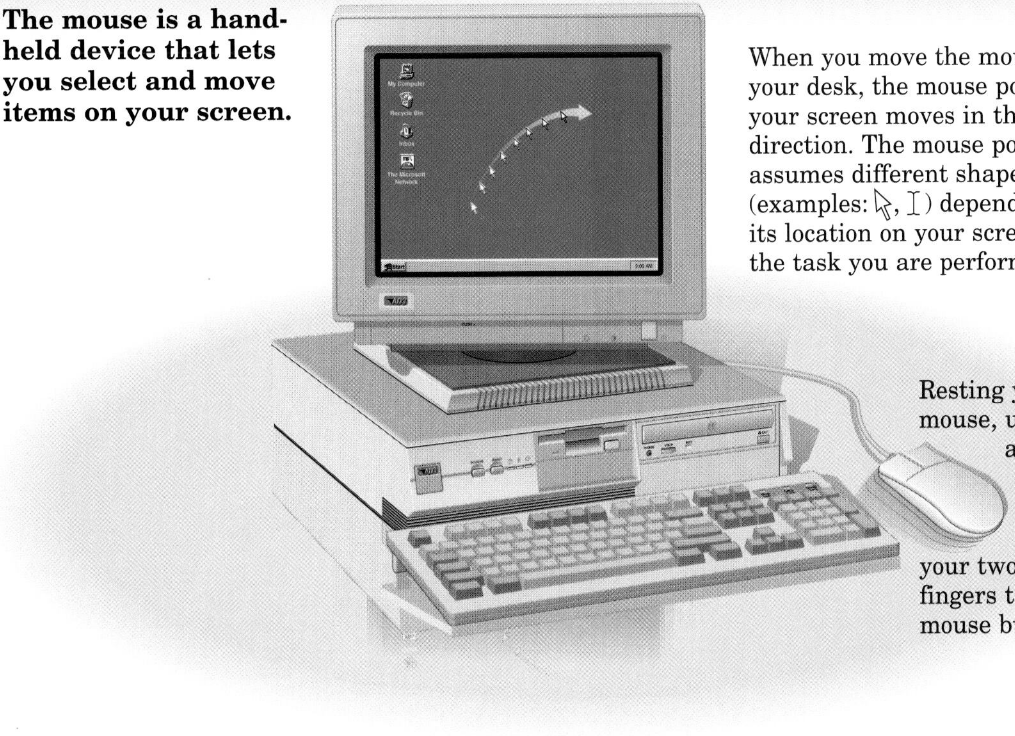

When you move the mouse on your desk, the mouse pointer on your screen moves in the same direction. The mouse pointer assumes different shapes (examples: ↖, I) depending on its location on your screen and the task you are performing.

Resting your hand on the mouse, use your thumb and two rightmost fingers to move the mouse on your desk. Use your two remaining fingers to press the mouse buttons.

REMEMBER THESE MOUSE TERMS

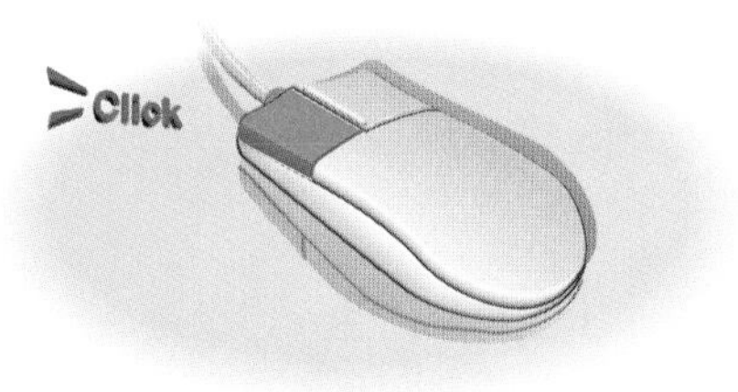

CLICK
Press and release the left mouse button.

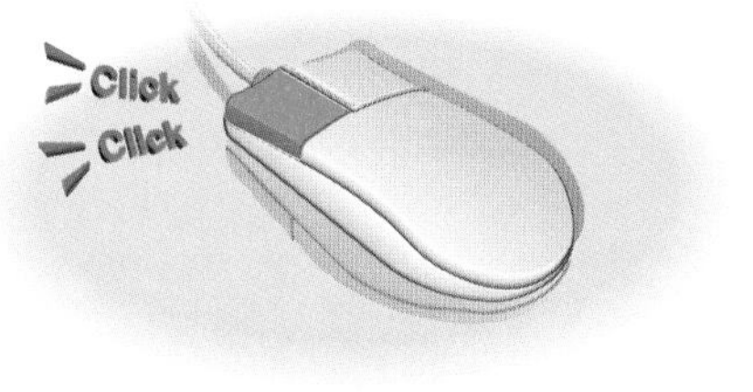

DOUBLE-CLICK
Quickly press and release the left mouse button twice.

DRAG
When the mouse pointer is over an object on your screen, press and hold down the left mouse button. Still holding down the button, move the mouse to where you want to place the object and then release the button.

START WINDOWS

Windows provides an easy, graphical way for you to use your computer.

START WINDOWS

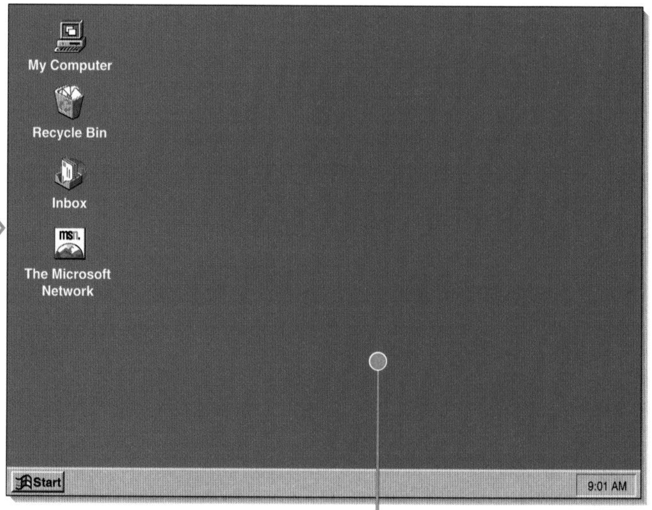

■ When you start Windows, the **Welcome** dialog box appears. It displays a tip about using Windows.

1 If you do not want this dialog box to appear every time you start Windows, click this option (☑ changes to ☐).

2 To close the dialog box, click **Close**.

■ The dialog box disappears and you can clearly view your desktop. The **desktop** is the background area of your screen.

THE WINDOWS 95 SCREEN

The Windows screen displays various items. The items that appear depend on how your computer is set up.

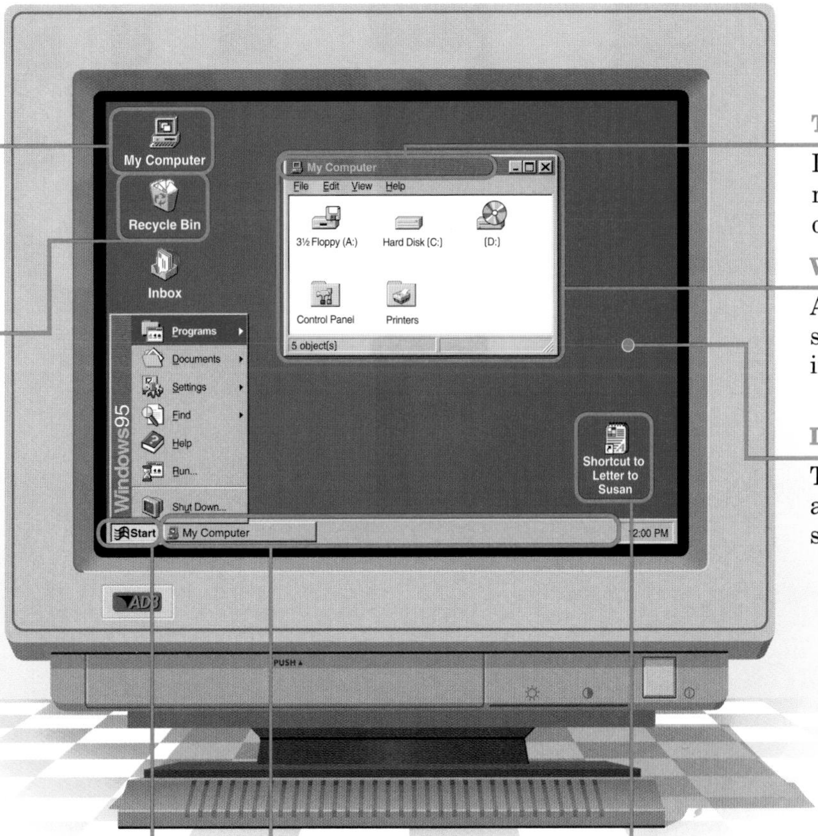

MY COMPUTER

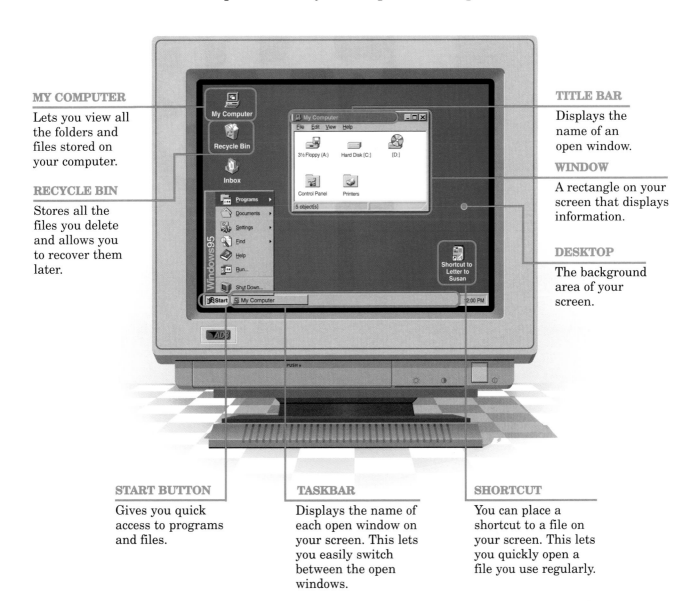

Lets you view all the folders and files stored on your computer.

RECYCLE BIN

Stores all the files you delete and allows you to recover them later.

TITLE BAR

Displays the name of an open window.

WINDOW

A rectangle on your screen that displays information.

DESKTOP

The background area of your screen.

START BUTTON

Gives you quick access to programs and files.

TASKBAR

Displays the name of each open window on your screen. This lets you easily switch between the open windows.

SHORTCUT

You can place a shortcut to a file on your screen. This lets you quickly open a file you use regularly.

DISPLAY THE DATE

You can easily display the date on your screen.

DISPLAY THE DATE

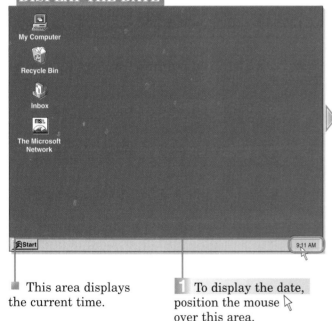

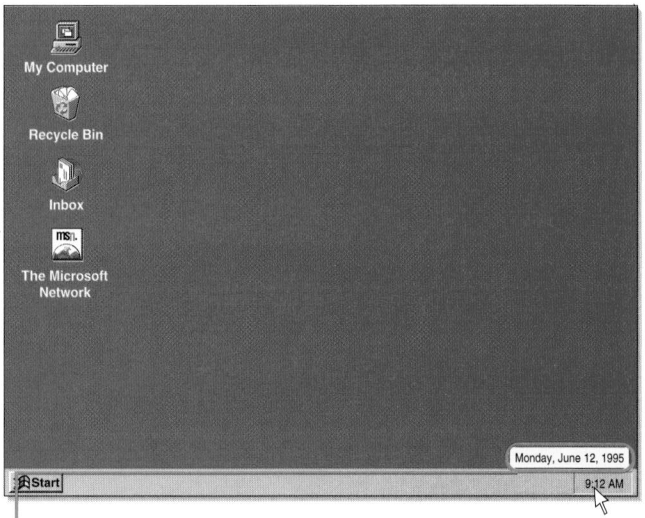

■ This area displays the current time.

1 To display the date, position the mouse over this area.

■ After a few seconds, the date appears.

Note: If Windows displays the wrong date or time, you can change the date or time set in your computer. For more information, refer to page 102.

SHUT DOWN WINDOWS

When you finish using your computer, you should shut down Windows before turning off the computer.

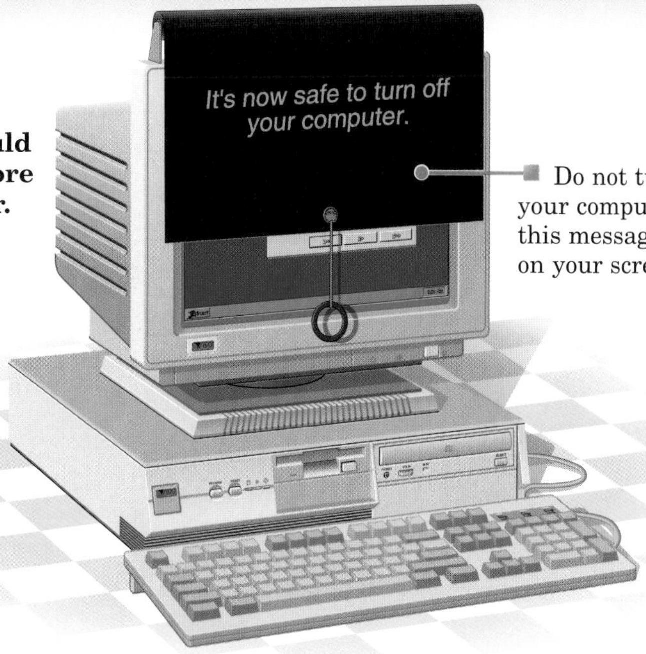

■ Do not turn off your computer until this message appears on your screen.

SHUT DOWN WINDOWS

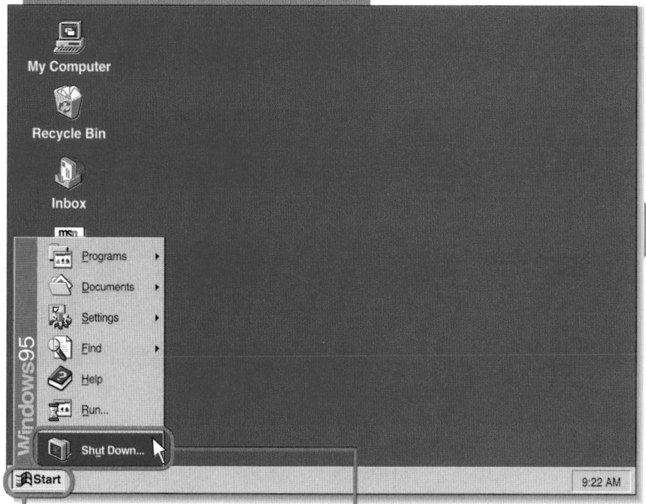

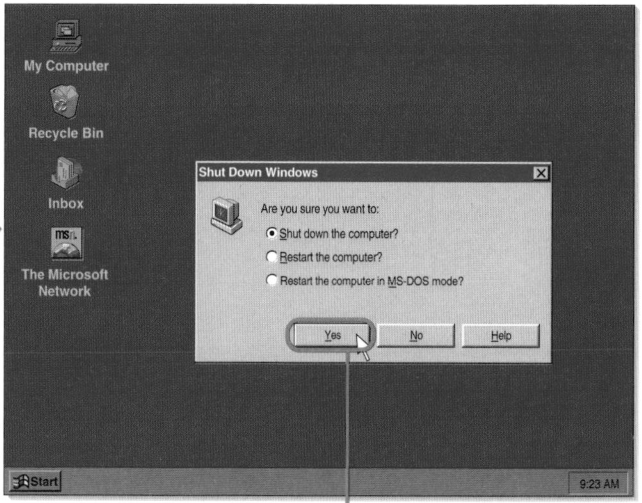

1 Click **Start**.

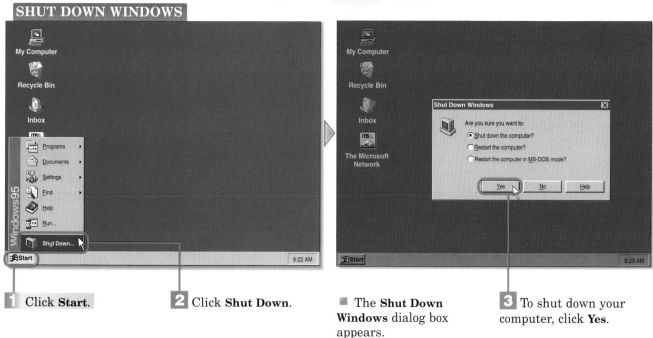

2 Click **Shut Down**.

■ The **Shut Down Windows** dialog box appears.

3 To shut down your computer, click **Yes**.

In this chapter you will learn the basic skills you need to work in Windows 95.

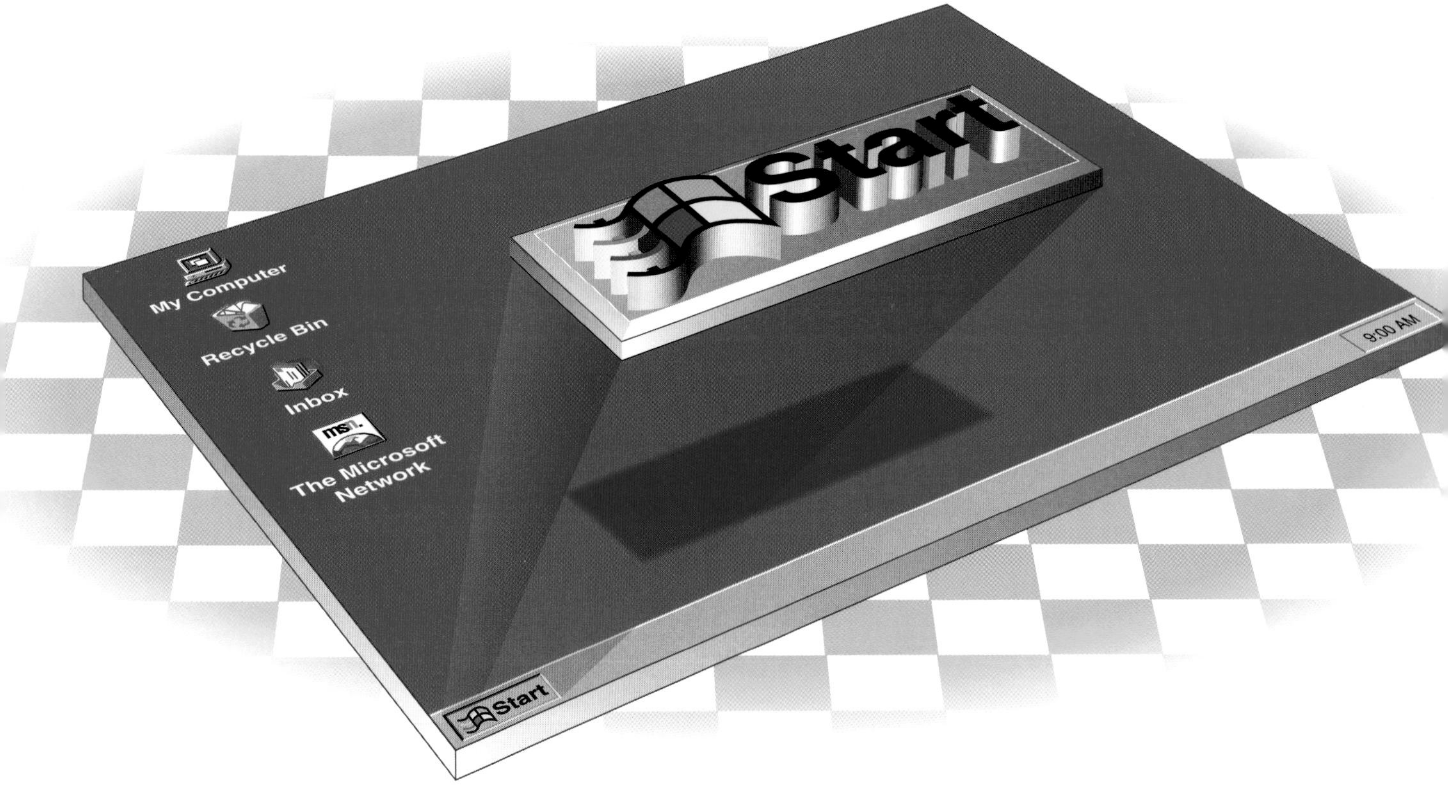

CHAPTER 2: WINDOWS BASICS

Start a Program 10

Minimize a Window 12

Maximize a Window .13

Move a Window 14

Size a Window 15

Switch Between Windows 16

Cascade Windows 18

Tile Windows 19

Minimize All Windows 20

Close a Window 21

Getting Help 22

Scroll Through a Window 24

Using the MS-DOS Prompt 26

START A PROGRAM

You can use the Start button to start your programs.

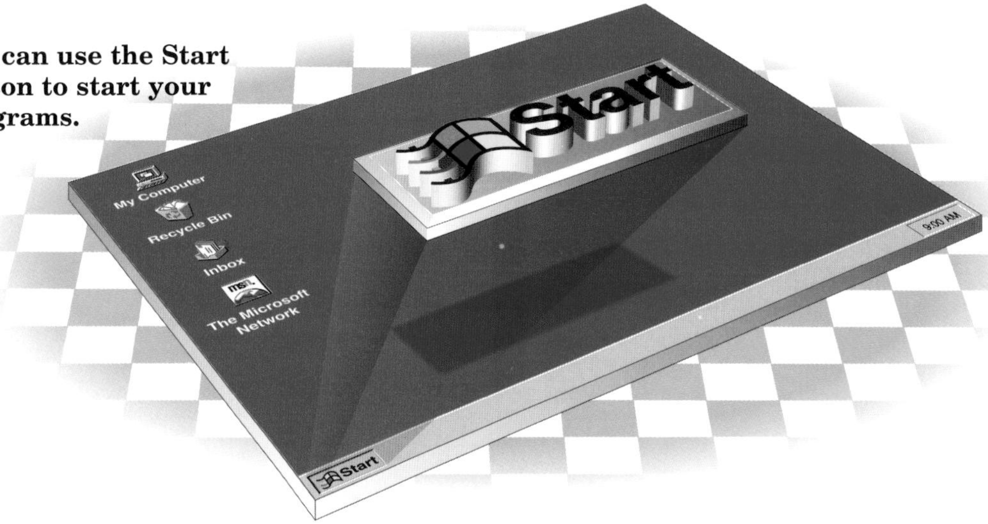

START A PROGRAM

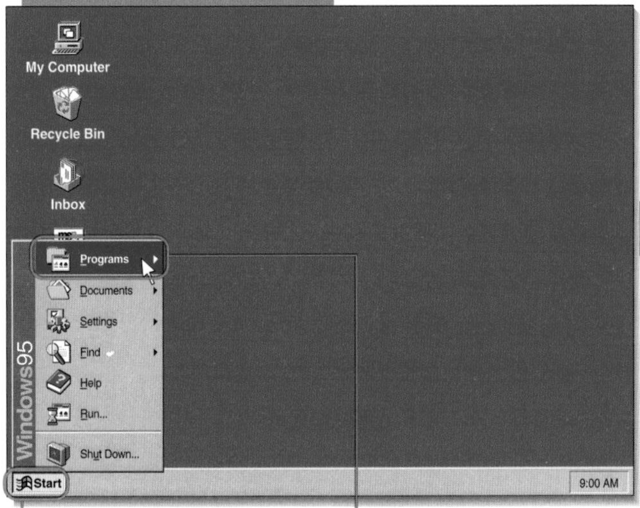

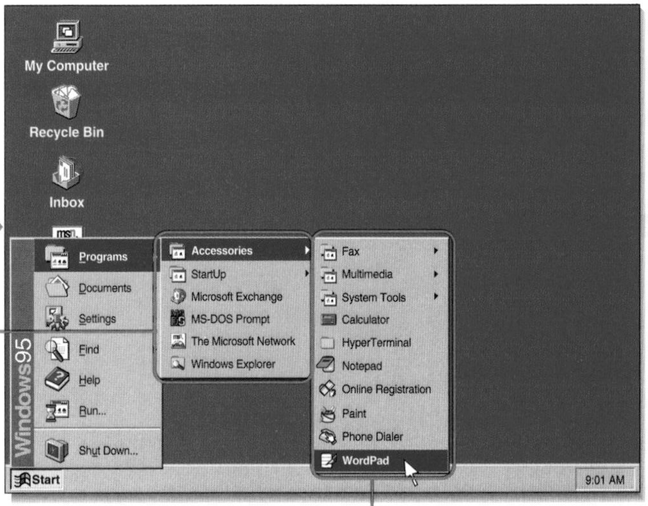

1 Click **Start**. A menu appears.

Note: To display the Start menu using the keyboard, press and hold down **Ctrl** *and then press* **Esc**.

2 Click **Programs**.

Note: To select a menu item using the keyboard, press the underlined letter (example: ***P*** *for* *Programs).*

■ A list of items appears.

3 To view the programs for an item displaying an arrow (▸), click the item (example: **Accessories**).

4 To start a program, click the program (example: **WordPad**).

Note: To close the Start menu without selecting a program, click outside the menu area or press **Alt** *on your keyboard.*

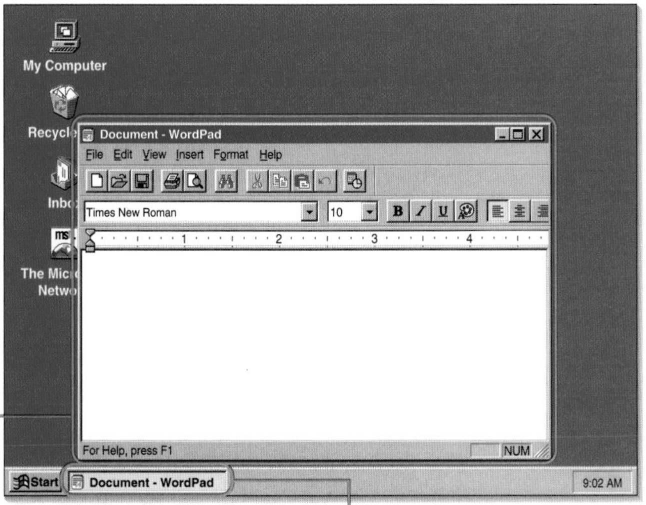

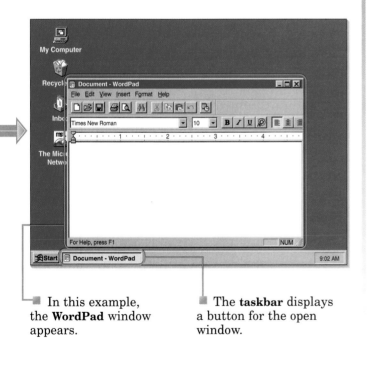

In this example, the **WordPad** window appears.

The **taskbar** displays a button for the open window.

TIP

Windows comes with many useful programs. Here are some examples:

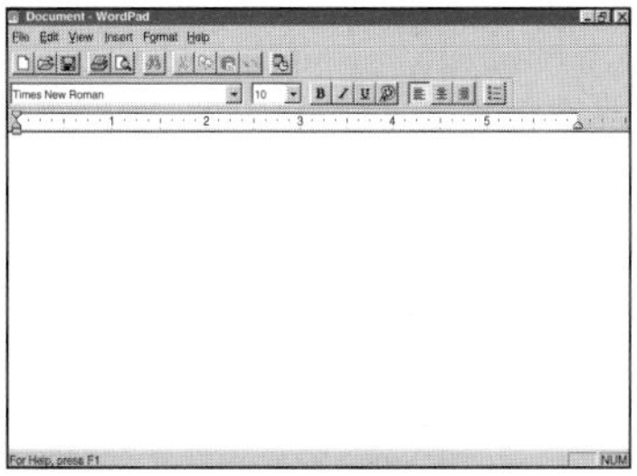

WordPad
is a word processing program that lets you create letters, reports and memos.

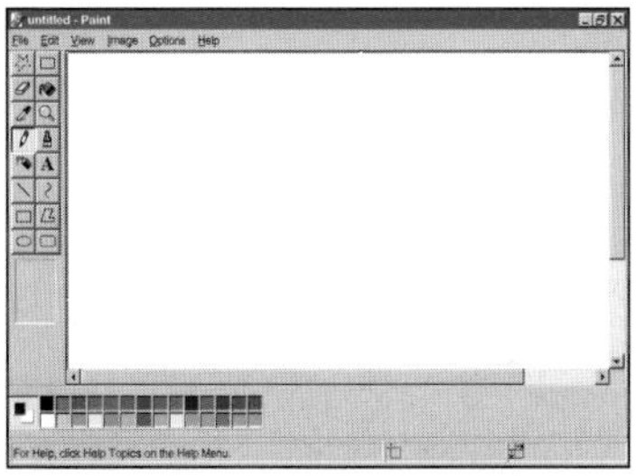

Paint
is a drawing program that lets you draw pictures and maps.

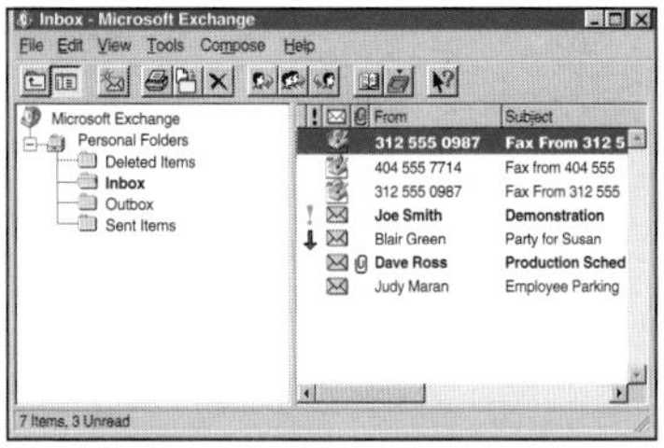

Microsoft Exchange
is a program that lets you exchange electronic mail and faxes.

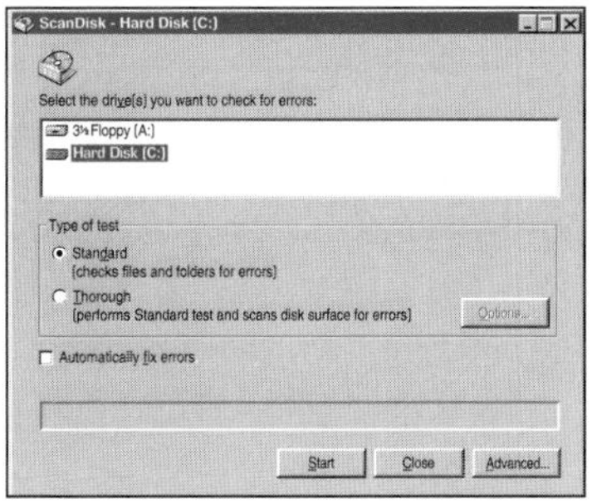

ScanDisk
is a program that searches for and repairs disk errors.

MINIMIZE A WINDOW

If you are not using a window, you can minimize the window to remove it from your screen. You can redisplay the window at any time.

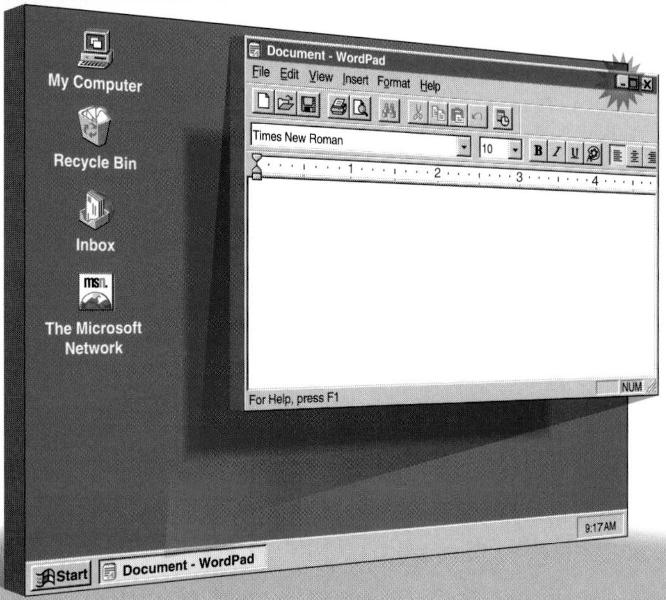

MINIMIZE A WINDOW

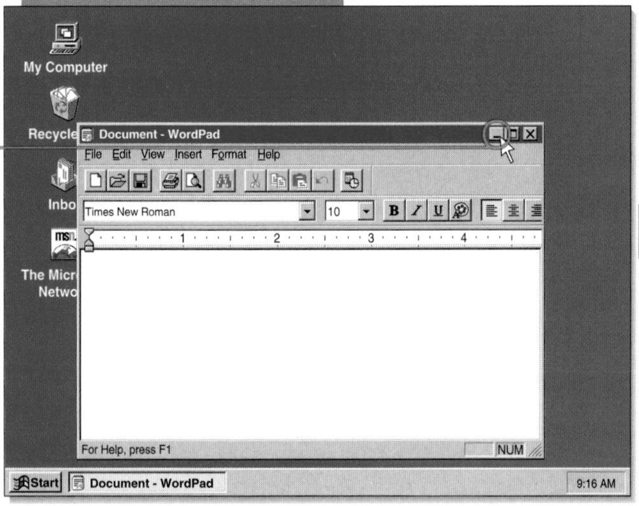

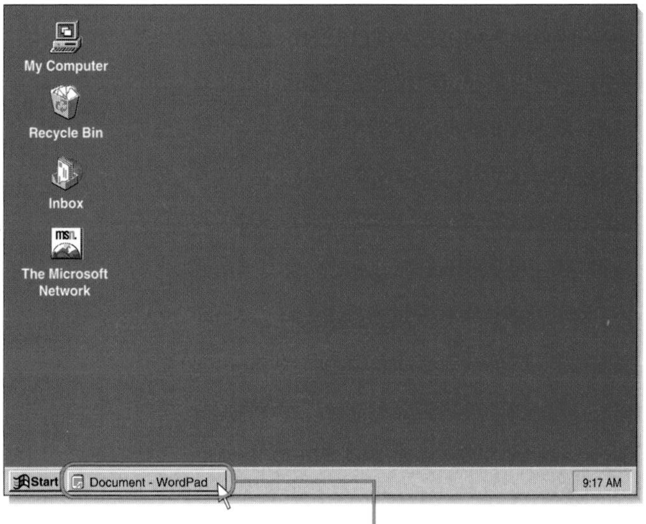

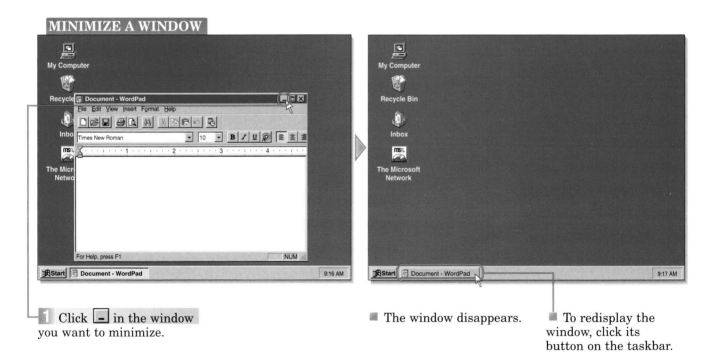

1 Click ▭ in the window you want to minimize.

■ The window disappears.

■ To redisplay the window, click its button on the taskbar.

MAXIMIZE A WINDOW

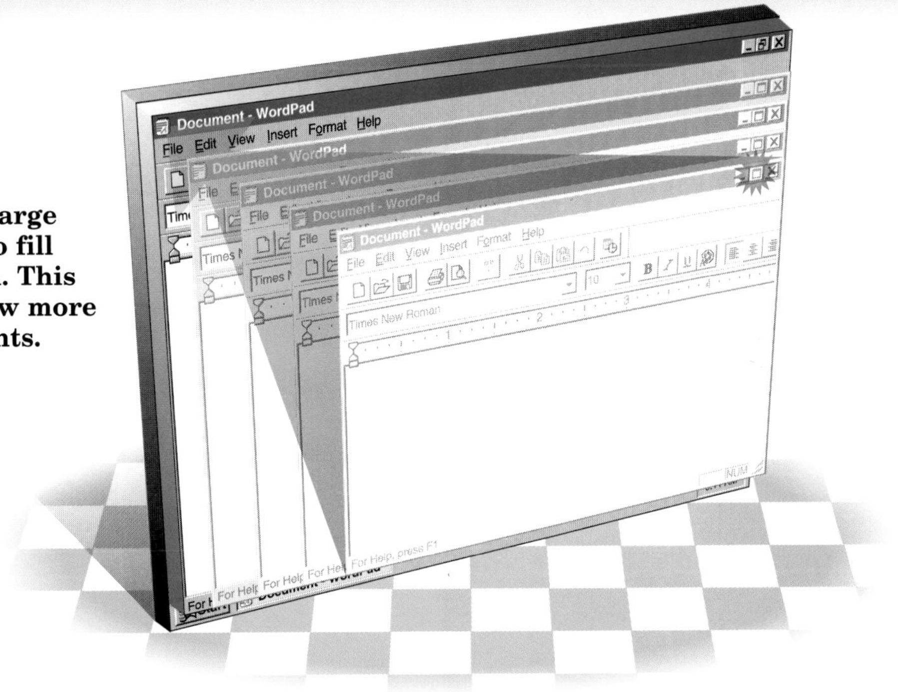

You can enlarge a window to fill your screen. This lets you view more of its contents.

MAXIMIZE A WINDOW

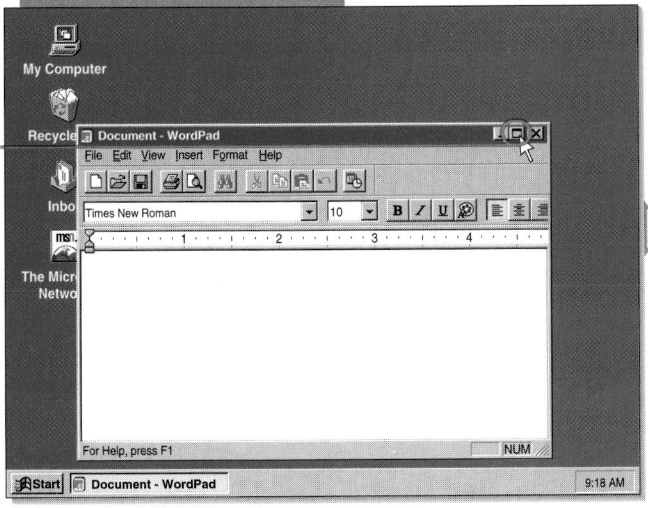

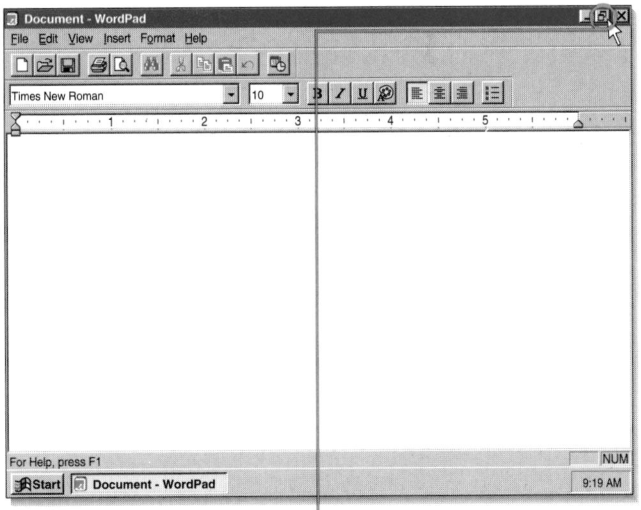

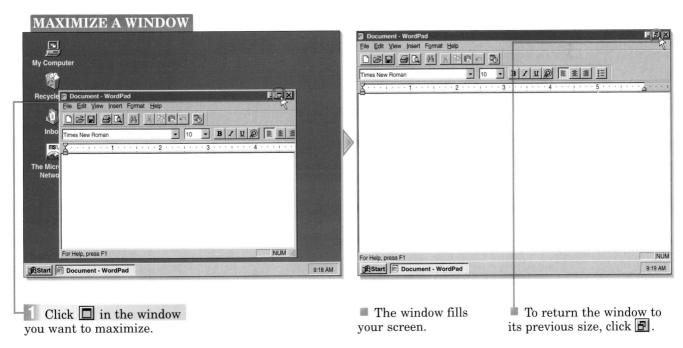

1 Click ☐ in the window you want to maximize.

■ The window fills your screen.

■ To return the window to its previous size, click 🗗.

MOVE A WINDOW

If a window covers items on your screen, you can move the window to a different location.

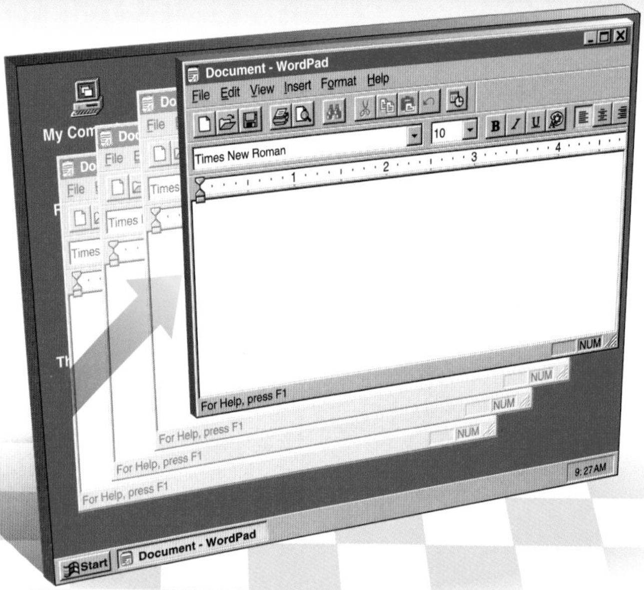

MOVE A WINDOW

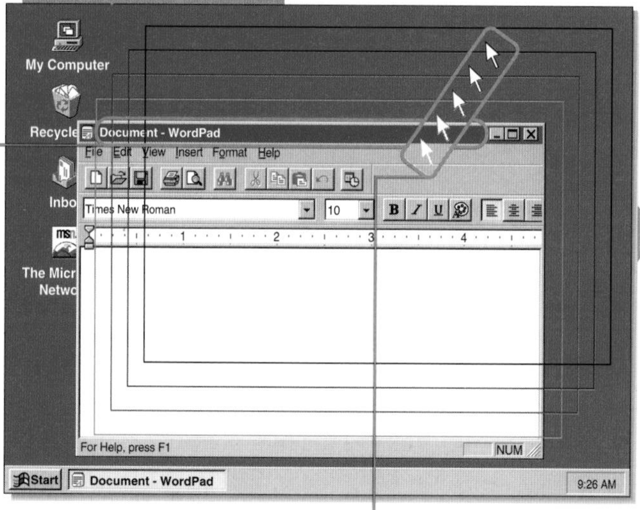

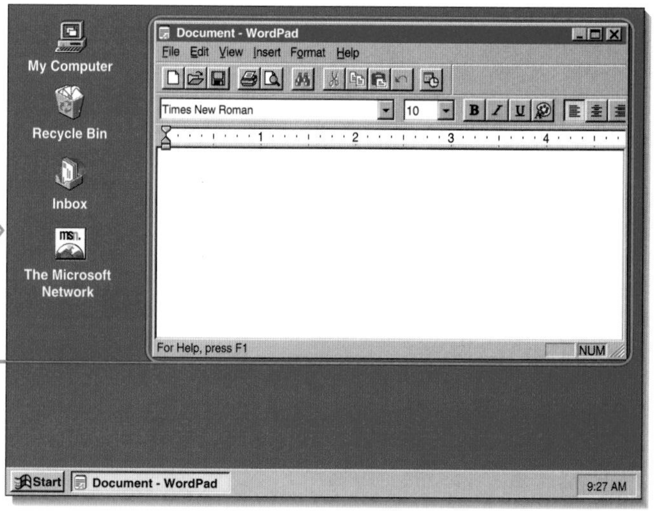

1 Position the mouse over the title bar of the window you want to move.

2 Drag the mouse to where you want to place the window.

- An outline of the window indicates the new location.

3 The window moves to the new location.

SIZE A WINDOW

You can easily change the size of a window displayed on your screen.

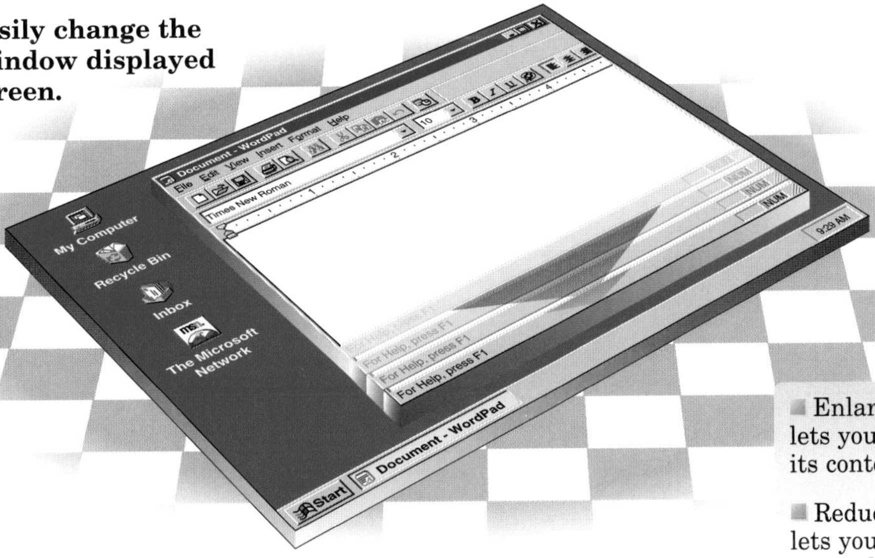

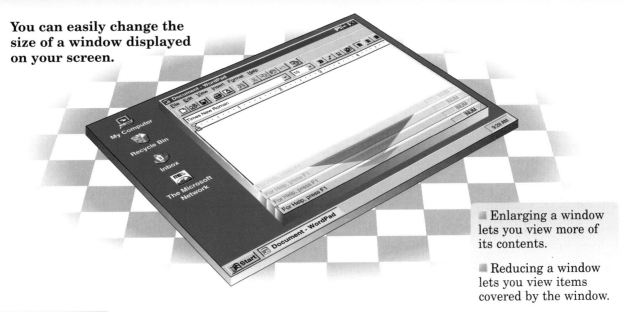

- Enlarging a window lets you view more of its contents.
- Reducing a window lets you view items covered by the window.

SIZE A WINDOW

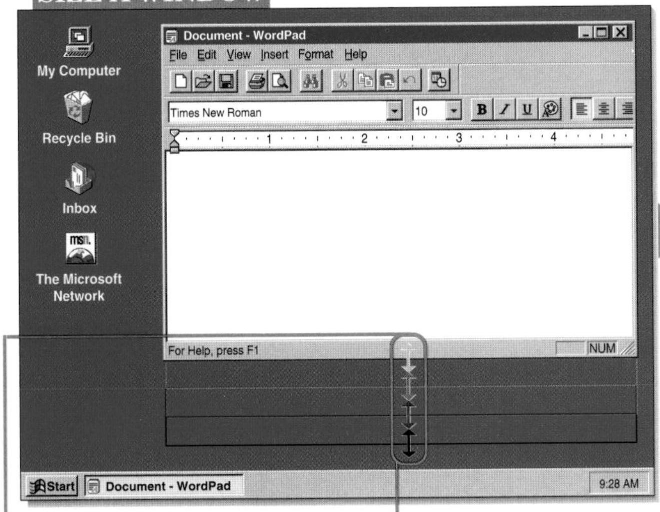

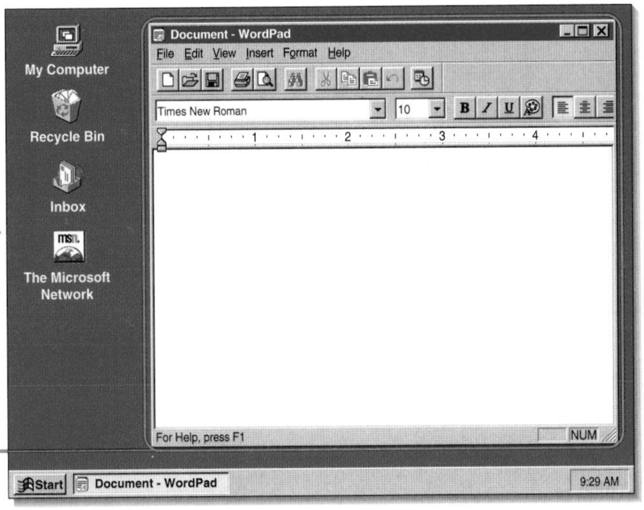

1 Position the mouse ↖ over an edge of the window you want to size (↖ changes to ↕ or ↔).

2 Drag the mouse ↕ until the outline of the window displays the size you want.

- The window changes to the new size.

SWITCH BETWEEN WINDOWS

You can have more than one window open at a time. You can easily switch between all open windows.

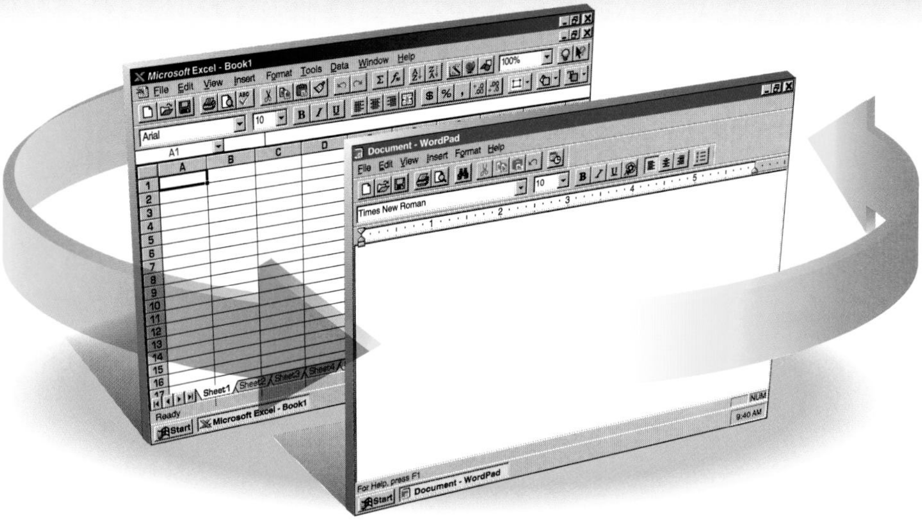

SWITCH BETWEEN WINDOWS

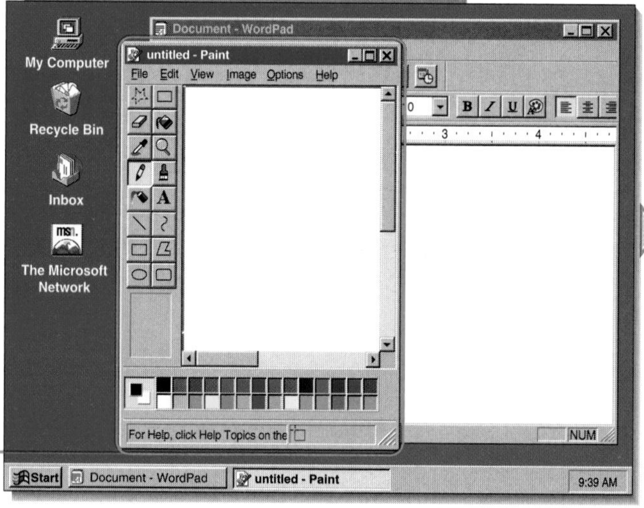

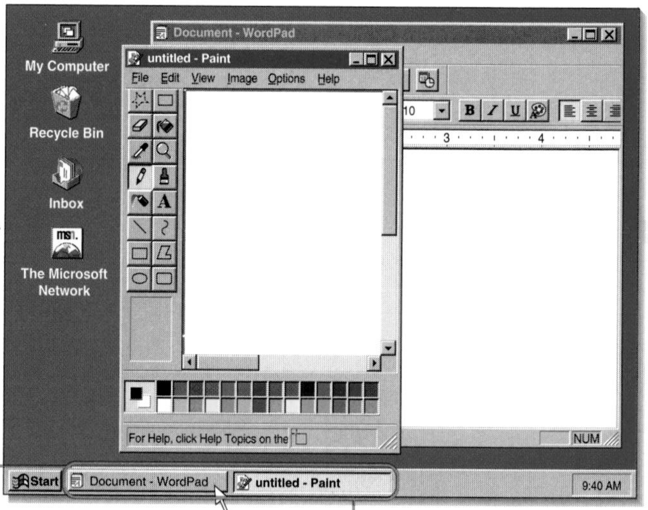

■ You can only work in one window at a time. The active window (example: **Paint**) appears in front of all other windows.

Note: To start a program, such as Paint, refer to page 10.

■ The taskbar displays a button for each open window on your screen.

1 To move the window you want to work with to the front, click its button on the taskbar.

TIP

Think of each window as a separate piece of paper. Switching between windows lets you place a different piece of paper at the top of the pile.

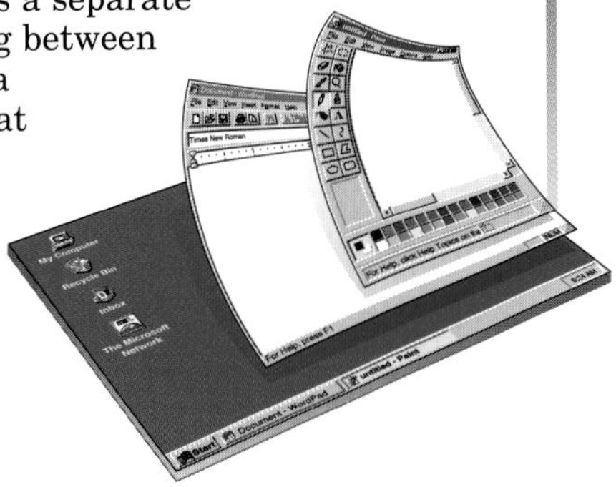

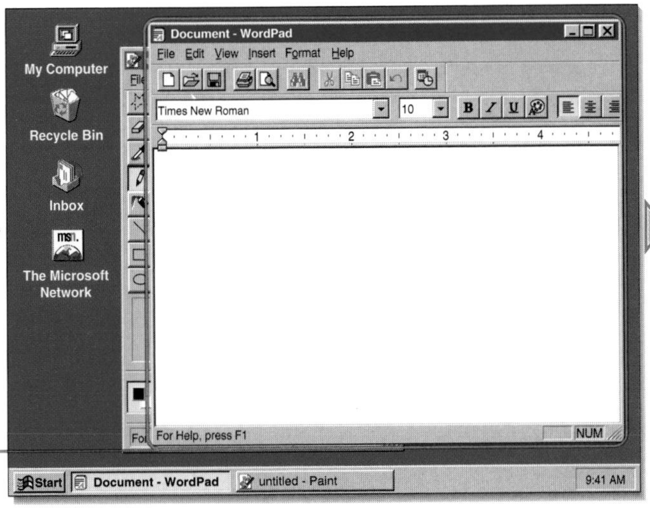

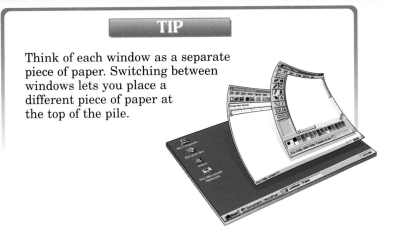

The window appears in front of all other windows. This lets you clearly view its contents.

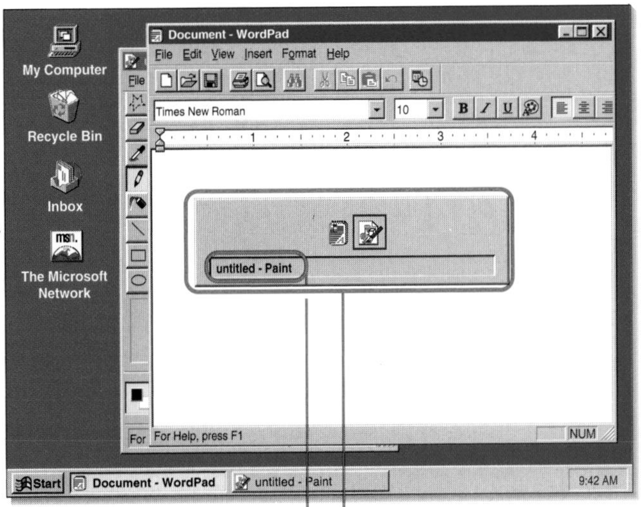

You can also use your keyboard to quickly switch between the open windows on your screen.

1 Press and hold down Alt on your keyboard.

2 Still holding down Alt, press Tab and a box appears.

3 Press Tab until this area displays the name of the window you want to work with. Then release Alt.

CASCADE WINDOWS

If you have several windows open, some of them may be hidden from view. The Cascade command lets you display your open windows one on top of the other.

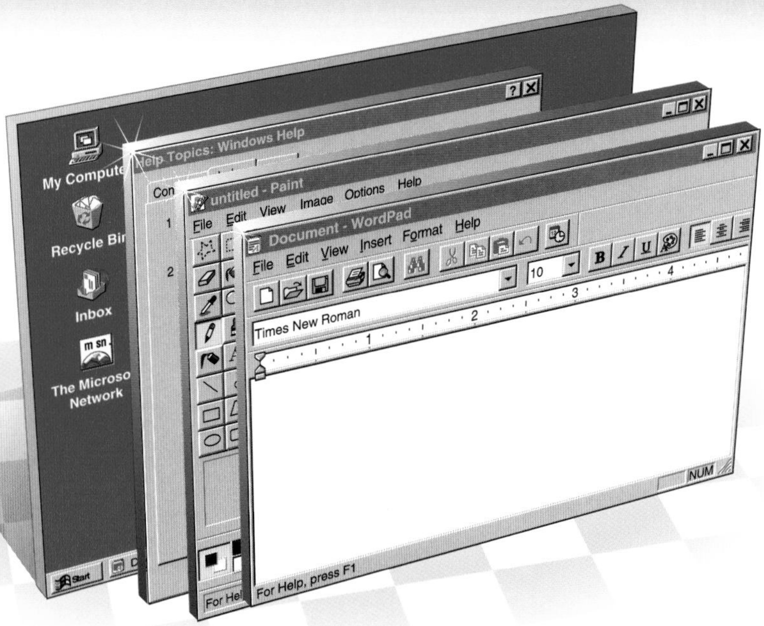

CASCADE WINDOWS

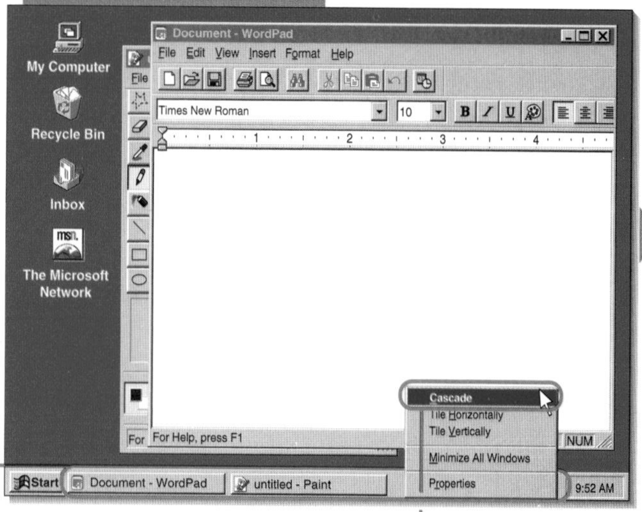

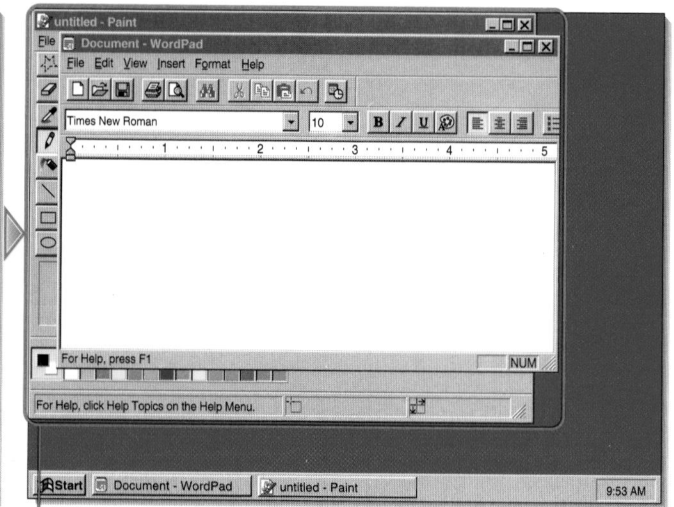

1 Click an empty area on the taskbar using the **right** button. A menu appears.

2 Click **Cascade**.

■ The windows neatly overlap each other.

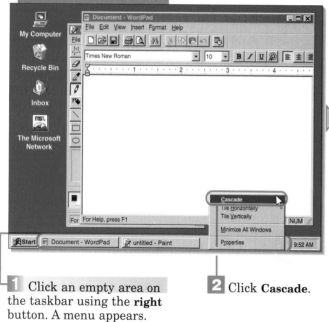

TILE WINDOWS

You can use the Tile command to view the contents of all your open windows at once.

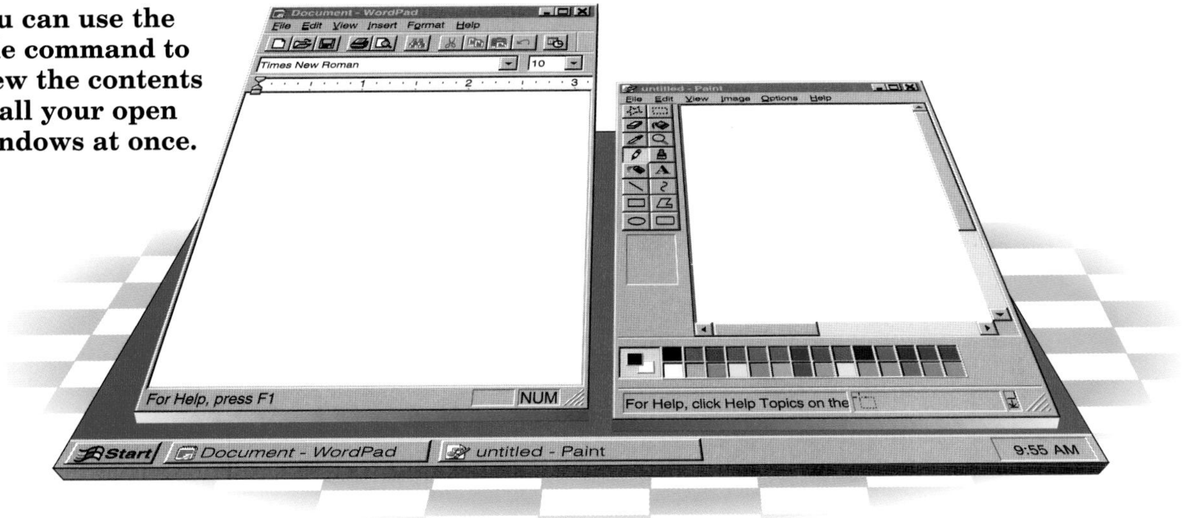

TILE WINDOWS

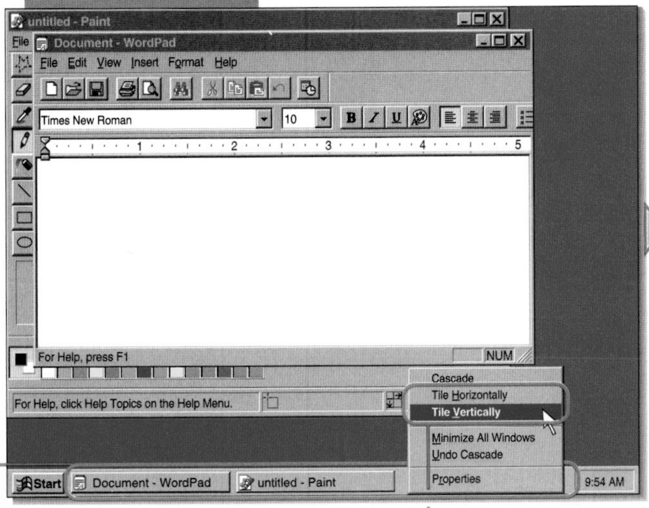

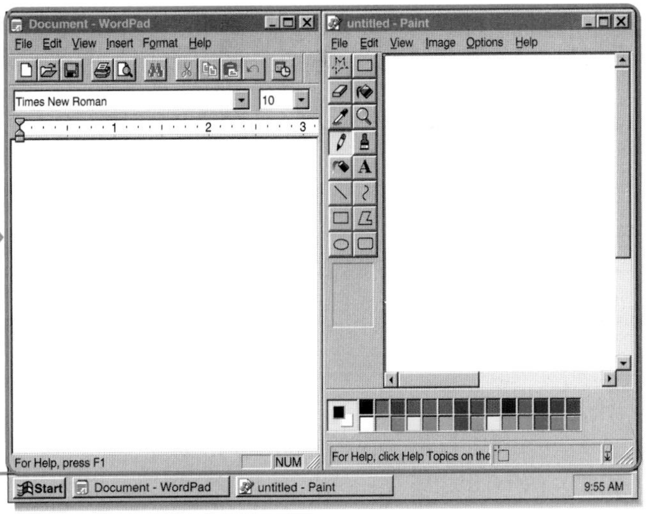

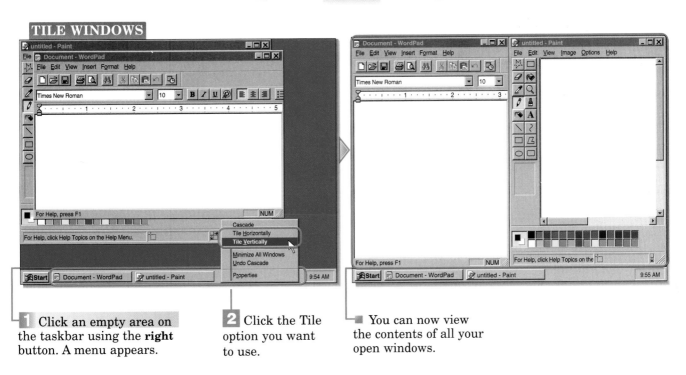

1 Click an empty area on the taskbar using the **right** button. A menu appears.

2 Click the Tile option you want to use.

■ You can now view the contents of all your open windows.

MINIMIZE ALL WINDOWS

You can minimize all your open windows to remove them from your screen. You can redisplay a window at any time.

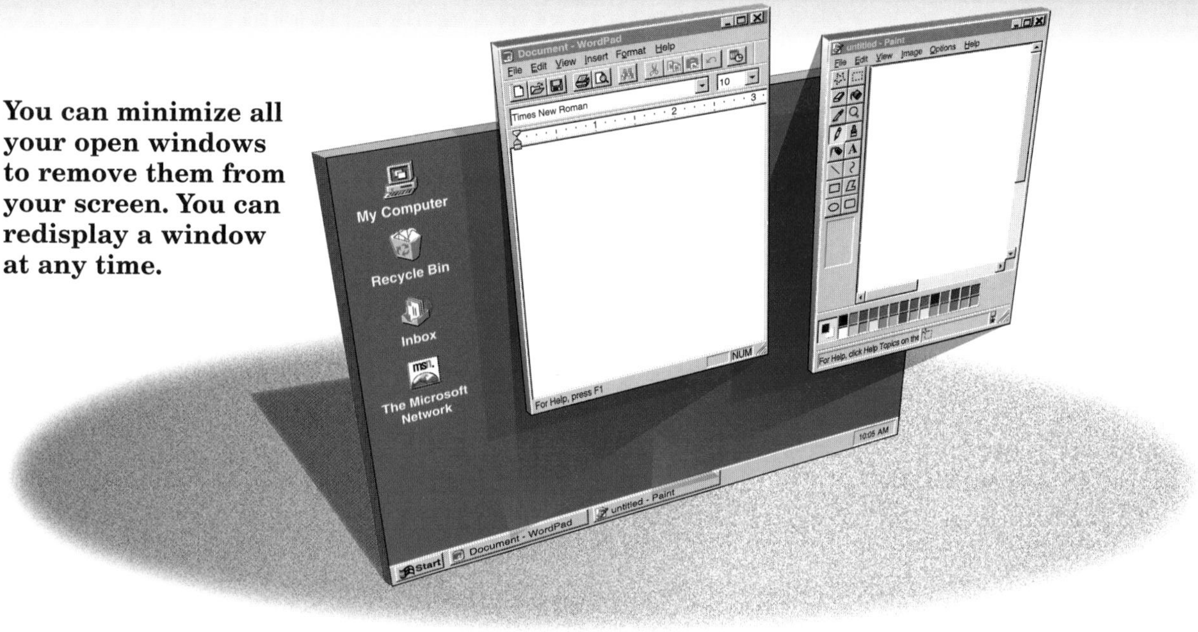

MINIMIZE ALL WINDOWS

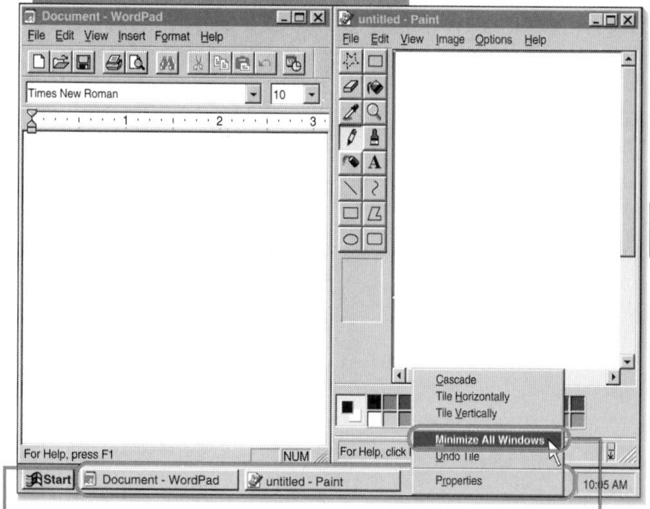

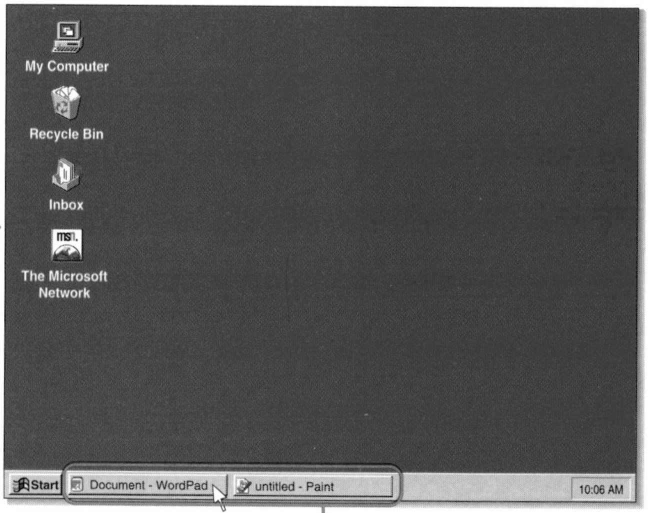

1 Click an empty area on the taskbar using the **right** button. A menu appears.

2 Click **Minimize All Windows**.

■ All the windows disappear.

3 To redisplay a window, click its button on the taskbar.

CLOSE A WINDOW

When you finish working with a window, you can close the window to remove it from your screen.

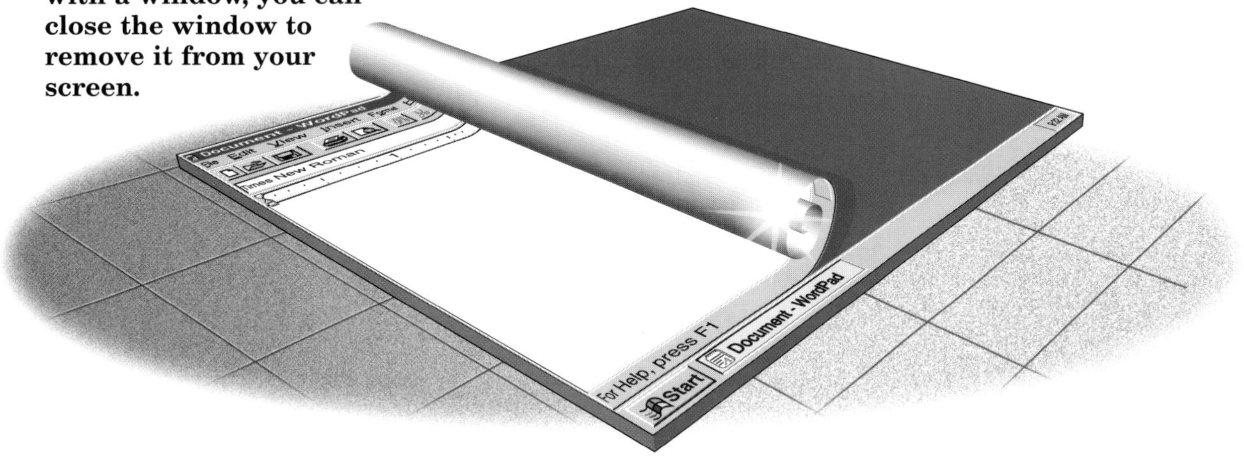

CLOSE A WINDOW

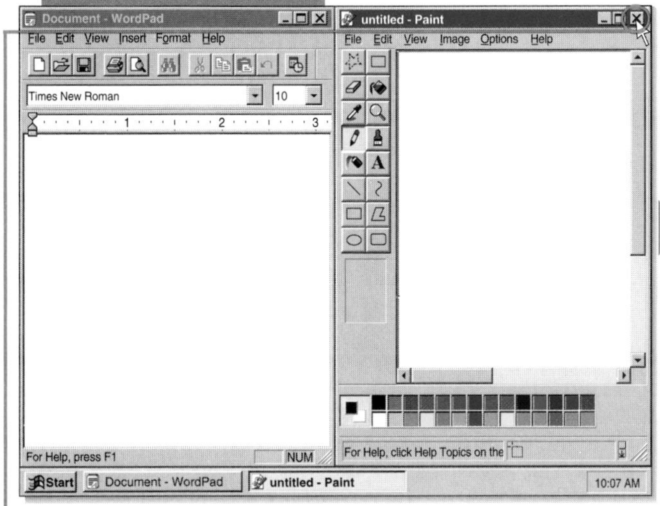

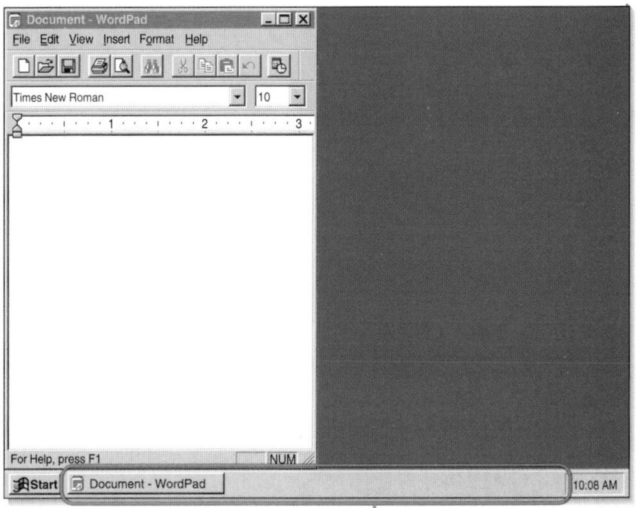

1 Click ☒ in the window you want to close.

■ The window disappears from your screen.

■ The button for the window disappears from the taskbar.

GETTING HELP

If you do not know how to perform a task, you can use the Help feature to get information.

GETTING HELP

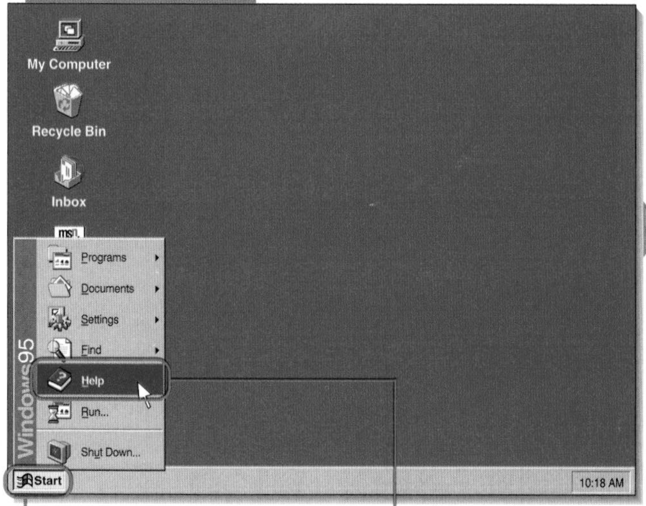

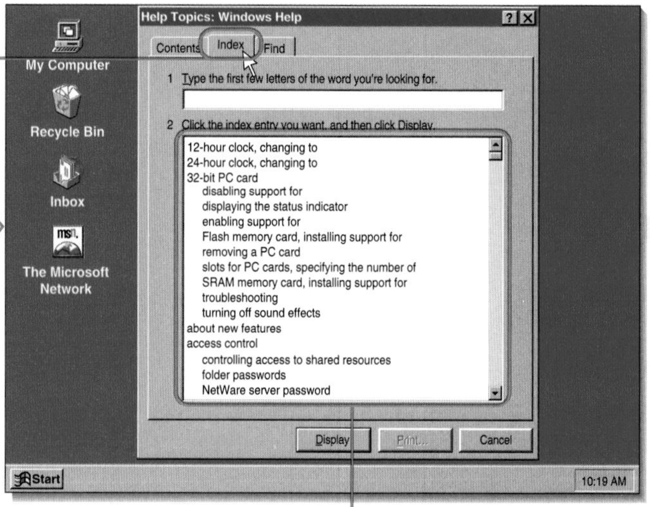

1 Click **Start**.

2 Click **Help**.

■ The **Help Topics** dialog box appears.

3 To display the help index, click the **Index** tab.

■ This area displays a list of all the available help topics.

Note: To browse through the topics, use the scroll bar. For more information, refer to page 24.

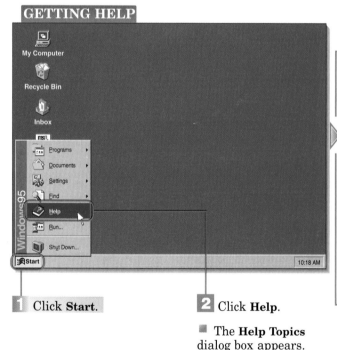

TIP

There are three ways to find information in the Help Topics dialog box.

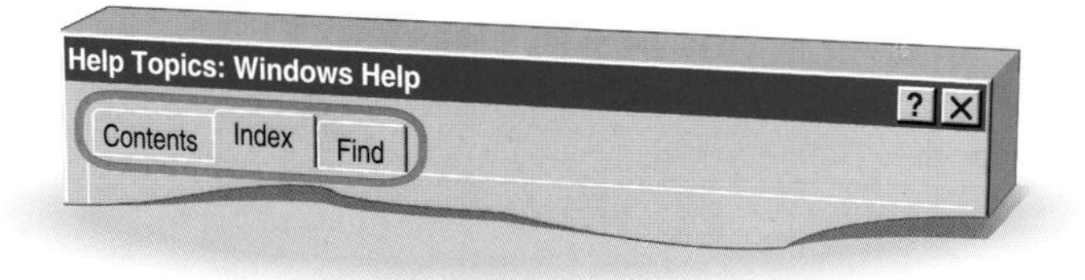

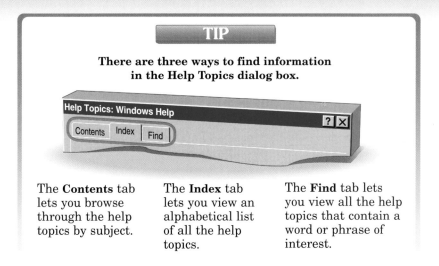

The **Contents** tab lets you browse through the help topics by subject.

The **Index** tab lets you view an alphabetical list of all the help topics.

The **Find** tab lets you view all the help topics that contain a word or phrase of interest.

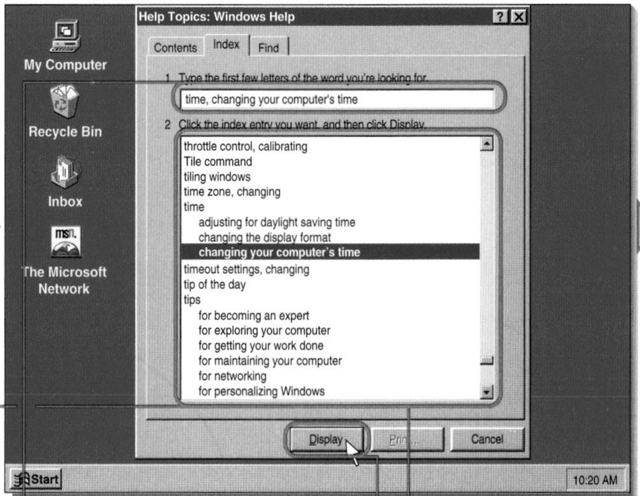

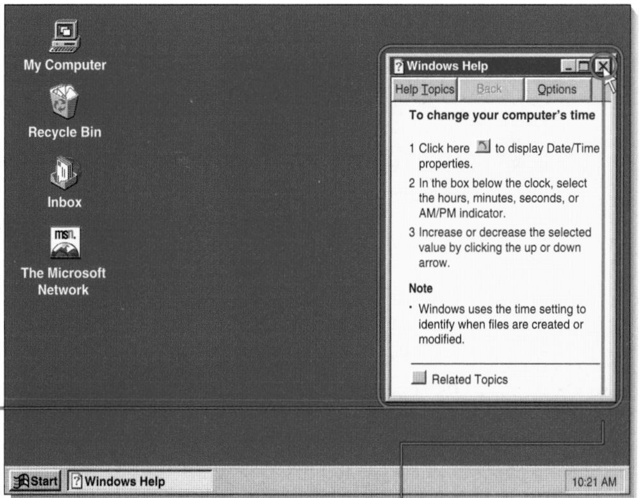

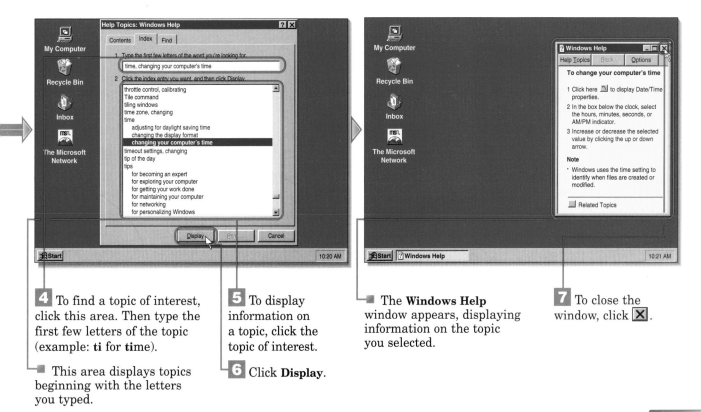

4 To find a topic of interest, click this area. Then type the first few letters of the topic (example: **ti** for **time**).

■ This area displays topics beginning with the letters you typed.

5 To display information on a topic, click the topic of interest.

6 Click **Display**.

■ The **Windows Help** window appears, displaying information on the topic you selected.

7 To close the window, click ☒.

SCROLL THROUGH A WINDOW

A scroll bar lets you browse through information in a window. This is useful when a window is not large enough to display all the information it contains.

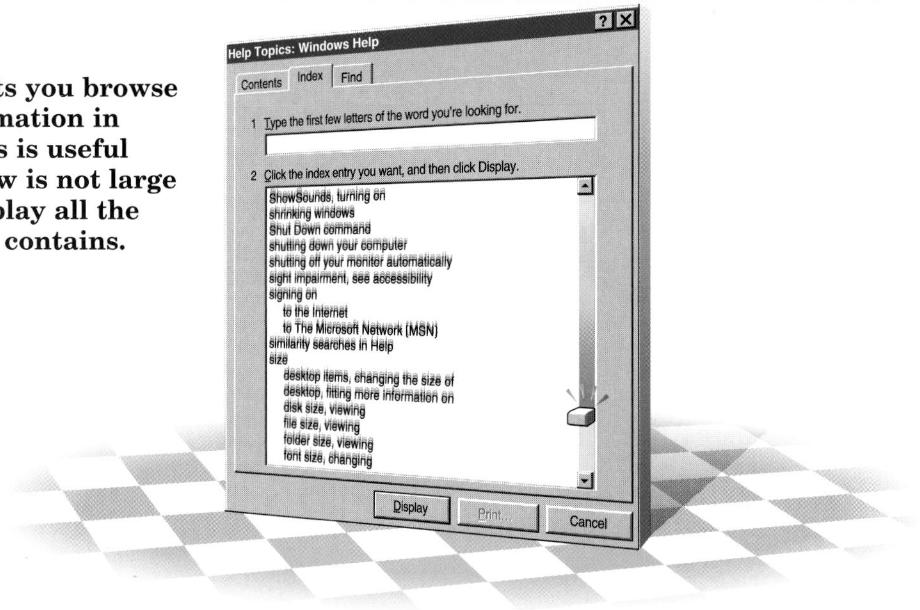

SCROLL DOWN

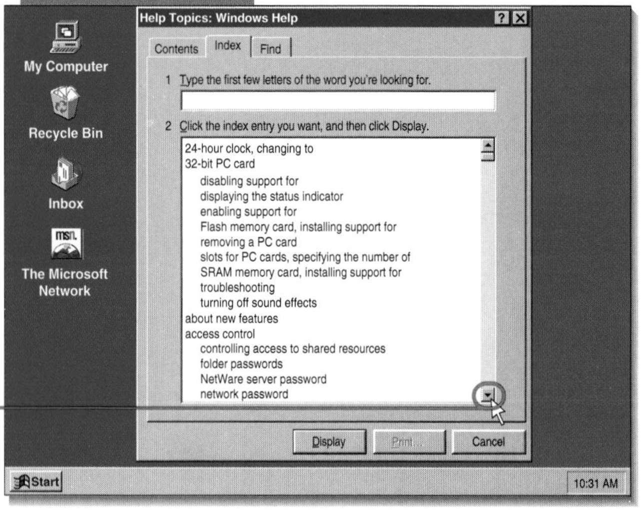

1 To scroll down, click ▼.

Note: In this example, we scroll through the ***Help Topics*** *dialog box. To display the dialog box, perform steps 1 and 2 on page 22.*

SCROLL UP

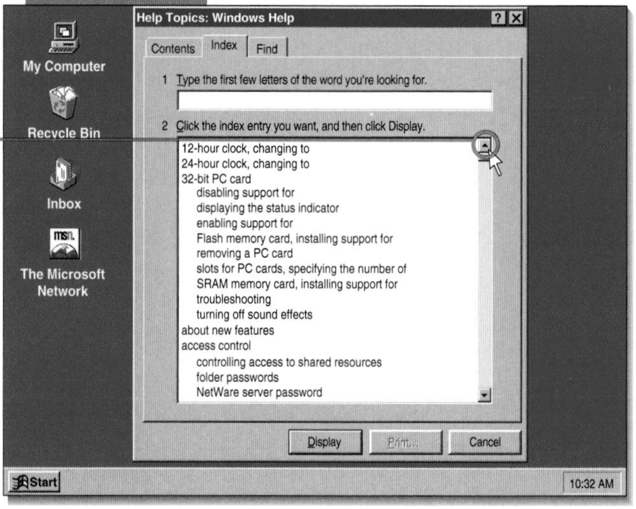

1 To scroll up, click ▲.

TIP

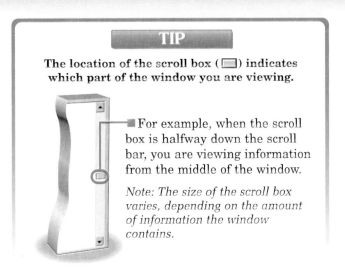

The location of the scroll box (▭) indicates which part of the window you are viewing.

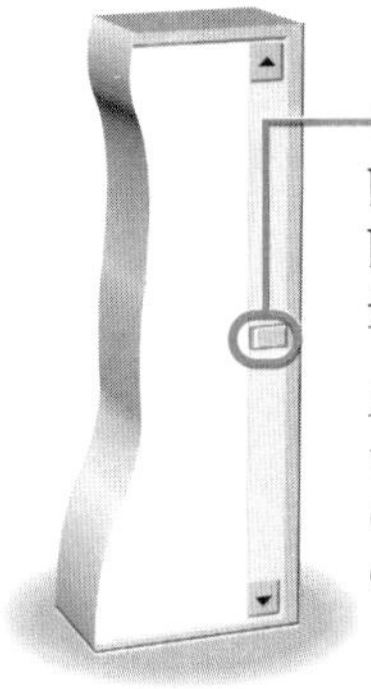

■ For example, when the scroll box is halfway down the scroll bar, you are viewing information from the middle of the window.

Note: The size of the scroll box varies, depending on the amount of information the window contains.

SCROLL TO ANY POSITION

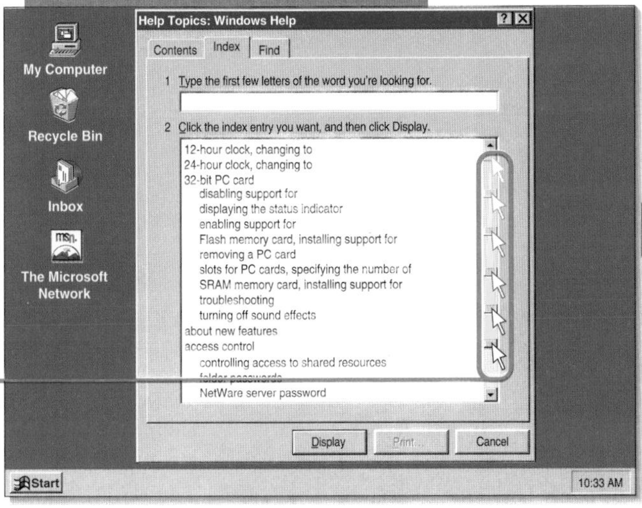

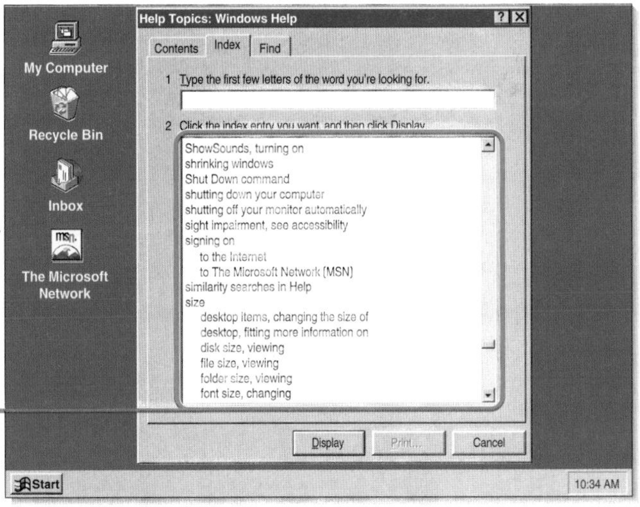

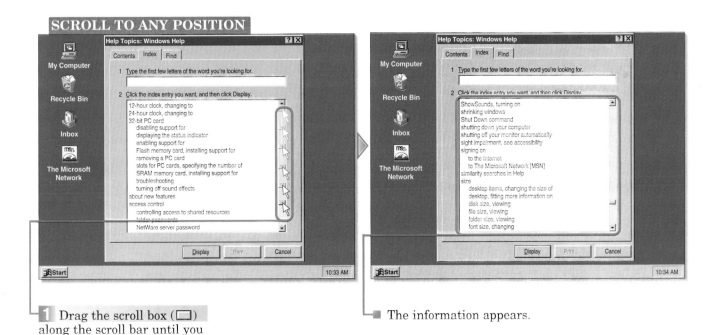

1 Drag the scroll box (▭) along the scroll bar until you see the information you want.

■ The information appears.

USING THE MS-DOS PROMPT

You can work with DOS programs and commands in Windows.

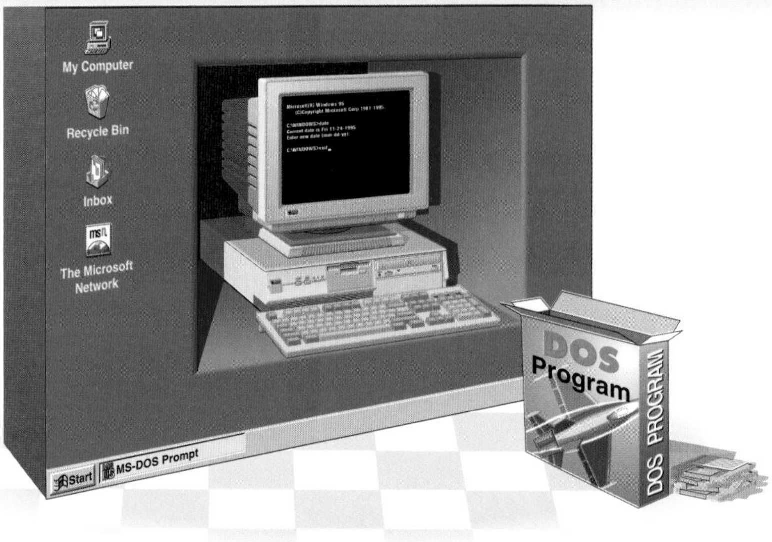

USING THE MS-DOS PROMPT

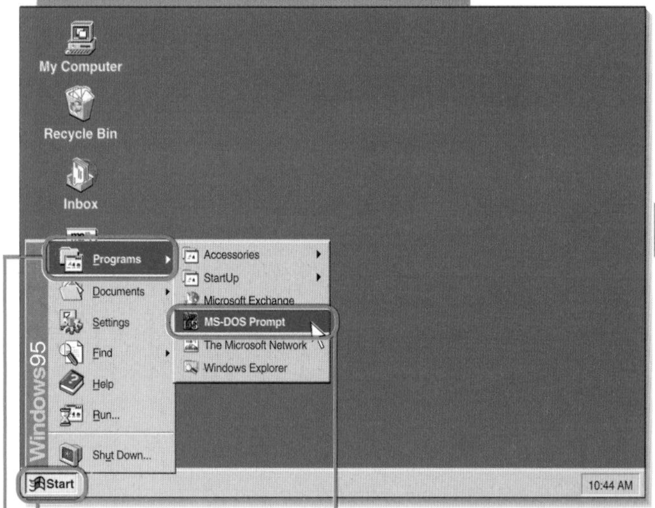

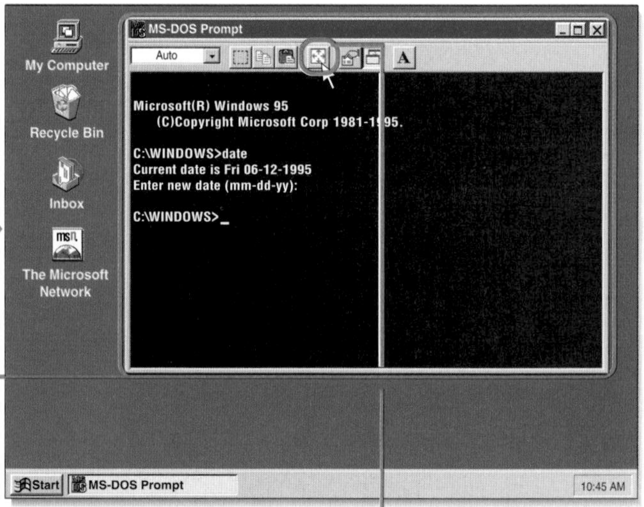

1 Click **Start**.

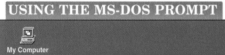

2 Click **Programs**.

3 Click **MS-DOS Prompt**.

■ The **MS-DOS Prompt** window appears. You can enter DOS commands and start DOS programs in the window.

*Note: In this example, we use the **date** command to display the date set in the computer.*

4 To fill your screen with the MS-DOS prompt, click .

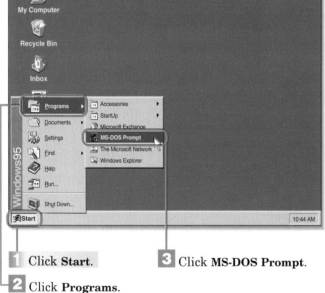

TIP

If a DOS program will not run in a window, try restarting the computer in MS-DOS mode.

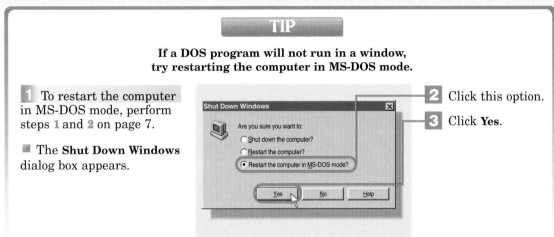

1 To restart the computer in MS-DOS mode, perform steps 1 and 2 on page 7.

■ The **Shut Down Windows** dialog box appears.

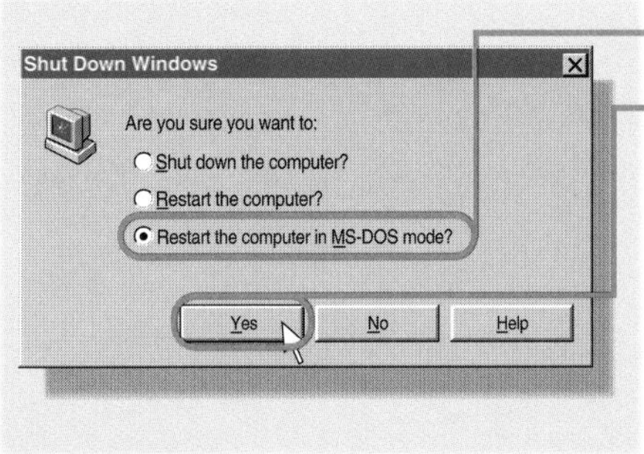

2 Click this option.

3 Click **Yes**.

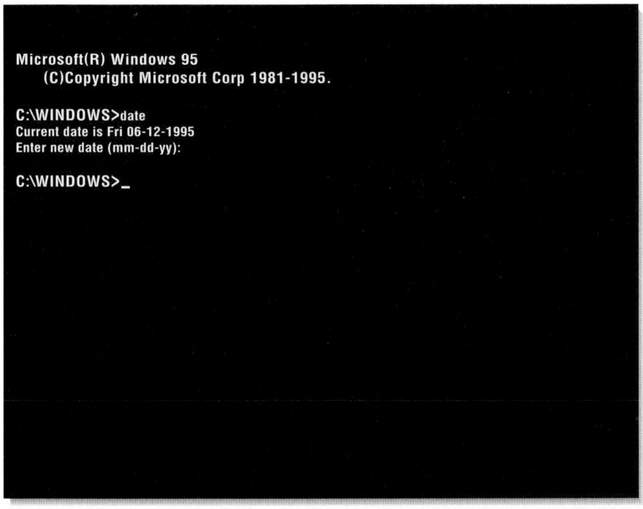

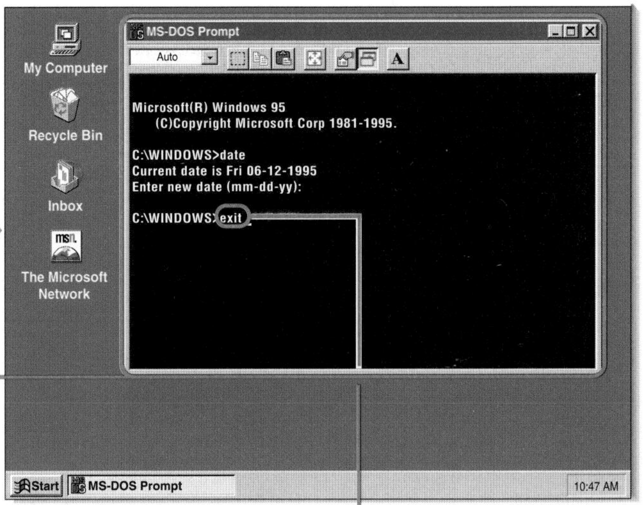

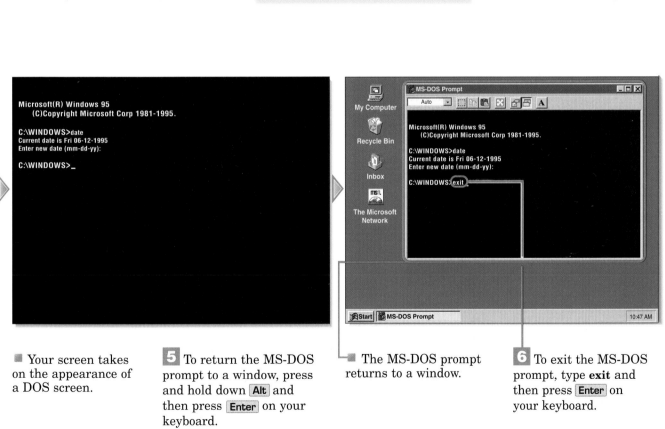

■ Your screen takes on the appearance of a DOS screen.

5 To return the MS-DOS prompt to a window, press and hold down Alt and then press Enter on your keyboard.

■ The MS-DOS prompt returns to a window.

6 To exit the MS-DOS prompt, type **exit** and then press Enter on your keyboard.

In this chapter you will learn how to create drawings using the Paint program.

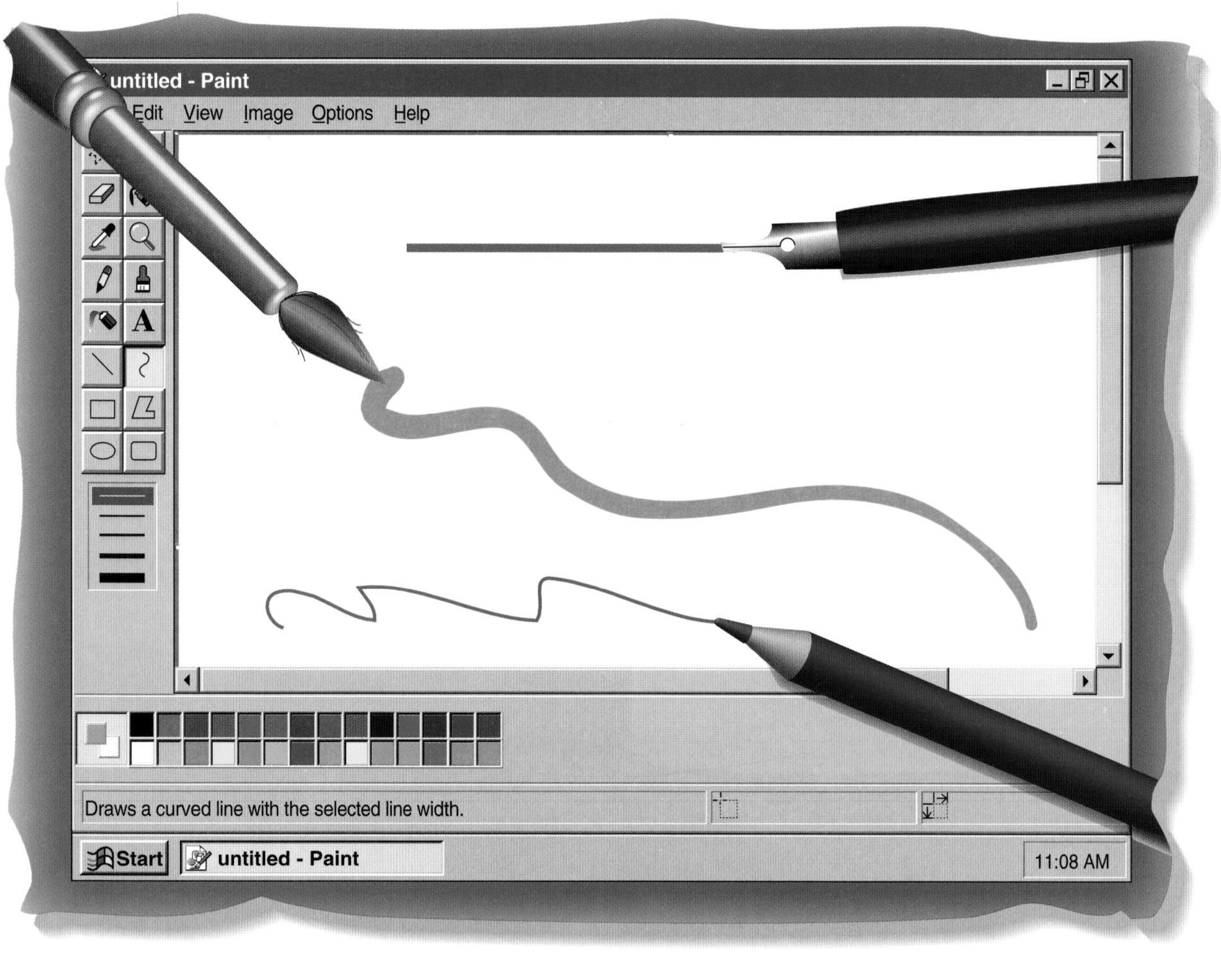

CHAPTER 3: PAINT

Start Paint 30

Draw Shapes 32

Draw Lines 34

Erase an Area 36

Undo Last Change 37

Add Text 38

Save a Drawing 40

Exit Paint 41

Open a Drawing 42

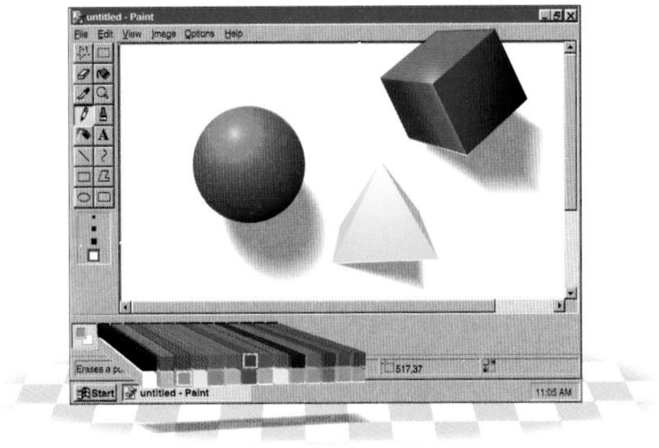

START PAINT

Paint lets you use your artistic abilities to draw pictures and maps on your computer.

START PAINT

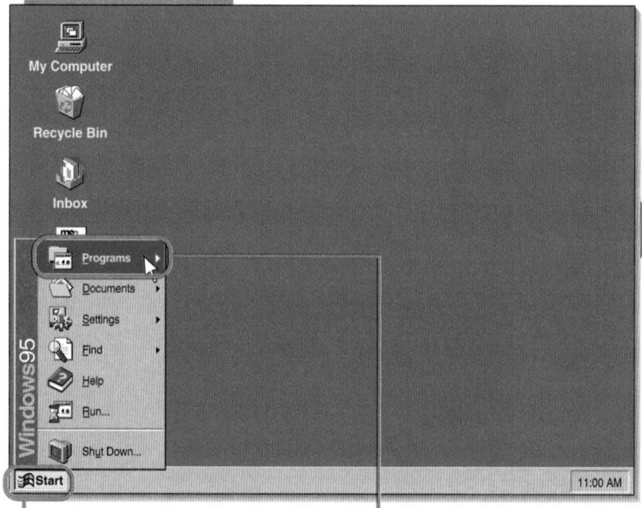

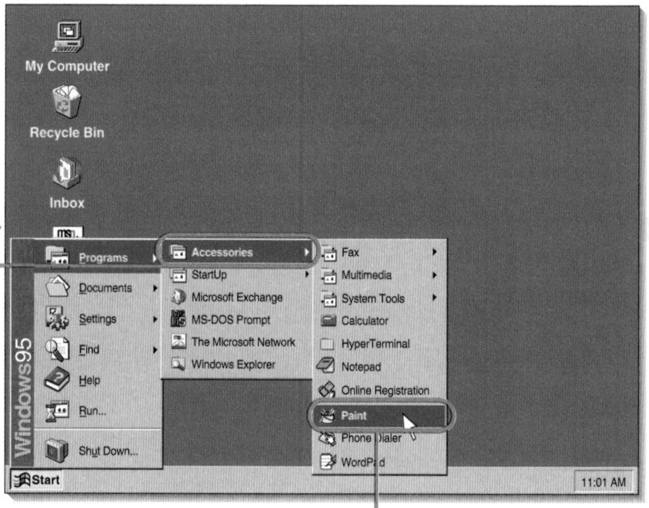

1 Click **Start**.

2 Click **Programs**.

3 Click **Accessories**.

4 Click **Paint**.

TIP

You can place Paint drawings in other programs. For example, you can add your company logo to a business letter you created.

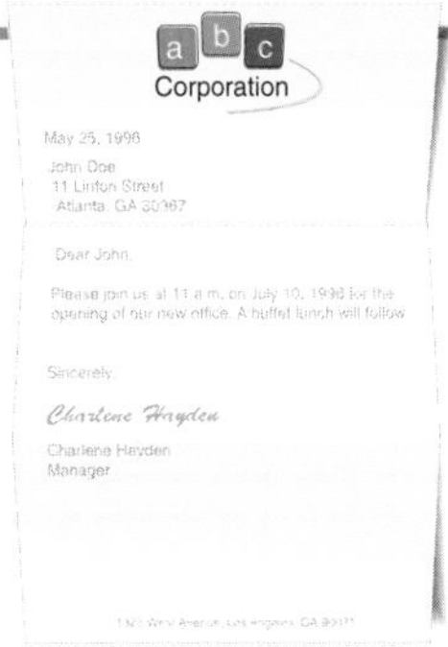

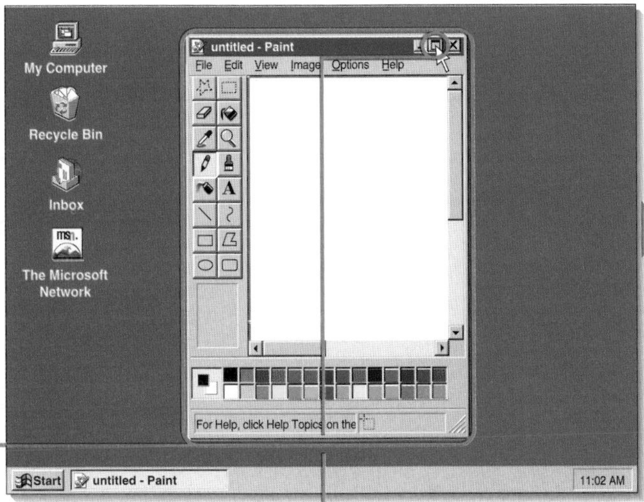

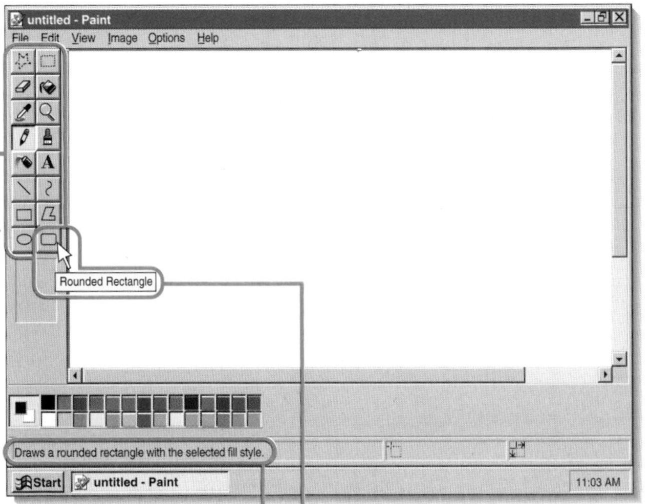

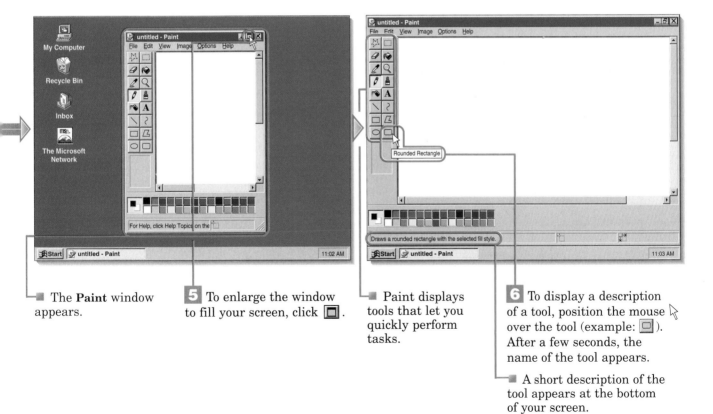

■ The **Paint** window appears.

5 To enlarge the window to fill your screen, click ▢.

■ Paint displays tools that let you quickly perform tasks.

6 To display a description of a tool, position the mouse over the tool (example: ▢). After a few seconds, the name of the tool appears.

■ A short description of the tool appears at the bottom of your screen.

DRAW SHAPES

You can draw shapes such as circles and squares in any color displayed at the bottom of your screen.

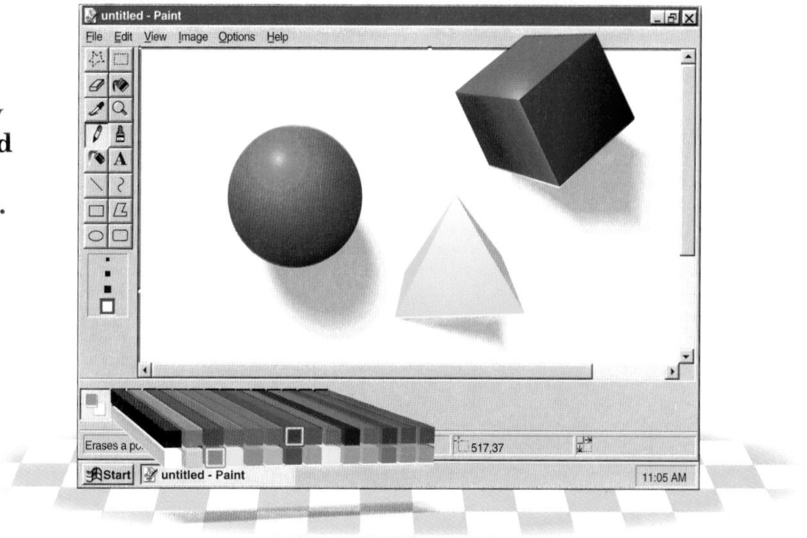

DRAW SHAPES

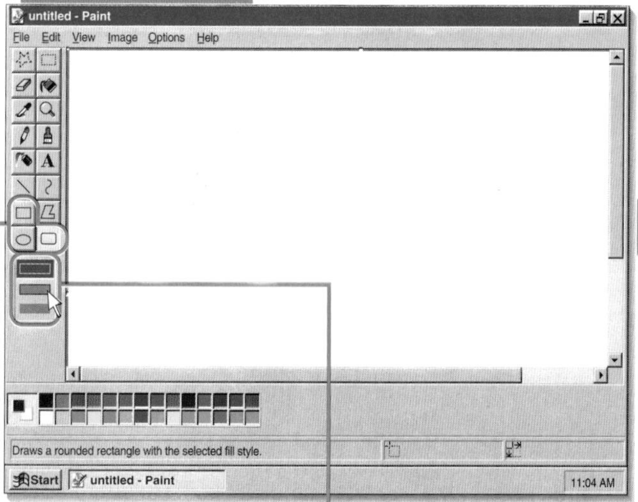

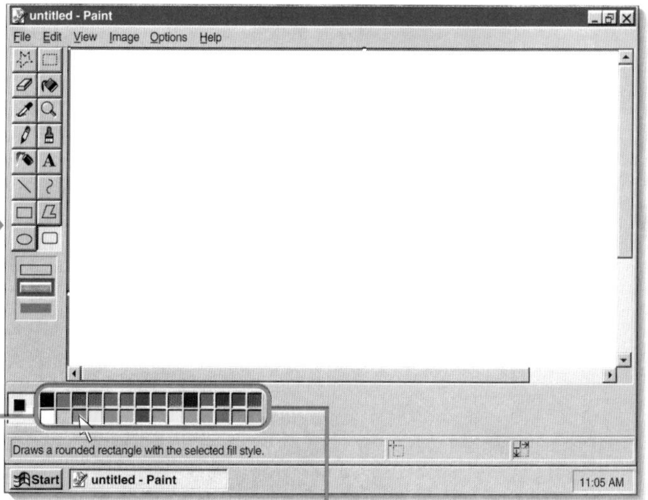

1 Click the tool displaying the shape you want to draw (example:).

2 To select how you want the shape to appear, click one of the options in this area.

Note: For more information, refer to the top of page 33.

3 To select a color for the outline of the shape, click the color (example:).

4 To select a color for the inside of the shape, click the color using the **right** button (example:).

Paint offers three options for drawing a shape.

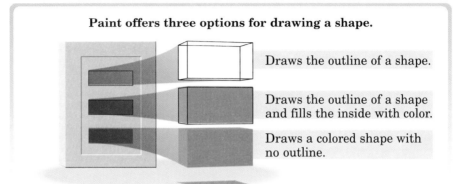

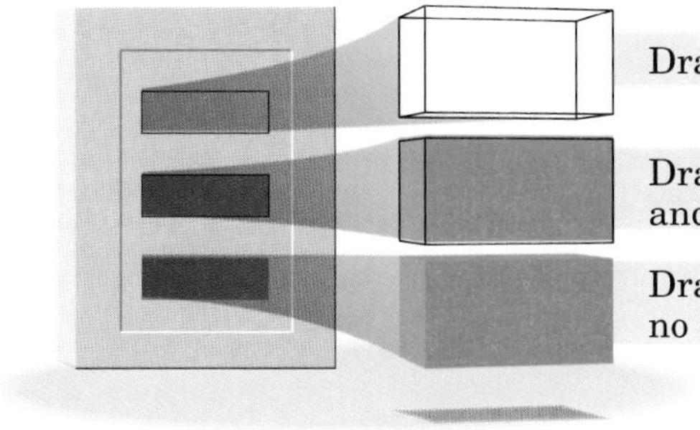

Draws the outline of a shape.

Draws the outline of a shape and fills the inside with color.

Draws a colored shape with no outline.

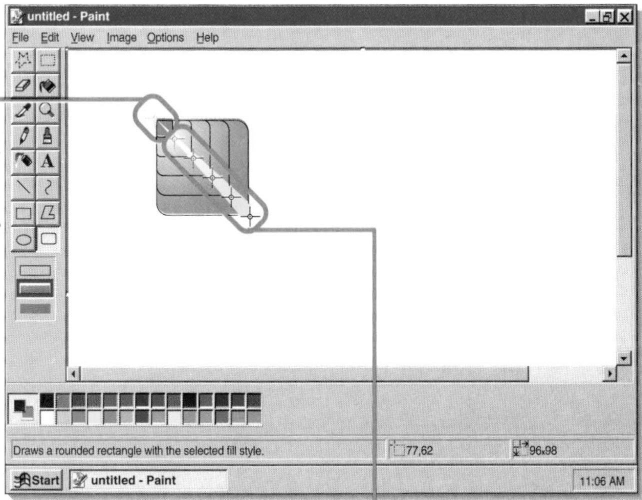

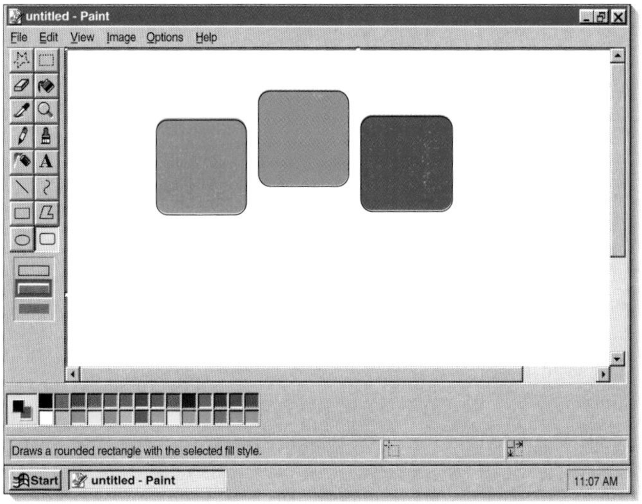

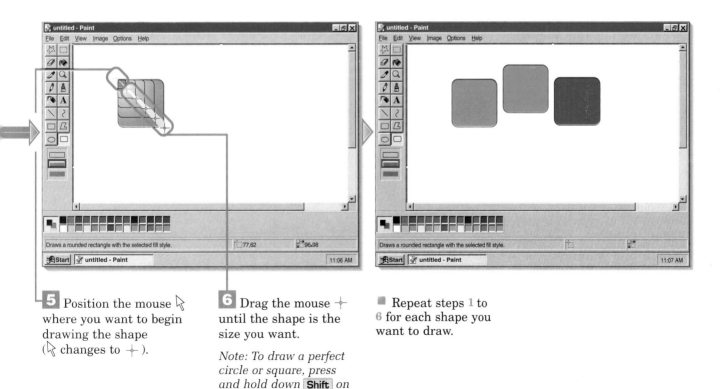

5 Position the mouse ↖ where you want to begin drawing the shape (↖ changes to ✛).

6 Drag the mouse ✛ until the shape is the size you want.

Note: To draw a perfect circle or square, press and hold down **Shift** *on your keyboard before and during step 6.*

■ Repeat steps 1 to 6 for each shape you want to draw.

DRAW LINES

You can draw straight, wavy and curved lines in any color displayed at the bottom of your screen.

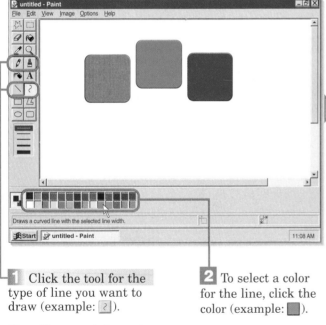

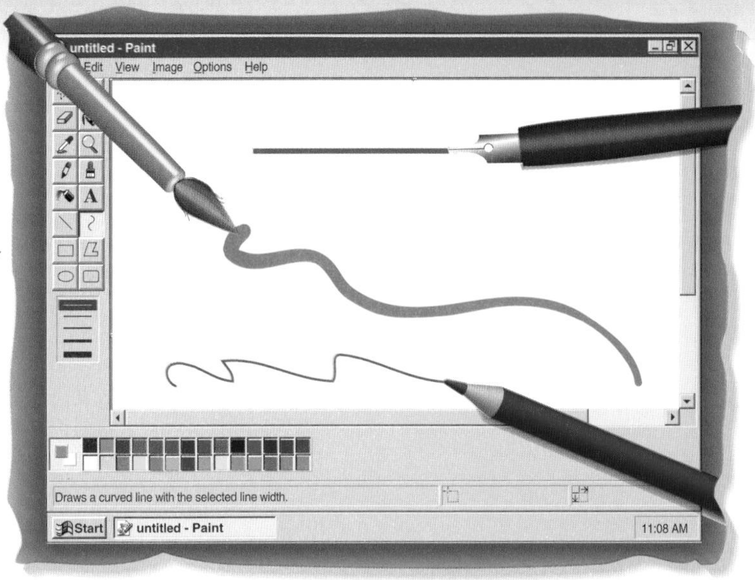

DRAW LINES

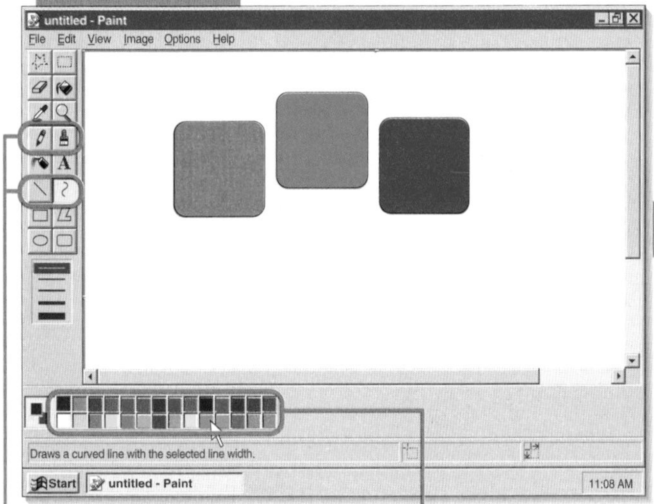

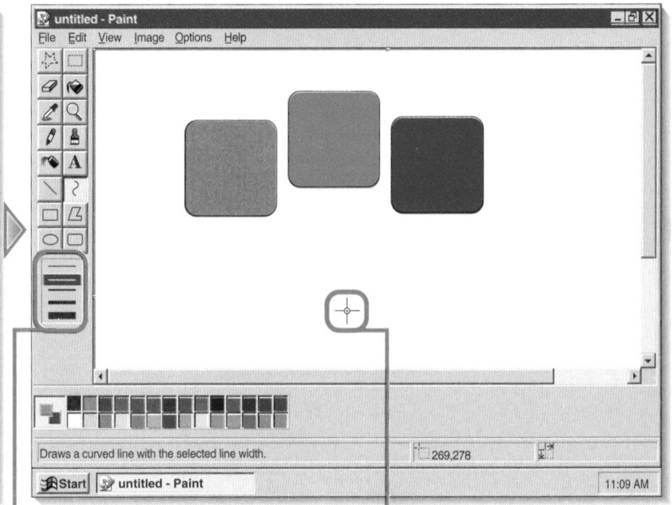

1 Click the tool for the type of line you want to draw (example:).

Note: For more information, refer to the top of page 35.

2 To select a color for the line, click the color (example:).

3 To select a line thickness, click one of the options in this area.

Note: The tool does not provide any line thickness options. The tool provides a different set of options.

4 Position the mouse where you want to begin drawing the line (changes to or).

Paint lets you draw these types of lines.

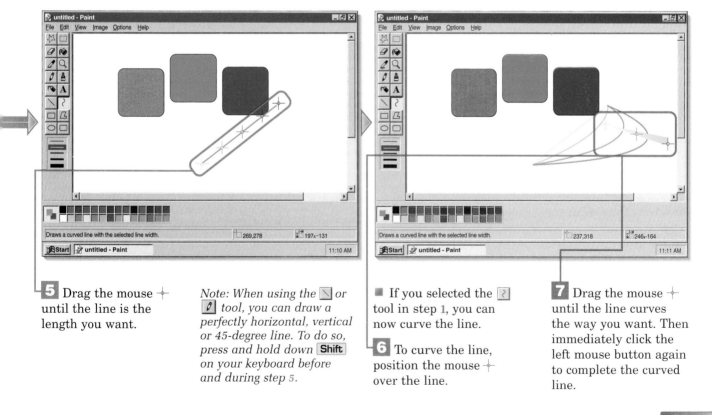

- Draws thin, wavy lines.
- Draws wavy lines of different thicknesses.
- Draws straight lines of different thicknesses.
- Draws curved lines of different thicknesses.

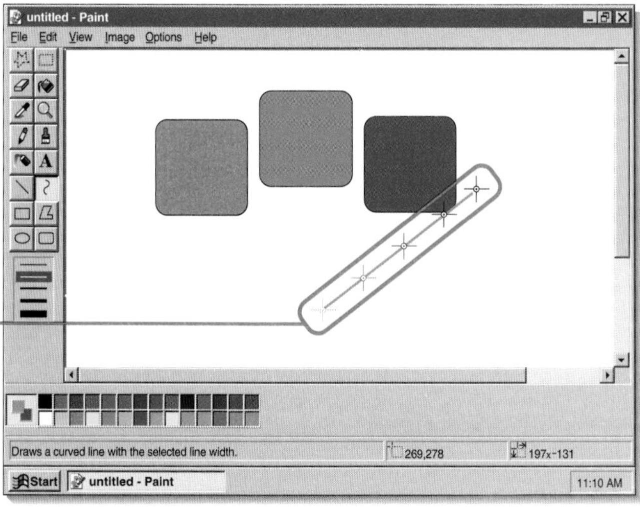

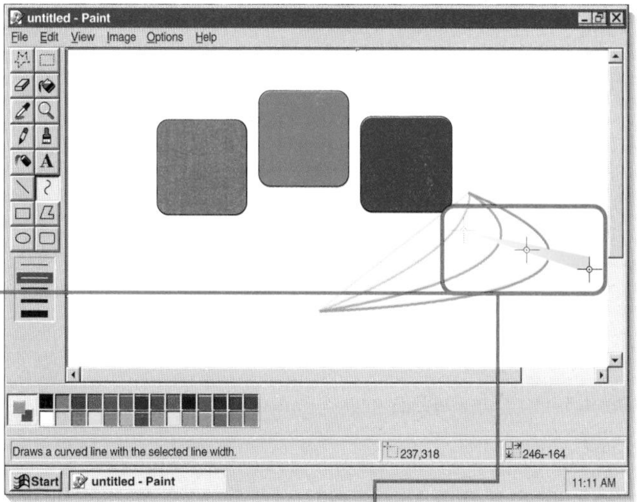

5 Drag the mouse until the line is the length you want.

Note: When using the or tool, you can draw a perfectly horizontal, vertical or 45-degree line. To do so, press and hold down **Shift** *on your keyboard before and during step 5.*

■ If you selected the tool in step 1, you can now curve the line.

6 To curve the line, position the mouse over the line.

7 Drag the mouse until the line curves the way you want. Then immediately click the left mouse button again to complete the curved line.

ERASE AN AREA

You can use the Eraser tool to remove part of your drawing.

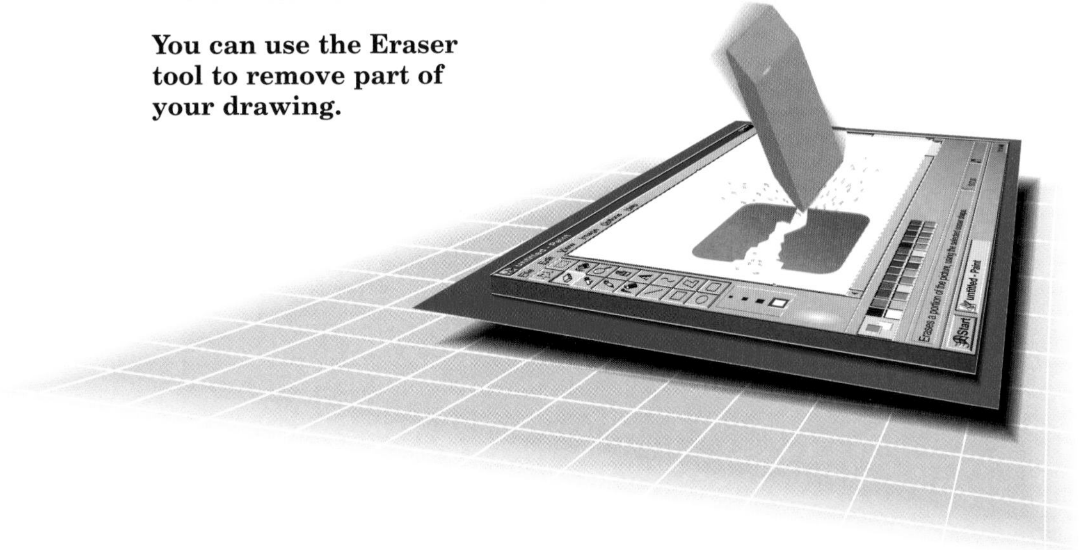

ERASE AN AREA

You can use any color to erase an area on your screen.

Use a white eraser when the area you want to erase has a white background.

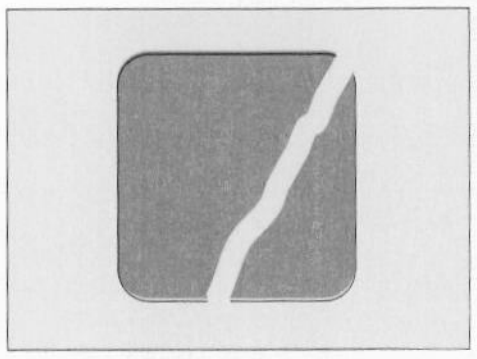

Use a colored eraser when the area you want to erase has a colored background.

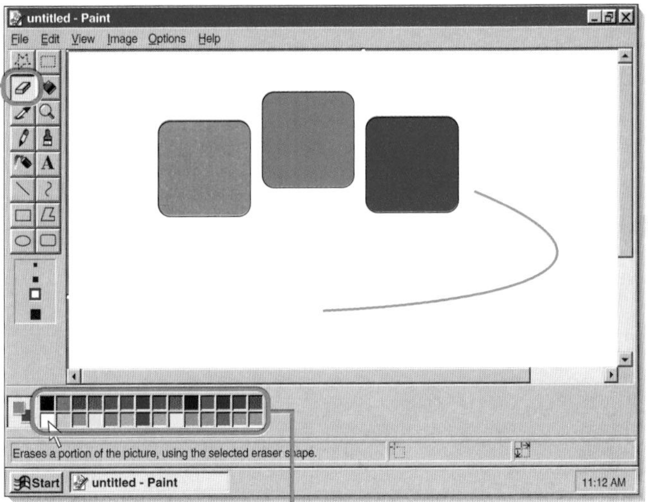

1 Click [eraser icon].

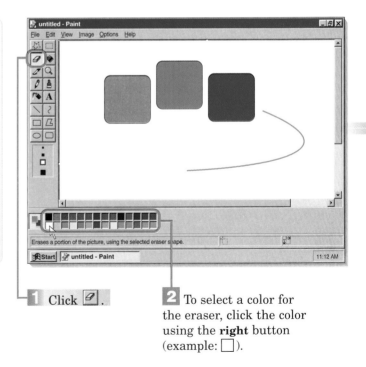

2 To select a color for the eraser, click the color using the **right** button (example: □).

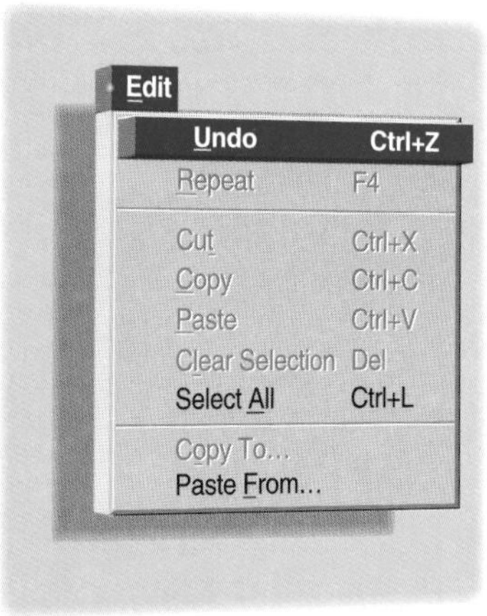

Paint remembers the last change you made to your drawing. If you regret this change, you can cancel it by using the Undo feature.

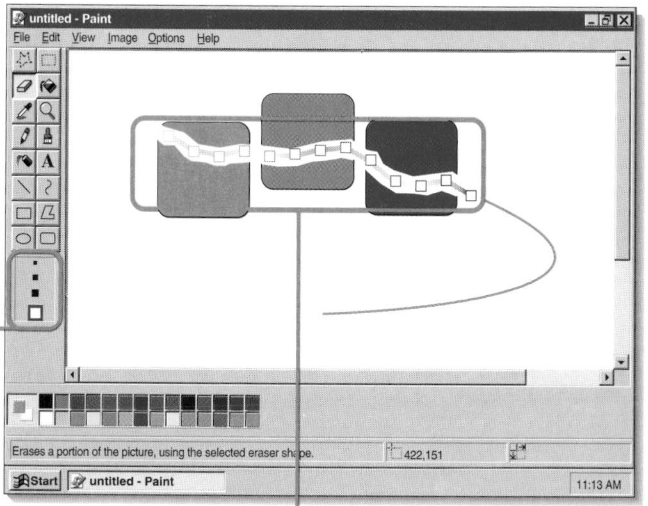

UNDO LAST CHANGE

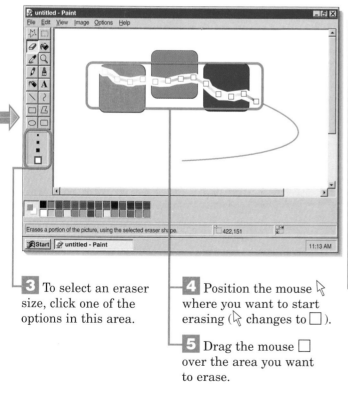

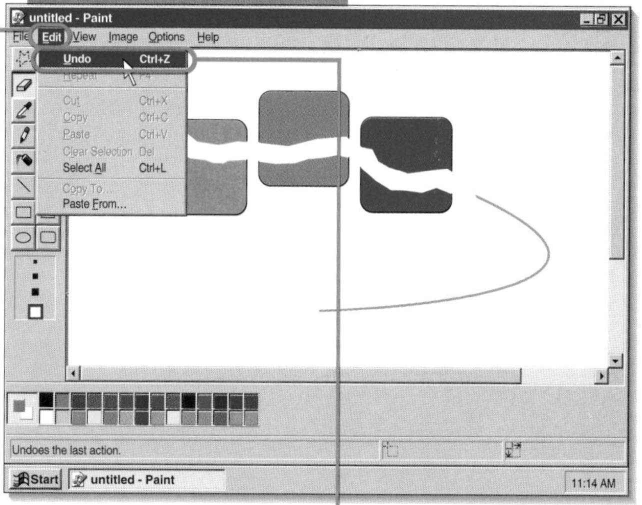

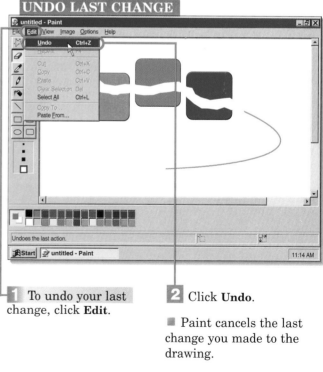

3 To select an eraser size, click one of the options in this area.

4 Position the mouse where you want to start erasing (changes to □).

5 Drag the mouse □ over the area you want to erase.

1 To undo your last change, click **Edit**.

2 Click **Undo**.

■ Paint cancels the last change you made to the drawing.

ADD TEXT

You can add a title or explanation to your drawing.

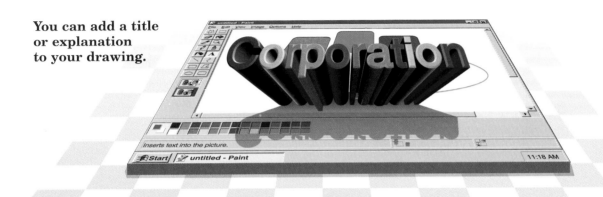

ADD TEXT

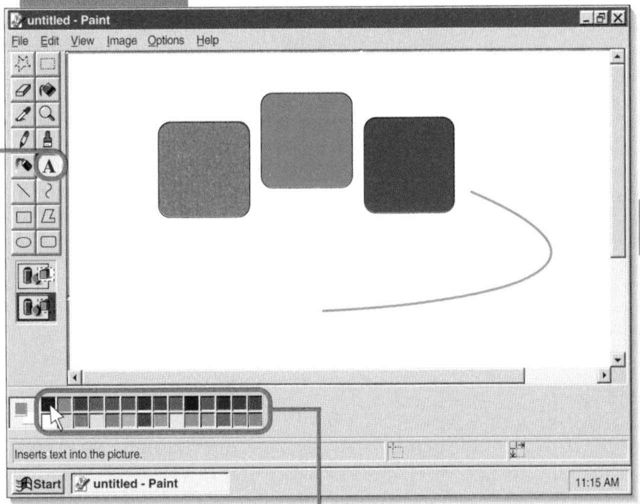

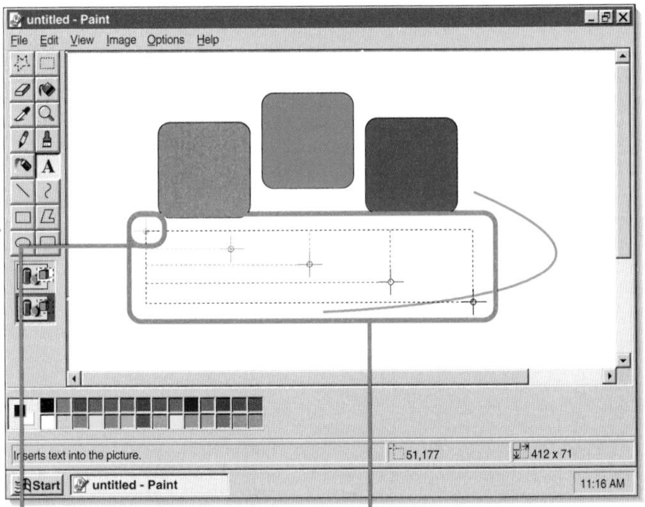

1 Click A.

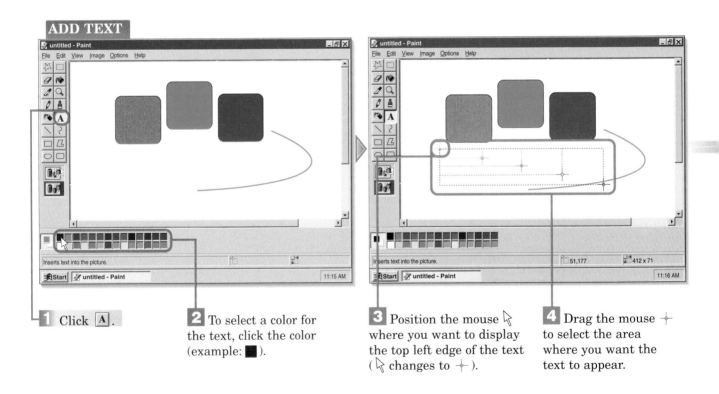

2 To select a color for the text, click the color (example: ■).

3 Position the mouse ↖ where you want to display the top left edge of the text (↖ changes to +).

4 Drag the mouse + to select the area where you want the text to appear.

TIP

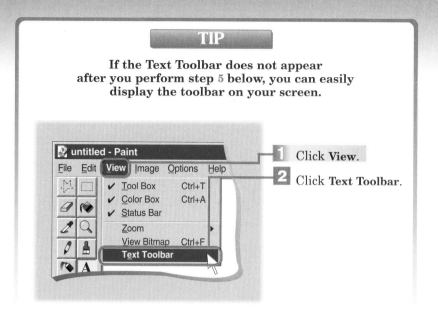

If the Text Toolbar does not appear after you perform step 5 below, you can easily display the toolbar on your screen.

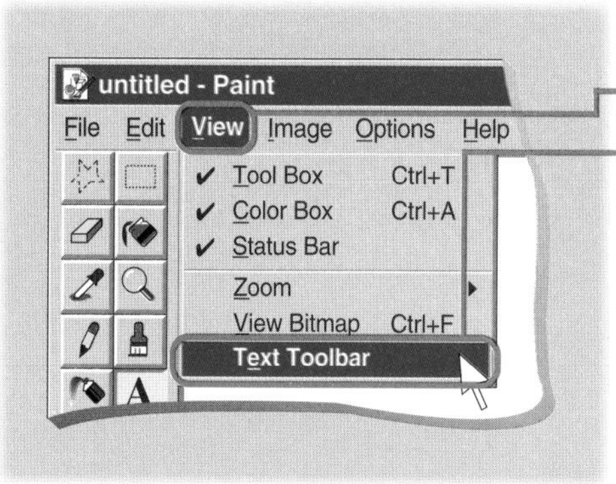

1 Click **View**.

2 Click **Text Toolbar**.

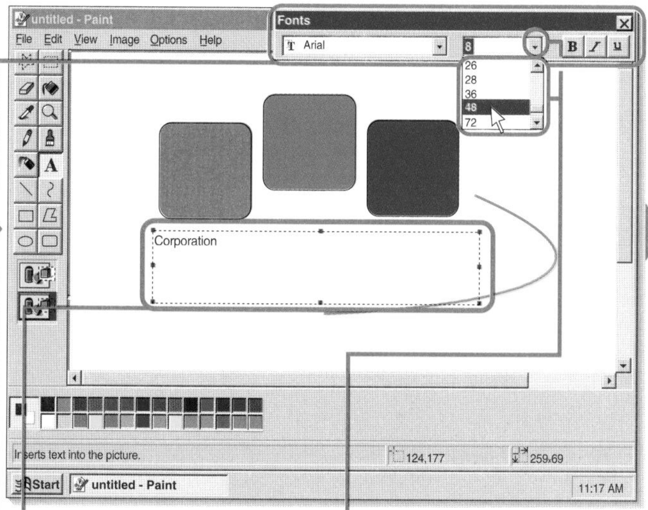

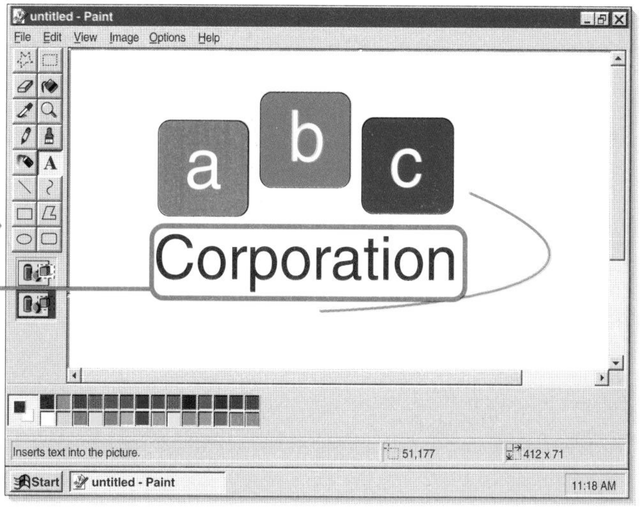

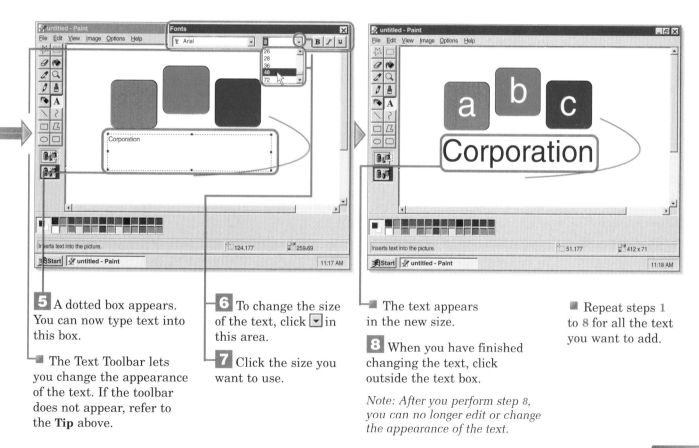

5 A dotted box appears. You can now type text into this box.

■ The Text Toolbar lets you change the appearance of the text. If the toolbar does not appear, refer to the **Tip** above.

6 To change the size of the text, click ▼ in this area.

7 Click the size you want to use.

■ The text appears in the new size.

8 When you have finished changing the text, click outside the text box.

Note: After you perform step 8, you can no longer edit or change the appearance of the text.

■ Repeat steps 1 to 8 for all the text you want to add.

SAVE A DRAWING

You should save your drawing to store it for future use. This lets you later review and make changes to the drawing.

SAVE A DRAWING

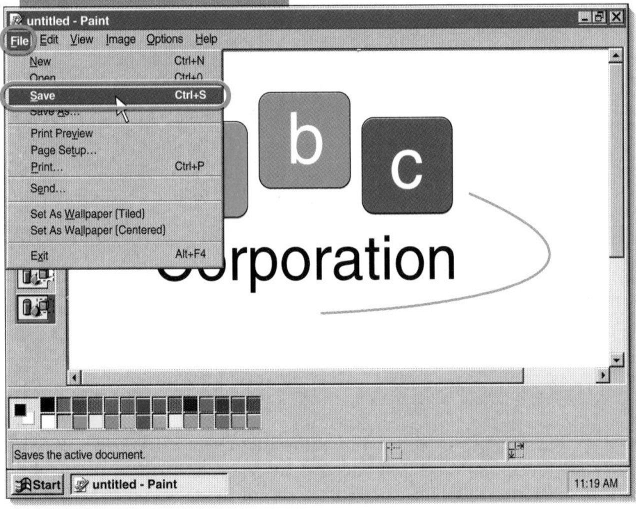

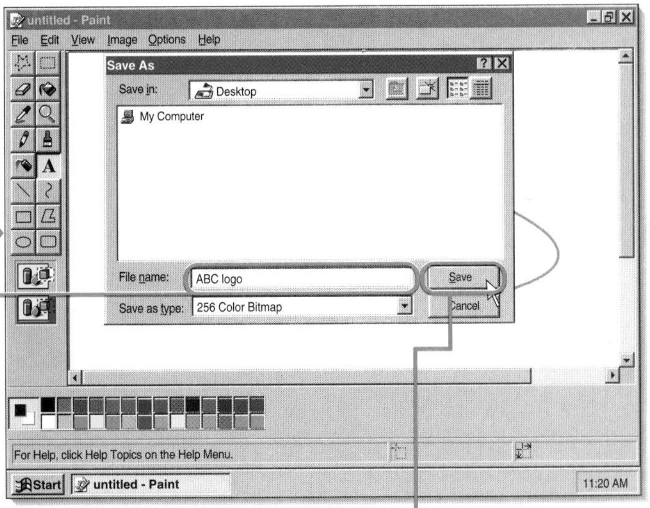

1 Click **File**.

2 Click **Save**.

■ The **Save As** dialog box appears.

Note: If you previously saved your drawing, the ***Save As*** *dialog box will not appear, since you have already named the drawing.*

3 Type a name for your drawing.

*Note: You can use up to 255 characters to name your drawing. The name cannot contain the characters \ ? : * " < > or |.*

4 Click **Save**.

EXIT PAINT

When you finish using Paint, you can exit the program.

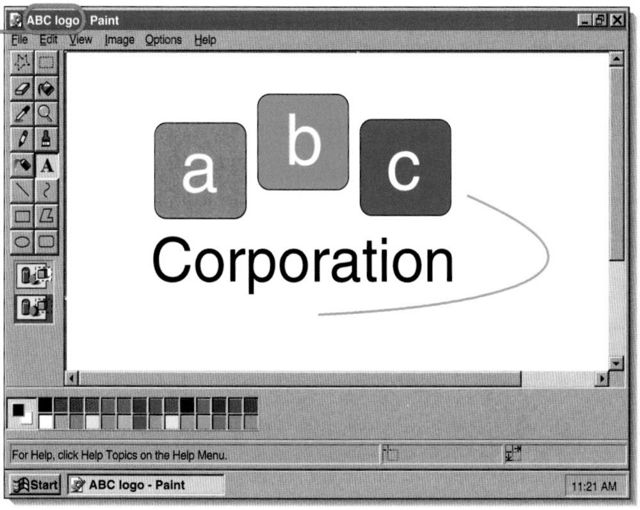

■ Paint saves your drawing and displays the name at the top of your screen.

SAVE CHANGES

To avoid losing your work, you should save your drawing every 5 to 10 minutes.

■ To save changes, repeat steps 1 and 2 on page 40.

EXIT PAINT

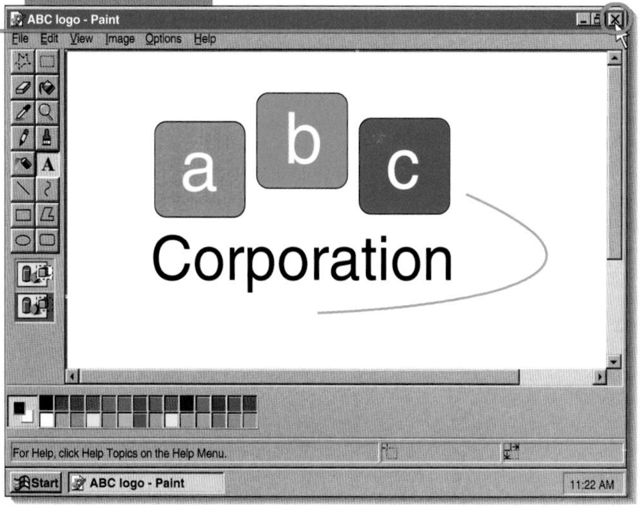

1 To exit Paint, click ☒.

Note: To restart Paint, refer to page 30.

OPEN A DRAWING

You can open a saved drawing and display it on your screen. This lets you view and make changes to the drawing.

OPEN A DRAWING

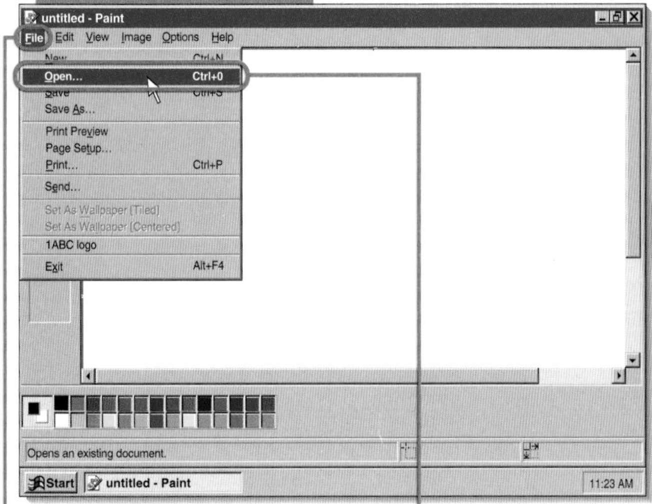

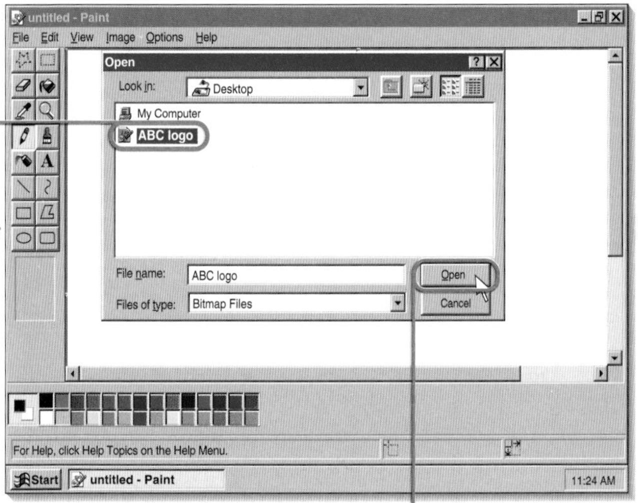

1 Click **File**.

2 Click **Open**.

■ The **Open** dialog box appears.

3 Click the name of the drawing you want to open.

Note: If you cannot find the drawing you want to open, refer to page 90 to find the drawing.

4 Click **Open**.

IMPORTANT

Paint only lets you work with one drawing at a time. If you are currently working with a drawing, save the drawing before opening another.

Note: For information on saving a drawing, refer to page 40.

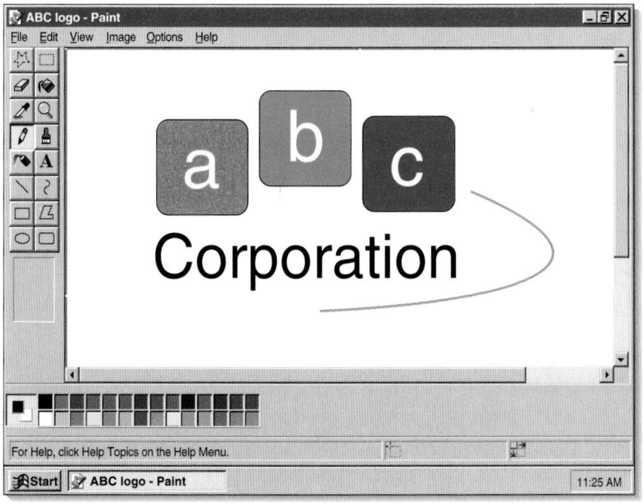

■ Paint opens the drawing and displays it on your screen. You can now review and make changes to the drawing.

QUICKLY OPEN A DRAWING

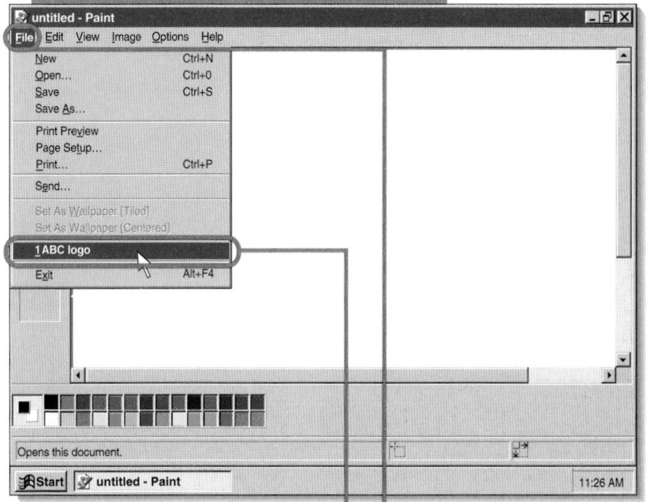

The File menu displays the names of the last four drawings you opened.

Note: In this example, only one drawing has been opened.

1 To quickly open a drawing, click **File**.

2 Click the name of the drawing you want to open.

In this chapter you will learn how to view the information stored on your computer.

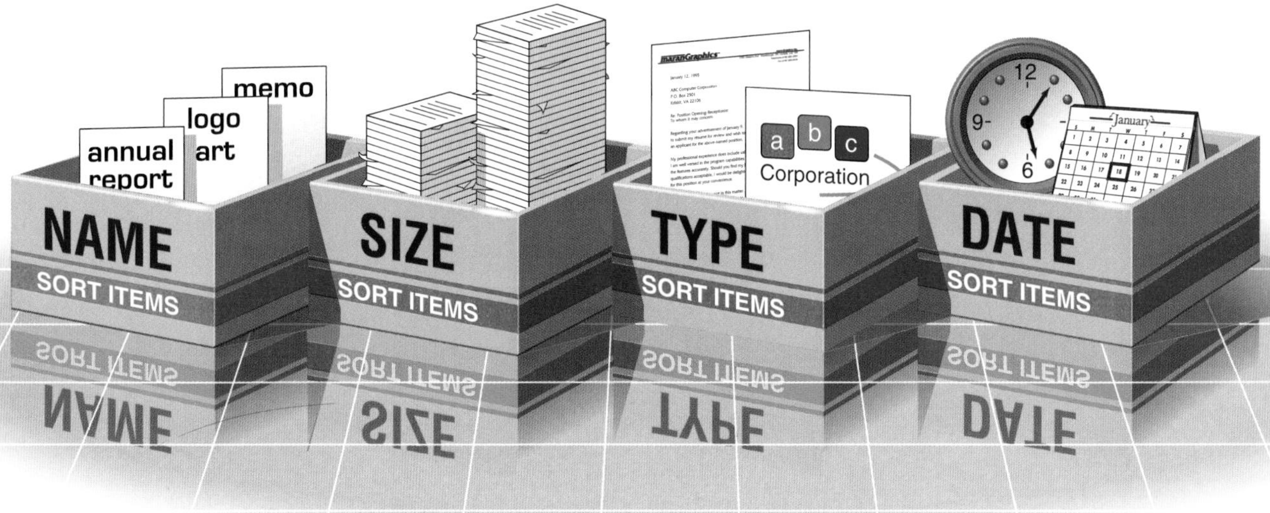

CHAPTER 4: VIEW CONTENTS OF COMPUTER

Storage Devices . . . . *.46*

View Contents of Computer . . . . *.48*

Change Size of Items . . . . *.50*

Move an Item . . . . *.51*

Arrange Items . . . . *.52*

Display File Information . . . . *.54*

Sort Items . . . . *.56*

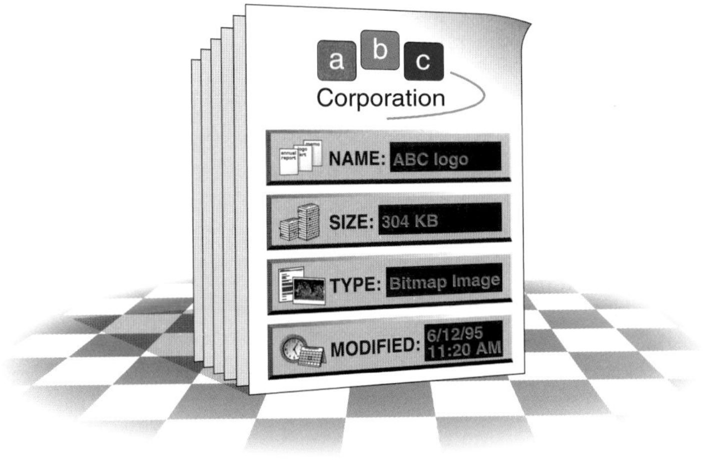

STORAGE DEVICES

HARD DRIVE (C:)

The hard drive is the primary device your computer uses to store information.

Most computers come with one hard drive, located inside the computer case. The hard drive is usually called drive C.

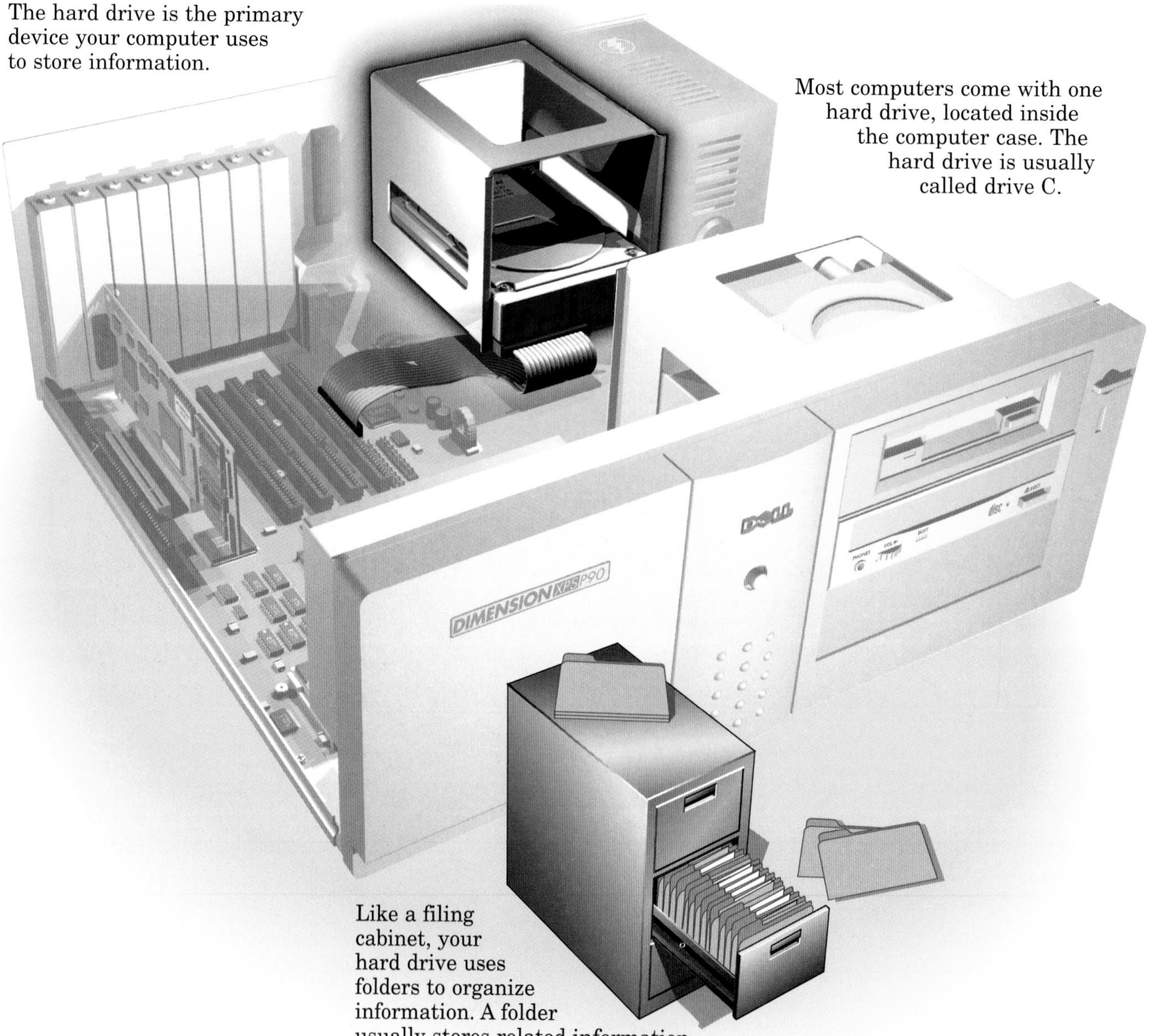

Like a filing cabinet, your hard drive uses folders to organize information. A folder usually stores related information and can contain documents and other folders.

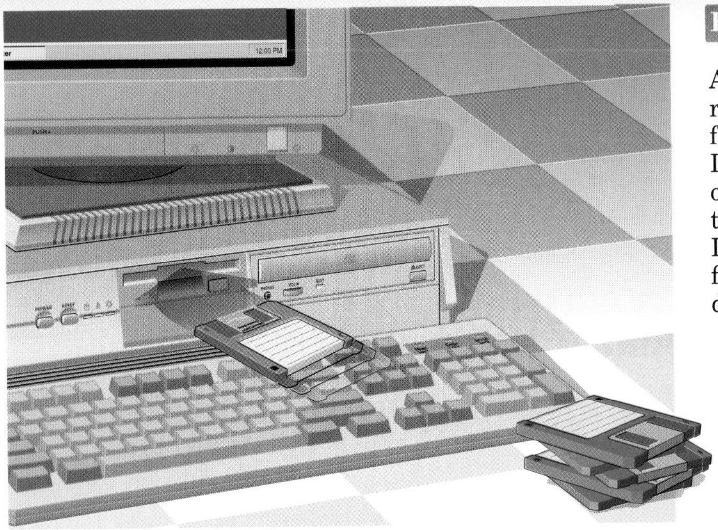

FLOPPY DRIVE (A:)

A floppy drive stores and retrieves information on floppy disks (diskettes). If your computer has only one floppy drive, the drive is called drive A. If your computer has two floppy drives, the second drive is called drive B.

CD-ROM DRIVE (D:)

A CD-ROM drive is a device that reads information stored on compact discs. You cannot change information stored on a compact disc.

Note: Your computer may not have a CD-ROM drive.

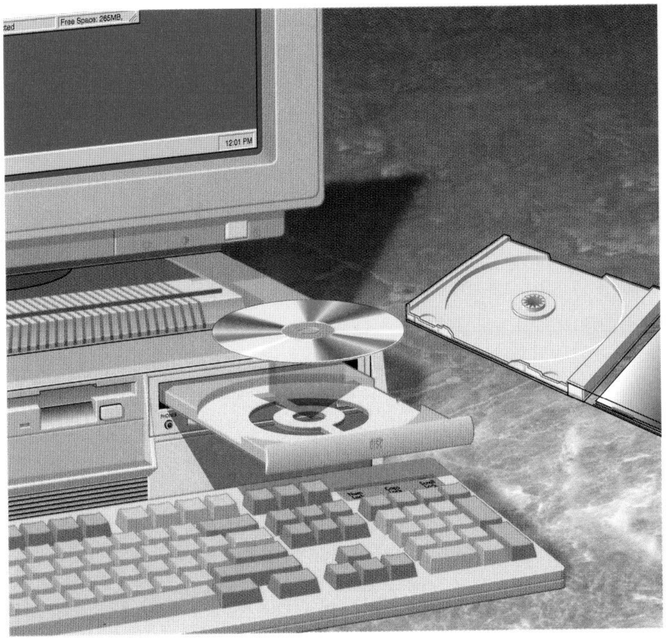

VIEW CONTENTS OF COMPUTER

You can easily view the folders and files stored on your computer.

VIEW CONTENTS OF COMPUTER

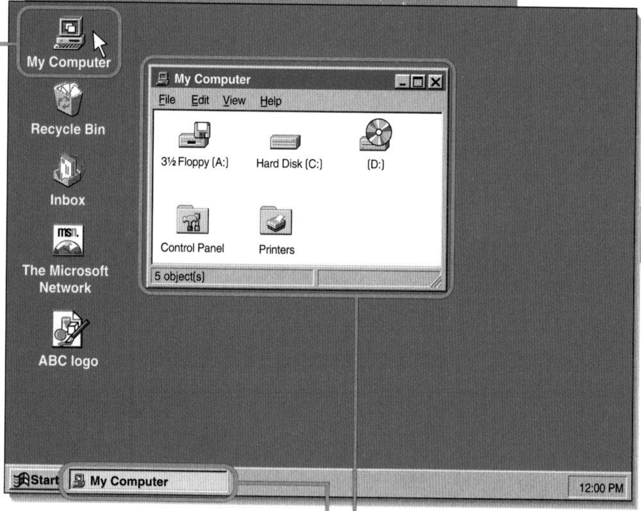

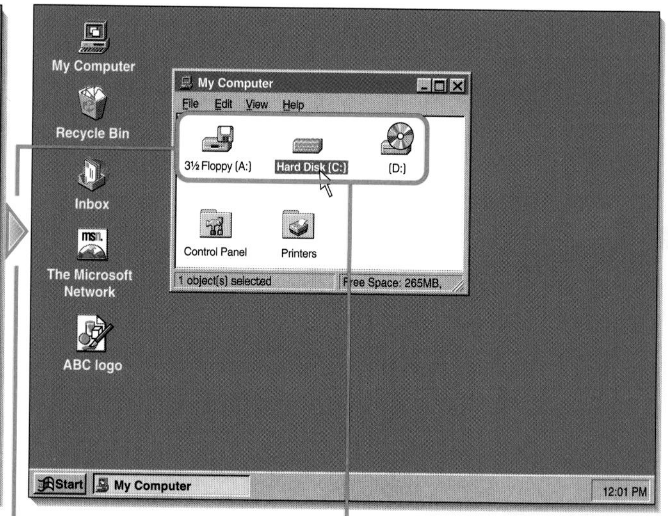

1 To view the contents of your computer, double-click **My Computer**.

■ The **My Computer** window appears.

■ The taskbar displays the name of the open window.

■ These objects represent the drives on your computer.

2 To display the contents of a drive, double-click the drive.

Note: If you want to view the contents of a floppy or CD-ROM drive, make sure you insert a floppy disk or CD-ROM disc before performing step 2.

TIP

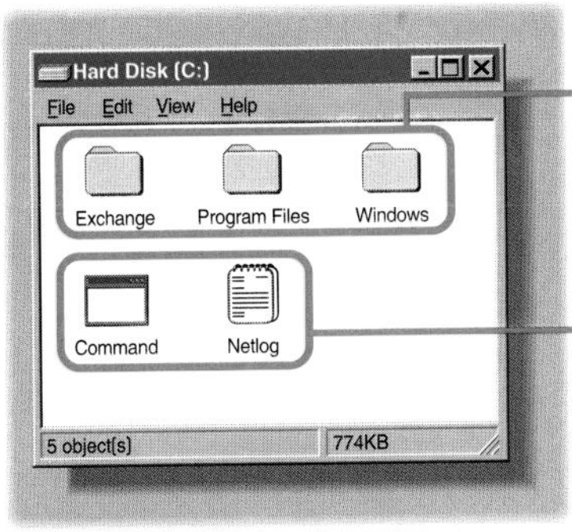

Folder

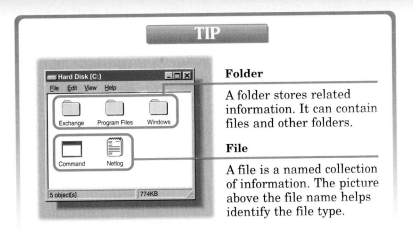

A folder stores related information. It can contain files and other folders.

File

A file is a named collection of information. The picture above the file name helps identify the file type.

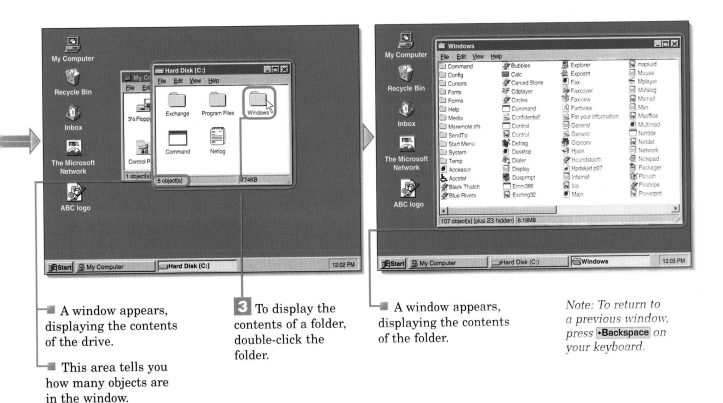

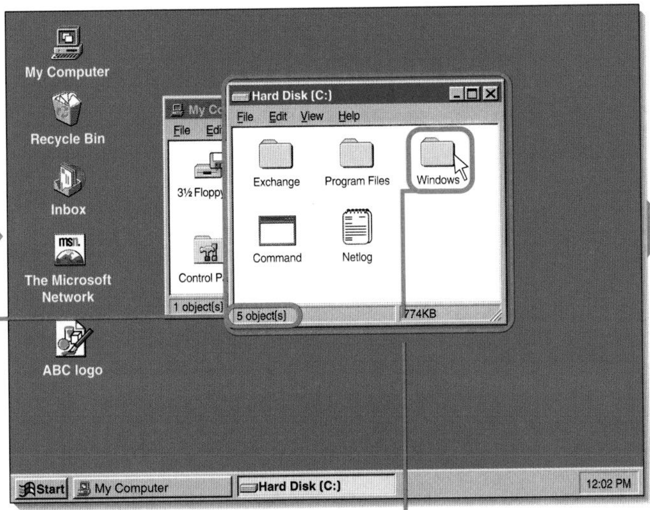

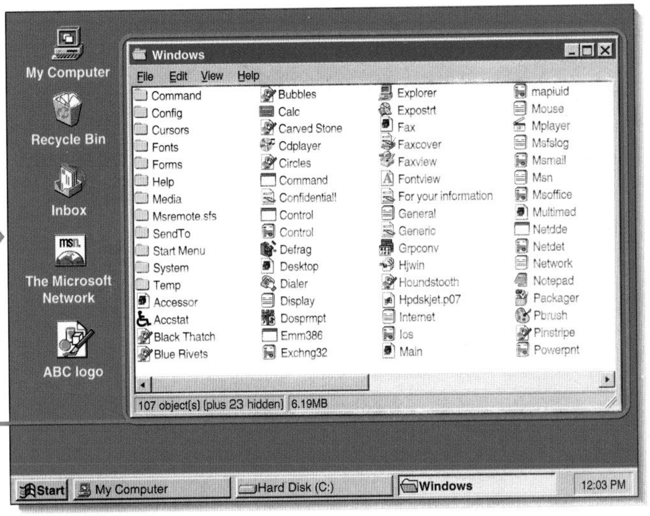

■ A window appears, displaying the contents of the drive.

■ This area tells you how many objects are in the window.

3 To display the contents of a folder, double-click the folder.

■ A window appears, displaying the contents of the folder.

Note: To return to a previous window, press **←Backspace** *on your keyboard.*

CHANGE SIZE OF ITEMS

You can change the size of items displayed in a window. Enlarging items lets you view the items more clearly.

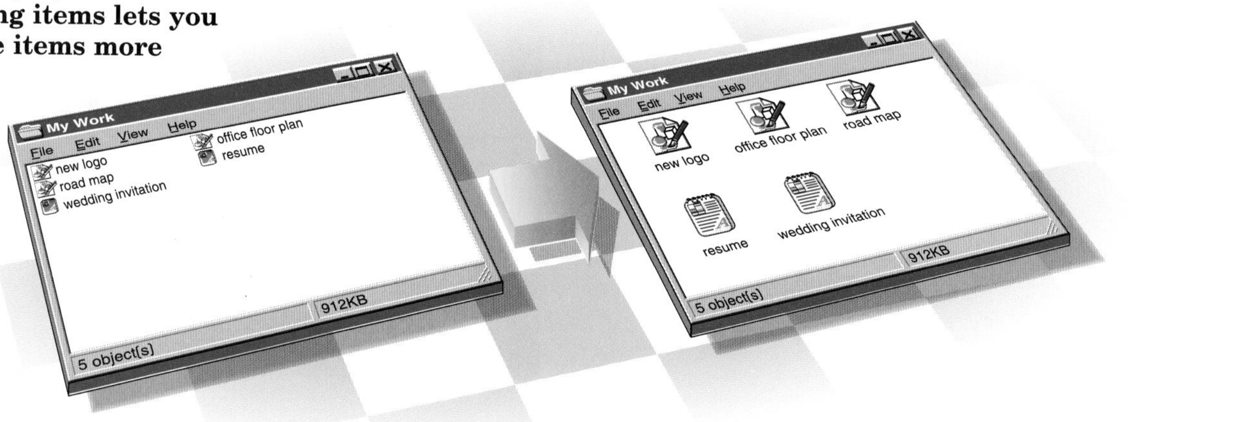

CHANGE SIZE OF ITEMS

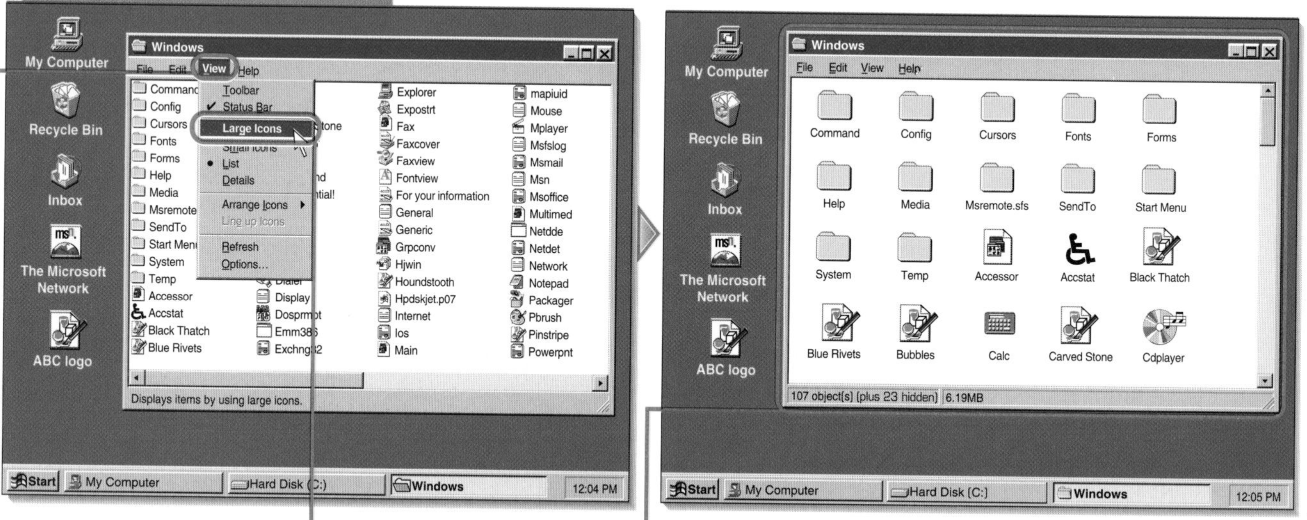

1 Click **View**.

2 To enlarge the items in a window, click **Large Icons**.

■ The items change to a larger size.

*Note: To return to the smaller item size, repeat steps 1 and 2, selecting **Small Icons** in step 2.*

You can move an item to a new location in a window. This lets you rearrange items as you would rearrange objects on your desk.

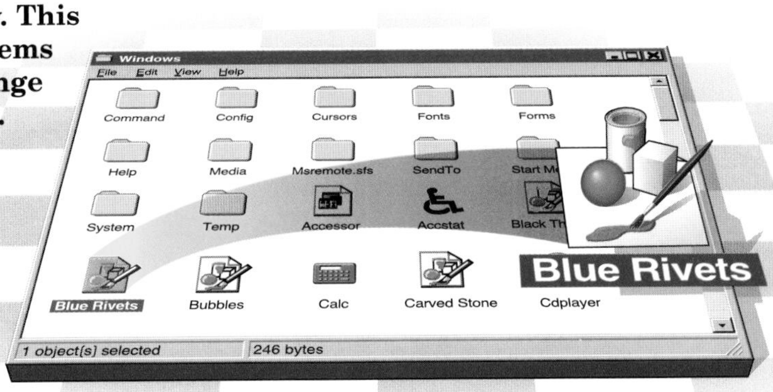

MOVE AN ITEM

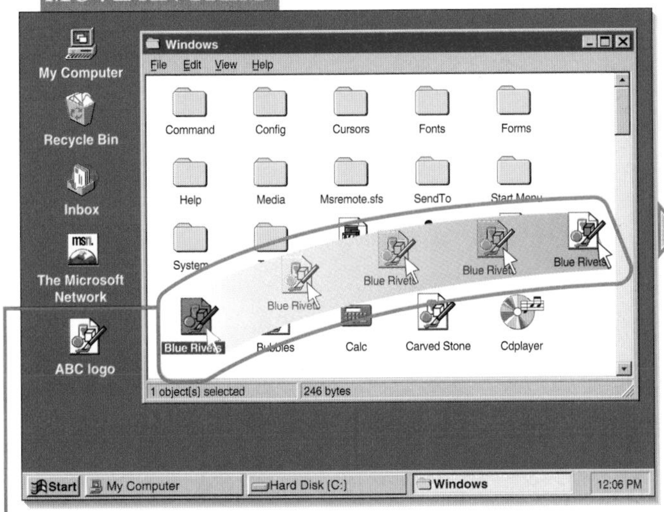

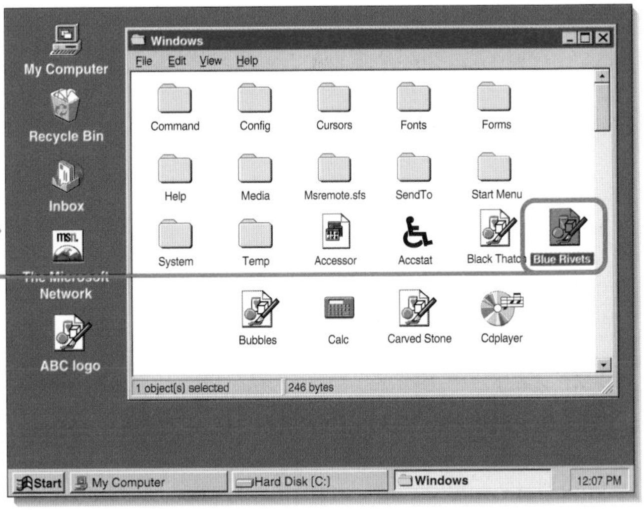

1 Drag the item you want to move to a new location.

2 The item moves to the new location.

Note: If the ***Auto Arrange*** *feature is on, other items will automatically adjust to make room for the item. For more information,* *refer to page 52.*

ARRANGE ITEMS

You can have Windows automatically arrange items to fit neatly in a window.

ARRANGE ITEMS

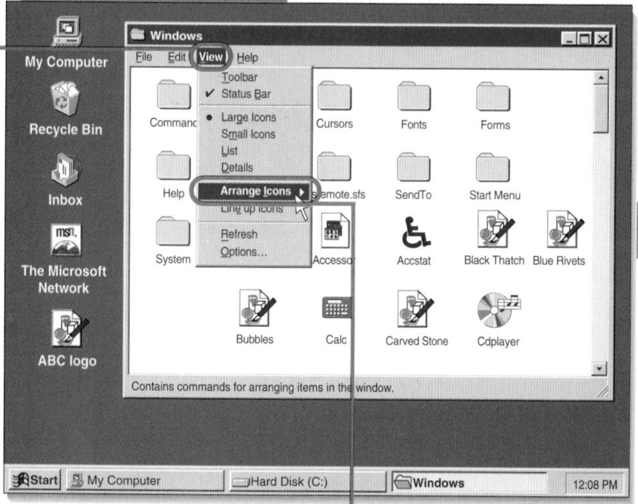

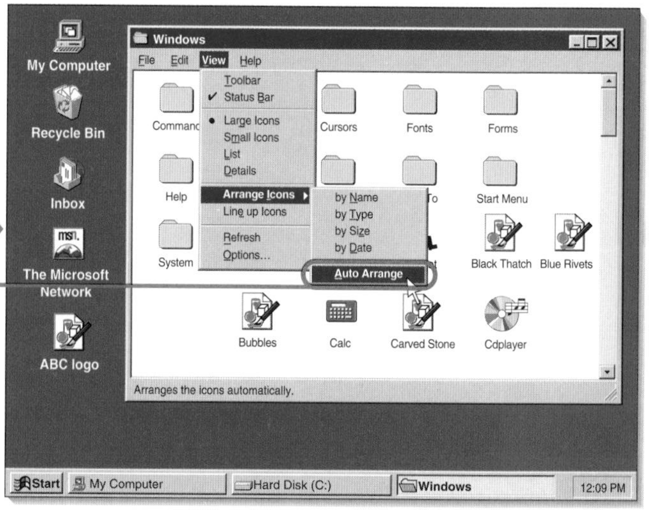

1 Click **View**.

2 Click **Arrange Icons**.

■ If this area does not display a check mark (✔), the Auto Arrange feature is off.

3 To turn on the feature, click **Auto Arrange**.

Note: If the area displays a check mark (✔) and you want to leave the feature on, press **Alt** *on your keyboard to close the menu.*

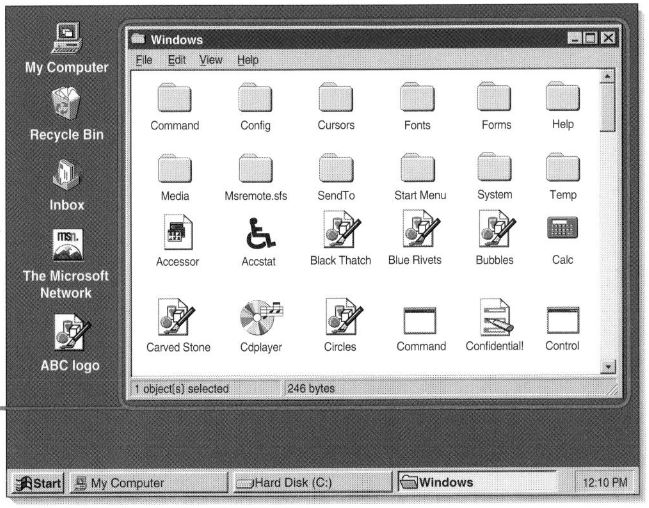

■ The items fit neatly in the window.

■ To turn off the Auto Arrange feature, repeat steps 1 to 3.

Note: You cannot move an item to a blank area in a window when the Auto Arrange feature is on.

TIP

If you change the size of a window when the Auto Arrange feature is on, Windows will automatically rearrange the items to fit the new size.

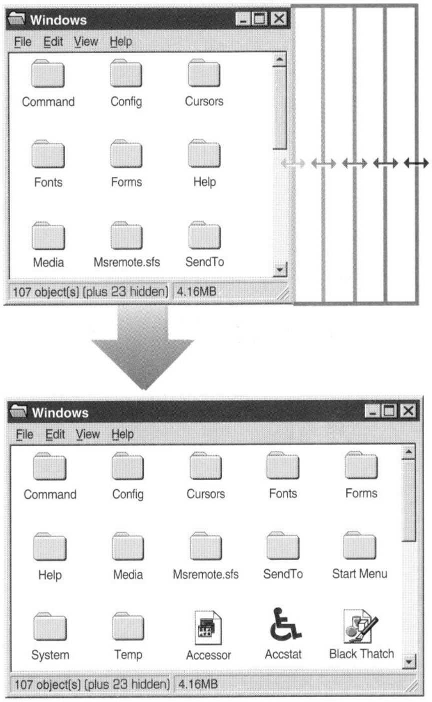

Note: For information on changing the size of a window, refer to page 15.

DISPLAY FILE INFORMATION

Windows lets you display information about the files listed in a window.

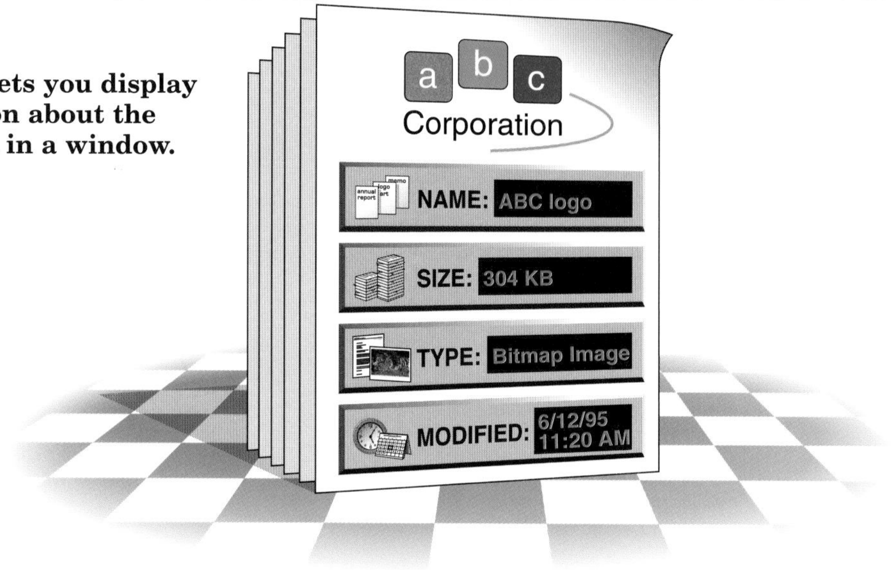

DISPLAY FILE INFORMATION

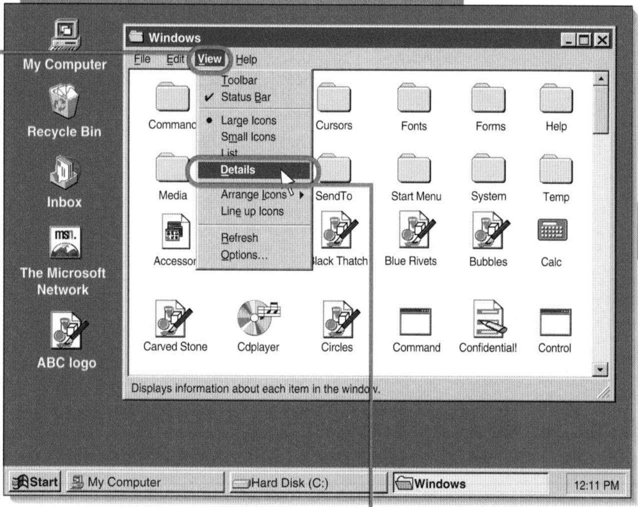

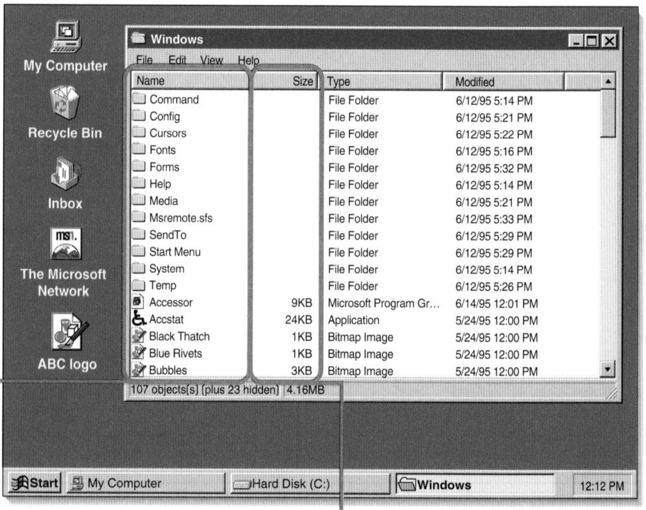

1 Click **View**.

2 Click **Details**.

■ This column displays the name of each file.

■ This column displays the size of each file.

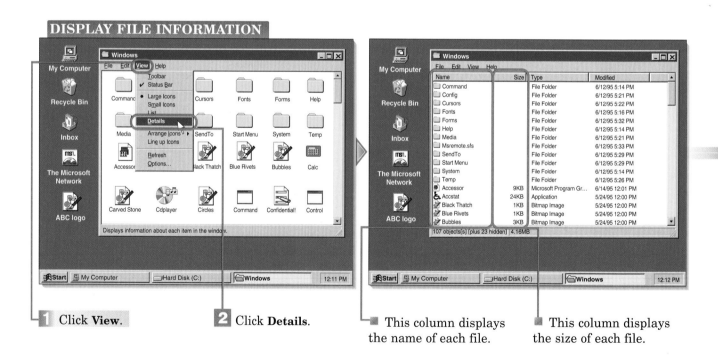

TIP

The size of a file is measured in kilobytes (KB). A kilobyte is approximately 1,000 characters, or one page of double-spaced text.

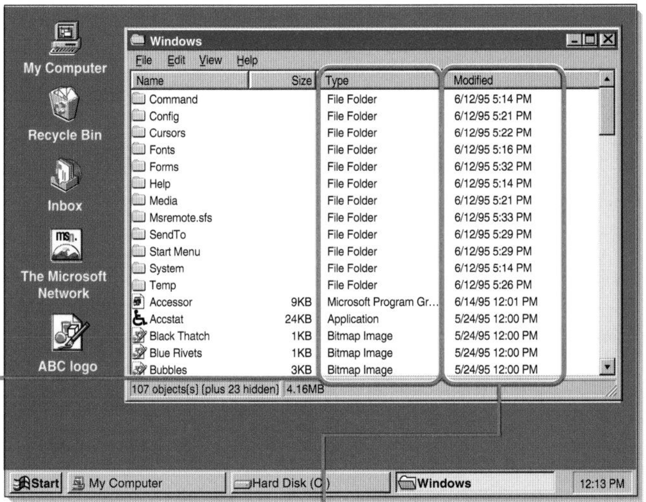

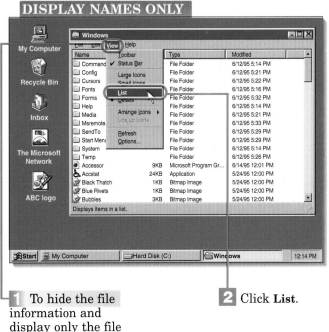

- This column displays the file types.
- This column displays the date and time each file was last changed.

DISPLAY NAMES ONLY

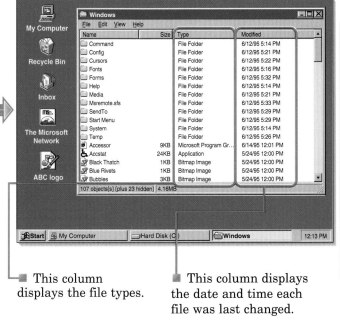

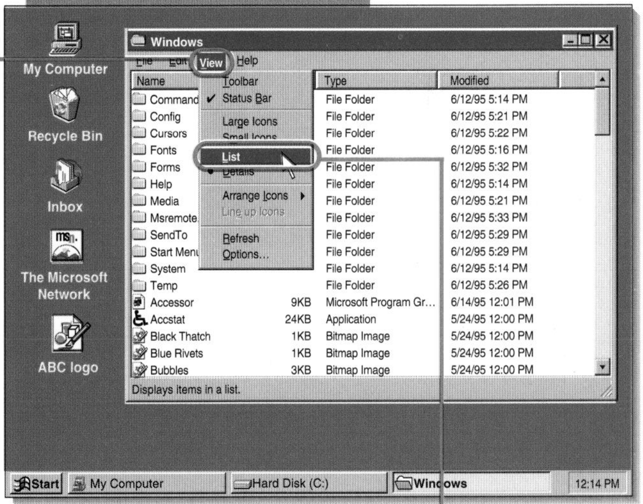

1 To hide the file information and display only the file names, click **View**.

2 Click **List**.

SORT ITEMS

You can sort the items displayed in a window. This can help you find files and folders more easily.

SORT BY NAME

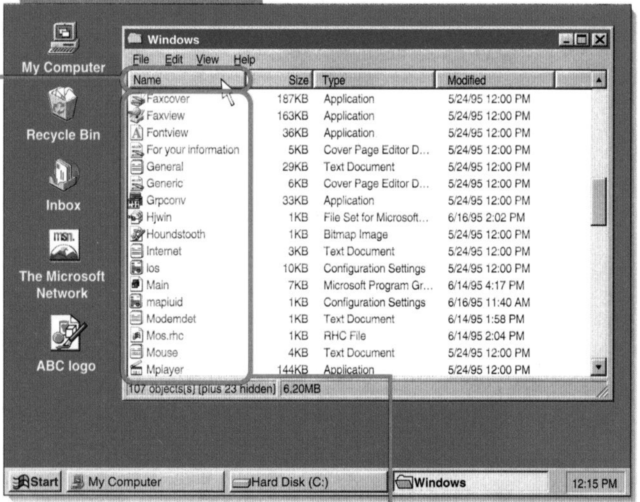

1 To sort the item names from A to Z, click **Name**.

Note: If the **Name** *button is not displayed, perform steps 1 and 2 on page 54.*

■ The items in the window are sorted.

■ To sort the item names from Z to A, repeat step 1.

SORT BY SIZE

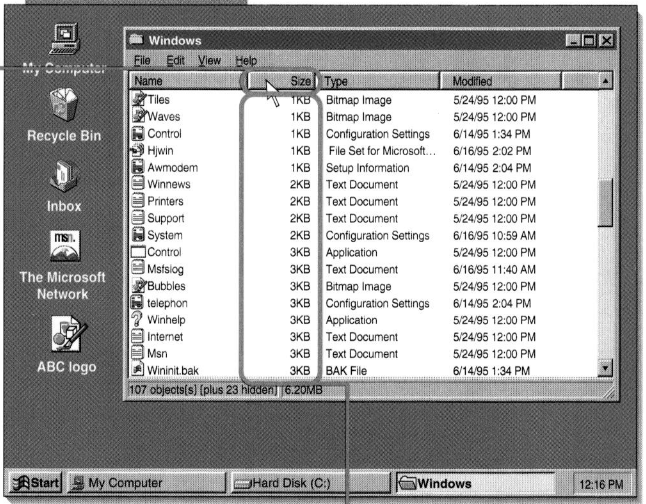

1 To sort the items from smallest to largest, click **Size**.

Note: If the **Size** *button is not displayed, perform steps 1 and 2 on page 54.*

■ The items in the window are sorted.

■ To sort the items from largest to smallest, repeat step 1.

TIP

No matter how you sort items, Windows always lists the folders separately from the files.

SORT BY TYPE

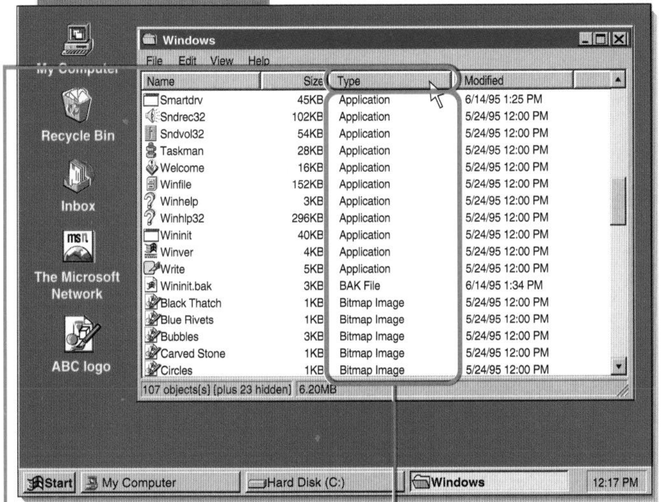

1 To sort the item types from A to Z, click **Type**.

*Note: If the **Type** button is not displayed, perform steps 1 and 2 on page 54.*

■ The items in the window are sorted.

■ To sort the item types from Z to A, repeat step 1.

SORT BY DATE

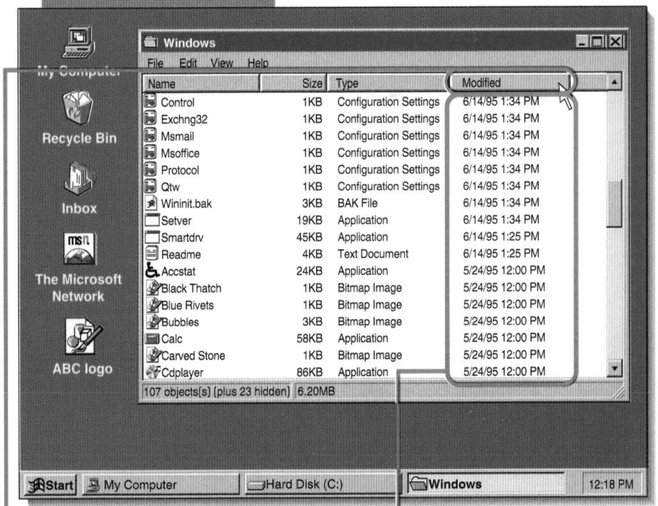

1 To sort the items from newest to oldest, click **Modified**.

*Note: If the **Modified** button is not displayed, perform steps 1 and 2 on page 54.*

■ The items in the window are sorted.

■ To sort the items from oldest to newest, repeat step 1.

In this chapter you will learn how to work with files and folders stored on your computer.

CHAPTER 5: WORK WITH FILES AND FOLDERS

Select Files 60

Create a New Folder .62

Move a File to a Folder 64

Copy a File to a Floppy Disk 66

Rename a File 68

Open a File 70

Open a Recently Used File 71

Preview a File 72

Print a File 74

View Files Sent to the Printer 75

Pause the Printer 76

Cancel Printing 77

Delete a File 78

Restore a Deleted File 80

Empty the Recycle Bin 82

Start Windows Explorer 84

Display or Hide Folders 86

SELECT FILES

Before working with files, you must first select the files you want to work with. Selected files appear highlighted on your screen.

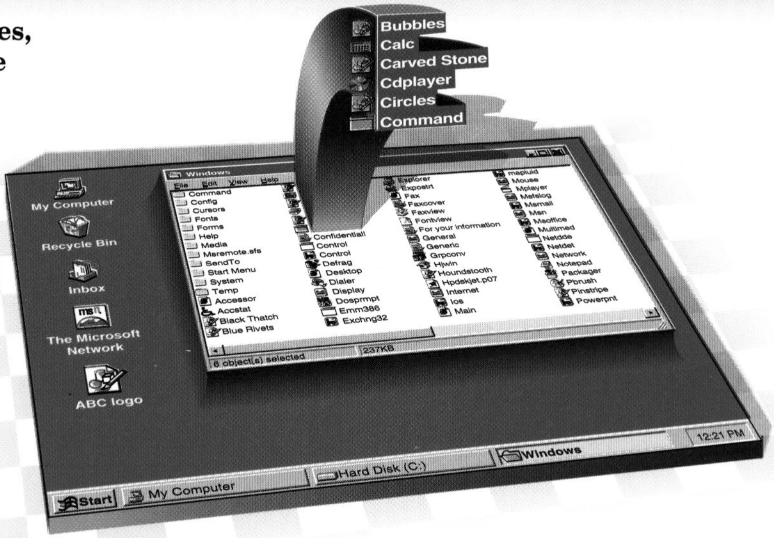

SELECT A FILE

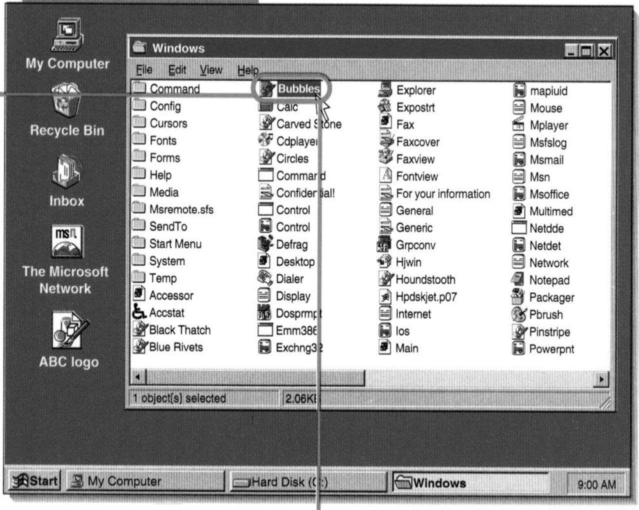

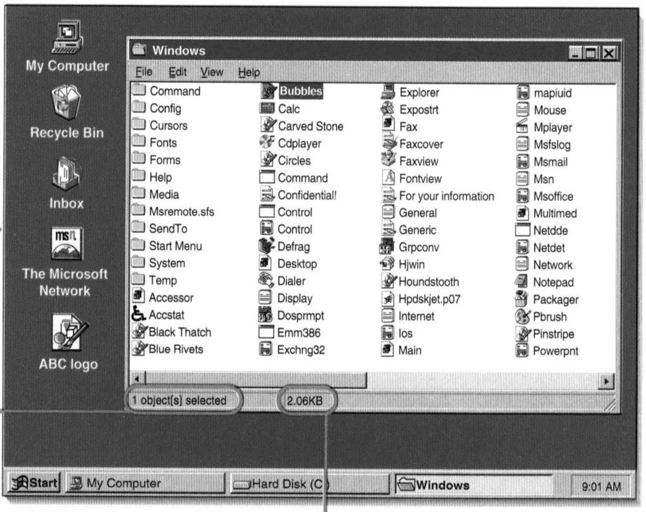

1 Click the file you want to select.

■ The file is highlighted.

Note: To deselect files, click a blank area in the window.

■ This area displays the number of files you selected.

■ This area displays the total size of the files you selected.

Note: One byte equals one character. One kilobyte (KB) equals approximately one page of double-spaced text.

TIP

SELECT FOLDERS

You can select folders the same way you select files.

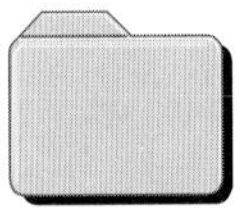

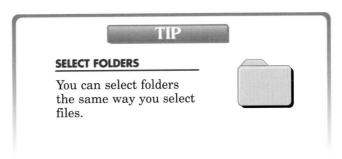

SELECT A GROUP OF FILES

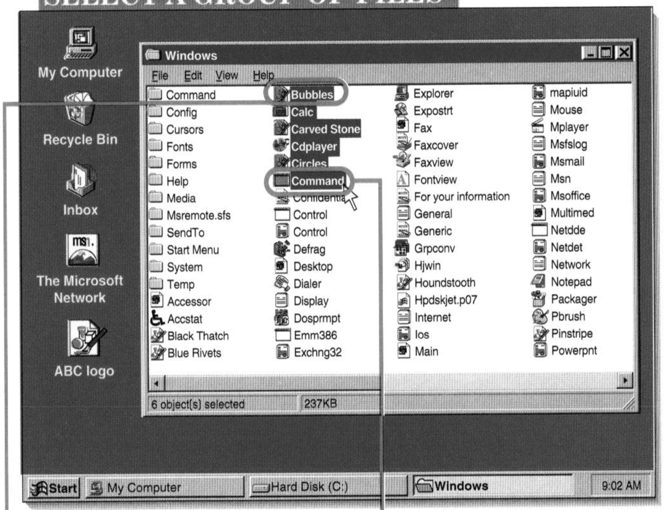

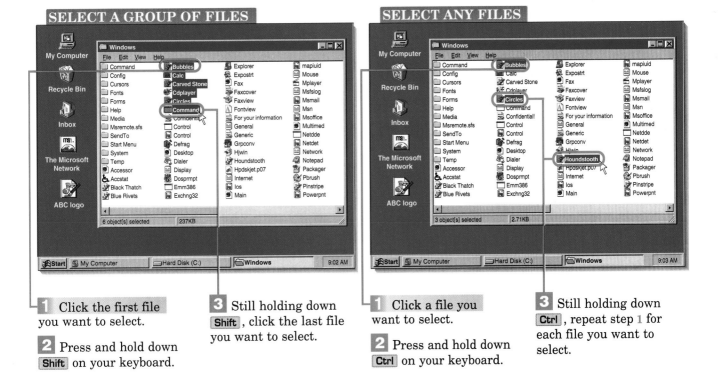

1 Click the first file you want to select.

2 Press and hold down **Shift** on your keyboard.

3 Still holding down **Shift**, click the last file you want to select.

SELECT ANY FILES

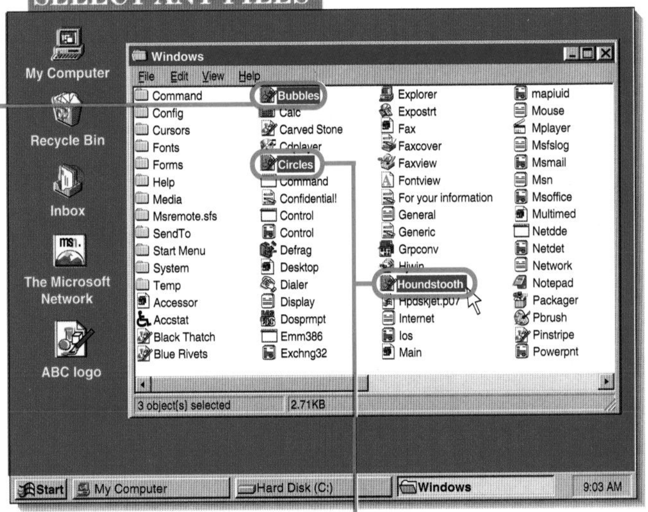

1 Click a file you want to select.

2 Press and hold down **Ctrl** on your keyboard.

3 Still holding down **Ctrl**, repeat step 1 for each file you want to select.

CREATE A NEW FOLDER

You can create a new folder to better organize the information stored on your computer. Creating a folder is like placing a new folder in a filing cabinet.

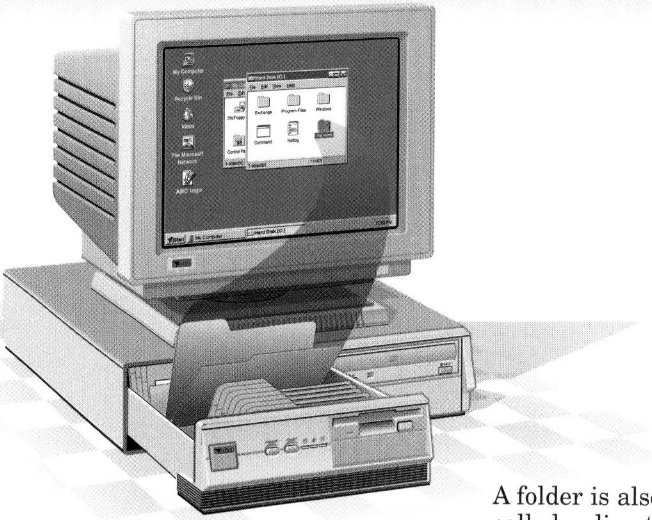

A folder is also called a directory.

CREATE A NEW FOLDER

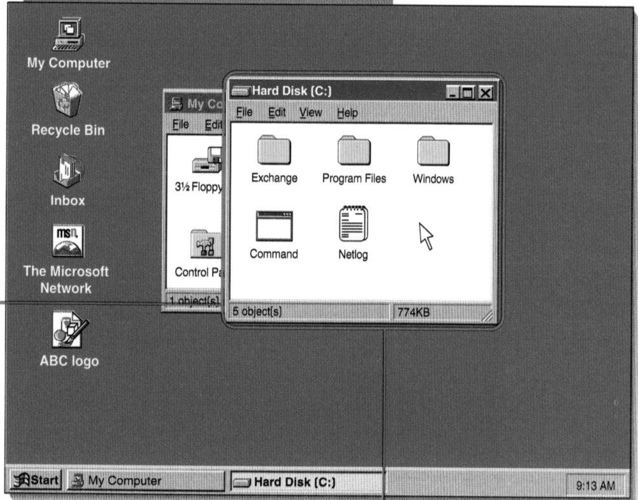

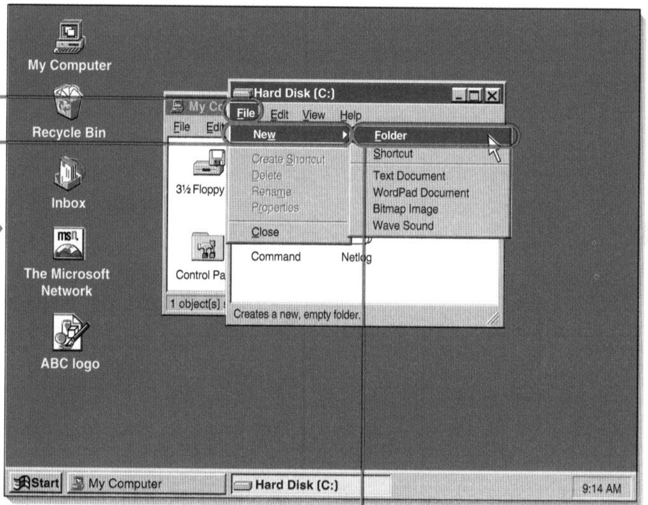

1 Display the contents of the drive or folder where you want to place the new folder.

Note: For more information, refer to page 48.

2 To deselect any selected files, click a blank area in the window.

3 Click **File**.

4 Click **New**.

5 Click **Folder**.

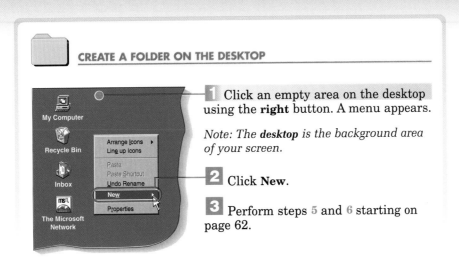

CREATE A FOLDER ON THE DESKTOP

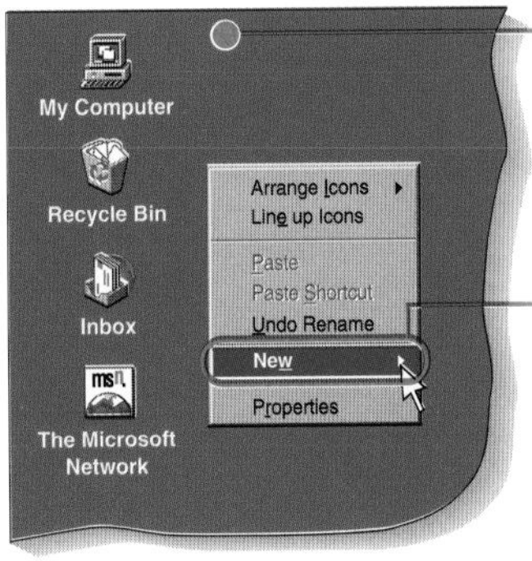

1 Click an empty area on the desktop using the **right** button. A menu appears.

*Note: The **desktop** is the background area of your screen.*

2 Click **New**.

3 Perform steps 5 and 6 starting on page 62.

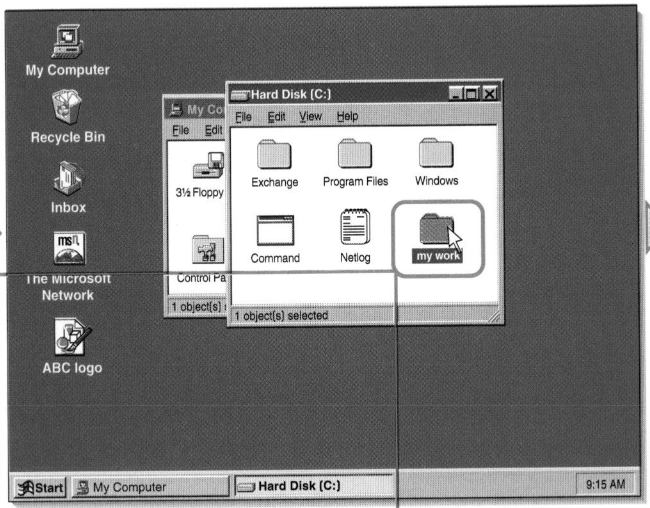

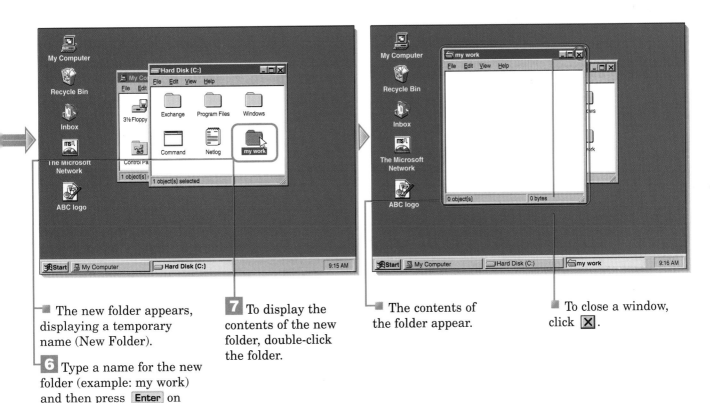

■ The new folder appears, displaying a temporary name (New Folder).

6 Type a name for the new folder (example: my work) and then press **Enter** on your keyboard.

7 To display the contents of the new folder, double-click the folder.

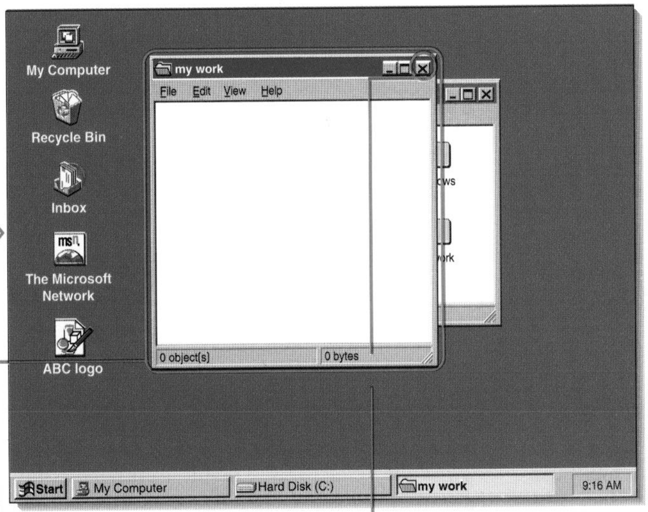

■ The contents of the folder appear.

■ To close a window, click ☒.

MOVE A FILE TO A FOLDER

You can organize the files stored on your computer by placing them in folders.

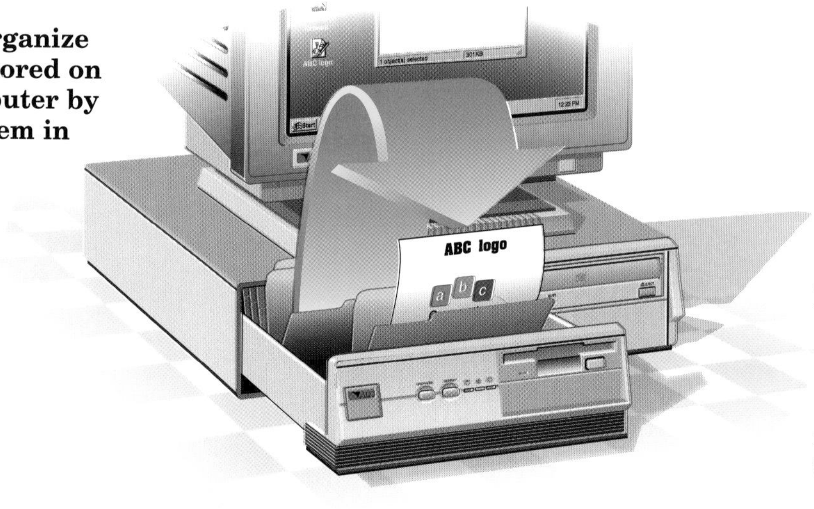

Moving files to folders is similar to rearranging documents in a filing cabinet to make them easier to find.

MOVE A FILE TO A FOLDER

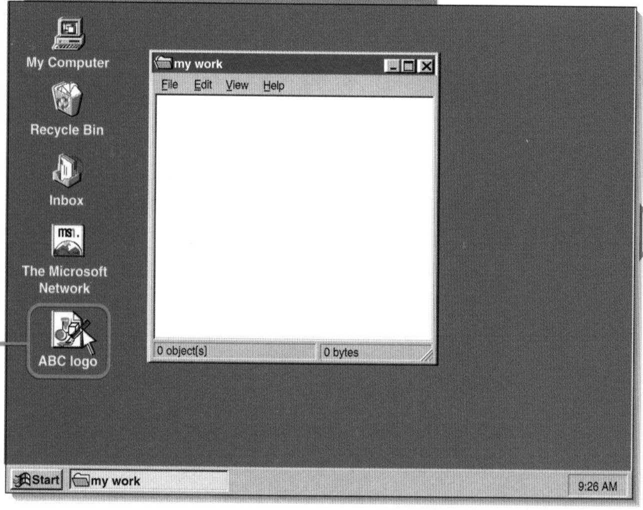

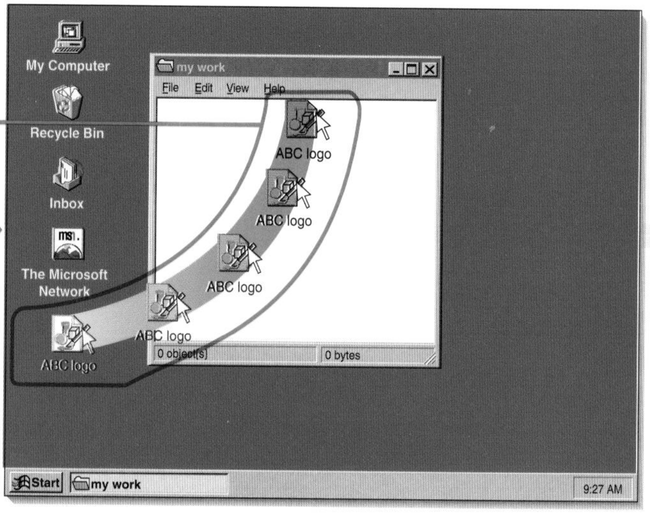

1 Position the mouse over the file you want to move.

■ To move more than one file, select all the files you want to move. Then position the mouse over one of the files.

Note: To select multiple files, refer to page 61.

2 Drag the file to a folder.

TIP

You can move a folder and all the files it contains.

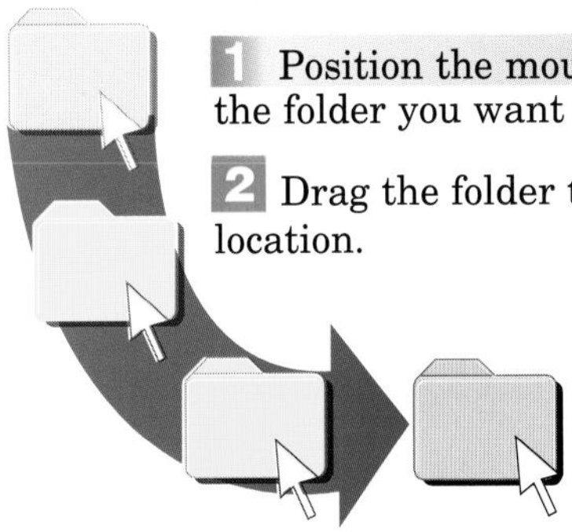

1 Position the mouse over the folder you want to move.

2 Drag the folder to a new location.

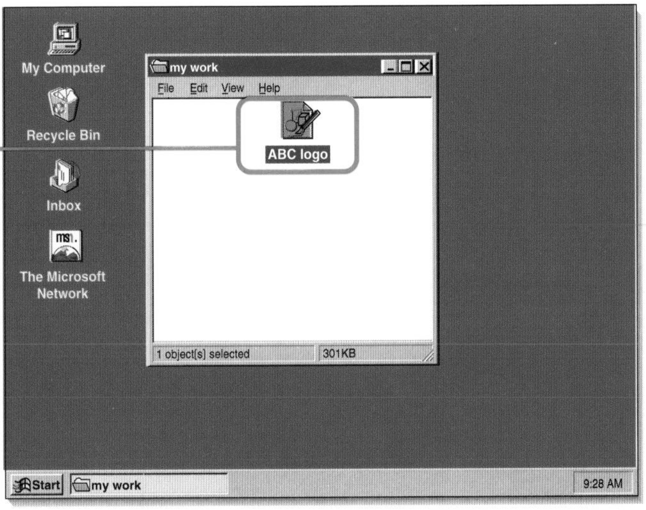

■ The file moves to the folder.

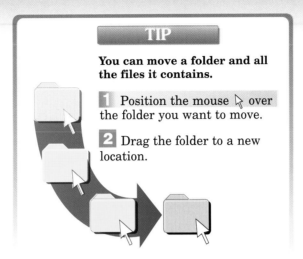

COPY A FILE TO A FOLDER

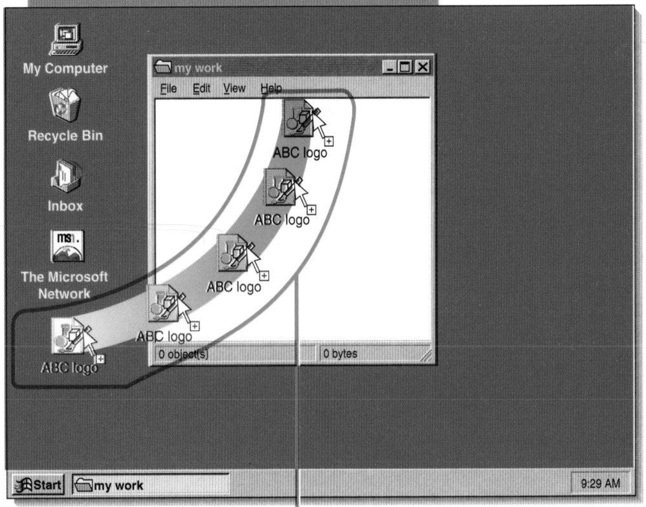

You can make an exact copy of a file and then place the copy in a folder. This lets you store the file in two locations.

1 Press and hold down Ctrl on your keyboard.

2 Still holding down Ctrl, drag the file to the folder.

COPY A FILE TO A FLOPPY DISK

You can make an exact copy of a file and then place the copy on a floppy disk. This is useful if you want to give a copy of a file to a colleague.

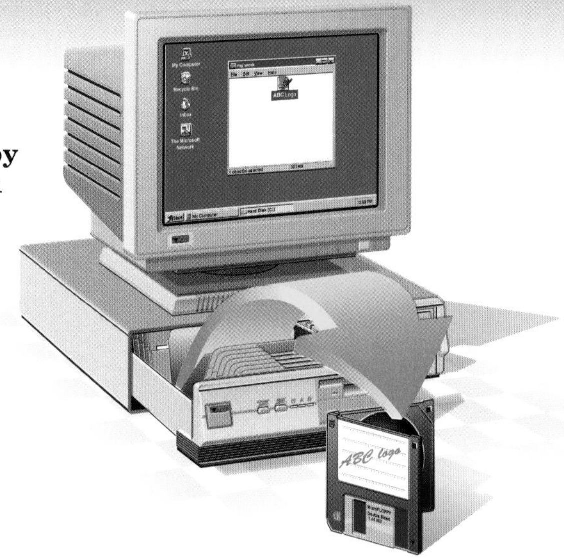

COPY A FILE TO A FLOPPY DISK

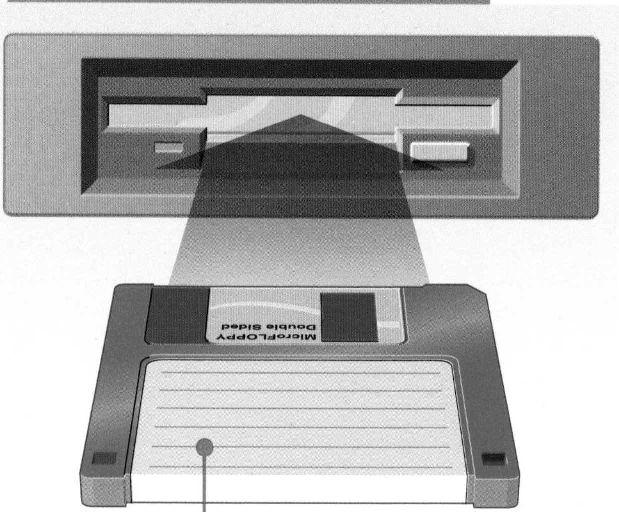

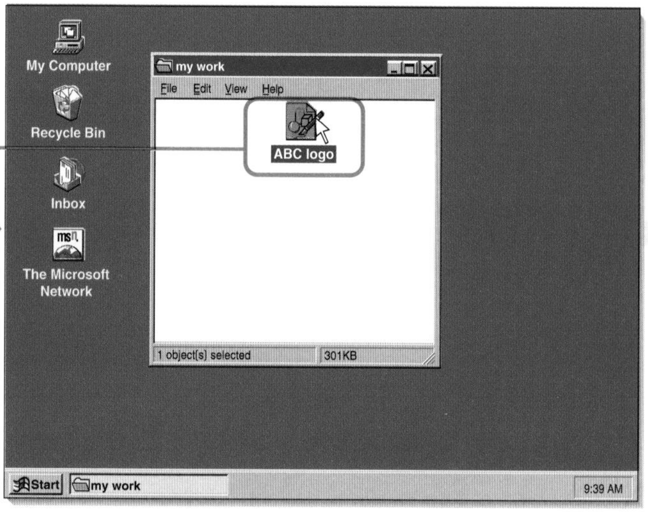

1 Insert a floppy disk into a drive.

2 Click the file you want to copy.

■ To copy more than one file, select all the files you want to copy.

Note: To select multiple files, refer to page 61.

TIP

Windows provides a backup program that helps you copy all your important files to floppy disks. This provides you with extra copies in case the original files are lost or damaged.

Note: To back up files, refer to the Back Up Your Files chapter starting on page 228.

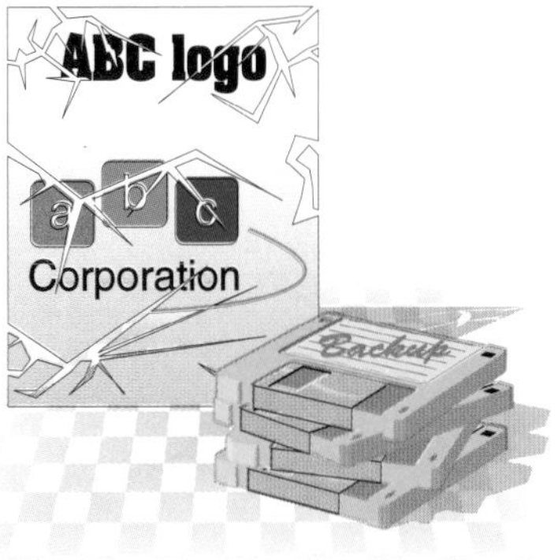

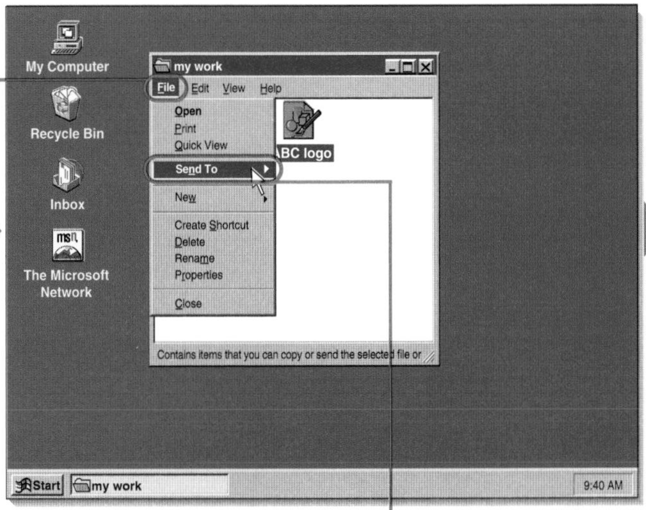

3 Click **File**.

4 Click **Send To**.

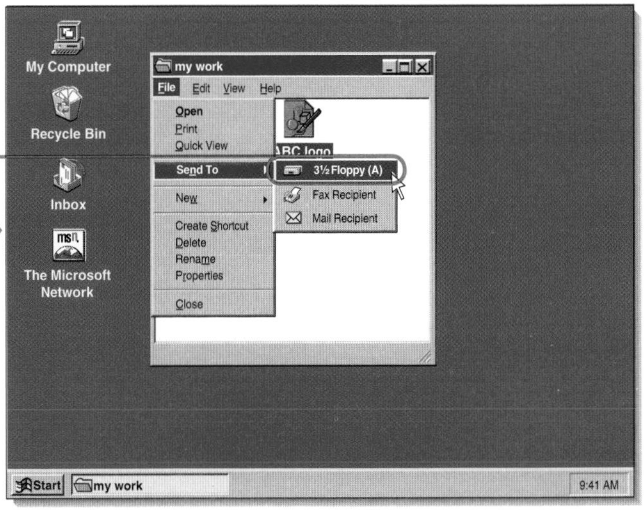

■ This area lists the floppy drive(s) on your computer.

5 Click the drive where you want to place a copy of the file.

COPY A FOLDER

You can copy a folder and all the files it contains to a floppy disk.

1 Perform steps 1 to 5 starting on page 66, except click the folder you want to copy in step 2.

RENAME A FILE

You can give a file a new name to better describe its contents. This makes it easier to find the file.

RENAME A FILE

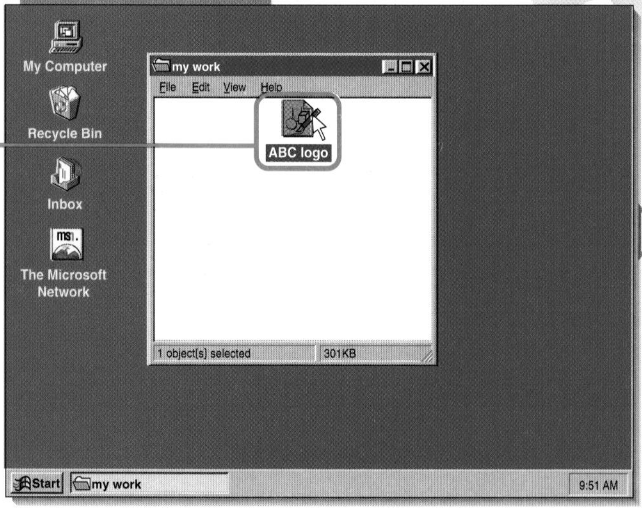

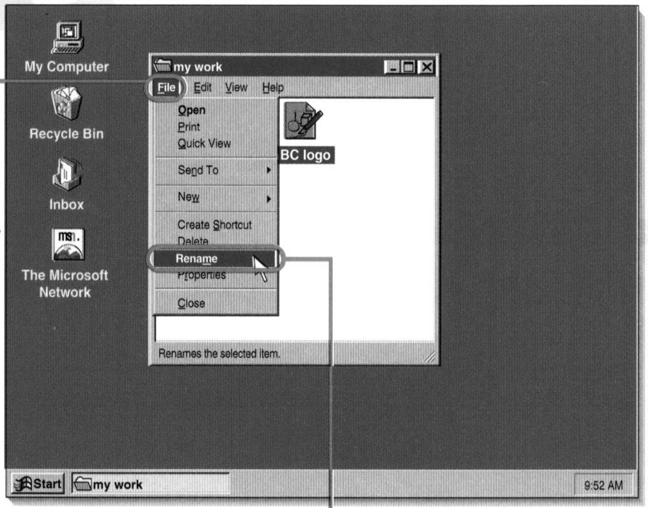

1 Click the file you want to rename.

2 Click **File**.

3 Click **Rename**.

TIP

You can easily rename a file on the desktop.

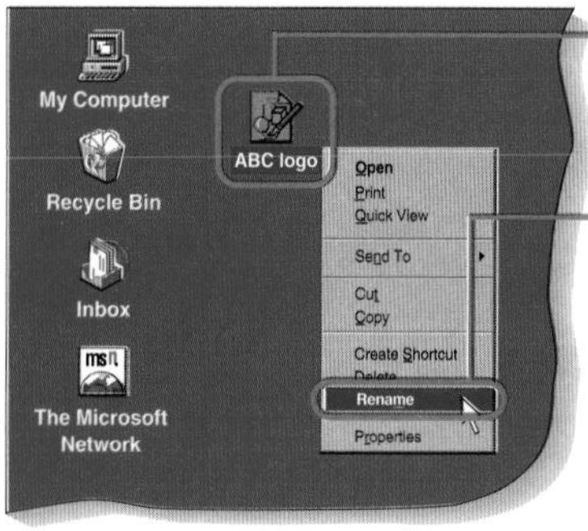

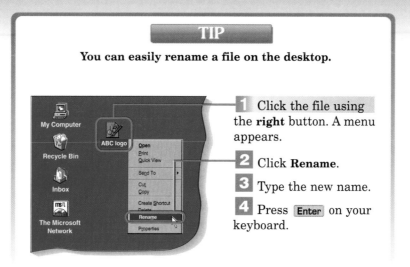

1 Click the file using the **right** button. A menu appears.

2 Click **Rename**.

3 Type the new name.

4 Press Enter on your keyboard.

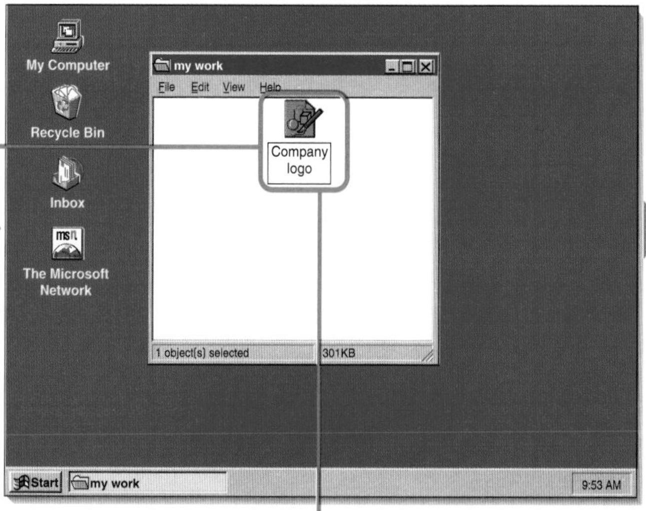

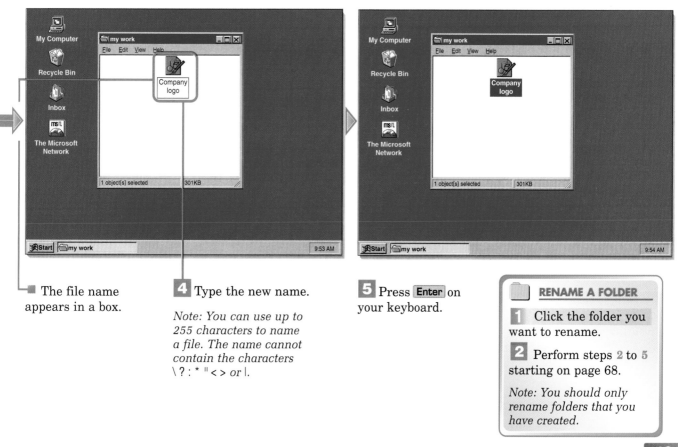

■ The file name appears in a box.

4 Type the new name.

Note: You can use up to 255 characters to name a file. The name cannot contain the characters \ ? : * " < > *or* |.

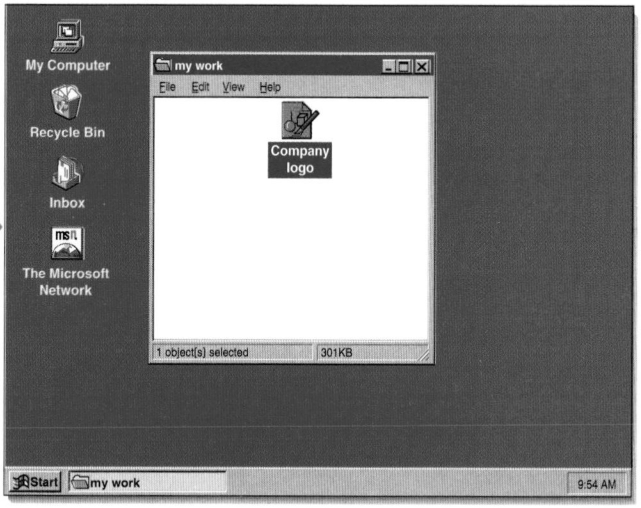

5 Press Enter on your keyboard.

RENAME A FOLDER

1 Click the folder you want to rename.

2 Perform steps 2 to 5 starting on page 68.

Note: You should only rename folders that you have created.

OPEN A FILE

You can open a file to display its contents on your screen. This lets you review and make changes to the file.

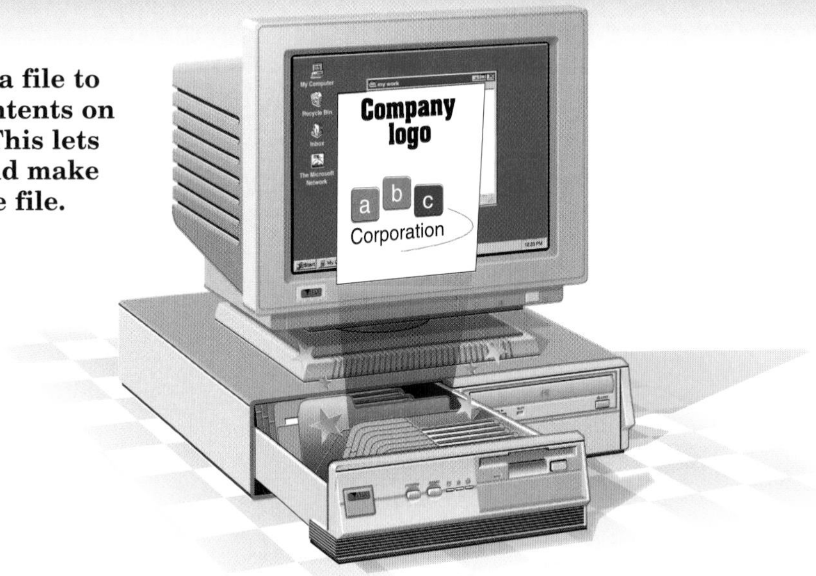

OPEN A FILE

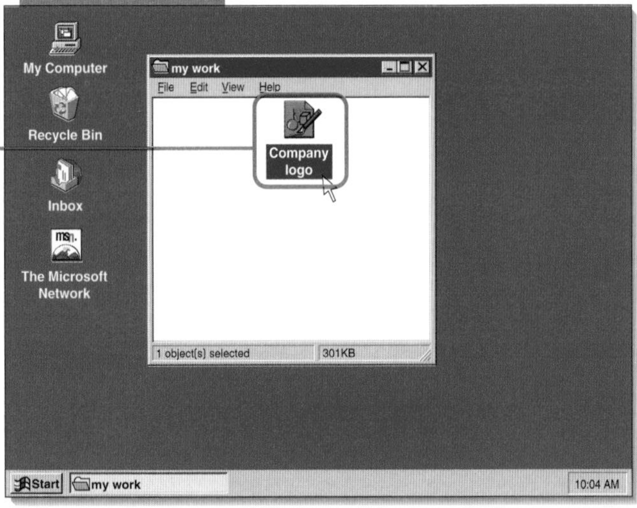

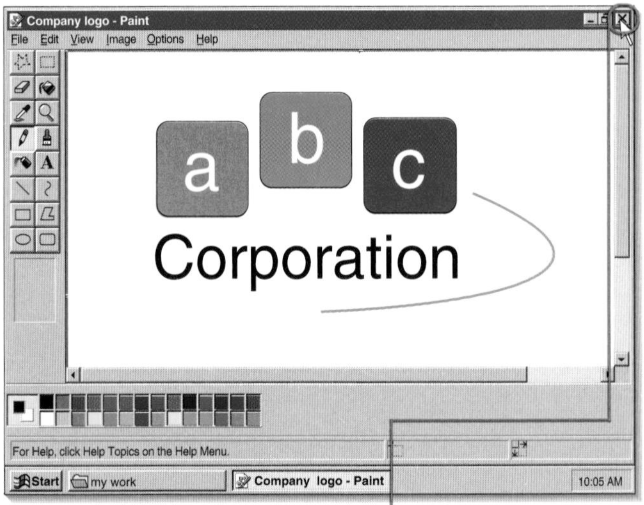

1 Double-click the file you want to open.

■ The file opens. You can review and make changes to the file.

2 To close the file, click ☒ .

OPEN A RECENTLY USED FILE

Windows remembers the files you most recently used. You can quickly open any of these files.

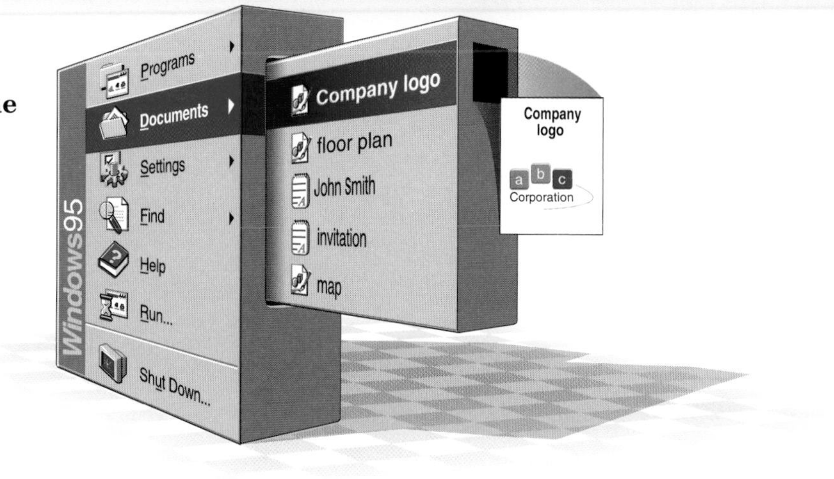

OPEN A RECENTLY USED FILE

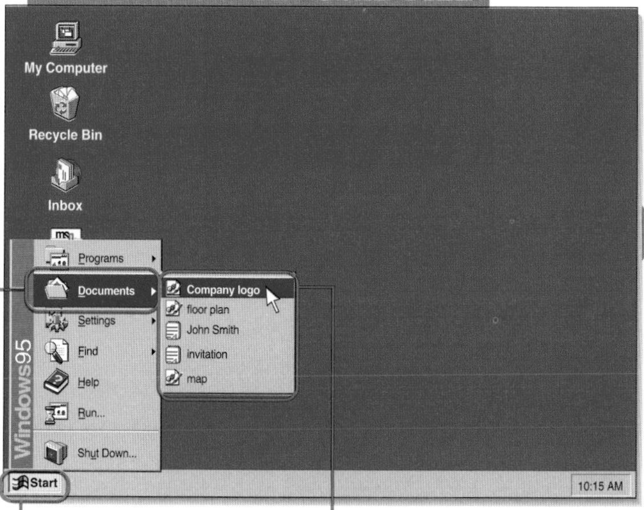

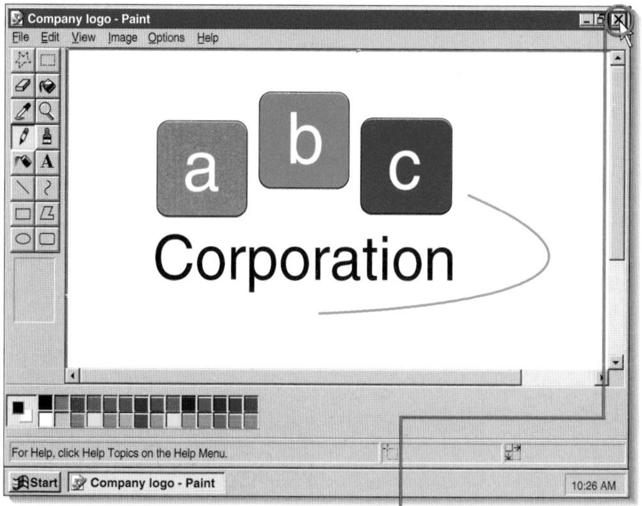

1 Click **Start**.

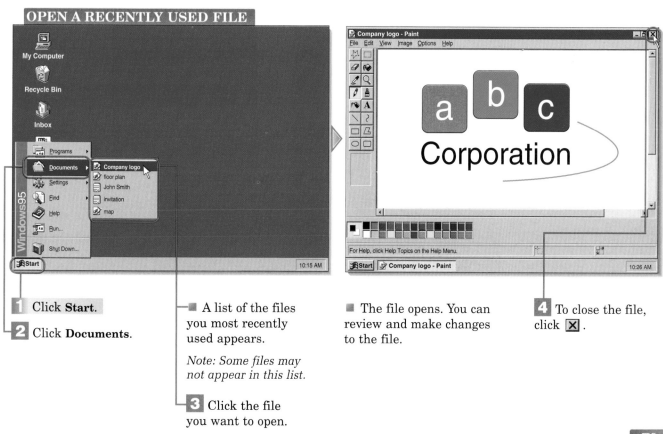

2 Click **Documents**.

■ A list of the files you most recently used appears.

Note: Some files may not appear in this list.

3 Click the file you want to open.

■ The file opens. You can review and make changes to the file.

4 To close the file, click ☒.

PREVIEW A FILE

You can quickly view the contents of a file without starting the program that created the file.

PREVIEW A FILE

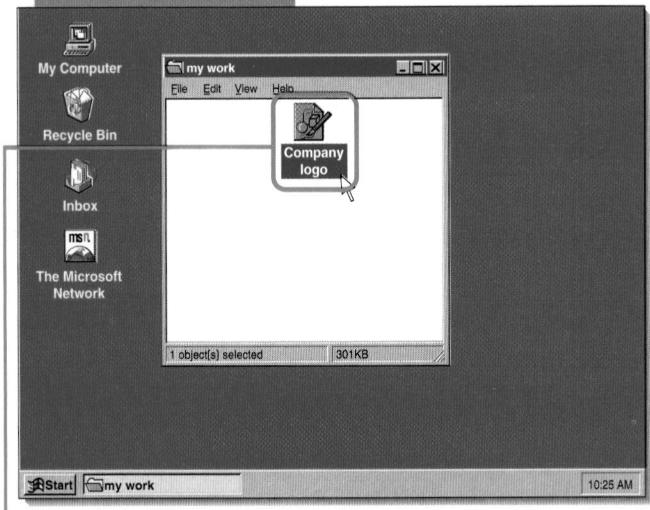

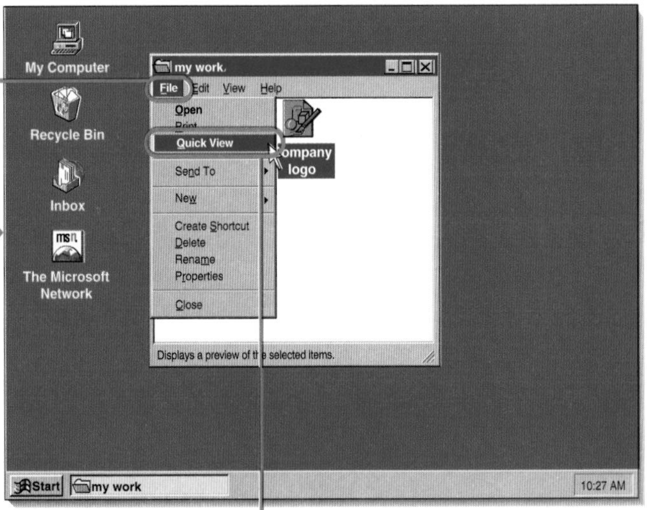

1 Click the file you want to preview.

2 Click **File**.

3 Click **Quick View**.

*Note: If **Quick View** is not available, either you cannot preview the type of file you selected or you must add the **Quick View** component. To add the component, which is found in the Accessories category on the Windows 95 CD-ROM, refer to page 186.*

TIP

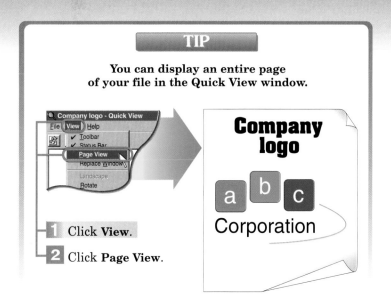

You can display an entire page of your file in the Quick View window.

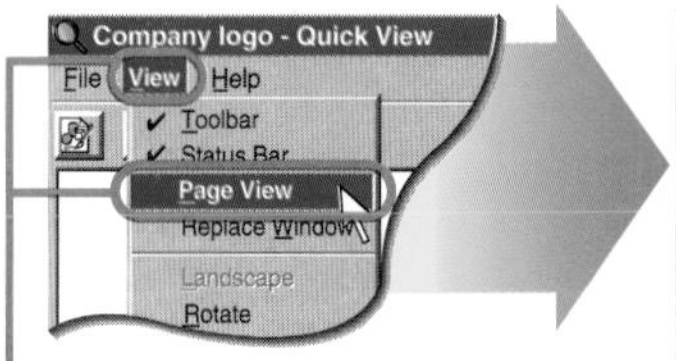

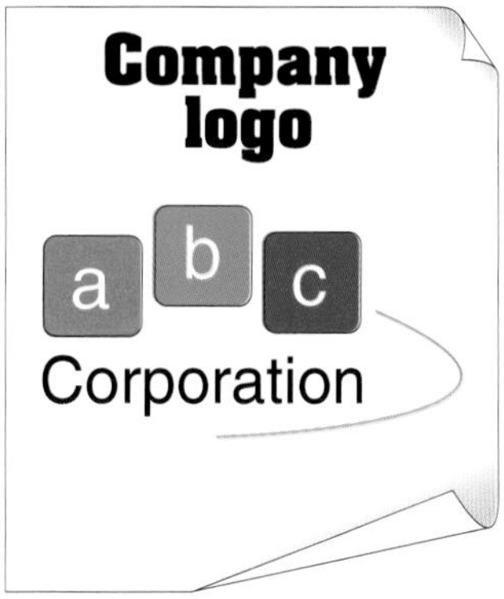

1 Click **View**.

2 Click **Page View**.

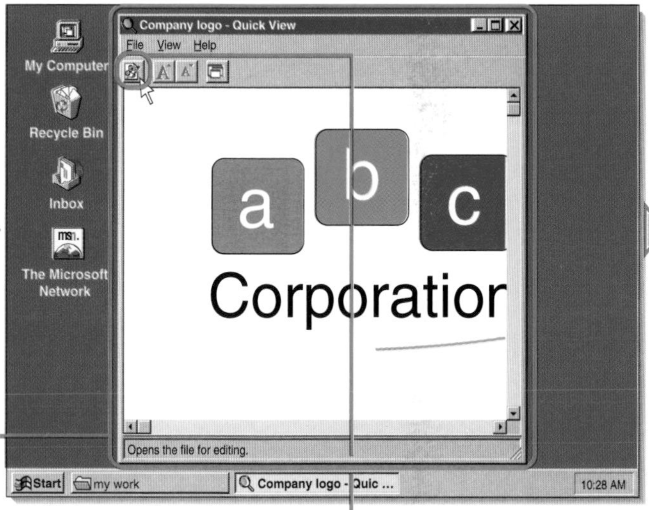

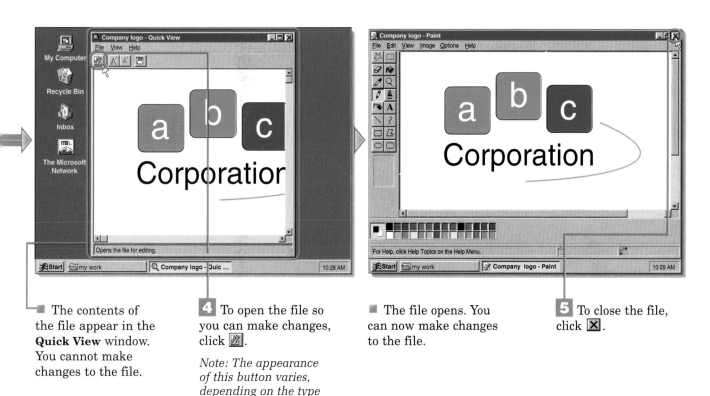

■ The contents of the file appear in the **Quick View** window. You cannot make changes to the file.

4 To open the file so you can make changes, click .

Note: The appearance of this button varies, depending on the type of file you are viewing.

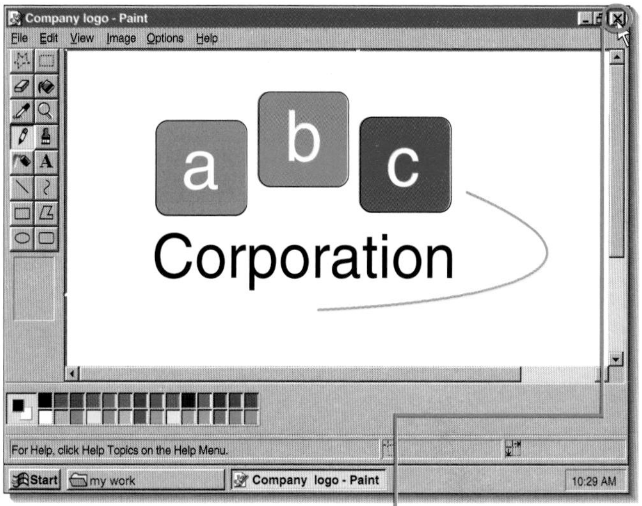

■ The file opens. You can now make changes to the file.

5 To close the file, click .

PRINT A FILE

You can produce a paper copy of a file stored on your computer. Before printing, make sure your printer is turned on and contains paper.

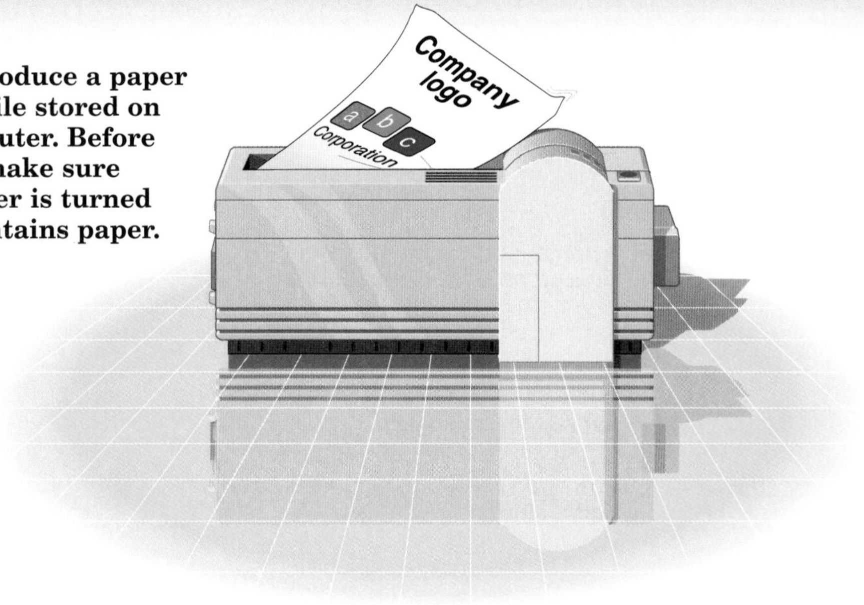

PRINT A FILE

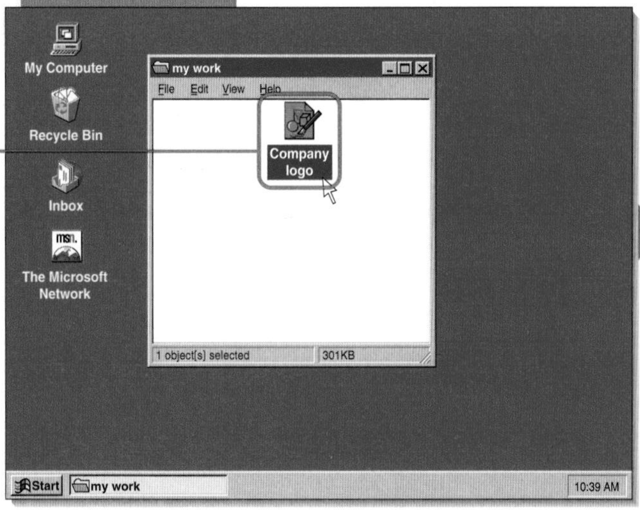

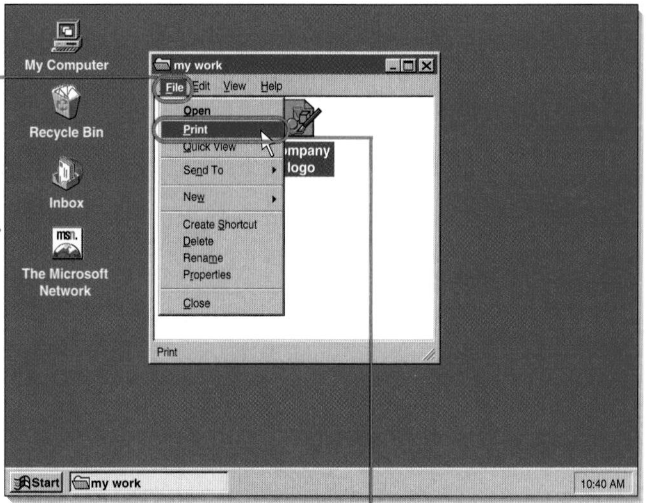

1 Click the file you want to print.

■ To print more than one file, select the files.

Note: To select multiple files, refer to page 61.

2 Click **File**.

3 Click **Print**.

VIEW FILES SENT TO THE PRINTER

You can view information about the files you send to the printer.

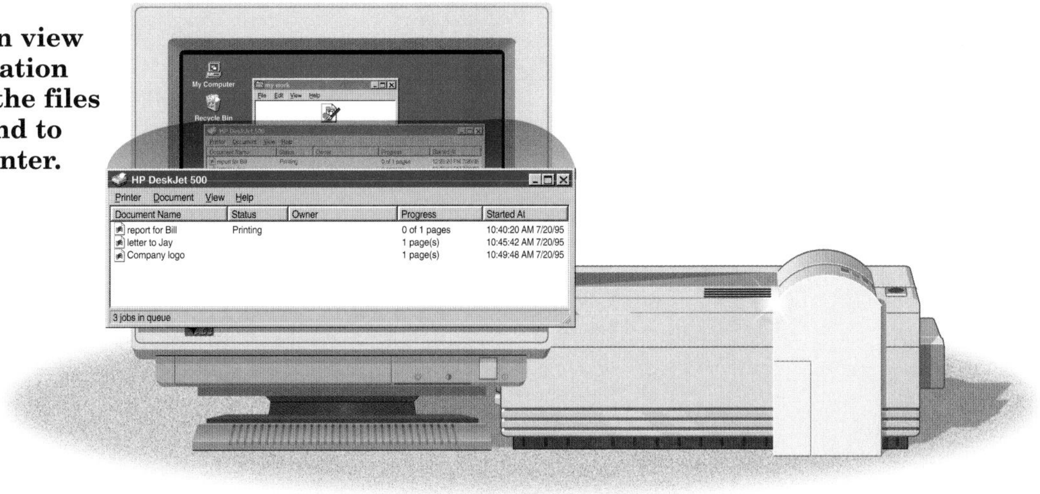

VIEW FILES SENT TO THE PRINTER

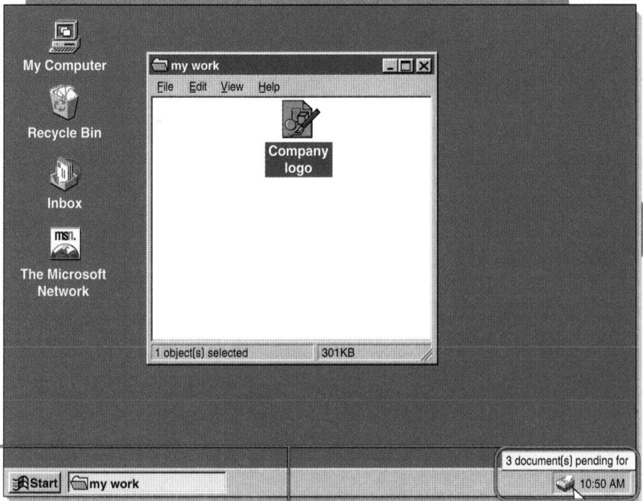

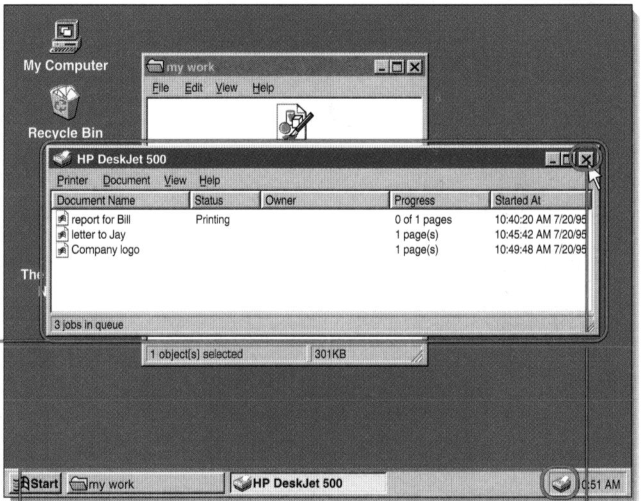

■ When you print a file, the printer icon (🖨) appears in this area.

Note: The printer icon disappears when the file is finished printing.

1 To see how many files are waiting to print, position the mouse over the printer icon (🖨).

■ A box appears, displaying the number of files.

2 To view information about the files waiting to print, double-click the printer icon (🖨).

■ A window appears, displaying information about the files. The file at the top of the list will print first.

3 To close the window, click **X**.

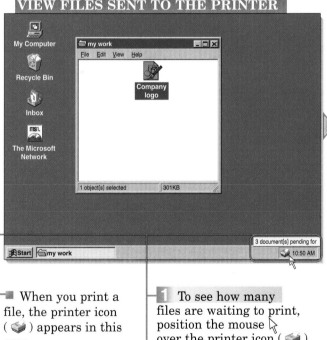

PAUSE THE PRINTER

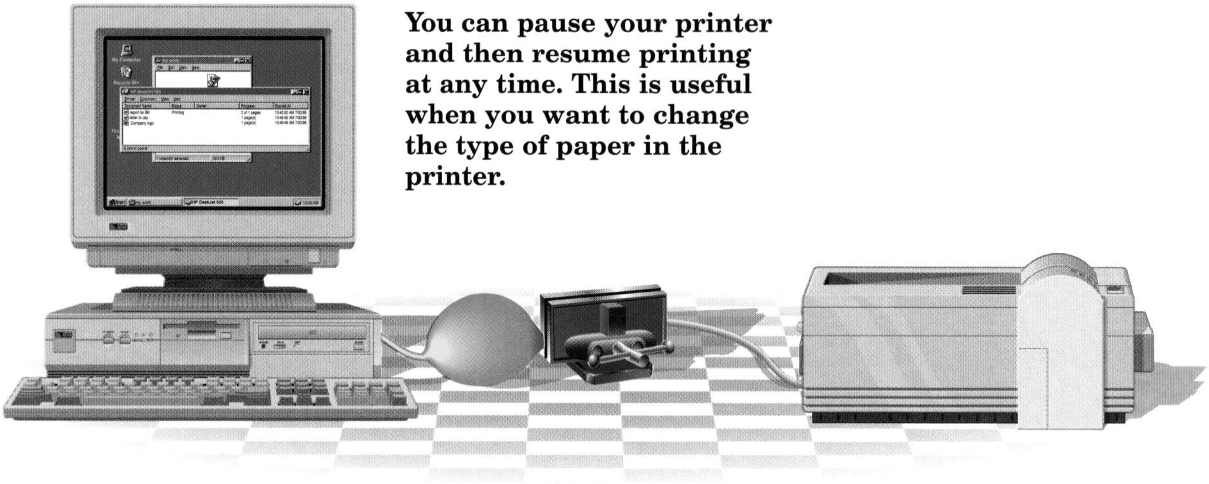

You can pause your printer and then resume printing at any time. This is useful when you want to change the type of paper in the printer.

PAUSE THE PRINTER

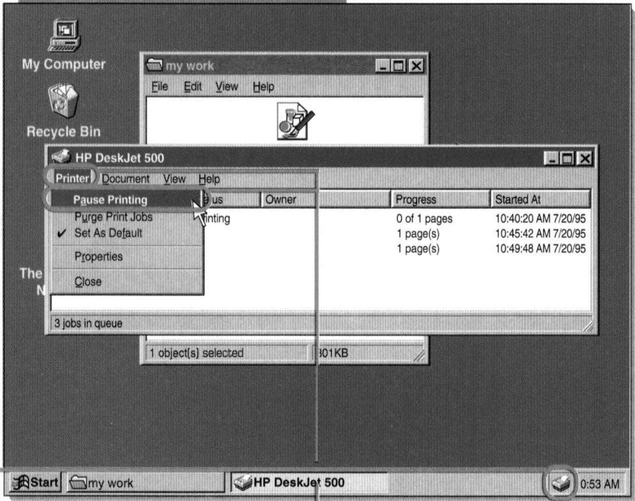

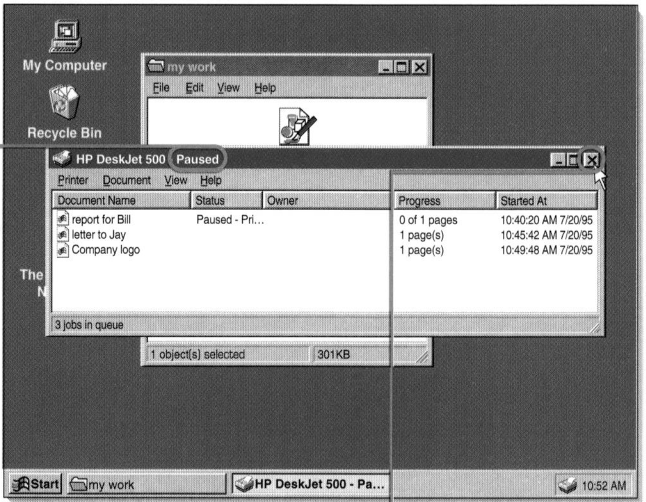

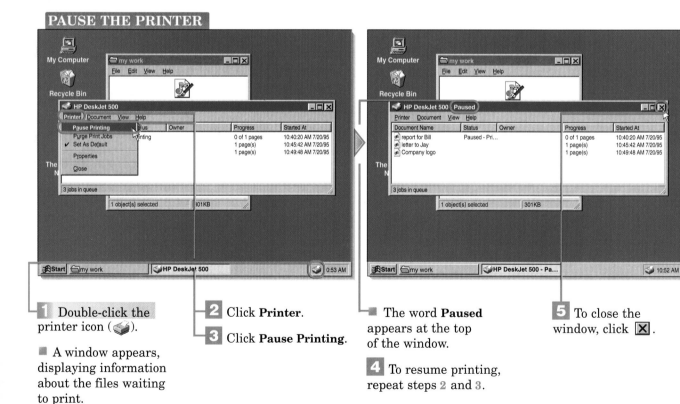

1 Double-click the printer icon ( ).

■ A window appears, displaying information about the files waiting to print.

2 Click **Printer**.

3 Click **Pause Printing**.

■ The word **Paused** appears at the top of the window.

4 To resume printing, repeat steps 2 and 3.

5 To close the window, click ☒.

CANCEL PRINTING

You can cancel the printing of a file if you forgot to make last-minute changes.

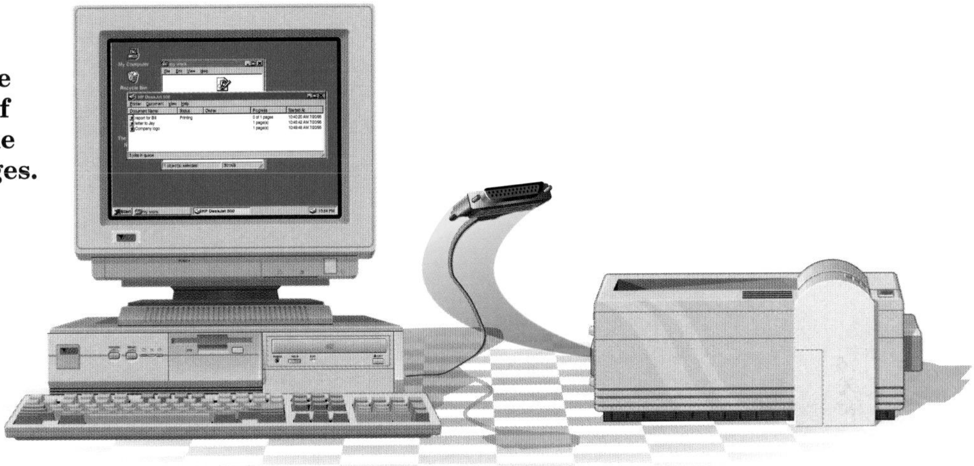

CANCEL PRINTING

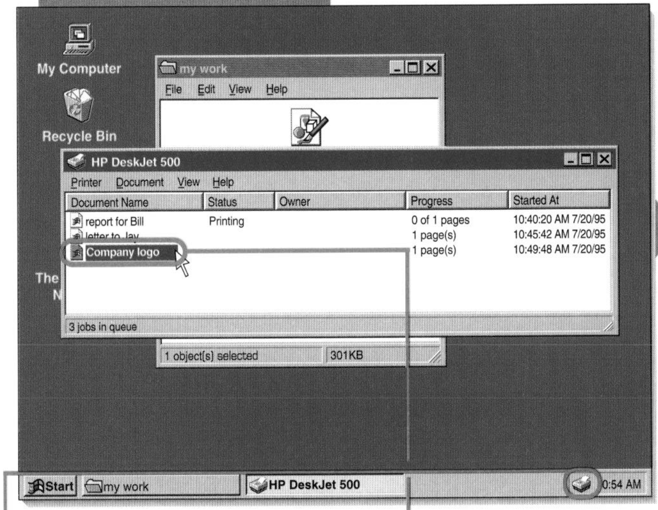

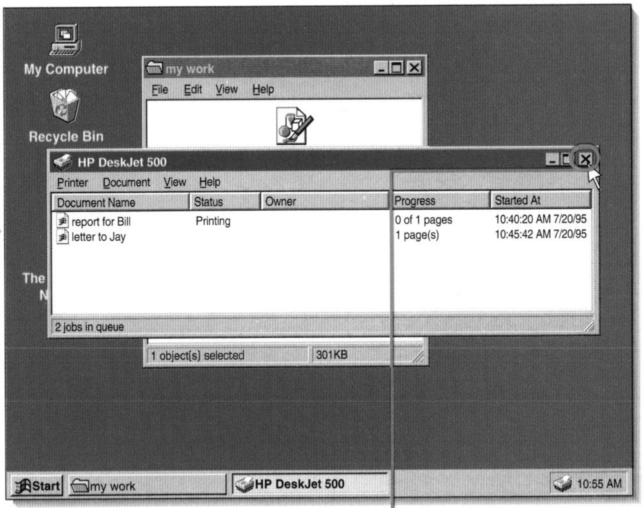

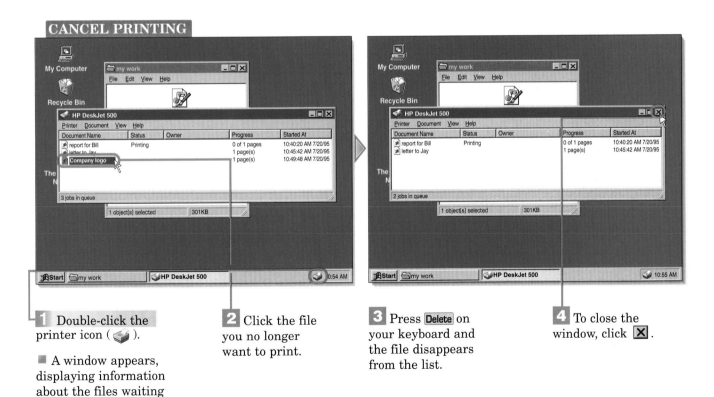

1 Double-click the printer icon (🖨).

■ A window appears, displaying information about the files waiting to print.

2 Click the file you no longer want to print.

3 Press **Delete** on your keyboard and the file disappears from the list.

4 To close the window, click **[X]**.

DELETE A FILE

You can delete a file you no longer need.

DELETE A FILE

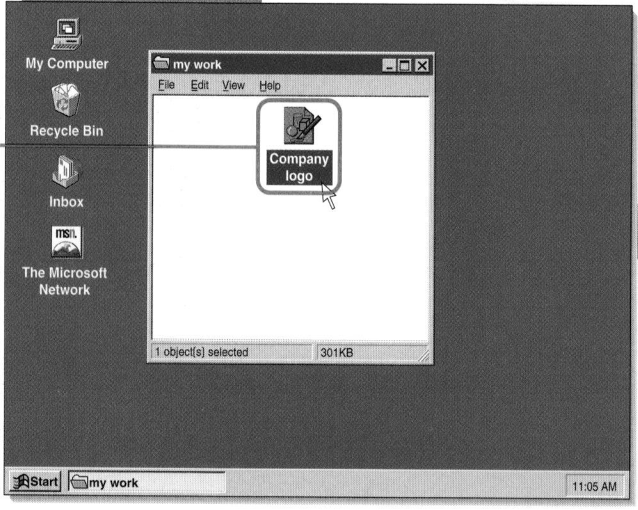

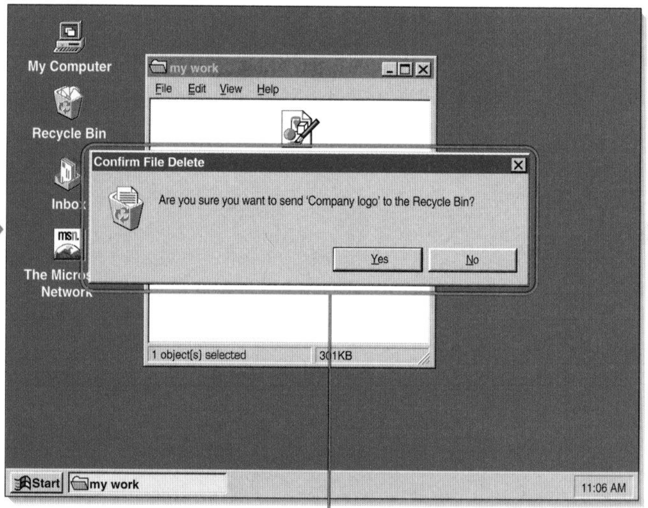

1 Click the file you want to delete.

■ To delete more than one file, select the files.

Note: To select multiple files, refer to page 61.

2 Press Delete on your keyboard.

■ The **Confirm File Delete** dialog box appears.

TIP

You can restore a file you have deleted.

Note: For more information, refer to page 80.

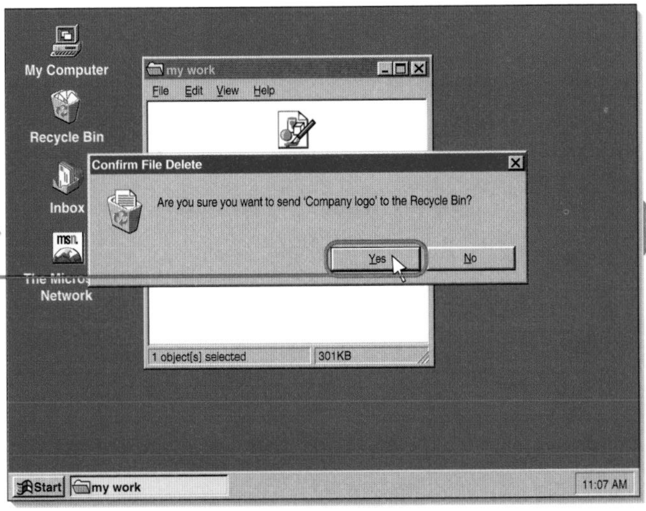

3 To delete the file, click **Yes**.

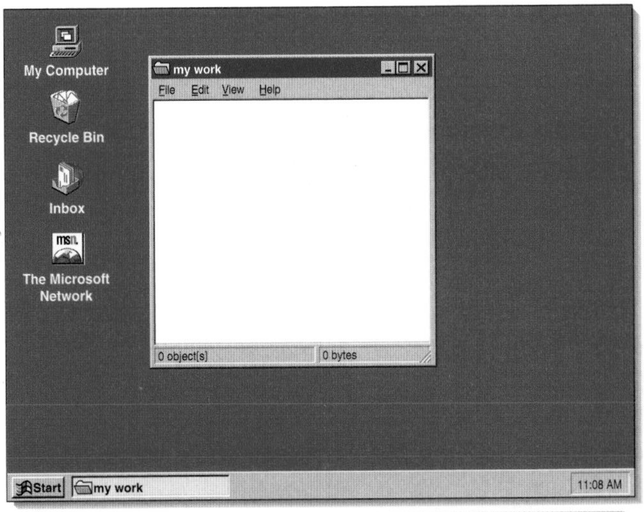

■ The file disappears.

DELETE A FOLDER

You can delete a folder and all the files it contains.

1 Click the folder you want to delete.

2 Perform steps 2 and 3 starting on page 78.

RESTORE A DELETED FILE

The Recycle Bin stores all the files you have deleted. You can easily restore any of these files.

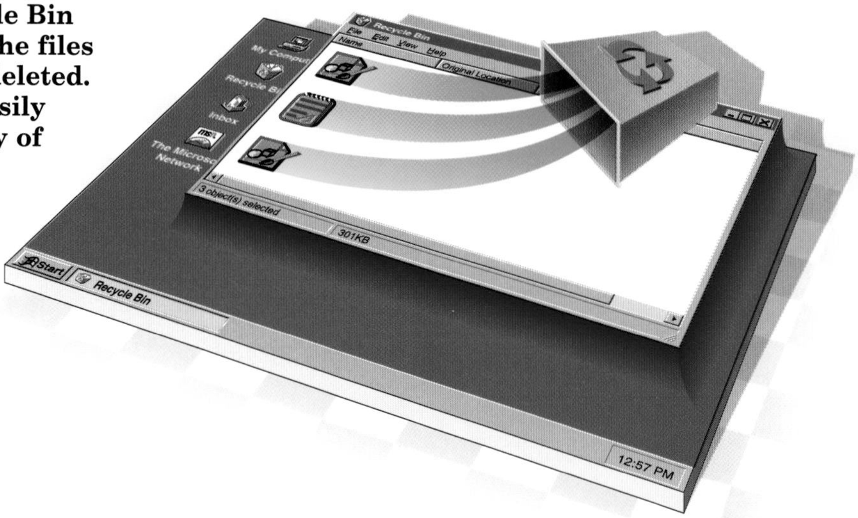

RESTORE A DELETED FILE

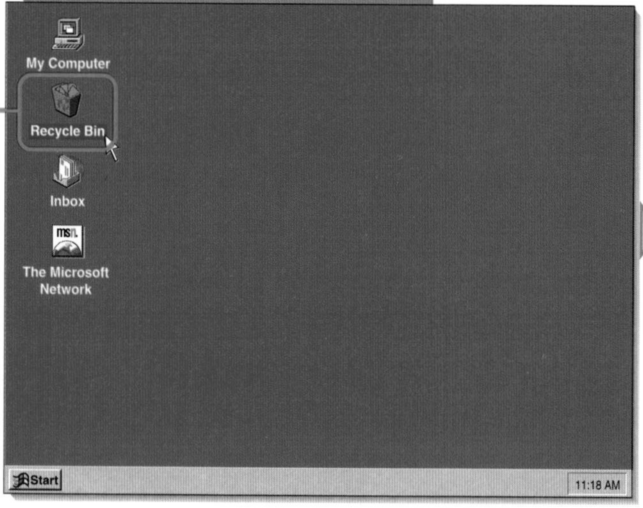

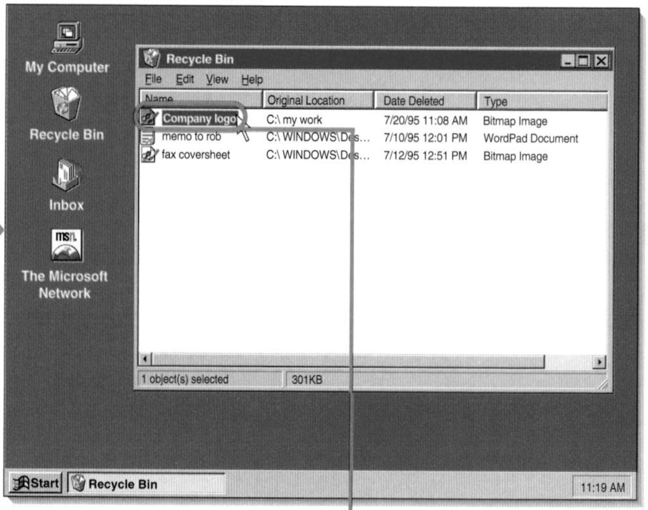

1 To display all the files you have deleted, double-click **Recycle Bin**.

■ The **Recycle Bin** window appears, listing all the files you have deleted.

2 Click the file you want to restore.

■ To restore more than one file, select the files.

Note: To select multiple files, refer to page 61.

TIP

The appearance of the Recycle Bin indicates whether or not the bin contains deleted files.

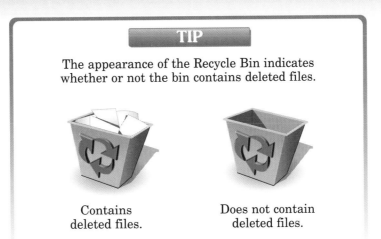

Contains deleted files.

Does not contain deleted files.

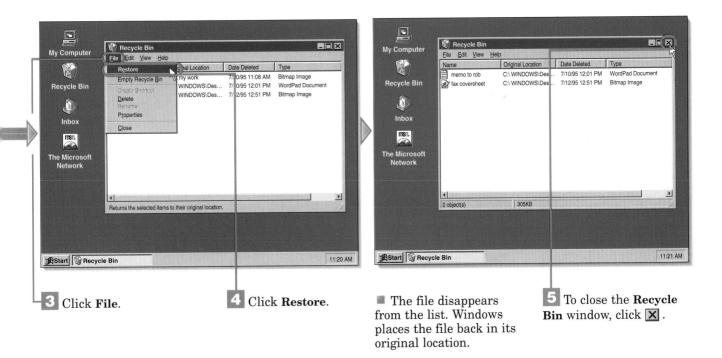

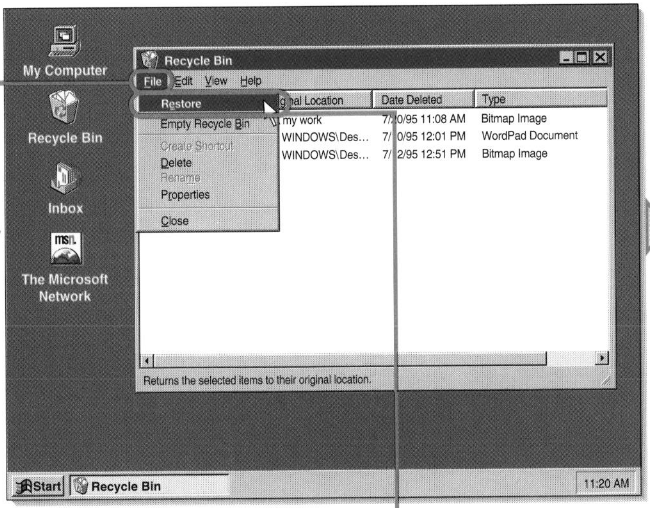

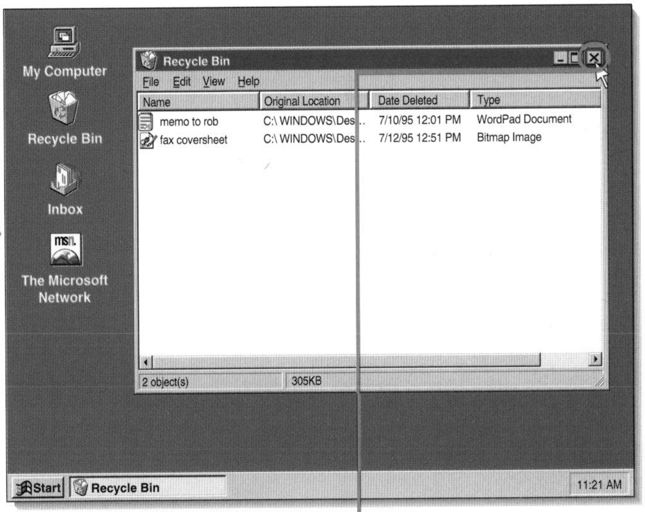

3 Click **File**.

4 Click **Restore**.

■ The file disappears from the list. Windows places the file back in its original location.

5 To close the **Recycle Bin** window, click ☒.

EMPTY THE RECYCLE BIN

You can create more space on your computer by permanently removing all the files from the Recycle Bin.

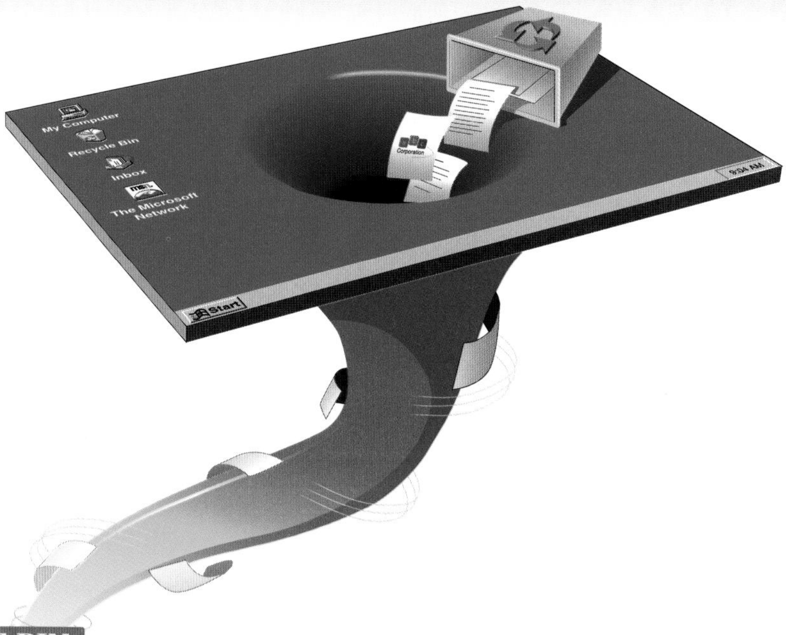

EMPTY THE RECYCLE BIN

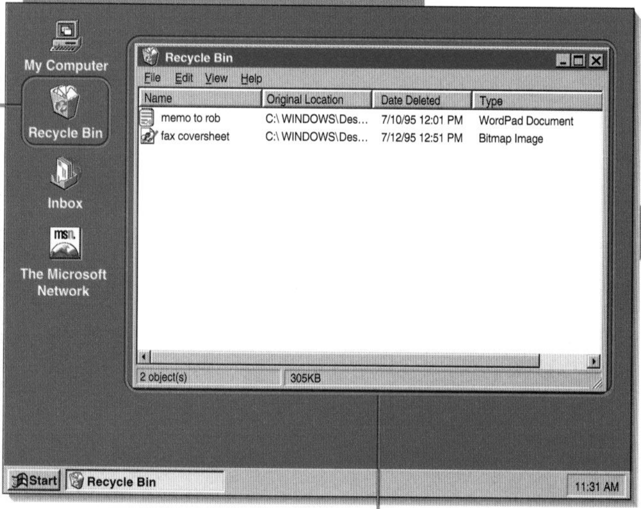

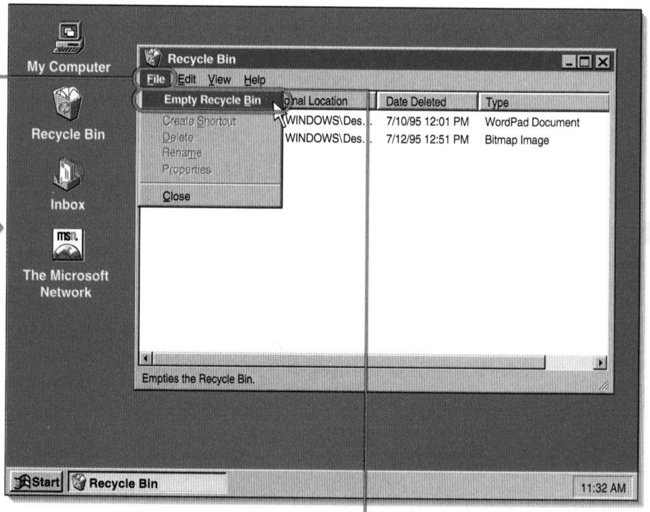

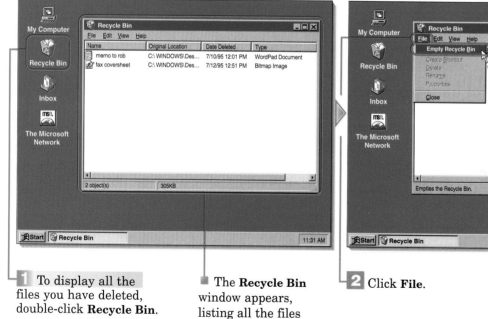

1 To display all the files you have deleted, double-click **Recycle Bin**.

■ The **Recycle Bin** window appears, listing all the files you have deleted.

2 Click **File**.

3 Click **Empty Recycle Bin**.

IMPORTANT

Before emptying the Recycle Bin, make sure it does not contain files you may need in the future.

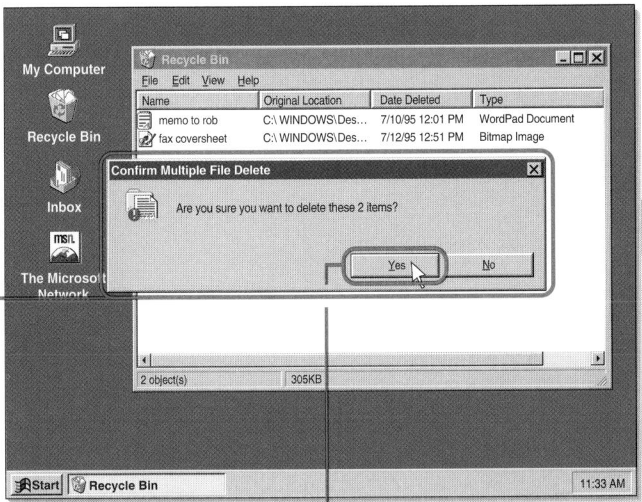

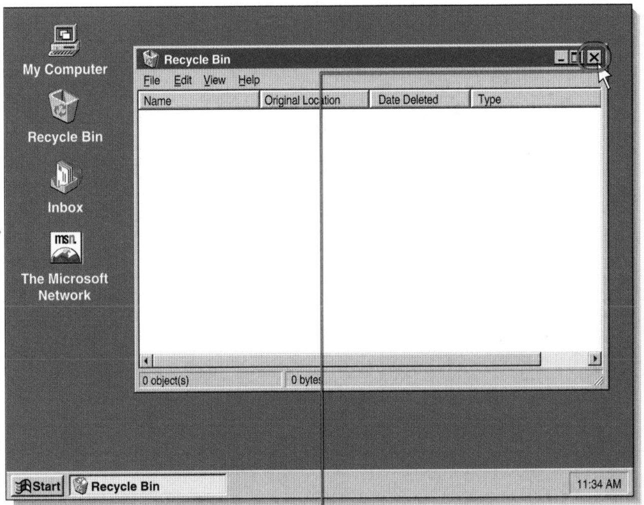

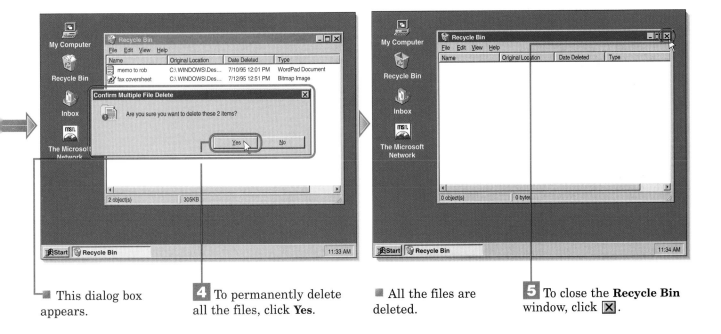

■ This dialog box appears.

4 To permanently delete all the files, click **Yes**.

■ All the files are deleted.

5 To close the **Recycle Bin** window, click ☒.

START WINDOWS EXPLORER

Like a map, Windows Explorer shows the location of every folder and file on your computer.

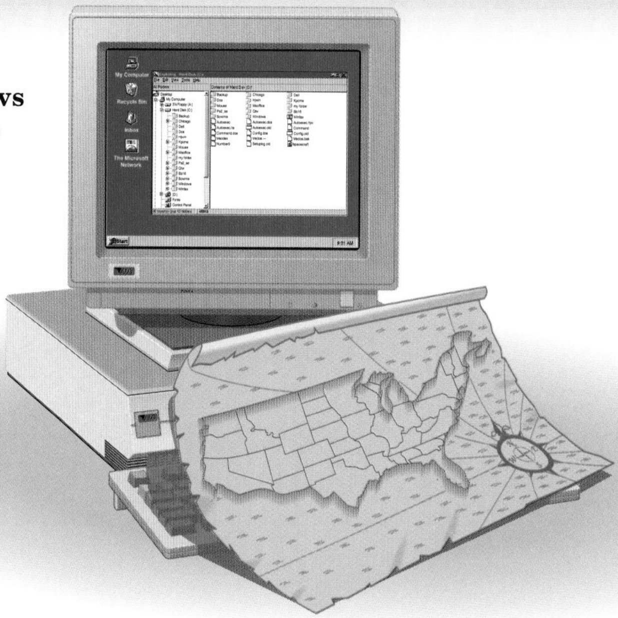

START WINDOWS EXPLORER

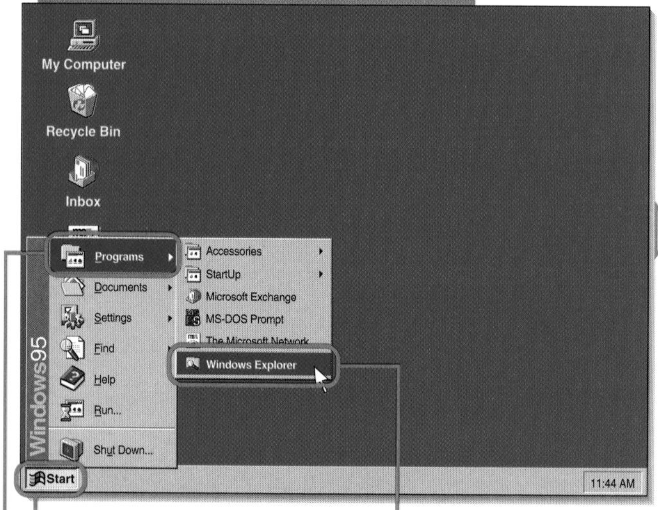

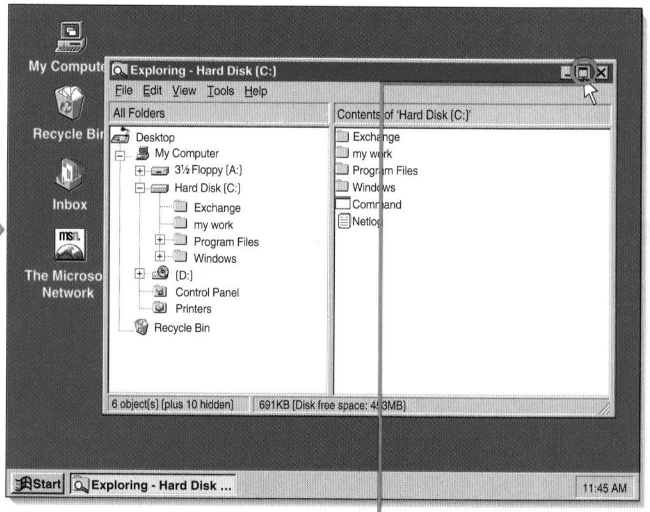

1 Click **Start**.

2 Click **Programs**.

3 Click **Windows Explorer**.

■ The **Exploring** window appears.

4 To enlarge the window to fill your screen, click .

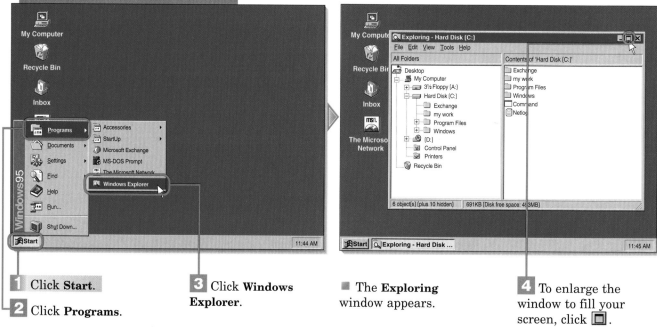

TIP

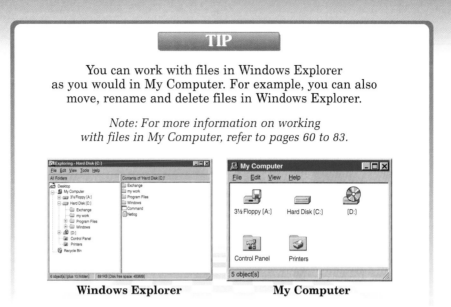

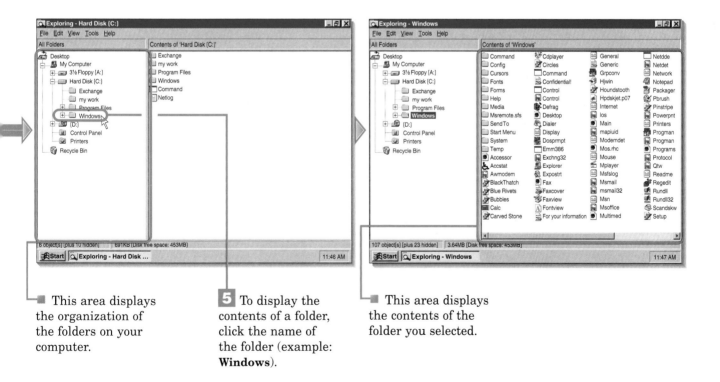

You can work with files in Windows Explorer as you would in My Computer. For example, you can also move, rename and delete files in Windows Explorer.

Note: For more information on working with files in My Computer, refer to pages 60 to 83.

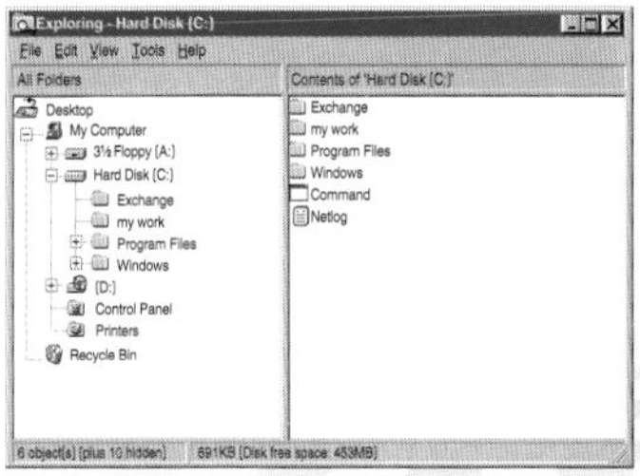

Windows Explorer

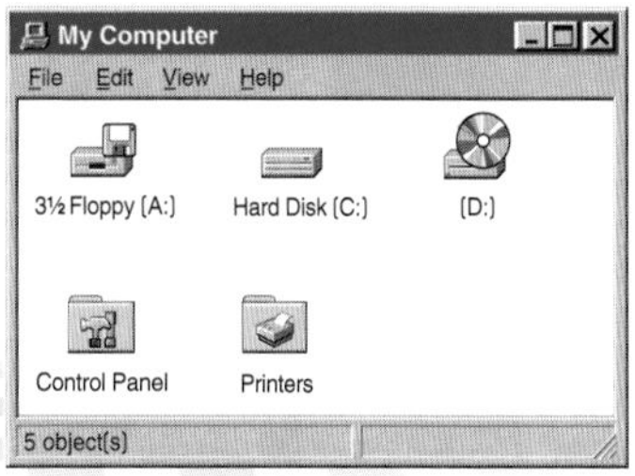

My Computer

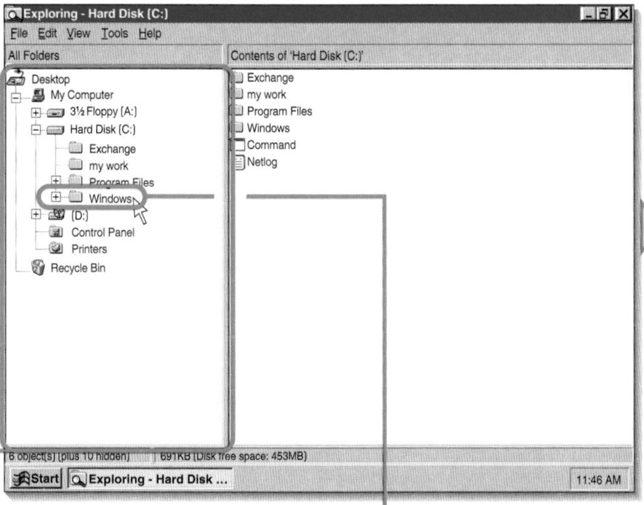

■ This area displays the organization of the folders on your computer.

5 To display the contents of a folder, click the name of the folder (example: **Windows**).

■ This area displays the contents of the folder you selected.

DISPLAY OR HIDE FOLDERS

A folder may contain other folders. You can easily display or hide these folders at any time.

DISPLAY HIDDEN FOLDERS

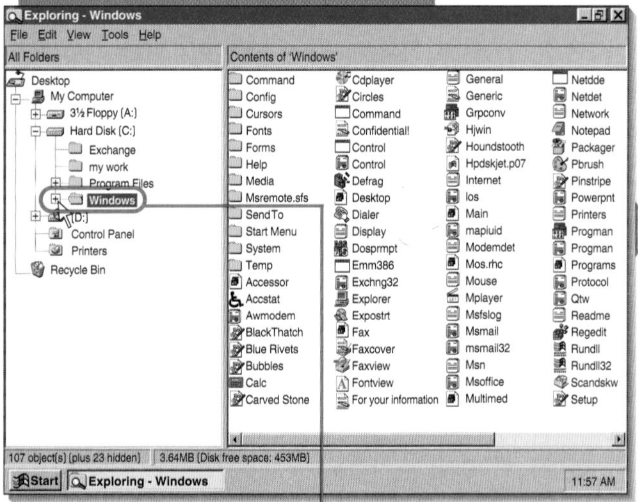

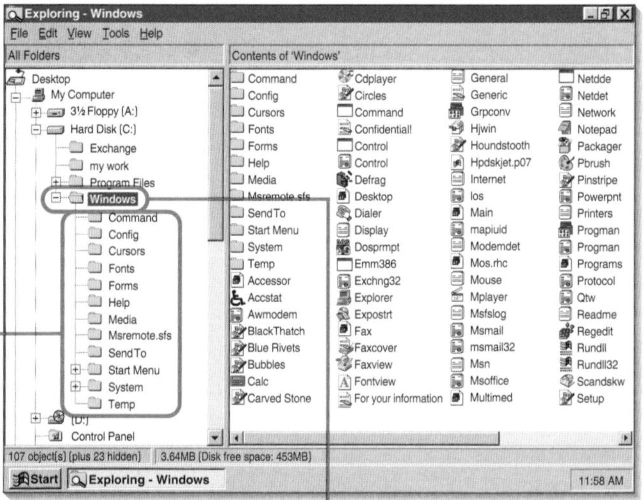

You can display hidden folders to view more of the contents of your computer.

1 To display the hidden folders within a folder, click the plus sign (⊞) beside the folder.

■ The hidden folders appear.

■ The plus sign (⊞) beside the folder changes to a minus sign (⊟). This indicates that all the folders within the folder are now displayed.

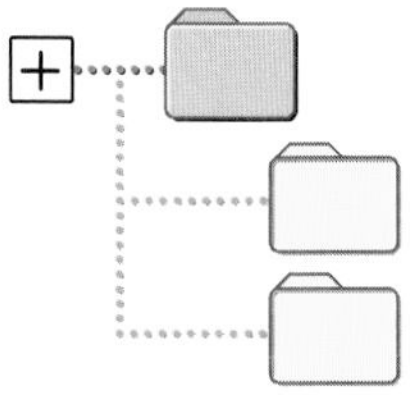

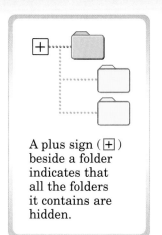

A plus sign (⊞) beside a folder indicates that all the folders it contains are hidden.

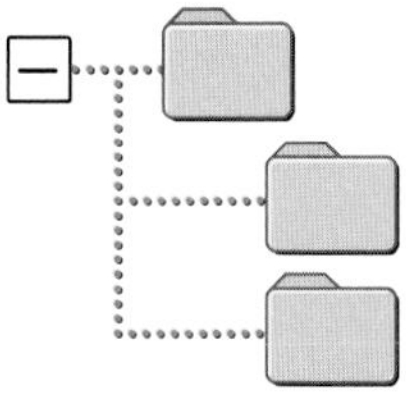

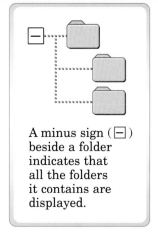

A minus sign (⊟) beside a folder indicates that all the folders it contains are displayed.

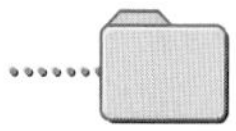

No sign beside a folder indicates that the folder does not contain any folders, although it may contain files.

HIDE FOLDERS

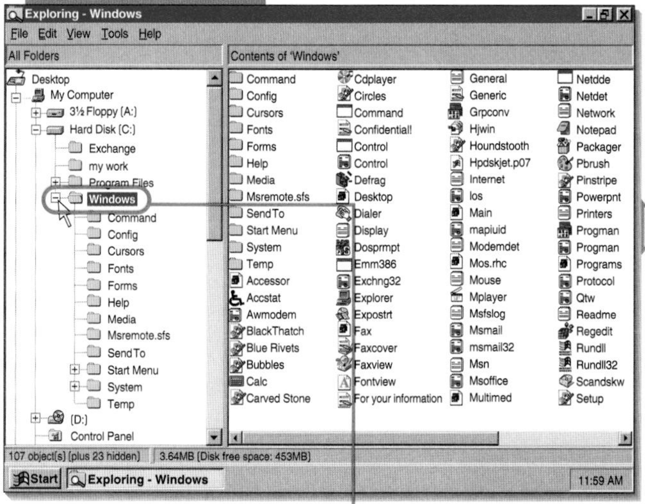

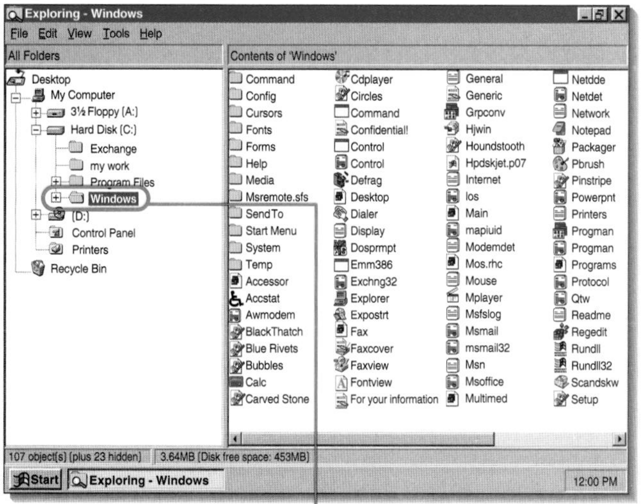

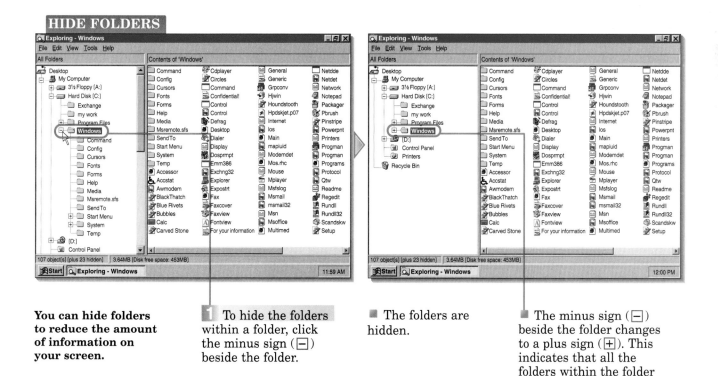

You can hide folders to reduce the amount of information on your screen.

1 To hide the folders within a folder, click the minus sign (⊟) beside the folder.

■ The folders are hidden.

■ The minus sign (⊟) beside the folder changes to a plus sign (⊞). This indicates that all the folders within the folder are now hidden.

In this chapter you will learn how to use several Windows features that will save you time.

CHAPTER 6: TIME-SAVING FEATURES

Find a File . . . . *.90*

Add a Shortcut to the Desktop . . . . *.92*

Put Part of a Document on the Desktop . . . . *.94*

Add a Program to the Start Menu . . . . *.96*

Have a Program Start Automatically . . . . . . *.98*

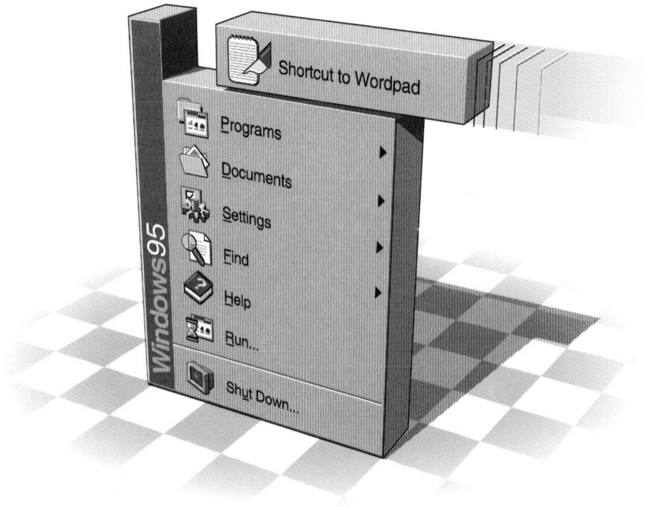

FIND A FILE

If you cannot remember the name or location of a file you want to work with, you can have Windows search for the file.

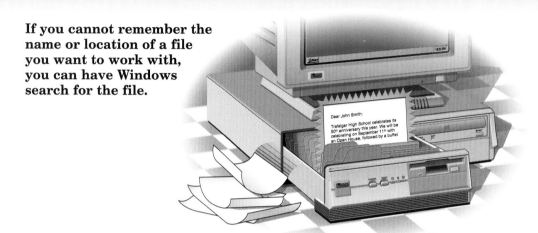

FIND A FILE

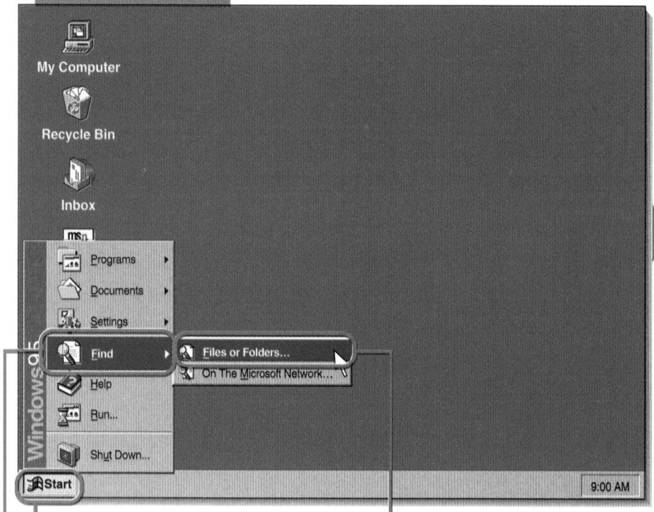

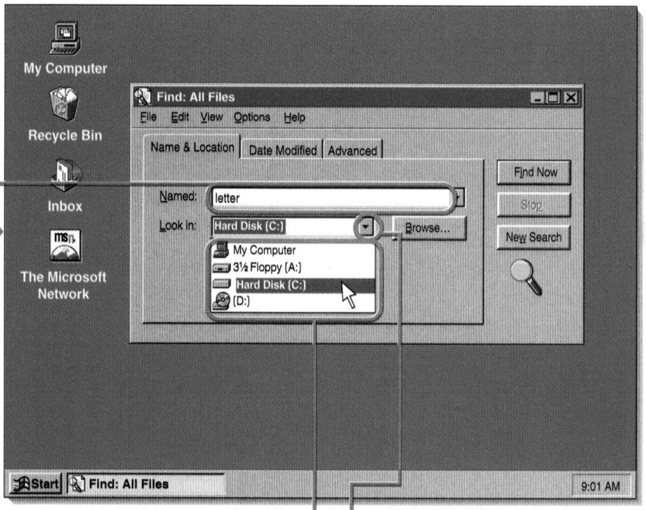

1 Click **Start**.

2 Click **Find**.

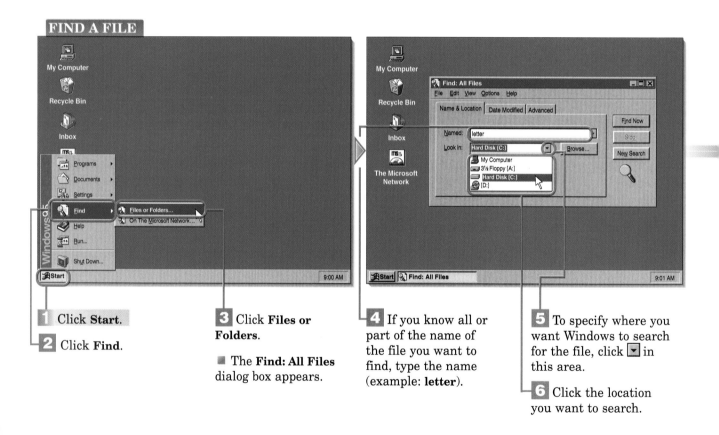

3 Click **Files or Folders**.

■ The **Find: All Files** dialog box appears.

4 If you know all or part of the name of the file you want to find, type the name (example: **letter**).

5 To specify where you want Windows to search for the file, click ▼ in this area.

6 Click the location you want to search.

TIP

You can search for a specific type of file, such as an application.

Note: An application is a program that lets you perform tasks (example: ***WordPad****).*

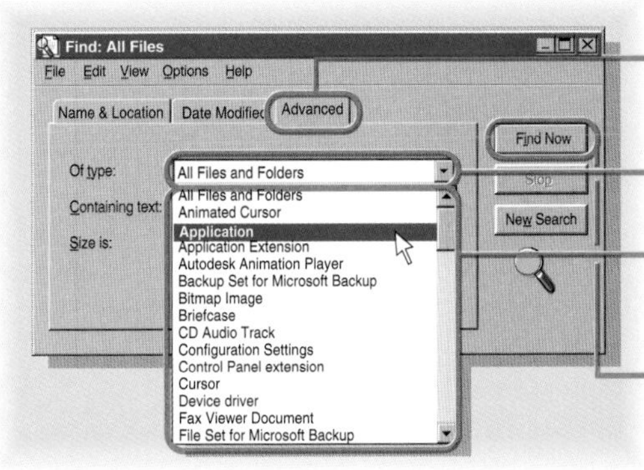

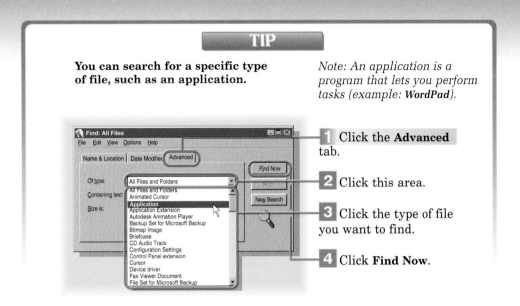

1 Click the **Advanced** tab.

2 Click this area.

3 Click the type of file you want to find.

4 Click **Find Now**.

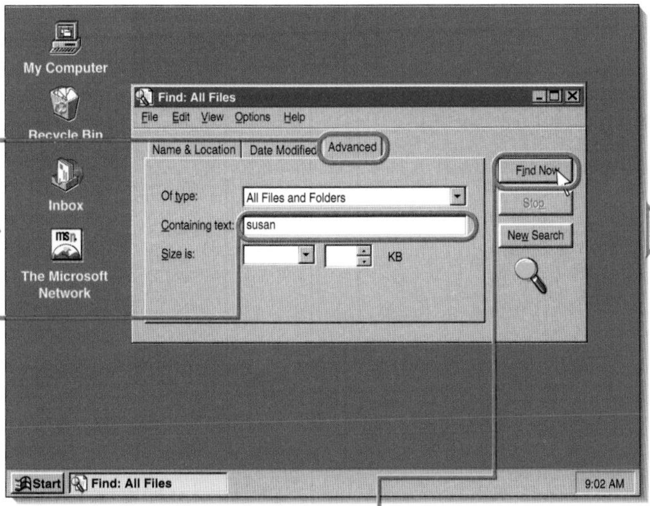

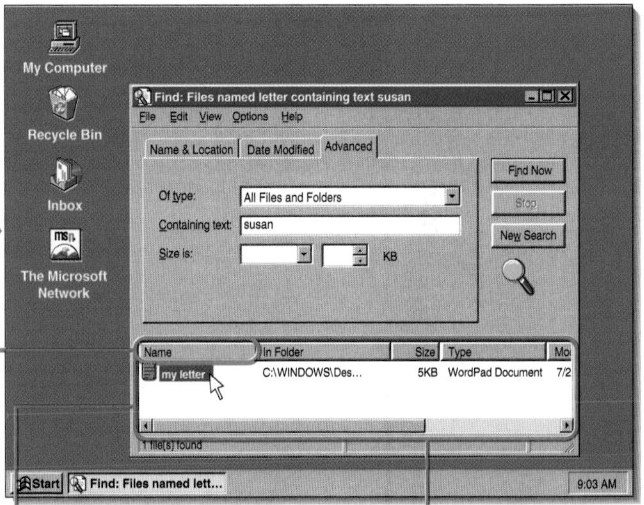

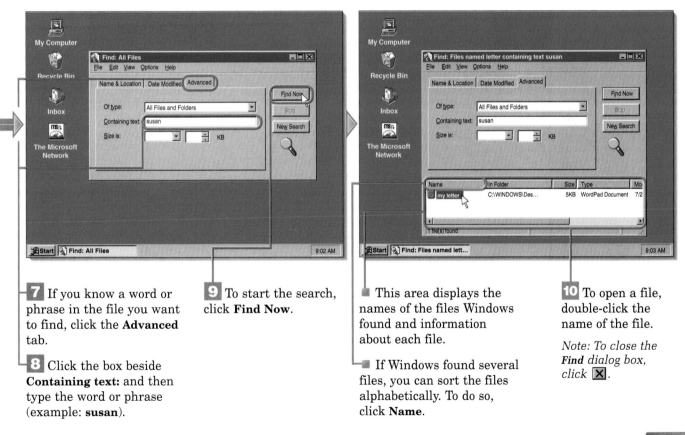

7 If you know a word or phrase in the file you want to find, click the **Advanced** tab.

8 Click the box beside **Containing text:** and then type the word or phrase (example: **susan**).

9 To start the search, click **Find Now**.

■ This area displays the names of the files Windows found and information about each file.

■ If Windows found several files, you can sort the files alphabetically. To do so, click **Name**.

10 To open a file, double-click the name of the file.

Note: To close the ***Find*** *dialog box, click* ☒.

ADD A SHORTCUT TO THE DESKTOP

You can add a shortcut to the desktop to provide a quick way of opening a file you use regularly.

ADD A SHORTCUT TO THE DESKTOP

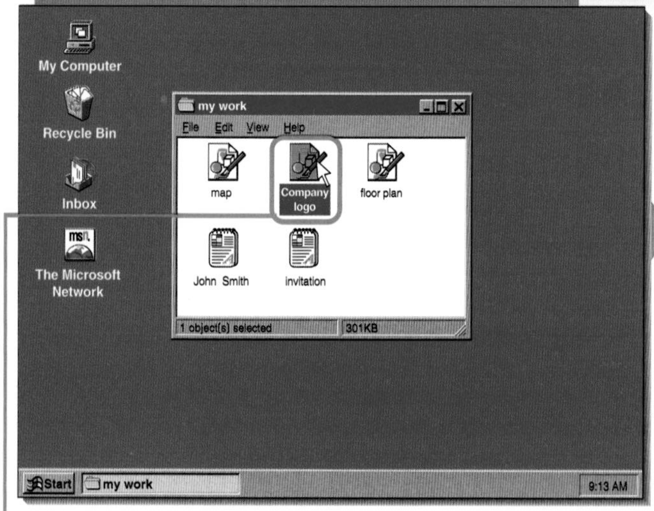

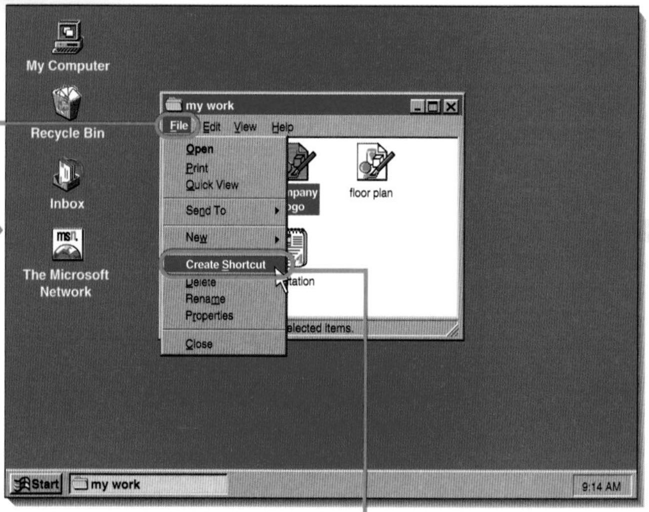

1 Click the file you want to create a shortcut to.

2 Click **File**.

3 Click **Create Shortcut**.

TIP

You can easily tell the difference between the original file and the shortcut.

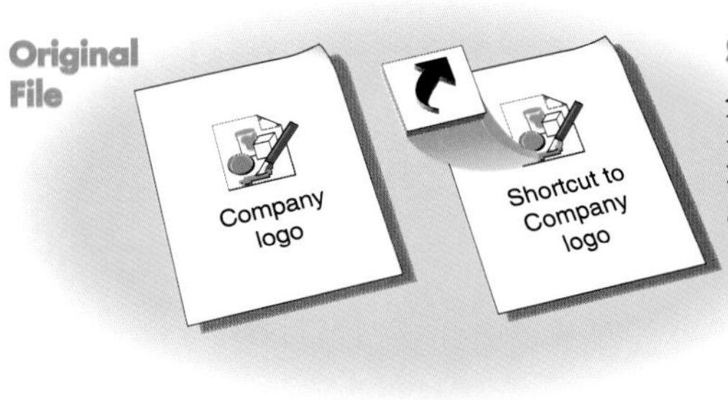

Shortcut
A shortcut looks like the original file, but displays an arrow (↗).

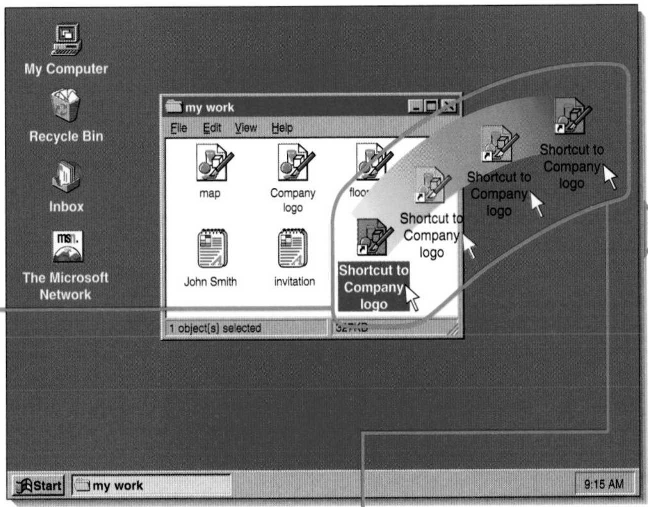

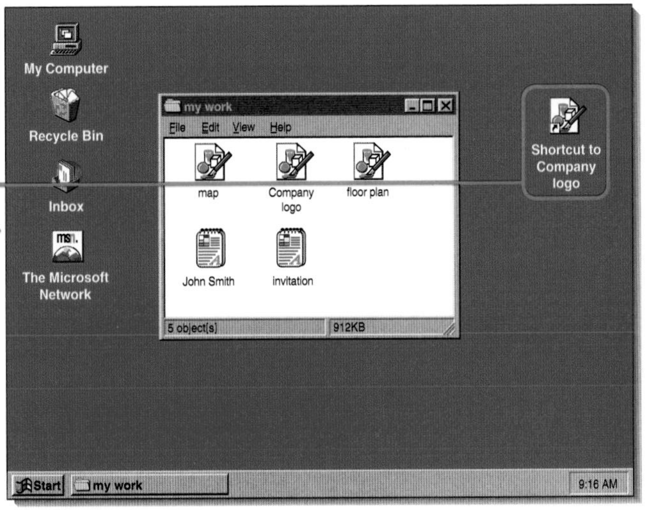

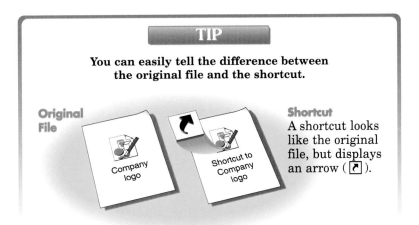

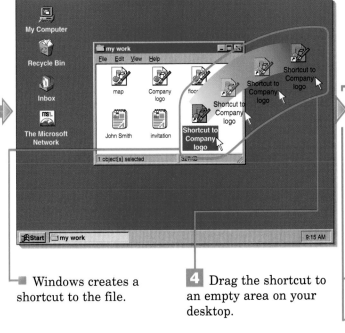

■ Windows creates a shortcut to the file.

4 Drag the shortcut to an empty area on your desktop.

■ The shortcut appears on the desktop.

■ To open the file and display its contents on your screen, double-click the shortcut.

Note: When you add a shortcut to the desktop, the original file does not move. The original file remains in the same place on your hard disk.

PUT PART OF A DOCUMENT ON THE DESKTOP

You can place frequently used information on your desktop. This gives you quick access to the information.

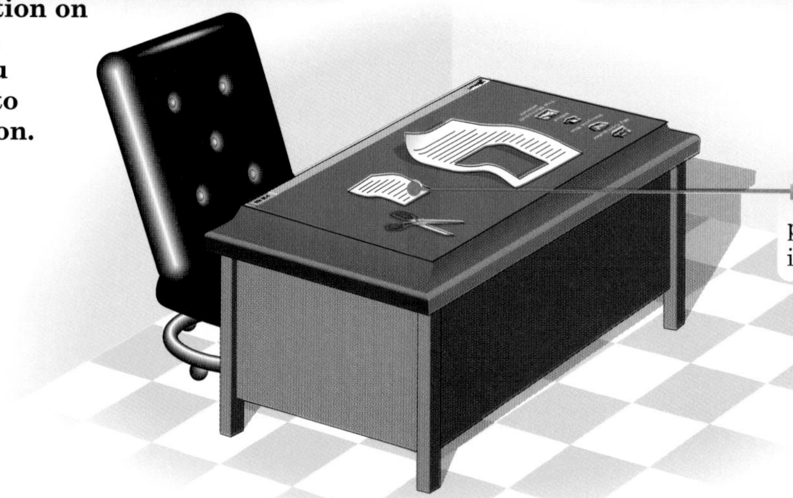

Information you place on the desktop is called a scrap.

PUT PART OF A DOCUMENT ON THE DESKTOP

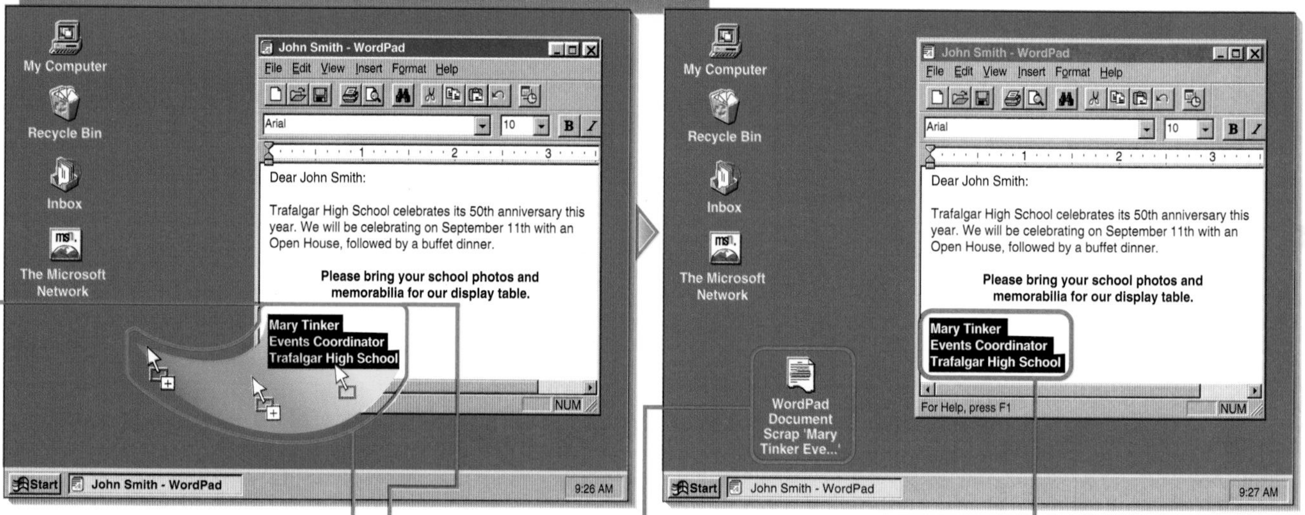

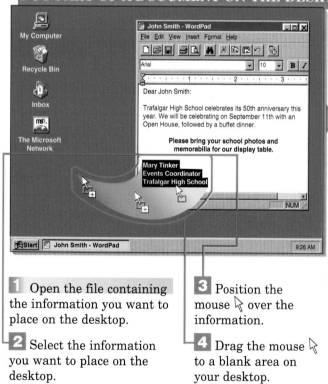

1 Open the file containing the information you want to place on the desktop.

2 Select the information you want to place on the desktop.

3 Position the mouse over the information.

4 Drag the mouse to a blank area on your desktop.

Windows creates an icon, called a scrap, to represent the information from the document.

Note: Some programs cannot create scraps.

The information does not move from the document.

TIP

You can create scraps for information you frequently use in documents, such as your name and address or company logo.

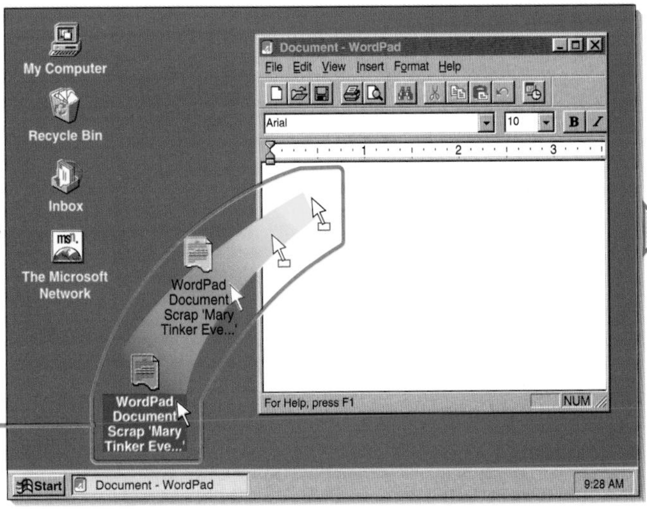

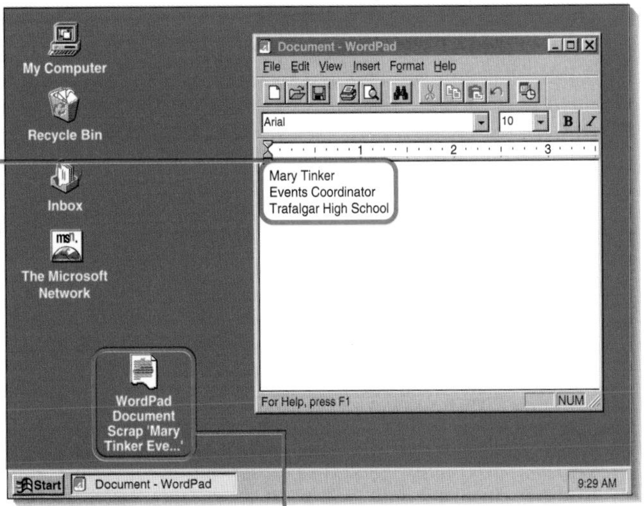

USING SCRAPS

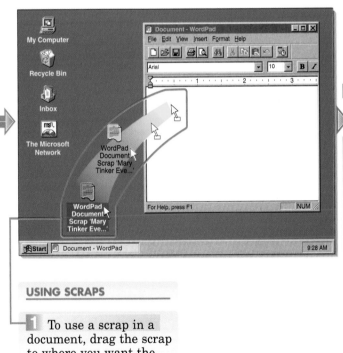

1 To use a scrap in a document, drag the scrap to where you want the information to appear.

■ The information appears in the document.

■ The scrap remains on your desktop. This lets you place the information in as many documents as you wish.

Note: You can delete a scrap from your screen as you would delete any file. To delete a file, refer to page 78.

ADD A PROGRAM TO THE START MENU

You can add your favorite programs to the Start menu so you can quickly open them.

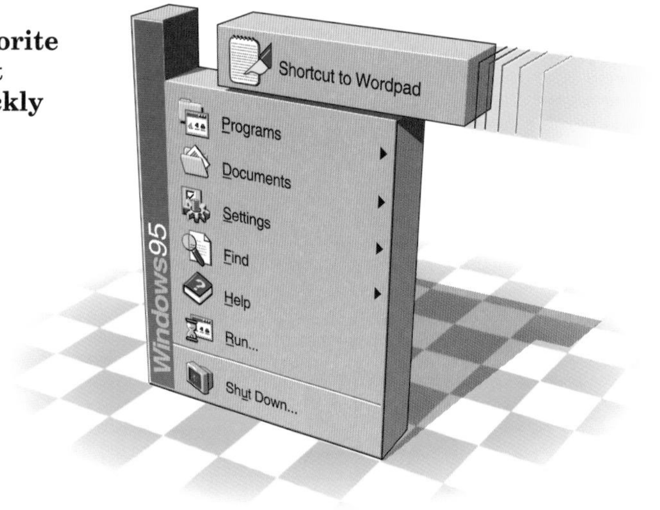

ADD A PROGRAM TO THE START MENU

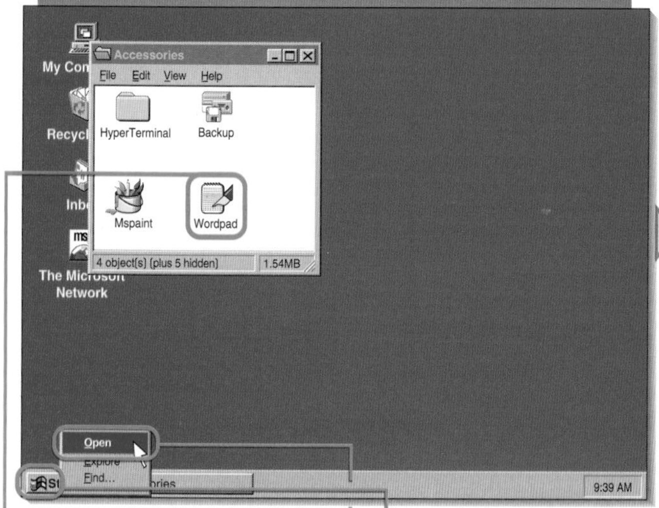

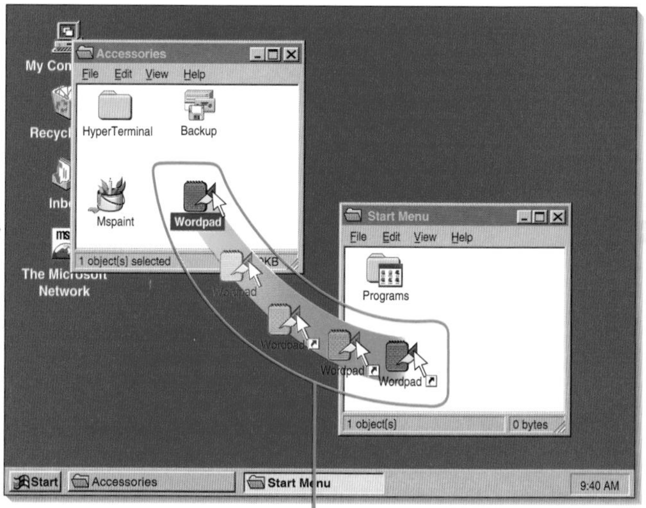

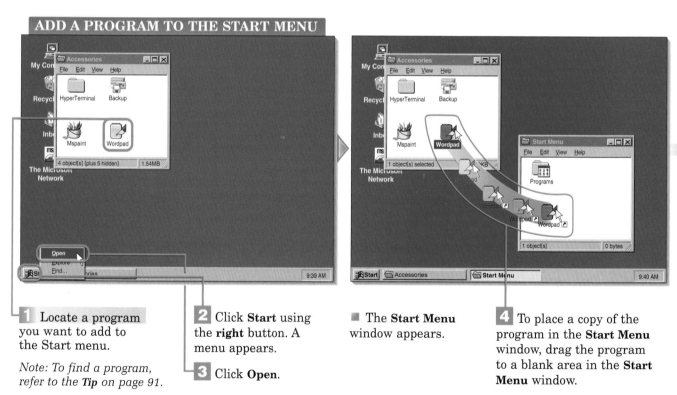

1 Locate a program you want to add to the Start menu.

*Note: To find a program, refer to the **Tip** on page 91.*

2 Click **Start** using the **right** button. A menu appears.

3 Click **Open**.

■ The **Start Menu** window appears.

4 To place a copy of the program in the **Start Menu** window, drag the program to a blank area in the **Start Menu** window.

TIP

If you no longer want a program to appear on the Start menu, delete the program from the **Start Menu** window as you would delete any file.

Note: To delete a file, refer to page 78.

Removing a program from the **Start Menu** window does not delete the program from your hard disk.

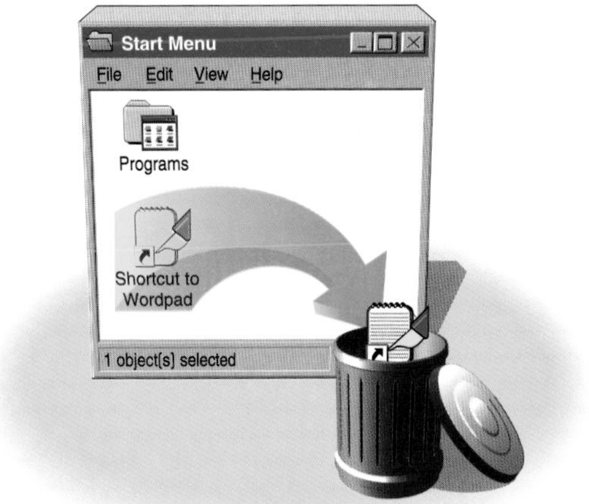

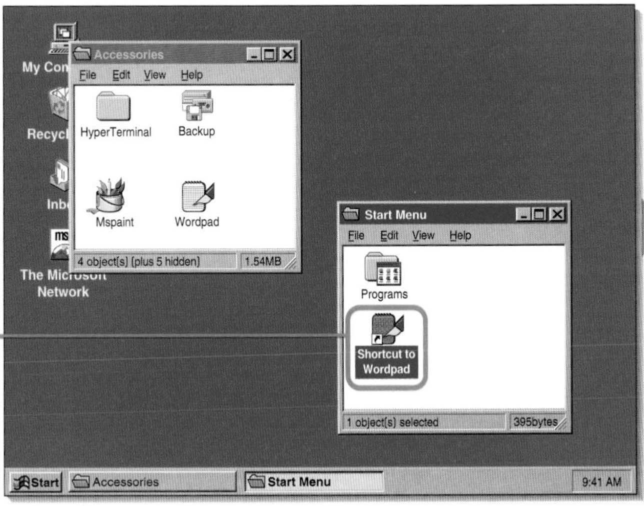

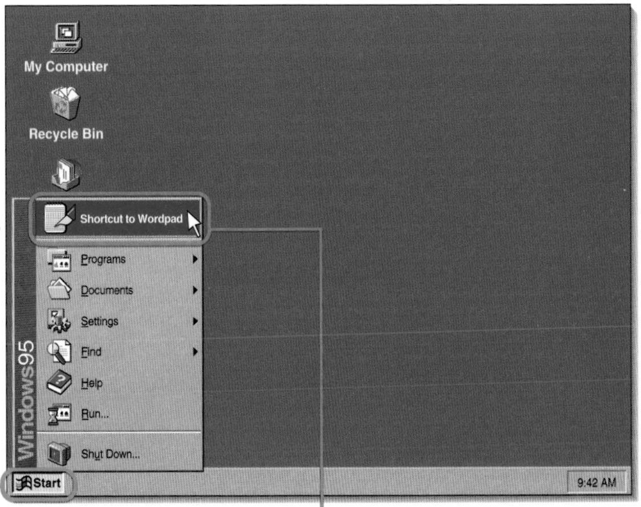

■ A copy of the program appears in the **Start Menu** window.

■ When you copy a program to the **Start Menu** window, you do not change the location of the program on your hard disk.

START THE PROGRAM

1 Click **Start**.

■ The program you added to the Start menu appears at the top of the menu.

2 To start the program, click the name of the program.

HAVE A PROGRAM START AUTOMATICALLY

If you use the same program every day, you can have the program start automatically every time you turn on your computer.

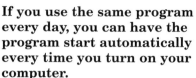

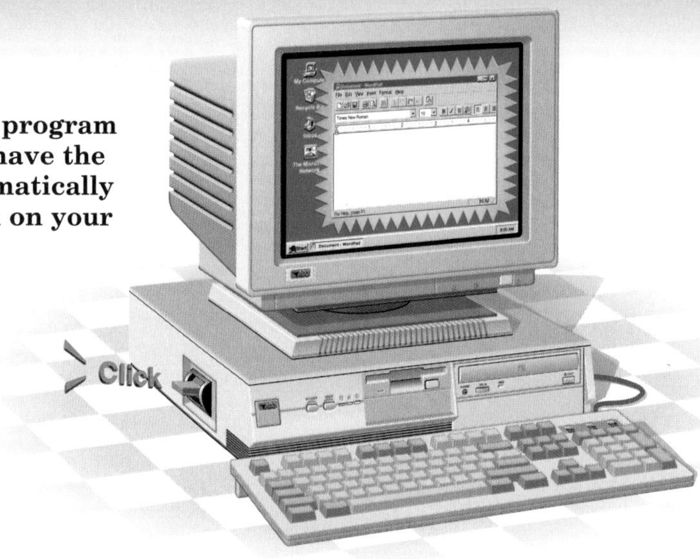

HAVE A PROGRAM START AUTOMATICALLY

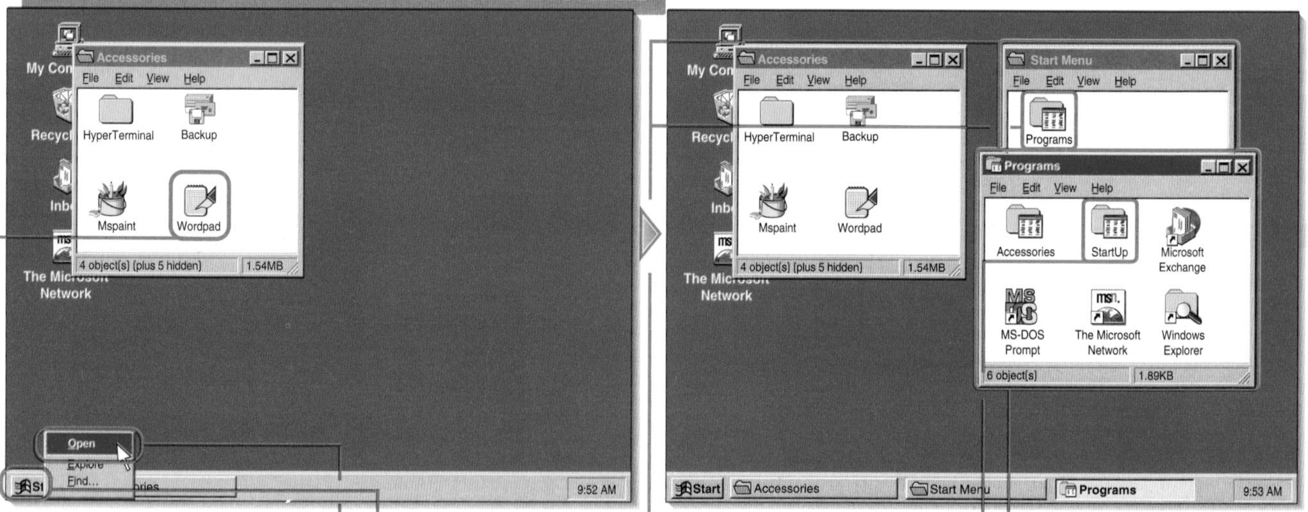

1 Locate the program you want to start automatically.

*Note: To find a program, refer to the **Tip** on page 91.*

2 Click **Start** using the **right** button. A menu appears.

3 Click **Open**.

■ The **Start Menu** window appears.

4 To display the contents of the **Programs** folder, double-click the folder.

■ The **Programs** window appears.

■ The **StartUp** folder contains all the programs that start automatically when you turn on your computer.

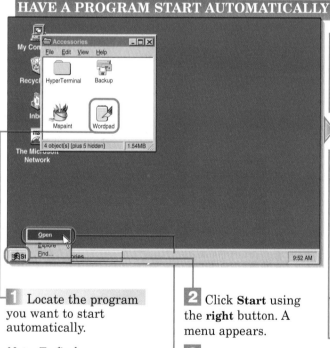

TIP

The items in the Programs menu match the items in the Programs window.

If you add or remove items in the Programs window, the Programs menu will display the changes.

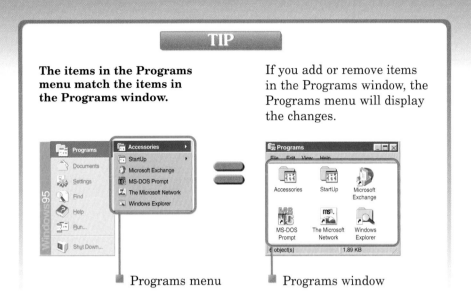

Programs menu

Programs window

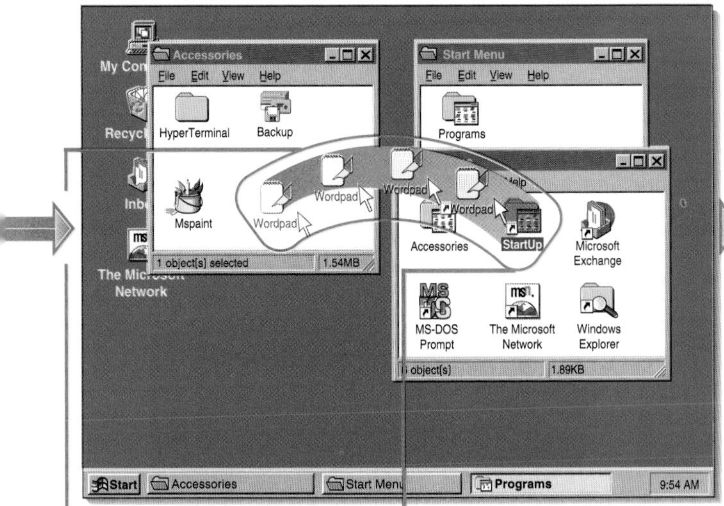

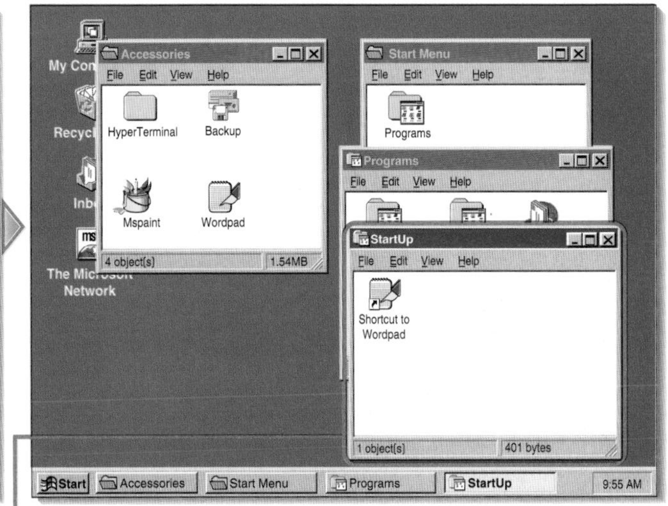

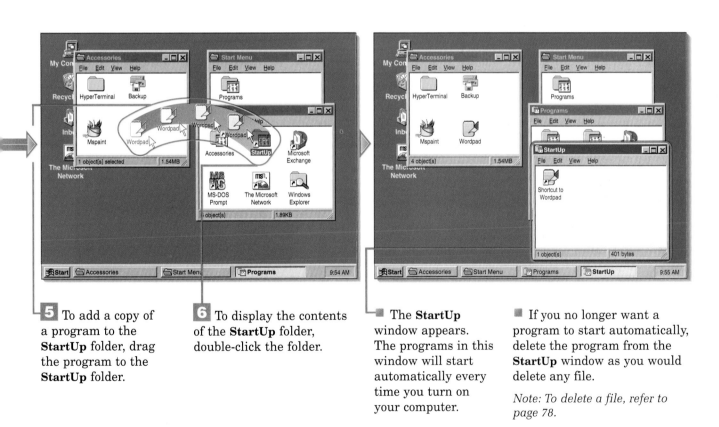

5 To add a copy of a program to the **StartUp** folder, drag the program to the **StartUp** folder.

6 To display the contents of the **StartUp** folder, double-click the folder.

■ The **StartUp** window appears. The programs in this window will start automatically every time you turn on your computer.

■ If you no longer want a program to start automatically, delete the program from the **StartUp** window as you would delete any file.

Note: To delete a file, refer to page 78.

In this chapter you will learn how to change Windows settings to suit your needs.

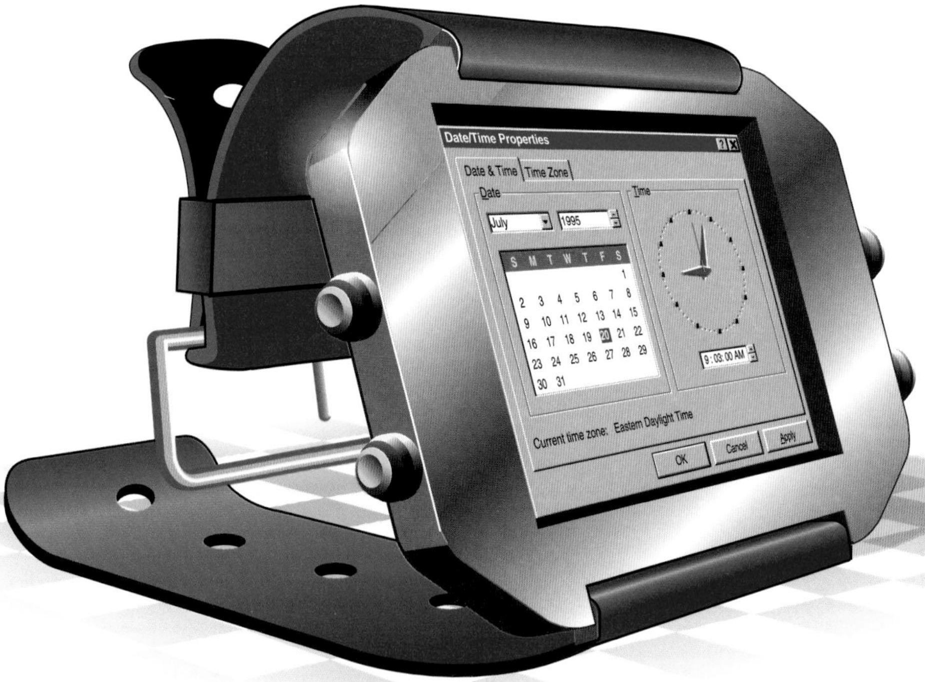

CHAPTER 7: PERSONALIZE WINDOWS

Change the Date and Time 102

Add Wallpaper 104

Change Screen Colors 106

Set Up a Screen Saver 108

Change Mouse Settings 110

Move the Taskbar 114

Size the Taskbar 115

Hide the Taskbar 116

Change Screen Resolution 118

Change Color Depth 120

CHANGE THE DATE AND TIME

It is important to have the correct date and time set in your computer. Windows uses this information to identify each document you create or update.

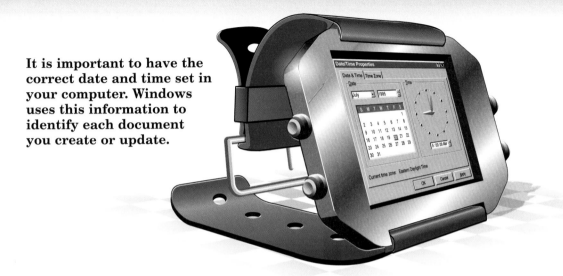

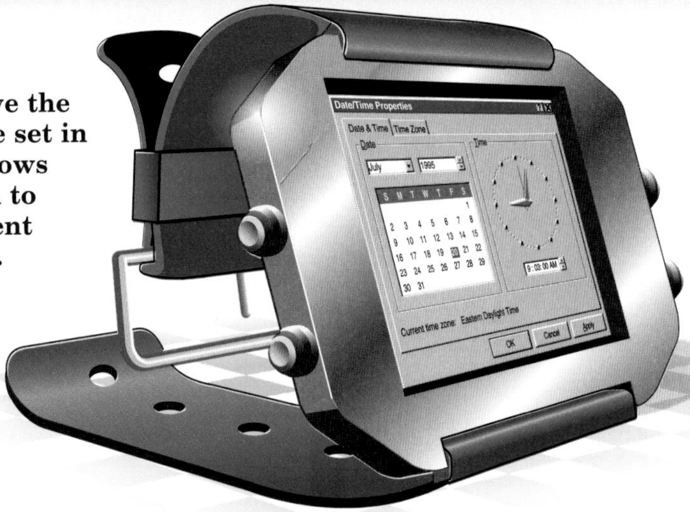

CHANGE THE DATE AND TIME

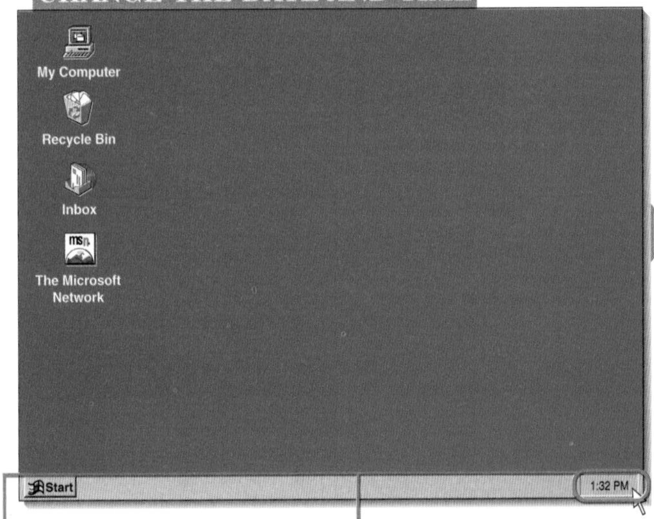

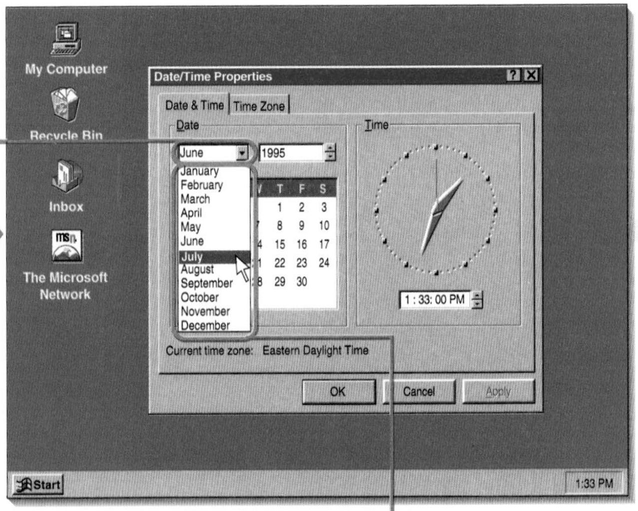

■ This area displays the time set in your computer.

1 To change the date or time set in your computer, double-click this area.

■ The **Date/Time Properties** dialog box appears.

■ This area displays the month set in your computer.

2 To change the month, click this area.

3 Click the correct month.

TIP

Your computer has a built-in clock that keeps track of the date and time even when you turn off the computer.

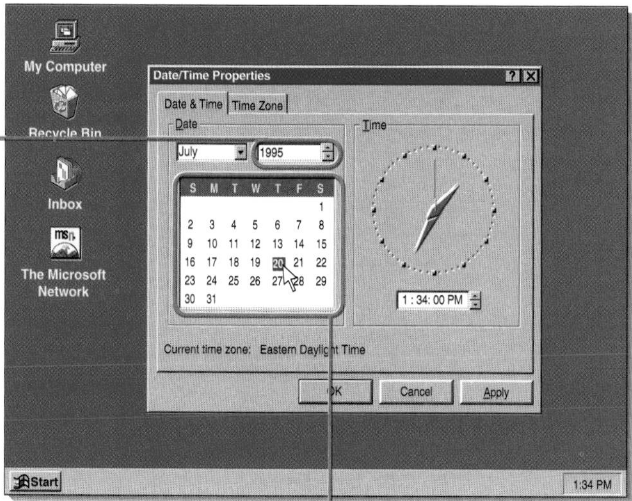

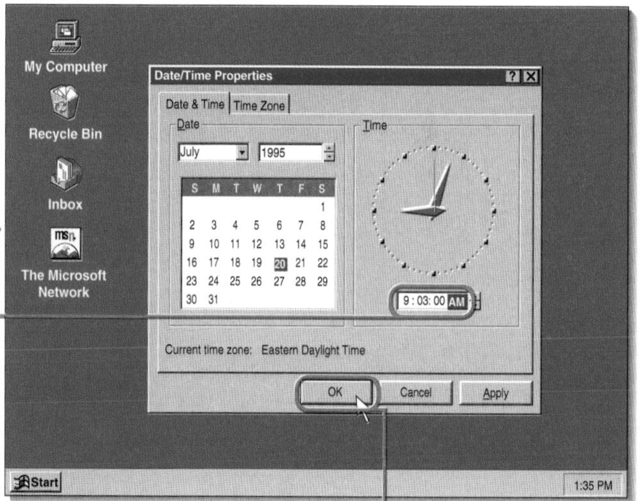

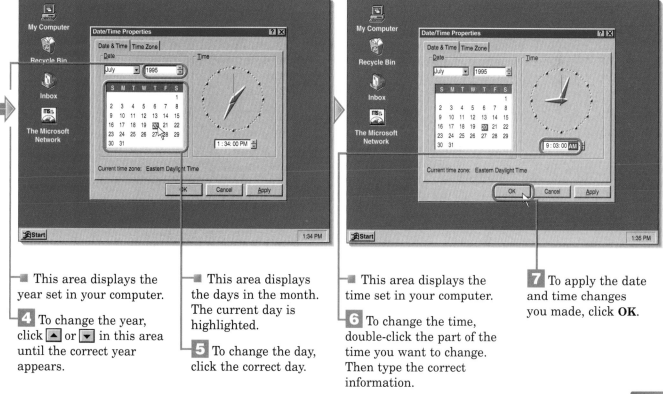

■ This area displays the year set in your computer.

4 To change the year, click ▲ or ▼ in this area until the correct year appears.

■ This area displays the days in the month. The current day is highlighted.

5 To change the day, click the correct day.

■ This area displays the time set in your computer.

6 To change the time, double-click the part of the time you want to change. Then type the correct information.

7 To apply the date and time changes you made, click **OK**.

ADD WALLPAPER

You can decorate your screen by adding wallpaper.

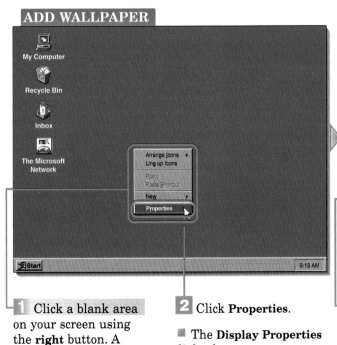

ADD WALLPAPER

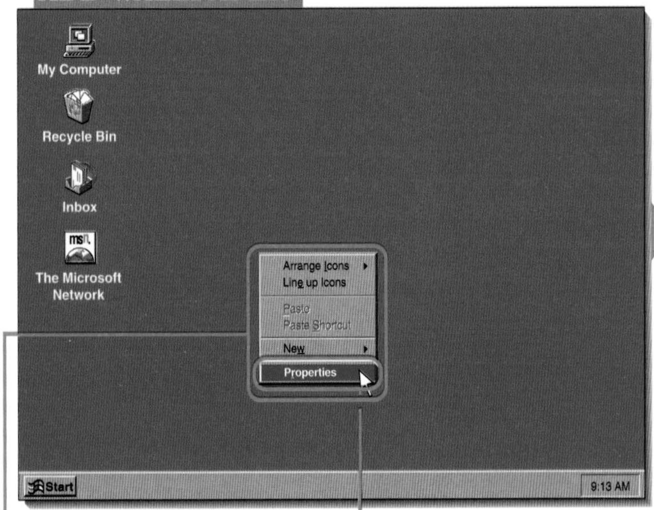

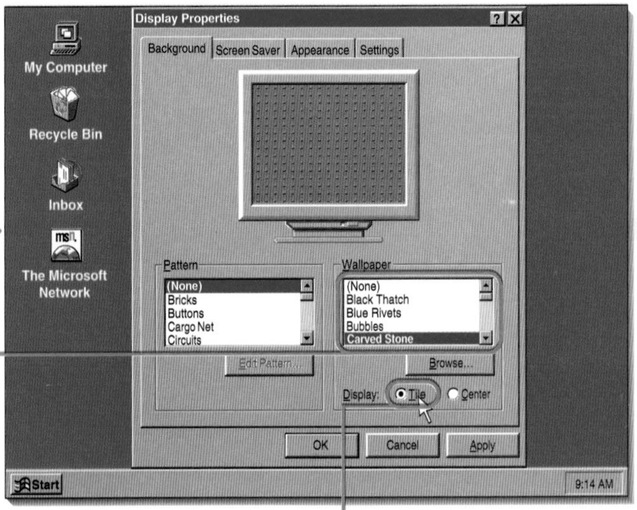

1 Click a blank area on your screen using the **right** button. A menu appears.

2 Click **Properties**.

■ The **Display Properties** dialog box appears.

3 Click the wallpaper you want to display.

Note: To view all the available wallpapers, use the scroll bar. For more information, refer to page 24.

4 To cover your entire screen with the wallpaper you selected, click **Tile** (○ changes to ◉).

*Note: To place a small wallpaper image in the middle of your screen, click **Center**.*

These are a few of the available wallpapers.

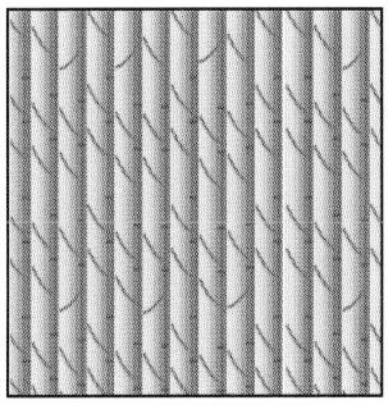

Straw Mat

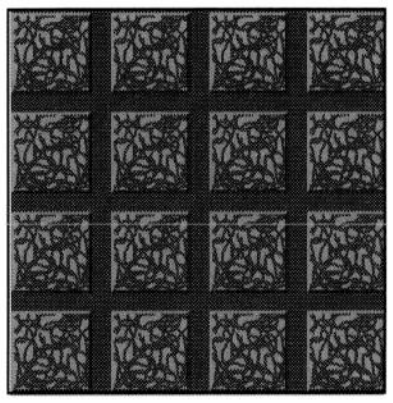

Tiles

Triangles

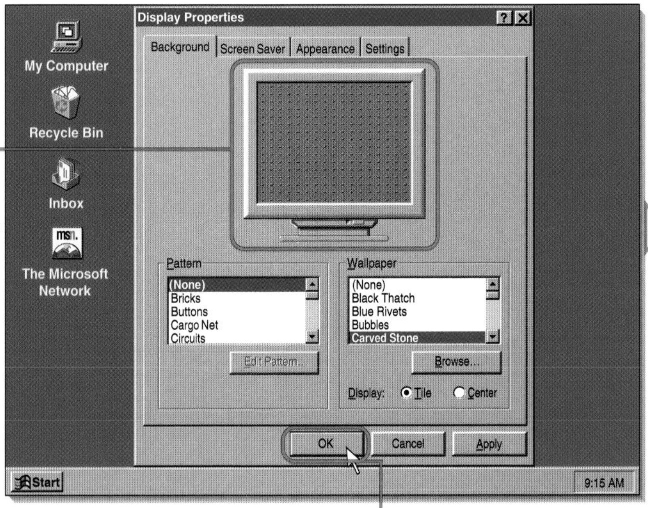

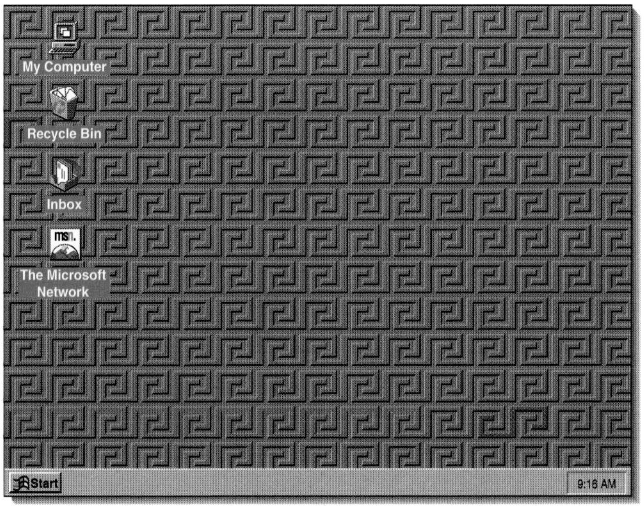

■ This area displays how the wallpaper you selected will look on your screen.

5 To display the wallpaper on your screen, click **OK**.

■ Your screen displays the wallpaper you selected.

*Note: To remove wallpaper from your screen, perform steps 1 to 3, selecting (**None**) in step 3. Then perform step 5.*

CHANGE SCREEN COLORS

You can change the colors displayed on your screen to suit your preferences.

CHANGE SCREEN COLORS

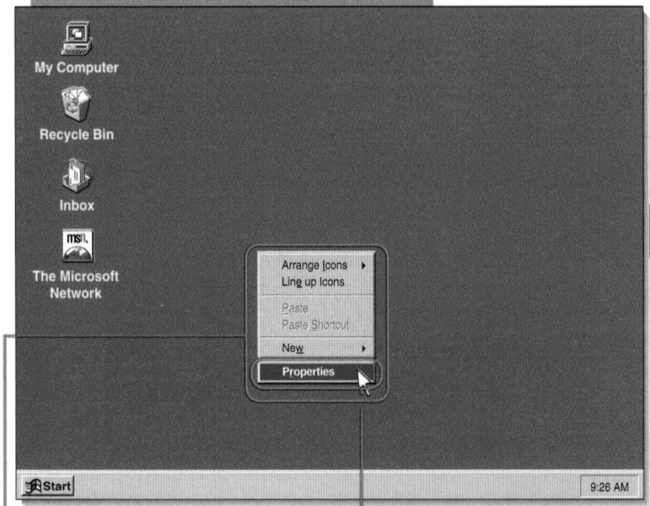

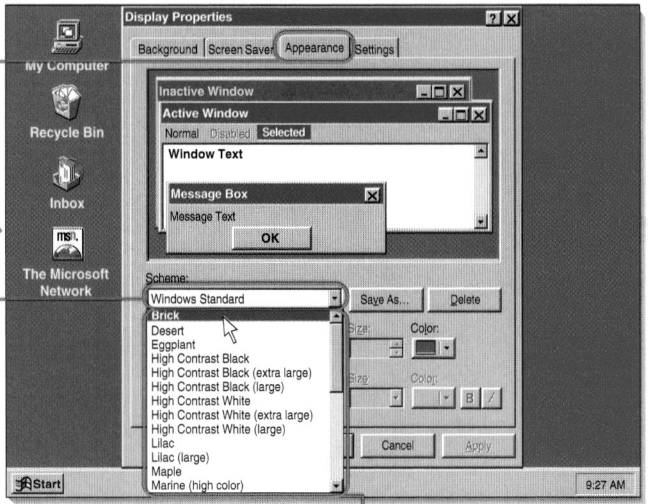

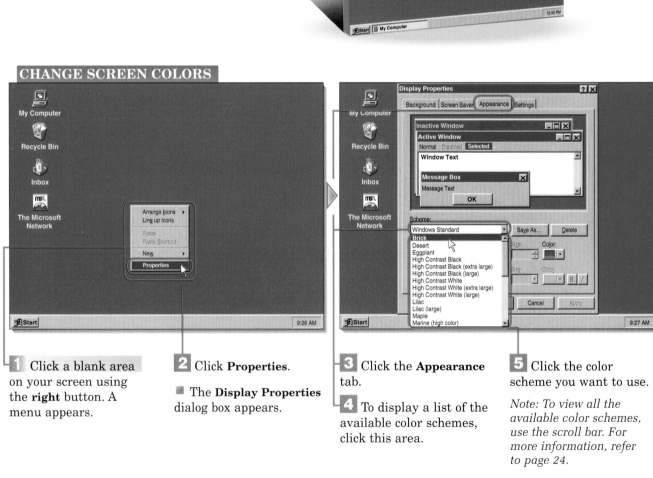

1 Click a blank area on your screen using the **right** button. A menu appears.

2 Click **Properties**.

■ The **Display Properties** dialog box appears.

3 Click the **Appearance** tab.

4 To display a list of the available color schemes, click this area.

5 Click the color scheme you want to use.

Note: To view all the available color schemes, use the scroll bar. For more information, refer to page 24.

These are a few of the available color schemes.

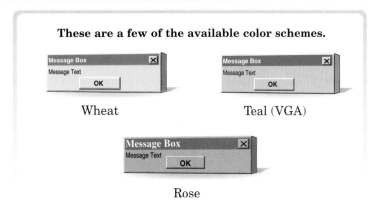

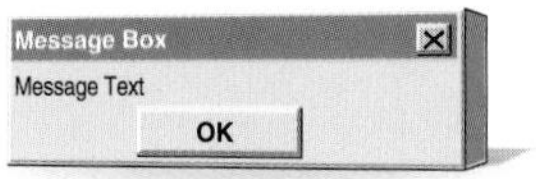

Wheat

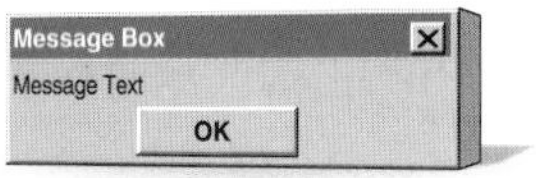

Teal (VGA)

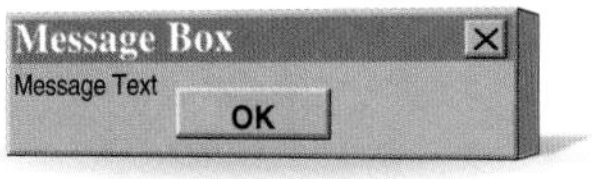

Rose

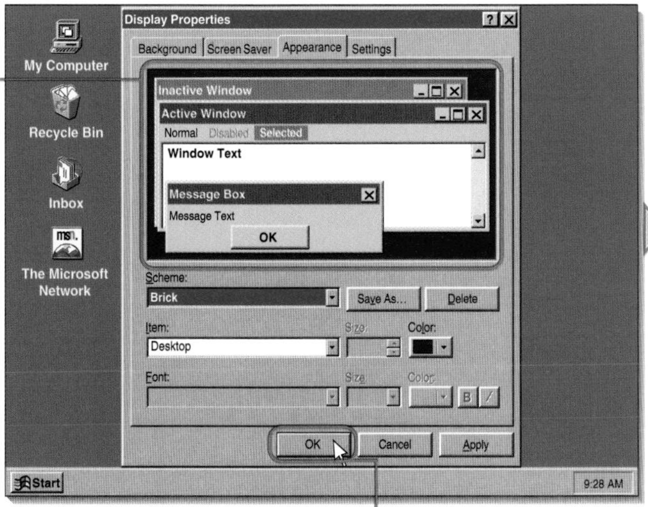

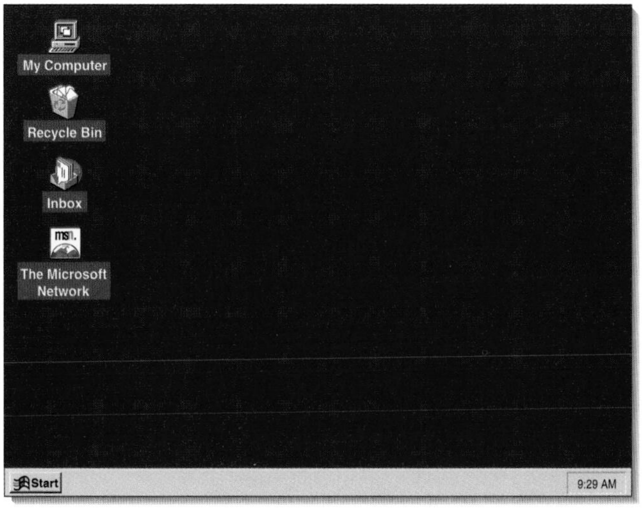

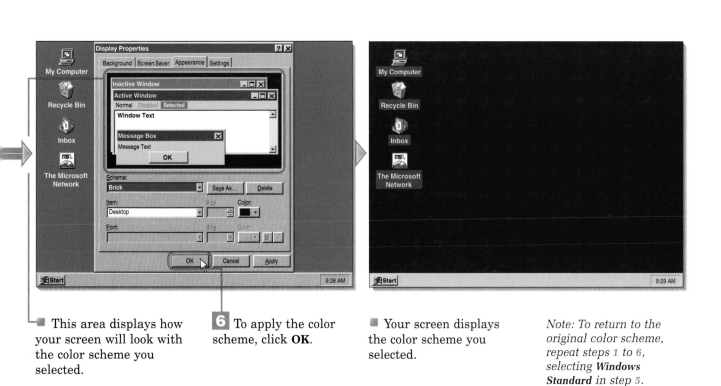

■ This area displays how your screen will look with the color scheme you selected.

6 To apply the color scheme, click **OK**.

■ Your screen displays the color scheme you selected.

*Note: To return to the original color scheme, repeat steps 1 to 6, selecting **Windows Standard** in step 5.*

SET UP A SCREEN SAVER

A screen saver is a moving picture or pattern that appears on the screen when you do not use your computer for a period of time.

SET UP A SCREEN SAVER

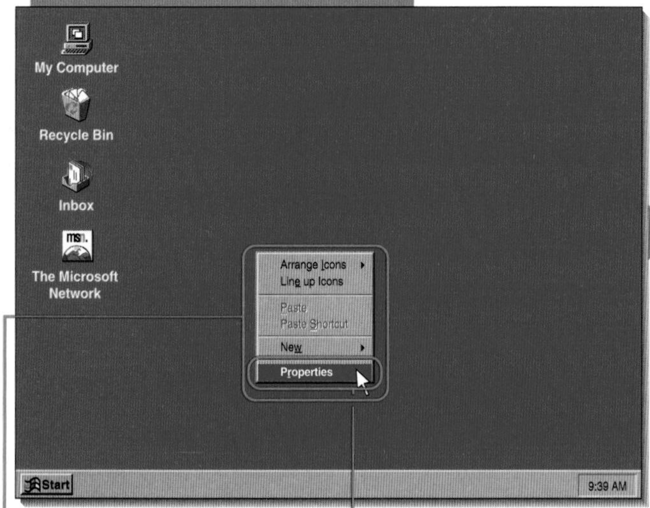

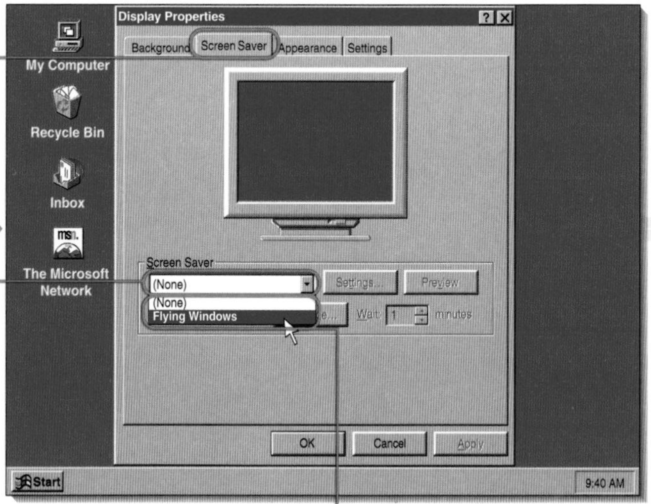

1 Click a blank area on your screen using the **right** button. A menu appears.

2 Click **Properties**.

■ The **Display Properties** dialog box appears.

3 Click the **Screen Saver** tab.

4 To display a list of the available screen savers, click this area.

5 Click the screen saver you want to use.

Note: To install additional screen savers that come with Windows, refer to page 186.

TIP

Screen savers were originally designed to prevent screen burn, which occurs when an image appears in a fixed position for a period of time.

Today's monitors are better designed to prevent screen burn, but people still use screen savers for entertainment.

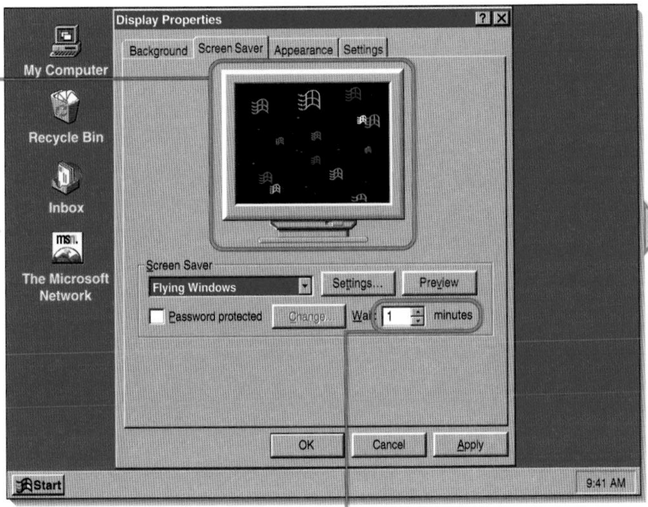

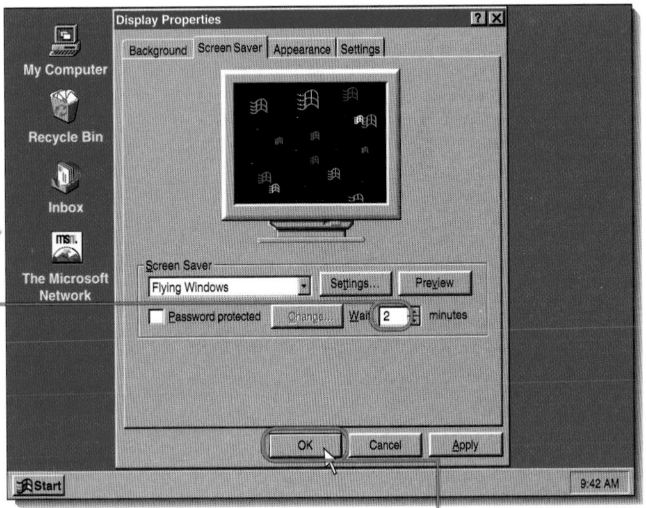

- This area displays how the screen saver will look on your screen.

- The screen saver will appear when you do not use your computer for the amount of time displayed in this area.

6 To change the amount of time, click this area.

7 Press ←Backspace or Delete on your keyboard to remove the existing number. Then type a new number.

8 Click **OK**.

CHANGE MOUSE SETTINGS

You can change the way your mouse works to suit your needs.

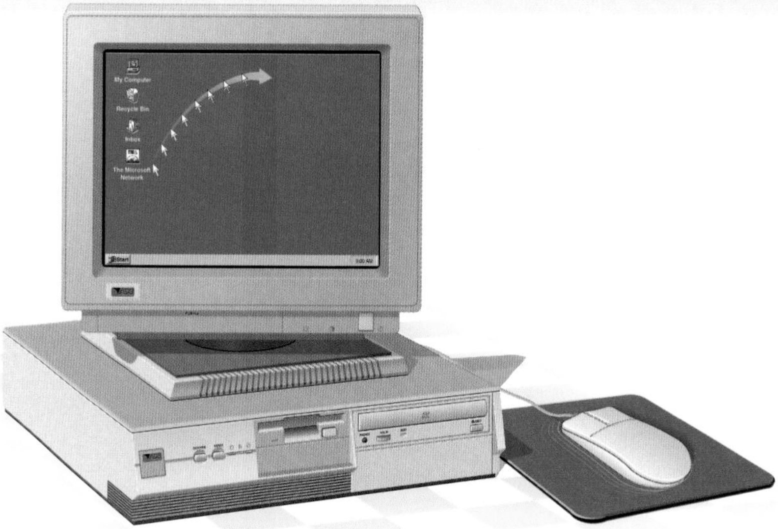

CHANGE MOUSE SETTINGS

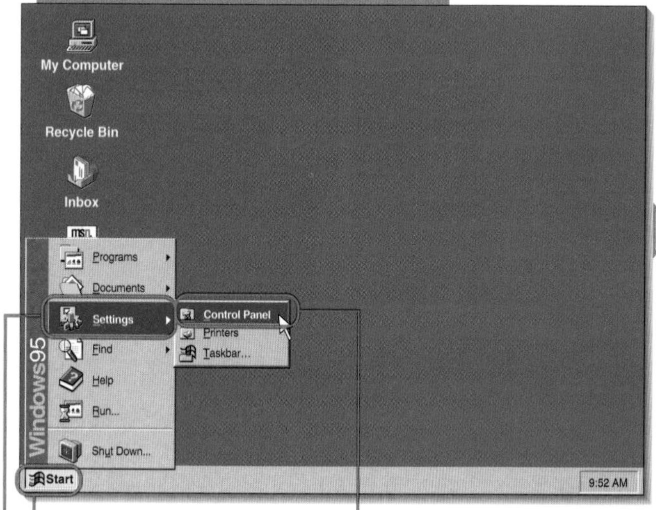

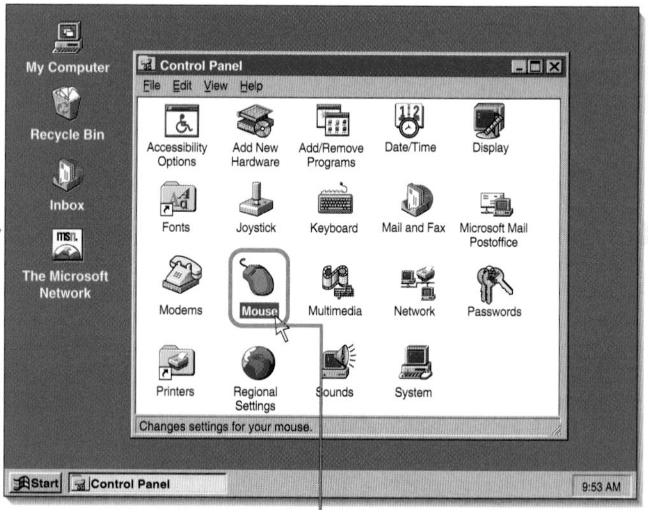

1 Click **Start**.

2 Click **Settings**.

3 Click **Control Panel**.

■ The **Control Panel** window appears.

4 To change the mouse settings, double-click **Mouse**.

■ The **Mouse Properties** dialog box appears.

TIP

A mouse pad provides a smooth surface for moving the mouse on your desk. You can buy mouse pads displaying interesting designs or pictures at most computer stores.

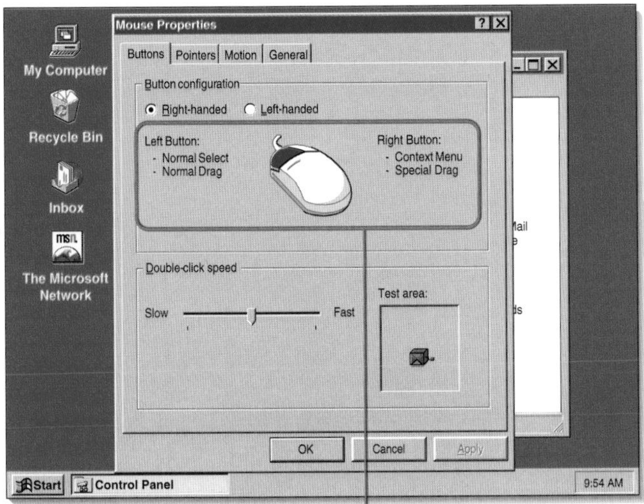

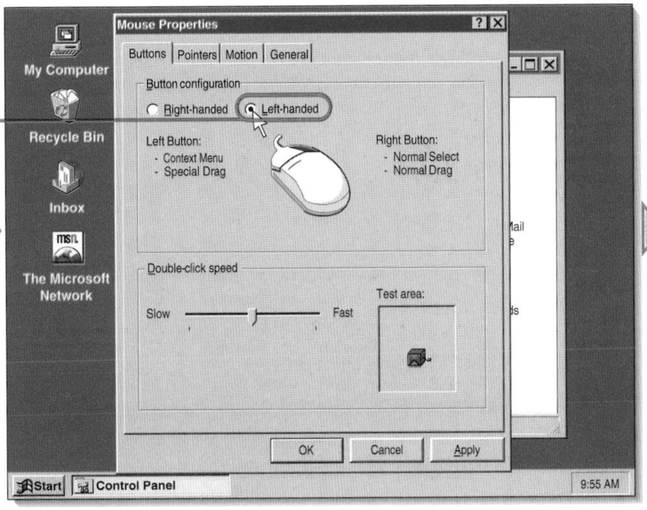

SWITCH BUTTONS

If you are left-handed, you can switch the functions of the left and right mouse buttons to make the mouse easier to use.

■ This area describes the current functions of the left and right mouse buttons.

1 To switch the functions of the buttons, click this option (○ changes to ◉).

Note: This change will not take effect until you confirm the changes. To do so, refer to page 113.

CONTINUED

CHANGE MOUSE SETTINGS

You can personalize your mouse by changing the double-click speed and the way the mouse pointer moves on your screen.

CHANGE MOUSE SETTINGS (CONTINUED)

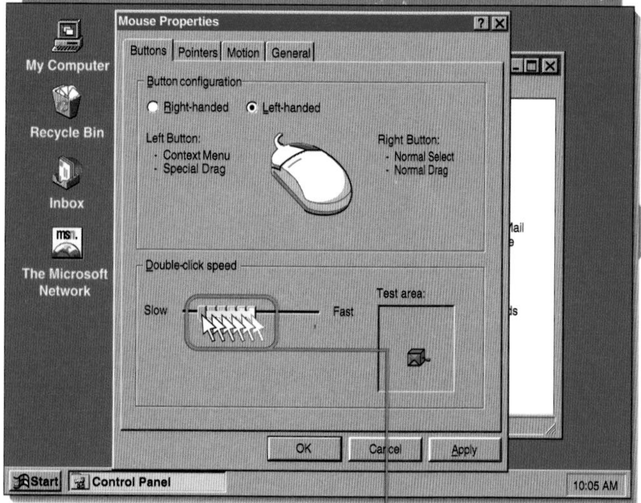

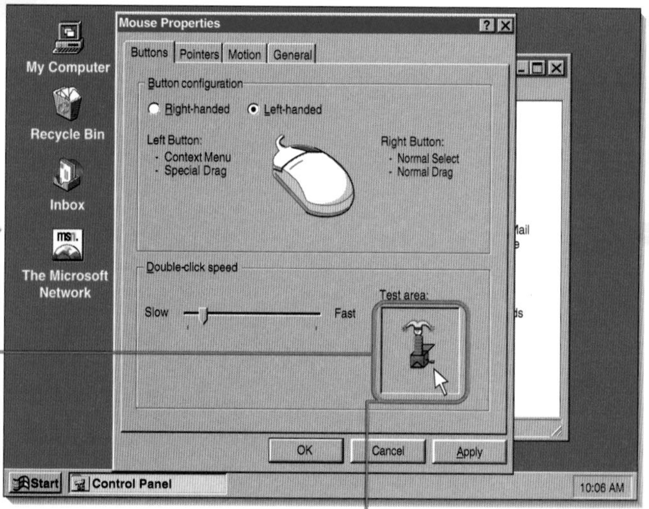

DOUBLE-CLICK SPEED

You can change the amount of time that can pass between two clicks of the mouse button for Windows to recognize a double-click.

1 To change the double-click speed, drag the slider (⛉) to a new position.

2 To test the double-click speed, double-click this area.

■ The jack-in-the-box appears if you clicked at the correct speed.

Note: If you are an inexperienced mouse user, you may find a slower speed easier to use.

TIP

Displaying mouse trails can help you follow the movement of the mouse on your screen. This is especially useful on portable computer screens, where the mouse can be difficult to follow.

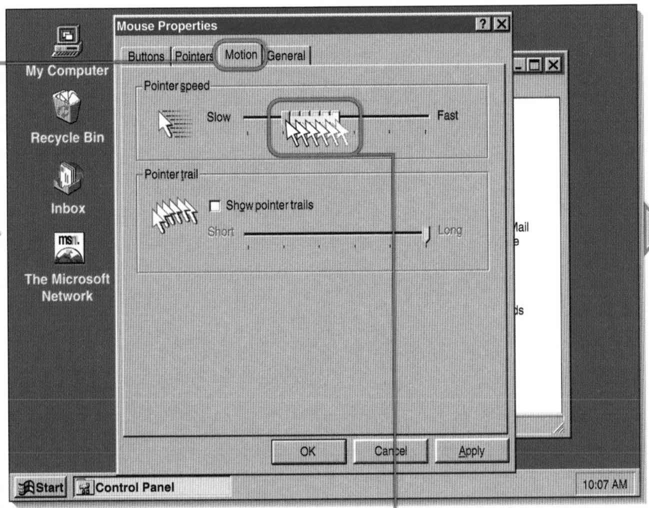

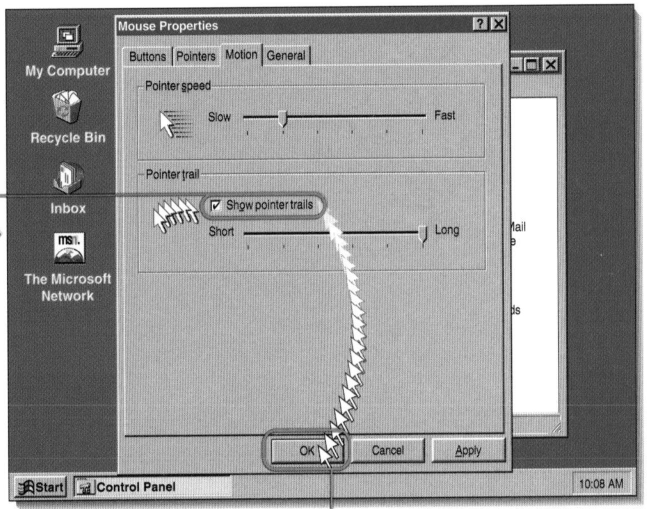

POINTER SPEED

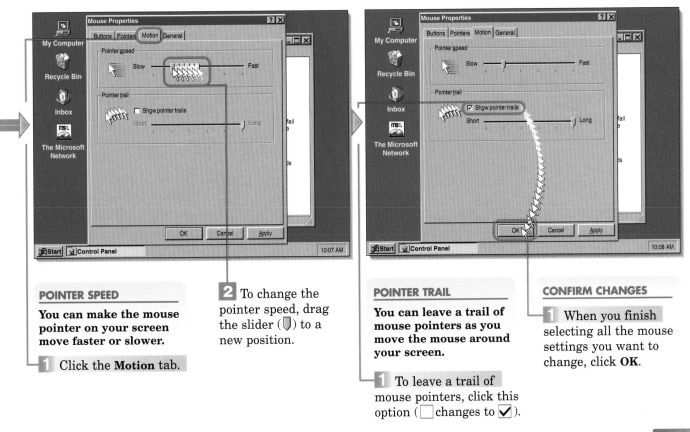

You can make the mouse pointer on your screen move faster or slower.

1 Click the **Motion** tab.

2 To change the pointer speed, drag the slider ( ) to a new position.

POINTER TRAIL

You can leave a trail of mouse pointers as you move the mouse around your screen.

1 To leave a trail of mouse pointers, click this option (changes to ✓).

CONFIRM CHANGES

1 When you finish selecting all the mouse settings you want to change, click **OK**.

MOVE THE TASKBAR

You can move the taskbar to a more convenient location on your screen.

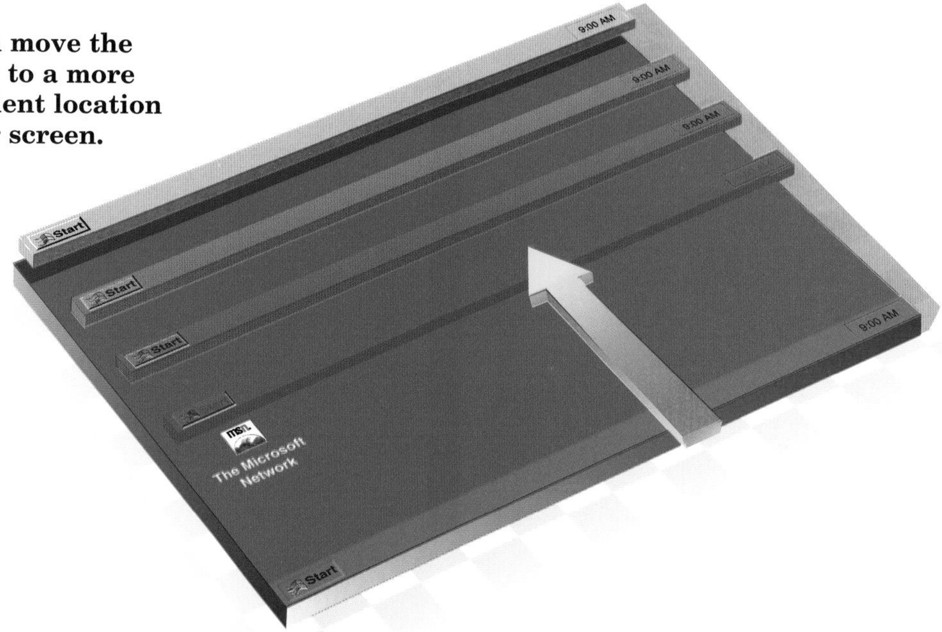

MOVE THE TASKBAR

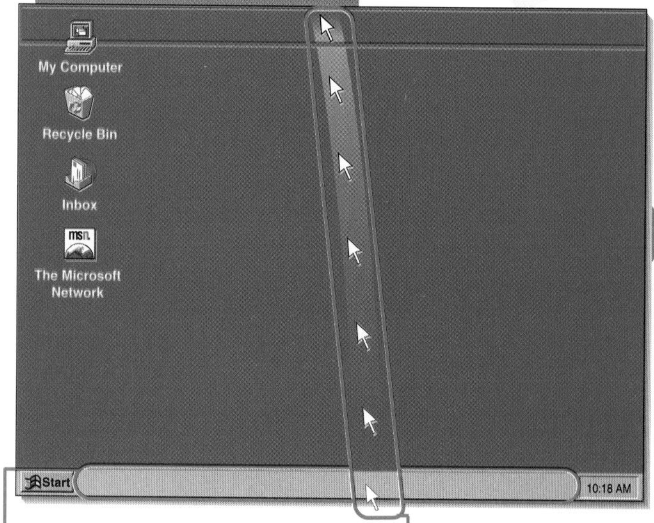

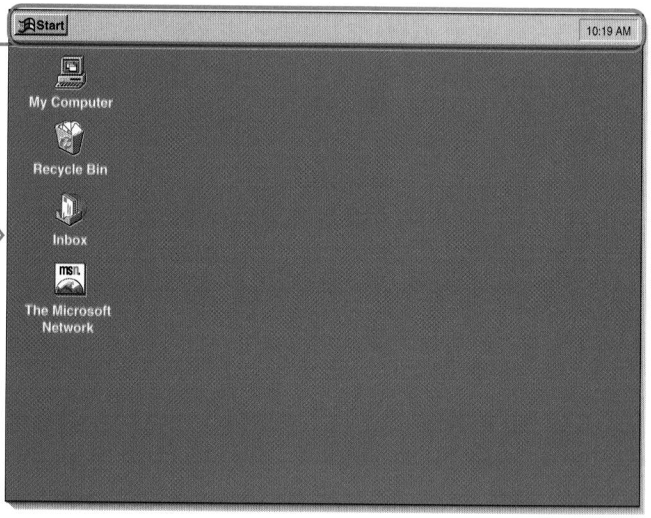

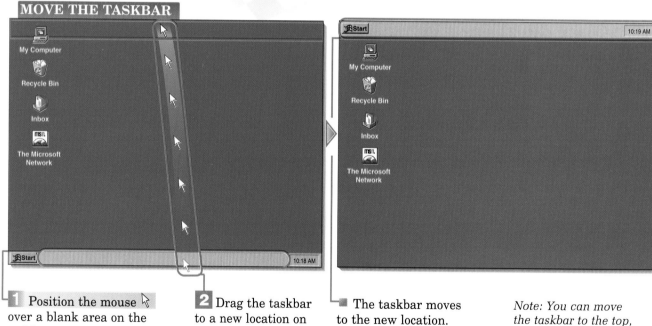

1 Position the mouse over a blank area on the taskbar.

2 Drag the taskbar to a new location on your screen.

■ The taskbar moves to the new location.

Note: You can move the taskbar to the top, bottom, left or right side of your screen.

SIZE THE TASKBAR

You can change the size of the taskbar so it can display more information.

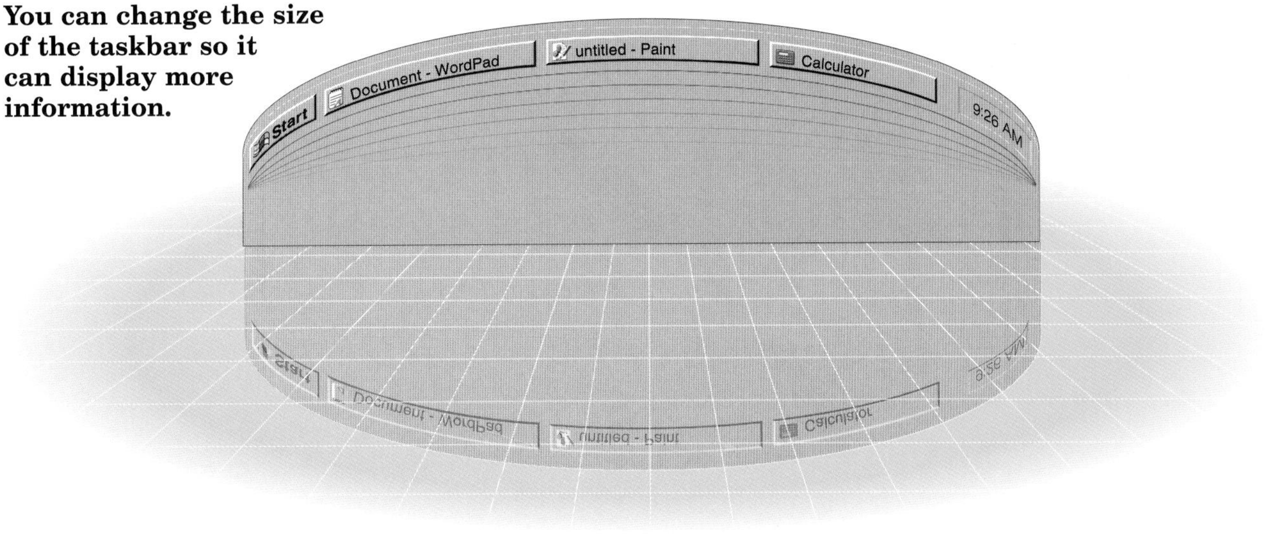

SIZE THE TASKBAR

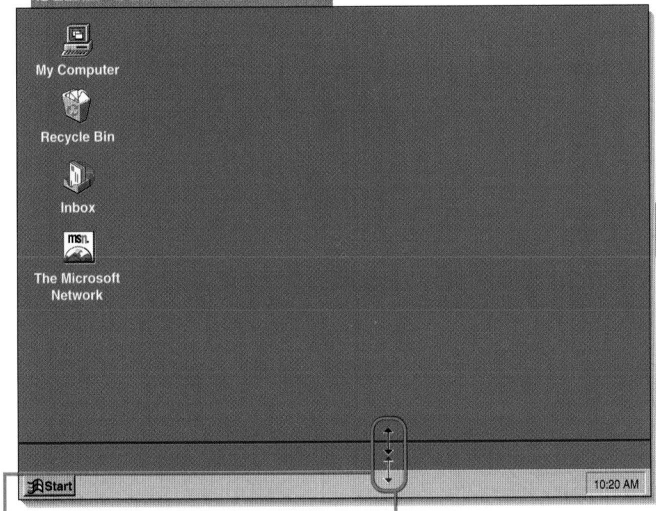

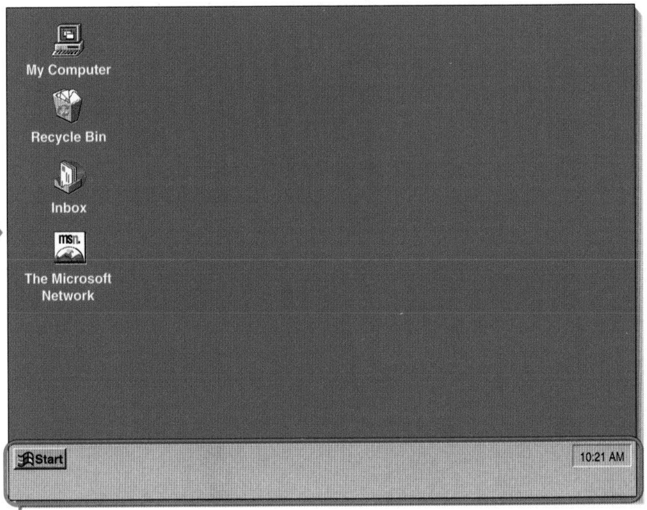

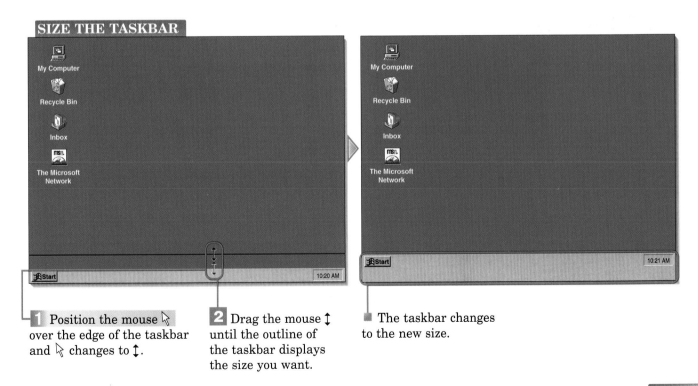

1 Position the mouse over the edge of the taskbar and changes to ↕.

2 Drag the mouse ↕ until the outline of the taskbar displays the size you want.

■ The taskbar changes to the new size.

HIDE THE TASKBAR

You can hide the taskbar to give you more room on the screen to accomplish your tasks.

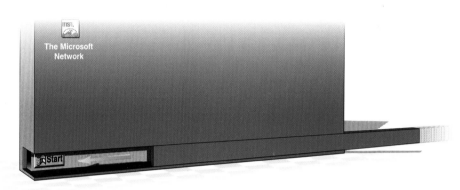

HIDE THE TASKBAR

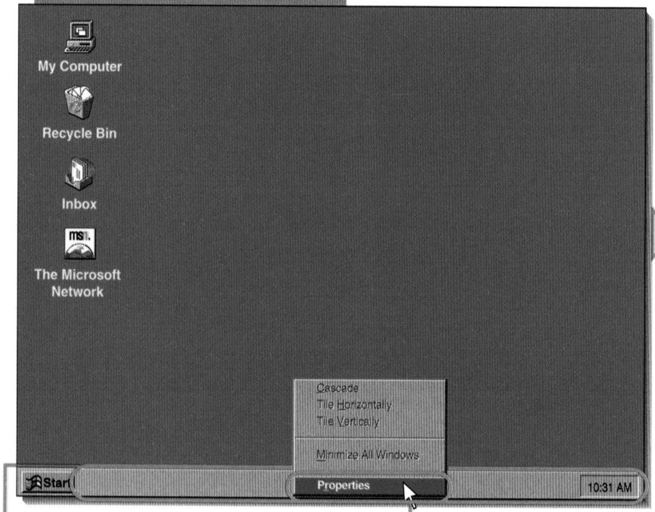

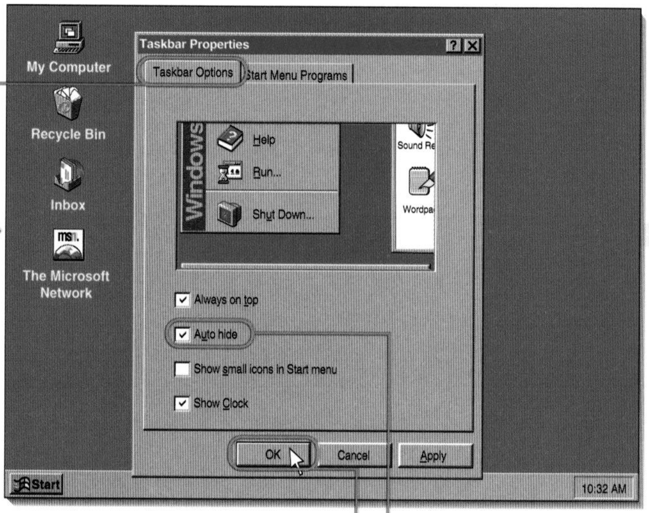

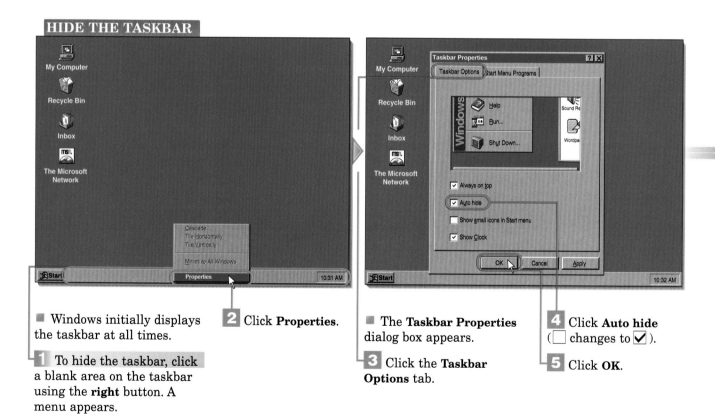

■ Windows initially displays the taskbar at all times.

1 To hide the taskbar, click a blank area on the taskbar using the **right** button. A menu appears.

2 Click **Properties**.

■ The **Taskbar Properties** dialog box appears.

3 Click the **Taskbar Options** tab.

4 Click **Auto hide** (☐ changes to ☑).

5 Click **OK**.

TIP

■ The taskbar contains the **Start** button, which gives you quick access to your programs and files.

■ The taskbar also displays the name of each open window on your screen and the current time.

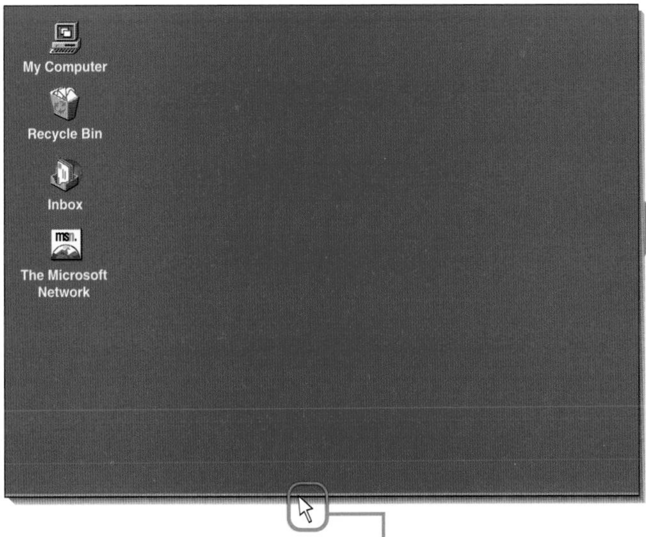

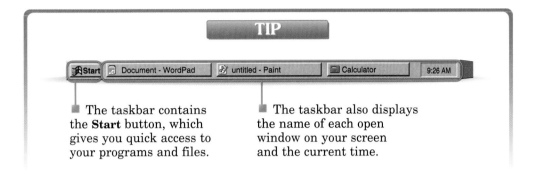

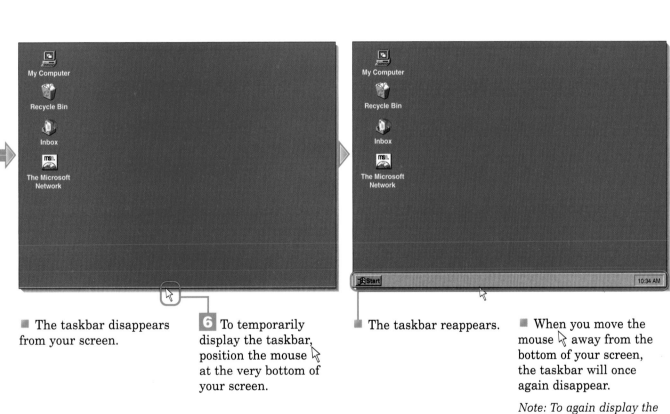

■ The taskbar disappears from your screen.

6 To temporarily display the taskbar, position the mouse at the very bottom of your screen.

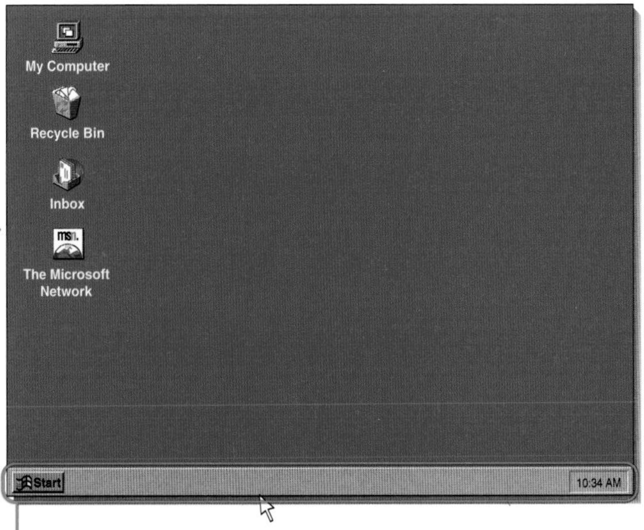

■ The taskbar reappears.

■ When you move the mouse away from the bottom of your screen, the taskbar will once again disappear.

Note: To again display the taskbar at all times, repeat steps 1 to 5 on page 116.

CHANGE SCREEN RESOLUTION

You can change the amount of information that can fit on your screen.

You cannot change the screen resolution for some monitors.

640 x 480
Lower resolutions display larger images on the screen. This lets you see information more clearly.

CHANGE SCREEN RESOLUTION

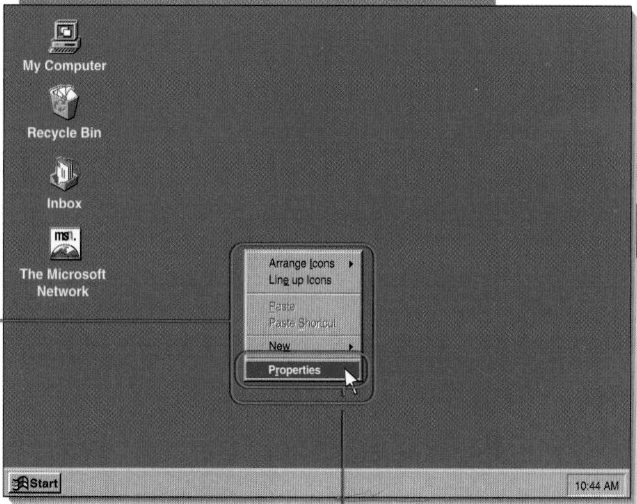

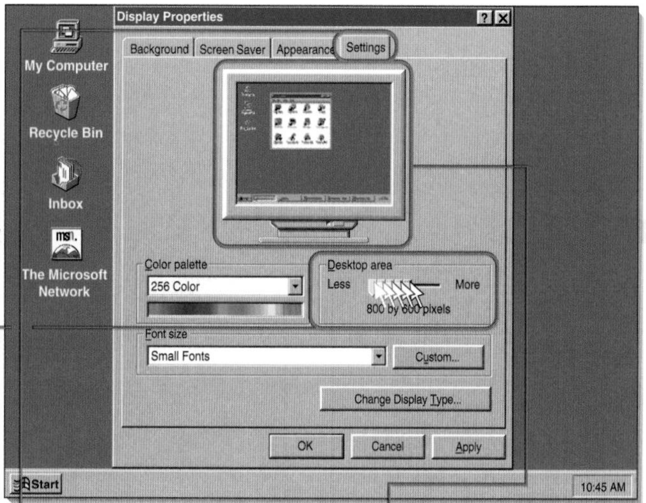

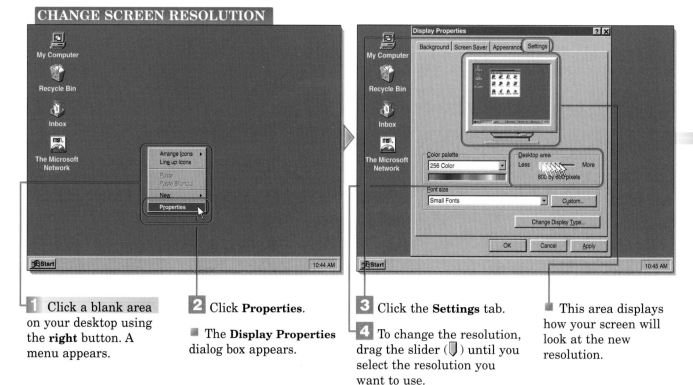

1 Click a blank area on your desktop using the **right** button. A menu appears.

2 Click **Properties**.

■ The **Display Properties** dialog box appears.

3 Click the **Settings** tab.

4 To change the resolution, drag the slider (▯) until you select the resolution you want to use.

■ This area displays how your screen will look at the new resolution.

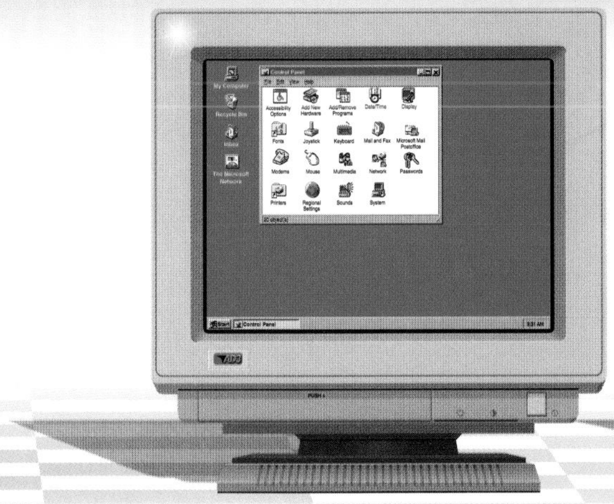

800 x 600

1024 x 768
Higher resolutions display smaller images on the screen. This lets you display more information at once.

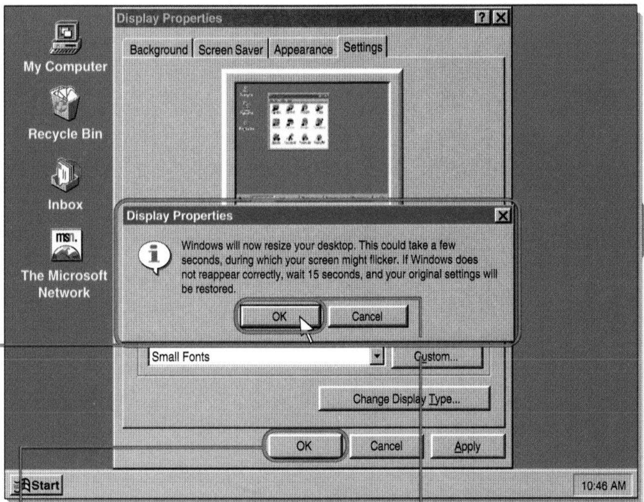

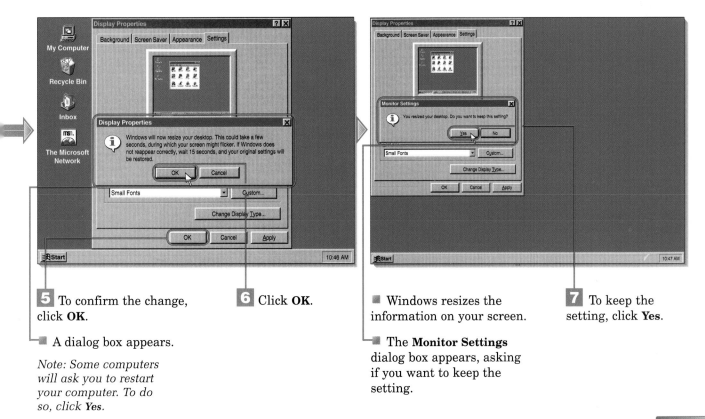

5 To confirm the change, click **OK**.

■ A dialog box appears.

Note: Some computers will ask you to restart your computer. To do so, click ***Yes****.*

6 Click **OK**.

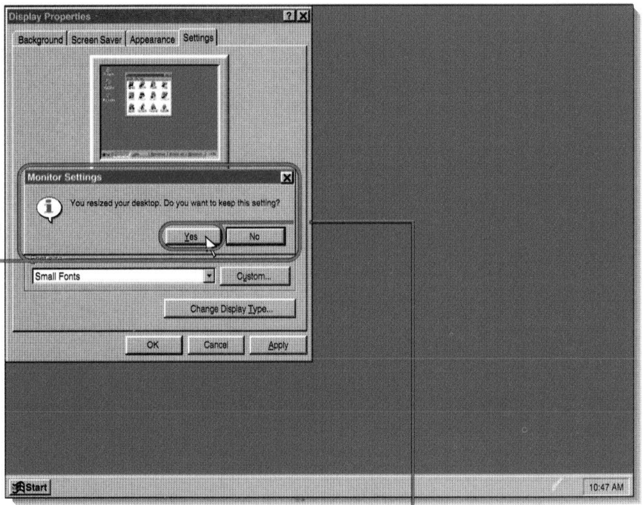

■ Windows resizes the information on your screen.

■ The **Monitor Settings** dialog box appears, asking if you want to keep the setting.

7 To keep the setting, click **Yes**.

CHANGE COLOR DEPTH

You can change the number of colors displayed on your screen. More colors result in more realistic images.

16 Color
Choppy-looking images.

256 Color
Ideal for most home and business applications.

CHANGE COLOR DEPTH

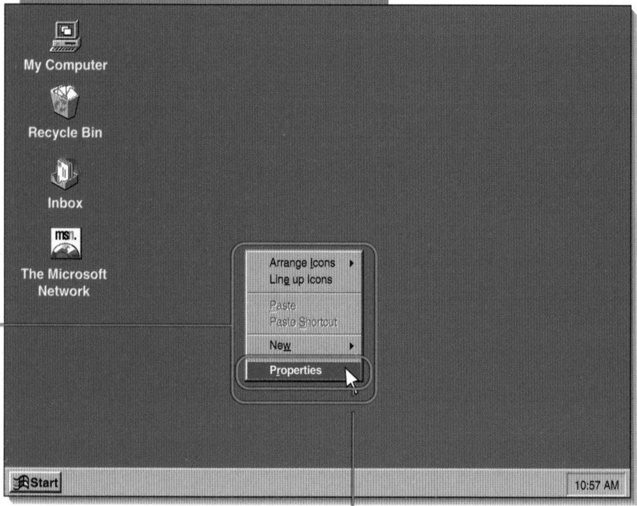

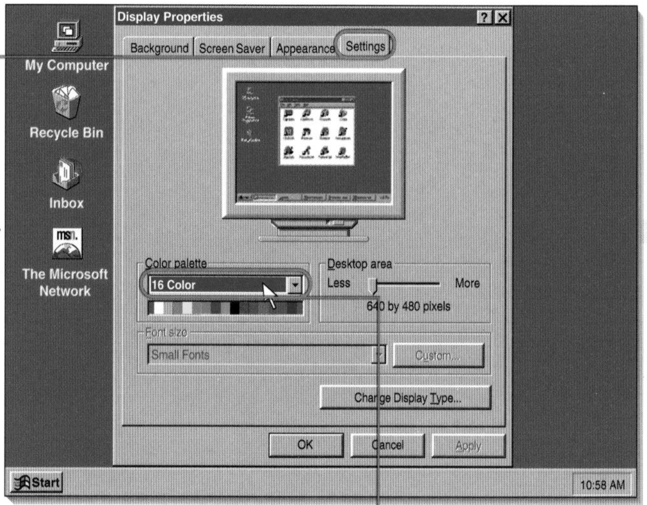

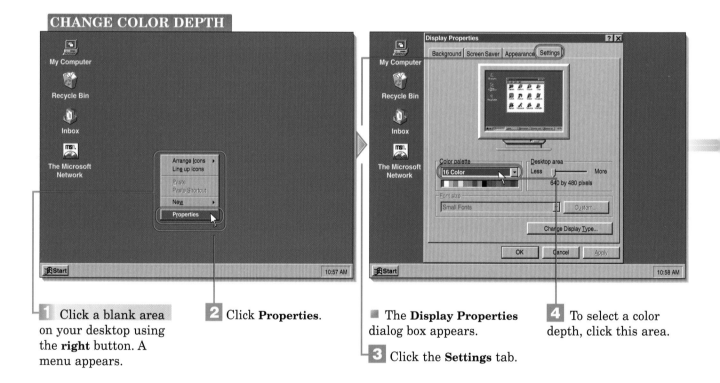

1 Click a blank area on your desktop using the **right** button. A menu appears.

2 Click **Properties**.

■ The **Display Properties** dialog box appears.

3 Click the **Settings** tab.

4 To select a color depth, click this area.

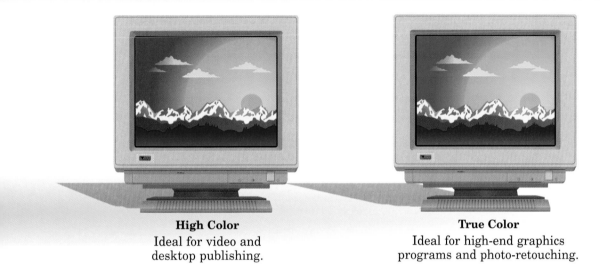

High Color
Ideal for video and desktop publishing.

True Color
Ideal for high-end graphics programs and photo-retouching.

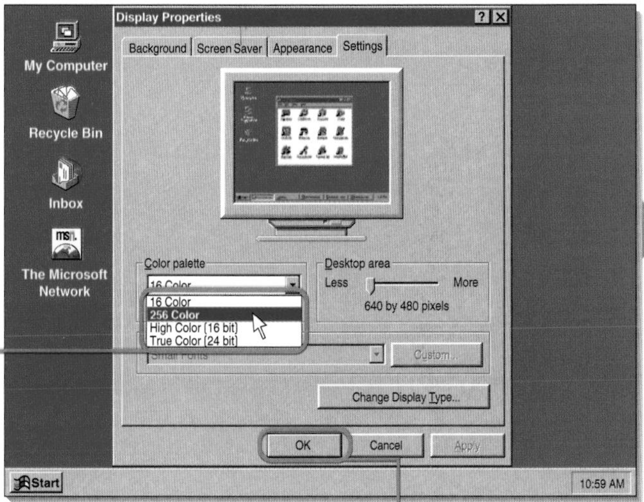

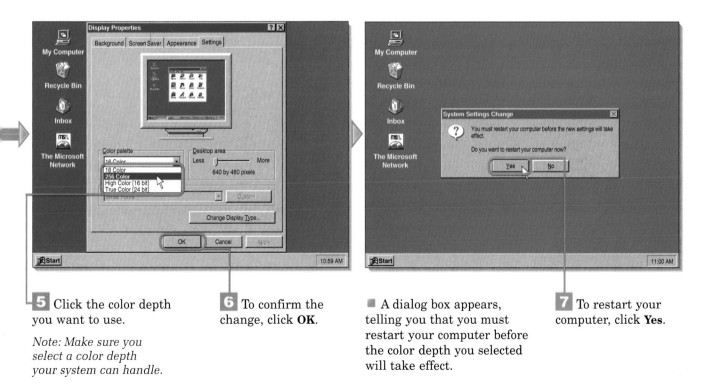

5 Click the color depth you want to use.

Note: Make sure you select a color depth your system can handle.

6 To confirm the change, click **OK**.

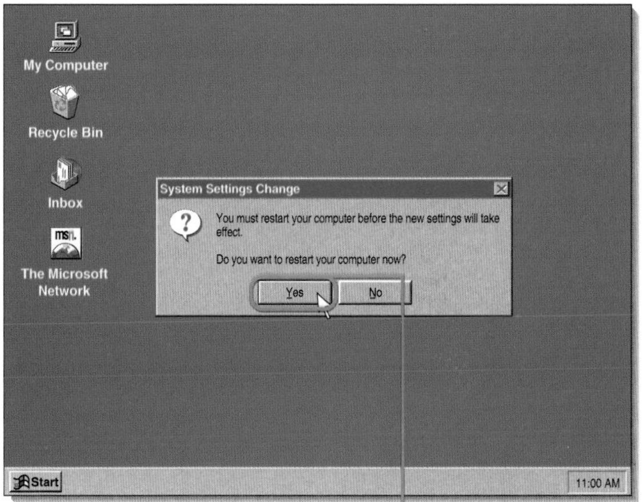

■ A dialog box appears, telling you that you must restart your computer before the color depth you selected will take effect.

7 To restart your computer, click **Yes**.

In this chapter you will learn how to view videos and hear and record sounds on your computer.

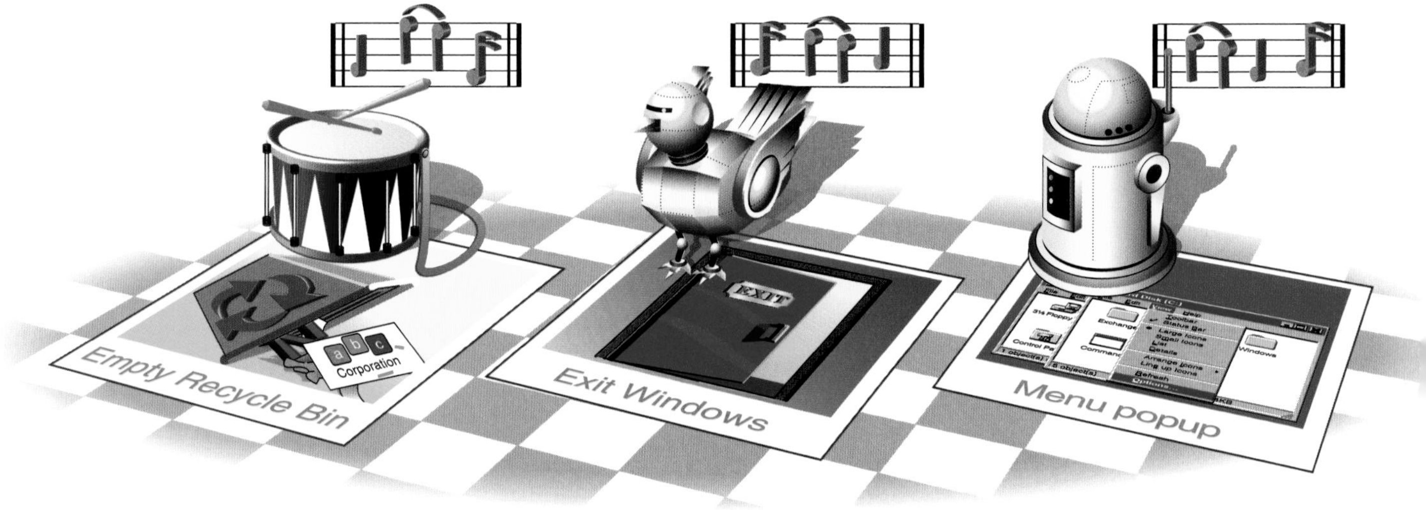

CHAPTER 8: ENTERTAINING FEATURES

Play a Music CD *124*

Adjust the Volume *127*

Assign Sounds to Program Events *128*

Record Sounds *132*

Using Media Player *136*

PLAY A MUSIC CD

You can use your computer to play music CDs while you work.

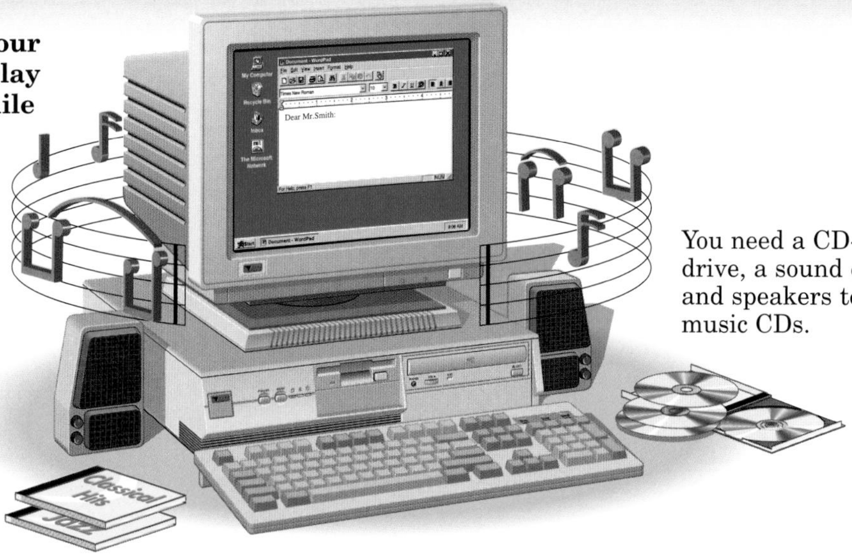

You need a CD-ROM drive, a sound card and speakers to play music CDs.

PLAY A MUSIC CD

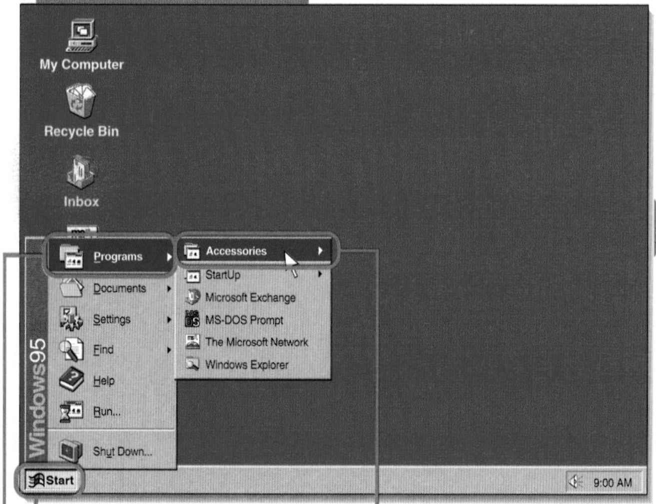

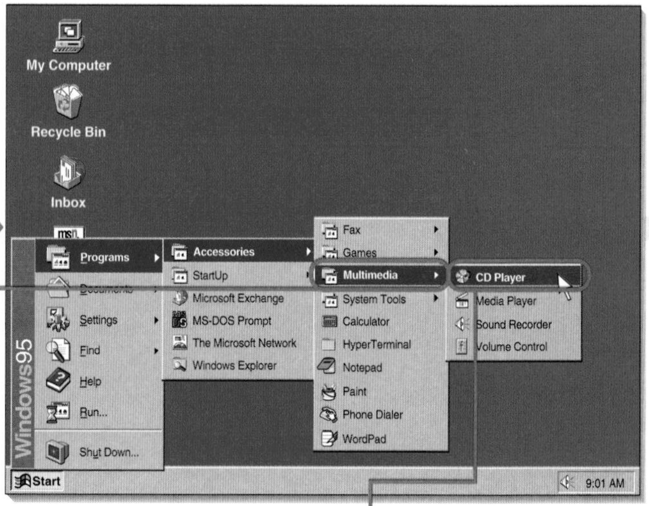

1 Click **Start**.

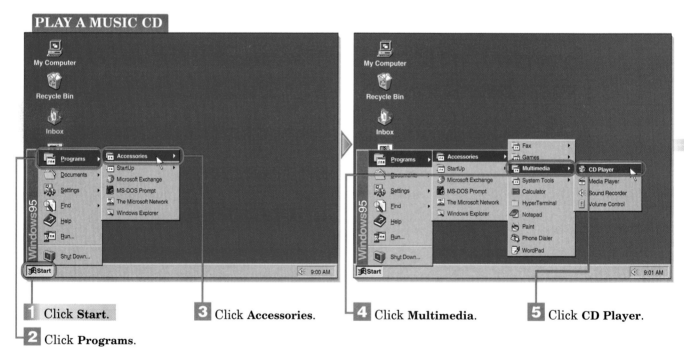

2 Click **Programs**.

3 Click **Accessories**.

4 Click **Multimedia**.

5 Click **CD Player**.

TIP

You can also listen to music privately by plugging a headset into your CD-ROM drive.

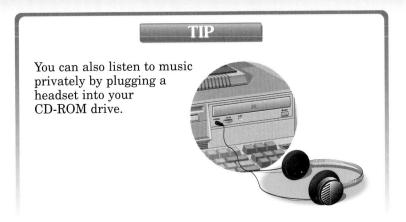

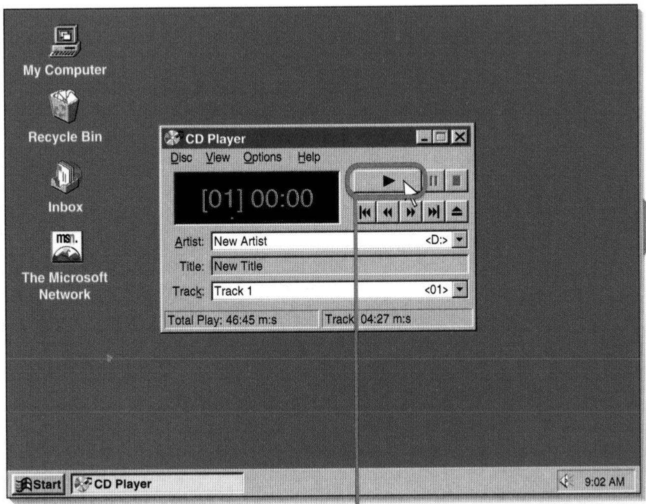

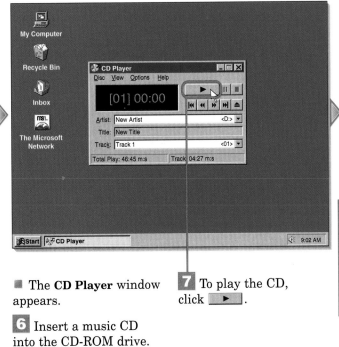

■ The **CD Player** window appears.

6 Insert a music CD into the CD-ROM drive.

7 To play the CD, click ▶.

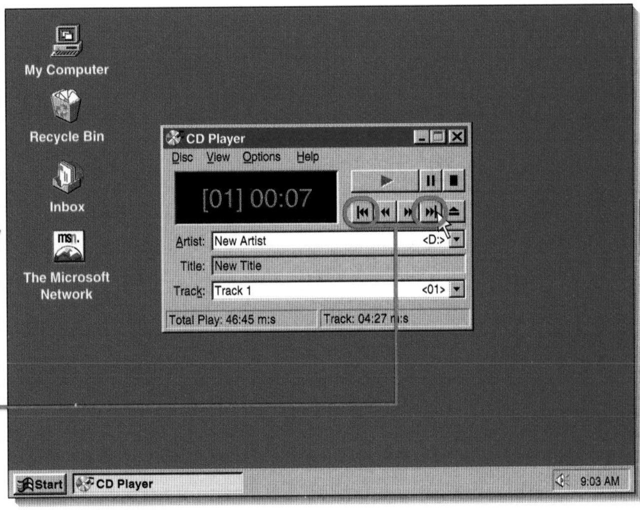

PLAY ANOTHER SONG

1 To play another song on the CD, click one of the following buttons.

⏮ Plays previous song.

⏭ Plays next song.

CONTINUED

PLAY A MUSIC CD

You can have Windows pause or stop the music at any time and play songs in random order.

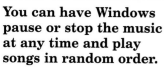

PLAY A MUSIC CD (CONTINUED)

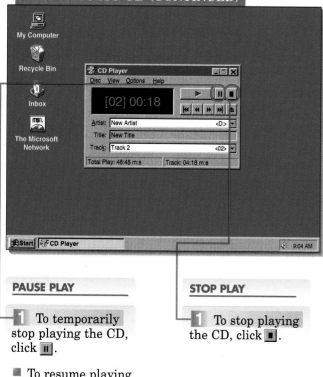

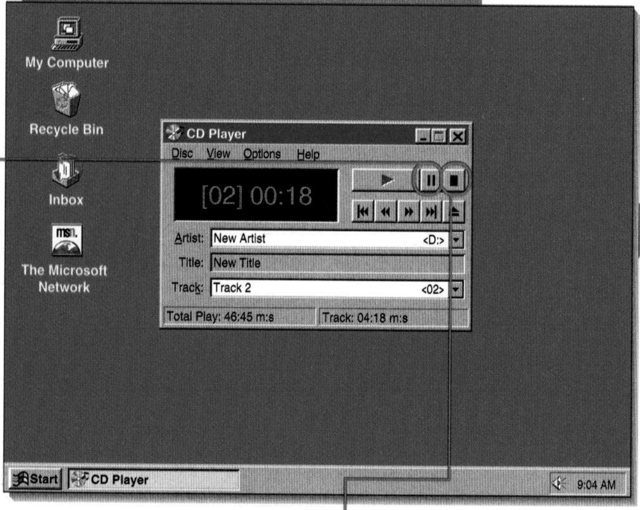

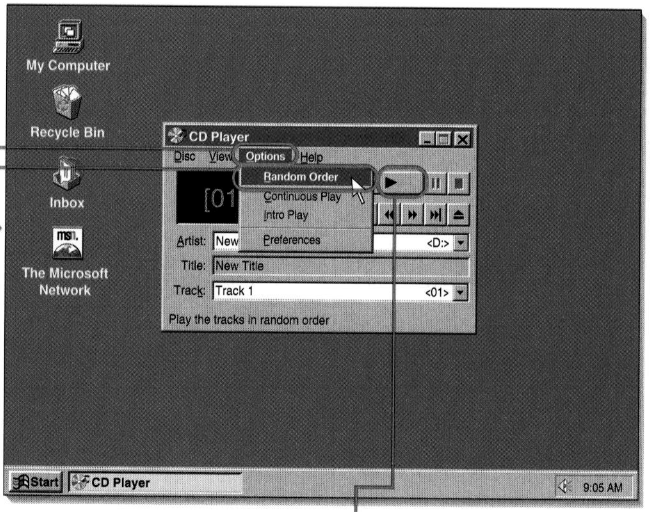

PAUSE PLAY

1 To temporarily stop playing the CD, click ⏸.

■ To resume playing the CD, repeat the step above.

STOP PLAY

1 To stop playing the CD, click ■.

PLAY SONGS IN RANDOM ORDER

1 To play the songs on a CD in random order, click **Options**.

2 Click **Random Order**.

3 To begin playing the songs in random order, click ▶.

Note: To once again play the songs in order, repeat steps 1 and 2.

ADJUST THE VOLUME

You can easily adjust the volume of sound coming from your speakers.

ADJUST THE VOLUME

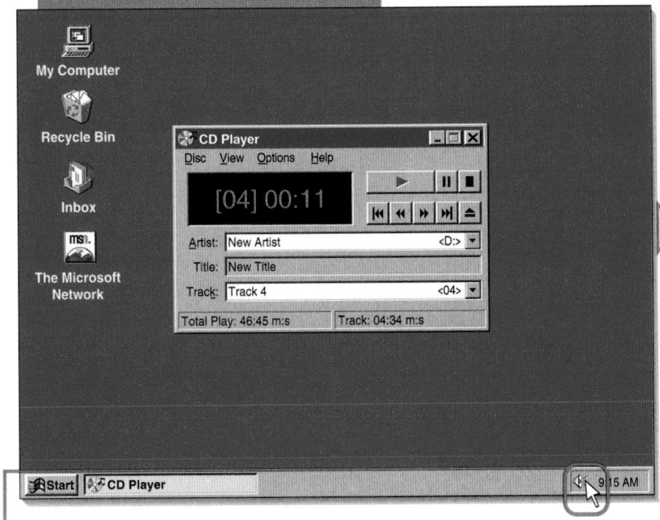

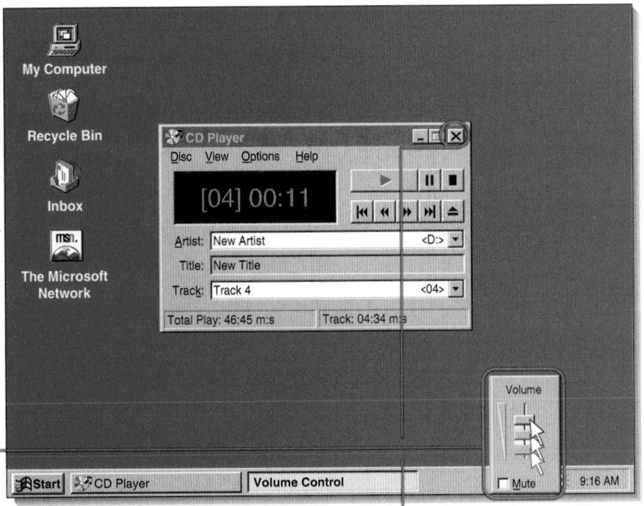

1 To display the **Volume** control box, click 🔈.

2 Drag the slider (▭) up or down to increase or decrease the volume.

3 To hide the **Volume** control box, click outside the box.

■ To close the **CD Player** window, click ☒.

ASSIGN SOUNDS TO PROGRAM EVENTS

You can have Windows play sound effects when you perform certain tasks on your computer.

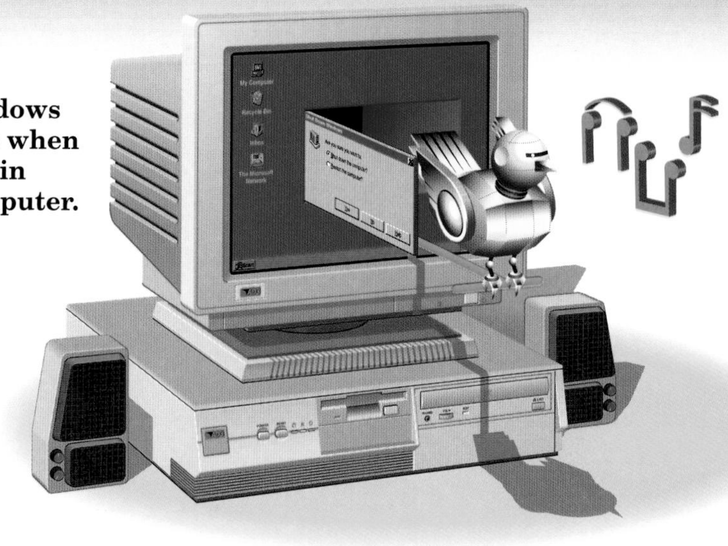

For example, you can hear a bird chirp when you close a program or a musical melody when you exit Windows.

ASSIGN SOUNDS TO PROGRAM EVENTS

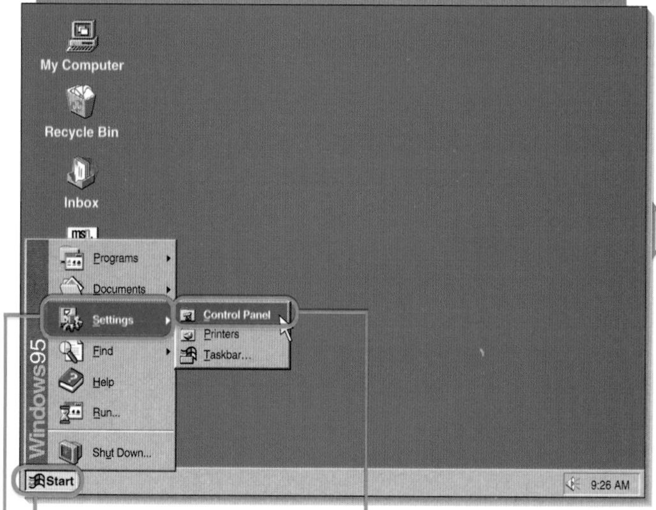

1 Click **Start.**

2 Click **Settings**.

3 Click **Control Panel**.

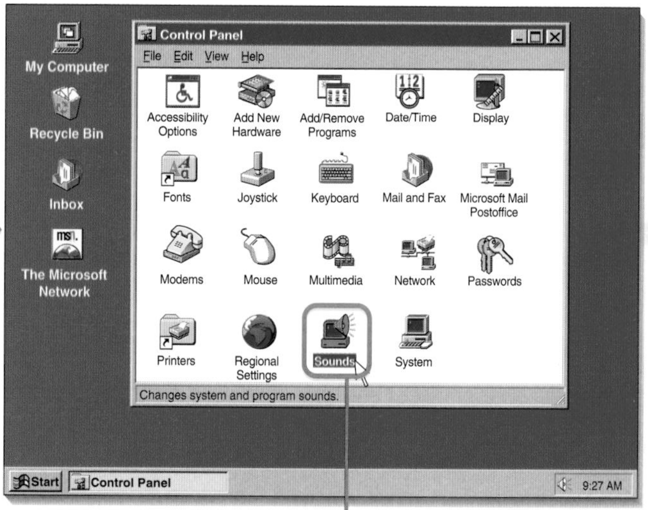

■ The **Control Panel** window appears.

4 Double-click **Sounds**.

IMPORTANT

When you first set up Windows, not all the sound schemes that come with Windows are added to your computer. The schemes you can add later include:

Jungle **Musica** **Robotz** **Utopia**

To add one or more sound schemes to your computer, refer to page 186. You can find these schemes in the Multimedia category.

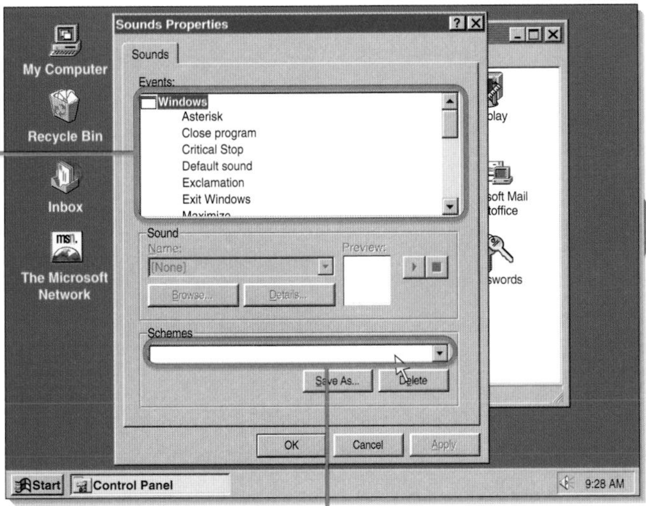

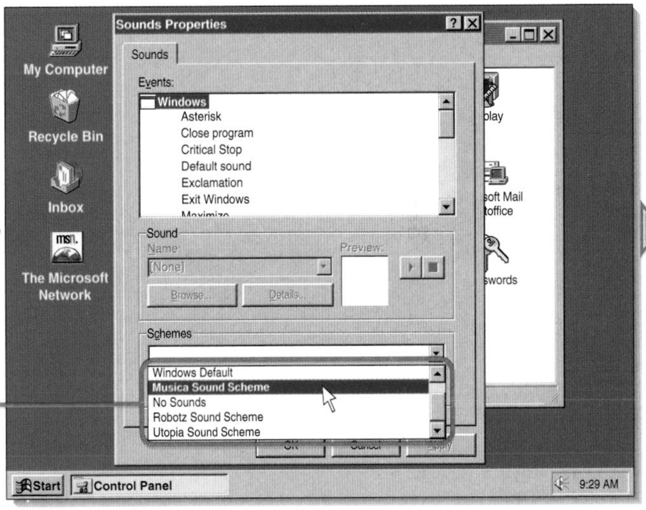

■ The **Sounds Properties** dialog box appears.

■ This area displays the events you can assign sounds to.

ASSIGN SOUNDS TO ALL EVENTS

1 To have Windows assign sounds to all program events at once, click this area.

Note: To assign a sound to only one event, refer to page 130.

2 Click the sound scheme you want to use.

Note: The available sound schemes depend on the schemes you have installed on your computer. For more information, refer to the top of this page.

CONTINUED

ASSIGN SOUNDS TO PROGRAM EVENTS

Assigning sounds to events can make Windows more fun and entertaining.

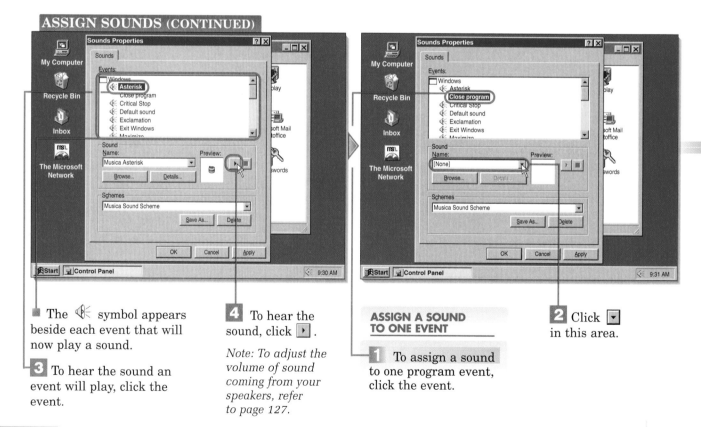

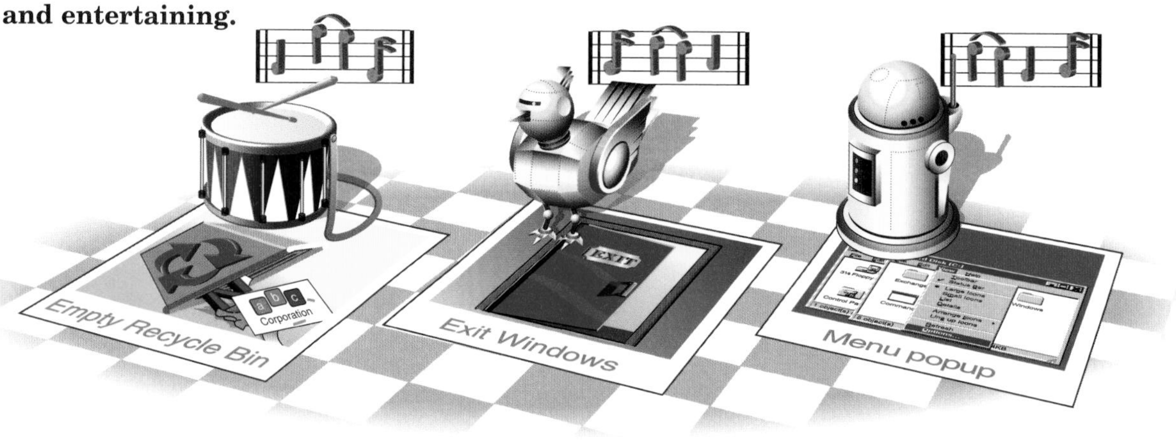

ASSIGN SOUNDS (CONTINUED)

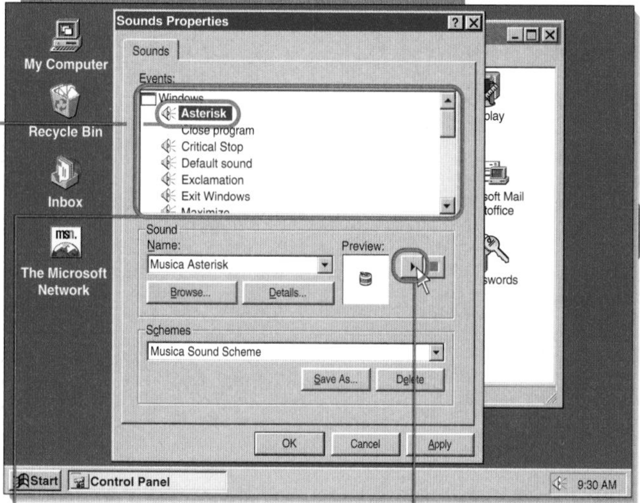

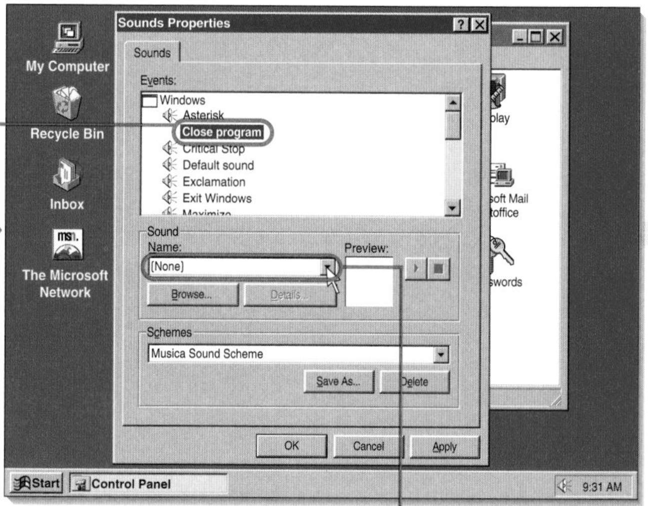

■ The 🔈 symbol appears beside each event that will now play a sound.

3 To hear the sound an event will play, click the event.

4 To hear the sound, click ▸.

Note: To adjust the volume of sound coming from your speakers, refer to page 127.

ASSIGN A SOUND TO ONE EVENT

1 To assign a sound to one program event, click the event.

2 Click ▾ in this area.

TIP

You need a sound card and speakers to hear sounds on your computer.

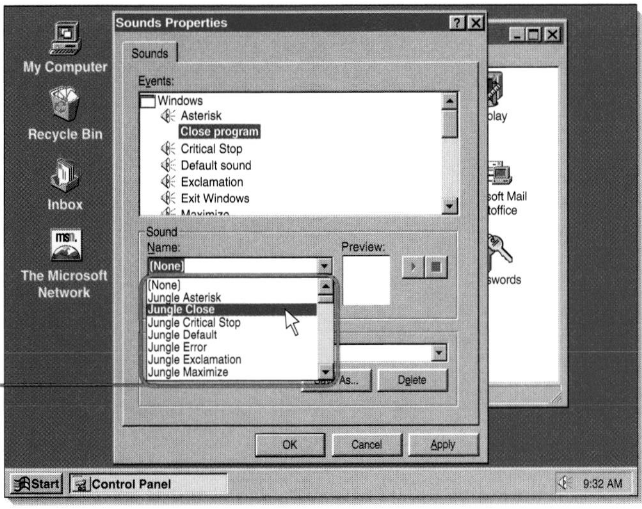

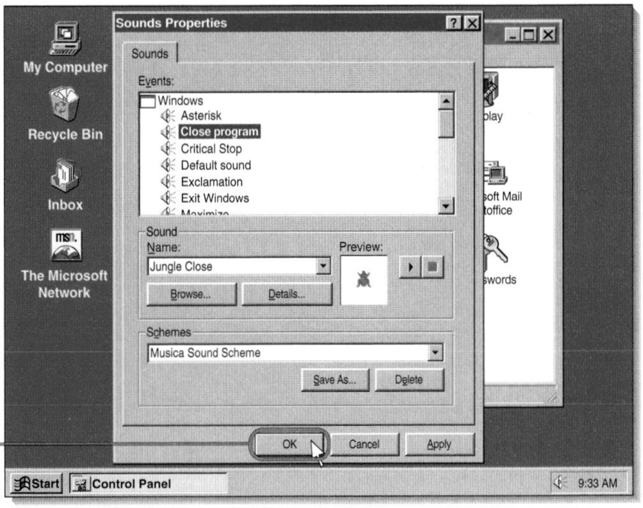

3 Click the sound you want to hear every time the event occurs.

4 To assign sounds to other events, repeat steps 1 to 3 starting on page 130 for each event.

5 To confirm the choices you have made, click **OK**.

RECORD SOUNDS

You can record your own sounds.

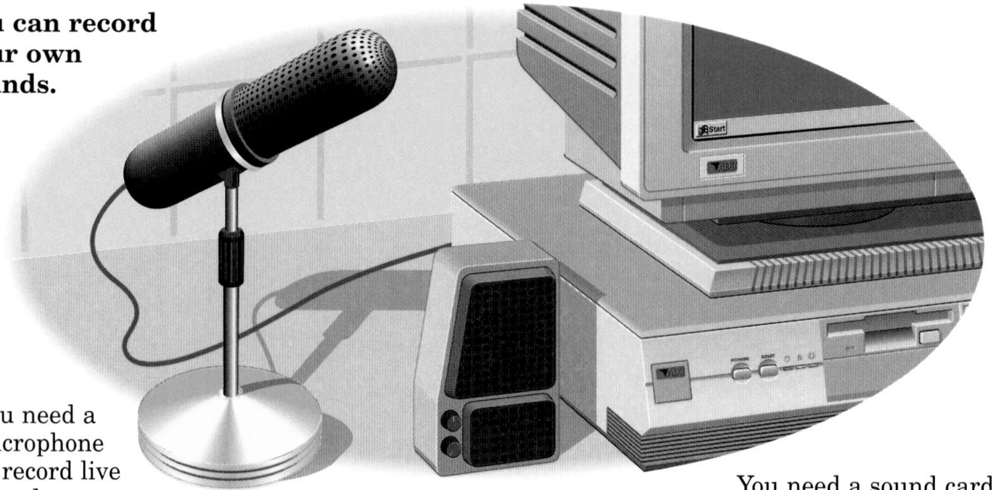

You need a microphone to record live sounds.

You need a sound card and speakers to record and play sounds.

RECORD SOUNDS

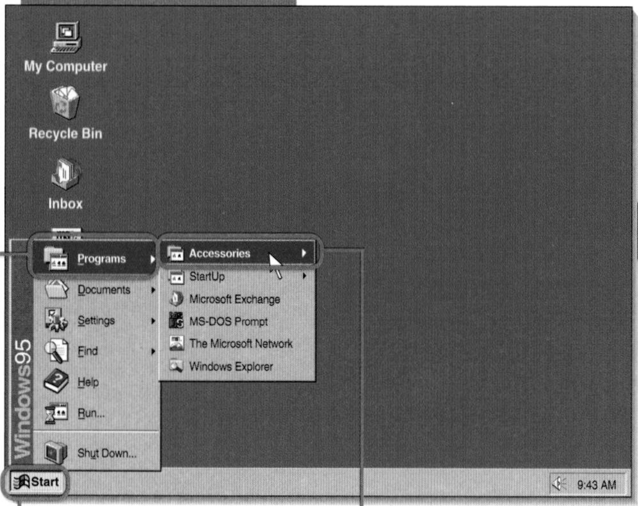

1 Click **Start**.

2 Click **Programs**.

3 Click **Accessories**.

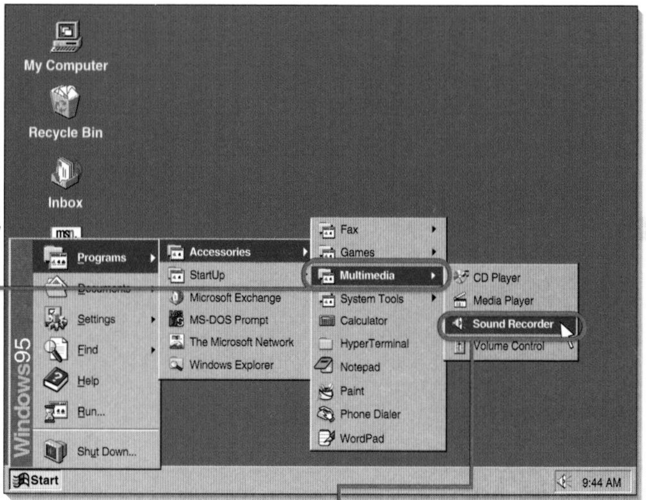

4 Click **Multimedia**.

5 Click **Sound Recorder**.

TIP

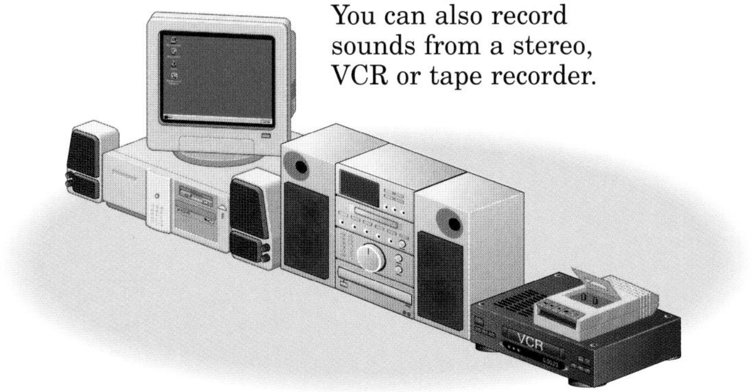

You can also record sounds from a stereo, VCR or tape recorder.

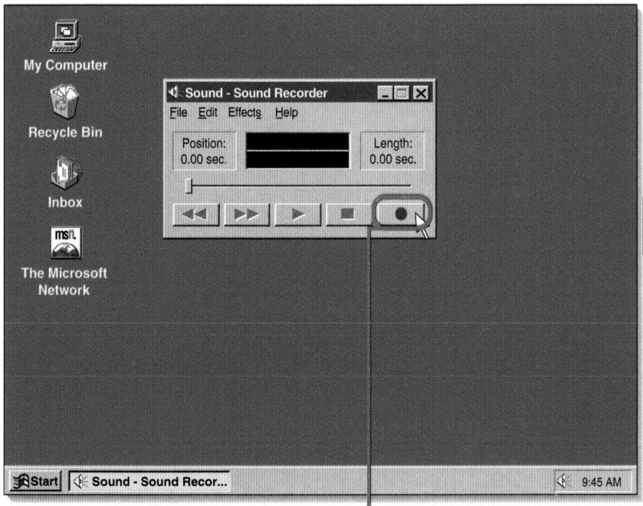

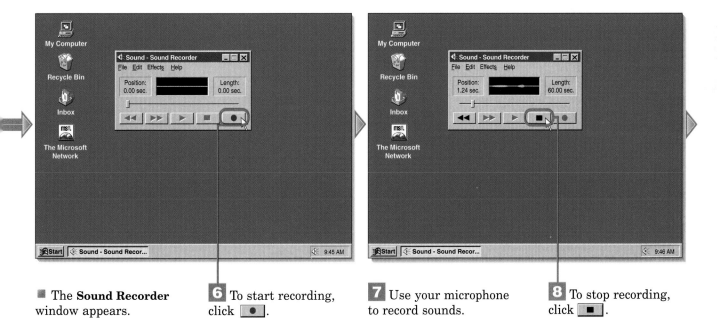

■ The **Sound Recorder** window appears.

6 To start recording, click ●.

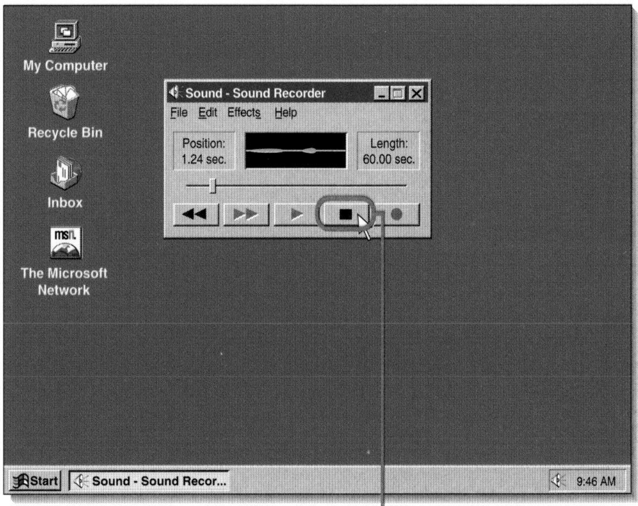

7 Use your microphone to record sounds.

8 To stop recording, click ■.

CONTINUED

RECORD SOUNDS

You can store sounds you record and listen to them later.

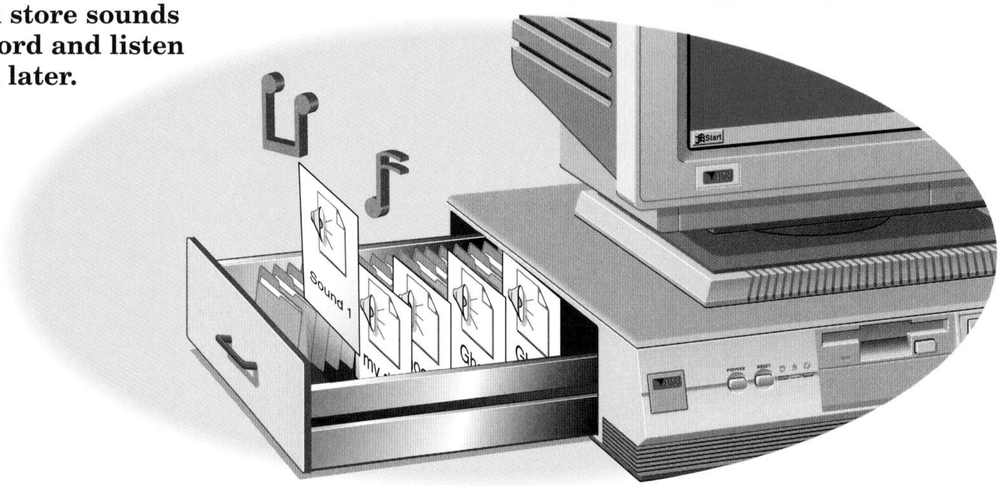

RECORD SOUNDS (CONTINUED)

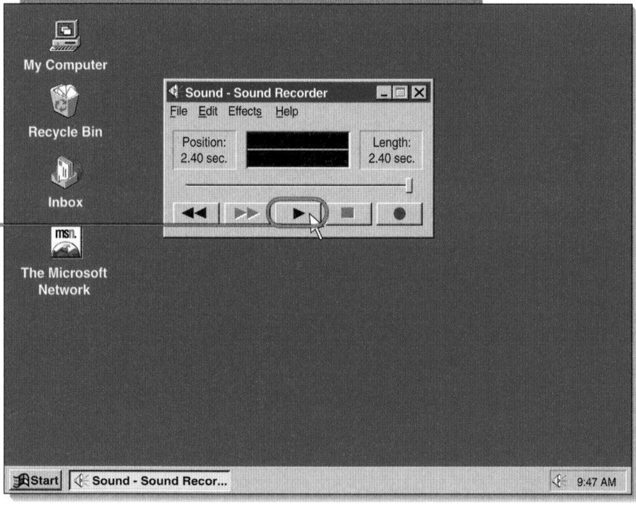

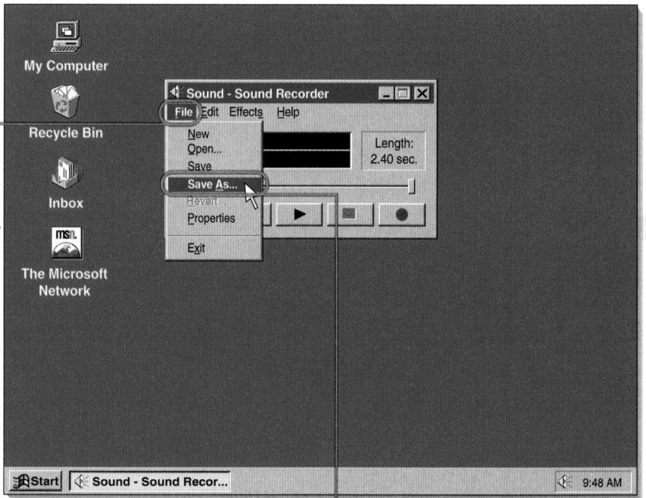

9 To play your recording, click ▶.

10 To save the recording, click **File**.

11 Click **Save As**.

■ The **Save As** dialog box appears.

TIP

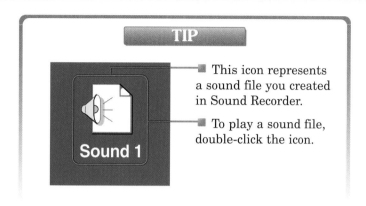

This icon represents a sound file you created in Sound Recorder.

To play a sound file, double-click the icon.

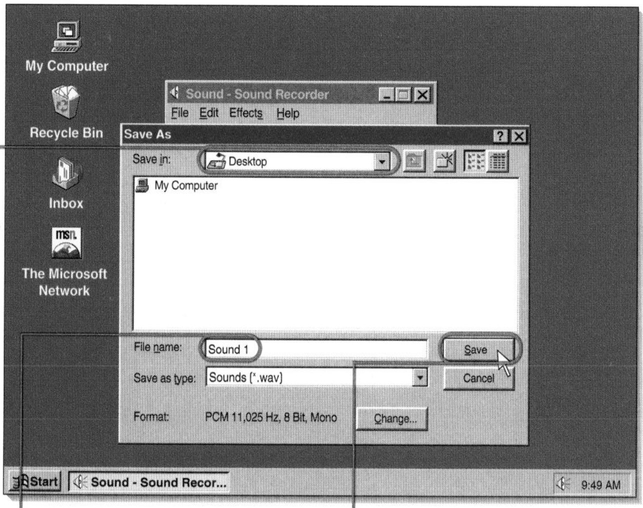

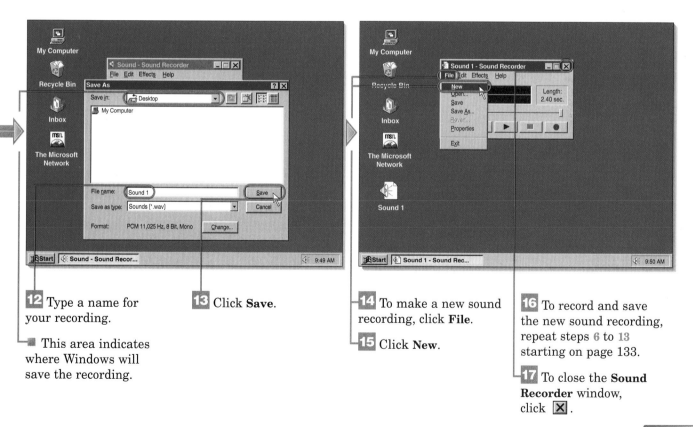

12 Type a name for your recording.

This area indicates where Windows will save the recording.

13 Click **Save**.

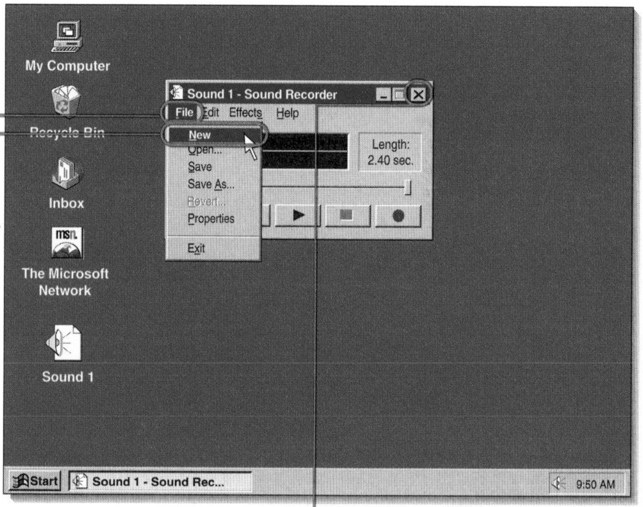

14 To make a new sound recording, click **File**.

15 Click **New**.

16 To record and save the new sound recording, repeat steps 6 to 13 starting on page 133.

17 To close the **Sound Recorder** window, click ☒.

USING MEDIA PLAYER

Media Player lets you play sound, video and animation files.

USING MEDIA PLAYER

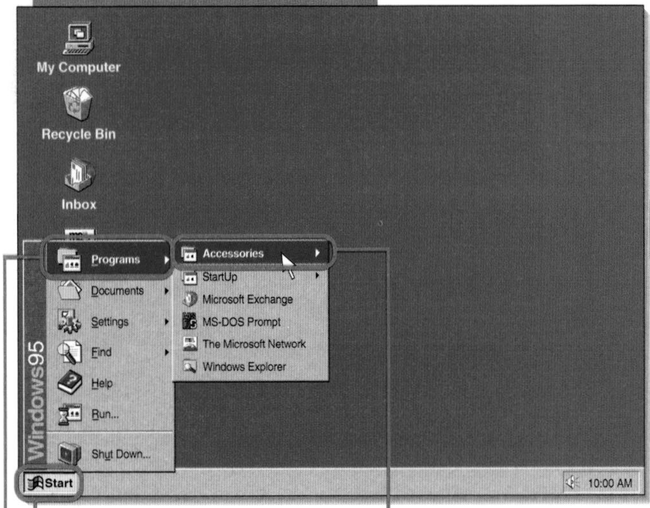

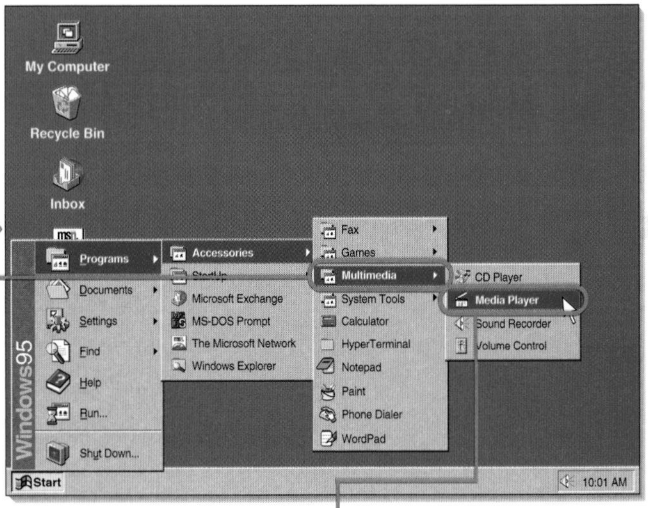

1 Click **Start**.

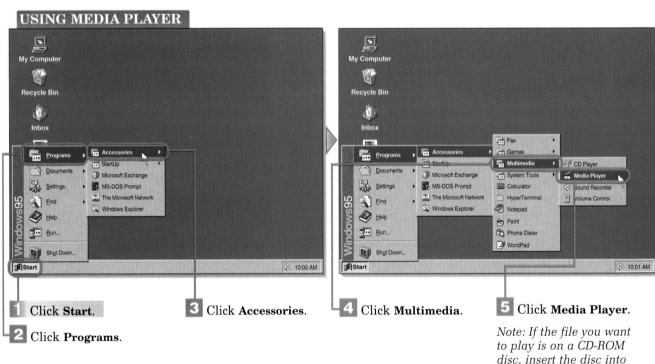

2 Click **Programs**.

3 Click **Accessories**.

4 Click **Multimedia**.

5 Click **Media Player**.

Note: If the file you want to play is on a CD-ROM disc, insert the disc into the CD-ROM drive.

TIP

The Windows 95 CD-ROM disc includes several video files you can play.

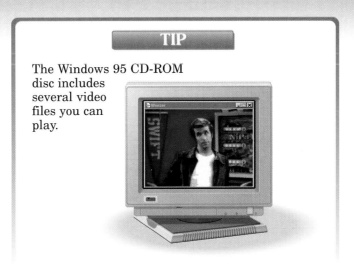

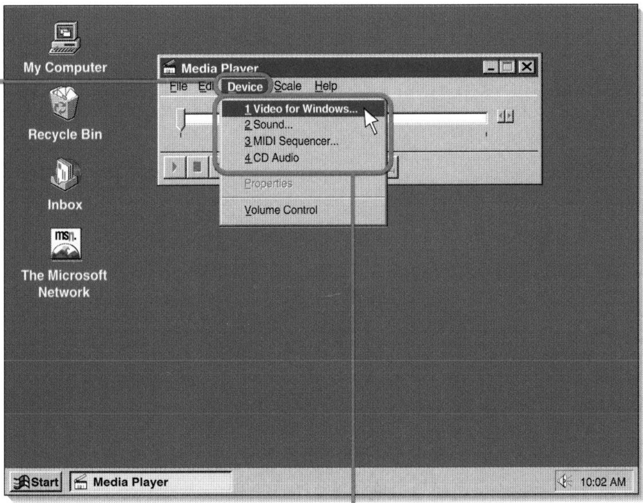

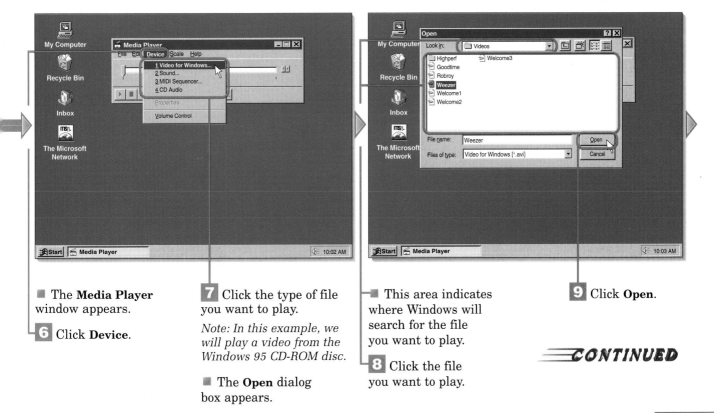

■ The **Media Player** window appears.

6 Click **Device**.

7 Click the type of file you want to play.

Note: In this example, we will play a video from the Windows 95 CD-ROM disc.

■ The **Open** dialog box appears.

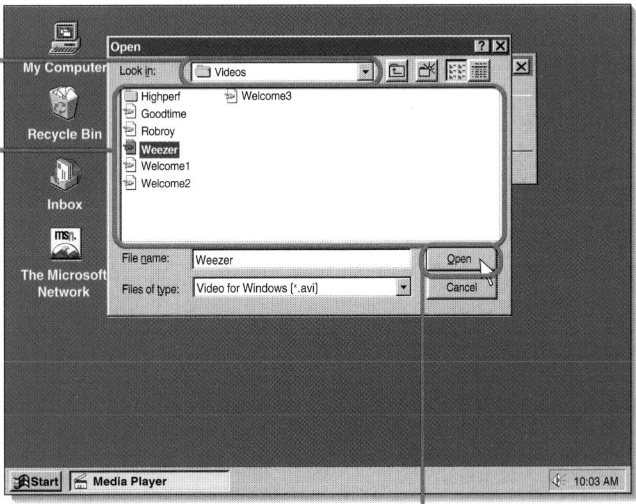

■ This area indicates where Windows will search for the file you want to play.

8 Click the file you want to play.

9 Click **Open**.

CONTINUED

USING MEDIA PLAYER

You can use Media Player to play files you get from the Internet.

USING MEDIA PLAYER (CONTINUED)

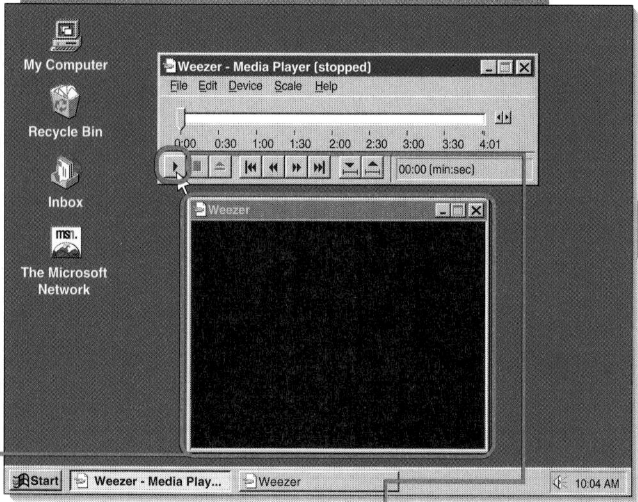

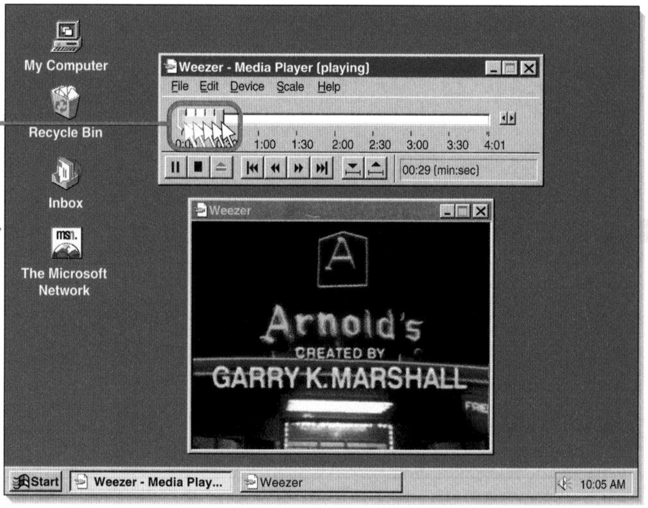

■ A window for viewing the file appears.

10 To play the file, click ▶.

11 To fast forward or rewind the file, drag the slider (⛉) to a new location.

TIP

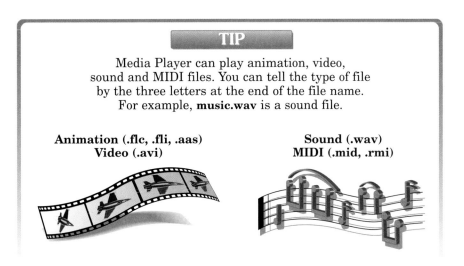

Media Player can play animation, video, sound and MIDI files. You can tell the type of file by the three letters at the end of the file name. For example, **music.wav** is a sound file.

Animation (.flc, .fli, .aas)
Video (.avi)

Sound (.wav)
MIDI (.mid, .rmi)

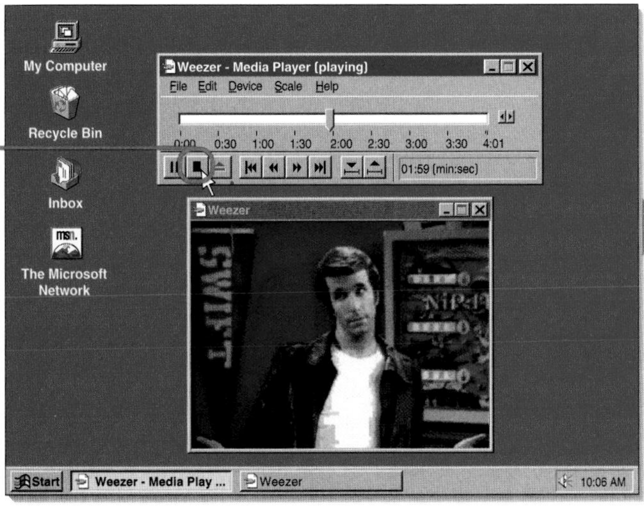

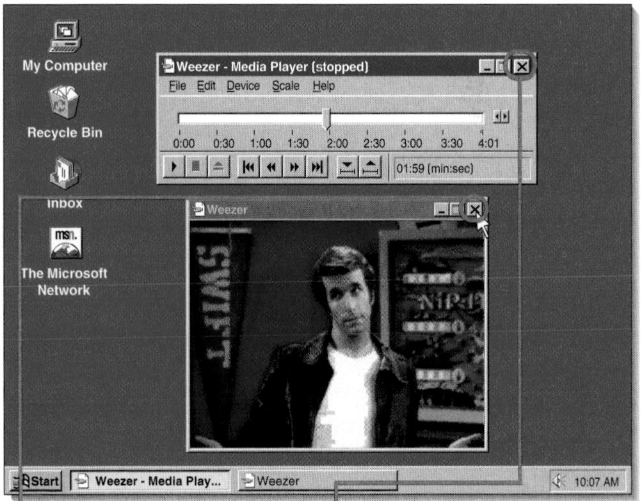

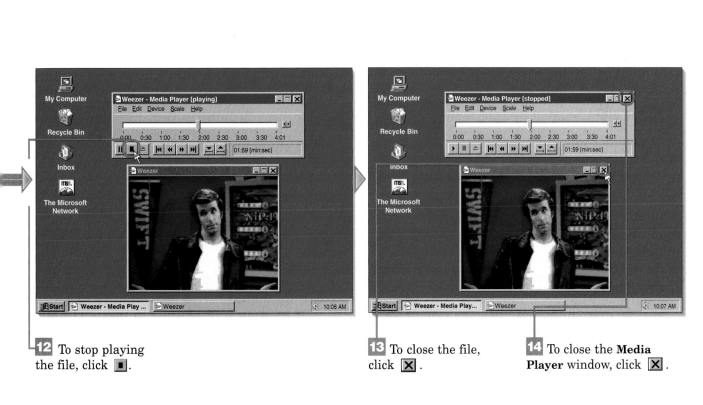

12 To stop playing the file, click ■.

13 To close the file, click ☒.

14 To close the **Media Player** window, click ☒.

In this chapter you will learn how to exchange information between documents.

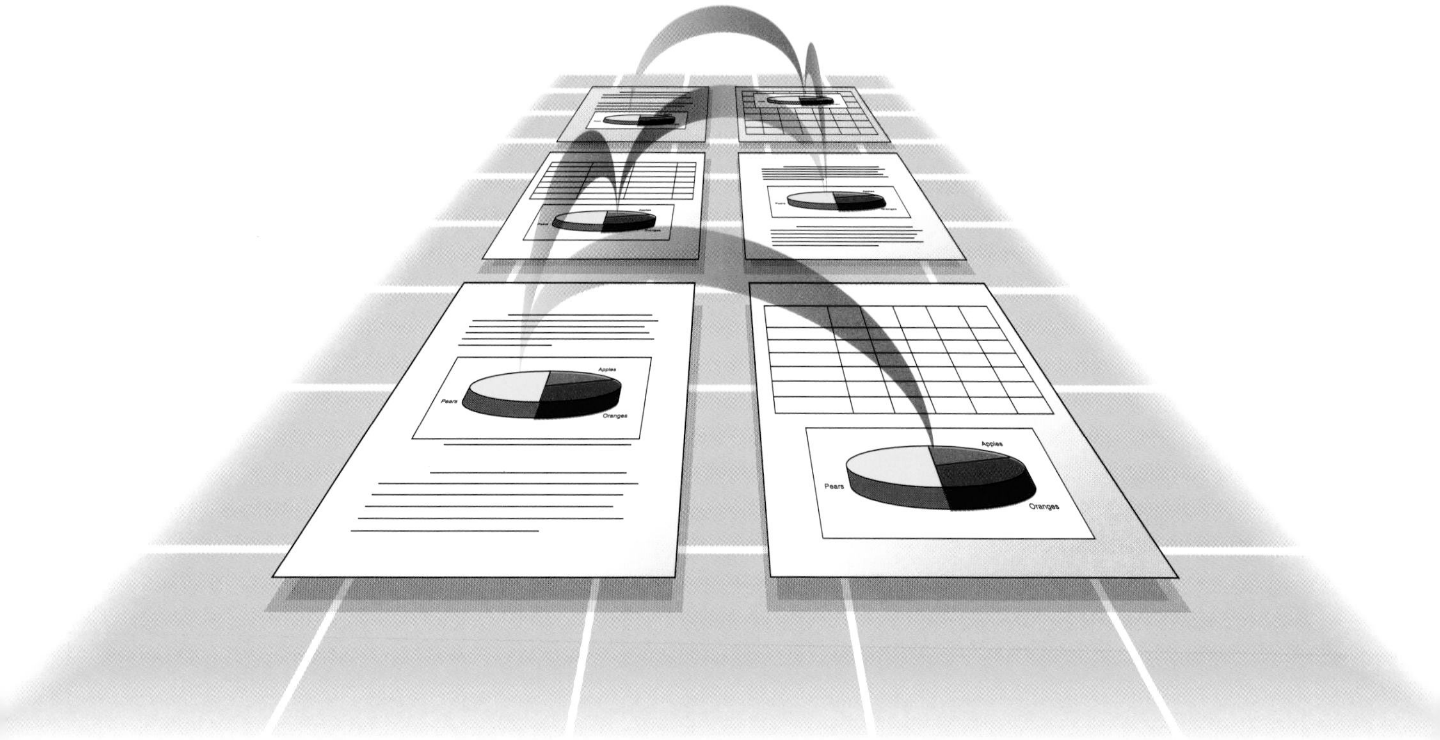

CHAPTER 9: OBJECT LINKING AND EMBEDDING

Embed or Link Information 142

Edit Embedded Information 146

Edit Linked Information 148

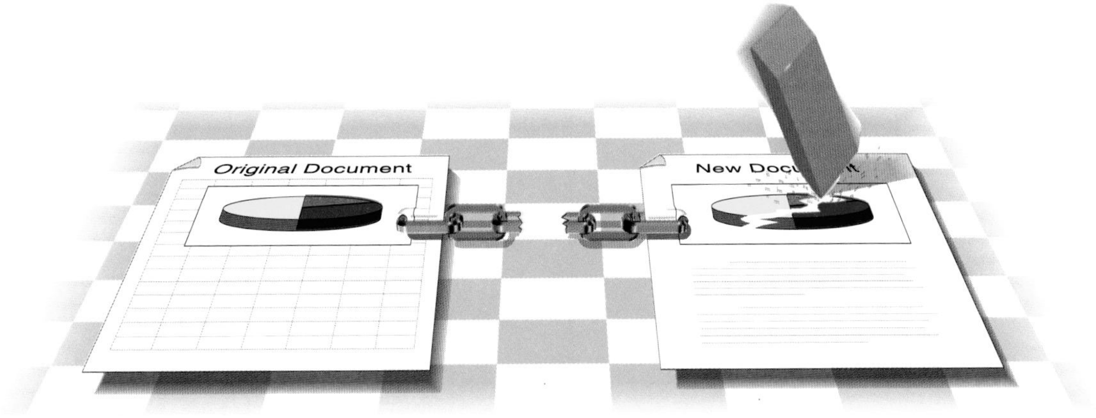

EMBED OR LINK INFORMATION

You can easily exchange information between documents.

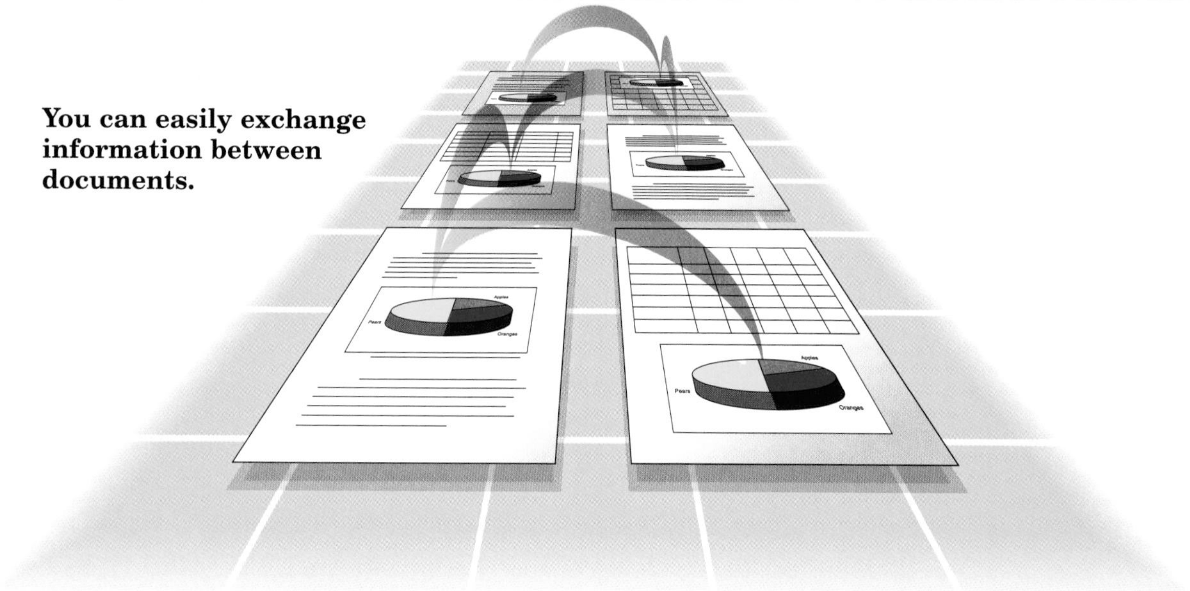

EMBED OR LINK INFORMATION

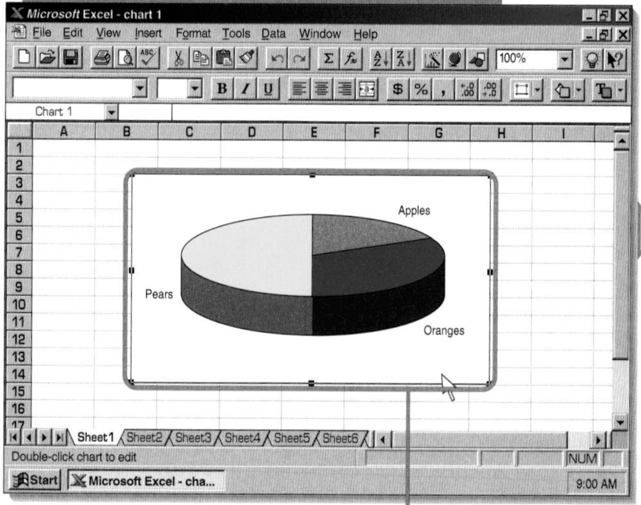

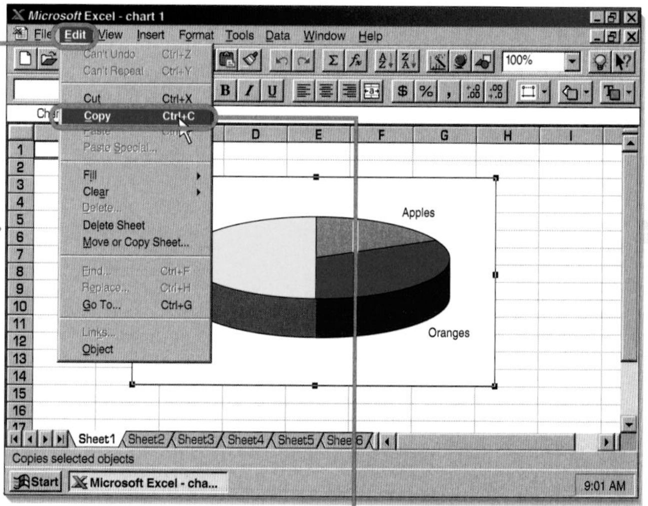

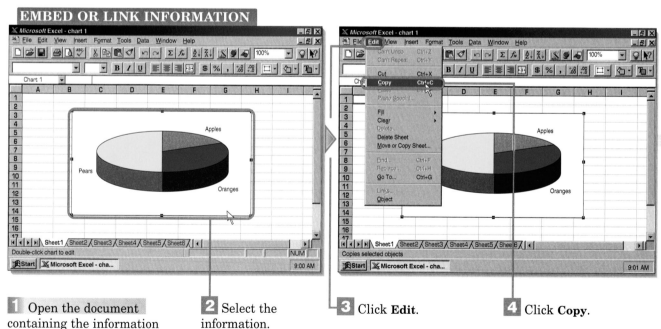

1 Open the document containing the information you want to place in another document.

2 Select the information.

3 Click **Edit**.

4 Click **Copy**.

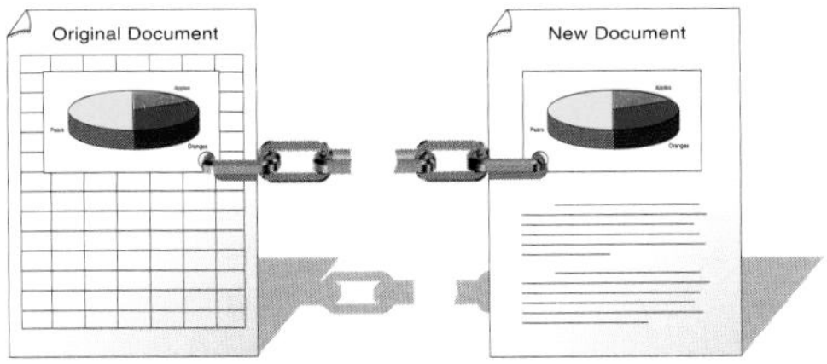

EMBED INFORMATION

When you embed information, the information becomes part of the new document.

The original document is no longer needed, since the new document now contains the information.

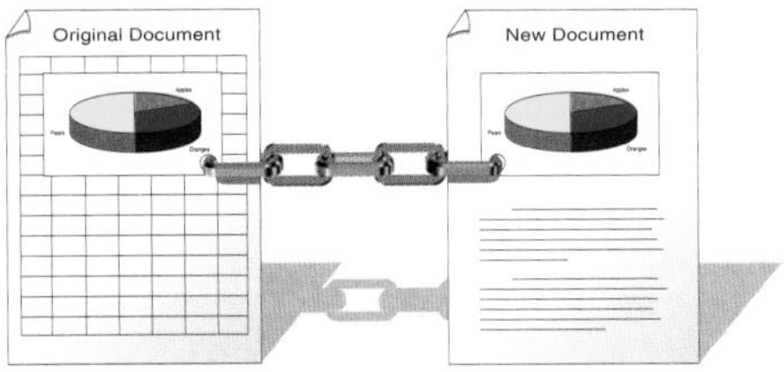

LINK INFORMATION

When you link information, the new document receives a "screen image" of the information. The information remains in the original document.

Since the new document only contains a "screen image" of the information, a connection exists between the two documents.

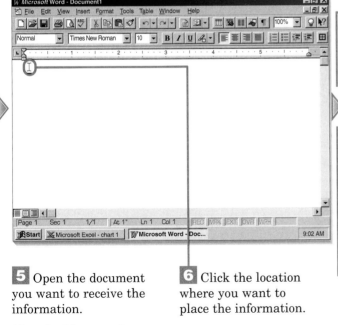

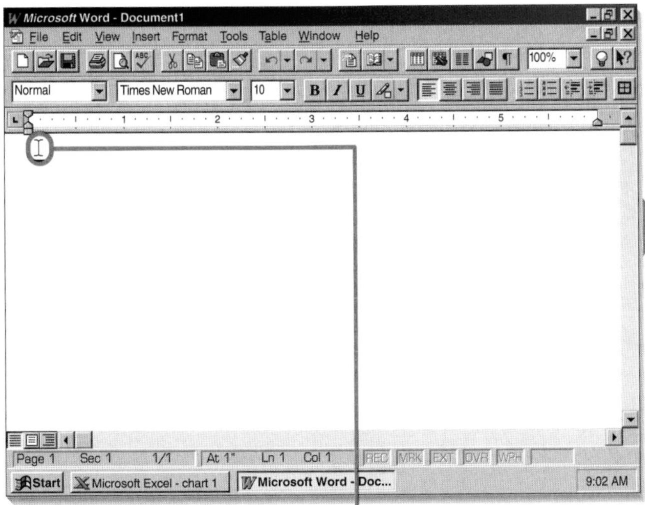

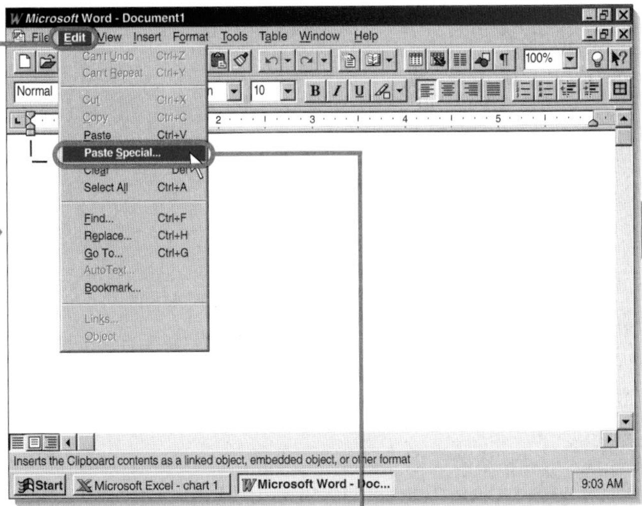

5 Open the document you want to receive the information.

Note: In this example, we opened a Word document using the Start button.

6 Click the location where you want to place the information.

7 Click **Edit**.

8 Click **Paste Special**.

CONTINUED

EMBED OR LINK INFORMATION

You can exchange pictures, charts, text, slides and spreadsheets between documents.

EMBED OR LINK INFORMATION (CONTINUED)

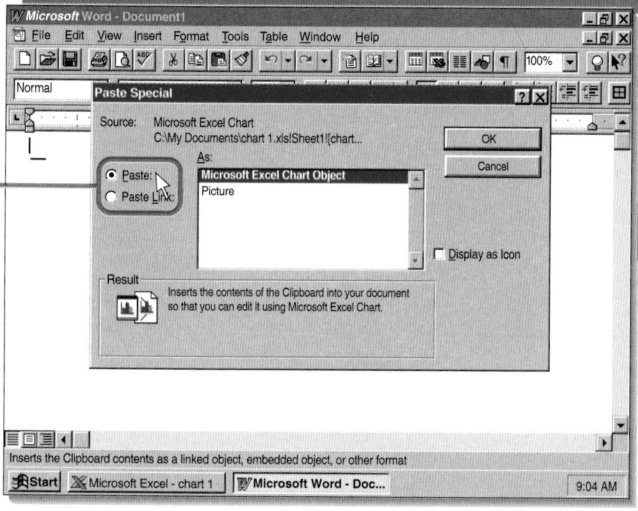

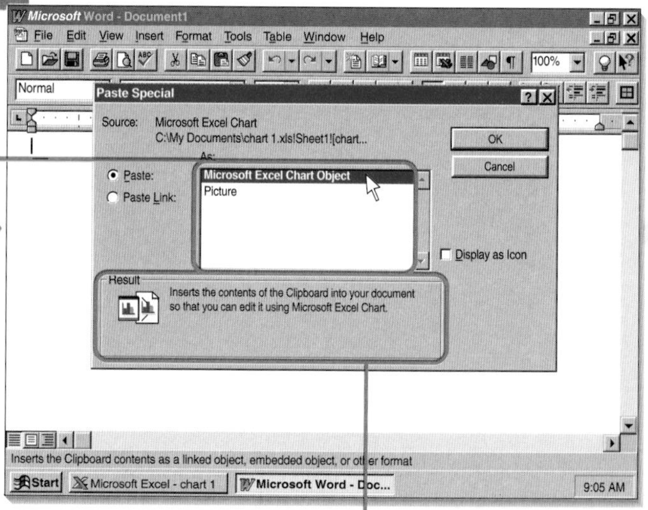

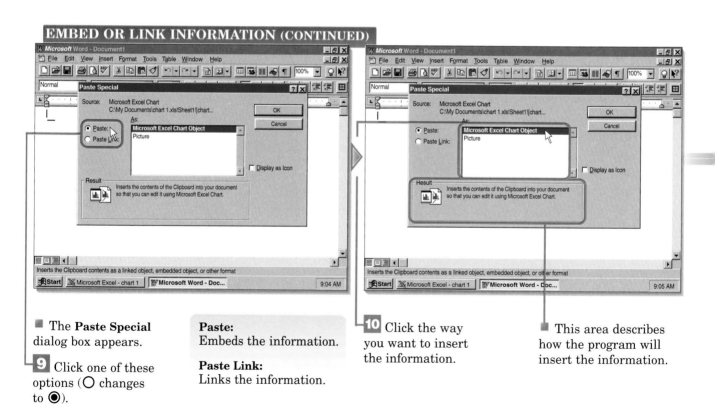

■ The **Paste Special** dialog box appears.

9 Click one of these options (○ changes to ◉).

Paste:
Embeds the information.

Paste Link:
Links the information.

10 Click the way you want to insert the information.

■ This area describes how the program will insert the information.

TIP

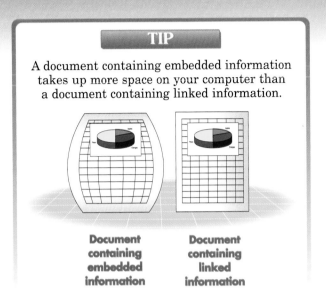

A document containing embedded information takes up more space on your computer than a document containing linked information.

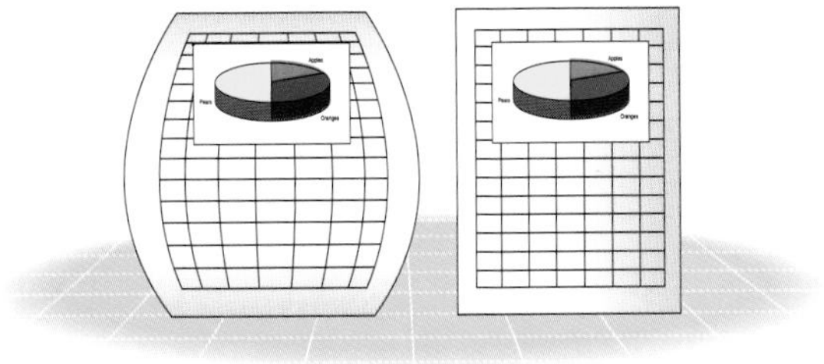

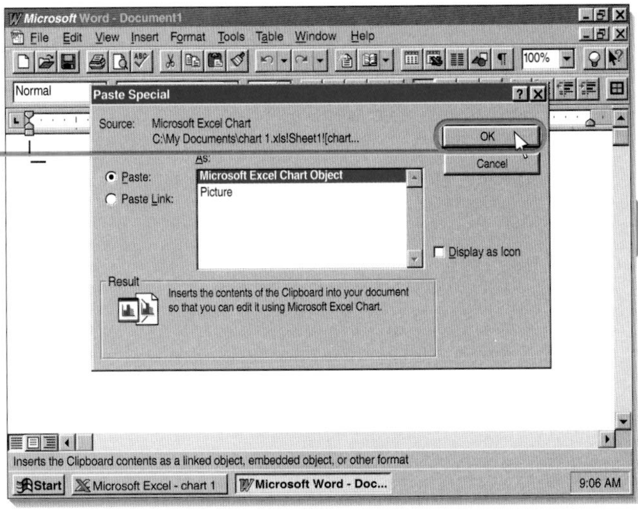

11 Click **OK**.

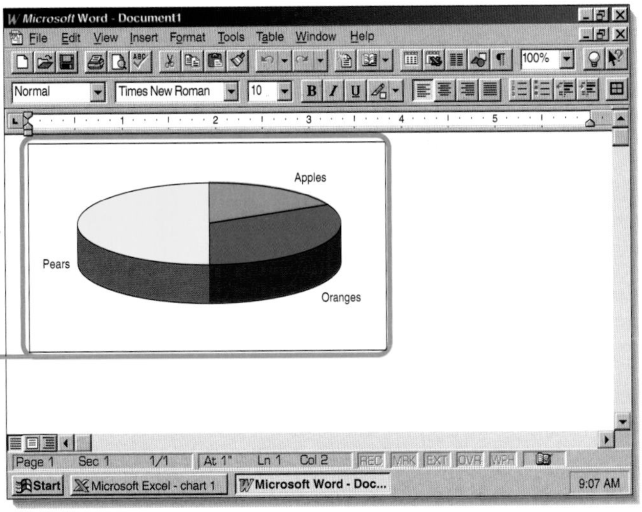

■ The information appears in the new document.

Note: To edit embedded information, refer to page 146. To edit linked information, refer to page 148.

EDIT EMBEDDED INFORMATION

When you change embedded information, the original document does not change.

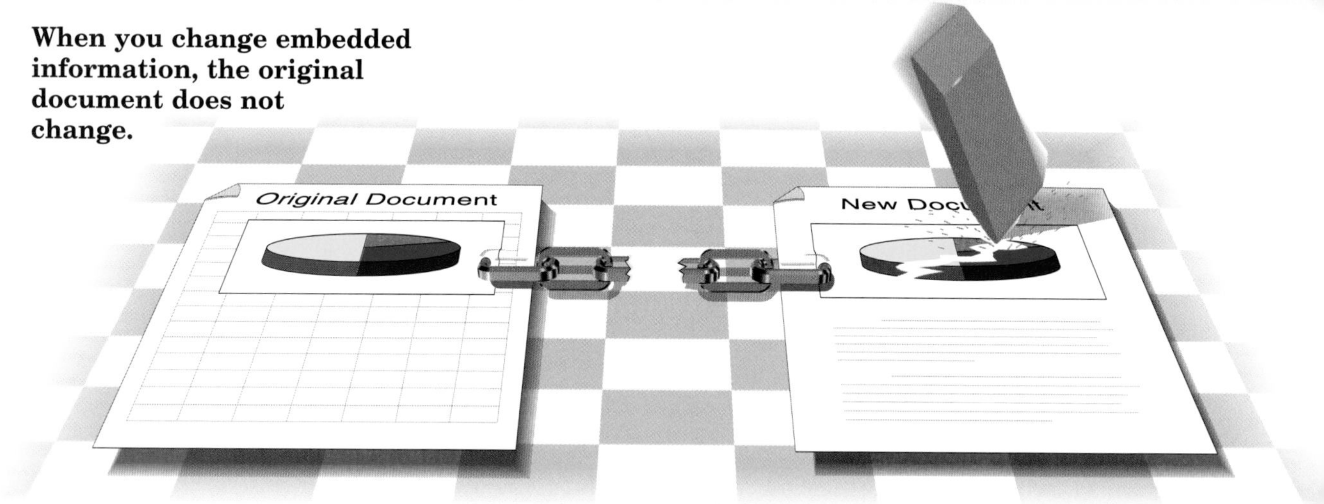

EDIT EMBEDDED INFORMATION

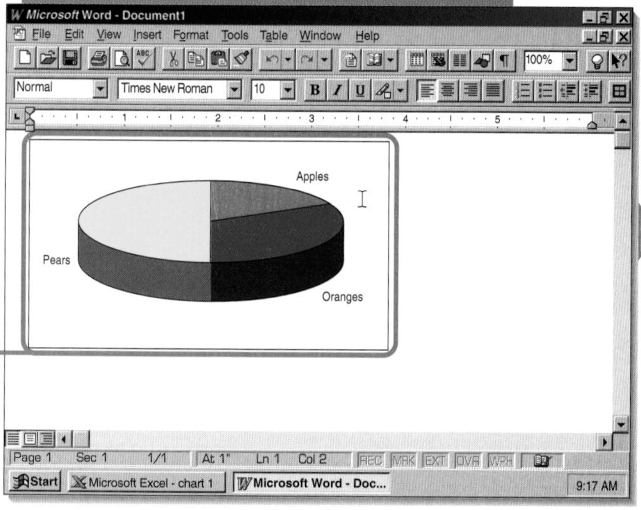

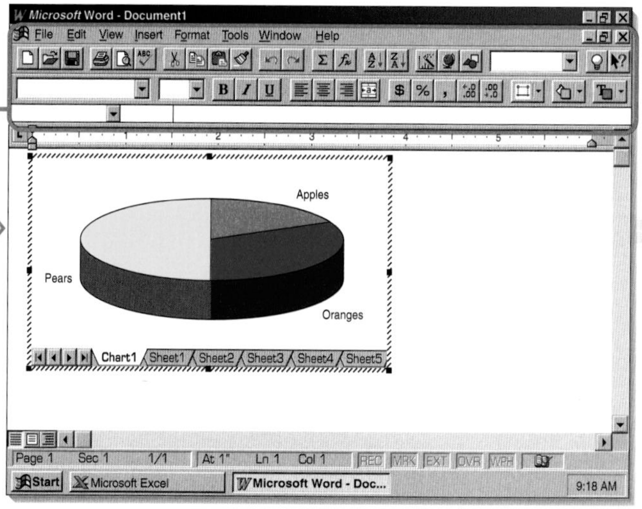

1 Double-click the embedded information you want to change.

■ The toolbars and menus from the program you used to create the information appear. This lets you access all the commands you need to make the necessary changes.

TIP

A program that can link and embed information supports OLE—Object Linking and Embedding.

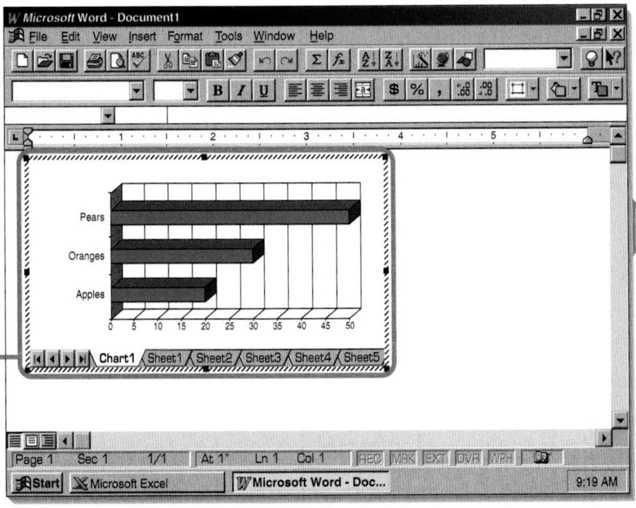

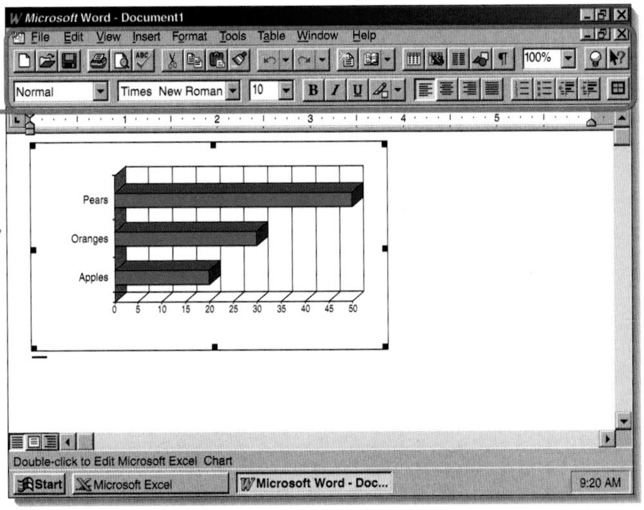

2 Edit the information.

Note: In this example, the pie chart is changed to a bar chart.

3 When you finish making the changes, click anywhere outside the information.

■ The original toolbars and menus reappear.

EDIT LINKED INFORMATION

When you change linked information, the original and new documents both display the changes.

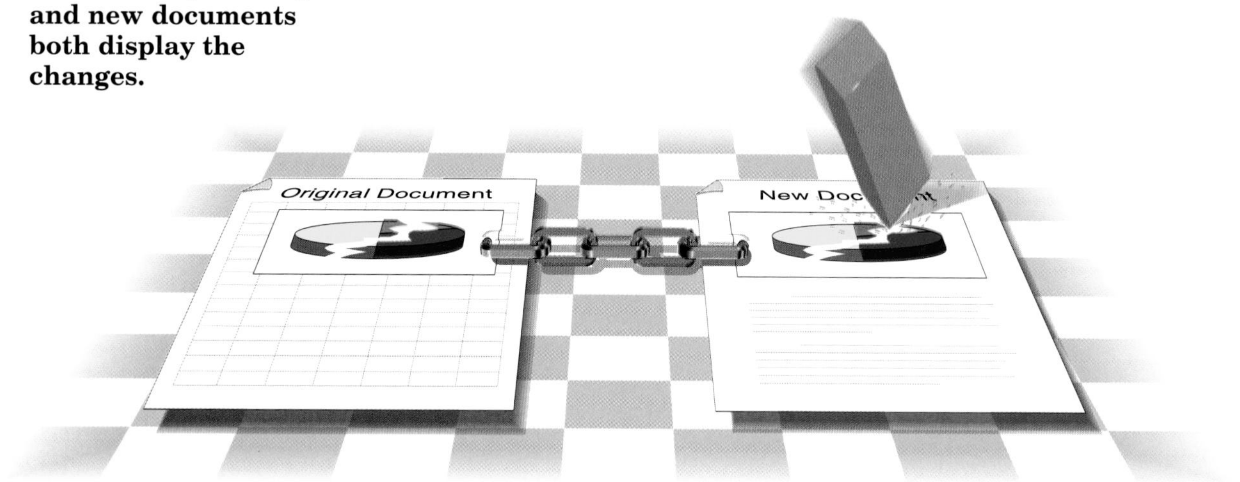

EDIT LINKED INFORMATION

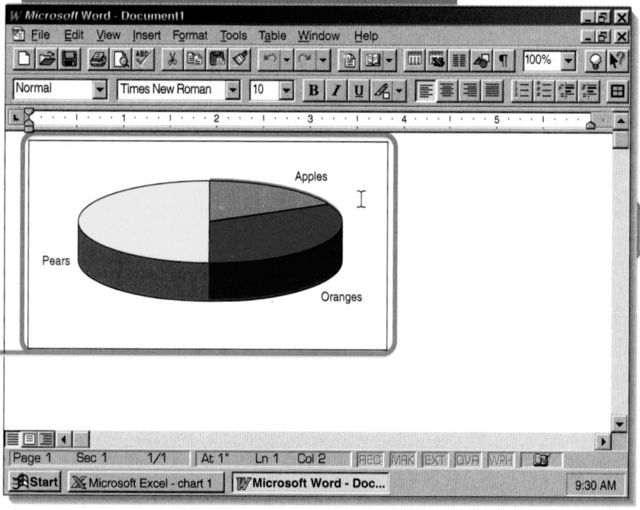

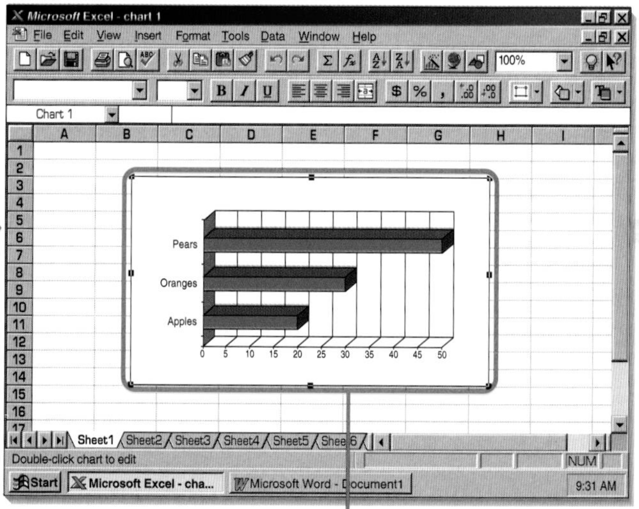

1 Double-click the linked information you want to change.

■ The program you used to create the information opens. This lets you access all the commands you need to make the necessary changes.

2 Edit the information.

Note: In this example, the pie chart is changed to a bar chart.

TIP

You can link information to several documents.

When you change linked information, the information changes in all linked documents. This is useful when you want several documents to display the same, up-to-date information.

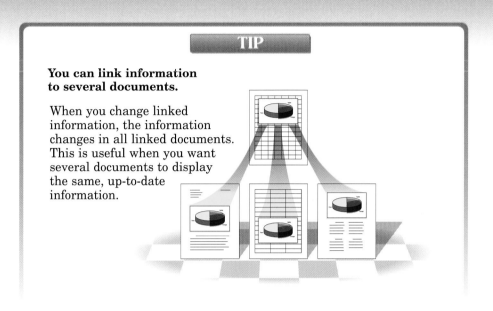

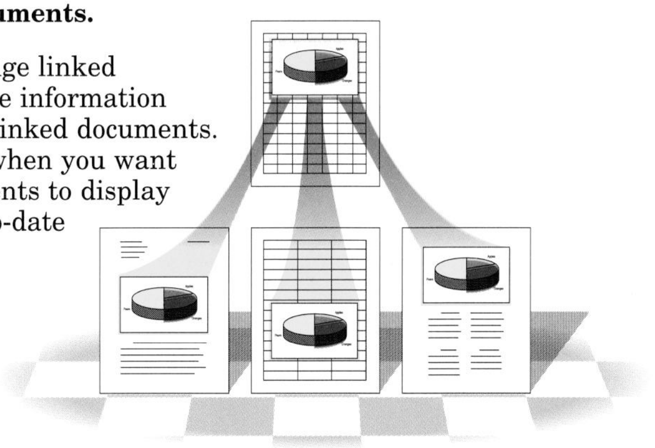

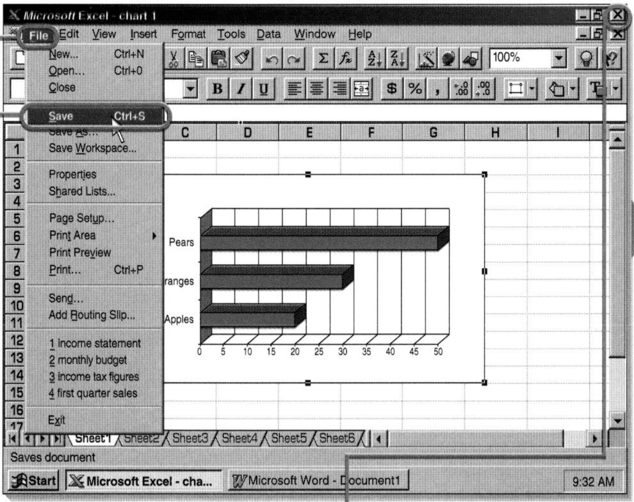

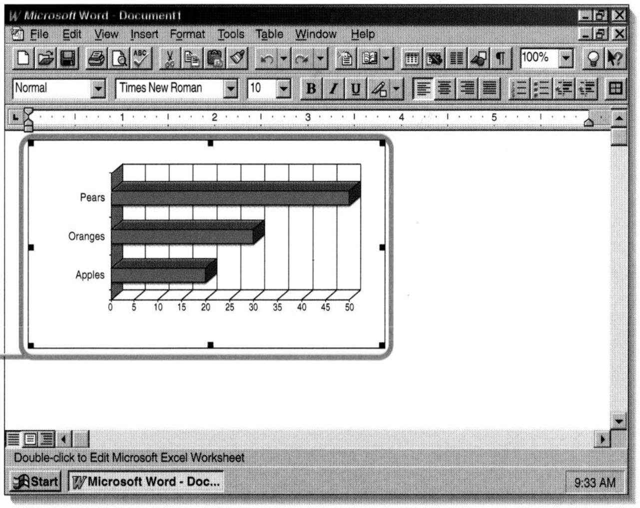

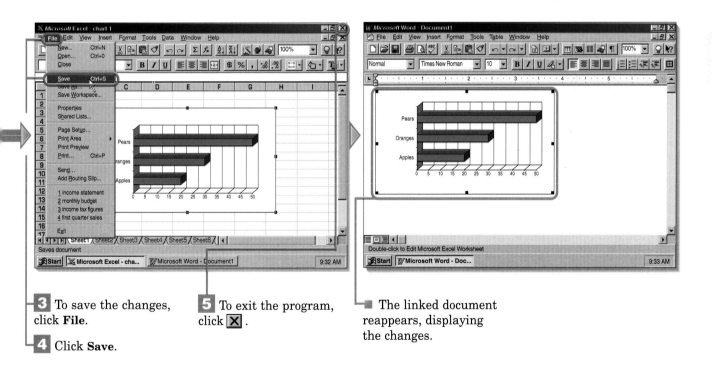

3 To save the changes, click **File**.

4 Click **Save**.

5 To exit the program, click ☒.

■ The linked document reappears, displaying the changes.

In this chapter you will learn how to send and receive faxes on your computer.

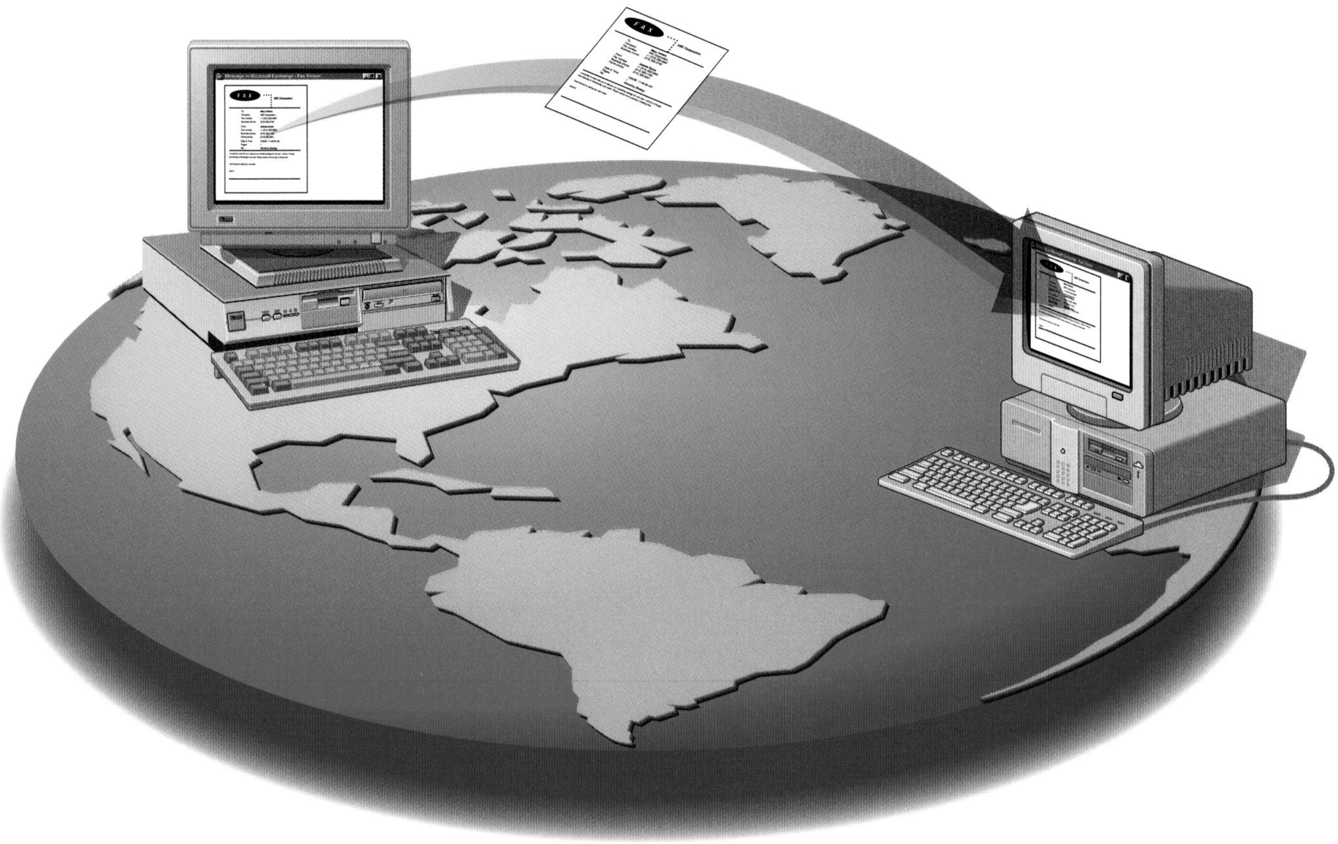

CHAPTER 10: FAXING

Start Microsoft Exchange 152

Send a Fax 154

Change How Modem Answers Faxes 158

View a Fax 160

Print a Fax 163

START MICROSOFT EXCHANGE

Microsoft Exchange lets you send and receive faxes and electronic mail (e-mail).

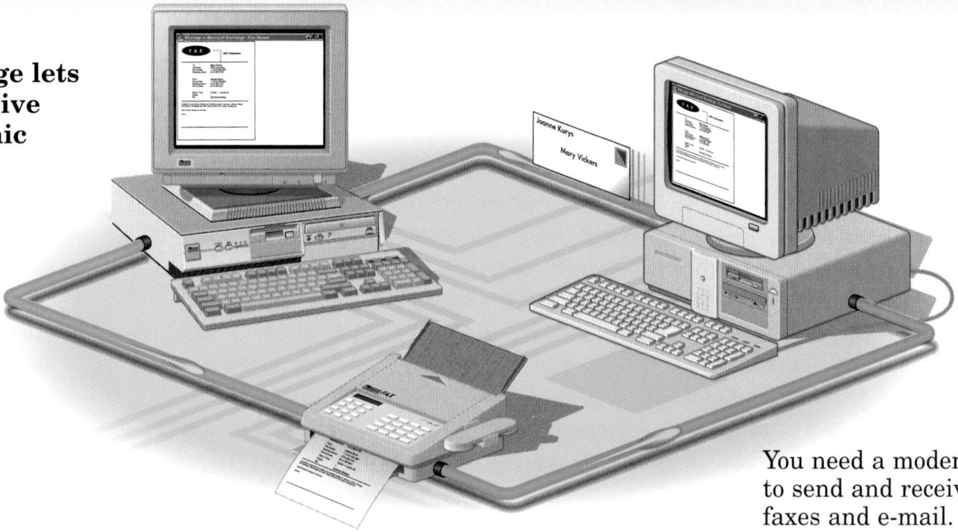

You need a modem to send and receive faxes and e-mail.

START MICROSOFT EXCHANGE

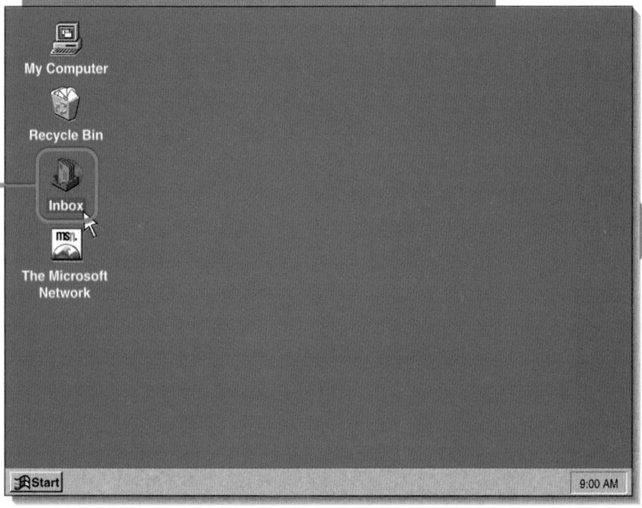

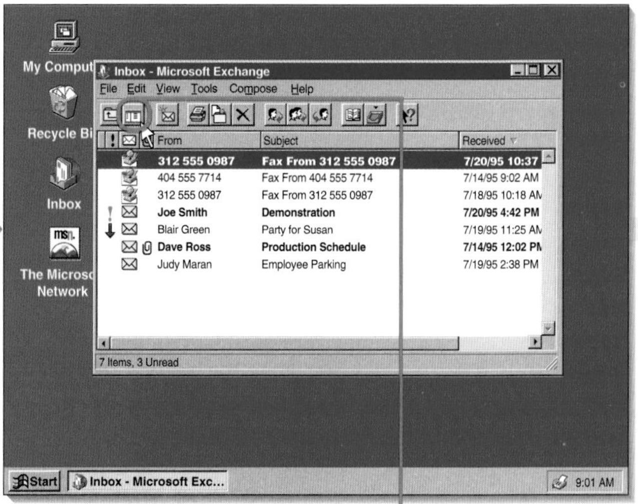

1 Double-click **Inbox**.

*Note: If your screen does not display **Inbox**, you must install the Microsoft Exchange and Microsoft Fax programs to continue.*

■ The **Microsoft Exchange** window appears.

2 To display the folders that store your messages, click ▤.

TIP

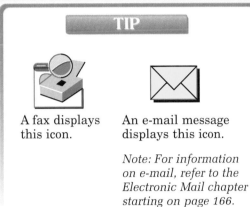

A fax displays this icon.

An e-mail message displays this icon.

Note: For information on e-mail, refer to the Electronic Mail chapter starting on page 166.

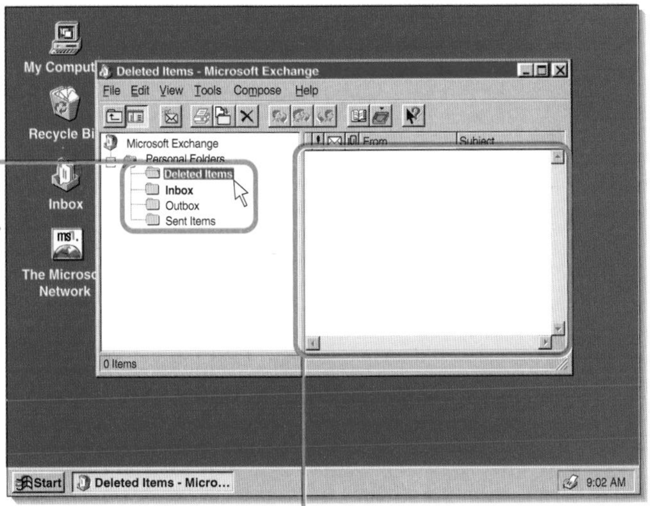

■ The folders appear.

3 To display the contents of a folder, click the folder.

■ This area displays the contents of the folder you selected. You can only display the contents of one folder at a time.

*Note: In this example, there are no messages in the **Deleted Items** folder.*

Microsoft Exchange provides four folders to store your messages.

DELETED ITEMS

Stores messages you have deleted.

INBOX

Stores messages sent to you.

OUTBOX

Temporarily stores messages you have sent until they are delivered.

SENT ITEMS

Stores copies of messages you have sent.

SEND A FAX

You can easily send a fax to a colleague across the city or around the world.

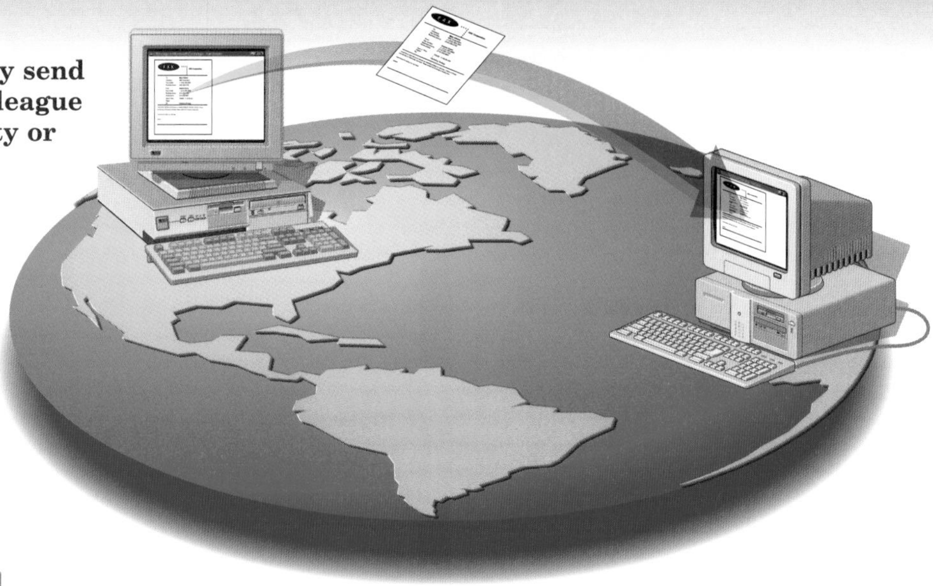

SEND A FAX

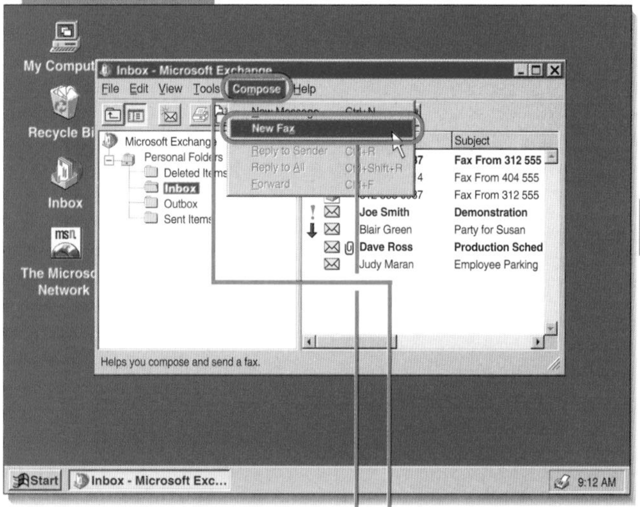

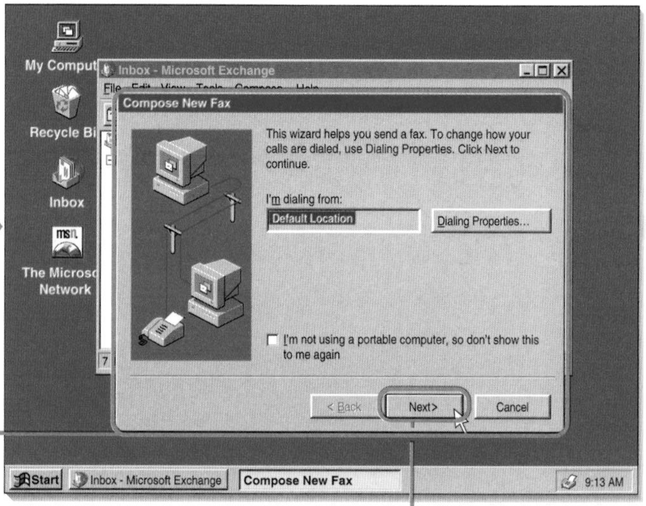

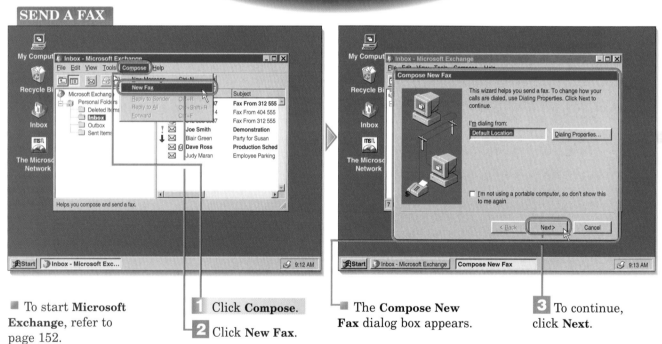

■ To start **Microsoft Exchange**, refer to page 152.

1 Click **Compose**.

2 Click **New Fax**.

■ The **Compose New Fax** dialog box appears.

3 To continue, click **Next**.

TIP

If you are sending a fax to another country, you must specify the country.

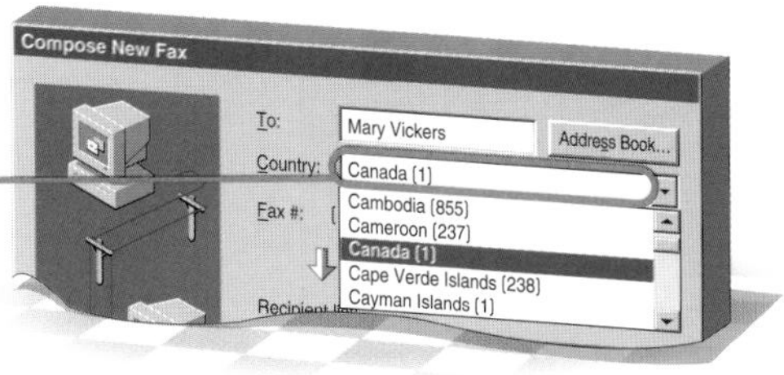

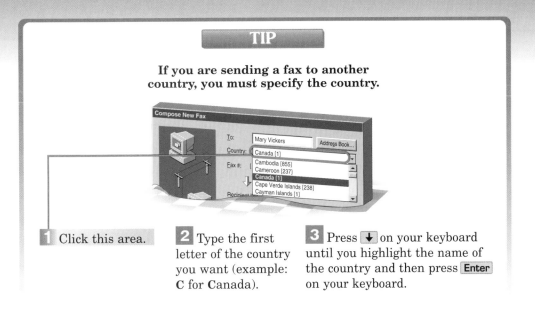

1 Click this area.

2 Type the first letter of the country you want (example: **C** for **C**anada).

3 Press ↓ on your keyboard until you highlight the name of the country and then press **Enter** on your keyboard.

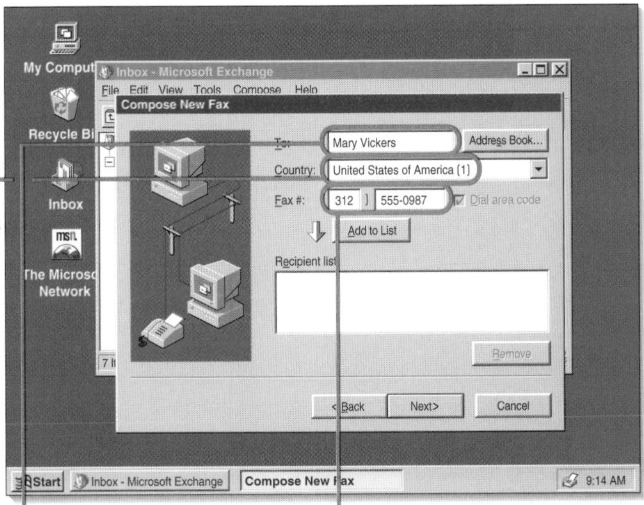

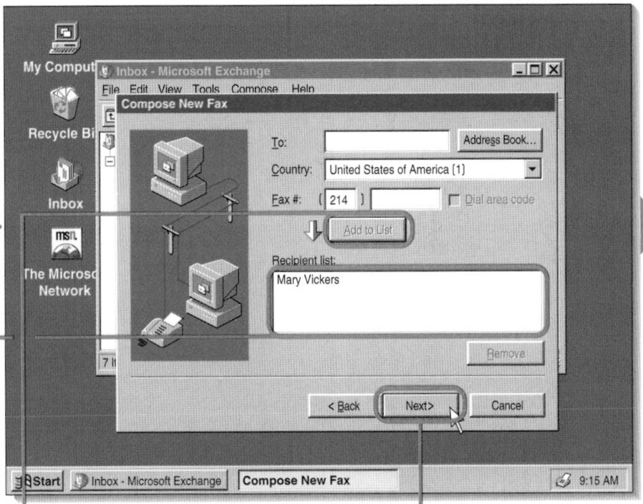

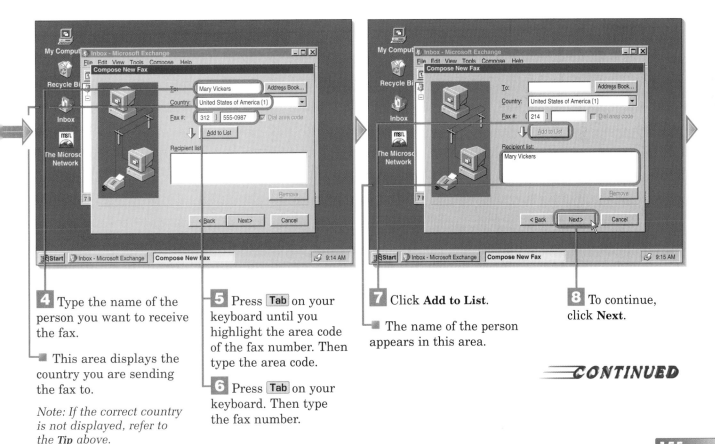

4 Type the name of the person you want to receive the fax.

■ This area displays the country you are sending the fax to.

Note: If the correct country is not displayed, refer to the ***Tip*** *above.*

5 Press **Tab** on your keyboard until you highlight the area code of the fax number. Then type the area code.

6 Press **Tab** on your keyboard. Then type the fax number.

7 Click **Add to List**.

■ The name of the person appears in this area.

8 To continue, click **Next**.

CONTINUED

SEND A FAX

Microsoft Exchange offers four types of cover pages you can include with your fax.

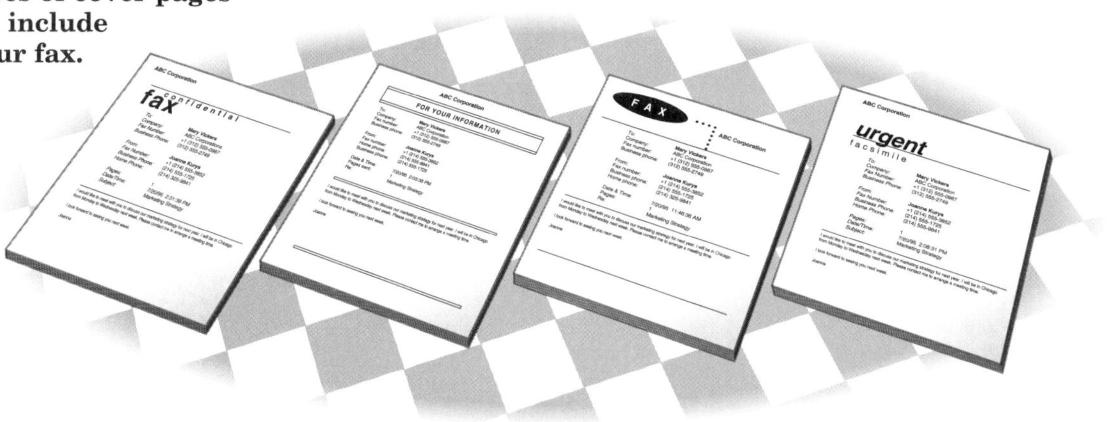

SEND A FAX (CONTINUED)

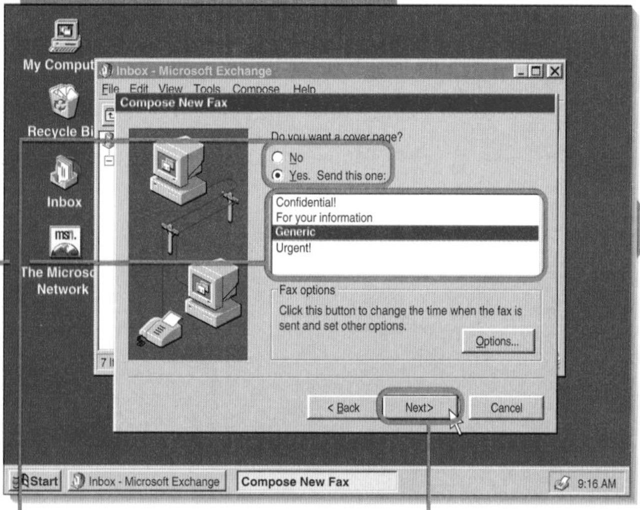

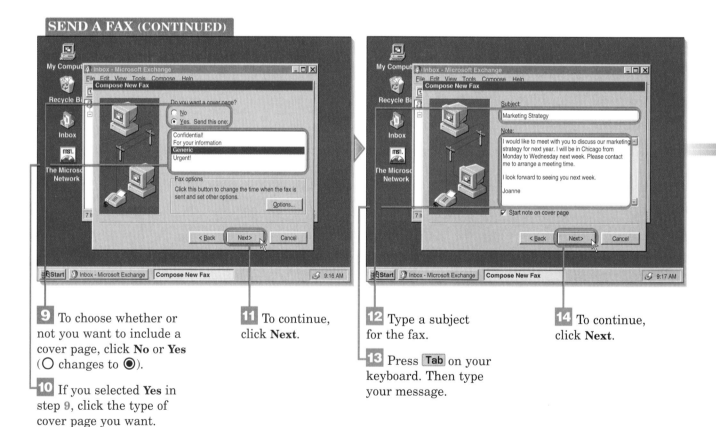

9 To choose whether or not you want to include a cover page, click **No** or **Yes** (○ changes to ◉).

10 If you selected **Yes** in step **9**, click the type of cover page you want.

11 To continue, click **Next**.

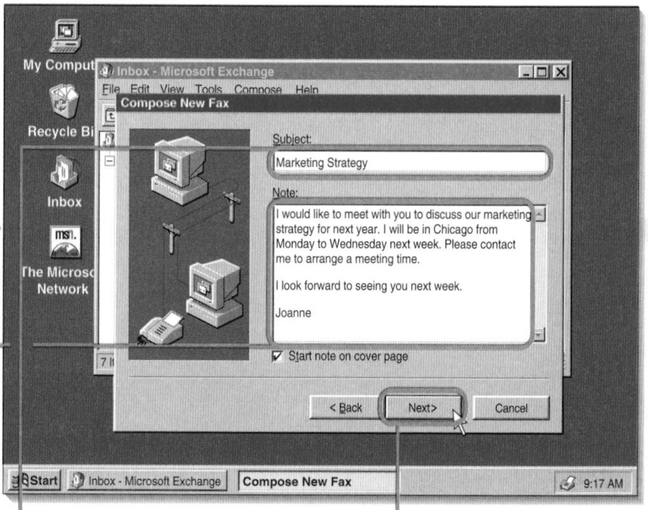

12 Type a subject for the fax.

13 Press Tab on your keyboard. Then type your message.

14 To continue, click **Next**.

TIP

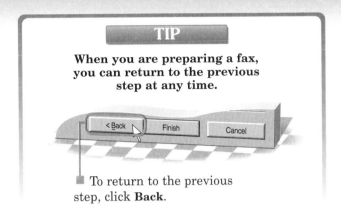

When you are preparing a fax, you can return to the previous step at any time.

■ To return to the previous step, click **Back**.

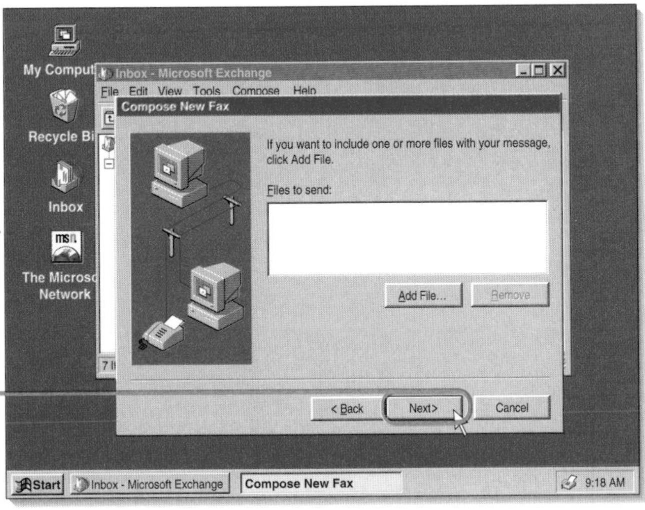

15 To continue, click **Next**.

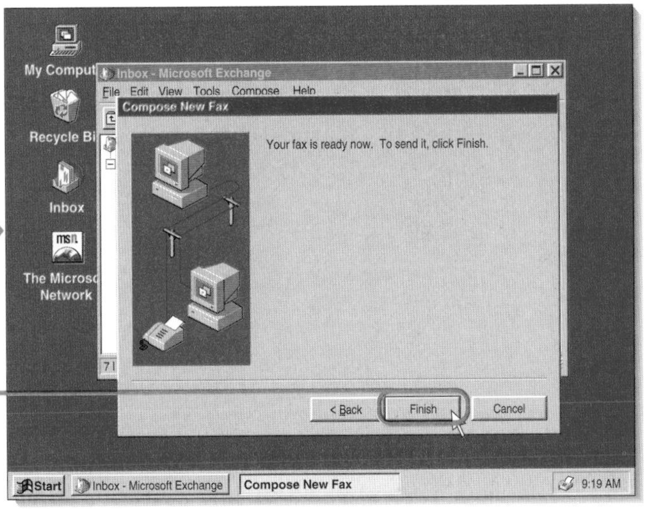

16 To send the fax, click **Finish**.

CHANGE HOW MODEM ANSWERS FAXES

You can instruct your modem to answer incoming faxes in the way that is most convenient for you.

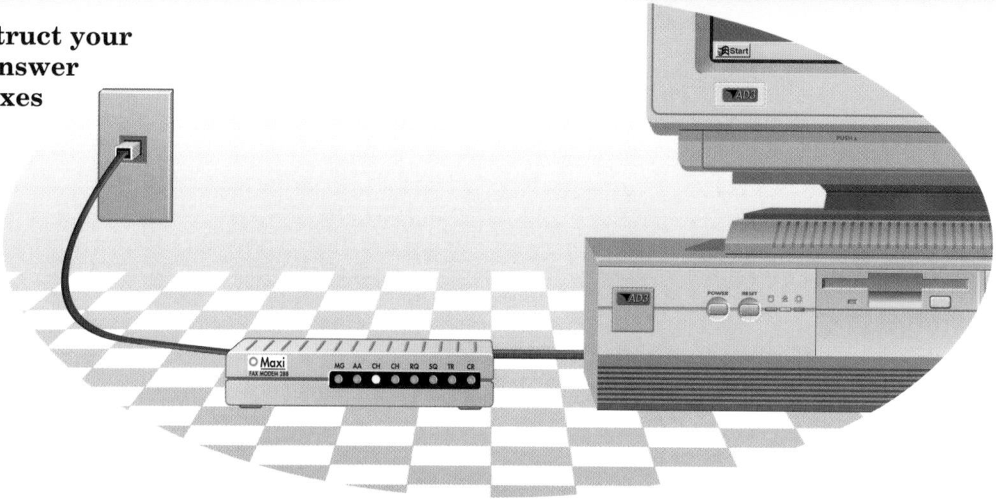

CHANGE HOW MODEM ANSWERS FAXES

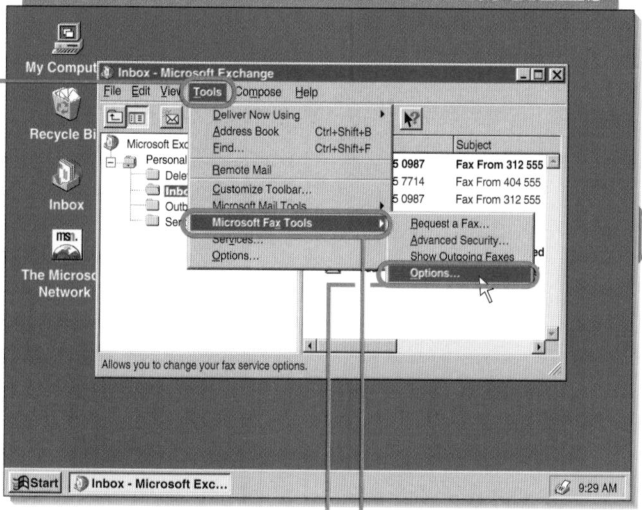

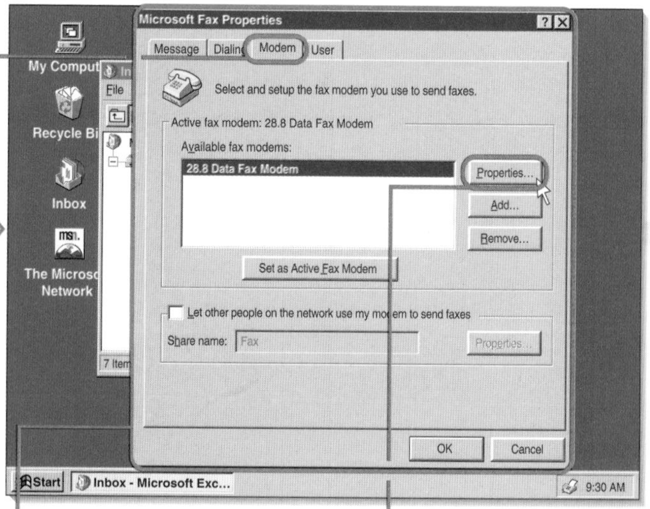

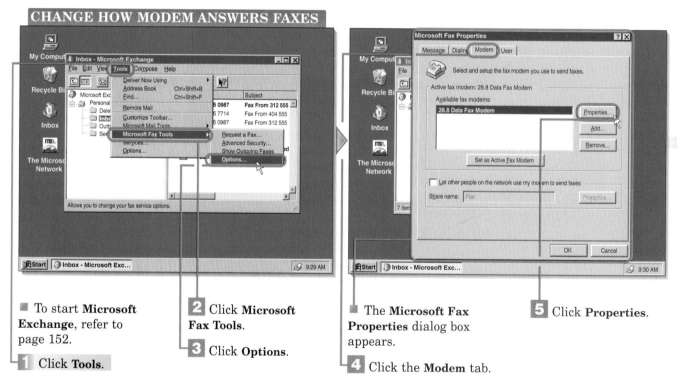

■ To start **Microsoft Exchange**, refer to page 152.

1 Click **Tools**.

2 Click **Microsoft Fax Tools**.

3 Click **Options**.

■ The **Microsoft Fax Properties** dialog box appears.

4 Click the **Modem** tab.

5 Click **Properties**.

ANSWER AFTER	MANUAL	DON'T ANSWER
The modem will answer all incoming faxes after the number of rings you specify. Select this option if you use the telephone line primarily for faxing.	The modem will only answer incoming faxes when you instruct it to. Select this option if you use the telephone line primarily for voice calls. *Note: A dialog box appears when someone is sending you a fax. To answer the fax, click* ***Yes****.*	The modem will not answer incoming faxes.

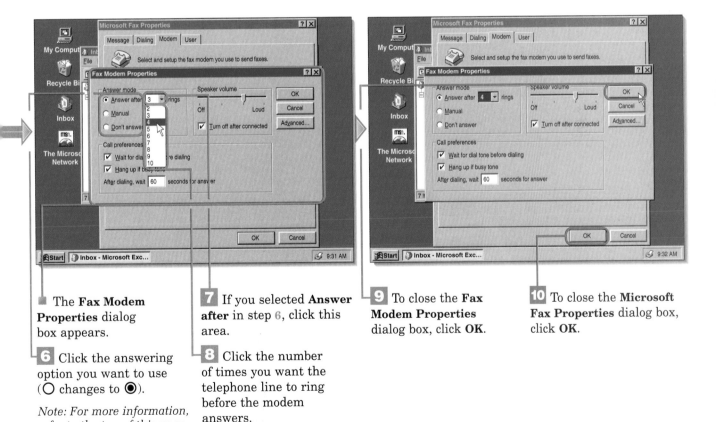

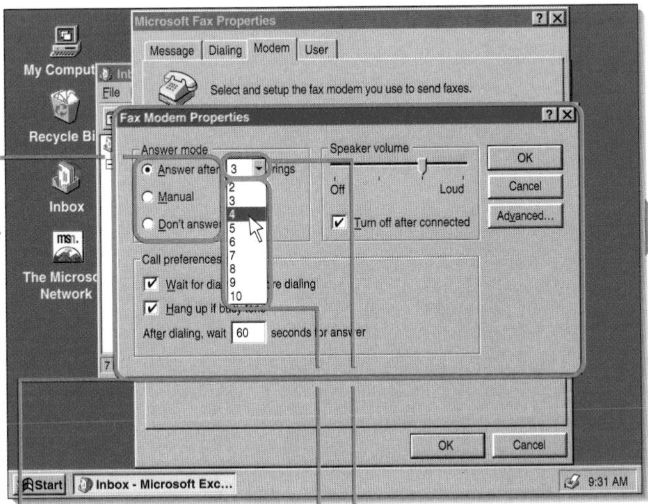

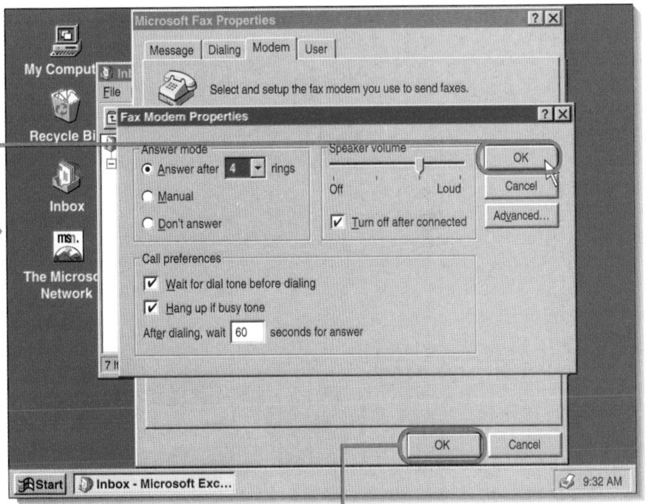

■ The **Fax Modem Properties** dialog box appears.

6 Click the answering option you want to use (○ changes to ◉).

Note: For more information, refer to the top of this page.

7 If you selected **Answer after** in step 6, click this area.

8 Click the number of times you want the telephone line to ring before the modem answers.

9 To close the **Fax Modem Properties** dialog box, click **OK**.

10 To close the **Microsoft Fax Properties** dialog box, click **OK**.

VIEW A FAX

You can display a fax on your screen so you can read the message.

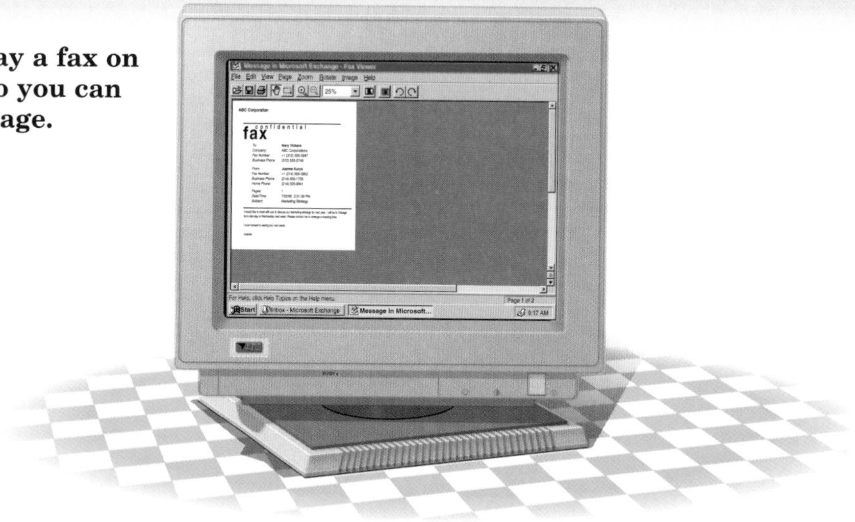

VIEW A FAX

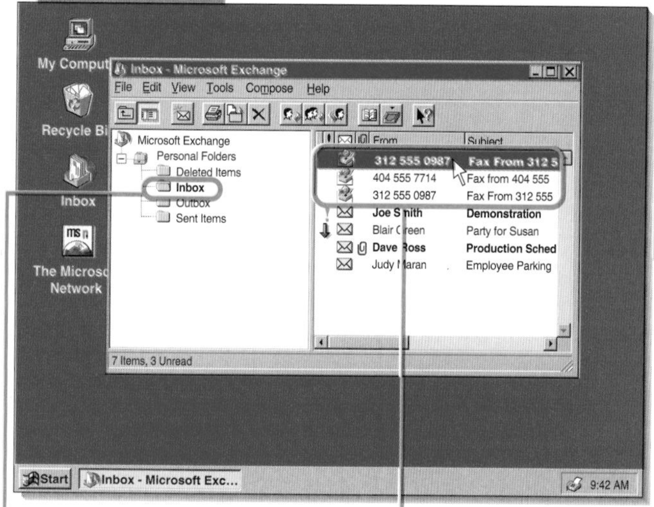

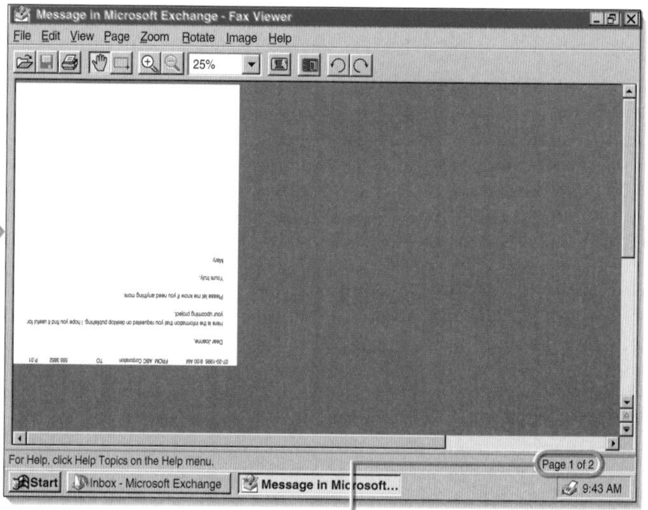

■ To start **Microsoft Exchange**, refer to page 152.

1 To display the faxes sent to you, click the **Inbox** folder.

2 Double-click the fax you want to view.

Note: A fax displays the icon.

■ The **Fax Viewer** window appears, displaying the first page of the fax.

Note: To enlarge the window to fill your screen, refer to page 13.

■ This area indicates which page is displayed and the total number of pages in the fax.

TIP

You can magnify or reduce a page displayed on your screen.

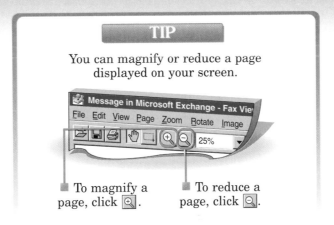

■ To magnify a page, click 🔍.

■ To reduce a page, click 🔍.

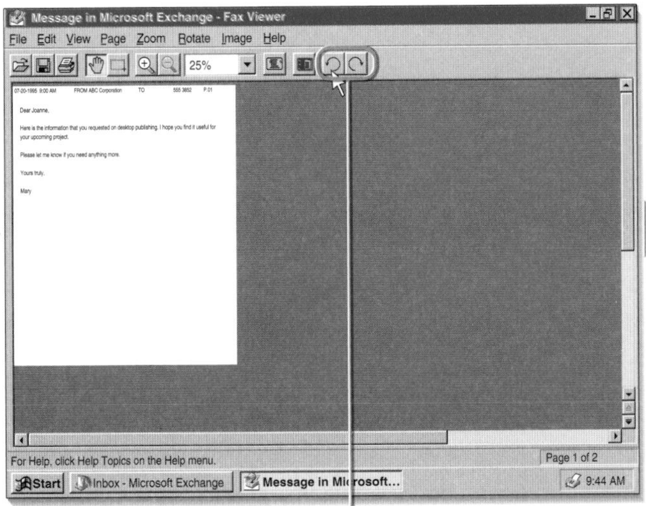

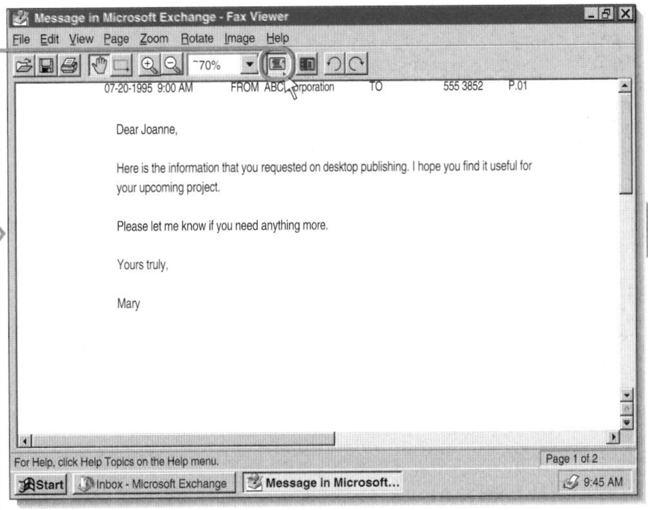

ROTATE A PAGE

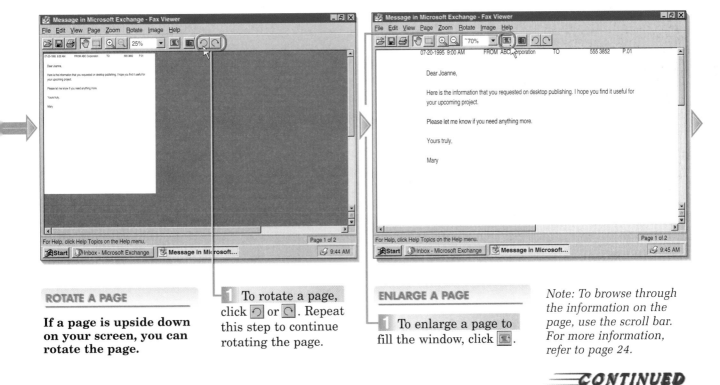

If a page is upside down on your screen, you can rotate the page.

1 To rotate a page, click ↺ or ↻. Repeat this step to continue rotating the page.

ENLARGE A PAGE

1 To enlarge a page to fill the window, click ▣.

Note: To browse through the information on the page, use the scroll bar. For more information, refer to page 24.

CONTINUED

VIEW A FAX

The Fax Viewer window lets you easily flip through the pages in your fax.

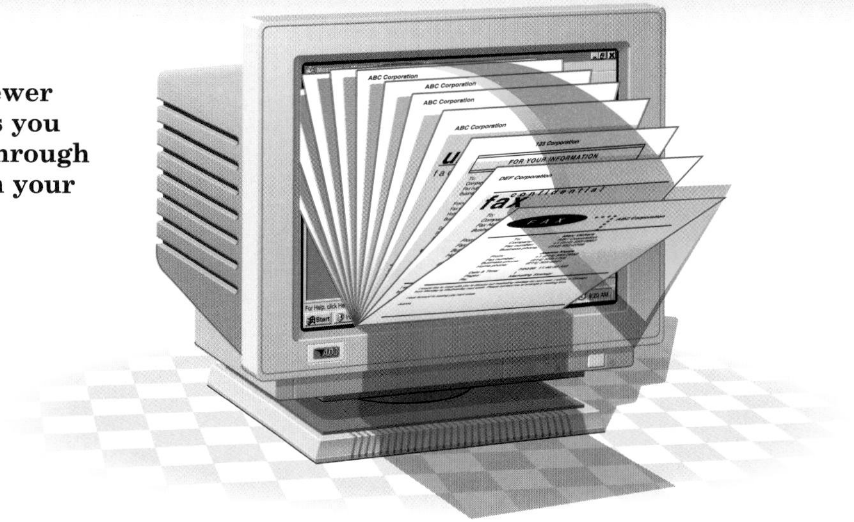

VIEW A FAX (CONTINUED)

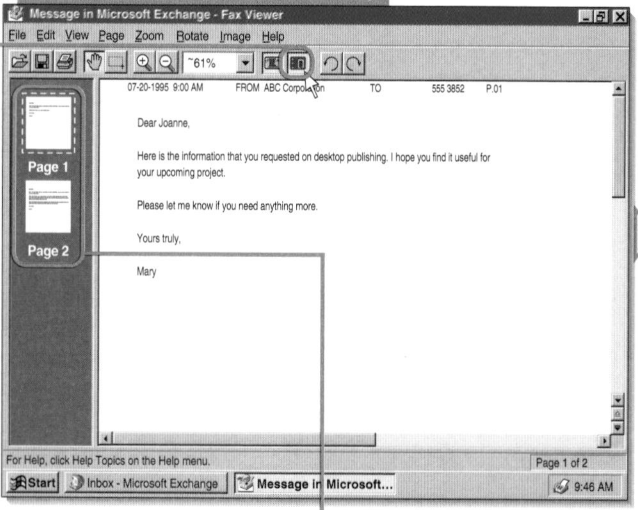

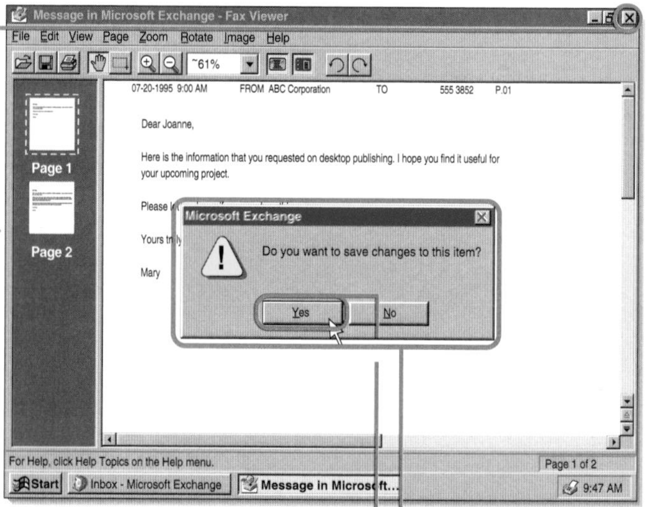

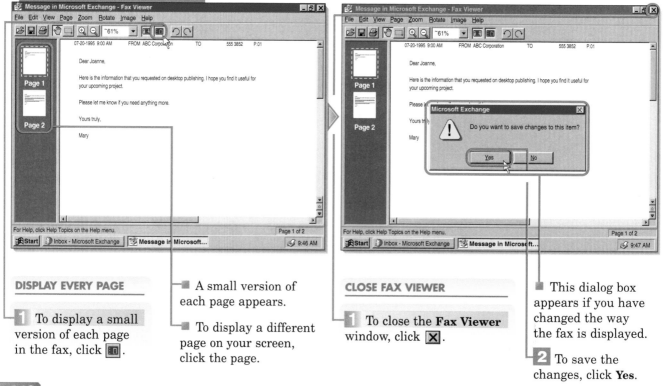

DISPLAY EVERY PAGE

1 To display a small version of each page in the fax, click ▣.

■ A small version of each page appears.

■ To display a different page on your screen, click the page.

CLOSE FAX VIEWER

1 To close the **Fax Viewer** window, click ☒.

■ This dialog box appears if you have changed the way the fax is displayed.

2 To save the changes, click **Yes**.

PRINT A FAX

You can easily produce a paper copy of a fax you received.

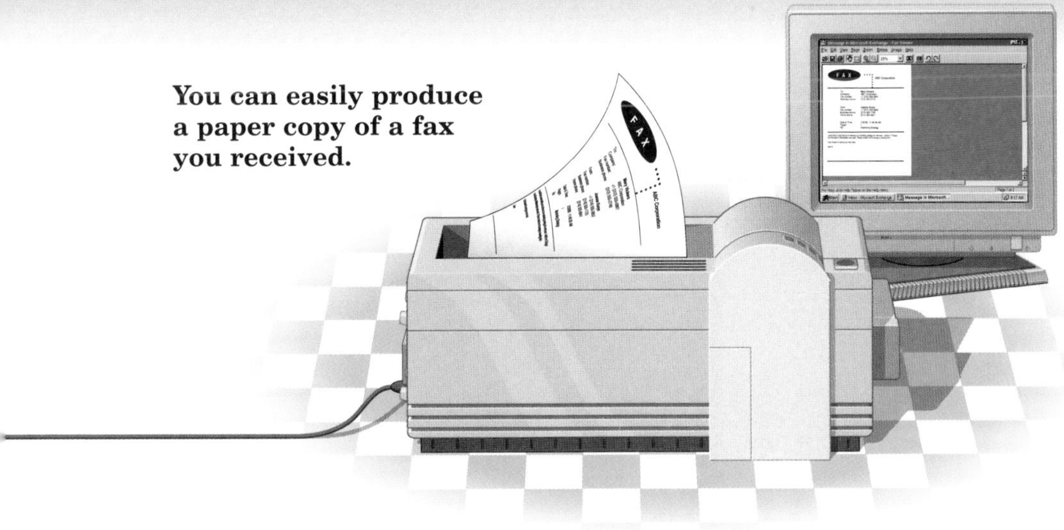

PRINT A FAX

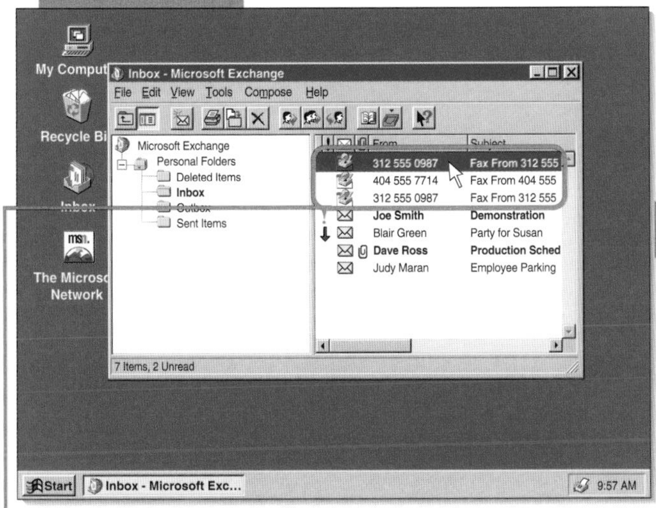

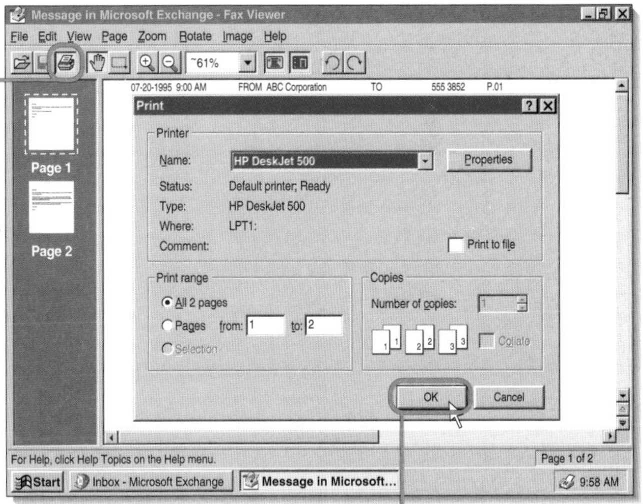

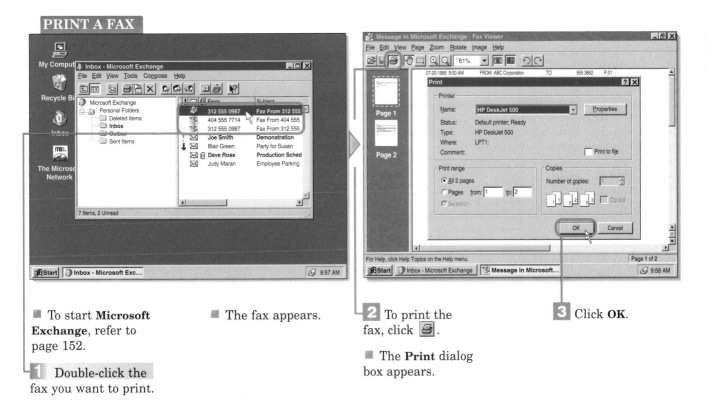

■ To start **Microsoft Exchange**, refer to page 152.

1 Double-click the fax you want to print.

■ The fax appears.

2 To print the fax, click 🖨.

■ The **Print** dialog box appears.

3 Click **OK**.

In this chapter you will learn how to send and receive electronic mail.

Subject :
Financial Statement
As you know, we are beginning to compile the figures for the company's financial statement. Please forward the information for the Chicago branch as soon as possible.
Thanks for your quick response.
Joanne Kurys - Head Office

CHAPTER 11: ELECTRONIC MAIL

Add a Name to the Address Book *166*

Send a Message *168*

Insert a File in a Message *172*

Read a Message *174*

Delete a Message *175*

Reply to a Message *176*

Forward a Message *178*

ADD A NAME TO THE ADDRESS BOOK

Microsoft Exchange provides a personal address book where you can store the names and addresses of people you frequently send messages to.

ADD A NAME TO THE ADDRESS BOOK

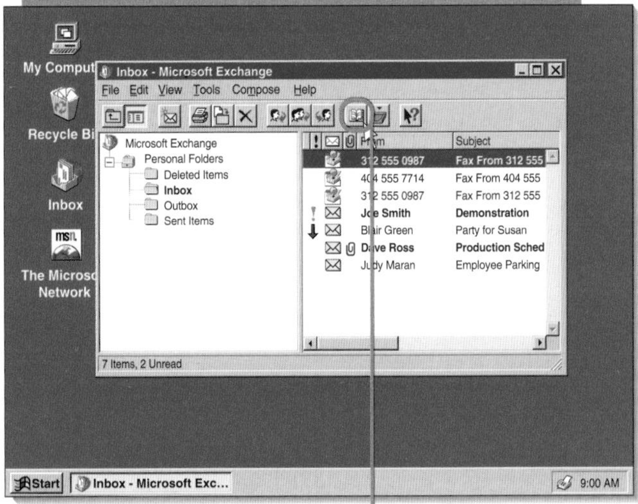

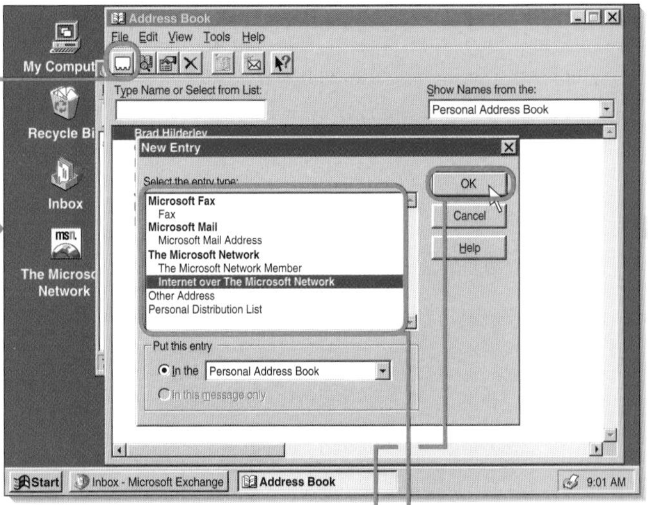

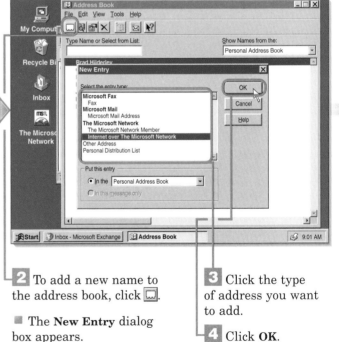

■ To start **Microsoft Exchange**, refer to page 152.

1 Click .

■ The **Address Book** window appears.

2 To add a new name to the address book, click .

■ The **New Entry** dialog box appears.

3 Click the type of address you want to add.

4 Click **OK**.

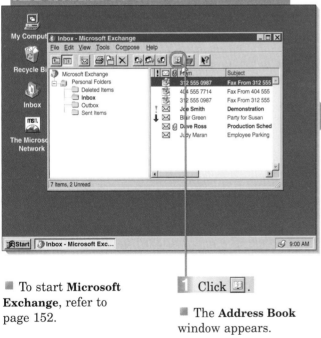

TIP

An Internet address consists of two parts, separated by the @ symbol.

dsmith @ maran.com

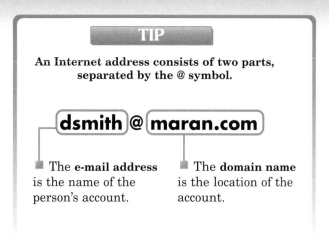

■ The **e-mail address** is the name of the person's account.

■ The **domain name** is the location of the account.

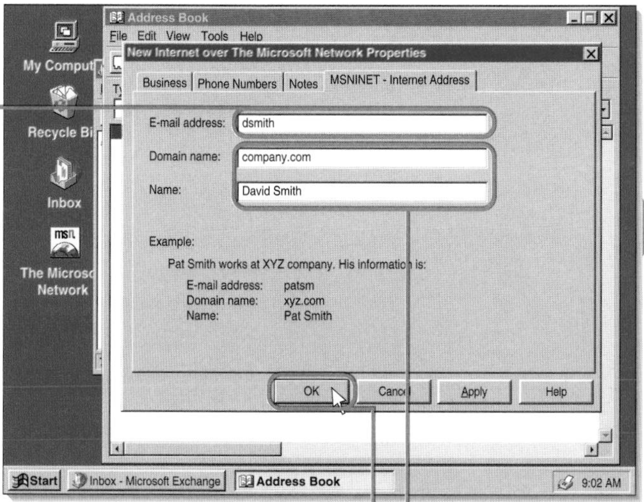

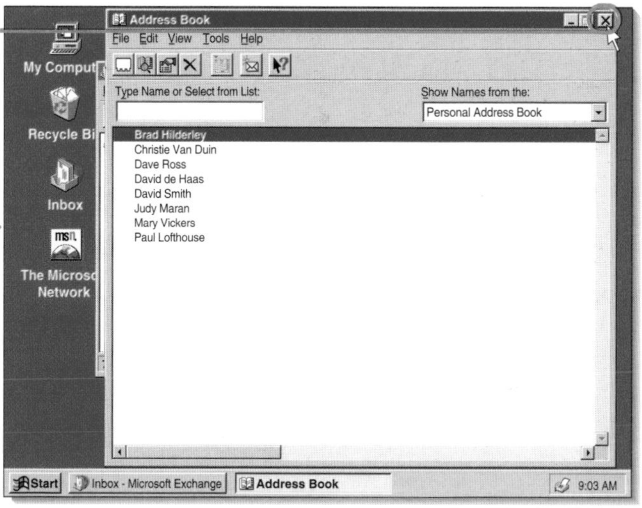

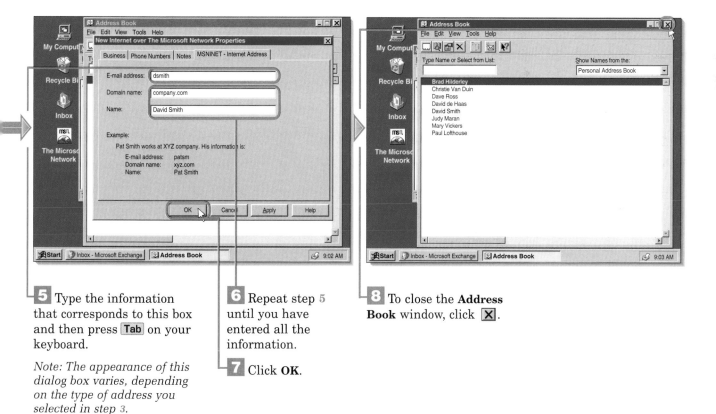

5 Type the information that corresponds to this box and then press **Tab** on your keyboard.

Note: The appearance of this dialog box varies, depending on the type of address you selected in step 3.

6 Repeat step 5 until you have entered all the information.

7 Click **OK**.

8 To close the **Address Book** window, click ☒.

SEND A MESSAGE

You can send a message to another person to exchange ideas or request information.

SEND A MESSAGE

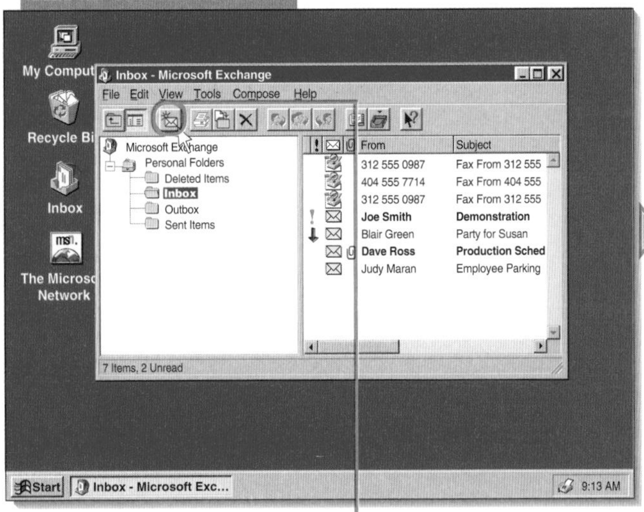

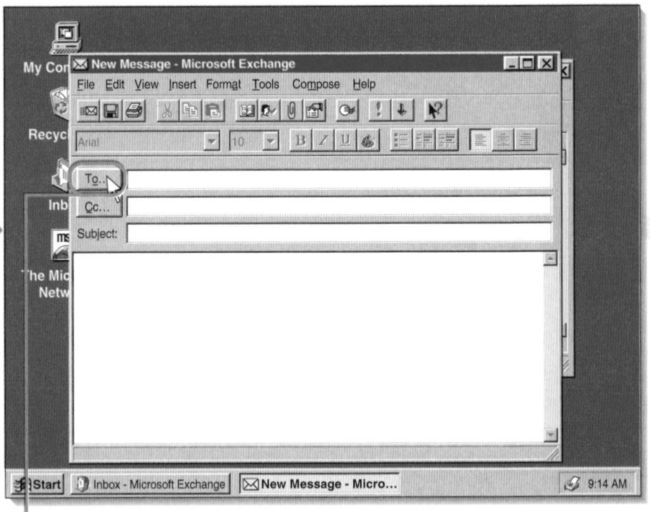

■ To start **Microsoft Exchange**, refer to page 152.

1 Click .

■ The **New Message** window appears.

2 To send the message to a person listed in an address book, click **To**.

*Note: You can also type the e-mail address of the person you want to receive the message in the **To** box (example: **dsmith@company.com**). This lets you skip steps 2 to 7.*

■ The **Address Book** dialog box appears.

TIP

Microsoft Exchange provides several address books to help you quickly find the person you want to send a message to.

Lists the address of each person you frequently send messages to.

Note: To add a name to the Personal Address Book, refer to page 166.

Lists the address of each person connected to The Microsoft Network.

Lists the address of each person connected to the network at your office.

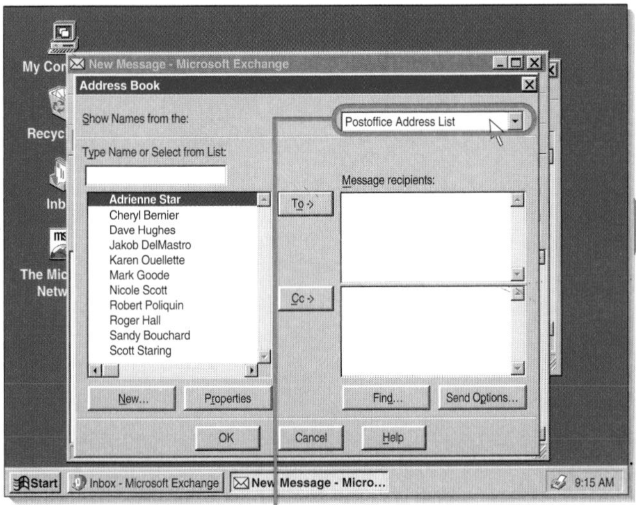

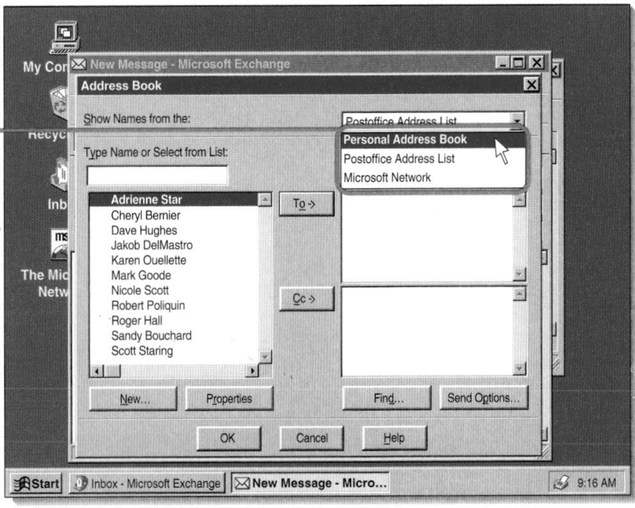

■ This area displays the name of the address book currently displayed.

*Note: For information on address books, refer to the **Tip** above.*

3 To display the names from a different address book, click this area.

4 Click the name of the address book you want to display.

CONTINUED

SEND A MESSAGE

When sending a message, you should enter a subject that will help the reader quickly identify the contents of your message.

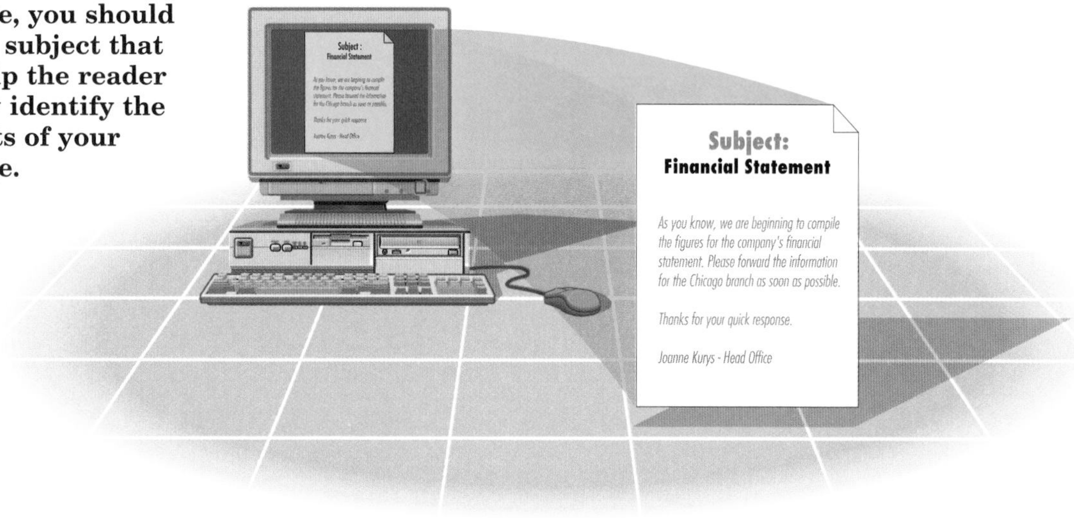
Subject:
Financial Statement
As you know, we are beginning to compile the figures for the company's financial statement. Please forward the information for the Chicago branch as soon as possible.
Thanks for your quick response.
Joanne Kurys - Head Office

SEND A MESSAGE (CONTINUED)

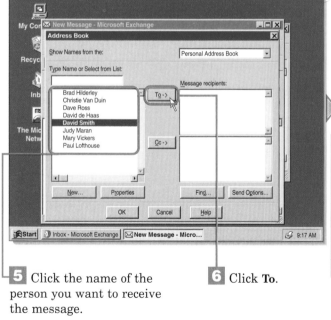

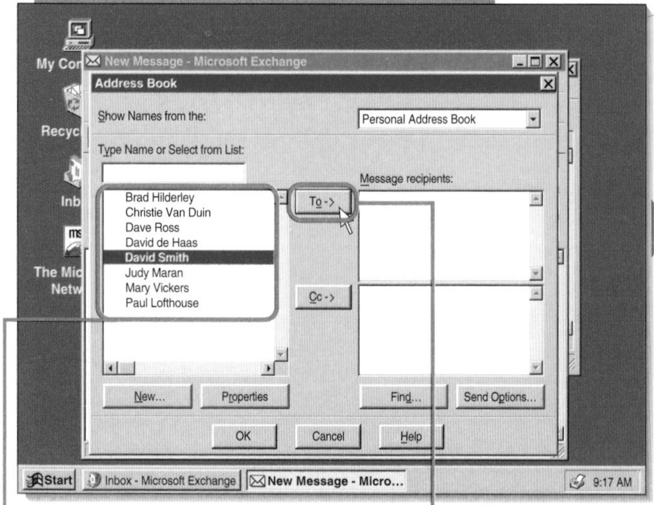

5 Click the name of the person you want to receive the message.

6 Click **To**.

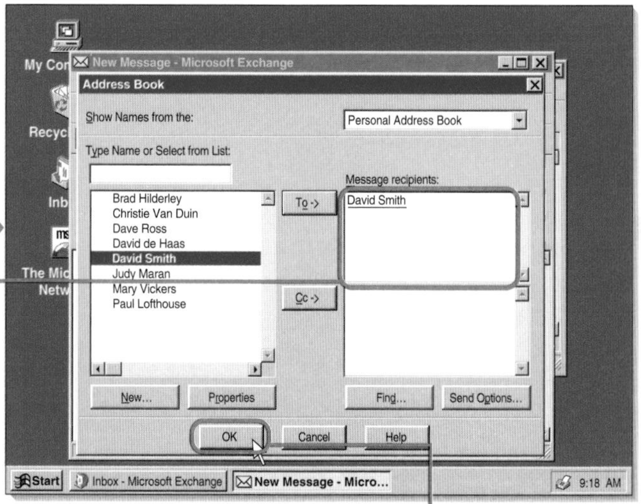

■ This area displays the name of the person you selected.

Note: To send the message to more than one person, repeat steps 5 and 6 for each person.

7 Click **OK**.

TIP

You can use Microsoft Exchange to send messages to co-workers, other members of The Microsoft Network, members of other online services and anyone using the Internet.

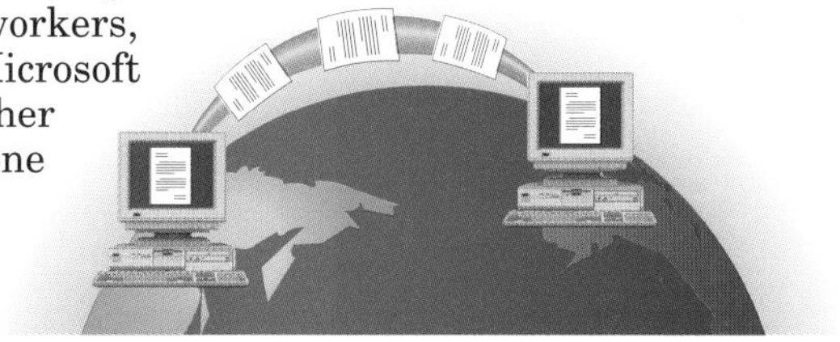

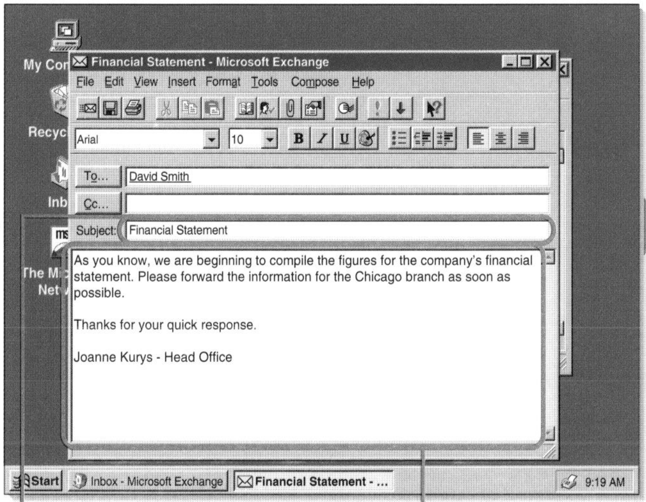

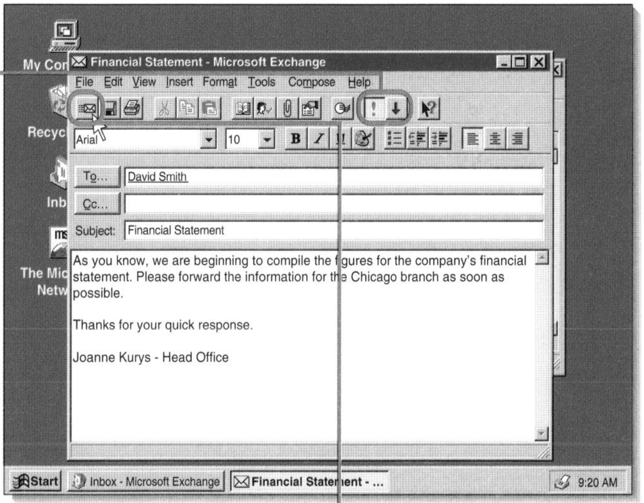

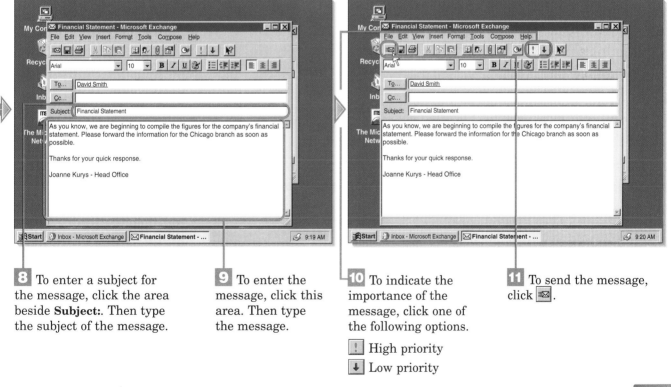

8 To enter a subject for the message, click the area beside **Subject:**. Then type the subject of the message.

9 To enter the message, click this area. Then type the message.

10 To indicate the importance of the message, click one of the following options.

 High priority

 Low priority

11 To send the message, click .

INSERT A FILE IN A MESSAGE

You can insert a file in a message. This is useful when you want to include additional information.

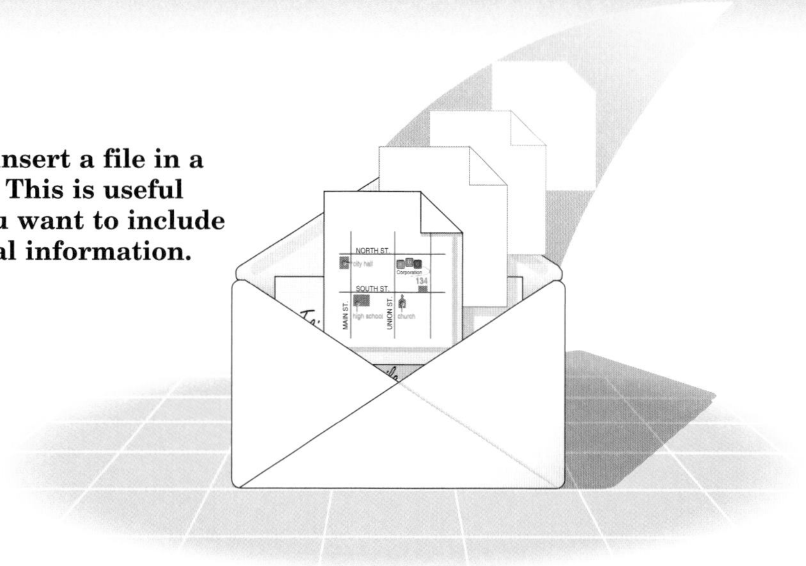

INSERT A FILE IN A MESSAGE

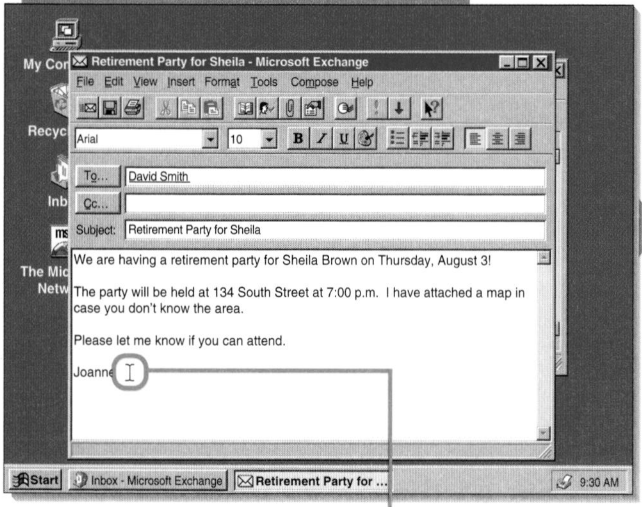

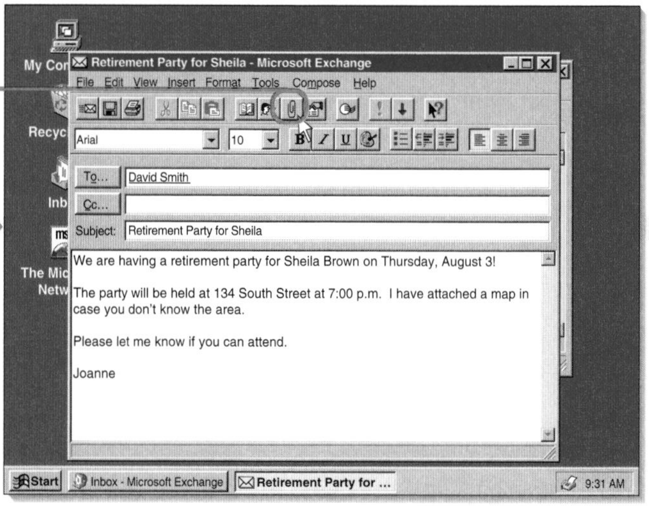

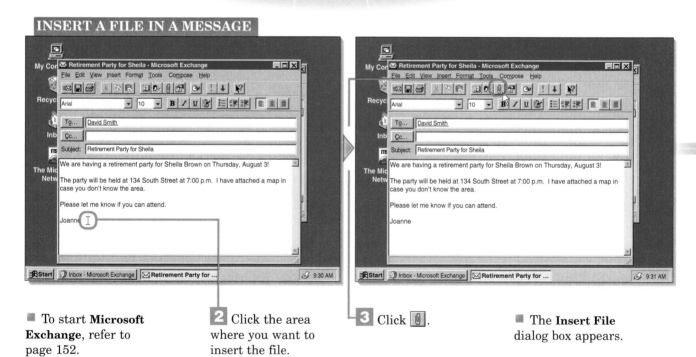

■ To start **Microsoft Exchange**, refer to page 152.

1 To create a message, perform steps 1 to 10 starting on page 168.

2 Click the area where you want to insert the file.

3 Click .

■ The **Insert File** dialog box appears.

TIP

To display the contents of a file in a message, double-click the file's icon.

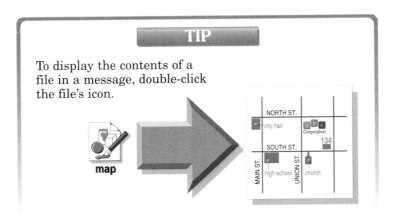

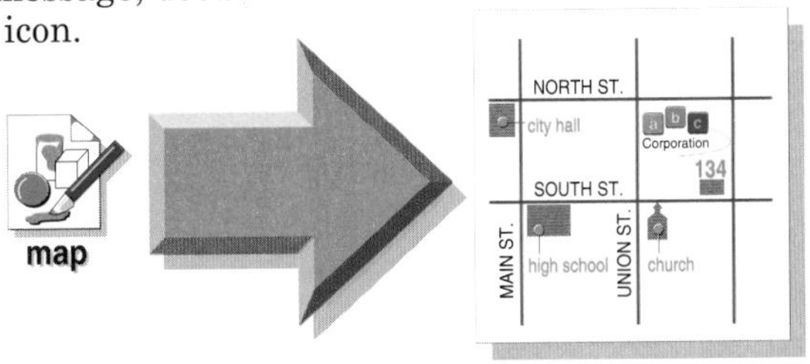

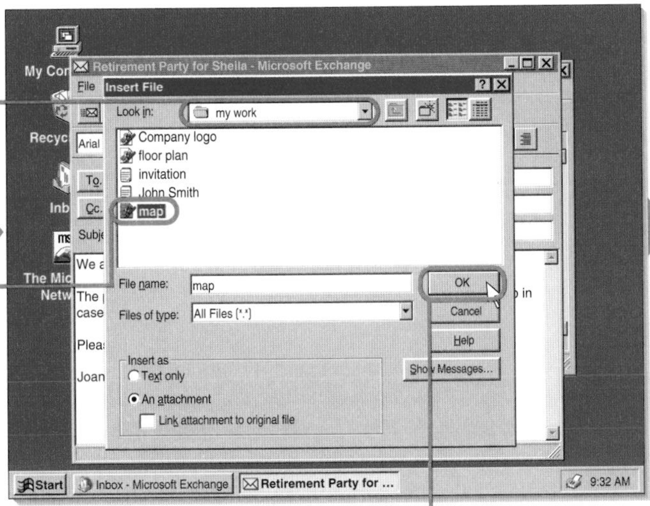

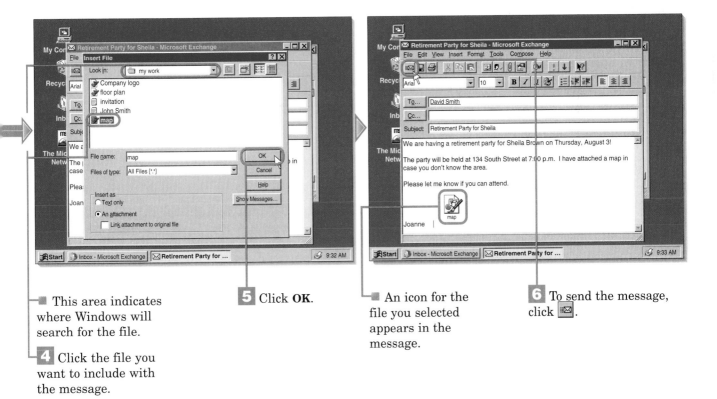

■ This area indicates where Windows will search for the file.

4 Click the file you want to include with the message.

5 Click **OK**.

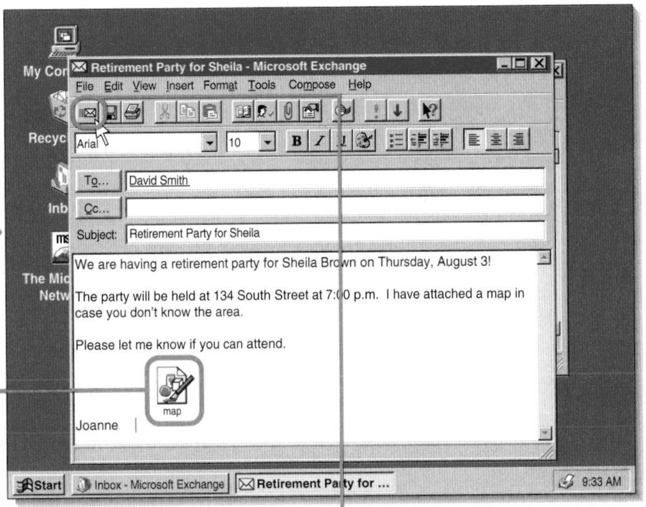

■ An icon for the file you selected appears in the message.

6 To send the message, click ✉.

READ A MESSAGE

You can easily display a message sent to you. Each message displays a symbol to provide additional information.

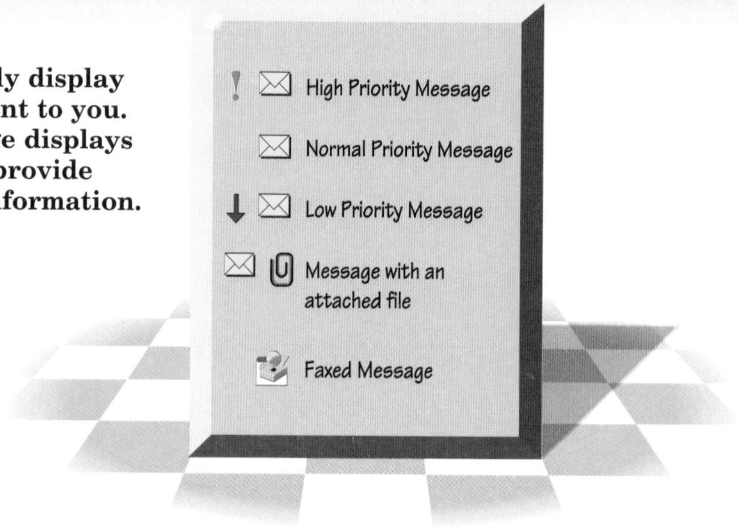

READ A MESSAGE

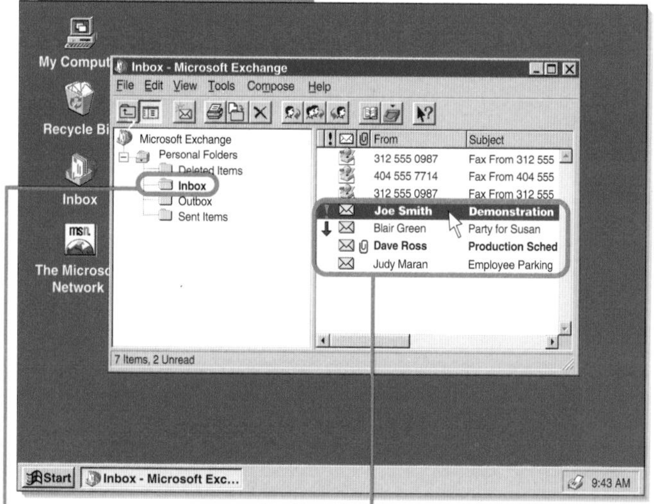

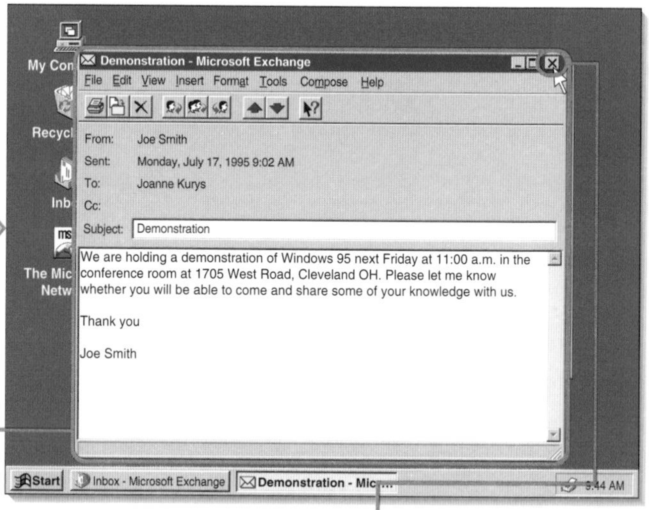

■ To start **Microsoft Exchange**, refer to page 152.

1 Click the **Inbox** folder.

■ This area displays a list of all your messages. Messages you have not read appear in **bold** type.

2 To read a message, double-click the message.

■ The message appears.

3 When you finish reading the message, click ☒.

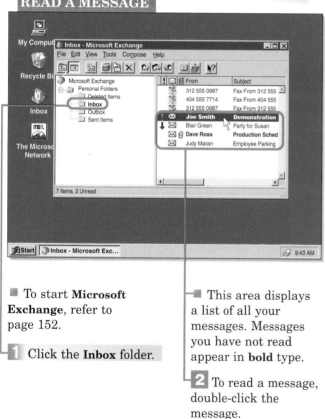

DELETE A MESSAGE

You can delete a message you no longer need.

DELETE A MESSAGE

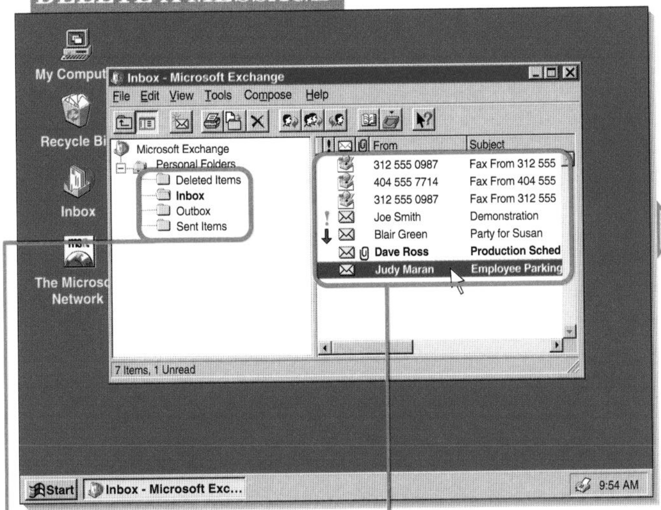

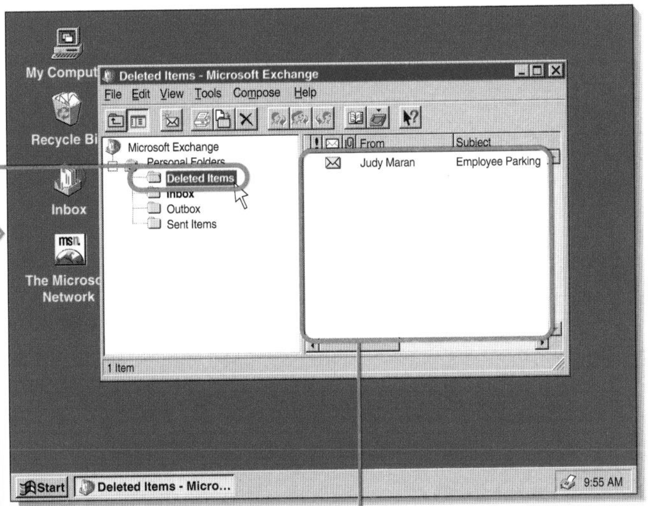

■ To start **Microsoft Exchange**, refer to page 152.

1 Click the folder containing the message you want to delete (example: **Inbox**).

2 Click the message you want to delete.

3 Press Delete on your keyboard and Microsoft Exchange places the message in the **Deleted Items** folder.

4 To view all the messages you have deleted, click the **Deleted Items** folder.

■ This area displays the messages you have deleted.

*Note: Deleting a message from the **Deleted Items** folder will permanently remove the message from your computer.*

REPLY TO A MESSAGE

After reading a message, you can send a reply. This lets you comment on the message or answer questions.

REPLY TO A MESSAGE

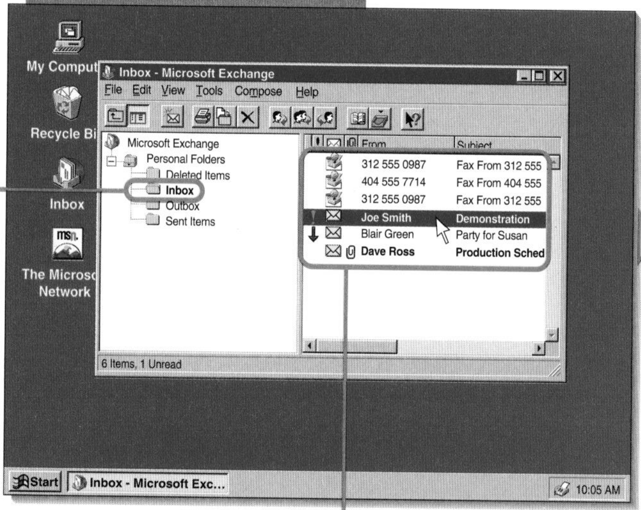

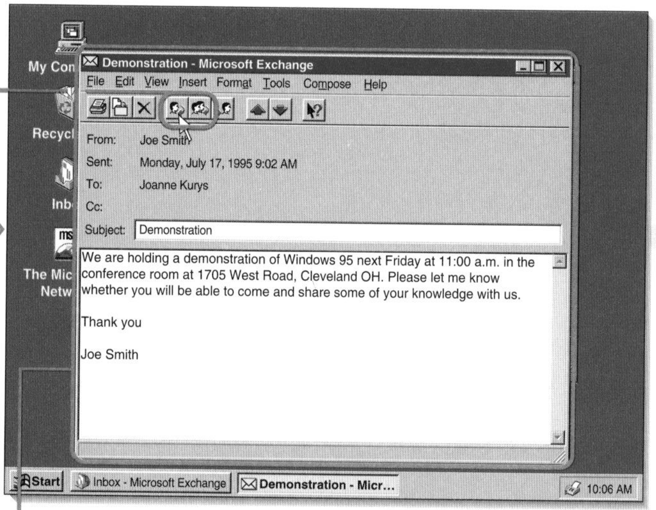

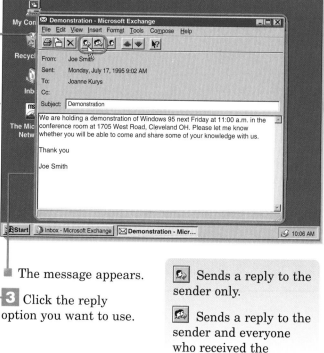

■ To start **Microsoft Exchange**, refer to page 152.

1 Click the **Inbox** folder.

2 To open a message you want to reply to, double-click the message.

■ The message appears.

3 Click the reply option you want to use.

Sends a reply to the sender only.

Sends a reply to the sender and everyone who received the original message.

TIP

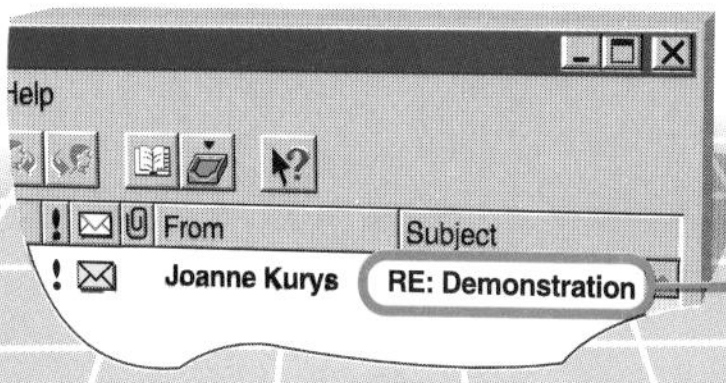

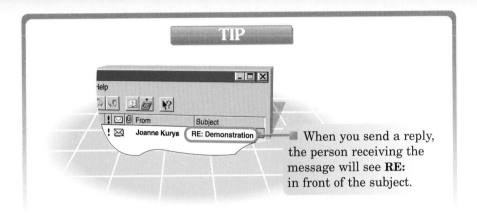

When you send a reply, the person receiving the message will see **RE:** in front of the subject.

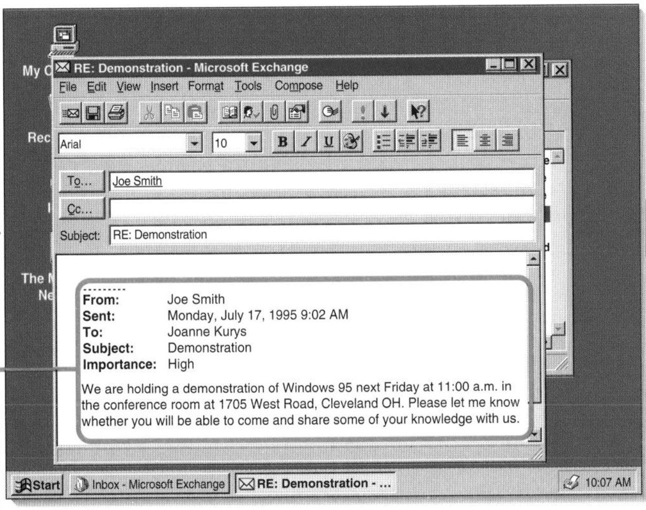

This area displays the original message.

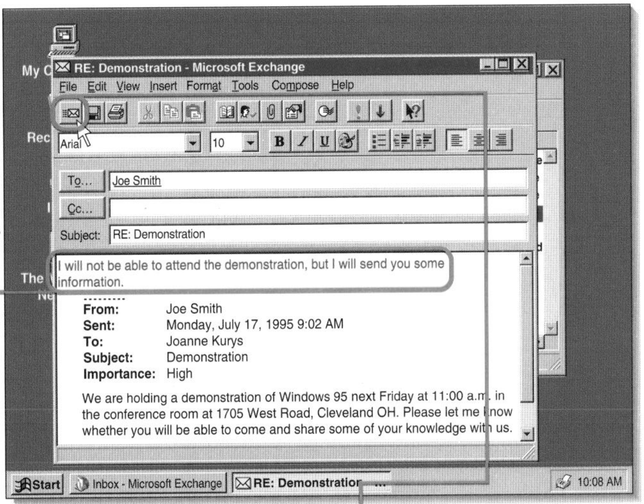

4 Type your reply.

5 To send the reply, click ✉.

FORWARD A MESSAGE

After reading a message, you can add comments and then forward the message to a colleague.

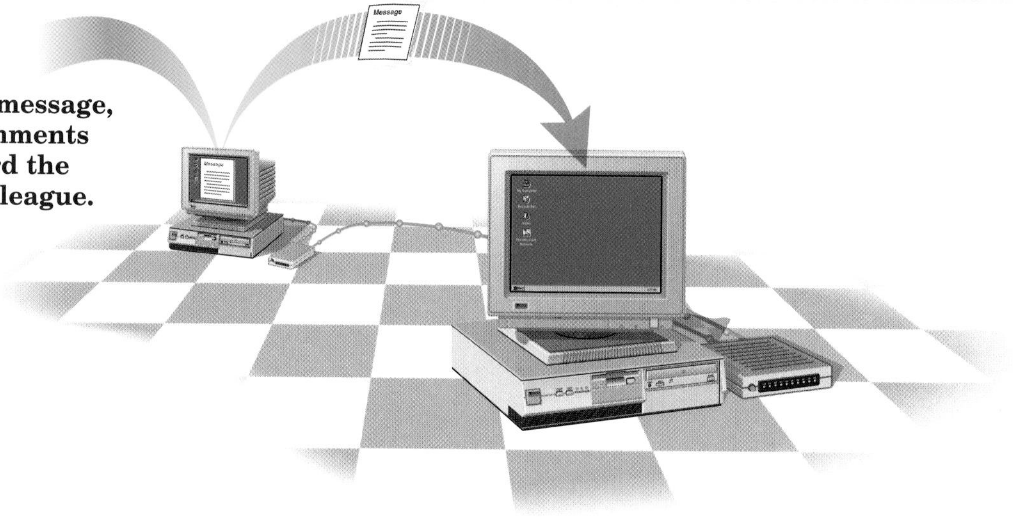

FORWARD A MESSAGE

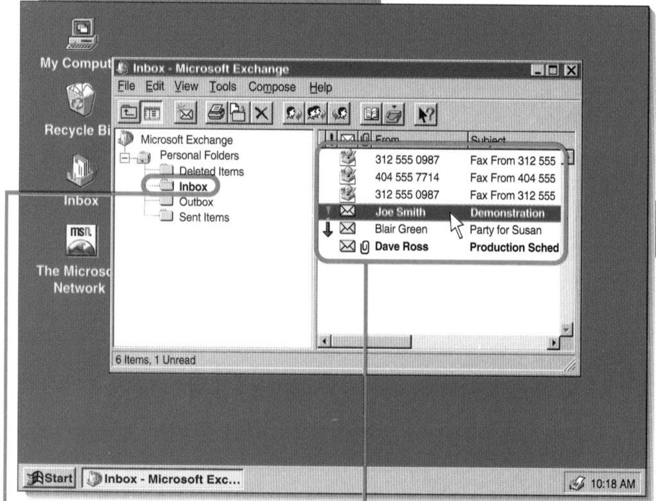

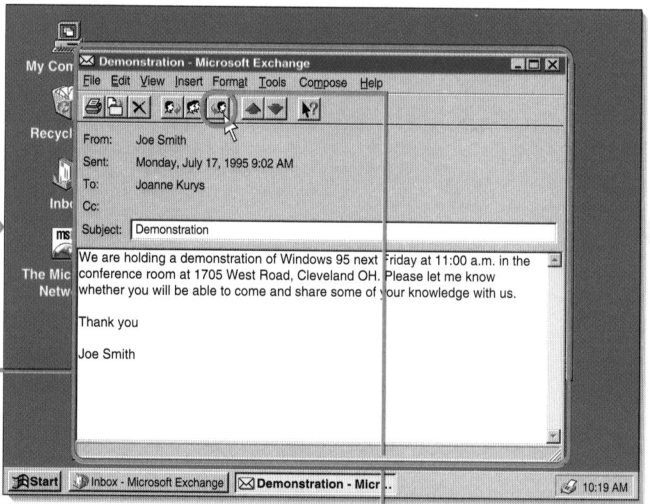

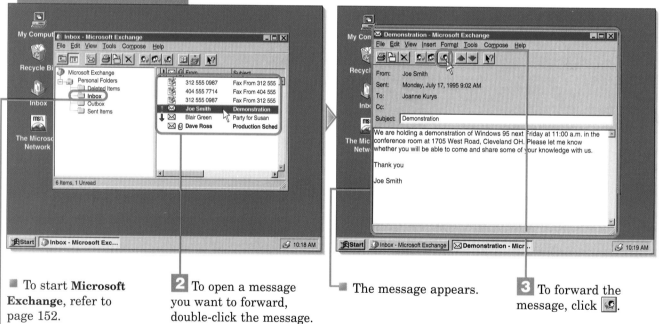

■ To start **Microsoft Exchange**, refer to page 152.

1 Click the **Inbox** folder.

2 To open a message you want to forward, double-click the message.

■ The message appears.

3 To forward the message, click .

TIP

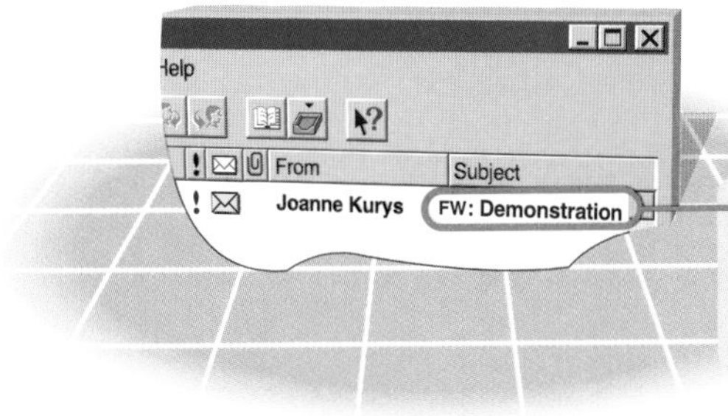

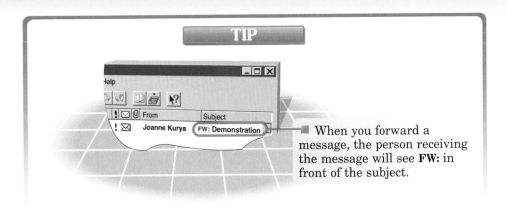

When you forward a message, the person receiving the message will see **FW:** in front of the subject.

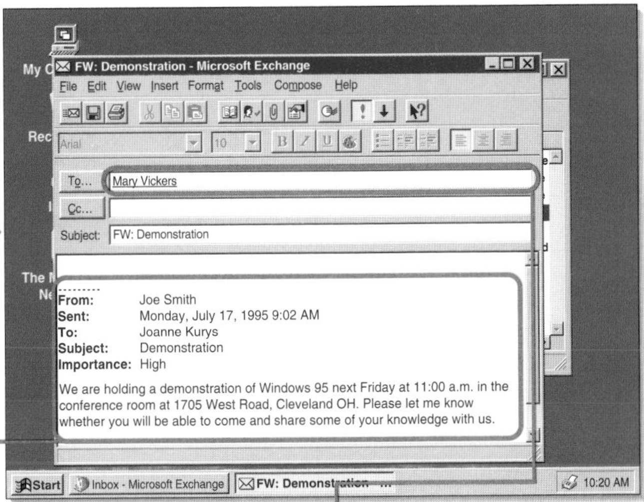

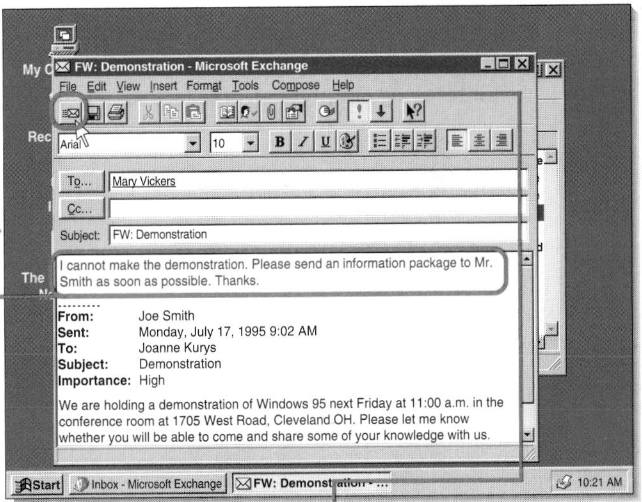

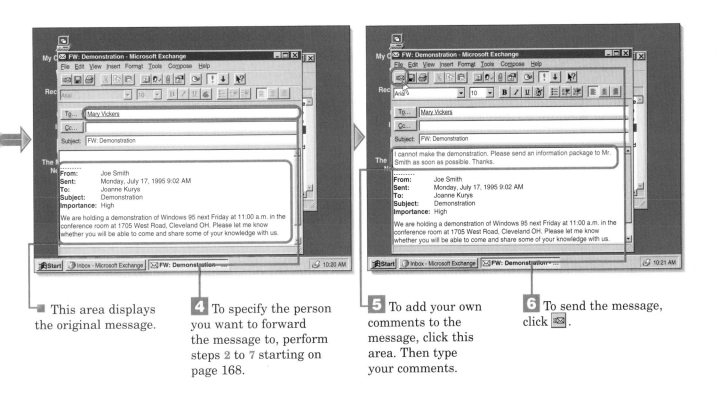

This area displays the original message.

4 To specify the person you want to forward the message to, perform steps 2 to 7 starting on page 168.

5 To add your own comments to the message, click this area. Then type your comments.

6 To send the message, click .

In this chapter you will learn how to add new fonts, Windows components, programs and hardware to your computer.

CHAPTER 12: ADD HARDWARE AND SOFTWARE

Add Fonts *182*

Add Windows Components *186*

Add a New Program *190*

Set Up New Hardware *194*

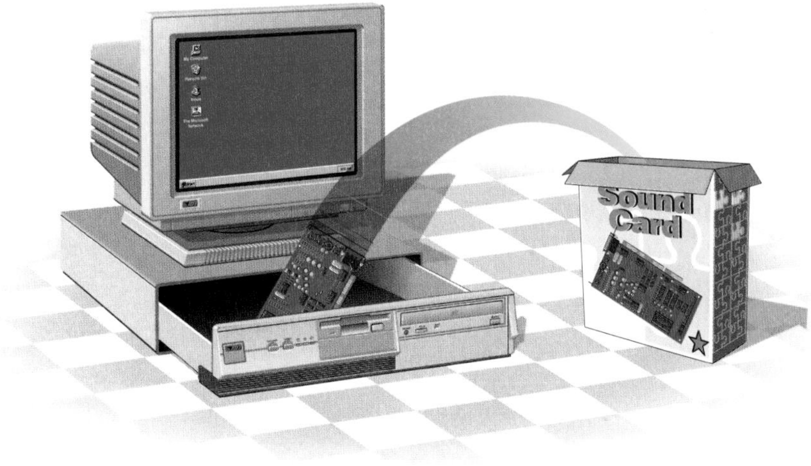

ADD FONTS

You can add fonts to your computer to give you more choices when creating documents.

ADD FONTS

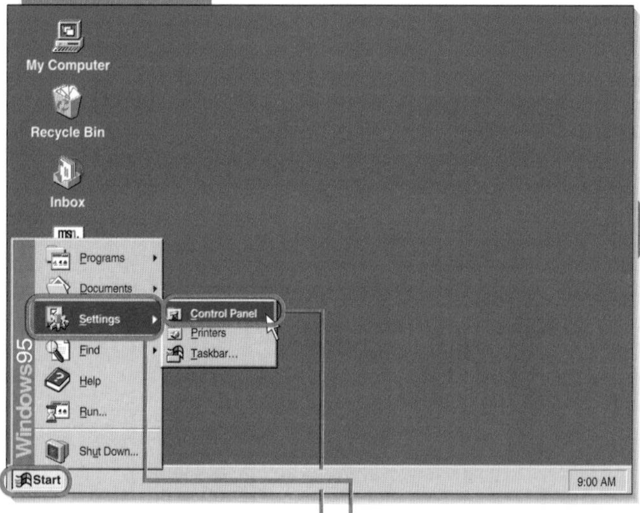

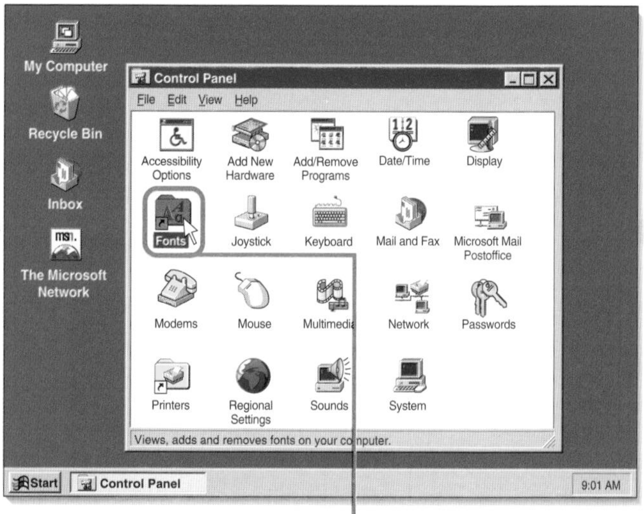

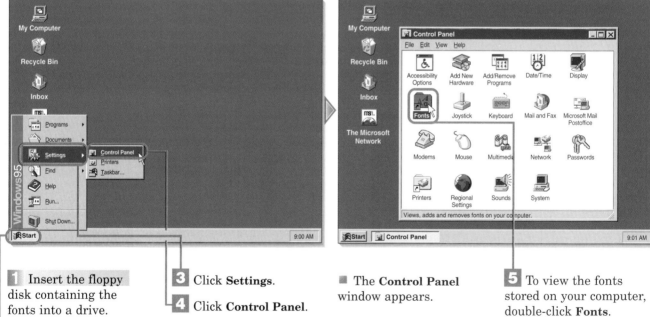

1 Insert the floppy disk containing the fonts into a drive.

2 Click **Start**.

3 Click **Settings**.

4 Click **Control Panel**.

■ The **Control Panel** window appears.

5 To view the fonts stored on your computer, double-click **Fonts**.

TIP

You can buy fonts to add to your computer at most computer stores.

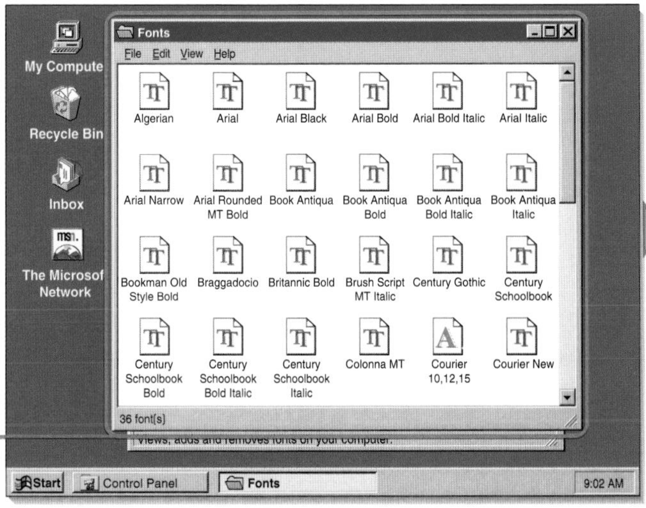

■ The **Fonts** window appears. Each icon represents a font stored on your computer.

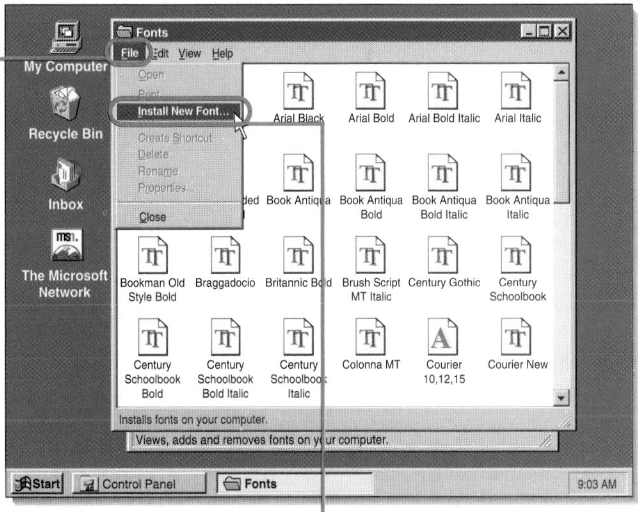

6 Click **File**.

7 Click **Install New Font**.

CONTINUED

ADD FONTS

When you add fonts to your computer, the fonts will be available for use in all your programs.

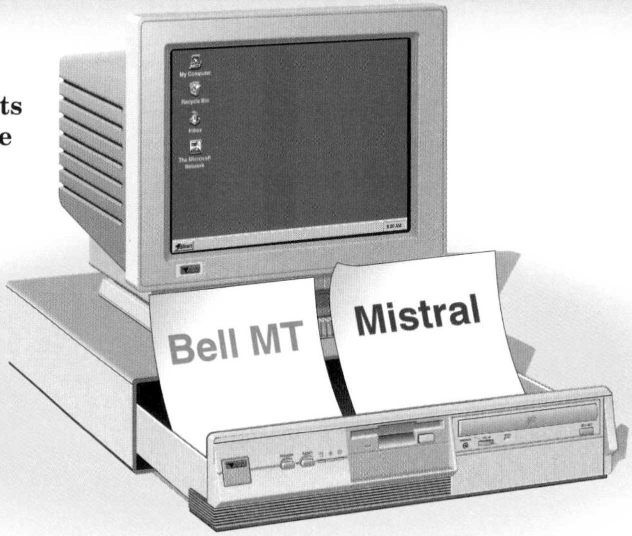

ADD FONTS (CONTINUED)

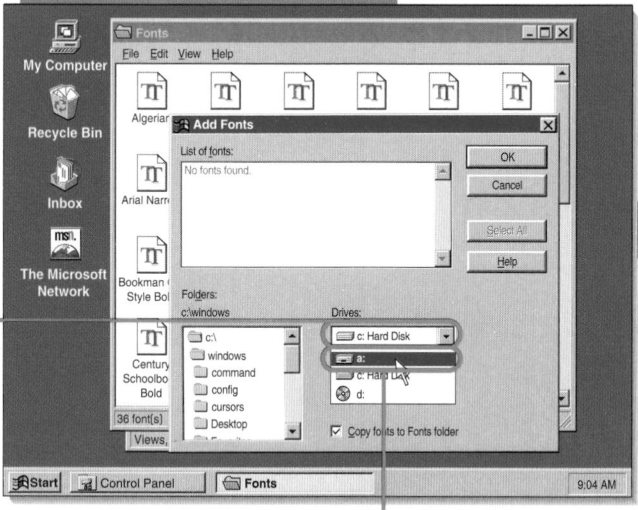

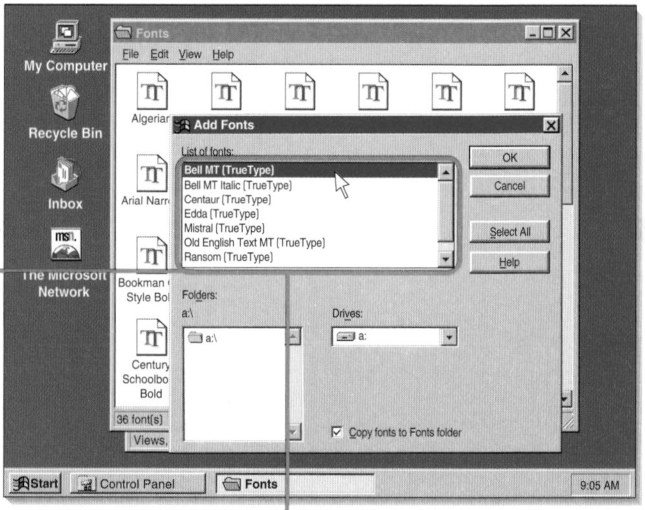

■ The **Add Fonts** dialog box appears.

8 To view the fonts stored on the floppy disk, click this area.

9 Click the drive containing the floppy disk.

■ This area now displays the fonts stored on the floppy disk.

10 To select a font you want to add to your computer, click the font.

TIP

Fonts take up space on your hard drive. If you do not use fonts you added to your computer, delete them as you would any file. Do not delete fonts that come with Windows.

Note: To delete a file, refer to page 78.

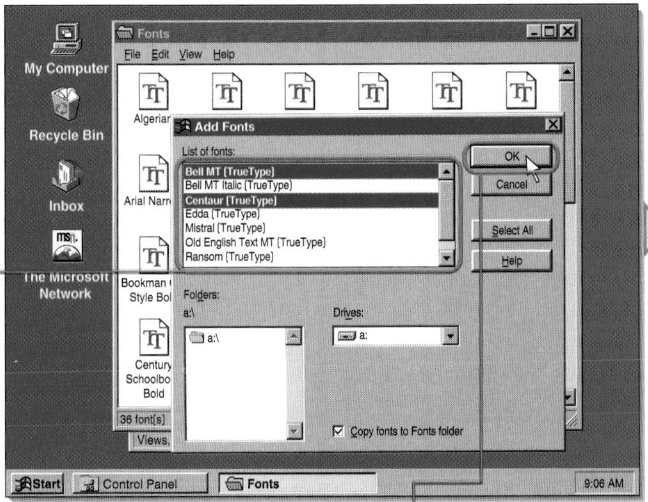

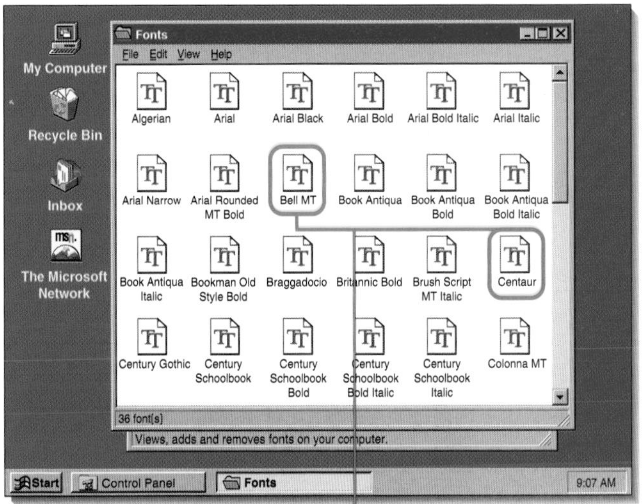

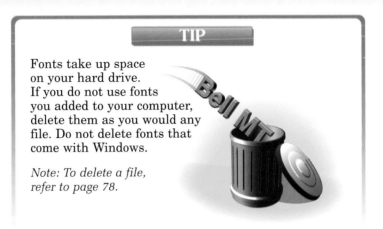

11 To select additional fonts, press and hold down **Ctrl** on your keyboard as you repeat step 10 for each font.

Note: To select all the fonts stored on the floppy disk, click Select All.

12 To add the fonts to your computer, click **OK**.

■ Windows copies the fonts to your computer.

■ The fonts now appear in the **Fonts** window.

ADD WINDOWS COMPONENTS

You can add components to your computer that you did not add when you first set up Windows.

When setting up Windows, most people do not install all the components that come with the program. This avoids taking up storage space with components they do not plan to use.

ADD WINDOWS COMPONENTS

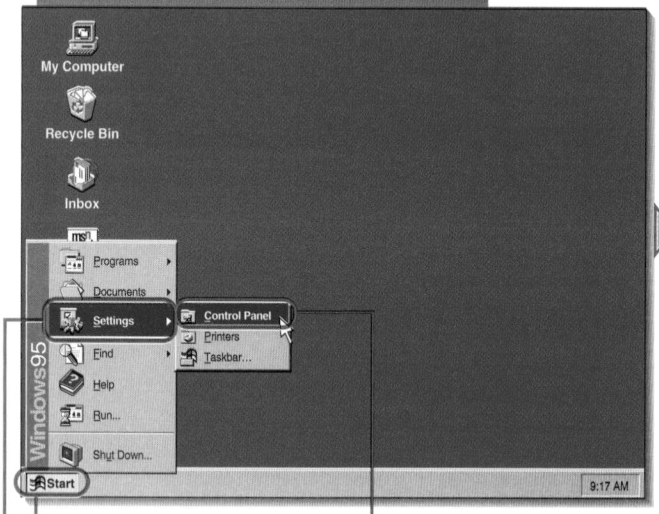

1 Click **Start**.

2 Click **Settings**.

3 Click **Control Panel**.

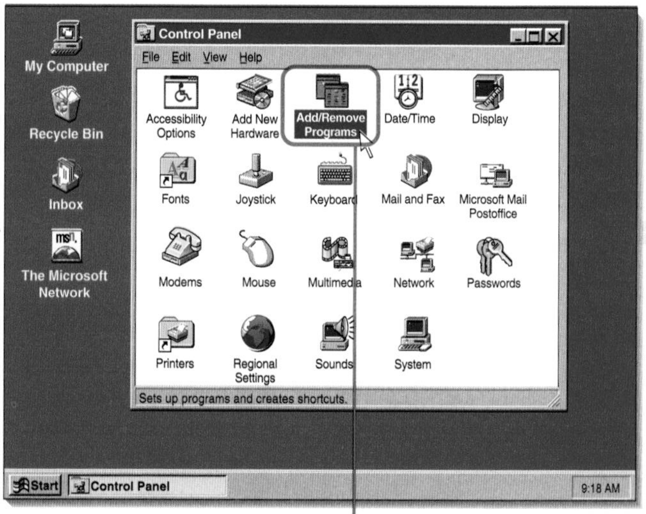

■ The **Control Panel** window appears.

4 Double-click **Add/Remove Programs**.

■ The **Add/Remove Programs Properties** dialog box appears.

TIP

Here are some Windows components you can add to your computer.

Games

Microsoft Exchange

Microsoft Fax

Screen Savers

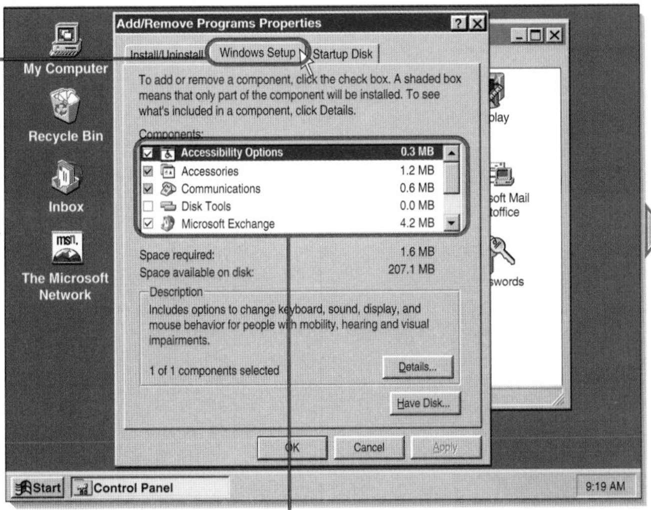

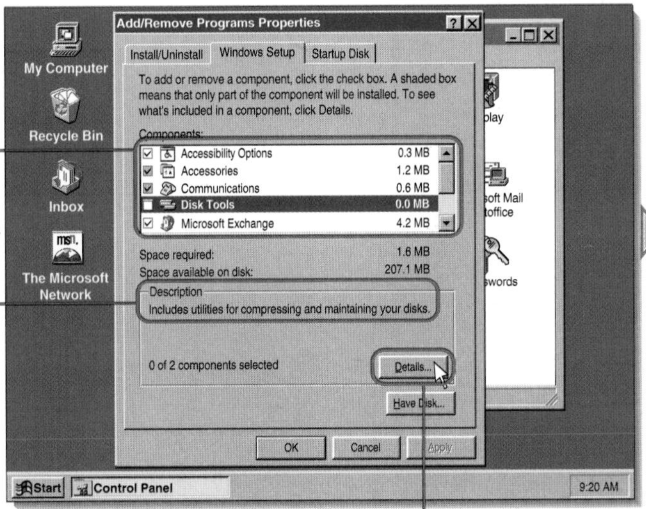

5 Click the **Windows Setup** tab.

■ This area displays the categories of components you can add to your computer.

■ The box beside each category indicates if all (☑), some (☑) or none (☐) of the components in the category exist on your computer.

6 To display a description of the components in a category, click the category (example: **Disk Tools**).

■ This area displays a description of the components in the category.

7 To display the components in the category, click **Details**.

CONTINUED

ADD WINDOWS COMPONENTS

When adding Windows components, you must insert the installation CD-ROM disc or floppy disks that come with Windows.

Some components, such as CD Player and Quick View, are available on the Windows CD-ROM disc but not on the Windows floppy disks.

ADD WINDOWS COMPONENTS (CONTINUED)

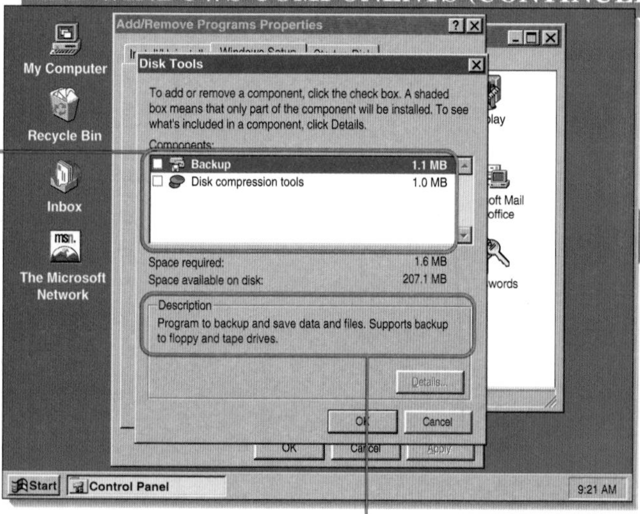

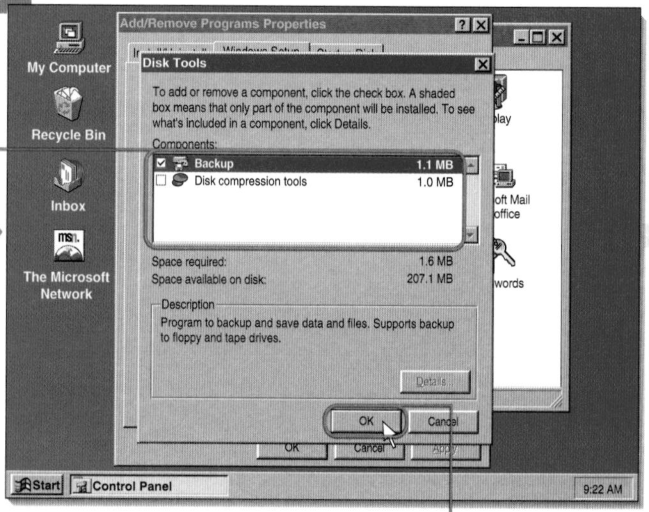

- The components in the category appear. The box beside each component indicates if the component exists (☑) or does not exist (☐) on your computer.

- This area displays a description of the highlighted component.

8 To select a component, click the box (☐) beside the component (☐ changes to ☑).

9 Repeat step 8 for each component in the category you want to add to your computer.

10 Click **OK**.

TIP

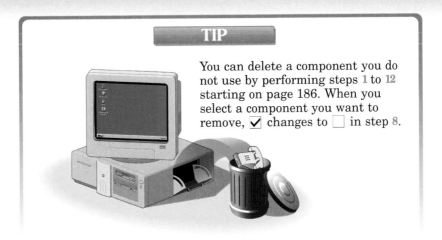

You can delete a component you do not use by performing steps 1 to 12 starting on page 186. When you select a component you want to remove, ☑ changes to ☐ in step 8.

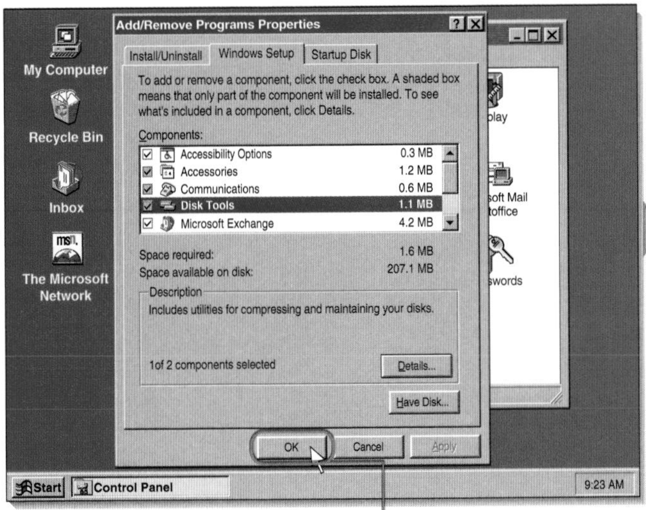

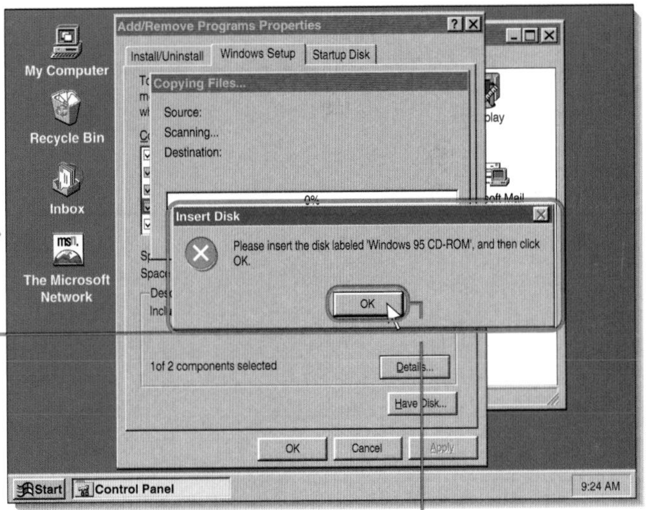

11 Repeat steps 6 to 10 starting on page 187 for any other component.

12 When you finish selecting all the components, click **OK**.

■ A dialog box appears, asking you to insert the Windows CD-ROM disc or floppy disk.

13 Insert the CD-ROM disc or floppy disk into the drive.

14 Click **OK**.

ADD A NEW PROGRAM

MAIN TYPES OF PROGRAMS

WORD PROCESSORS

A word processor helps you create documents quickly and efficiently. Popular word processors include Word and WordPerfect.

SPREADSHEETS

A spreadsheet program helps you manage, analyze and present financial information. Popular spreadsheet programs include Excel and Lotus 1-2-3.

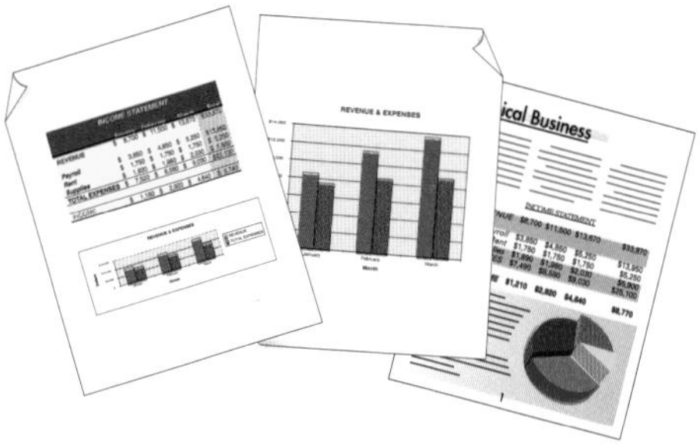

DATABASES

A database helps you manage large collections of information. Popular databases include Access and dBASE.

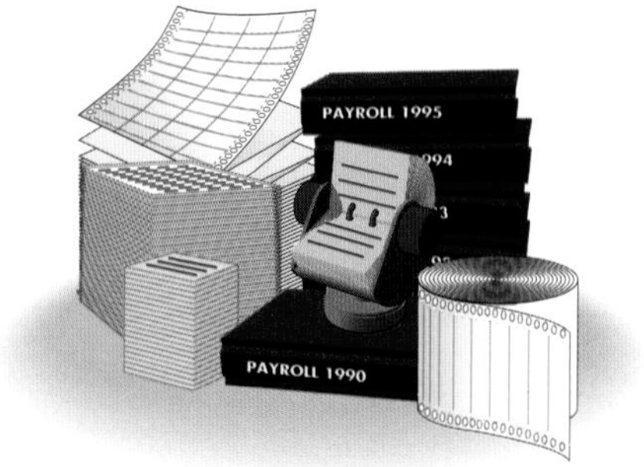

DESKTOP PUBLISHING

A desktop publishing program helps you create sophisticated documents by combining text and graphics on a page. Popular desktop publishing programs include PageMaker and QuarkXPress.

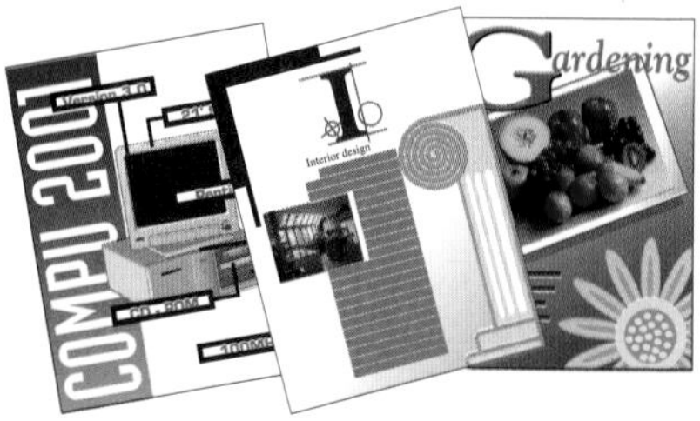

GAMES

There are thousands of games to entertain you. Popular games include Doom and Golf.

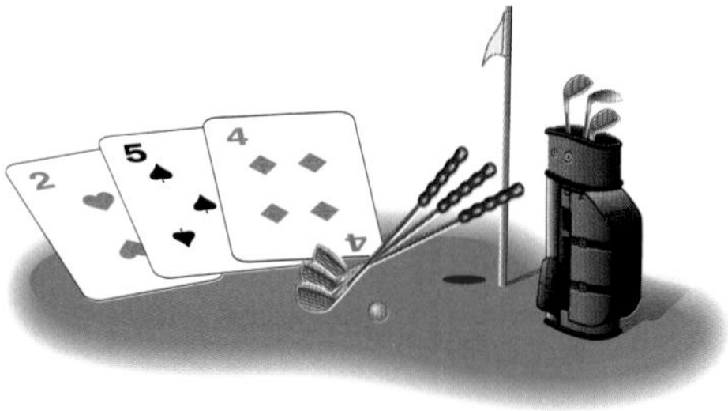

GRAPHICS

A graphics program helps you create and manipulate illustrations. Popular graphics programs include CorelDRAW! and Adobe Illustrator.

You can easily add a new program to your computer.

ADD A NEW PROGRAM

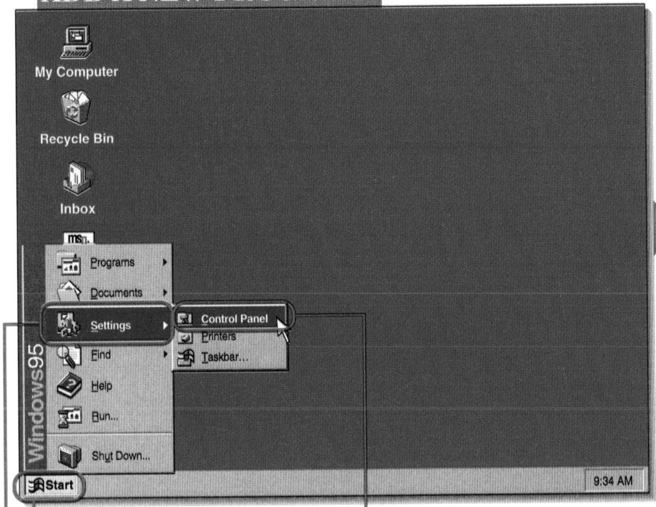

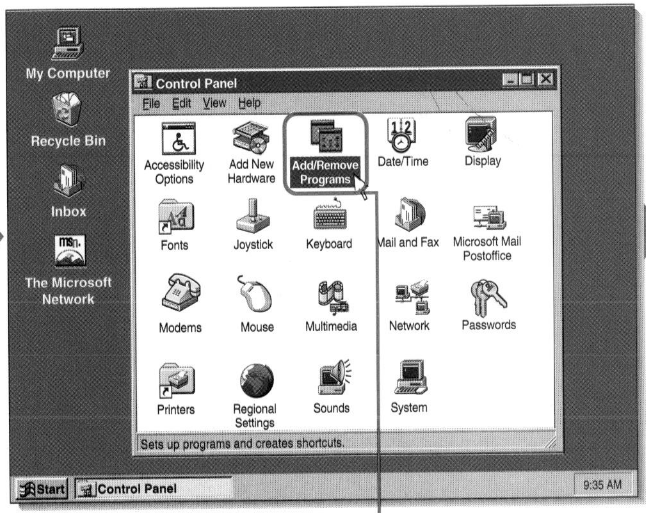

1 Click **Start.**

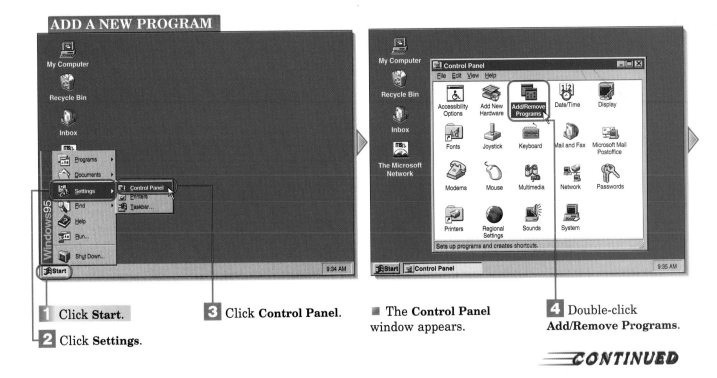

2 Click **Settings**.

3 Click **Control Panel**.

■ The **Control Panel** window appears.

4 Double-click **Add/Remove Programs**.

CONTINUED

ADD A NEW PROGRAM

Programs come on either a CD-ROM disc or floppy disks.

When you finish installing a program, make sure you keep the CD-ROM disc or floppy disks in a safe place. If your computer fails or if you accidentally erase the program files, you may need to install the program again.

ADD A NEW PROGRAM (CONTINUED)

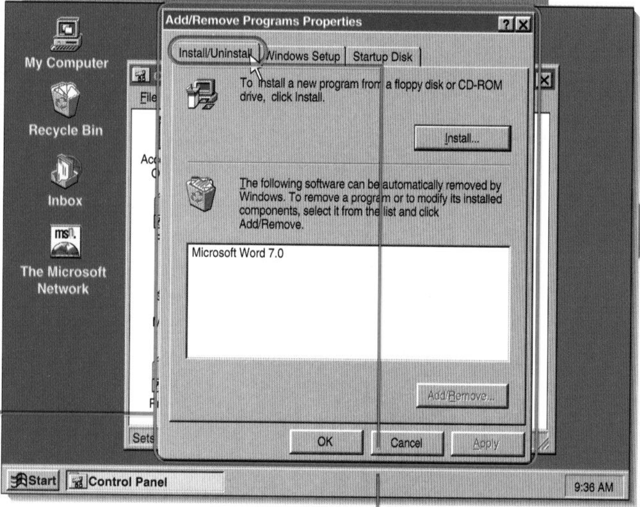

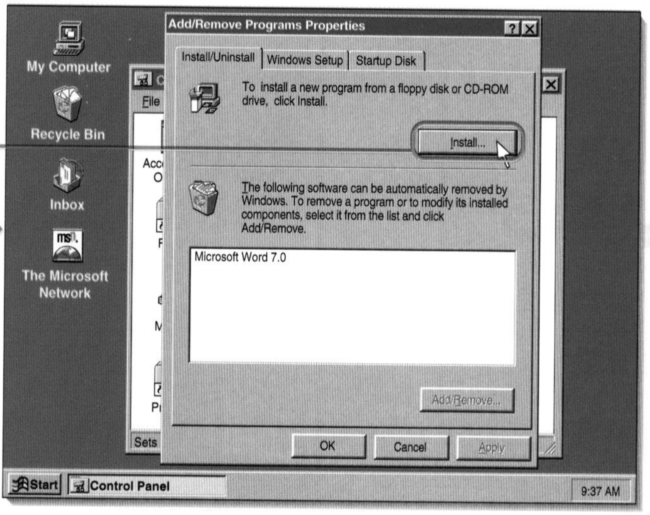

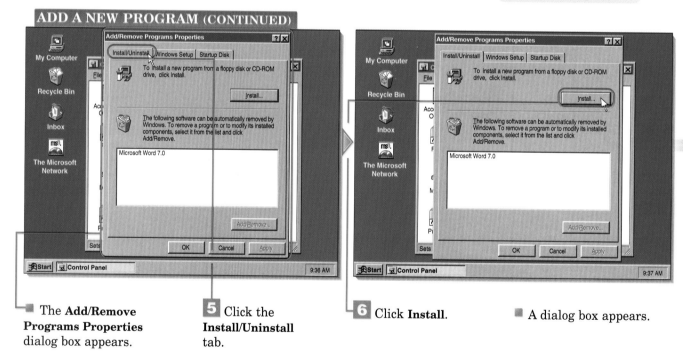

■ The **Add/Remove Programs Properties** dialog box appears.

5 Click the **Install/Uninstall** tab.

6 Click **Install**.

■ A dialog box appears.

TIP

You can often select the way you want to install a program. Common options include:

Typical—Installs the program as recommended for most people.

Custom—Lets you customize the program to suit your specific needs.

Minimum—Installs the minimum amount of the program needed. This is ideal for portable computers or computers with limited disk space.

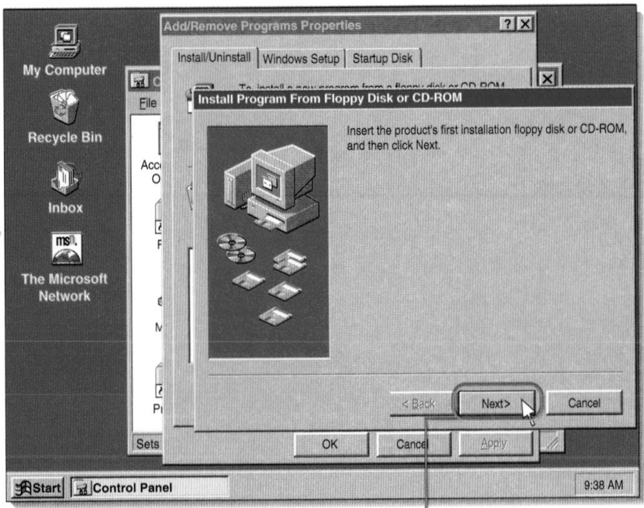

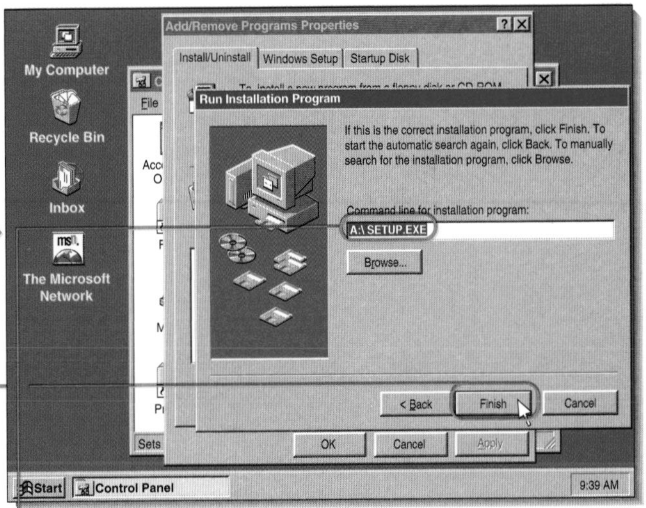

7 Insert the CD-ROM disc or the floppy disk labeled **Disk 1** into a drive.

8 To continue, click **Next**.

■ Windows locates the file needed to install the program.

9 To install the program, click **Finish**.

10 Follow the instructions on your screen. Every program sets itself up differently.

SET UP NEW HARDWARE

You can easily add new hardware to your computer.

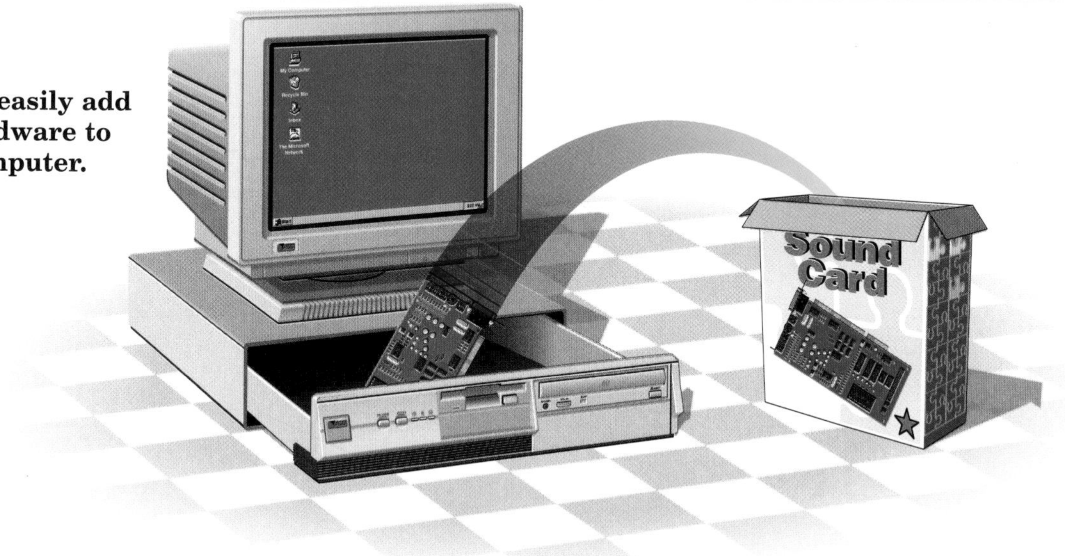

SET UP NEW HARDWARE

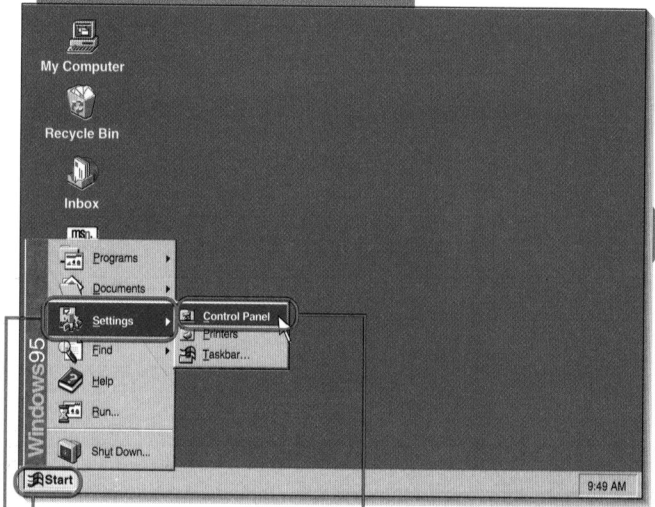

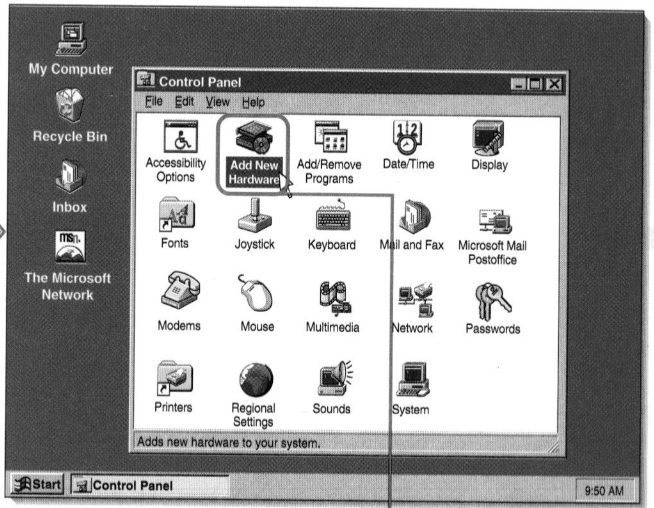

1 Click **Start**.

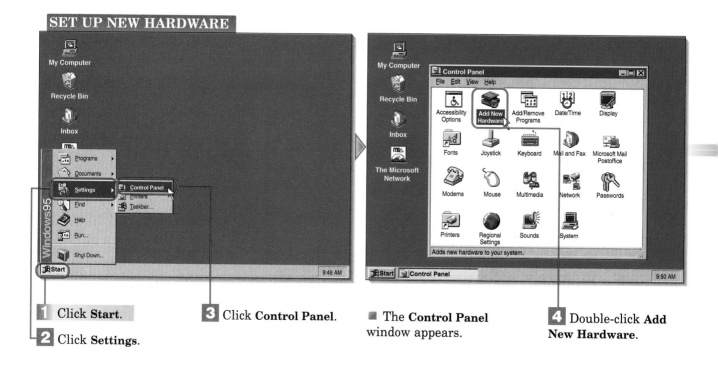

2 Click **Settings**.

3 Click **Control Panel**.

■ The **Control Panel** window appears.

4 Double-click **Add New Hardware**.

TIP

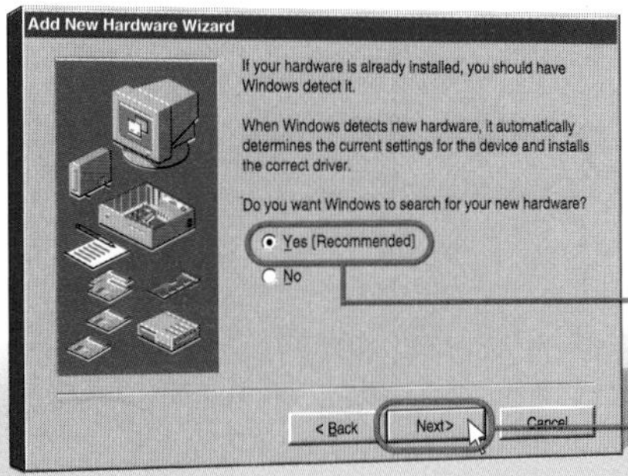

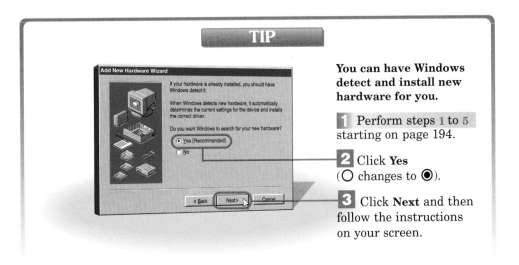

You can have Windows detect and install new hardware for you.

1 Perform steps 1 to 5 starting on page 194.

2 Click **Yes** (○ changes to ◉).

3 Click **Next** and then follow the instructions on your screen.

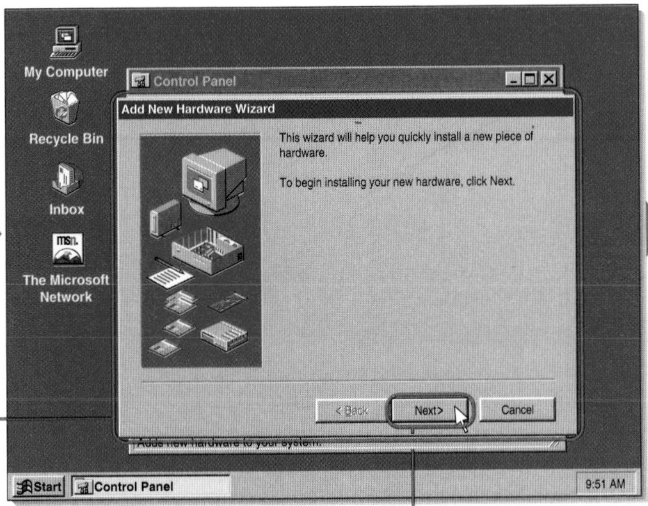

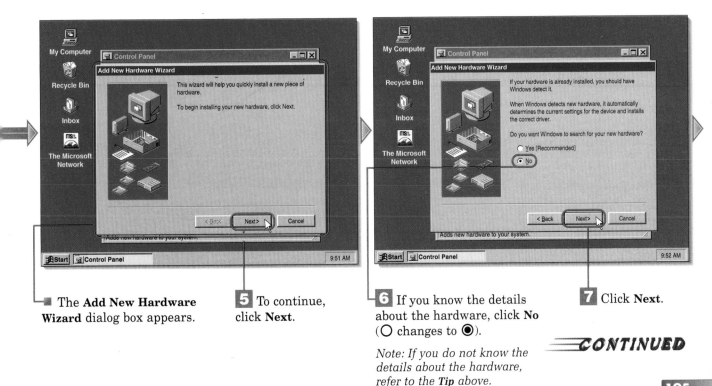

■ The **Add New Hardware Wizard** dialog box appears.

5 To continue, click **Next**.

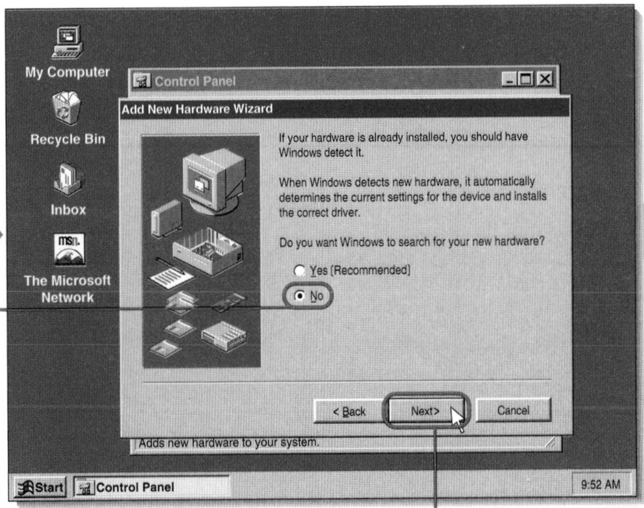

6 If you know the details about the hardware, click **No** (○ changes to ◉).

*Note: If you do not know the details about the hardware, refer to the **Tip** above.*

7 Click **Next**.

CONTINUED

SET UP NEW HARDWARE

When adding new hardware, you must specify the manufacturer and model of the hardware.

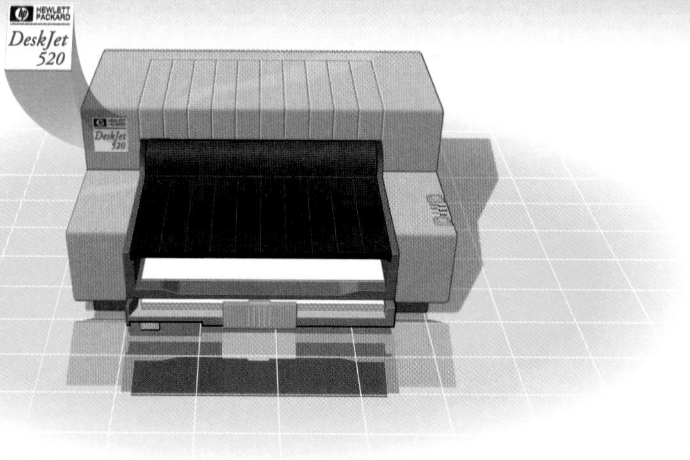

SET UP NEW HARDWARE (CONTINUED)

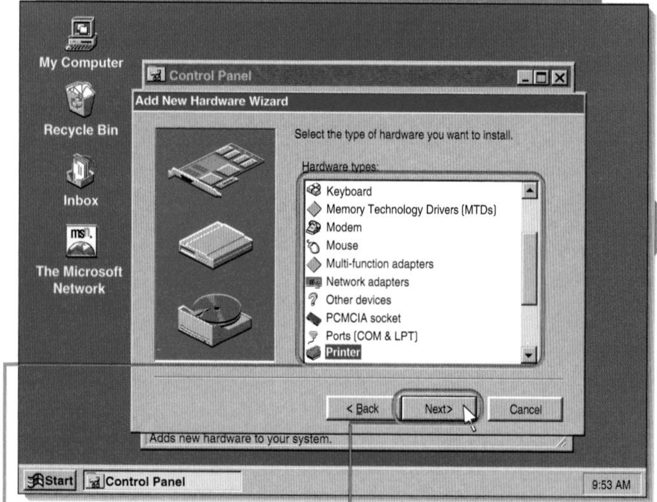

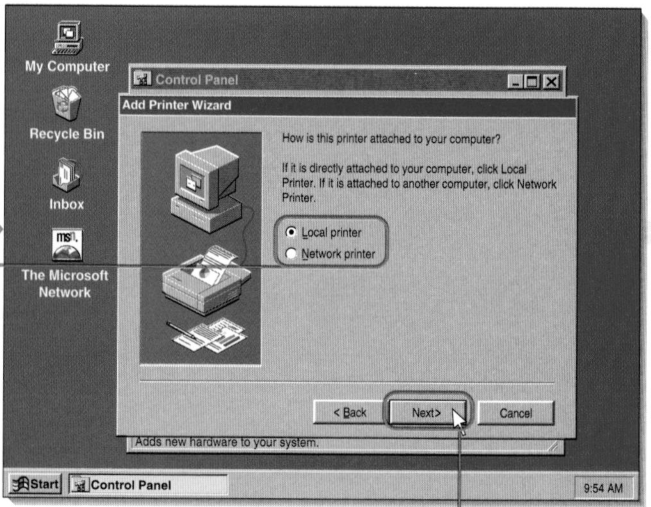

8 Click the type of hardware you want to install.

9 Click **Next**.

■ The remaining steps depend on the type of hardware you selected in step 8. In this example, we install a new printer.

10 You may be asked to tell Windows how the printer connects to your computer. To do so, click one of the following options (○ changes to ◉).

Local printer
Printer connects directly to your computer.

Network printer
Printer connects to another computer.

11 To continue, click **Next**.

TIP

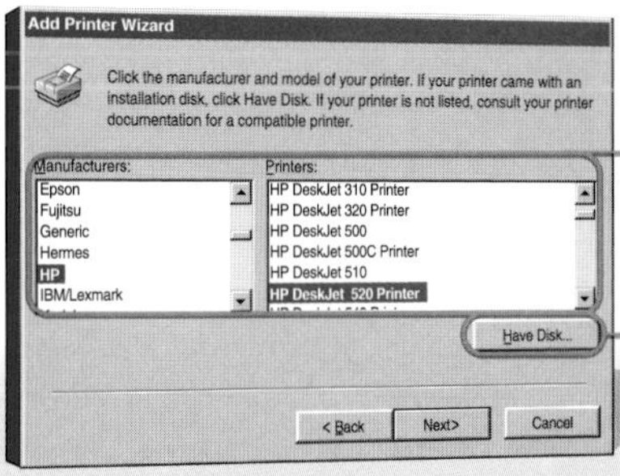

■ If the printer you want to use does not appear in the list, you can use the installation disk that came with the printer.

1 Insert the installation disk into a drive.

2 Click **Have Disk**. Then press Enter on your keyboard.

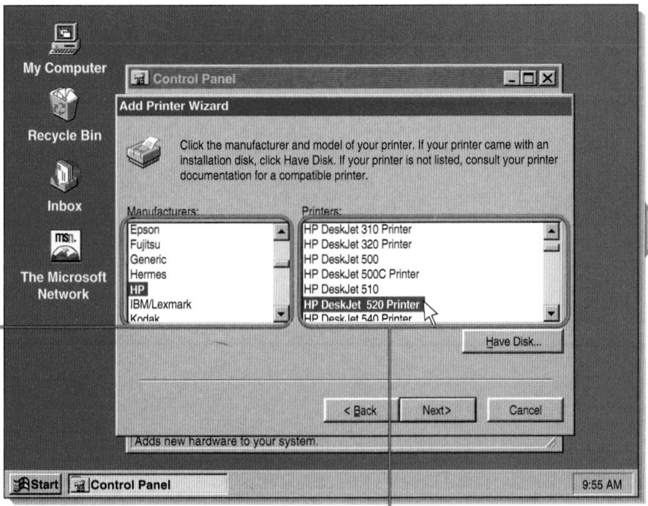

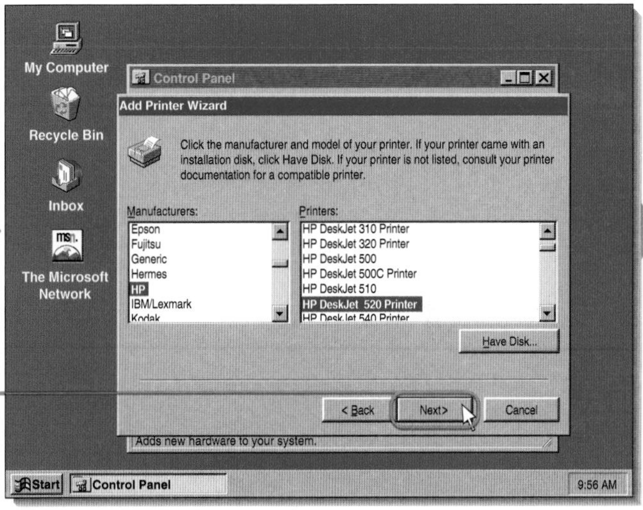

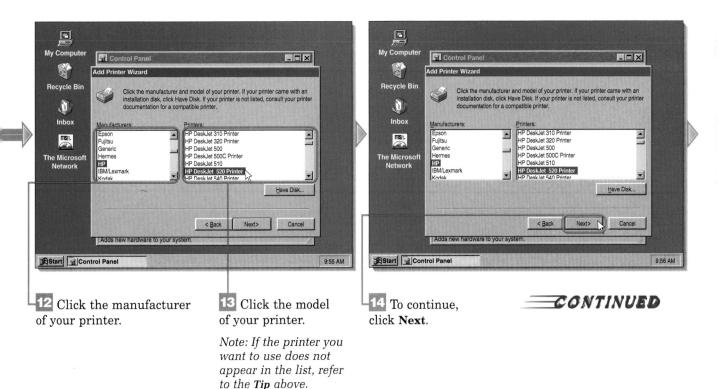

12 Click the manufacturer of your printer.

13 Click the model of your printer.

*Note: If the printer you want to use does not appear in the list, refer to the **Tip** above.*

14 To continue, click **Next**.

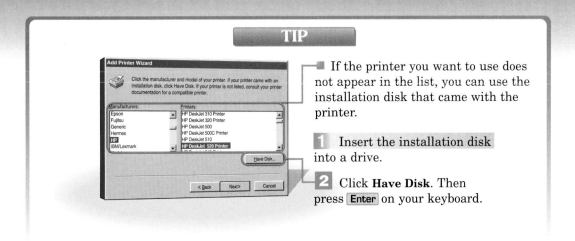

CONTINUED

SET UP NEW HARDWARE

Windows asks you questions about the new hardware. This helps Windows set up the hardware to suit your specific needs.

SET UP NEW HARDWARE (CONTINUED)

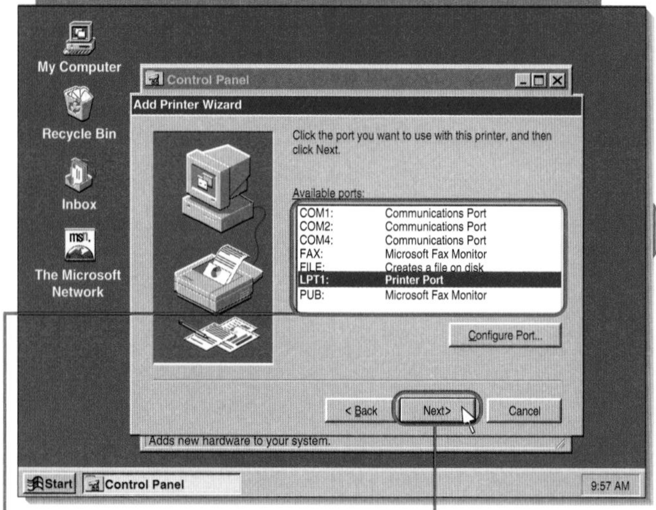

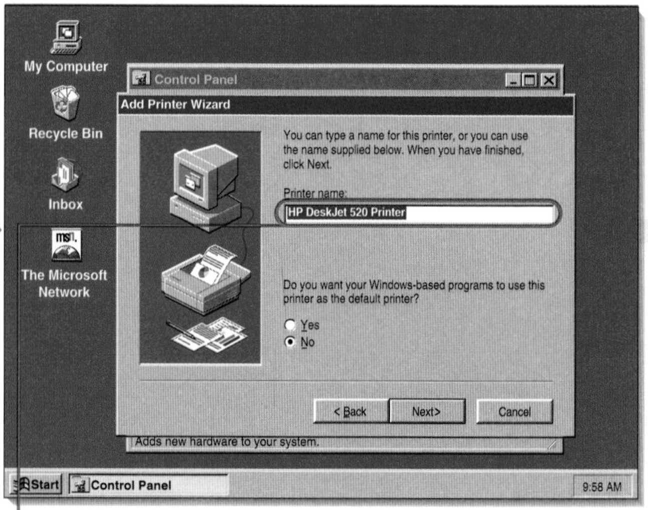

15 Click the port you want to use with the printer.

Note: A port is a socket at the back of a computer where you plug in a device. LPT1 is the most commonly used port for printers.

16 To continue, click **Next**.

17 Type a name for the printer.

Note: To use the name supplied by Windows, do not type a name.

TIP

Windows 95 supports Plug and Play. Before Plug and Play, adding new features to a computer was difficult and frustrating. Plug and Play lets you quickly and easily add new features to your computer.

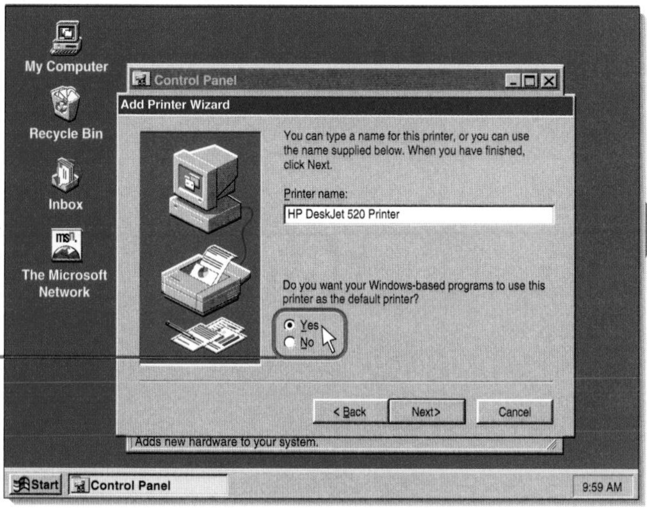

18 To specify if you want to use the printer as the default printer, click one of these options (○ changes to ◉).

Yes - Documents will always print to this printer.

No - Documents will print to this printer only when you select the printer.

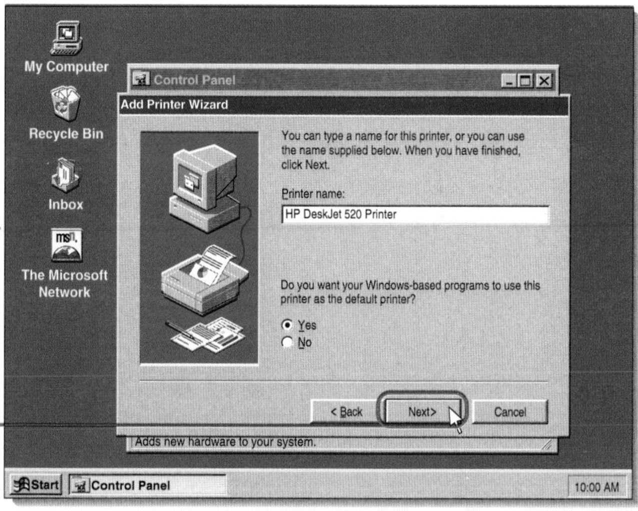

19 To continue, click **Next**.

CONTINUED

SET UP NEW HARDWARE

To complete the installation, Windows will ask you to insert the Windows 95 installation CD-ROM disc or floppy disks.

SET UP NEW HARDWARE (CONTINUED)

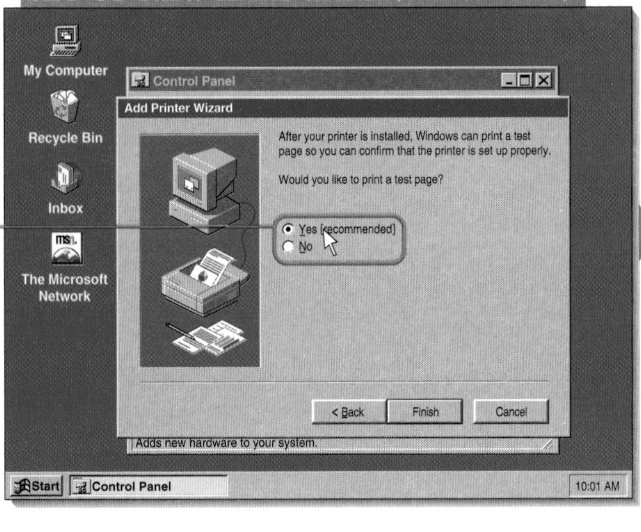

20 To specify if you want to print a test page, click **Yes** or **No**. A test page will confirm that your printer is set up properly.

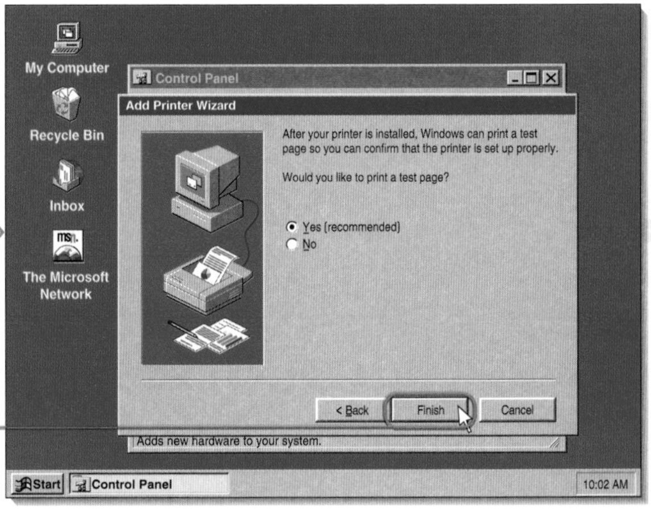

21 To complete the installation, click **Finish**.

TIP

For your computer to use new hardware, you have to install special software, called a **driver**. A driver is a program that helps the computer communicate with the hardware. Windows provides the most popular drivers and helps you install them.

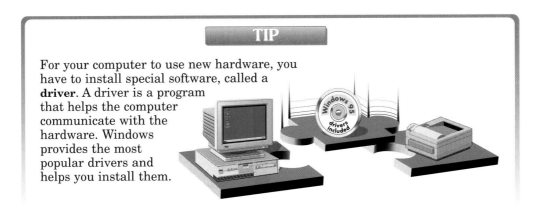

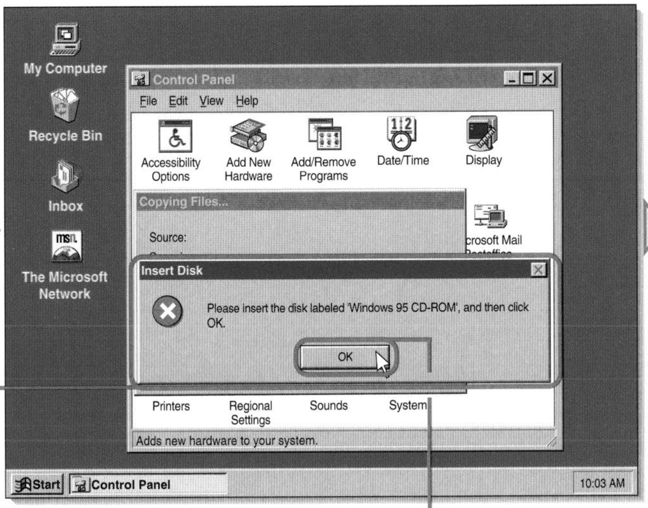

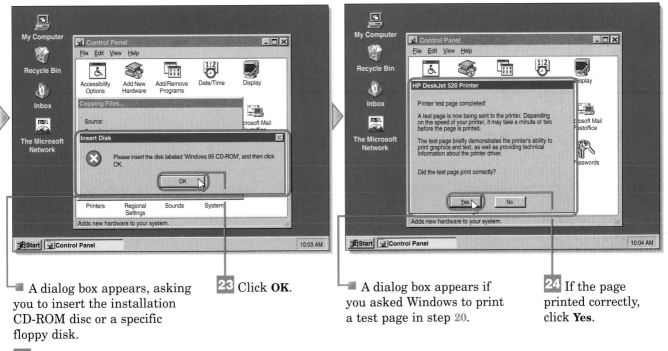

■ A dialog box appears, asking you to insert the installation CD-ROM disc or a specific floppy disk.

22 Insert the CD-ROM disc or floppy disk into a drive.

23 Click **OK**.

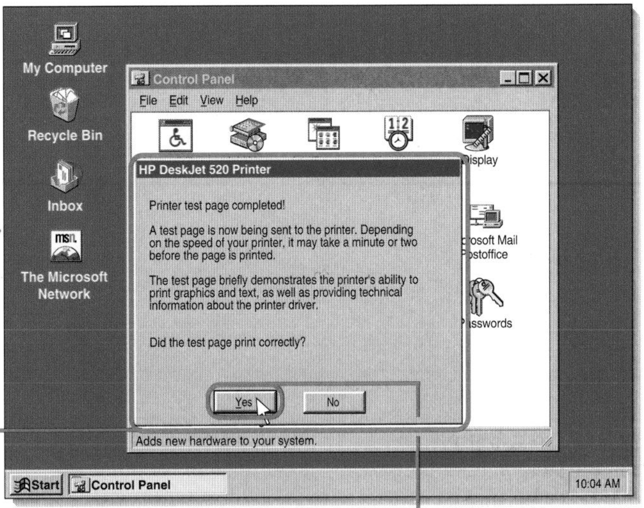

■ A dialog box appears if you asked Windows to print a test page in step 20.

24 If the page printed correctly, click **Yes**.

In this chapter you will learn how to format and copy disks and improve the performance of your computer.

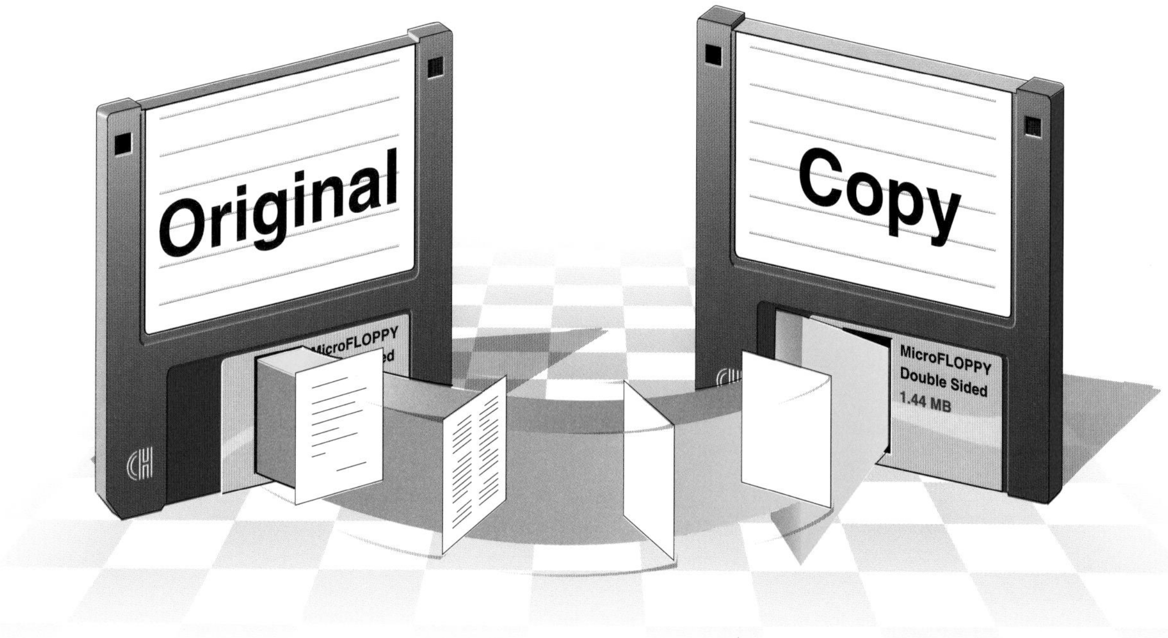

CHAPTER 13: MAINTAIN YOUR COMPUTER

Format a Disk . . . . *.204*

Detect and Repair Disk Errors . . . . *.208*

Defragment a Disk . . . . *.212*

Copy a Floppy Disk . . . . *.216*

Compress a Disk . . . . *.220*

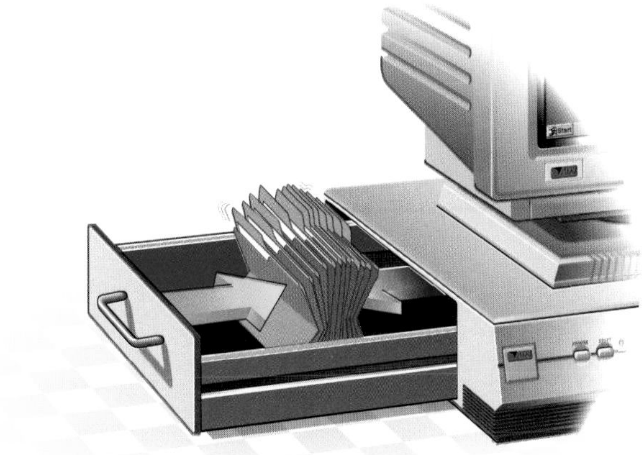

FORMAT A DISK

You must format a floppy disk before you can use it to store information.

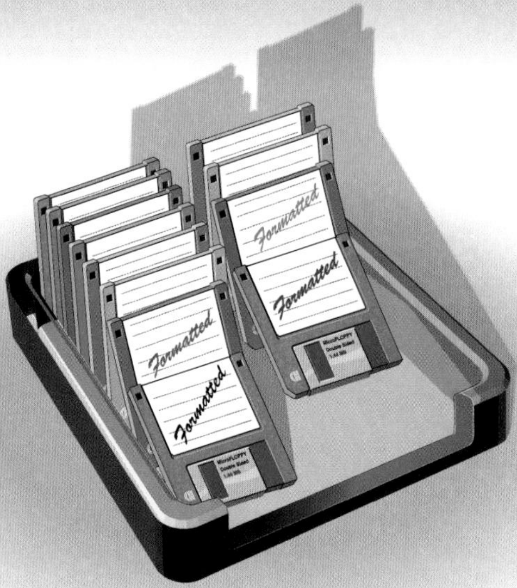

FORMAT A DISK

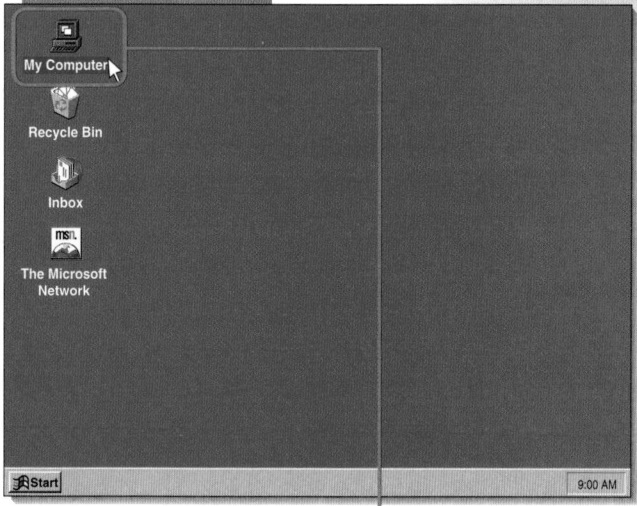

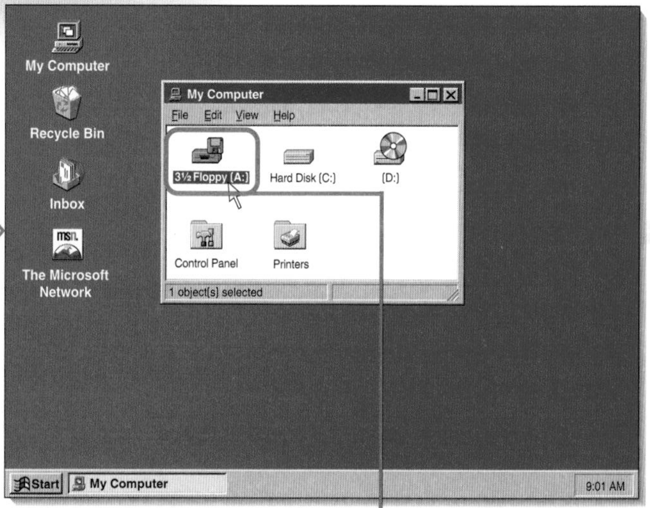

1 Insert the floppy disk you want to format into a drive.

2 Double-click **My Computer**.

■ The **My Computer** window appears.

3 Click the drive containing the floppy disk you want to format (example: **A:**).

IMPORTANT

Before formatting a floppy disk, make sure the disk does not contain information you want to keep. Formatting will remove all the information on the disk.

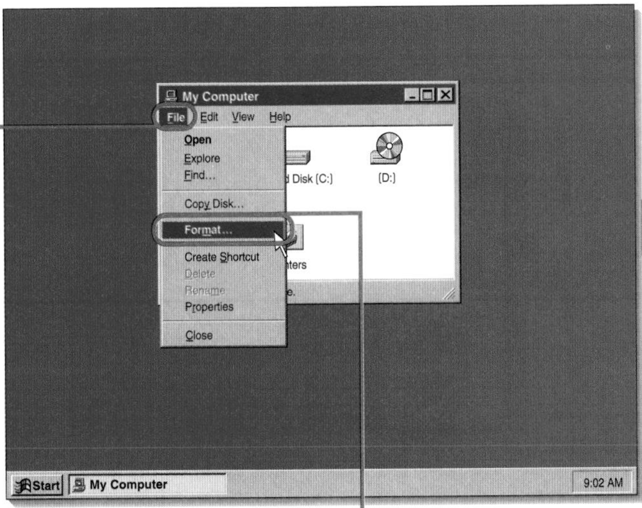

4 Click **File**.

5 Click **Format**.

■ The **Format** dialog box appears.

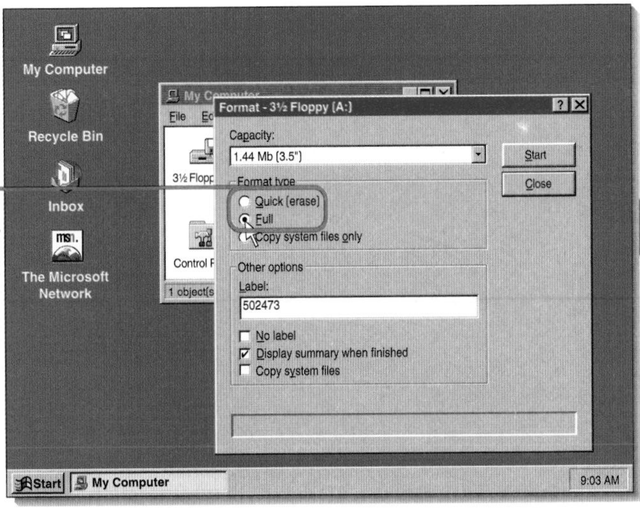

6 Click the type of format you want to perform (○ changes to ◉).

Note: If the floppy disk has never been formatted, select the ***Full*** *option.*

Quick (erase)
Removes all files but does not scan the disk for damaged areas.

Full
Removes all files and scans the disk for damaged areas.

CONTINUED

FORMAT A DISK

When formatting a floppy disk, you must tell Windows how much information the disk can hold.

DOUBLE-DENSITY 720 KB

A 3.5-inch floppy disk that has one hole can hold 720 Kb of information.

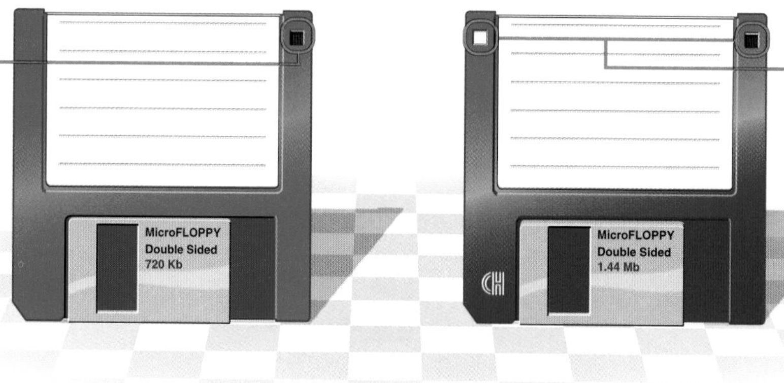

HIGH-DENSITY 1.44 MB

A 3.5-inch floppy disk that has two holes and displays the HD symbol can hold 1.44 Mb of information.

FORMAT A DISK (CONTINUED)

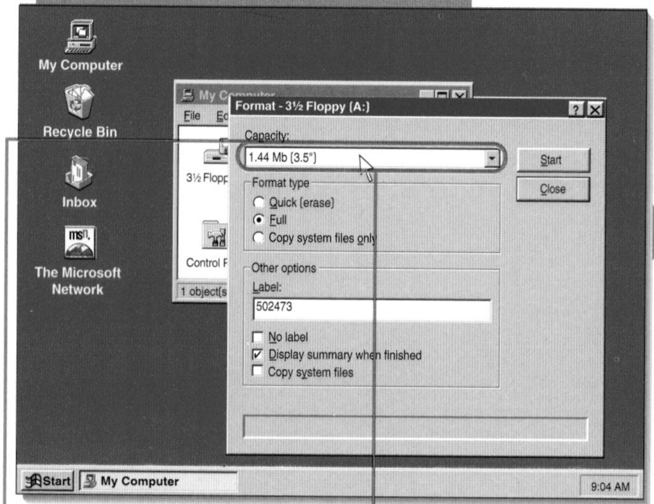

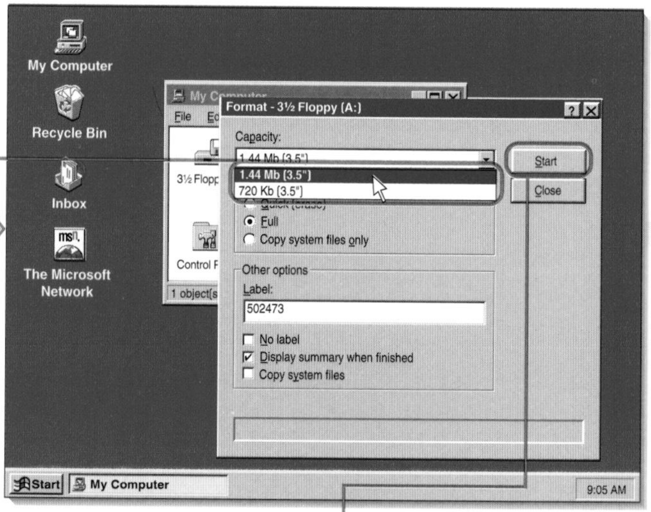

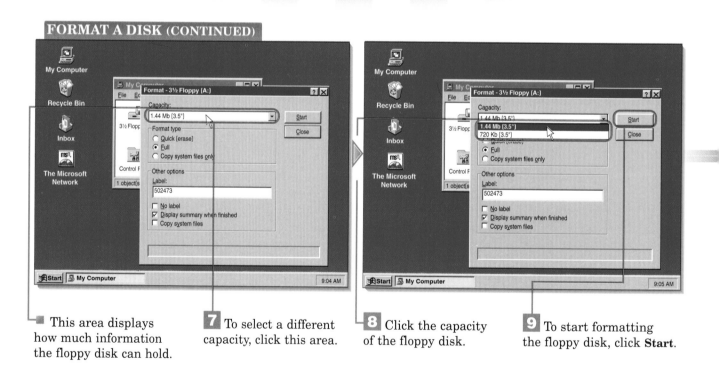

■ This area displays how much information the floppy disk can hold.

7 To select a different capacity, click this area.

8 Click the capacity of the floppy disk.

9 To start formatting the floppy disk, click **Start**.

DOUBLE-DENSITY 360 KB

A 5.25-inch floppy disk that has plastic around the center can hold 360 Kb of information.

HIGH-DENSITY 1.2 MB

A 5.25-inch floppy disk that does not have plastic around the center can hold 1.2 Mb of information.

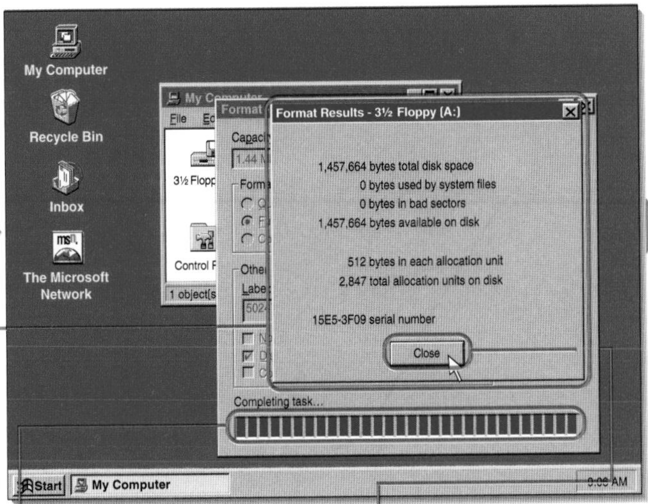

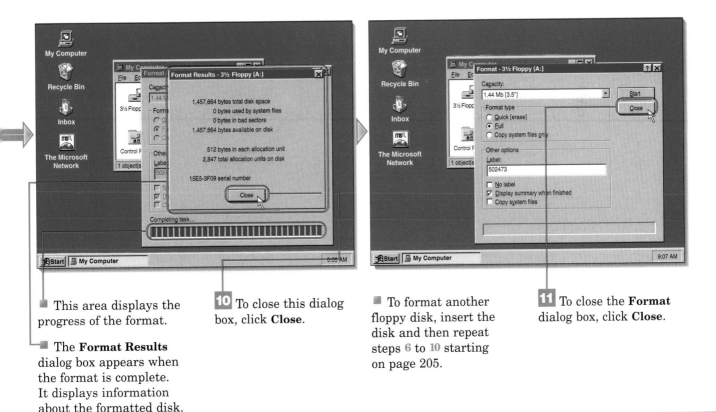

■ This area displays the progress of the format.

■ The **Format Results** dialog box appears when the format is complete. It displays information about the formatted disk.

10 To close this dialog box, click **Close**.

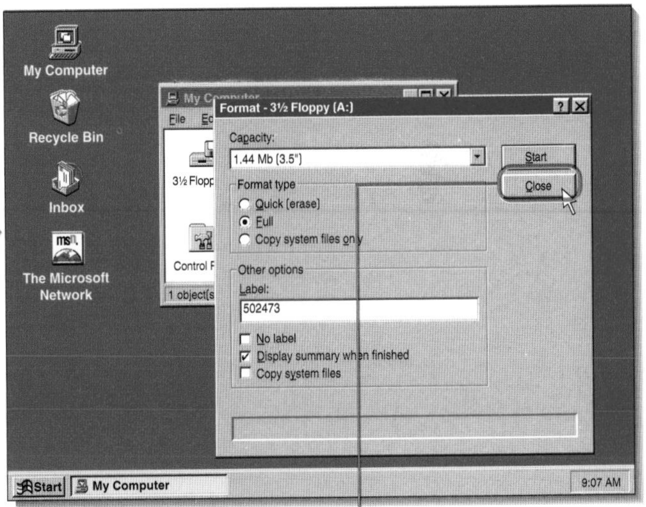

■ To format another floppy disk, insert the disk and then repeat steps 6 to 10 starting on page 205.

11 To close the **Format** dialog box, click **Close**.

DETECT AND REPAIR DISK ERRORS

You can improve the performance of your computer by using ScanDisk to search for and repair disk errors.

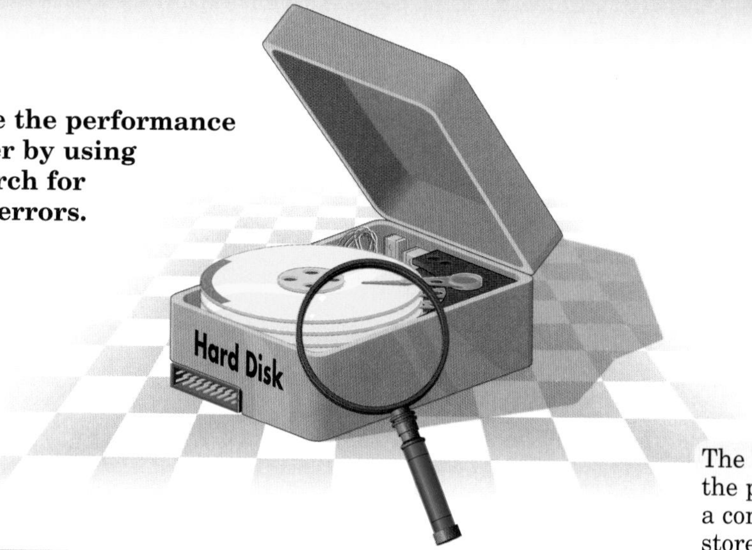

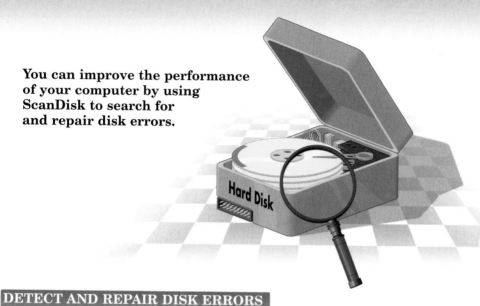

The hard disk is the primary device a computer uses to store information.

DETECT AND REPAIR DISK ERRORS

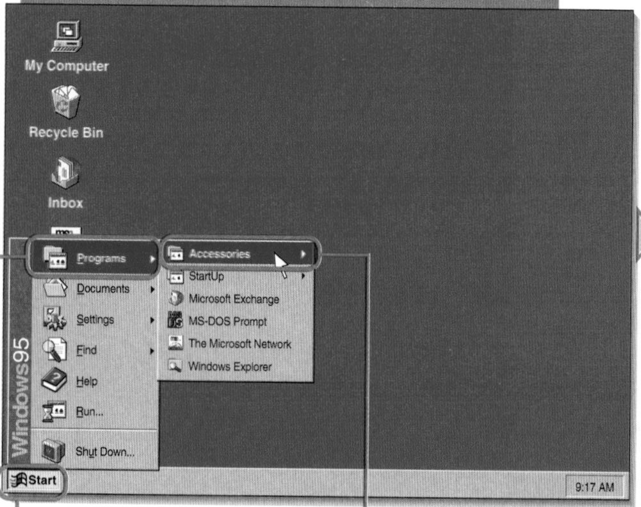

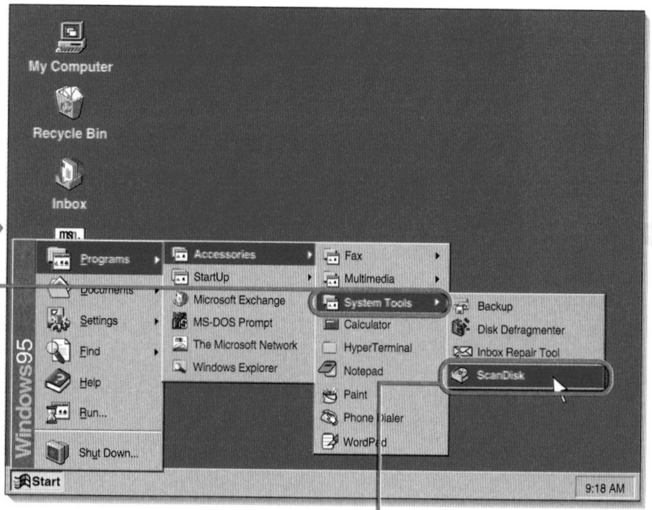

1 Click **Start**.

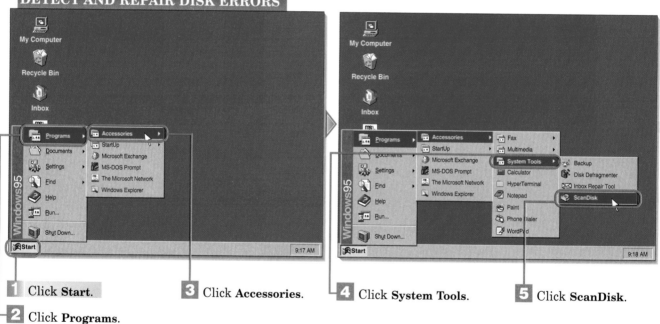

2 Click **Programs**.

3 Click **Accessories**.

4 Click **System Tools**.

5 Click **ScanDisk**.

TIP

You should check your hard disk for errors at least once a month.

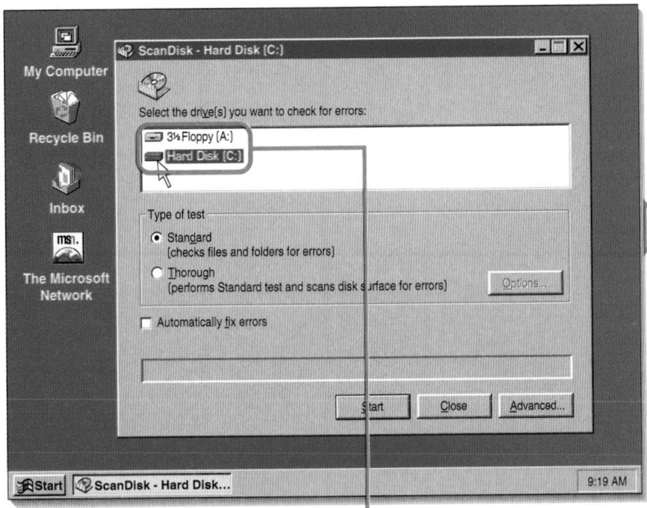

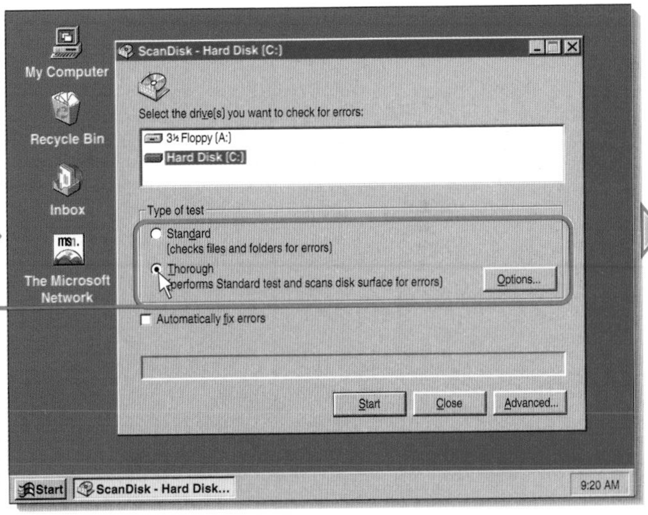

■ The **ScanDisk** dialog box appears.

6 Click the drive you want to check for errors (example: **C:**).

7 Click the type of test you want to perform (○ changes to ◉).

Standard
Checks files and folders for errors.

Thorough
Checks files, folders and the disk surface for errors.

CONTINUED

DETECT AND REPAIR DISK ERRORS

You can have Windows automatically repair any disk errors it finds.

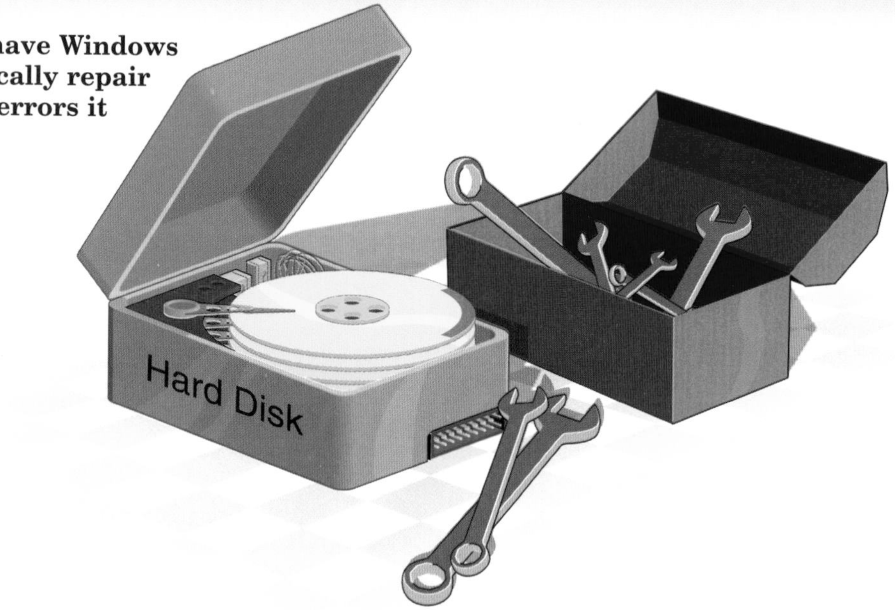

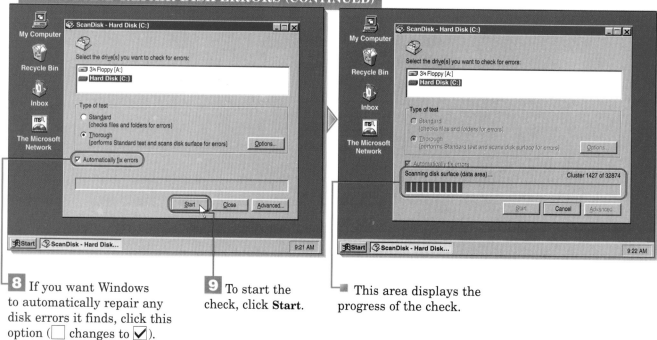

DETECT AND REPAIR DISK ERRORS (CONTINUED)

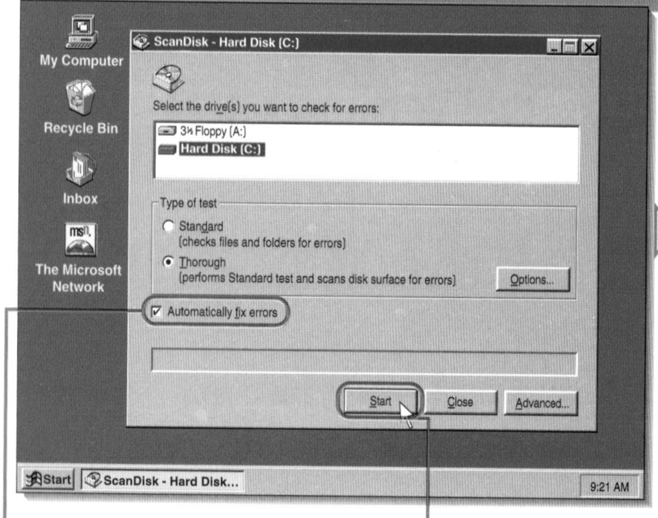

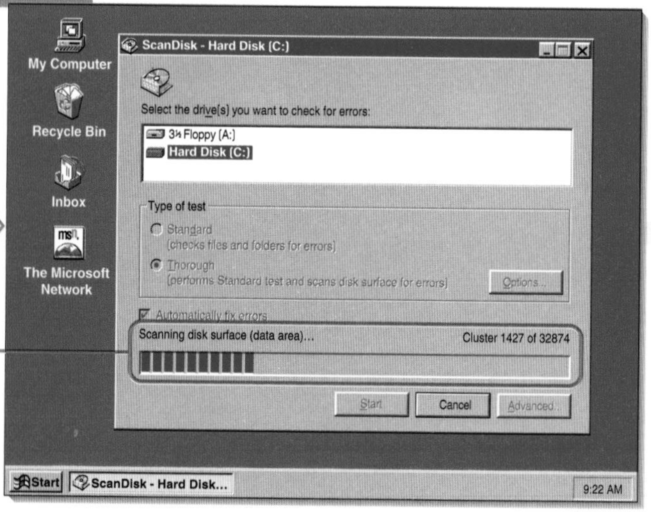

8 If you want Windows to automatically repair any disk errors it finds, click this option (☐ changes to ☑).

9 To start the check, click **Start**.

■ This area displays the progress of the check.

TIP

If you did not tell Windows to automatically repair any disk errors it finds, this dialog box will appear each time ScanDisk finds an error.

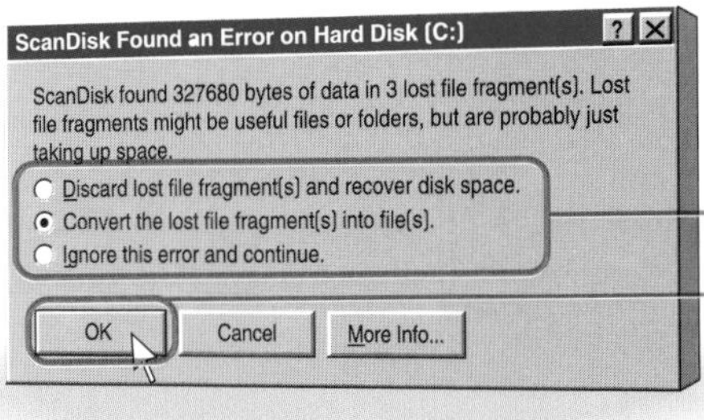

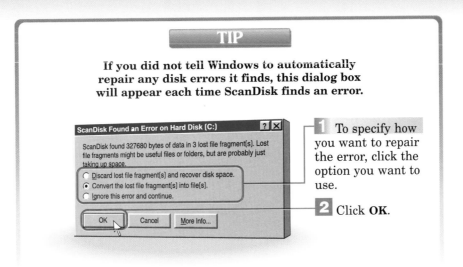

1 To specify how you want to repair the error, click the option you want to use.

2 Click **OK**.

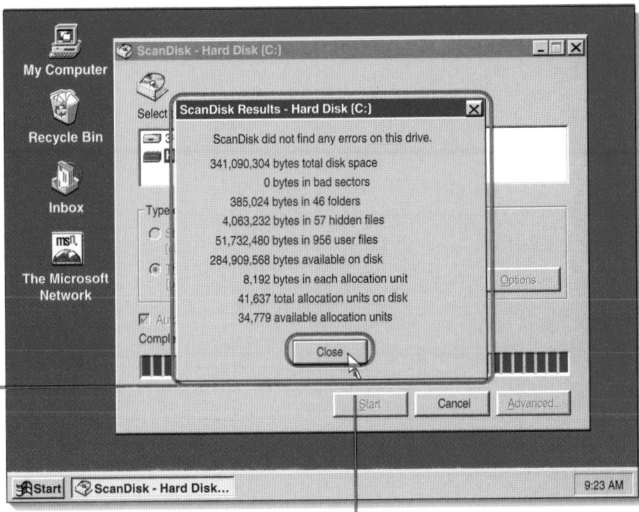

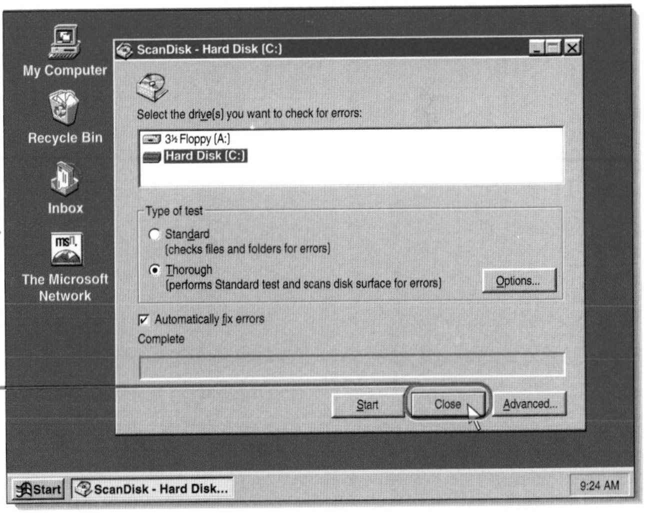

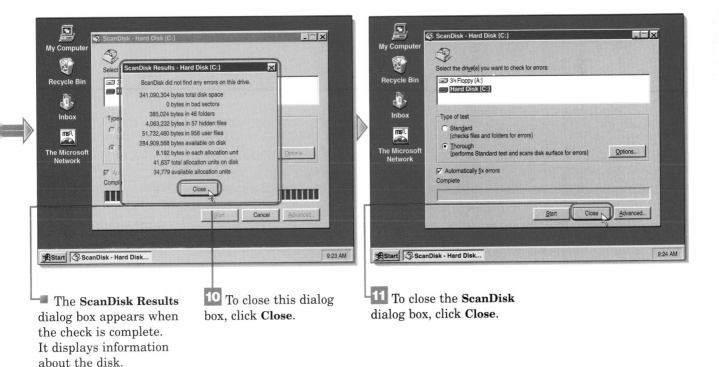

■ The **ScanDisk Results** dialog box appears when the check is complete. It displays information about the disk.

10 To close this dialog box, click **Close**.

11 To close the **ScanDisk** dialog box, click **Close**.

DEFRAGMENT A DISK

A fragmented hard disk stores parts of a file in many different locations. To retrieve a file, your computer must search many areas on the disk.

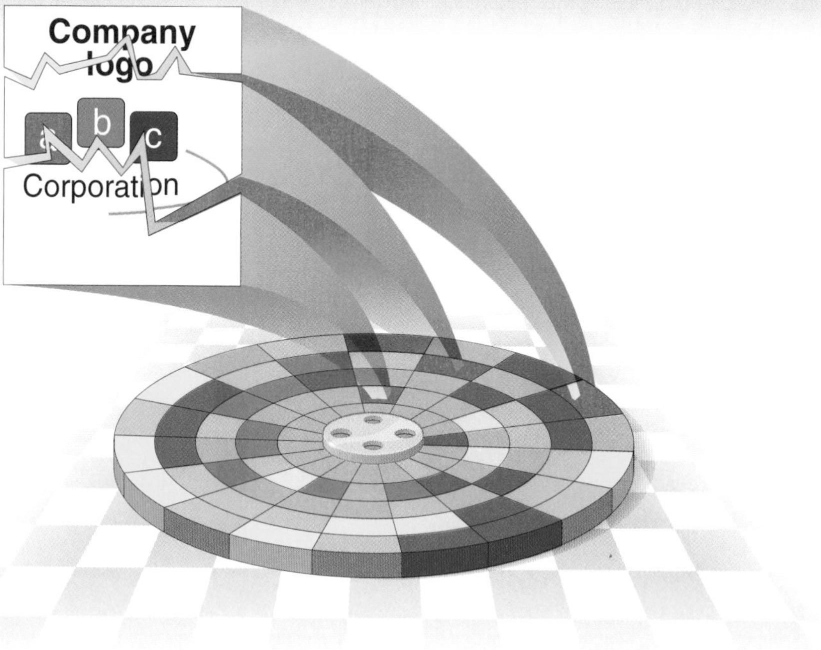

DEFRAGMENT A DISK

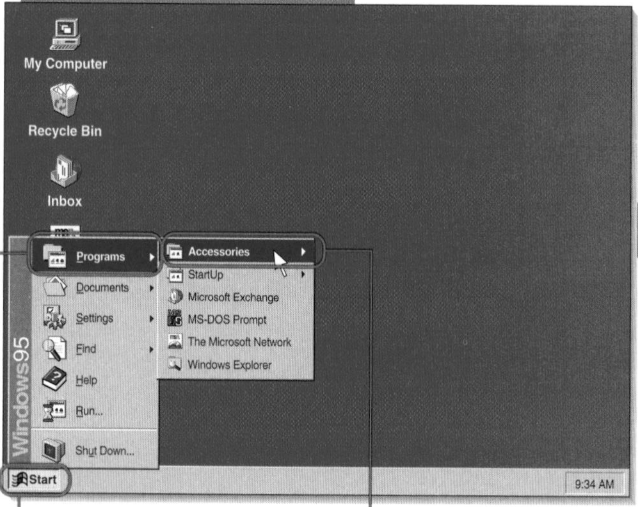

1 Click **Start**.

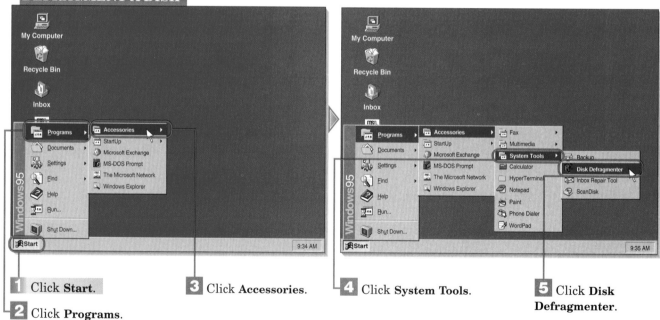

2 Click **Programs**.

3 Click **Accessories**.

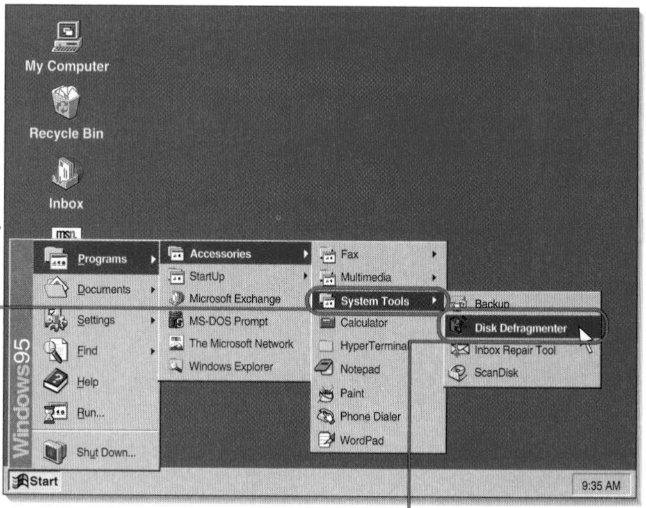

4 Click **System Tools**.

5 Click **Disk Defragmenter**.

You can improve the performance of your computer by using the Disk Defragmenter program.

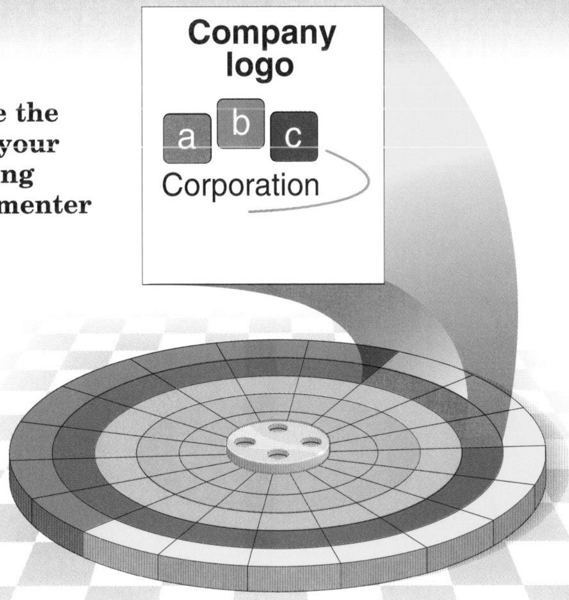

You can use the Disk Defragmenter program to place all the parts of a file in one location. This reduces the time your computer will spend locating the file.

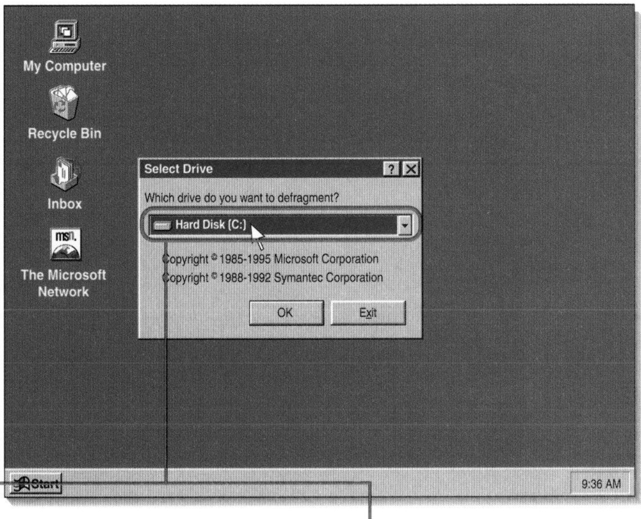

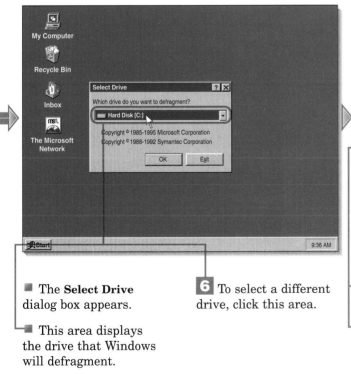

■ The **Select Drive** dialog box appears.

■ This area displays the drive that Windows will defragment.

6 To select a different drive, click this area.

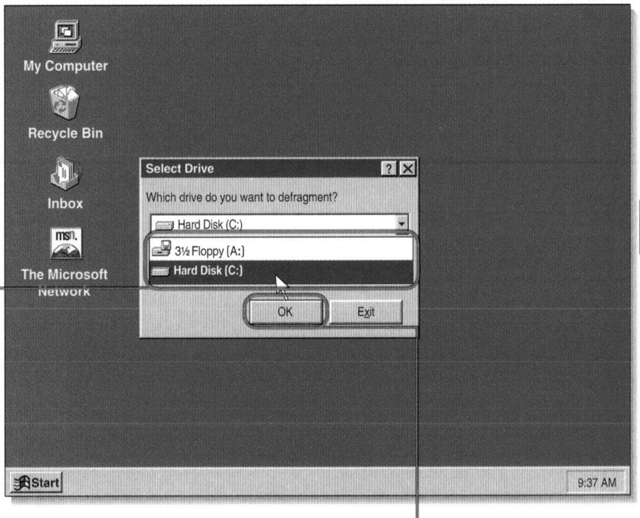

■ A list of the drives on your computer appears.

7 Click the drive you want to defragment (example: **C:**).

8 Click **OK**.

CONTINUED

DEFRAGMENT A DISK

You can perform other tasks on your computer while Windows defragments a disk, but your computer will operate slower.

DEFRAGMENT A DISK (CONTINUED)

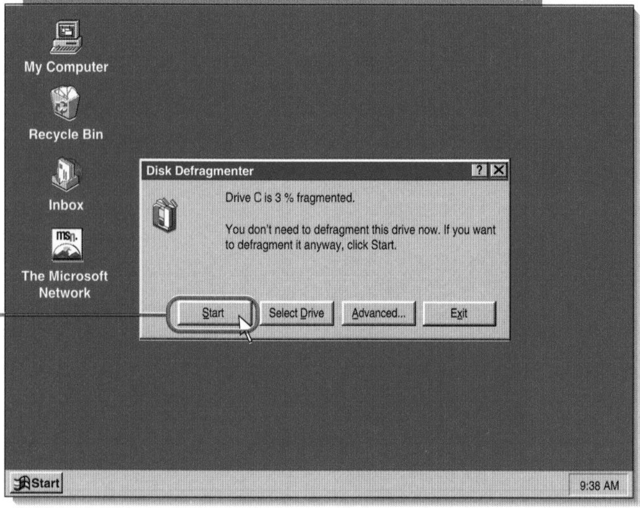

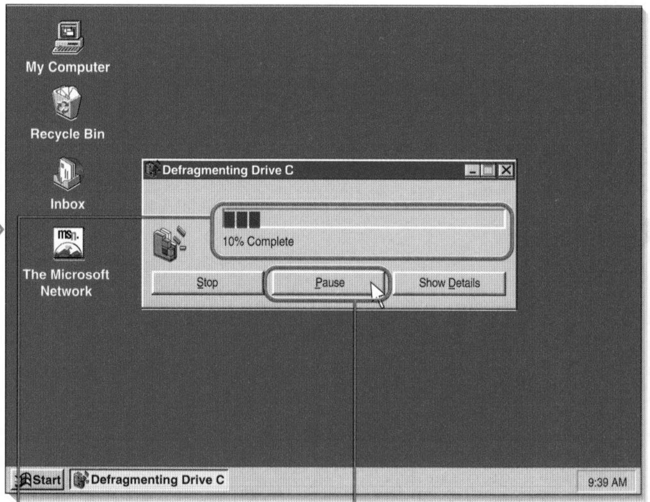

9 Click **Start**.

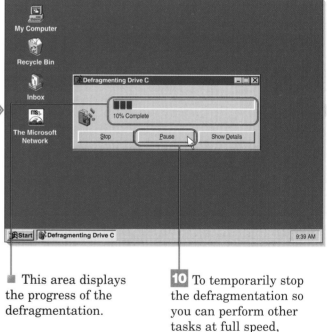

■ This area displays the progress of the defragmentation.

10 To temporarily stop the defragmentation so you can perform other tasks at full speed, click **Pause**.

TIP

You should defragment your hard disk at least once a month.

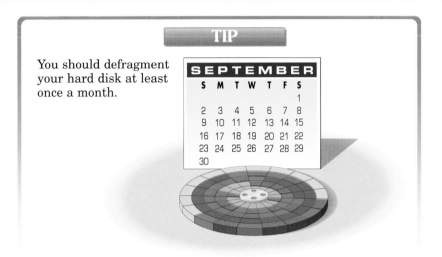

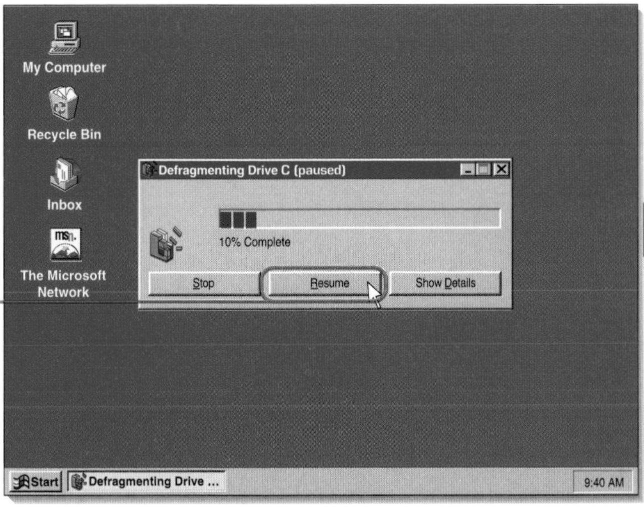

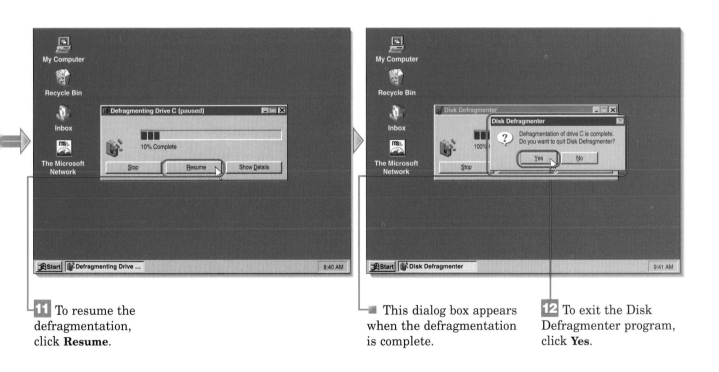

11 To resume the defragmentation, click **Resume**.

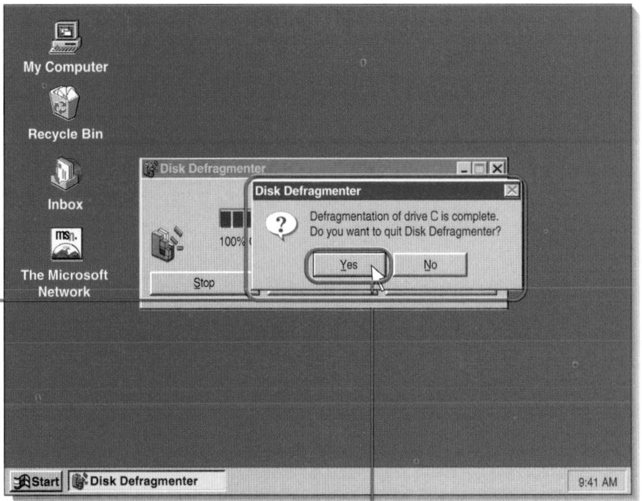

■ This dialog box appears when the defragmentation is complete.

12 To exit the Disk Defragmenter program, click **Yes**.

COPY A FLOPPY DISK

You can make an exact copy of a floppy disk. This is ideal when you want to make a backup copy of an important disk.

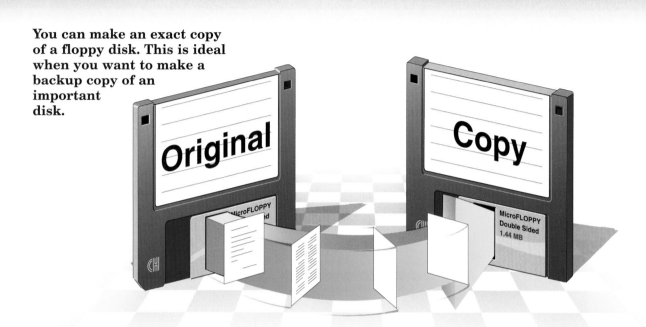

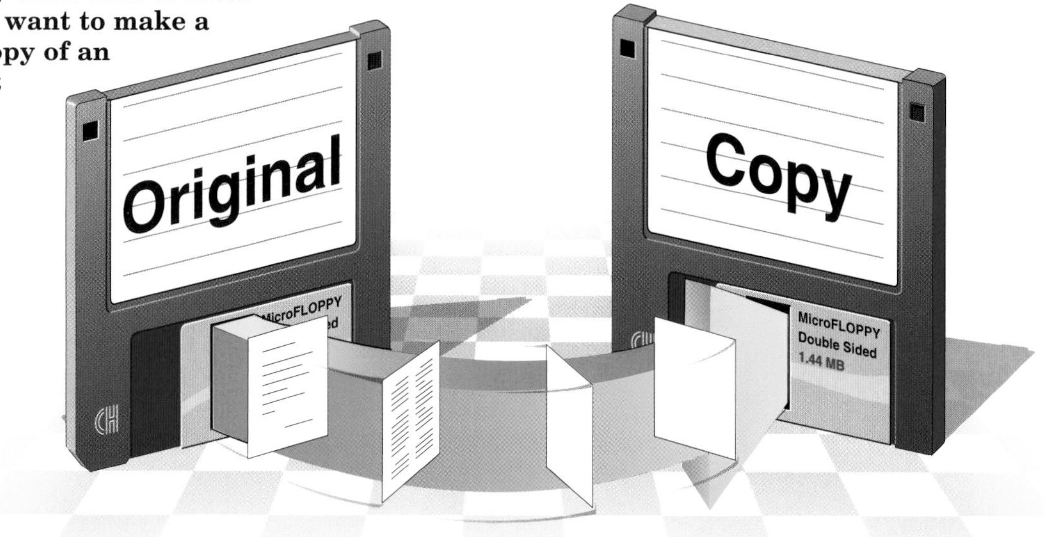

COPY A FLOPPY DISK

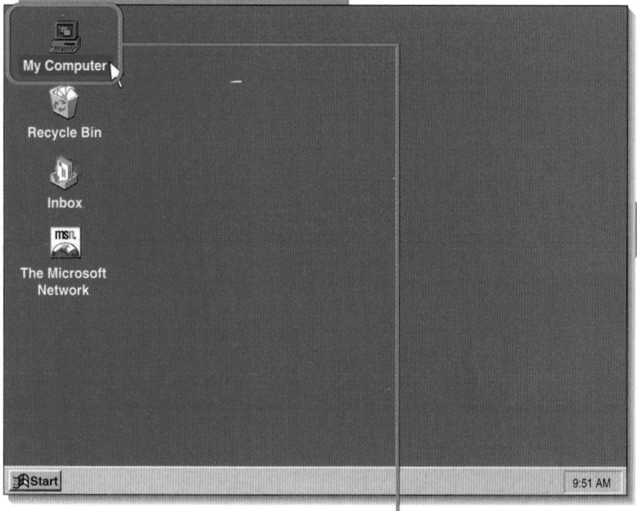

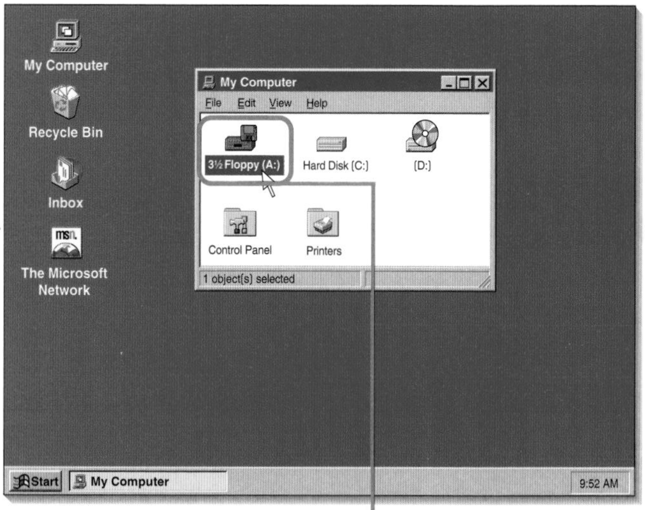

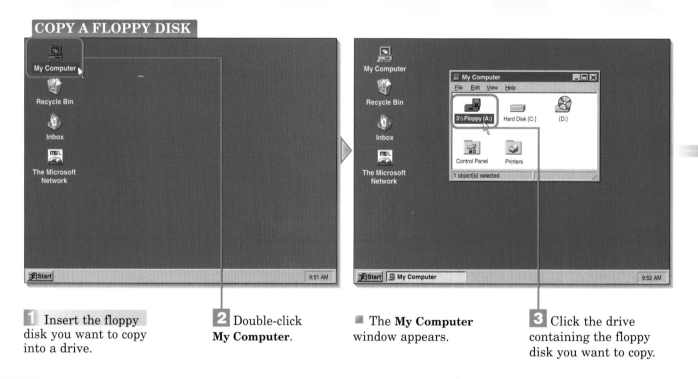

1 Insert the floppy disk you want to copy into a drive.

2 Double-click **My Computer**.

■ The **My Computer** window appears.

3 Click the drive containing the floppy disk you want to copy.

TIP

The original floppy disk and the disk that will receive the copy must be able to store the same amount of information.

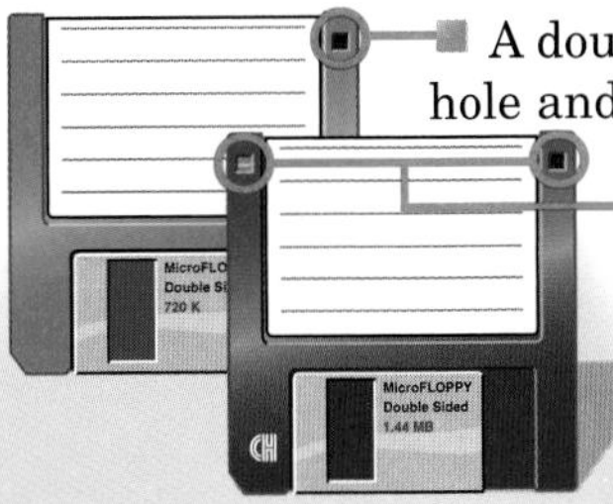

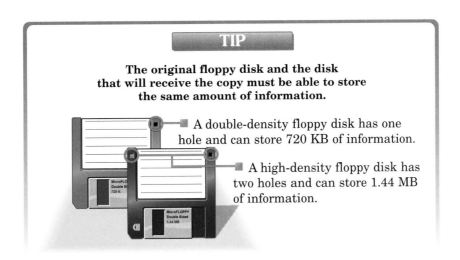

■ A double-density floppy disk has one hole and can store 720 KB of information.

■ A high-density floppy disk has two holes and can store 1.44 MB of information.

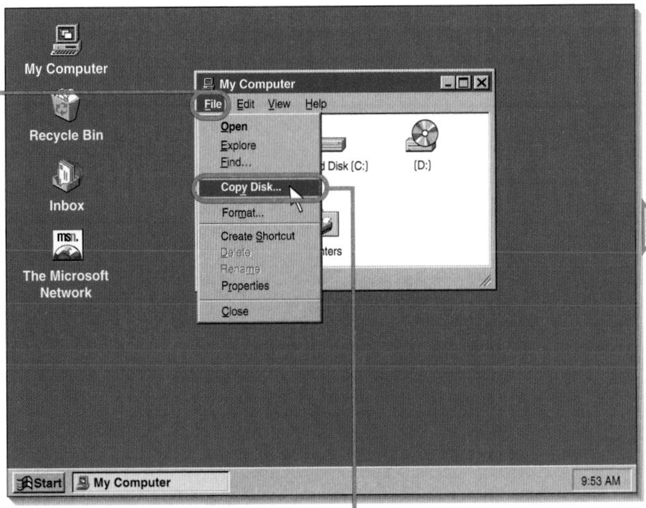

4 Click **File**.

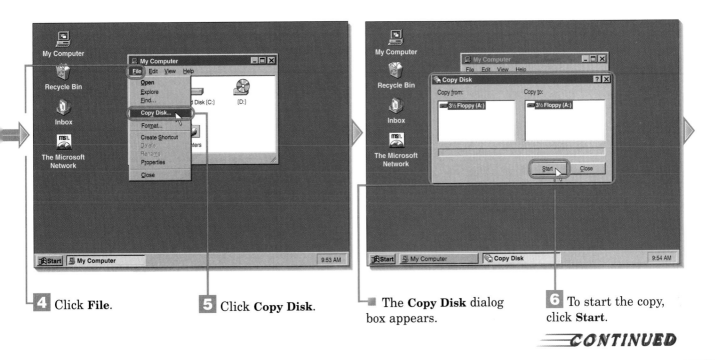

5 Click **Copy Disk**.

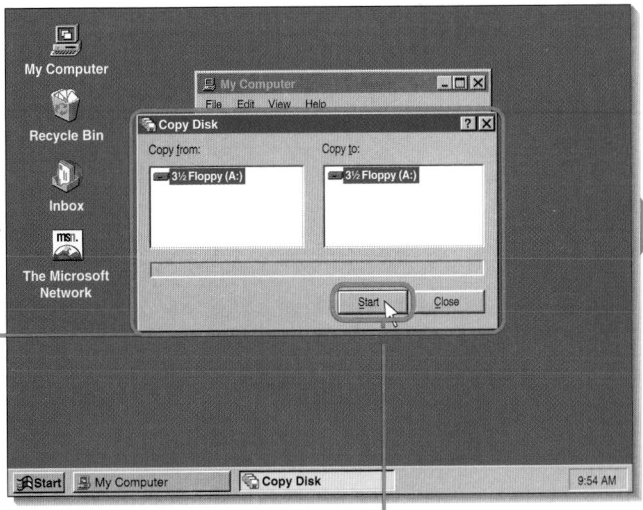

■ The **Copy Disk** dialog box appears.

6 To start the copy, click **Start**.

CONTINUED

COPY A FLOPPY DISK

Make sure the floppy disk receiving the copy does not contain information you want to keep. Copying will remove all the old information from the disk.

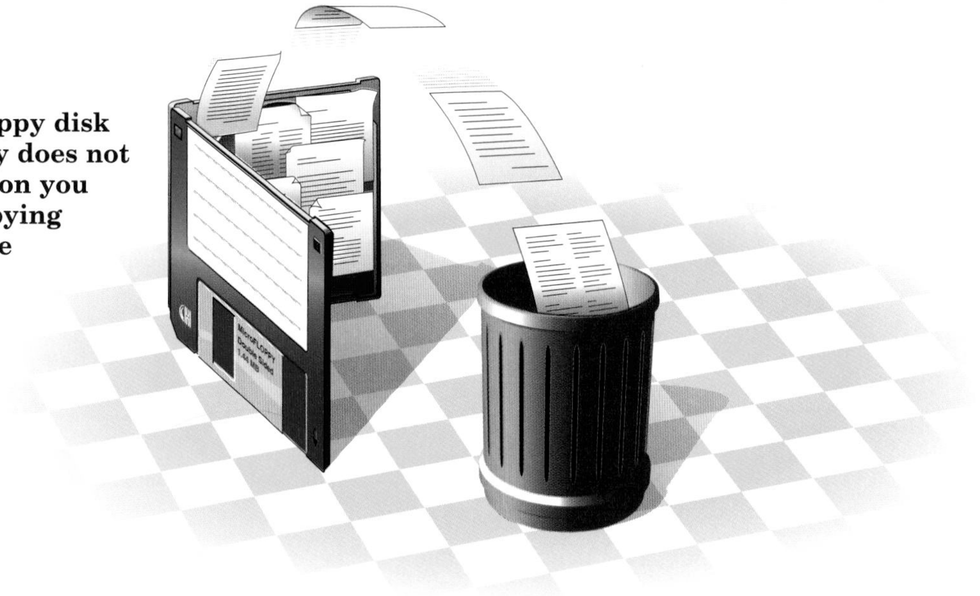

COPY A FLOPPY DISK (CONTINUED)

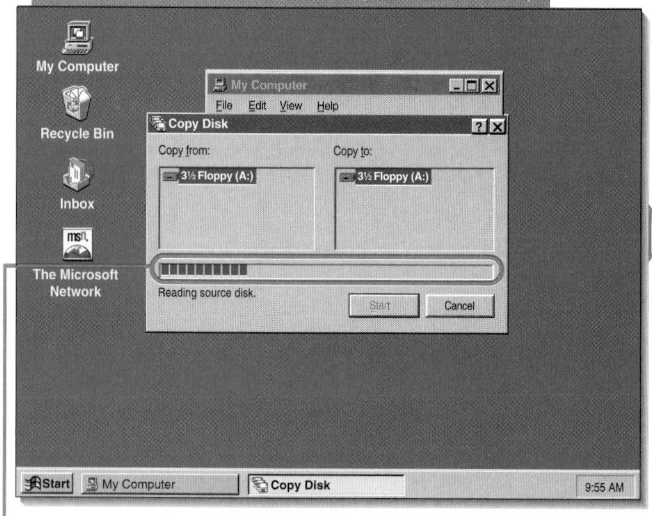

■ This area shows the progress of the copy.

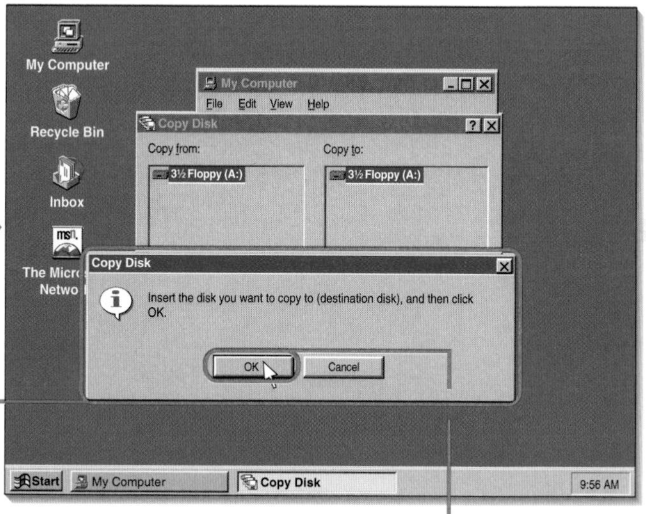

■ This dialog box appears, telling you to insert the floppy disk you want to receive the copy.

7 Remove the floppy disk from the drive and then insert the disk you want to receive the copy.

8 To continue, click **OK**.

TIP

Keep floppy disks away from magnets, which can damage the information stored on the disks. Also be careful not to spill liquids, such as coffee or soda, on the disks.

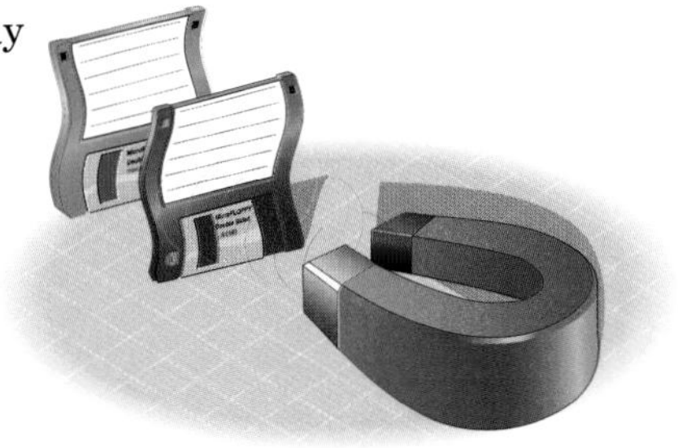

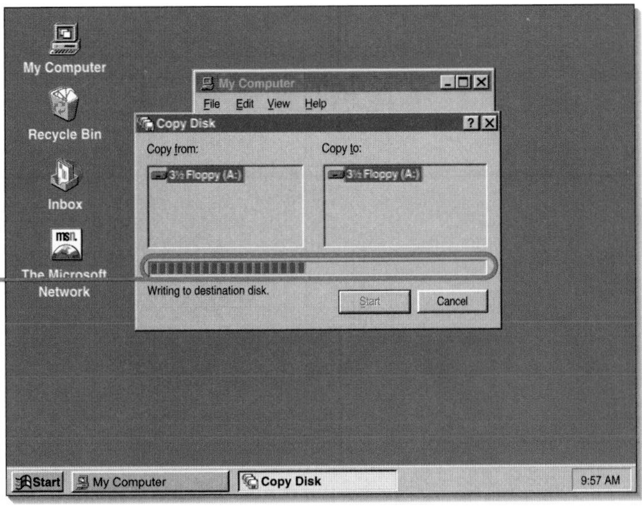

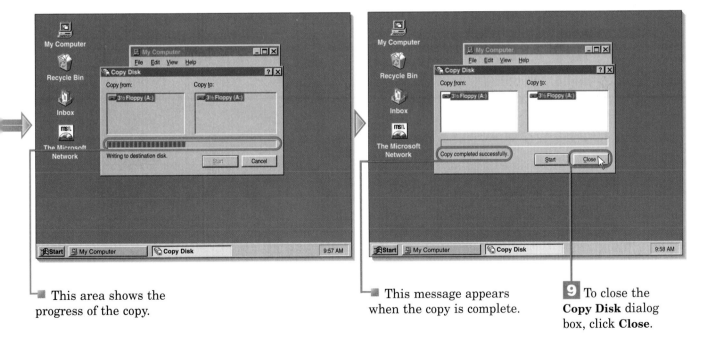

■ This area shows the progress of the copy.

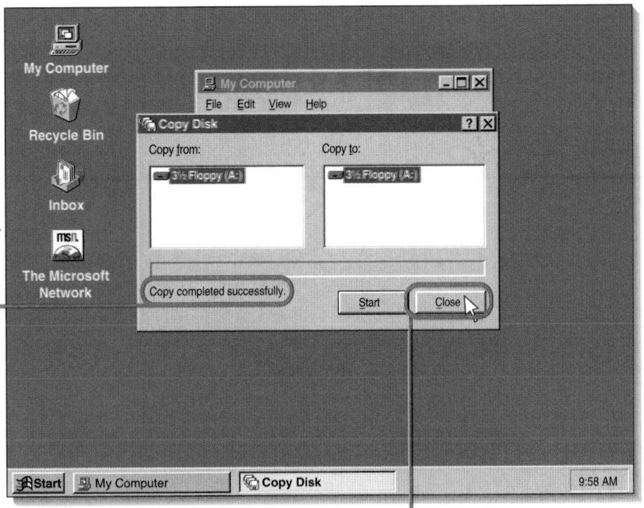

■ This message appears when the copy is complete.

9 To close the **Copy Disk** dialog box, click **Close**.

COMPRESS A DISK

You can compress, or squeeze together, the information stored on your hard disk. This can double the amount of information the disk can store.

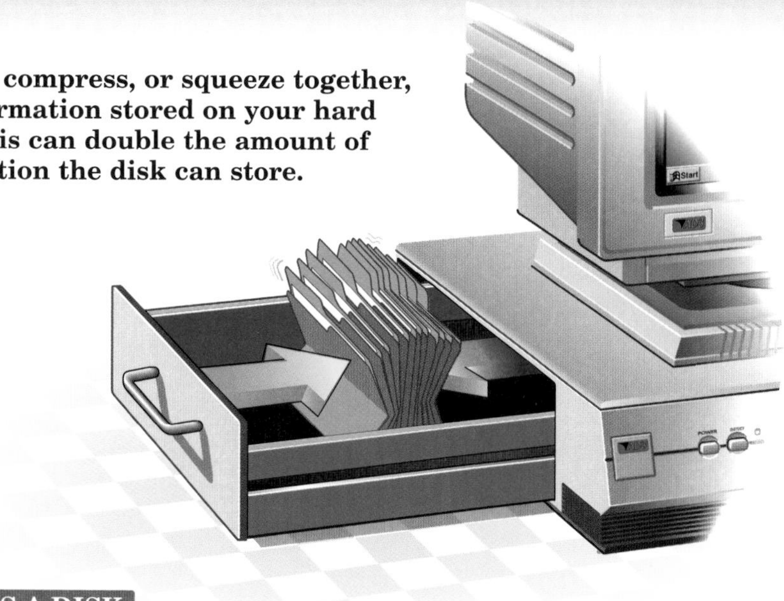

You can also compress floppy disks to store more information.

COMPRESS A DISK

Before compressing your hard disk, perform the following:

Exit all programs.

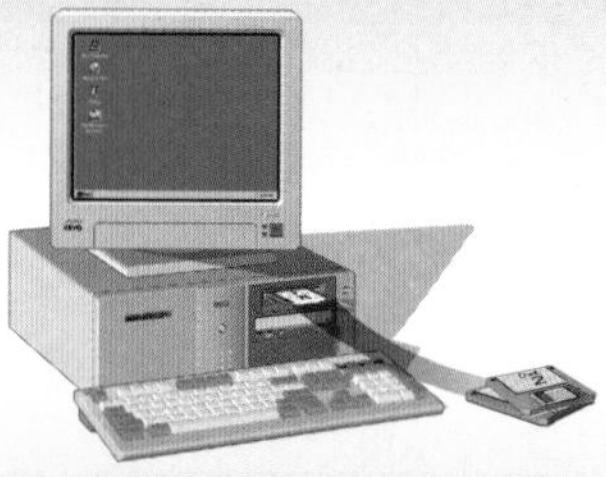

Back up the information on your hard disk.

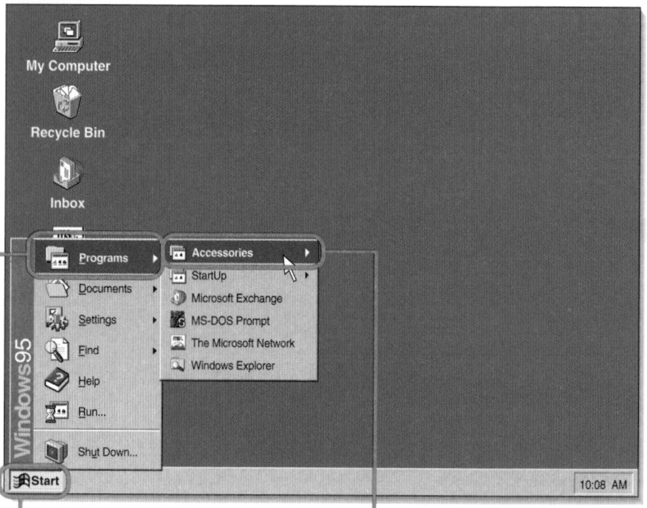

1 Click **Start**.

2 Click **Programs**.

3 Click **Accessories**.

IMPORTANT

You should only compress your hard disk if:

- The hard disk is running out of space to store new information.
- You have tried all other ways of increasing the available storage space, such as deleting all files you no longer need.

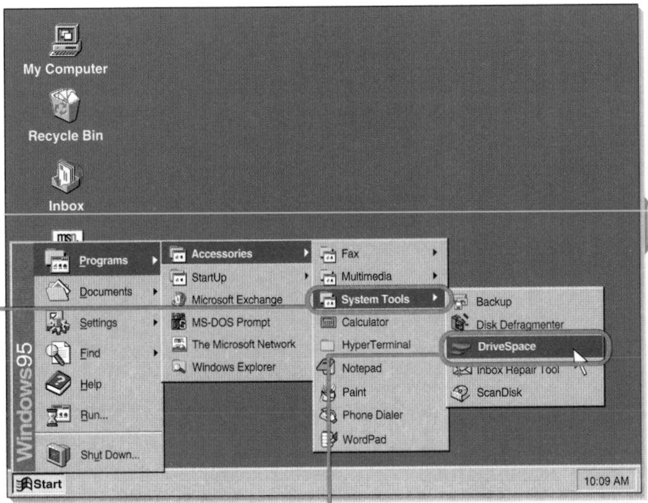

4 Click **System Tools**.

5 Click **DriveSpace**.

*Note: If **DriveSpace** is not available, you must add the Windows component called **Disk compression tools**. This component is found in the Disk Tools category. To add Windows components, refer to page 186.*

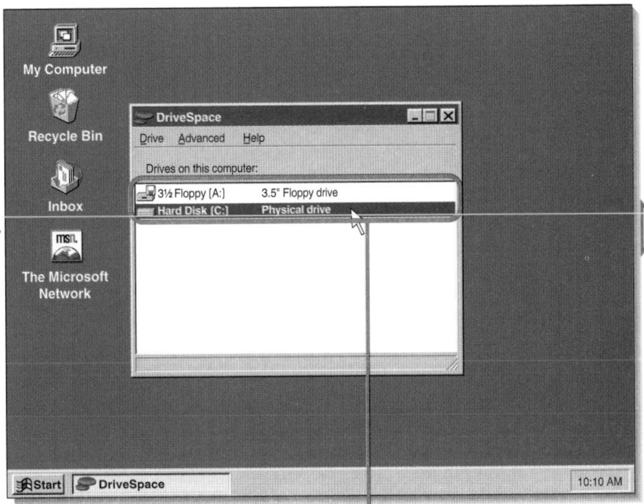

- The **DriveSpace** window appears.

6 Click the disk you want to compress.

CONTINUED

COMPRESS A DISK

Compressing your hard disk can take several hours. During this time, you cannot use your computer.

Compress your hard disk when you will not need your computer, such as after work.

COMPRESS A DISK (CONTINUED)

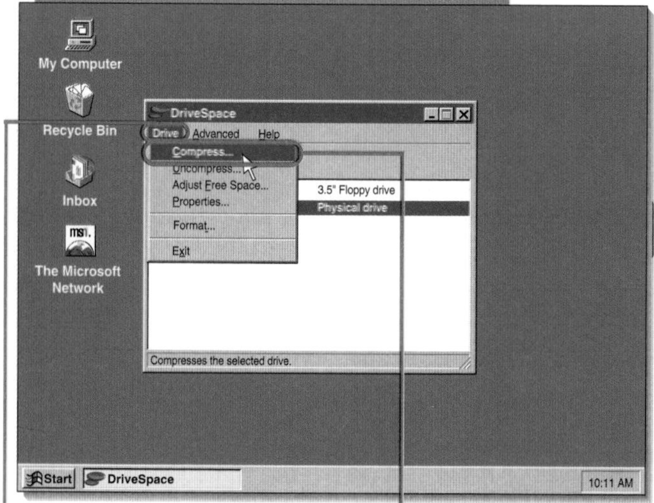

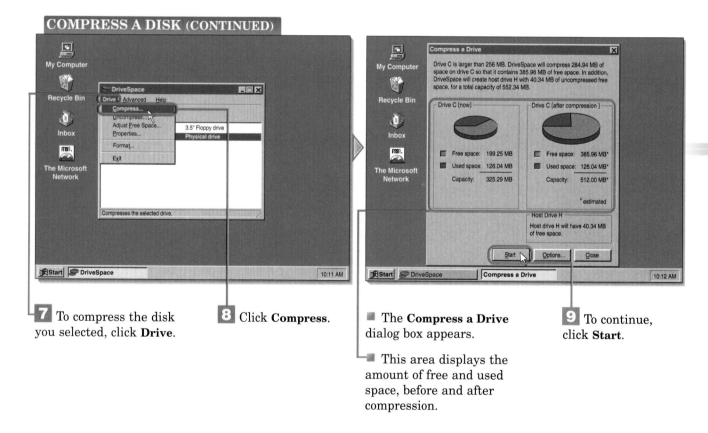

7 To compress the disk you selected, click **Drive**.

8 Click **Compress**.

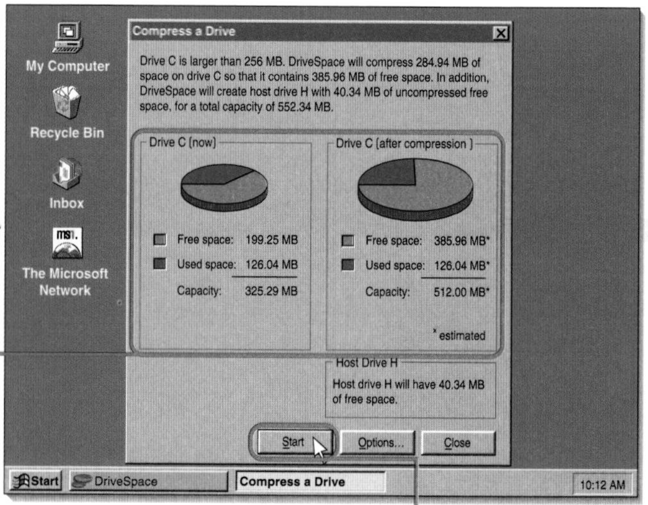

■ The **Compress a Drive** dialog box appears.

■ This area displays the amount of free and used space, before and after compression.

9 To continue, click **Start**.

TIP

Before Windows compresses your disk, it uses ScanDisk to search for and repair any disk errors.

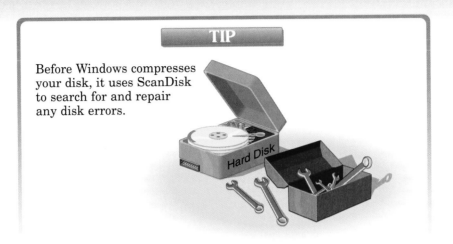

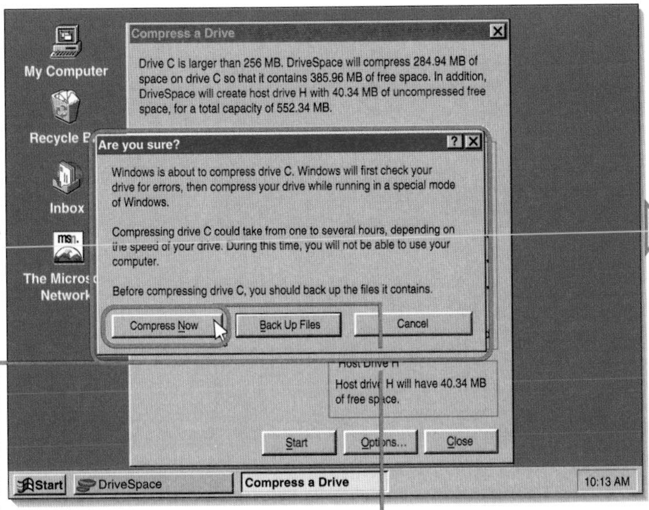

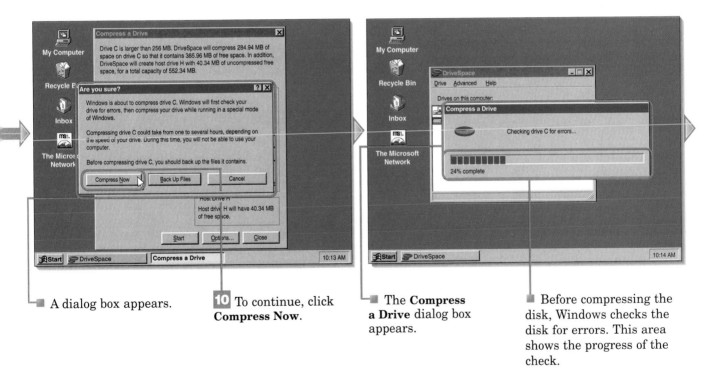

■ A dialog box appears.

10 To continue, click **Compress Now**.

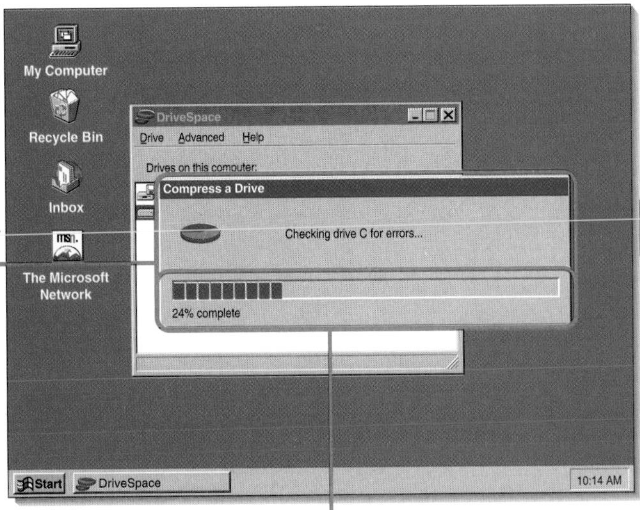

■ The **Compress a Drive** dialog box appears.

■ Before compressing the disk, Windows checks the disk for errors. This area shows the progress of the check.

CONTINUED

COMPRESS A DISK

When finished, Windows shows you the results of the compression.

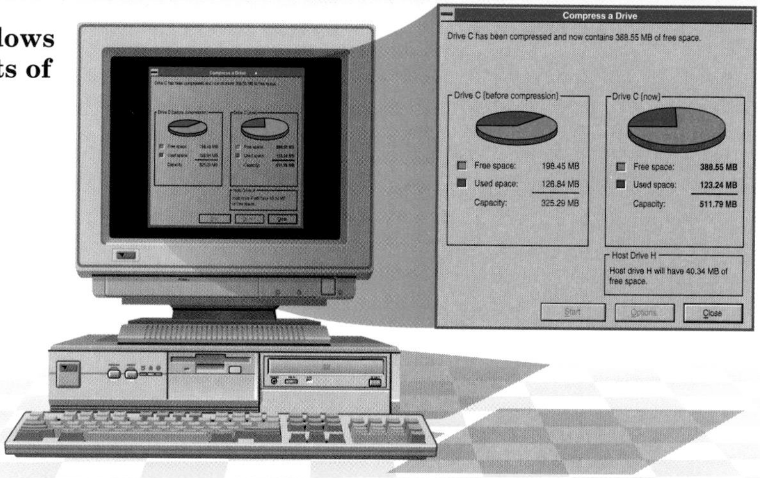

COMPRESS A DISK (CONTINUED)

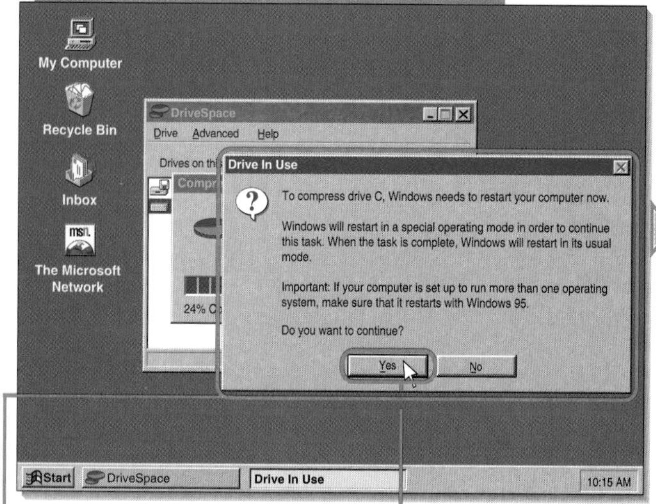

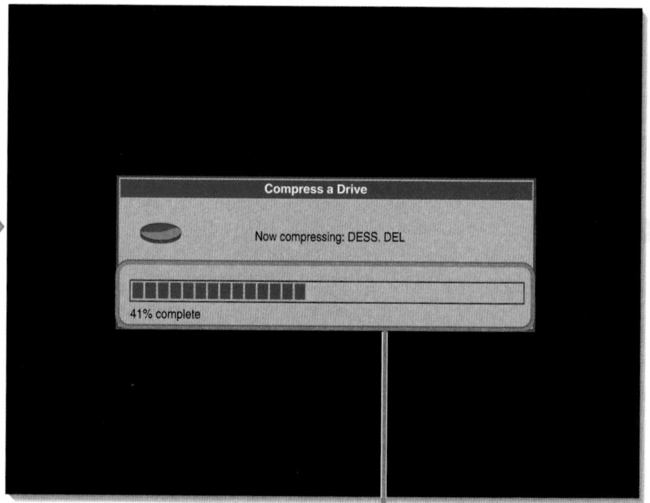

■ This dialog box appears if Windows needs to restart your computer before compressing the disk.

11 To continue, click **Yes**.

■ Windows restarts your computer and then begins compressing your disk.

■ This area displays the progress of the compression.

TIP

After you compress your hard disk, the amount of free space added to your computer depends on the type of information stored the disk.

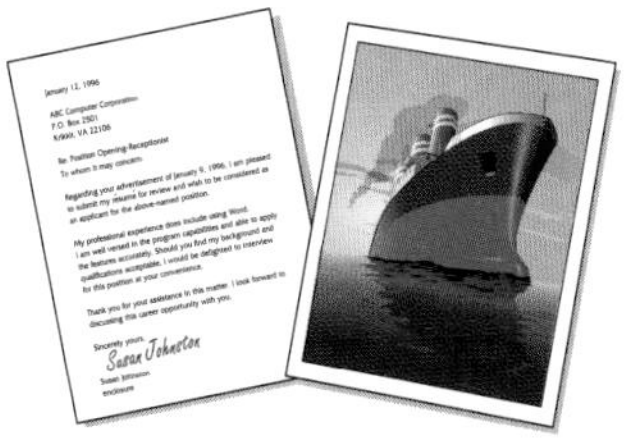

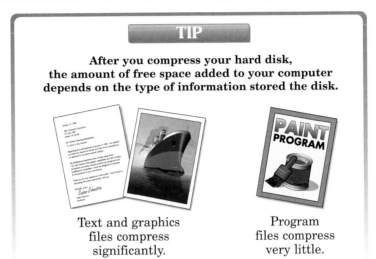

Text and graphics files compress significantly.

Program files compress very little.

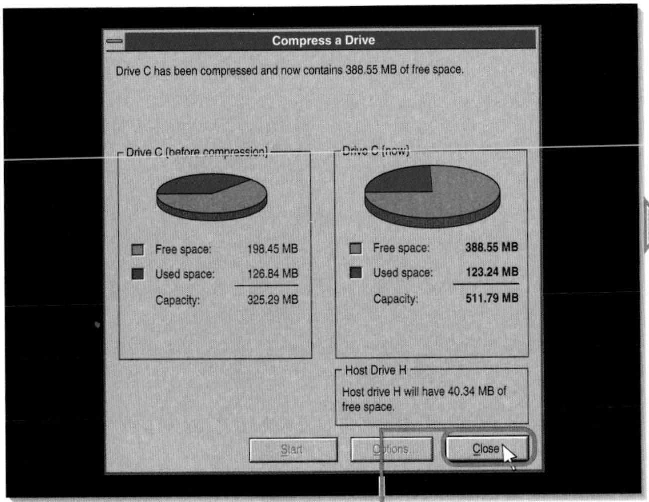

■ The **Compress a Drive** dialog box reappears when the compression is complete, displaying the results of the compression.

12 To close the dialog box, click **Close**.

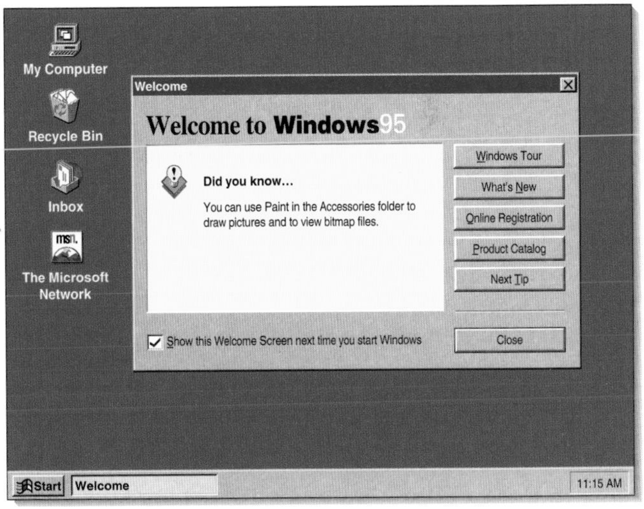

■ Windows restarts your computer.

■ You can now use your computer as usual.

In this chapter you will learn how to make backup copies of files stored on your computer.

CHAPTER 14: BACK UP YOUR FILES

Introduction 228

Start Microsoft Backup 230

Back Up Selected Files 232

Perform the Backup 236

Back Up Named Files 238

Restore Files 240

INTRODUCTION

You should regularly make backup copies of the files stored on your computer to protect them from theft, computer failure and viruses.

BACKUP DEVICES

Floppy Disks

You can use floppy disks to back up important files stored on your computer.

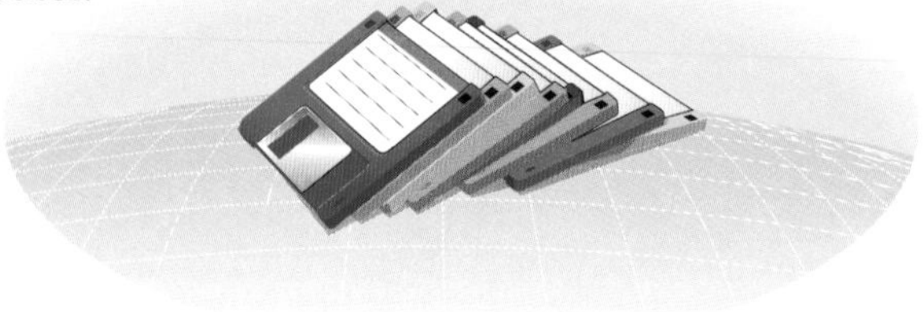

Tape Cartridges

You can use tape cartridges to back up large amounts of information, such as all the files on your hard drive.

Note: You must have a tape drive to use tape cartridges.

BACKUP STRATEGIES

Back up your work frequently. Consider how much work you can afford to lose. If you cannot afford to lose the work accomplished in one day, back up once a day. If your work does not change much during the week, back up once a week.

Create and then strictly follow a backup schedule. Hard drive disasters always seem to happen right after you miss a scheduled backup.

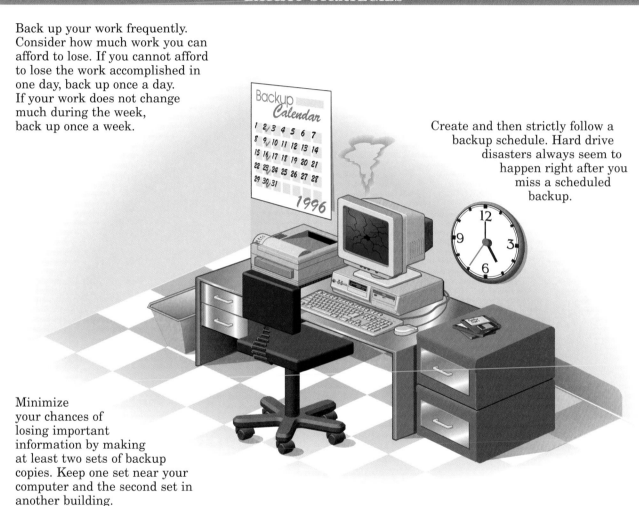

Minimize your chances of losing important information by making at least two sets of backup copies. Keep one set near your computer and the second set in another building.

Store backup copies in a cool, dry place, away from electrical equipment and magnetic devices.

START MICROSOFT BACKUP

Microsoft Backup helps you copy important information stored on your computer to floppy disks.

You can also copy files to tape cartridges. You must have a tape drive to use tape cartridges.

START MICROSOFT BACKUP

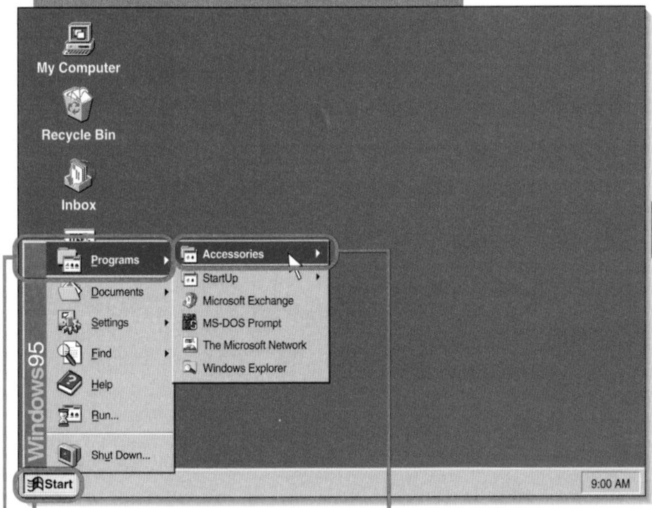

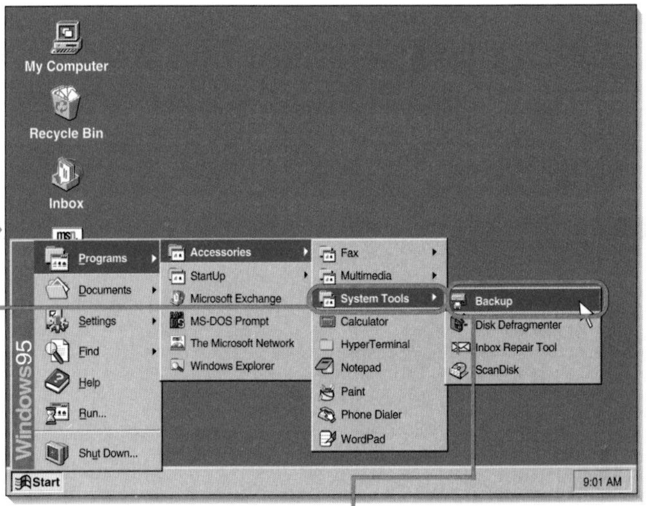

1 Click **Start**.

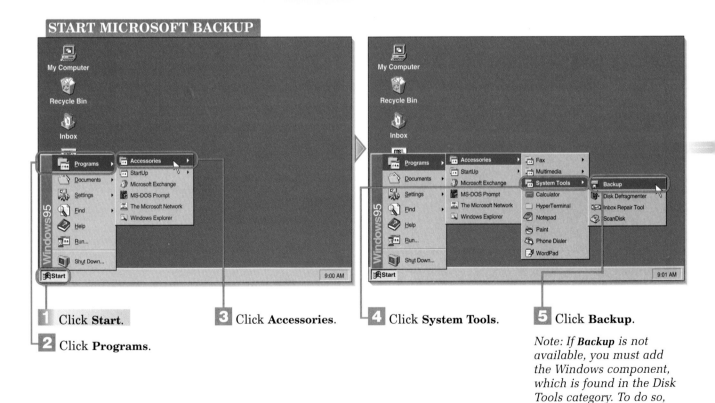

2 Click **Programs**.

3 Click **Accessories**.

4 Click **System Tools**.

5 Click **Backup**.

*Note: If **Backup** is not available, you must add the Windows component, which is found in the Disk Tools category. To do so, refer to page 186.*

TIP

You can also use Microsoft Backup to copy files you rarely use to floppy disks. You can then remove these files from your hard drive to create more storage space on your computer.

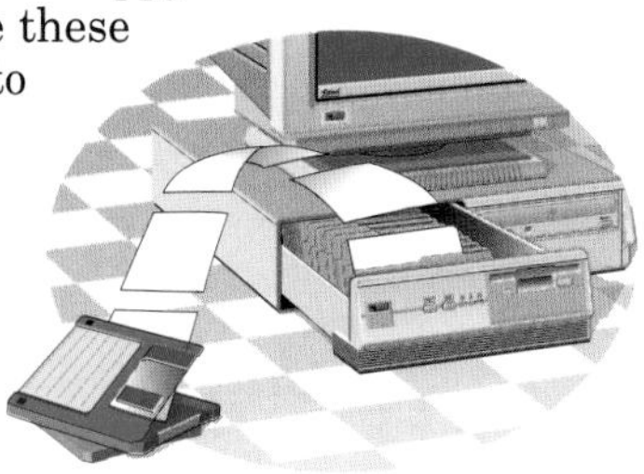

Note: To avoid losing the information, you should make two copies of these files and store the copies in different locations.

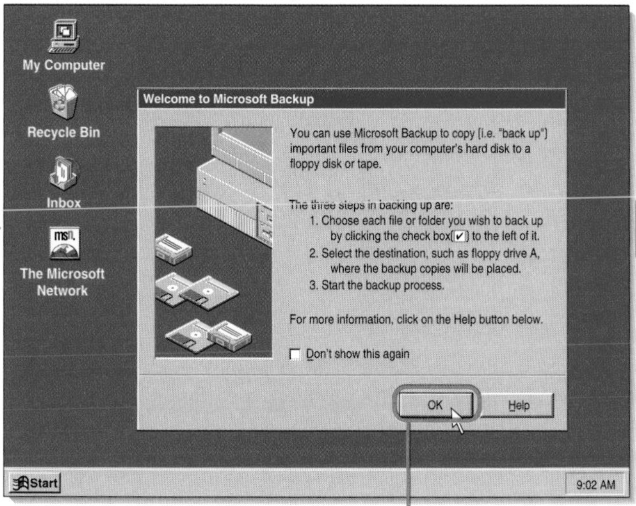

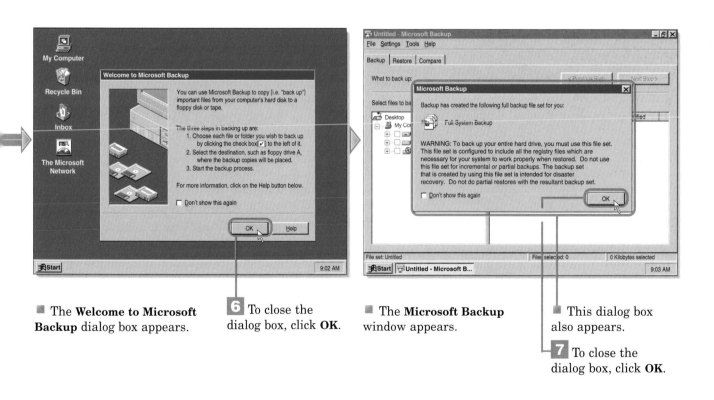

■ The **Welcome to Microsoft Backup** dialog box appears.

6 To close the dialog box, click **OK**.

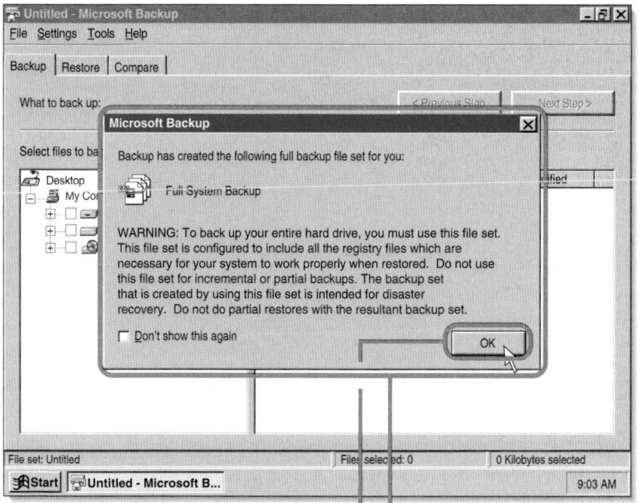

■ The **Microsoft Backup** window appears.

■ This dialog box also appears.

7 To close the dialog box, click **OK**.

BACK UP SELECTED FILES

To perform a backup, you must select the files you want to back up.

BACK UP SELECTED FILES

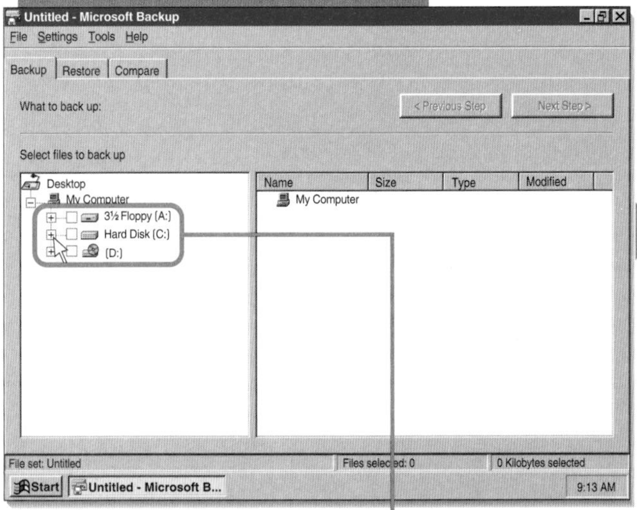

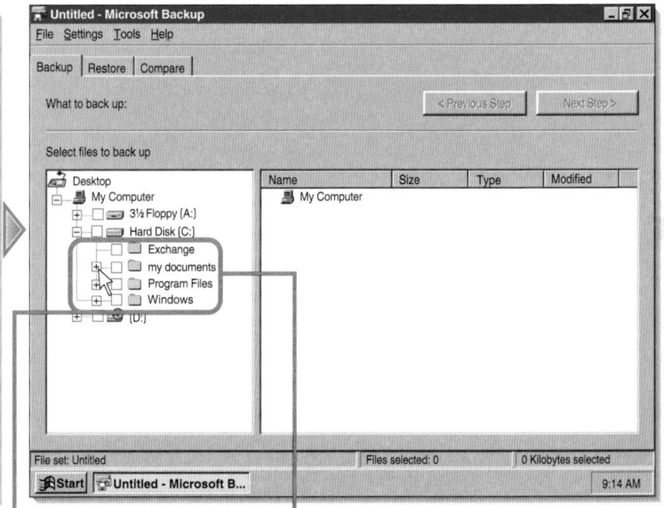

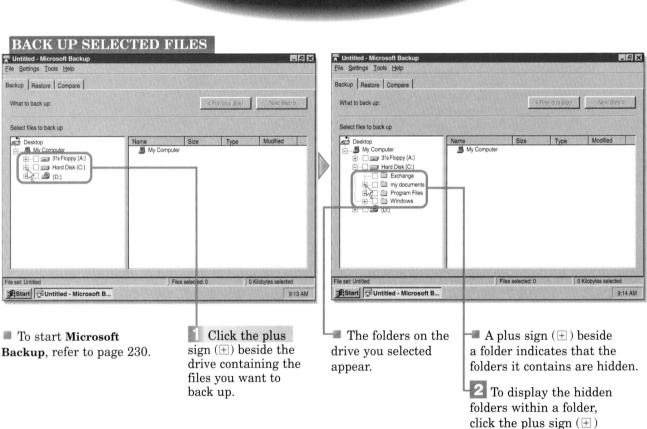

■ To start **Microsoft Backup**, refer to page 230.

1 Click the plus sign (⊞) beside the drive containing the files you want to back up.

■ The folders on the drive you selected appear.

■ A plus sign (⊞) beside a folder indicates that the folders it contains are hidden.

2 To display the hidden folders within a folder, click the plus sign (⊞) beside the folder.

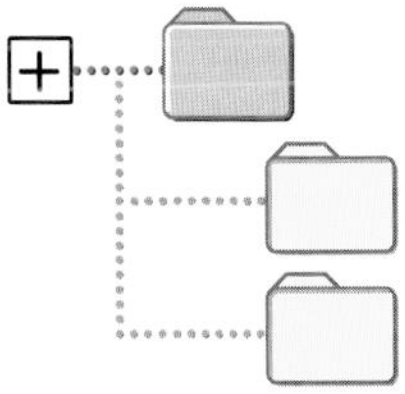

A plus sign (⊞) beside a folder indicates that all the folders it contains are hidden.

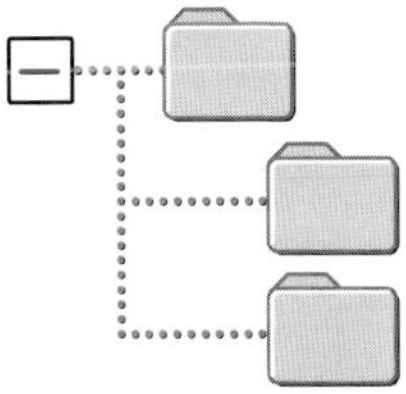

A minus sign (⊟) beside a folder indicates that all the folders it contains are displayed.

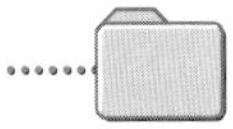

No sign beside a folder indicates that the folder does not contain any folders, although it may contain files.

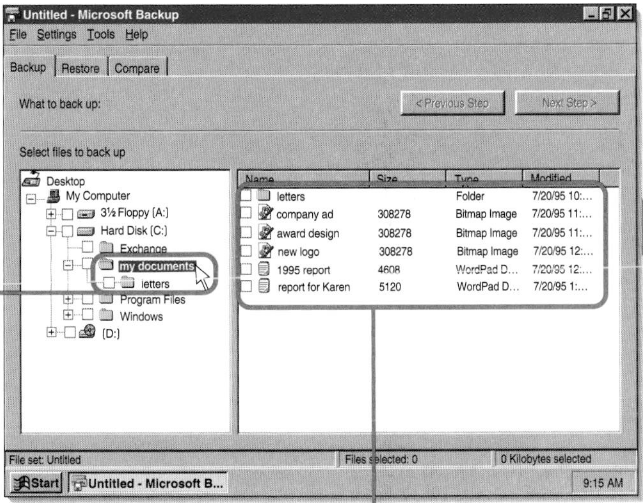

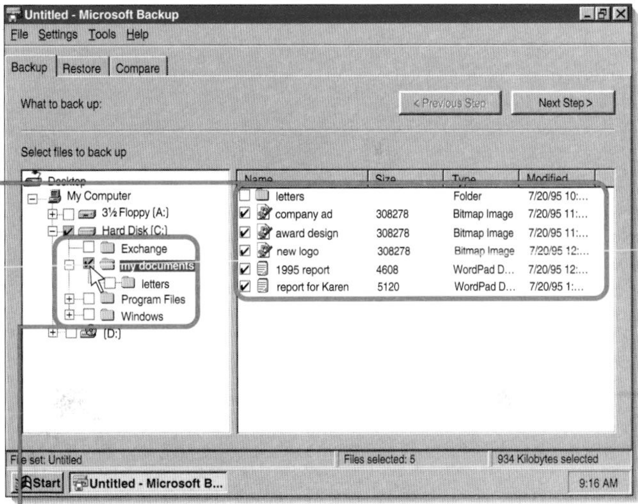

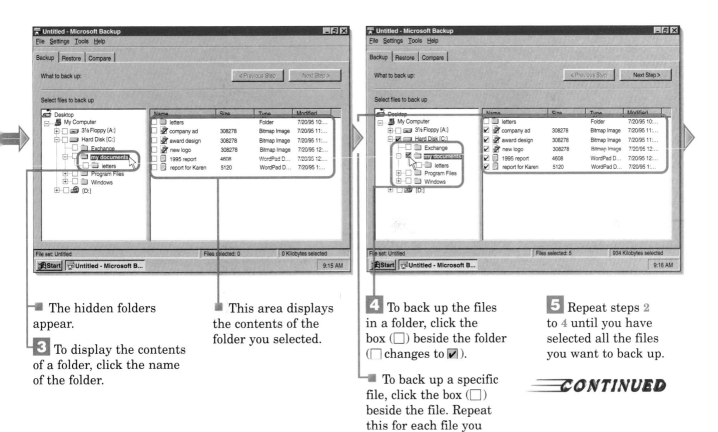

■ The hidden folders appear.

3 To display the contents of a folder, click the name of the folder.

■ This area displays the contents of the folder you selected.

4 To back up the files in a folder, click the box (☐) beside the folder (☐ changes to ☑).

■ To back up a specific file, click the box (☐) beside the file. Repeat this for each file you want to back up.

5 Repeat steps 2 to 4 until you have selected all the files you want to back up.

CONTINUED

BACK UP SELECTED FILES

If you often back up the same files, you can assign a name to the group of files. This saves you time in future backups.

BACK UP SELECTED FILES (CONTINUED)

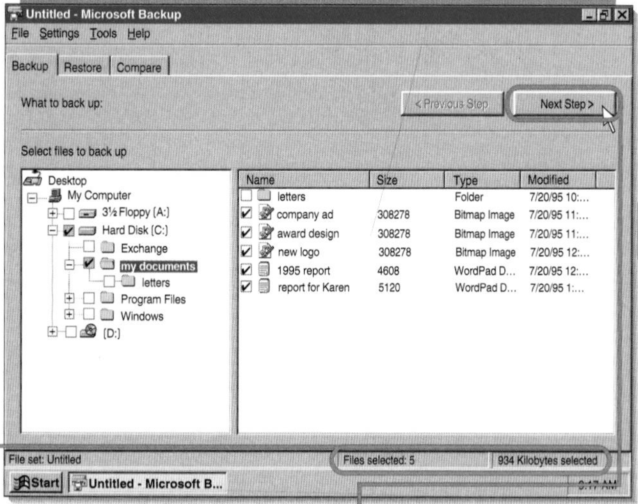

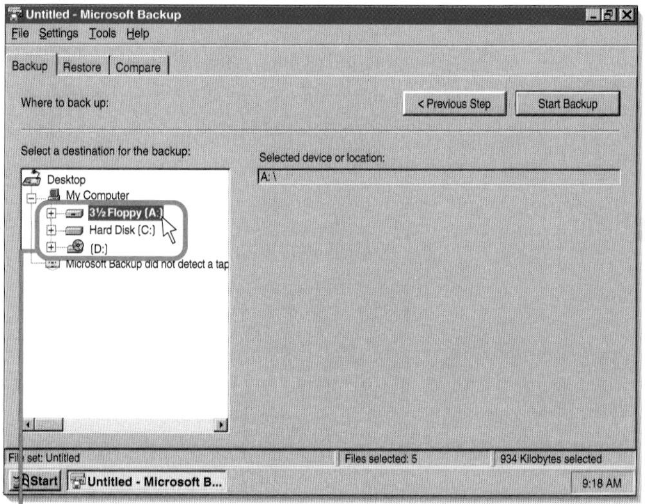

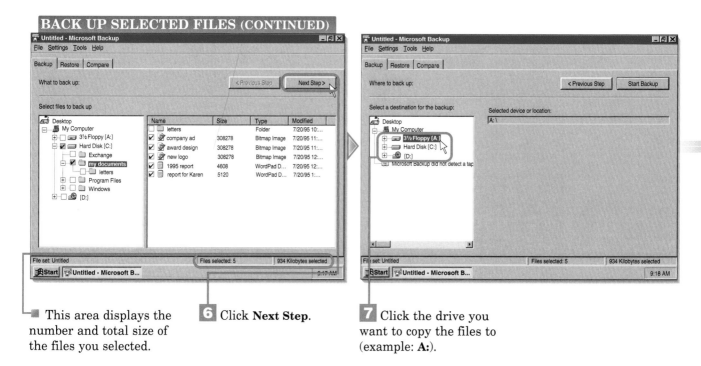

■ This area displays the number and total size of the files you selected.

6 Click **Next Step**.

7 Click the drive you want to copy the files to (example: **A:**).

TIP

Bytes are used to measure the size of files.

One byte equals one character.

Note: A character can be a number, letter or symbol.

One kilobyte equals approximately one thousand characters, or one page of double-spaced text.

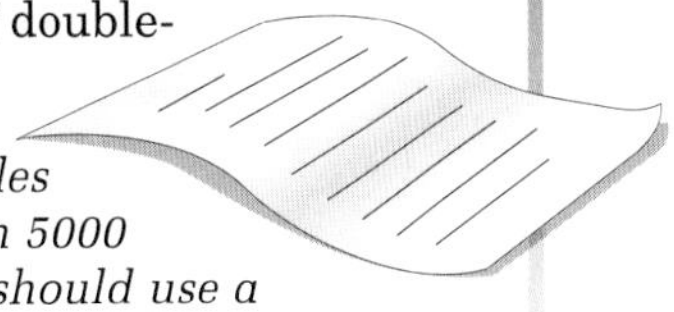

Note: If your files total more than 5000 kilobytes, you should use a tape cartridge to back up the files.

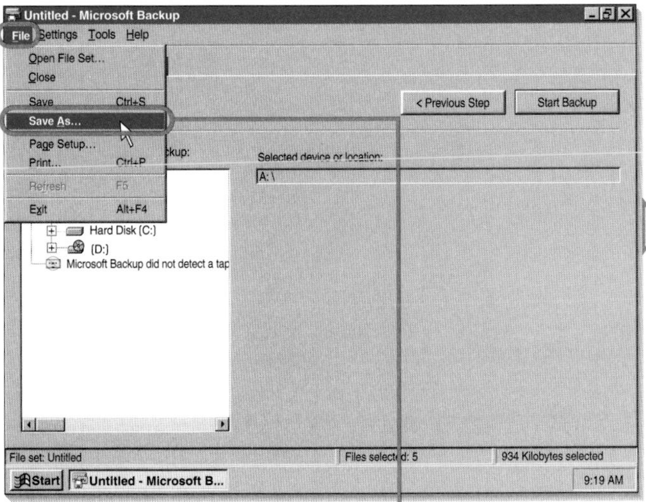

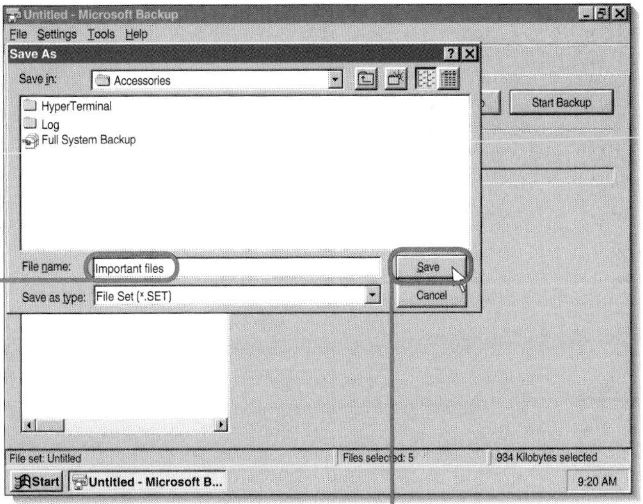

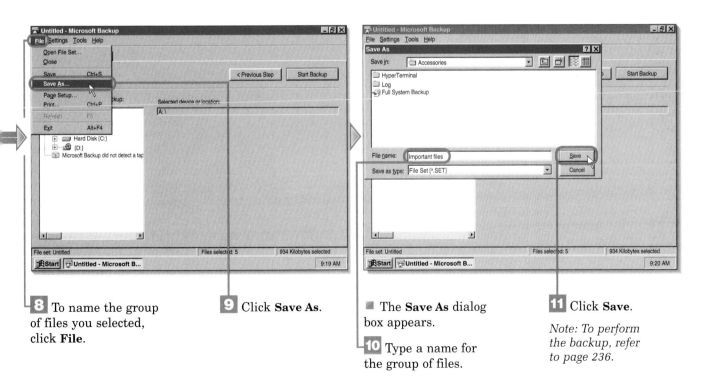

8 To name the group of files you selected, click **File**.

9 Click **Save As**.

■ The **Save As** dialog box appears.

10 Type a name for the group of files.

11 Click **Save**.

Note: To perform the backup, refer to page 236.

PERFORM THE BACKUP

After you have selected the files you want to back up, you can have Windows copy the files to floppy disks.

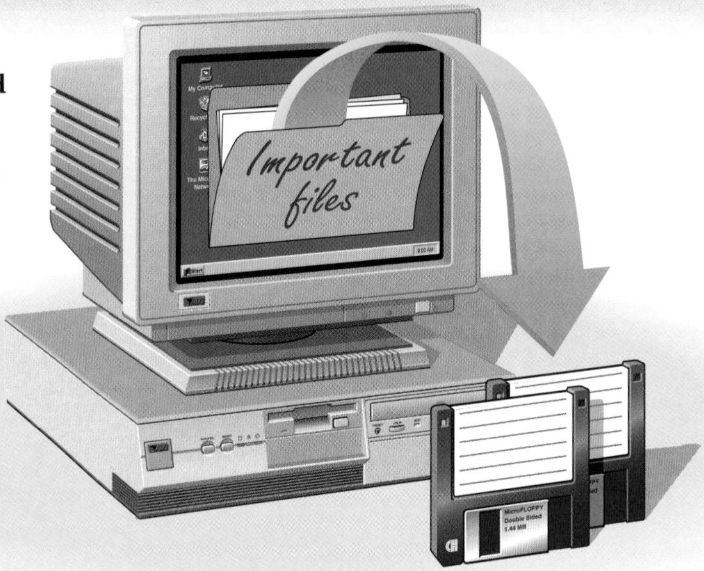

PERFORM THE BACKUP

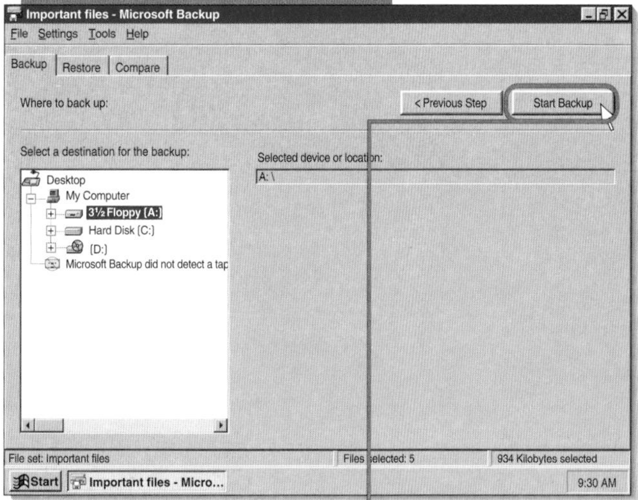

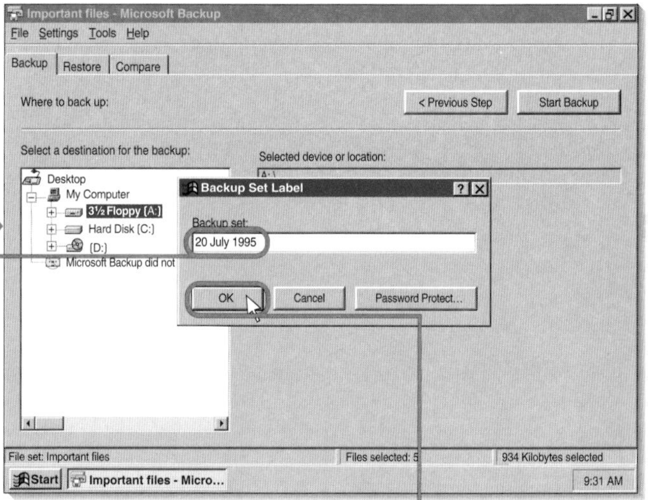

1 Insert a floppy disk into a drive.

2 Click **Start Backup**.

3 Type a name for the backup.

Note: To make it easier to identify the backup later, you can name the backup with the current date.

4 Click **OK**.

TIP

If the backup requires more than one floppy disk, this dialog box will appear when a disk is full.

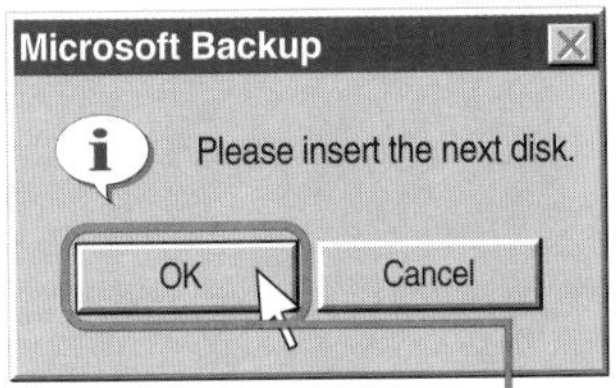

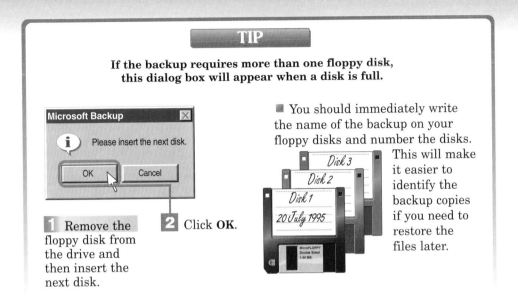

1 Remove the floppy disk from the drive and then insert the next disk.

2 Click **OK**.

■ You should immediately write the name of the backup on your floppy disks and number the disks.

This will make it easier to identify the backup copies if you need to restore the files later.

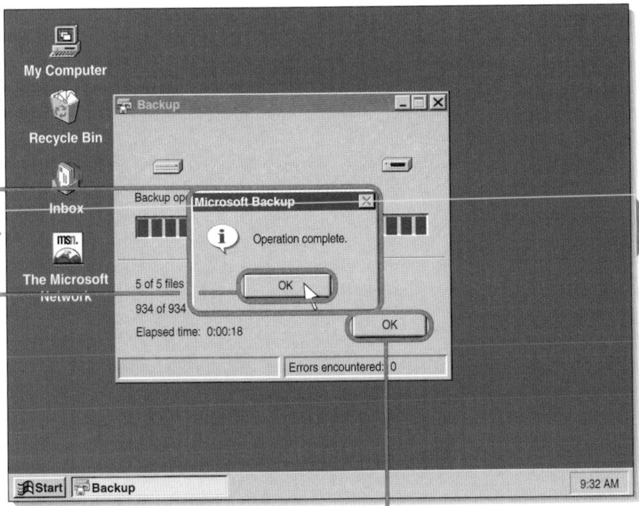

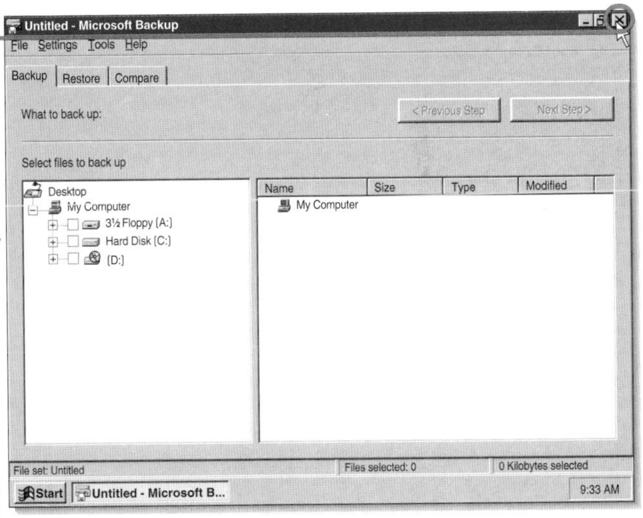

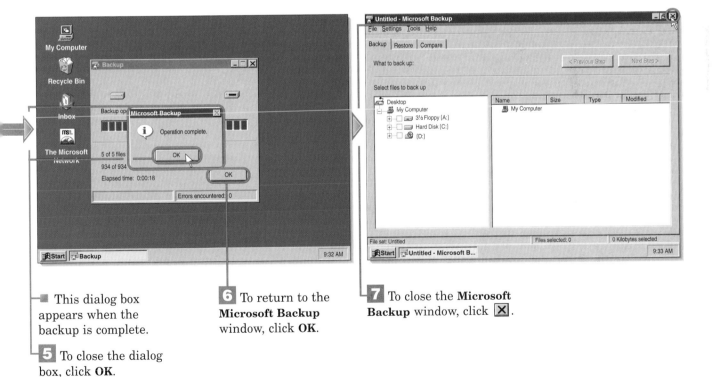

■ This dialog box appears when the backup is complete.

5 To close the dialog box, click **OK**.

6 To return to the **Microsoft Backup** window, click **OK**.

7 To close the **Microsoft Backup** window, click ☒.

BACK UP NAMED FILES

If you assigned a name to a group of files in a previous backup, Windows can save you time by selecting those files for you.

BACK UP NAMED FILES

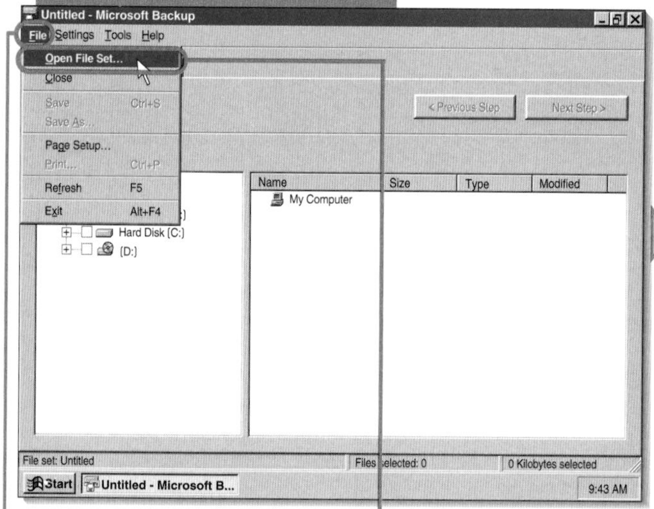

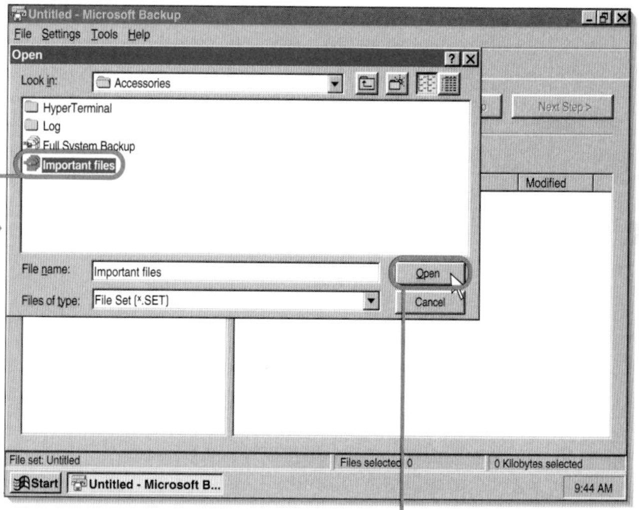

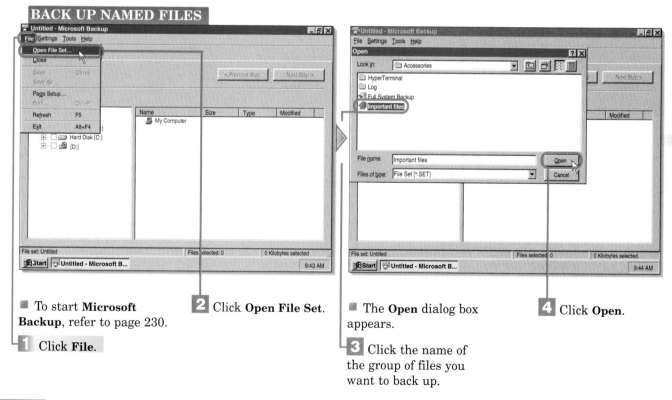

■ To start **Microsoft Backup**, refer to page 230.

1 Click **File**.

2 Click **Open File Set**.

■ The **Open** dialog box appears.

3 Click the name of the group of files you want to back up.

4 Click **Open**.

TIP

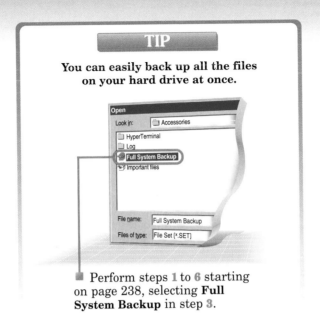

You can easily back up all the files on your hard drive at once.

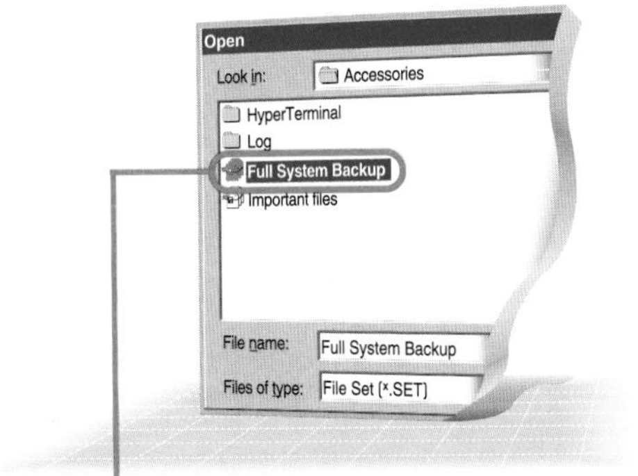

■ Perform steps 1 to 6 starting on page 238, selecting **Full System Backup** in step 3.

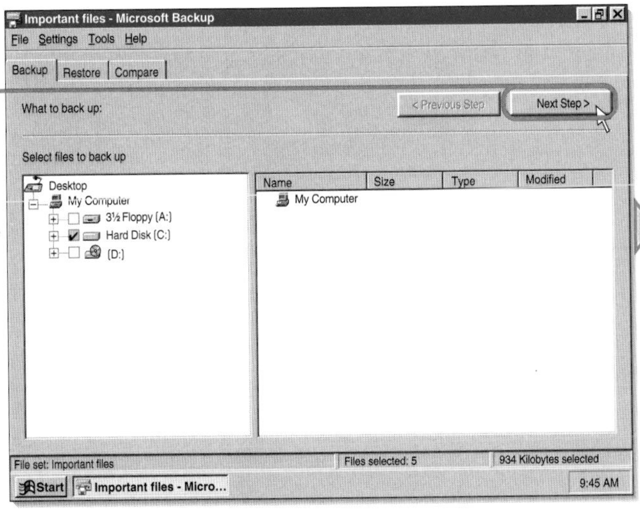

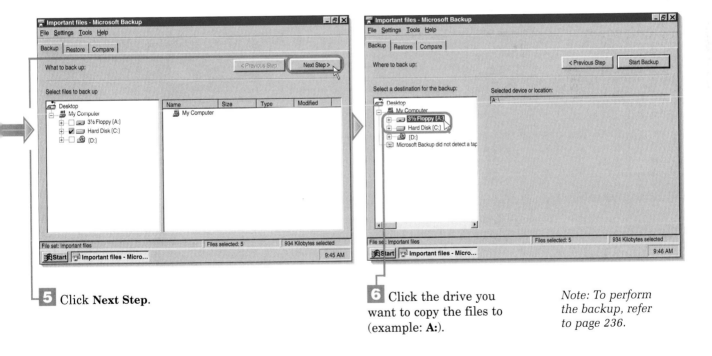

5 Click **Next Step**.

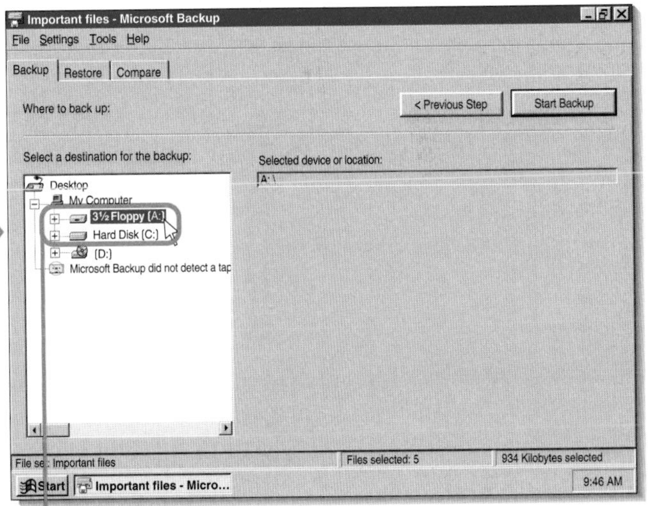

6 Click the drive you want to copy the files to (example: **A:**).

Note: To perform the backup, refer to page 236.

RESTORE FILES

If files on your computer are lost or damaged, you can use your backup copies to restore the files.

RESTORE FILES

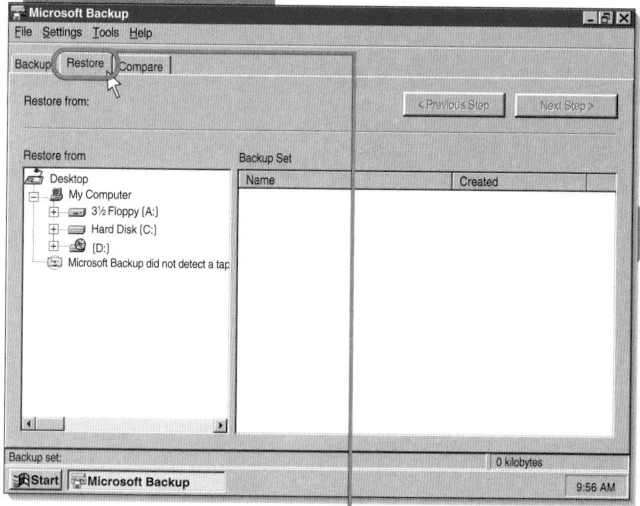

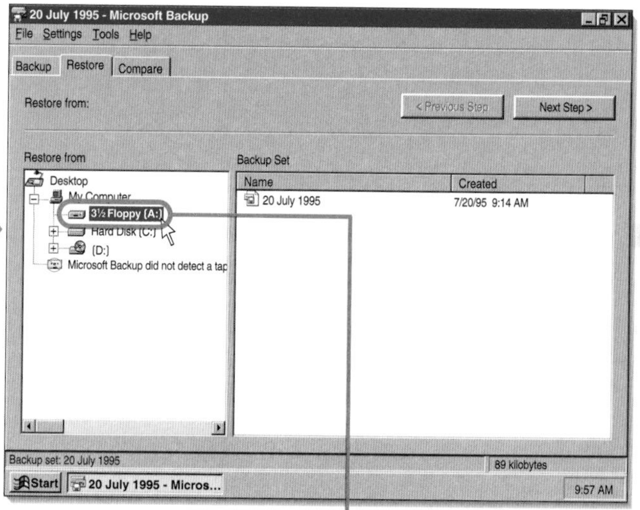

1 Start **Microsoft Backup**.

*Note: To start **Microsoft Backup**, refer to page 230.*

2 Click the **Restore** tab.

3 Insert the floppy disk containing the files you want to restore into a drive.

4 Click the drive containing the floppy disk (example: **A:**).

IMPORTANT

If your backup copies are stored on more than one floppy disk, you must insert the **last** disk into a drive in step 3 on page 240.

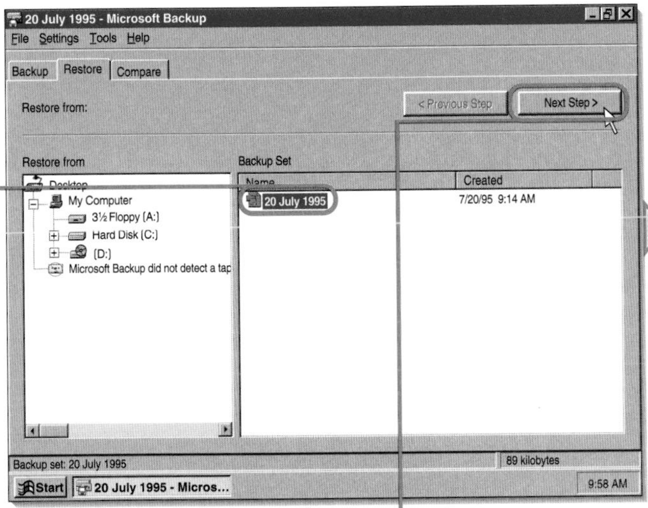

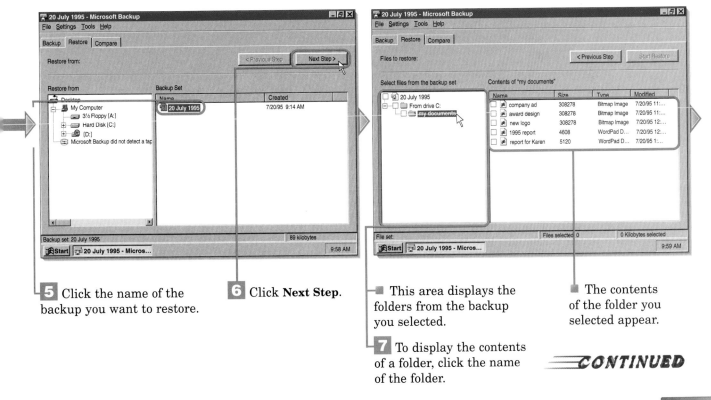

5 Click the name of the backup you want to restore.

6 Click **Next Step**.

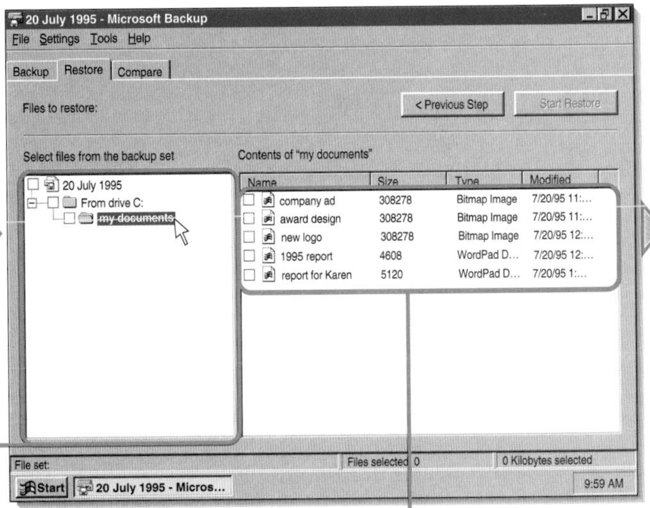

■ This area displays the folders from the backup you selected.

7 To display the contents of a folder, click the name of the folder.

■ The contents of the folder you selected appear.

CONTINUED

RESTORE FILES

If you do not need to restore all the files you backed up, you can select only the files you want to restore.

RESTORE FILES (CONTINUED)

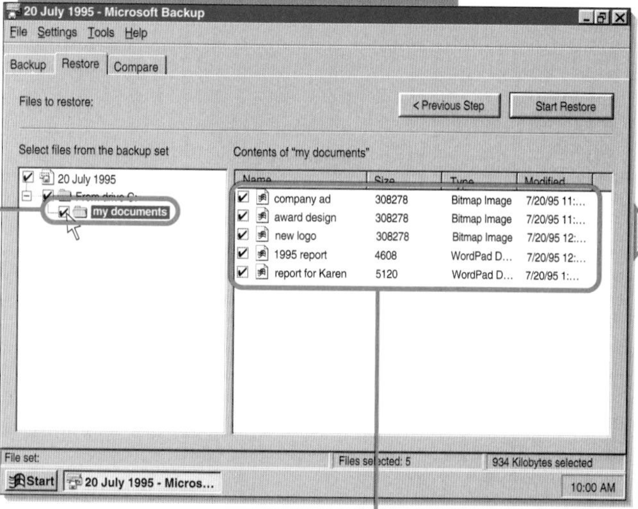

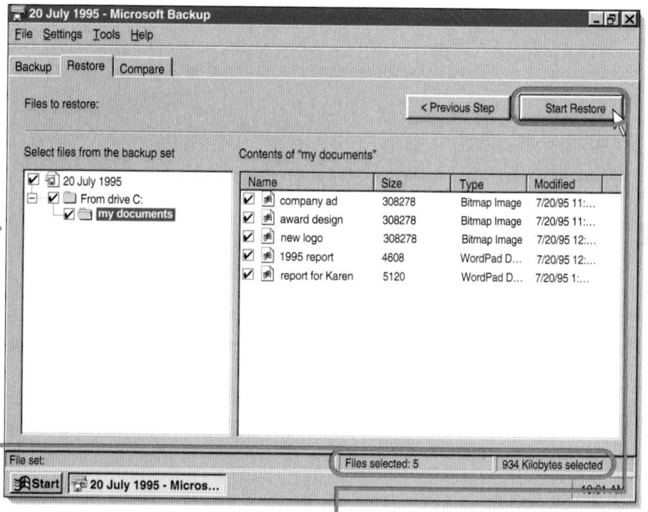

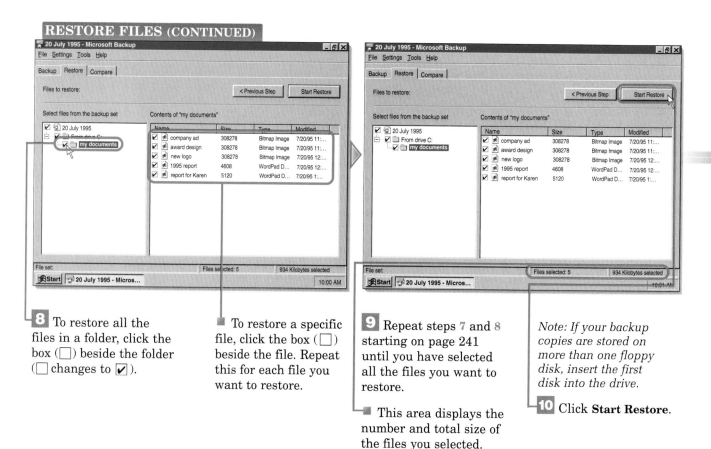

8 To restore all the files in a folder, click the box (☐) beside the folder (☐ changes to ☑).

■ To restore a specific file, click the box (☐) beside the file. Repeat this for each file you want to restore.

9 Repeat steps 7 and 8 starting on page 241 until you have selected all the files you want to restore.

■ This area displays the number and total size of the files you selected.

Note: If your backup copies are stored on more than one floppy disk, insert the first disk into the drive.

10 Click **Start Restore**.

TIP

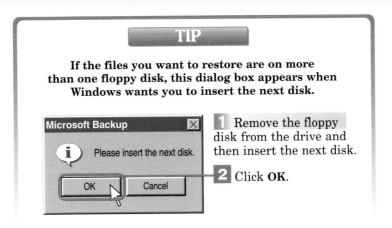

If the files you want to restore are on more than one floppy disk, this dialog box appears when Windows wants you to insert the next disk.

1 Remove the floppy disk from the drive and then insert the next disk.

2 Click **OK**.

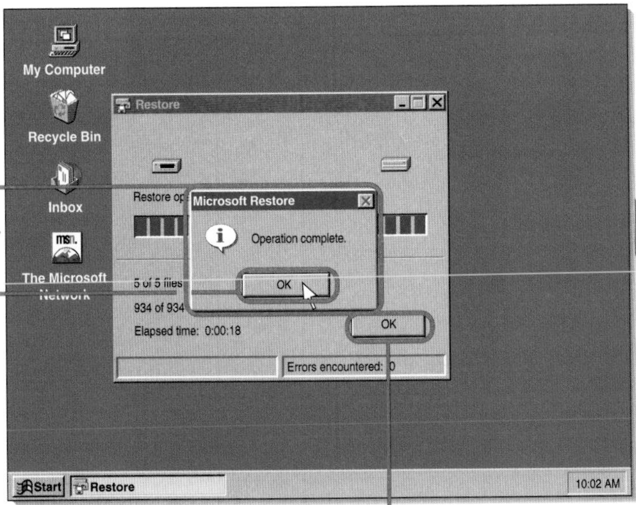

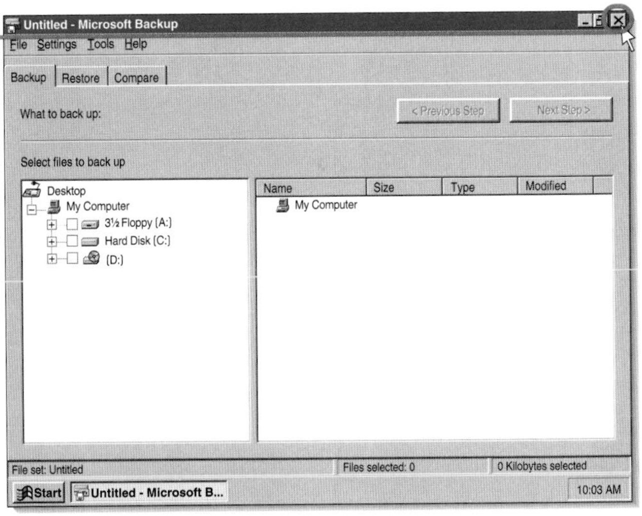

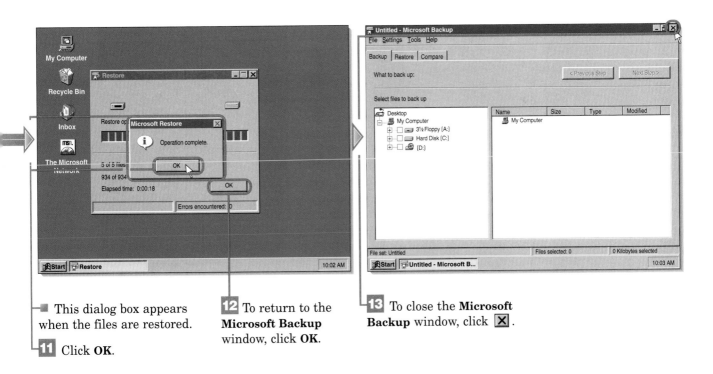

■ This dialog box appears when the files are restored.

11 Click **OK**.

12 To return to the **Microsoft Backup** window, click **OK**.

13 To close the **Microsoft Backup** window, click ☒.

In this chapter you will learn how to use The Microsoft Network to access information and communicate with people around the world.

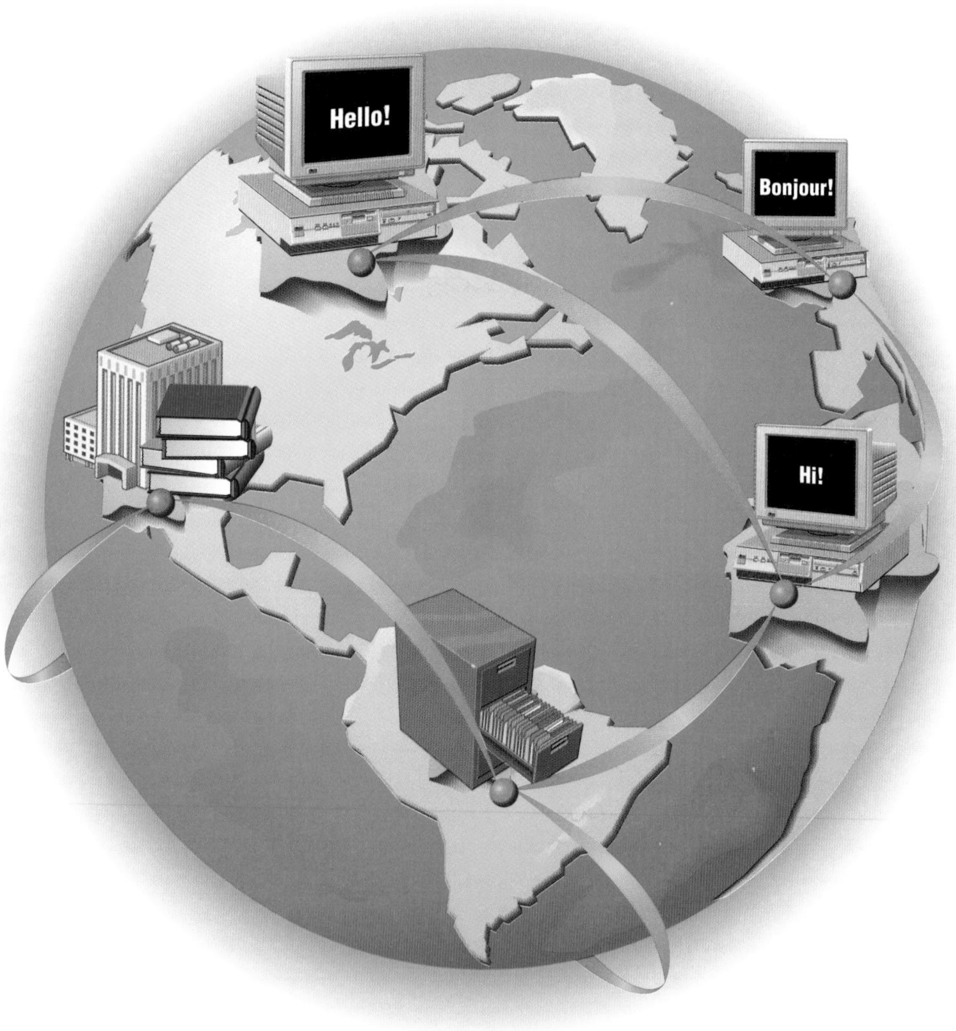

CHAPTER 15: THE MICROSOFT NETWORK

Introduction 246

Connect to The Microsoft Network 248

Browse Through Categories 250

Join a Chat Room 252

Display Bulletin Board Messages 254

Read Bulletin Board Messages 256

Reply to a Bulletin Board Message 258

Create a New Bulletin Board Message 260

Add an Item to Favorite Places 262

Sign Out of the MSN 263

INTRODUCTION

The Microsoft Network (MSN) provides a vast amount of information and allows you to communicate with people around the world.

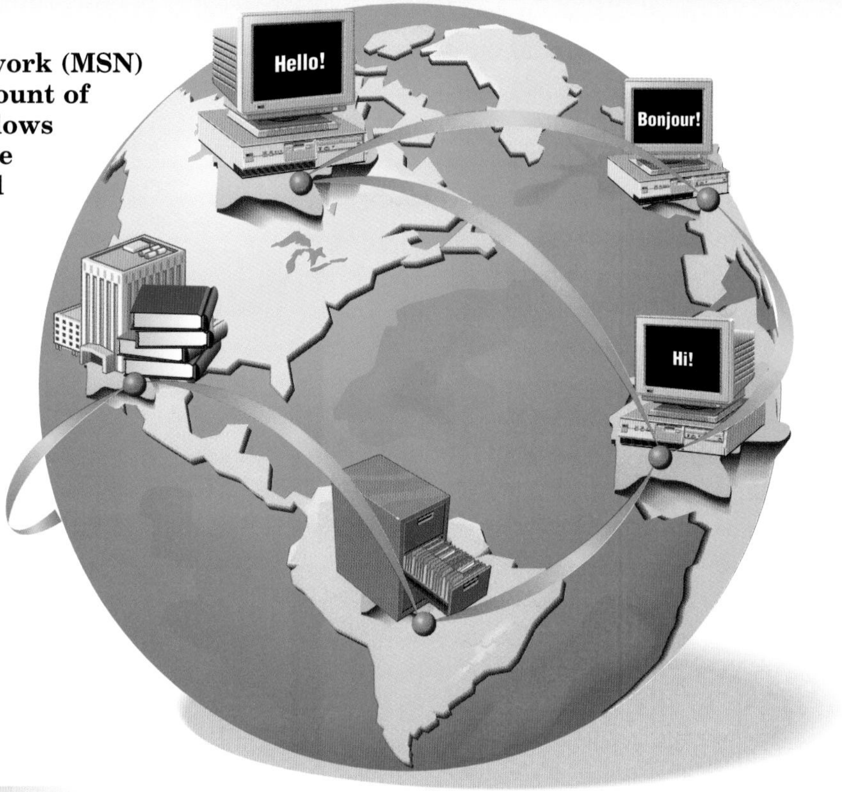

CHAT WITH OTHER MEMBERS

The Microsoft Network lets you have conversations with other members. You can observe ongoing conversations or make comments and ask questions other members will see immediately.

EXCHANGE ELECTRONIC MAIL

You can exchange private messages with millions of people around the world. This includes MSN members, members of other online services and anyone using the Internet.

USE BULLETIN BOARDS

You can read and post (send) messages on public bulletin boards. A bulletin board is an area where you can communicate with other MSN members with similar interests. Bulletin board topics include sports, education, science, business, entertainment, hobbies and much more.

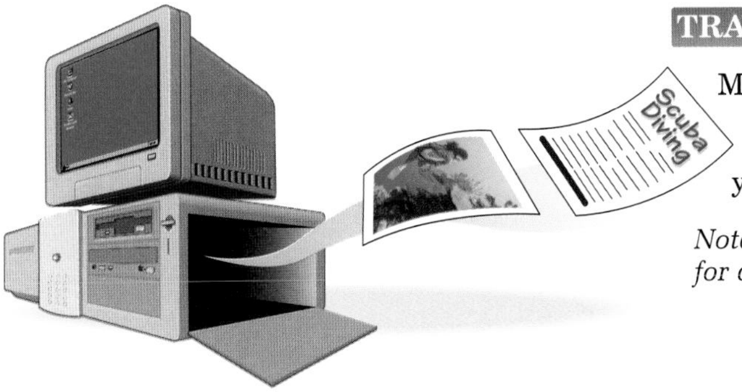

TRANSFER FILES

MSN provides useful files, such as documents, pictures and programs, that you can download (copy) to your computer.

Note: There may be a fee for copying some files.

USE THE INTERNET

You can exchange electronic messages with anyone connected to the Internet. You can also access thousands of newsgroups. Each newsgroup discusses a specific topic and allows people with common interests to communicate with each other. Windsurfing, politics, anthropology, religion, the environment, education and health are just a few of the newsgroup topics available.

Note: Newsgroups are similar to MSN bulletin boards, except they are available to everyone connected to the Internet.

CONNECT TO THE MICROSOFT NETWORK

You must connect to The Microsoft Network to use the services it provides.

CONNECT TO THE MICROSOFT NETWORK

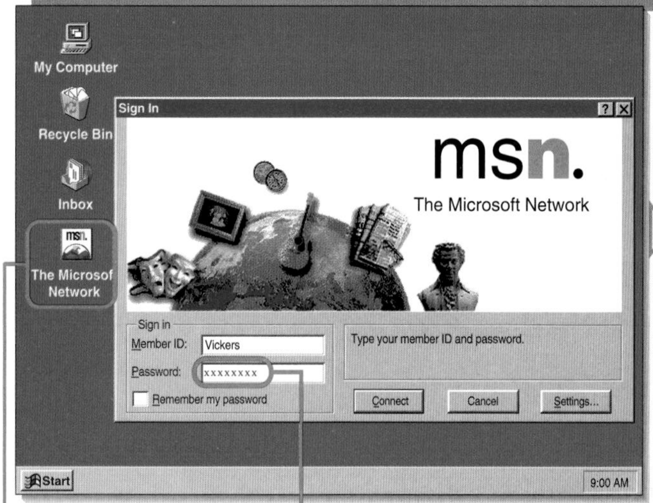

1 Double-click **The Microsoft Network**.

■ The **Sign In** dialog box appears.

2 To enter your password, click this area.

3 Type your password and then press **Enter** on your keyboard.

Note: A symbol (x) appears for each character you type.

■ The **MSN Today** window appears.

4 To close the window, click **☒**.

TIP

This dialog box appears if The Microsoft Network is not set up on your computer.

To set up The Microsoft Network, follow the instructions on your screen.

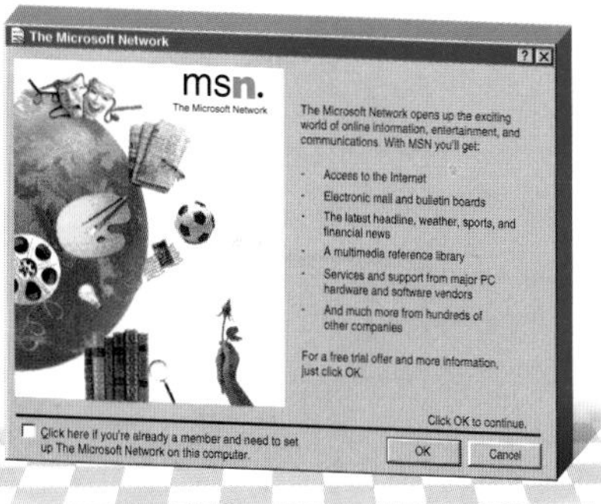

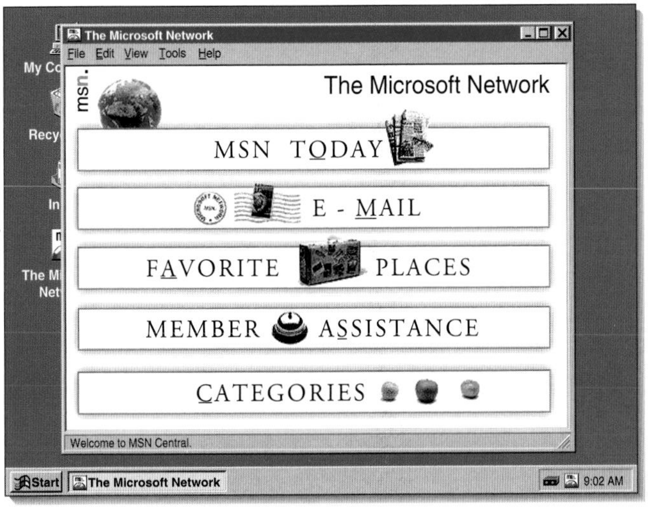

■ **The Microsoft Network** main window appears, displaying the five main areas on the network.

There are five main areas on The Microsoft Network.

MSN TODAY	Provides new information about The Microsoft Network.
E-MAIL	Lets you send and receive electronic mail.
FAVORITE PLACES	Lets you quickly access The Microsoft Network services you use most often.
MEMBER ASSISTANCE	Provides help to members of The Microsoft Network.
CATEGORIES	Lets you browse through the information on The Microsoft Network.

BROWSE THROUGH CATEGORIES

The Microsoft Network organizes information into categories. You can easily browse through the categories to find information of interest.

BROWSE THROUGH CATEGORIES

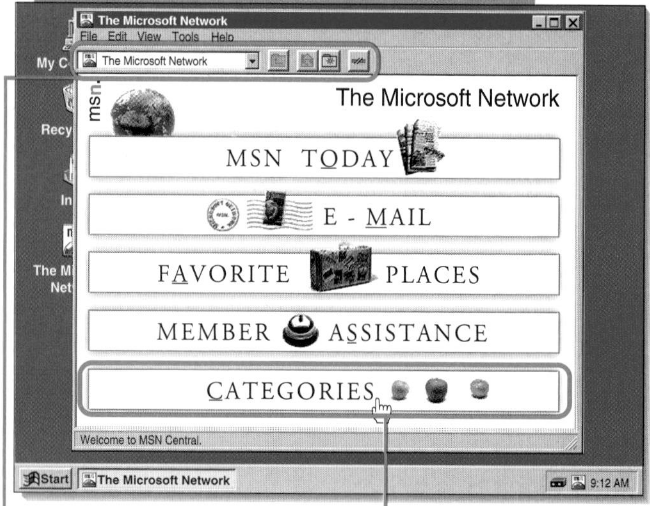

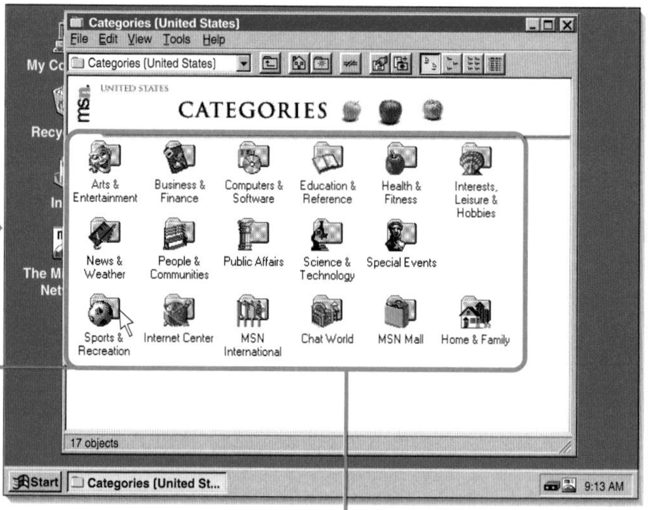

■ The toolbar displays buttons that let you quickly perform common tasks.

*Note: To display the toolbar, refer to the **Tip** on page 251.*

1 To display the main MSN categories, click **Categories**.

■ The main MSN categories appear.

2 To select a category of interest, double-click the category (example: **Sports & Recreation**).

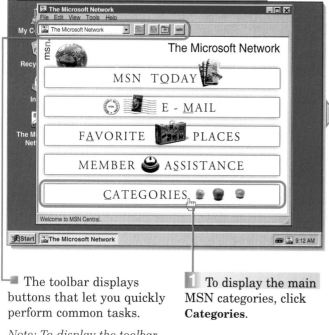

TIP

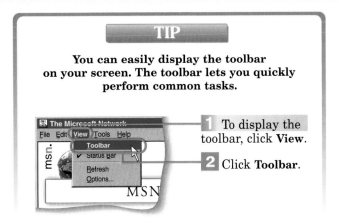

You can easily display the toolbar on your screen. The toolbar lets you quickly perform common tasks.

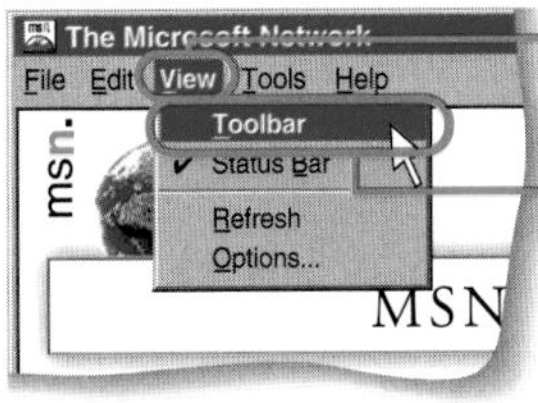

1 To display the toolbar, click **View**.

2 Click **Toolbar**.

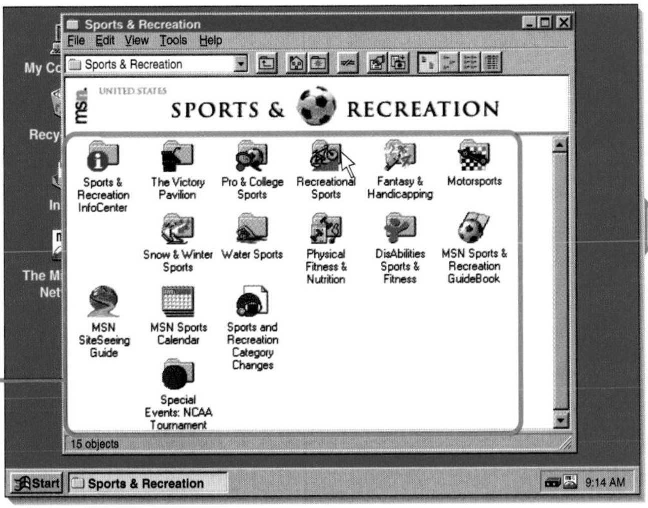

■ The topics in the category appear.

3 To select a topic of interest, double-click the topic (example: **Recreational Sports**).

Note: Topics displaying a folder ( ) contain subtopics.

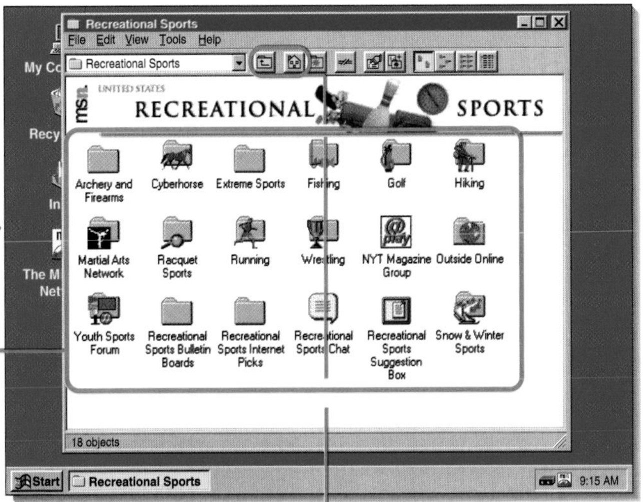

■ The subtopics of the topic appear.

4 Repeat step 3 until an item of interest appears.

■ To return to a previous window, click one of the following options.

- Returns to previous window.
- Returns to **The Microsoft Network** main window.

JOIN A CHAT ROOM

You can have conversations with other MSN members by simply typing back and forth.

JOIN A CHAT ROOM

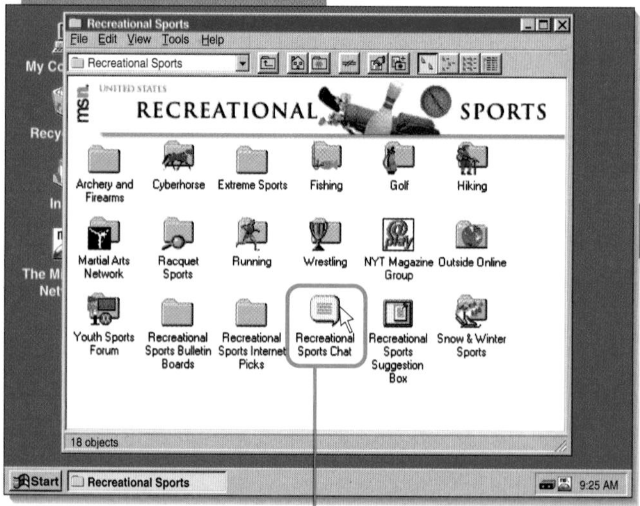

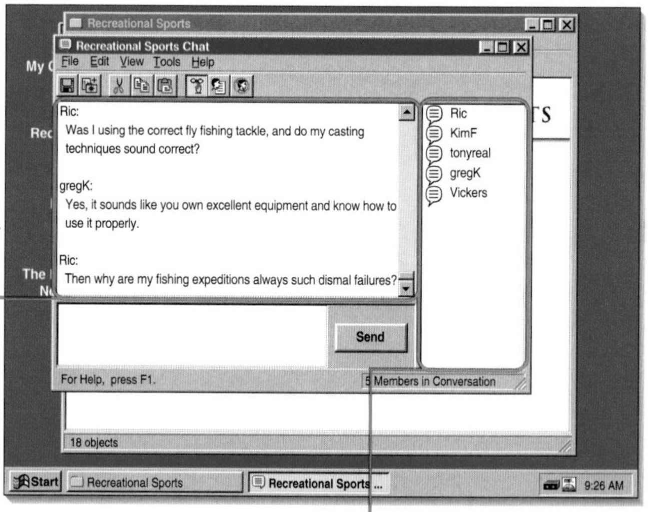

1 Browse through the categories until you find a chat room of interest.

Note: To browse through categories, refer to page 250.

■ A chat room usually displays a special symbol ( ) and has the word **Chat** in the title.

2 Double-click the chat room you want to join.

■ A chat window appears.

■ This area displays the current conversation.

■ This area displays all the participants in the conversation.

TIP

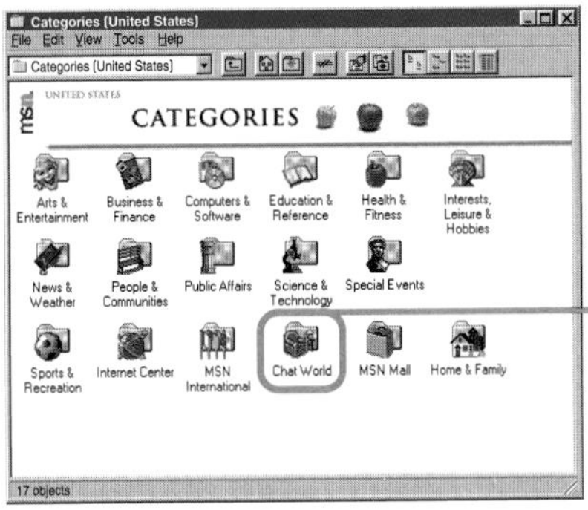

■ **Chat World** is a main MSN category devoted entirely to chatting.

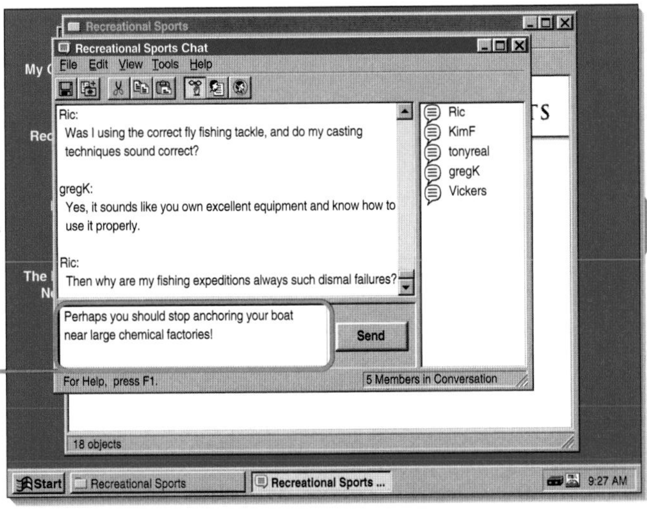

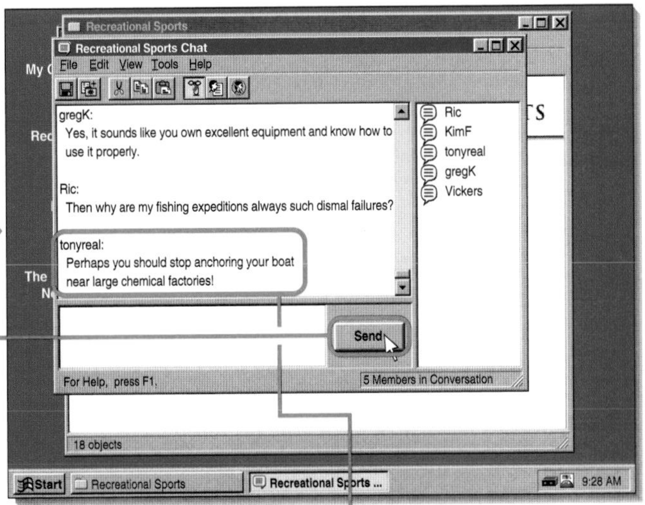

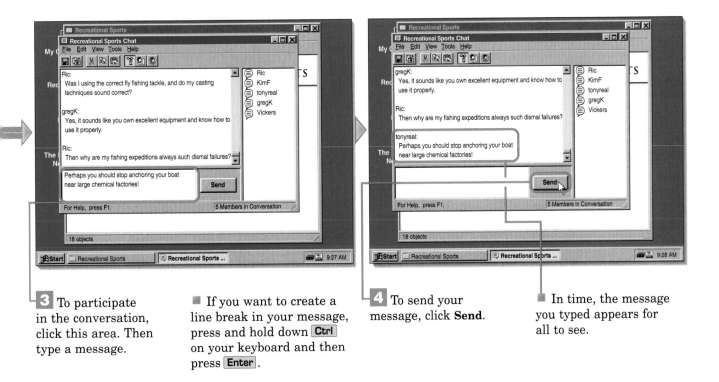

3 To participate in the conversation, click this area. Then type a message.

■ If you want to create a line break in your message, press and hold down **Ctrl** on your keyboard and then press **Enter**.

4 To send your message, click **Send**.

■ In time, the message you typed appears for all to see.

DISPLAY BULLETIN BOARD MESSAGES

The Microsoft Network offers hundreds of bulletin boards where people with similar interests exchange ideas, ask questions and share information.

DISPLAY BULLETIN BOARD MESSAGES

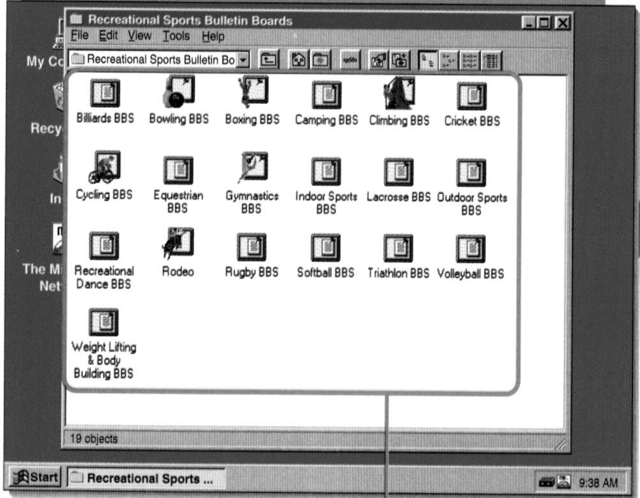

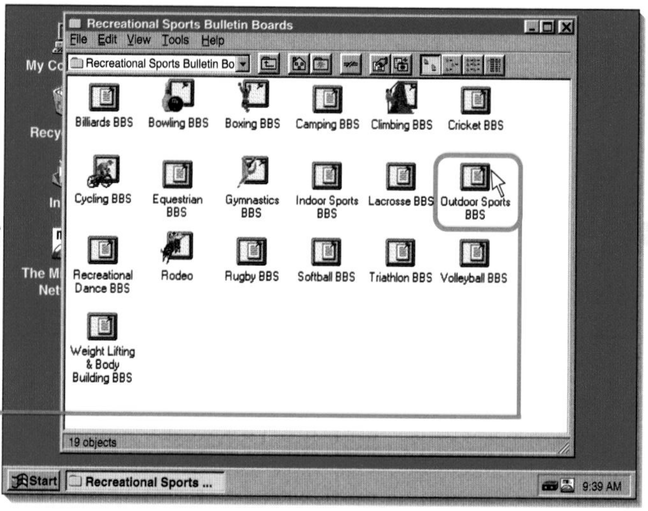

1 Browse through the categories until you find a bulletin board of interest.

Note: To browse through categories, refer to page 250.

■ A bulletin board usually displays a special symbol (📄) and has the letters **BBS** in the title.

2 Double-click the bulletin board of interest.

TIP

Here are some of the bulletin boards available on The Microsoft Network.

Arts & Crafts
Colleges and Universities
Jokes
Medicine
Mutual Funds
Outdoor Sports
Parenting in the 90's
Pets
Real Estate
Religion
Virtual Reality
Wine Guide

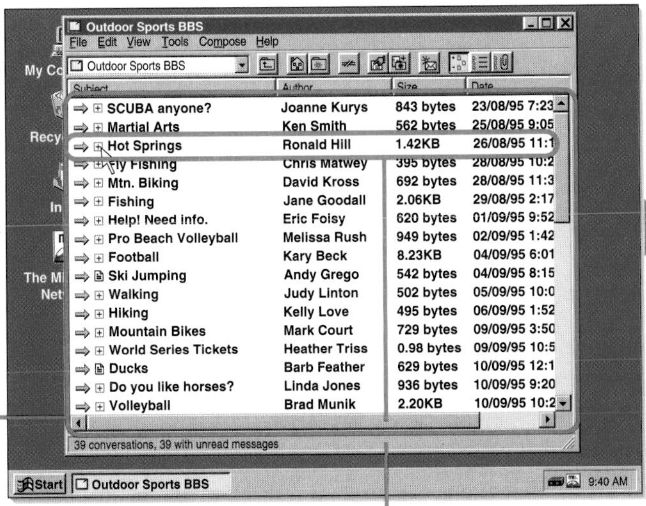

- A list of messages in the bulletin board appears.

- A message that has replies displays a plus sign (⊞). A message that has no replies displays a file symbol (🗎).

3 To view the replies to a message, click the plus sign (⊞) beside the message.

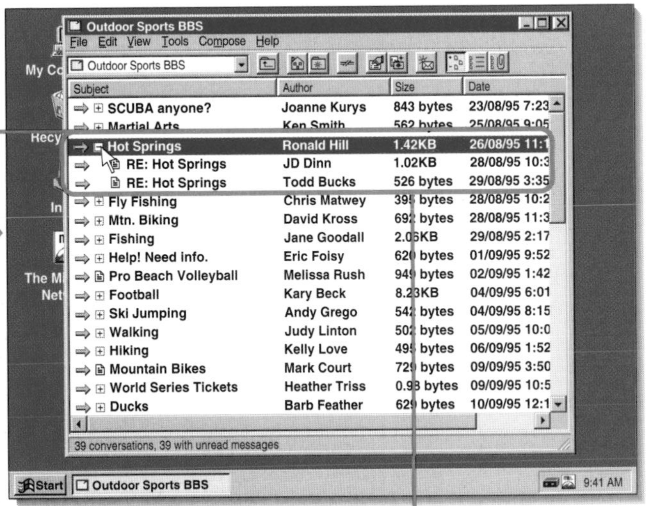

- The replies to the message appear. The replies are indented below the original message.

- The plus sign (⊞) changes to a minus sign (⊟) to indicate that the replies are now displayed.

- To once again hide the replies, click the minus sign (⊟).

Note: To read bulletin board messages, refer to page 256.

READ BULLETIN BOARD MESSAGES

You can read messages to learn the opinions and ideas of other MSN members.

READ BULLETIN BOARD MESSAGES

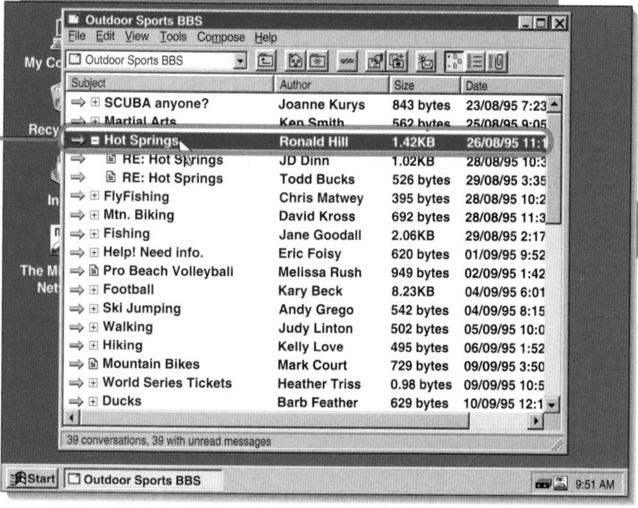

1 Double-click the message of interest.

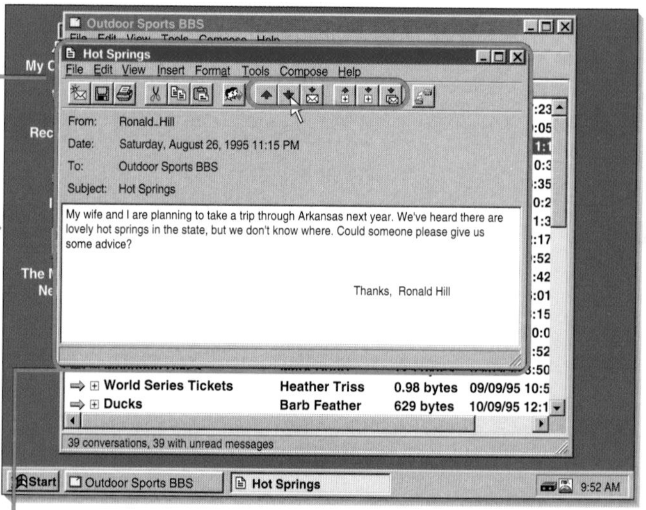

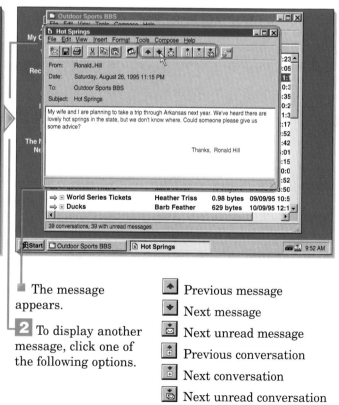

■ The message appears.

2 To display another message, click one of the following options.

- Previous message
- Next message
- Next unread message
- Previous conversation
- Next conversation
- Next unread conversation

TIP

The Microsoft Network organizes bulletin board messages into conversations.

A conversation is a series of messages on a particular subject. A conversation includes the original message and all replies to the message.

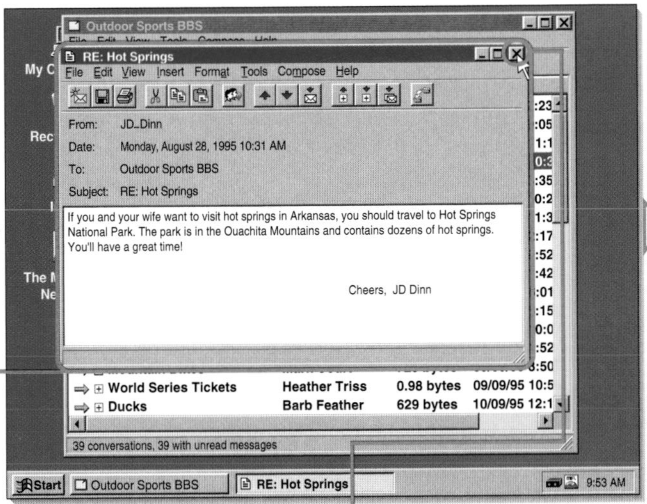

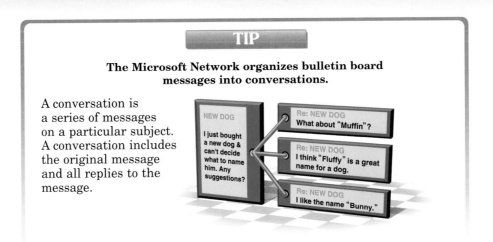

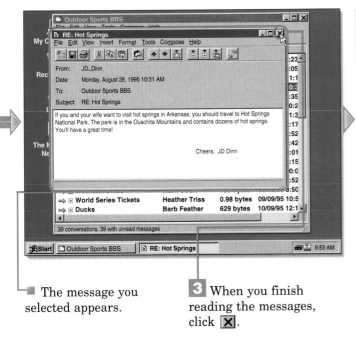

- The message you selected appears.

3 When you finish reading the messages, click ☒.

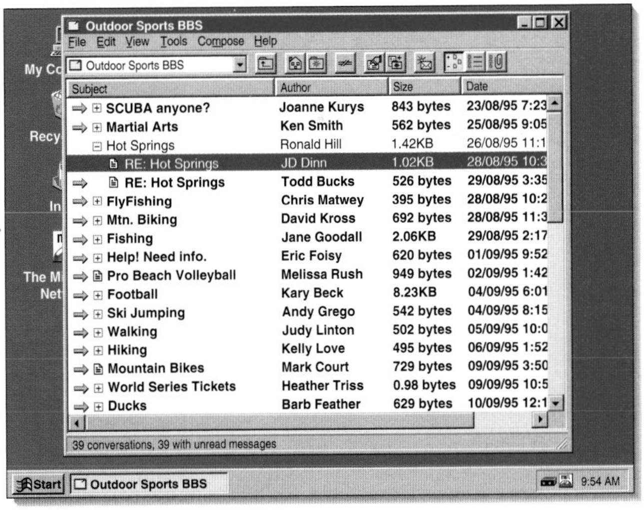

- Messages you have read appear in regular type. Messages you have not read appear in **bold type**.

REPLY TO A BULLETIN BOARD MESSAGE

You can reply to a message to answer a question, express an opinion or supply additional information.

REPLY TO A BULLETIN BOARD MESSAGE

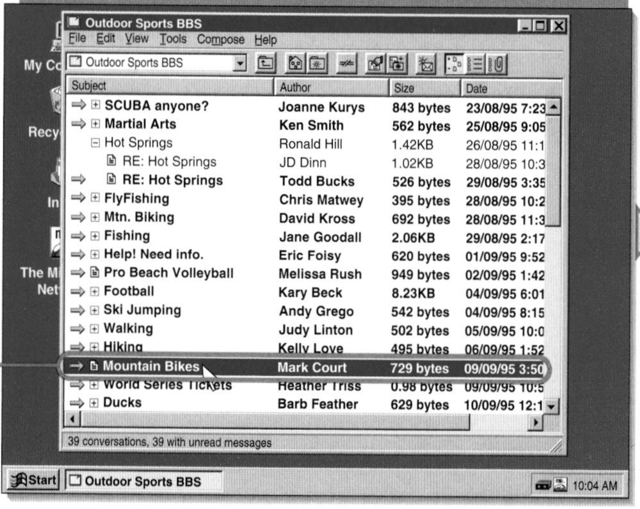

1 To open the message you want to reply to, double-click the message.

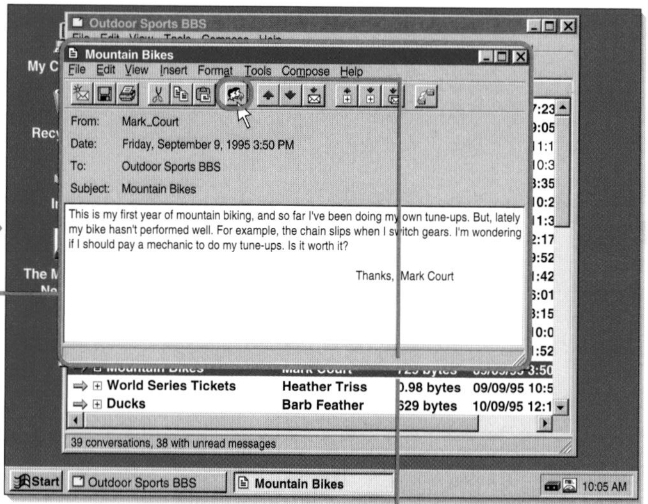

■ The message appears.

2 To reply to the message, click [icon].

TIP

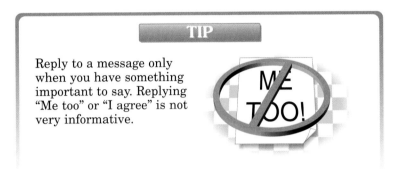

Reply to a message only when you have something important to say. Replying "Me too" or "I agree" is not very informative.

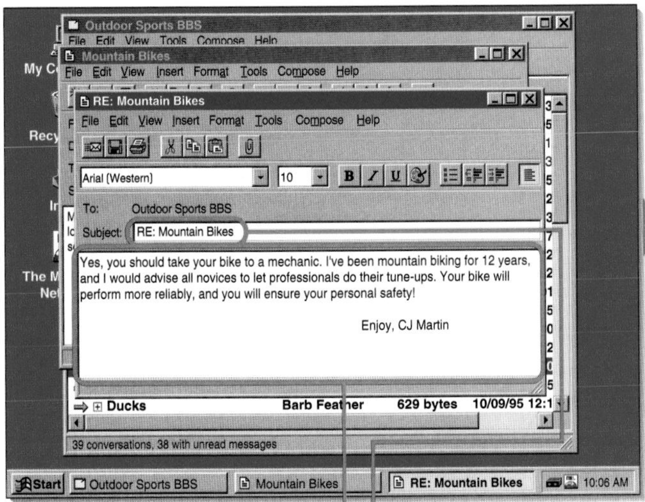

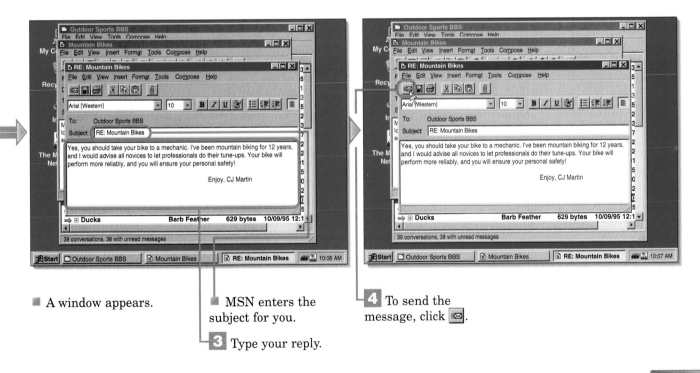

■ A window appears.

■ MSN enters the subject for you.

3 Type your reply.

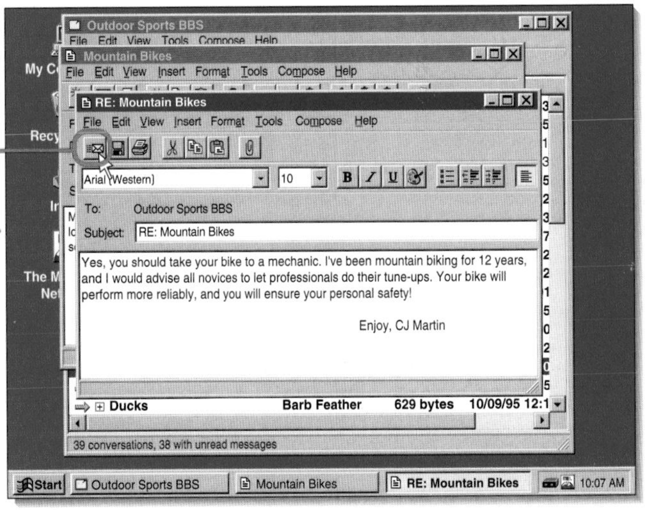

4 To send the message, click [send icon].

CREATE A NEW BULLETIN BOARD MESSAGE

You can create a new message to ask a question or express an opinion.

CREATE A NEW BULLETIN BOARD MESSAGE

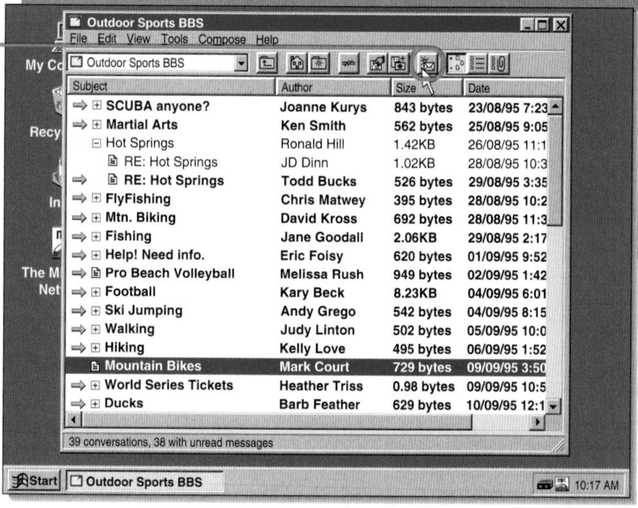

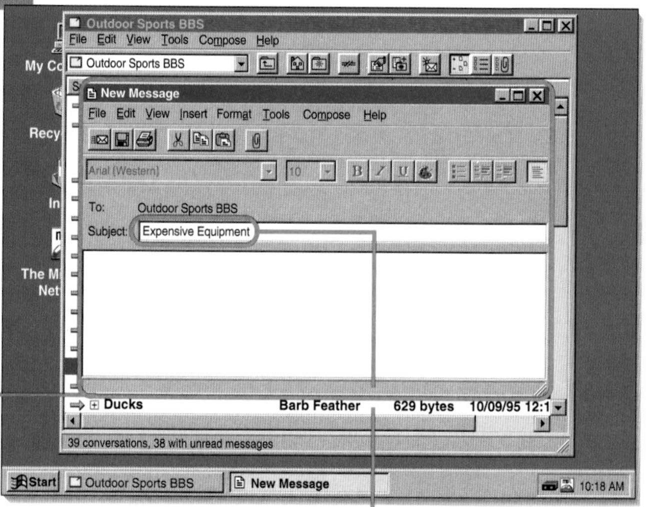

1 To create a new message, click .

*Note: If the New Message button ( ) is not available, refer to the **Tip** on page 251 to display the toolbar.*

■ A **New Message** window appears.

2 Type a subject for the message.

Note: Make sure your subject is descriptive and brief.

TIP

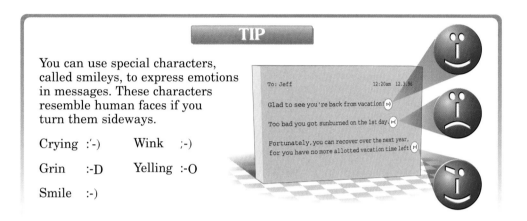

You can use special characters, called smileys, to express emotions in messages. These characters resemble human faces if you turn them sideways.

Crying	:'-)	Wink	;-)
Grin	:-D	Yelling	:-O
Smile	:-)		

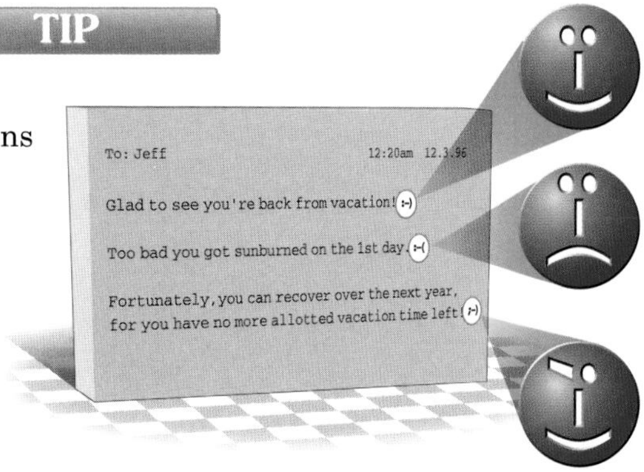

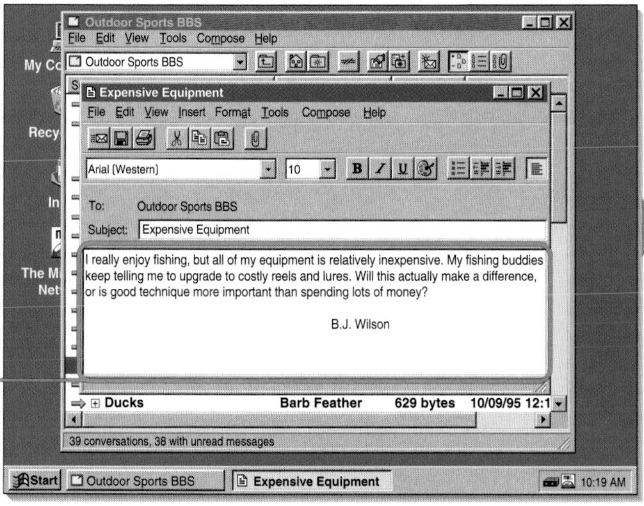

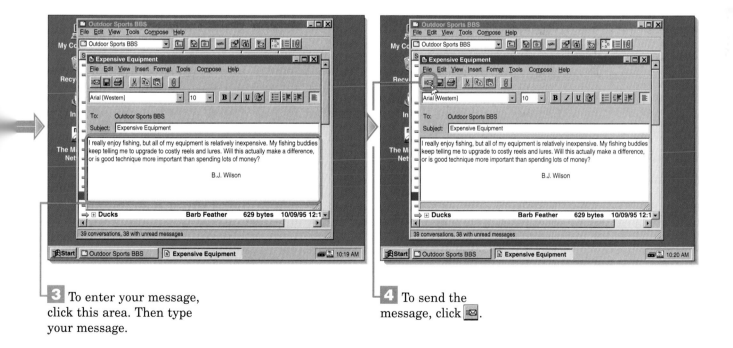

3 To enter your message, click this area. Then type your message.

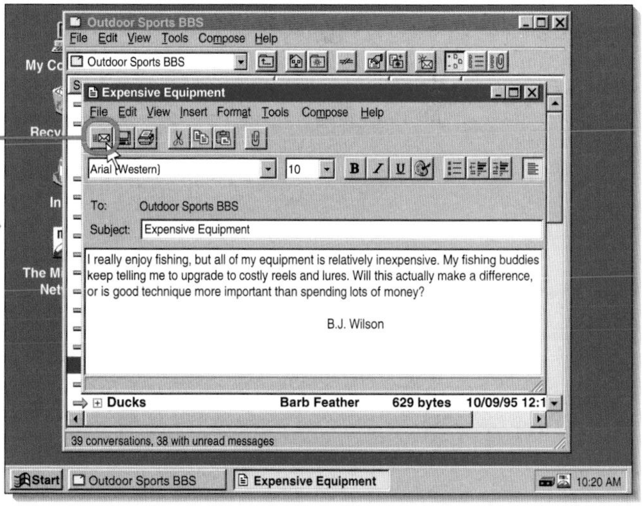

4 To send the message, click the Send button.

ADD AN ITEM TO FAVORITE PLACES

You can place all your favorite items in one location. This lets you quickly access information that interests you.

ADD AN ITEM TO FAVORITE PLACES

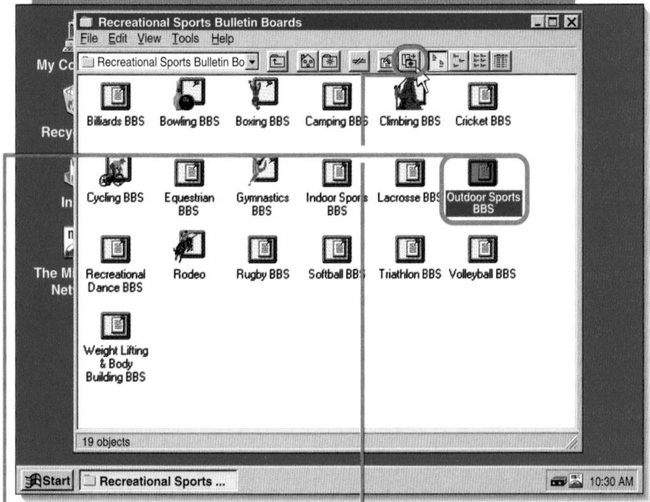

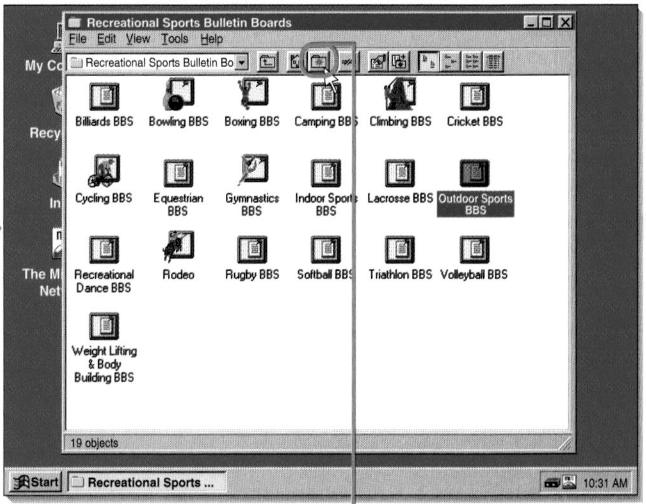

1 Click the item you want to add to **Favorite Places**.

2 To add the item, click .

*Note: If the Add to Favorite Places button ( ) is not available, refer to the **Tip** on page 251 to display the toolbar.*

You can display all your favorite places at any time.

1 Click .

SIGN OUT OF THE MSN

You should disconnect from The Microsoft Network when you no longer want to use the information and services it provides.

SIGN OUT OF THE MSN

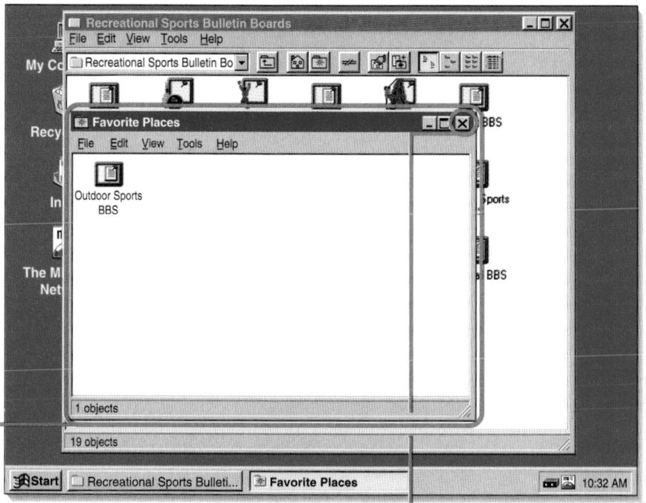

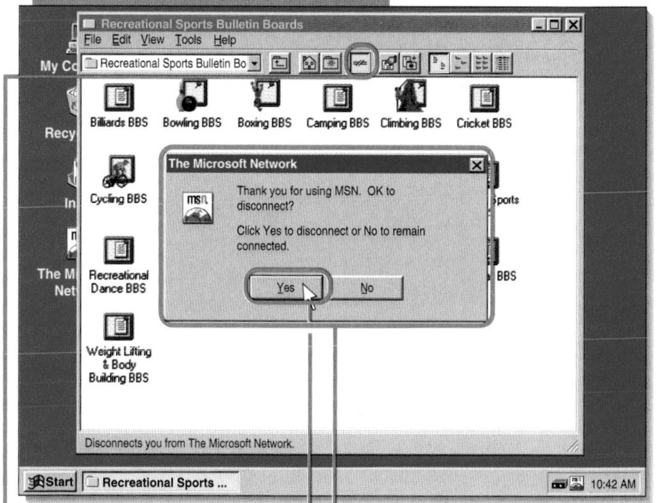

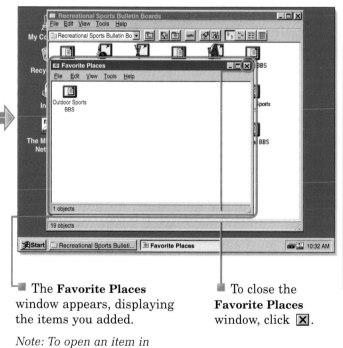

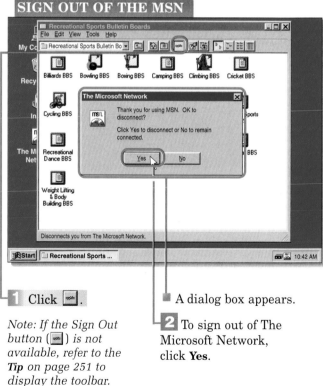

■ The **Favorite Places** window appears, displaying the items you added.

Note: To open an item in Favorite Places, double-click the item.

■ To close the **Favorite Places** window, click ☒.

1 Click ⊟.

Note: If the Sign Out button (⊟) is not available, refer to the ***Tip*** *on page 251 to display the toolbar.*

■ A dialog box appears.

2 To sign out of The Microsoft Network, click **Yes**.

In this chapter you will learn how to use Briefcase to work with files while you are away from the office.

CHAPTER 16: BRIEFCASE

Create a Briefcase .266

Work with Briefcase Files 270

Update Briefcase Files 272

CREATE A BRIEFCASE

Briefcase lets you work with files while you are away from the office. When you return, Briefcase will update all the files you changed.

CREATE A BRIEFCASE

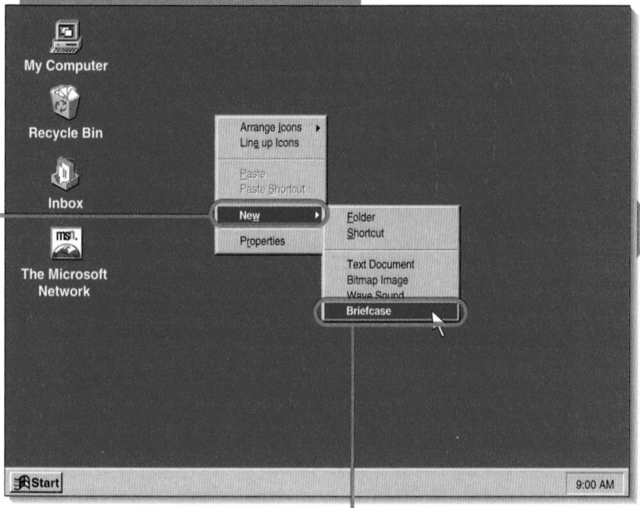

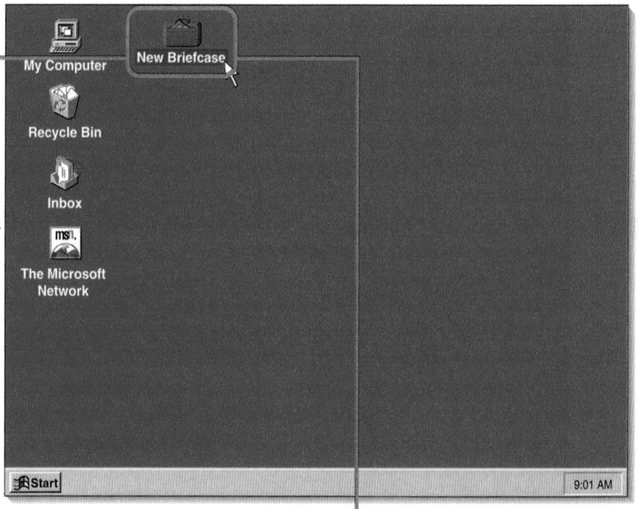

1 Click a blank area on your desktop using the **right** button. A menu appears.

2 Click **New**.

3 Click **Briefcase**.

*Note: If **Briefcase** is not available, you must add the Windows component, which is found in the Accessories category. To do so, refer to page 186.*

■ A briefcase appears.

Note: You can rename the briefcase as you would any file. To rename a file, refer to page 68.

4 To view the contents of the briefcase, double-click the briefcase.

TIP

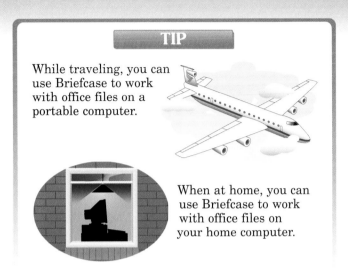

While traveling, you can use Briefcase to work with office files on a portable computer.

When at home, you can use Briefcase to work with office files on your home computer.

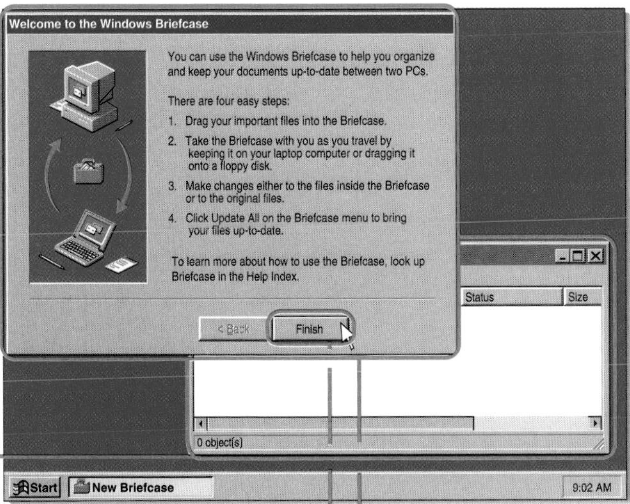

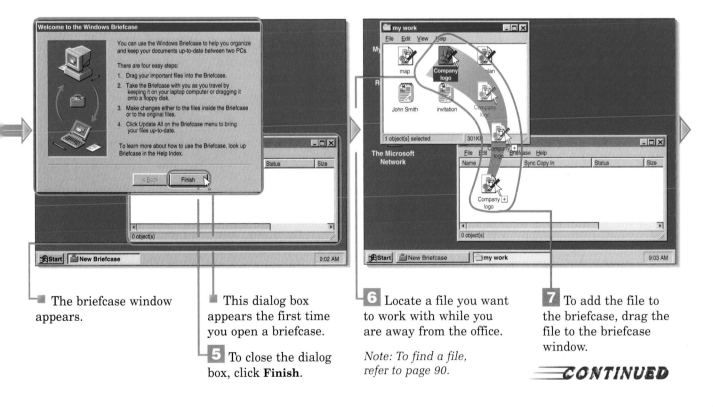

■ The briefcase window appears.

■ This dialog box appears the first time you open a briefcase.

5 To close the dialog box, click **Finish**.

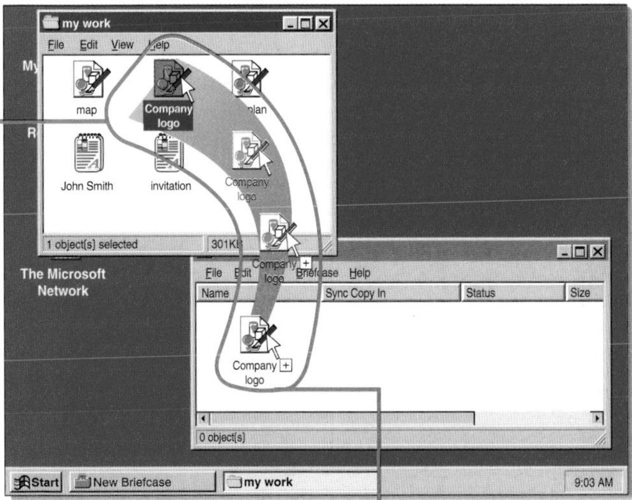

6 Locate a file you want to work with while you are away from the office.

Note: To find a file, refer to page 90.

7 To add the file to the briefcase, drag the file to the briefcase window.

CONTINUED

CREATE A BRIEFCASE

You can move a briefcase you created to a floppy disk. A floppy disk lets you transfer the briefcase files to your home or portable computer.

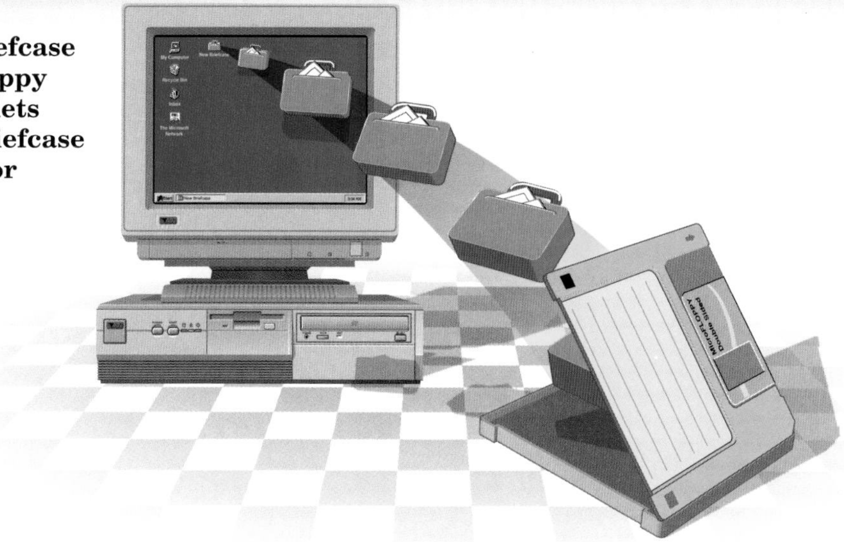

CREATE A BRIEFCASE (CONTINUED)

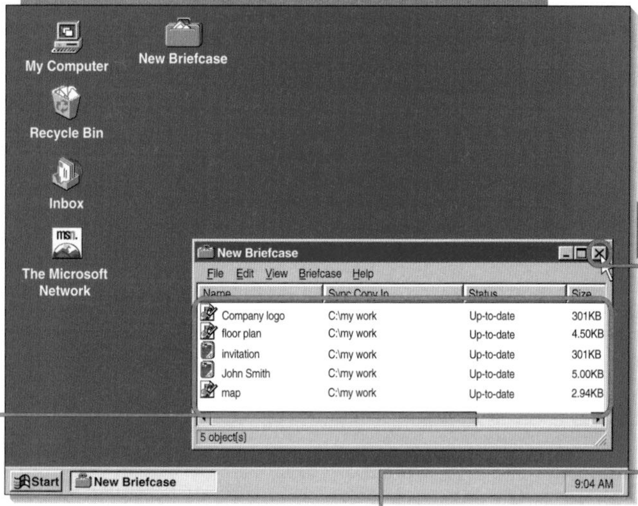

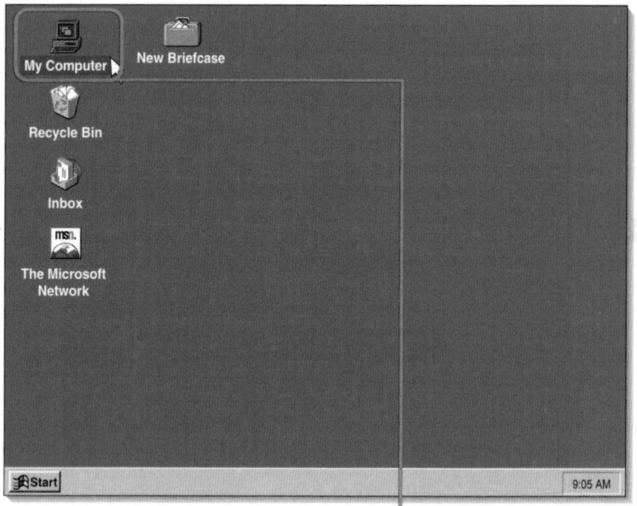

8 Repeat steps 6 and 7 on page 267 for each file you want to work with while you are away from the office.

9 To close the briefcase window, click ☒.

10 To place the briefcase on a floppy disk, insert a disk into a drive.

11 Double-click **My Computer**.

TIP

You can also use Direct Cable Connection to transfer office files to a briefcase on a portable computer. This is faster than using a floppy disk to transfer files and is ideal for transferring a large number of files.

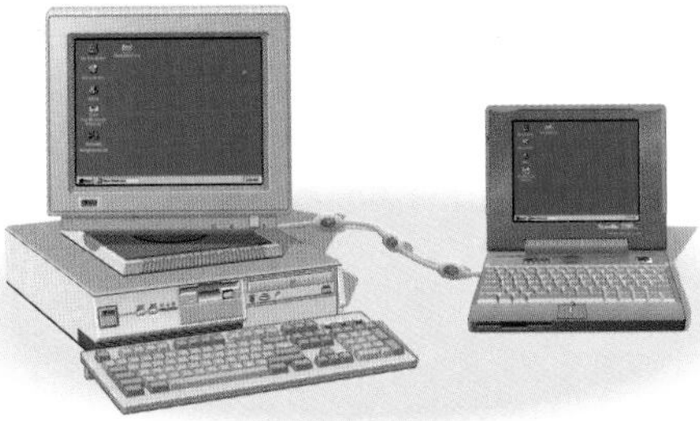

Note: For information on Direct Cable Connection, refer to the Direct Cable Connection chapter starting on page 310.

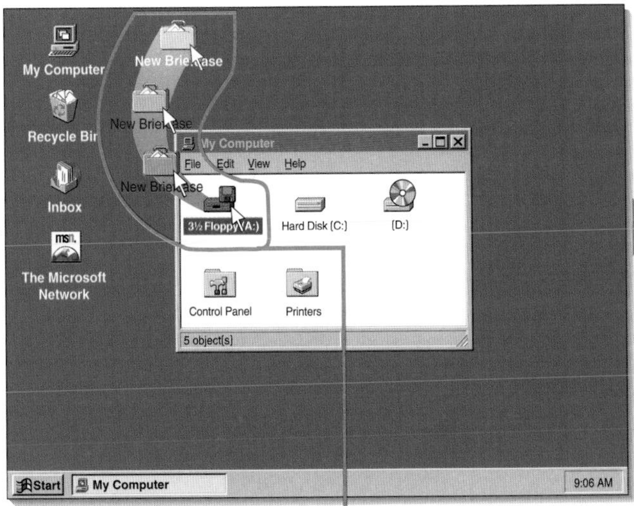

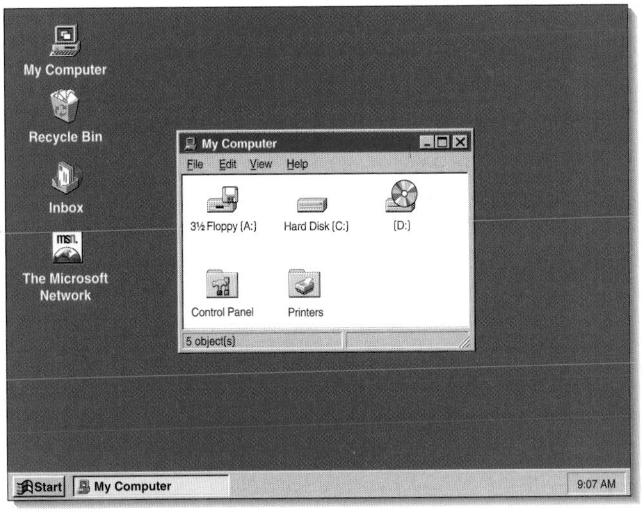

■ The **My Computer** window appears.

12 To place the briefcase on the floppy disk, drag the briefcase to the drive containing the disk.

■ The floppy disk now contains the briefcase.

■ The briefcase disappears from your screen.

13 Remove the floppy disk from the drive. You can now use the floppy disk to transfer the files to your home or portable computer.

Note: To work with briefcase files, refer to page 270.

WORK WITH BRIEFCASE FILES

When traveling or at home, you can work with briefcase files as you would any other files on your computer.

WORK WITH BRIEFCASE FILES

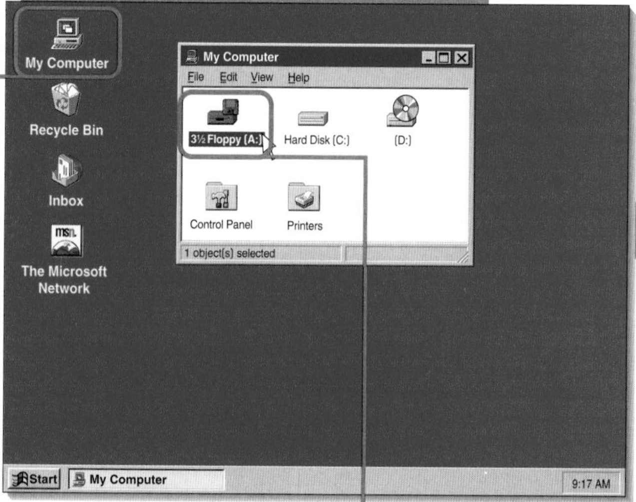

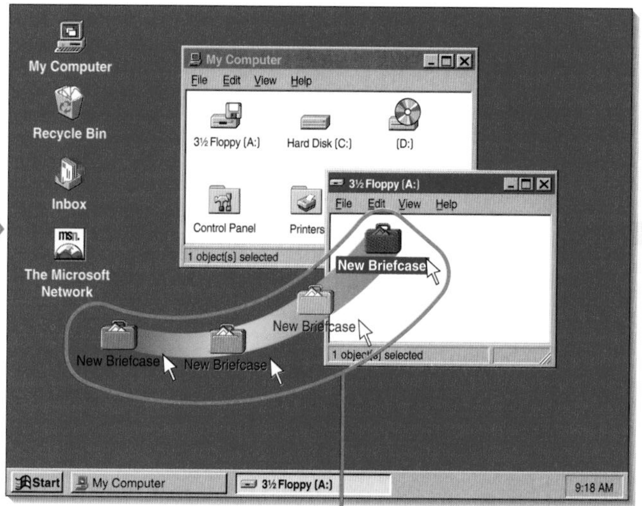

1 On your home or portable computer, insert the floppy disk containing the briefcase.

2 Double-click **My Computer**.

■ The **My Computer** window appears.

3 Double-click the drive containing the floppy disk.

■ The contents of the floppy disk appear.

4 To move the briefcase from the floppy disk to your desktop, drag the briefcase to a blank area on the desktop.

IMPORTANT

Do not rename the files in the briefcase or the original files on your office computer. If you do, Briefcase will not update the files.

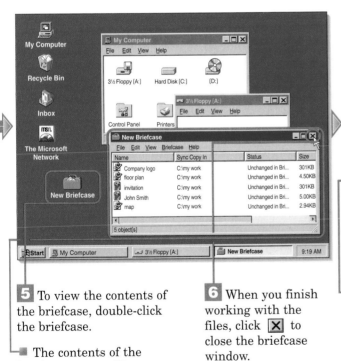

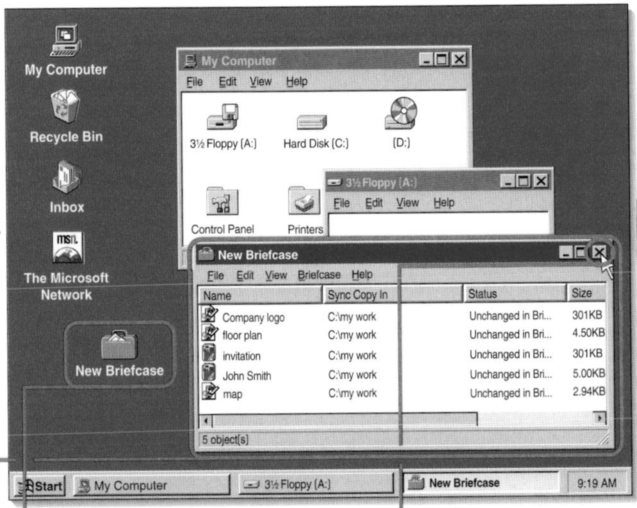

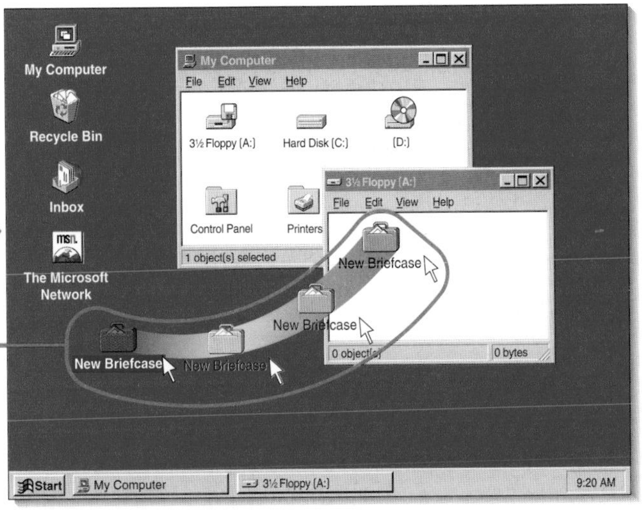

5 To view the contents of the briefcase, double-click the briefcase.

■ The contents of the briefcase appear. You can now work with files in the briefcase as you would any file.

6 When you finish working with the files, click ☒ to close the briefcase window.

7 To return the briefcase to the floppy disk, drag the briefcase to the floppy disk window.

8 Remove the floppy disk from the drive. You can now use the floppy disk to return the files to your office computer.

Note: To update the files you changed, refer to page 272.

UPDATE BRIEFCASE FILES

When you return to your office, you can quickly update the files you changed.

UPDATE BRIEFCASE FILES

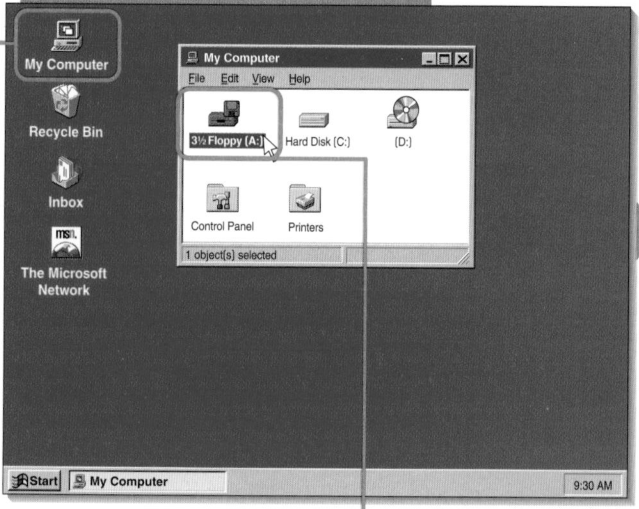

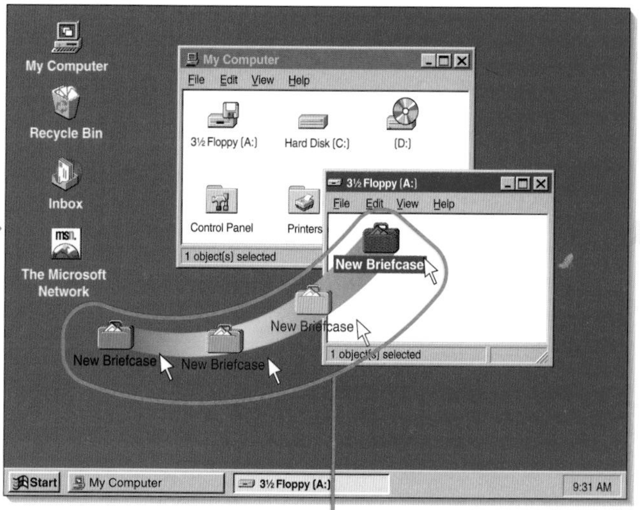

1 On your office computer, insert the floppy disk containing the briefcase.

2 Double-click **My Computer**.

■ The **My Computer** window appears.

3 Double-click the drive containing the floppy disk.

■ The contents of the floppy disk appear.

4 To move the briefcase from the floppy disk to your desktop, drag the briefcase to a blank area on the desktop.

TIP

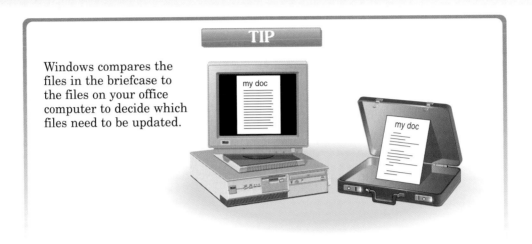

Windows compares the files in the briefcase to the files on your office computer to decide which files need to be updated.

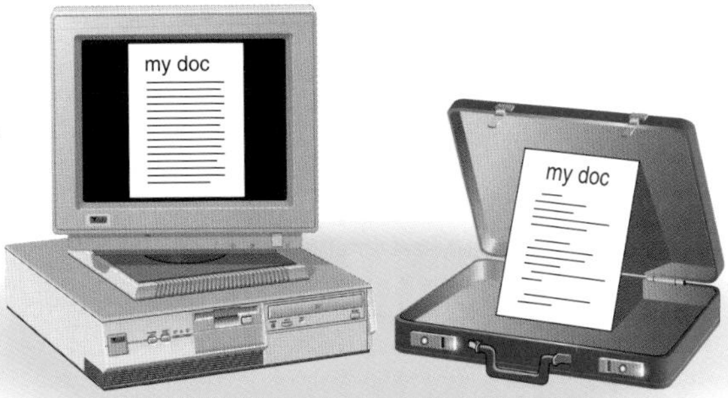

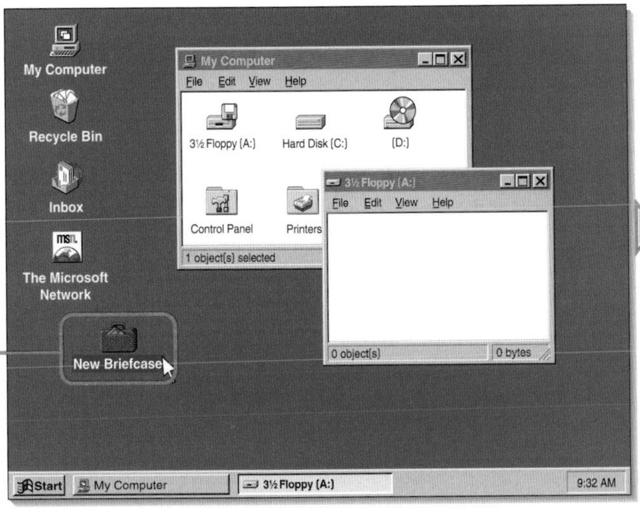

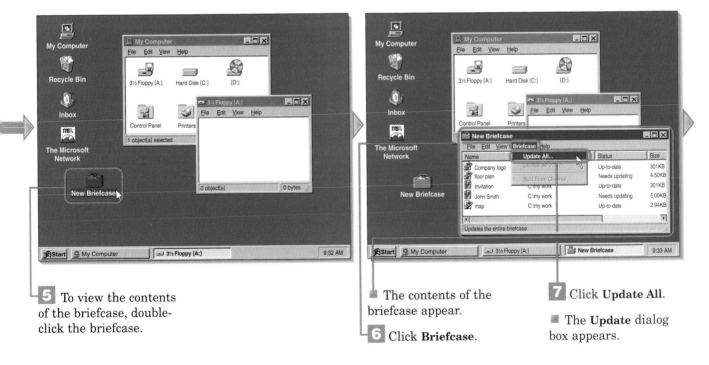

5 To view the contents of the briefcase, double-click the briefcase.

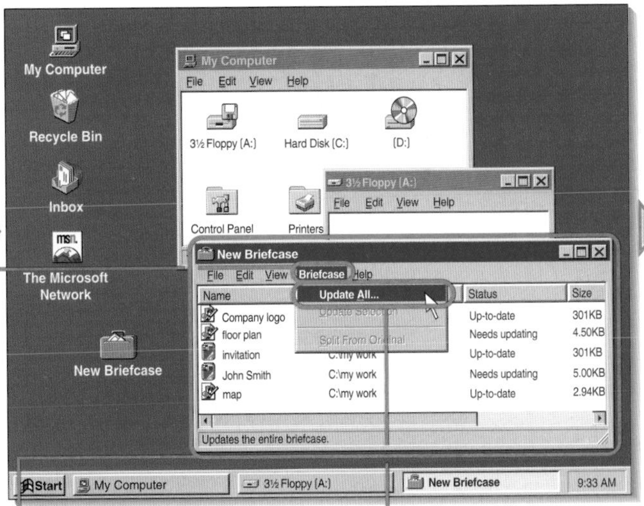

■ The contents of the briefcase appear.

6 Click **Briefcase**.

7 Click **Update All**.

■ The **Update** dialog box appears.

CONTINUED

UPDATE BRIEFCASE FILES

Windows tells you exactly which files need to be updated.

UPDATE BRIEFCASE FILES (CONTINUED)

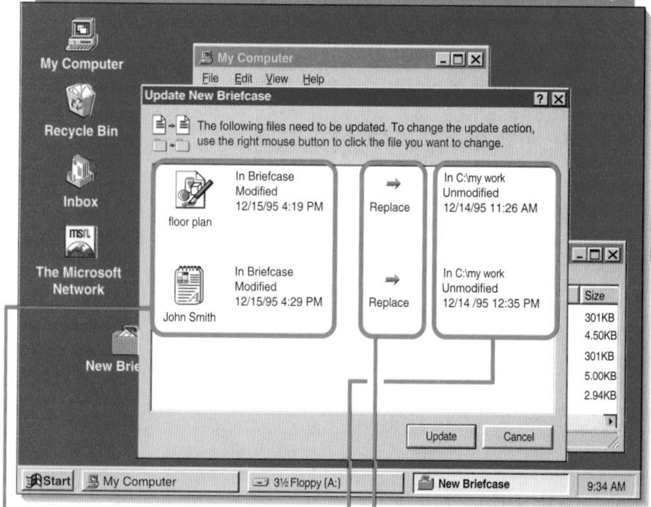

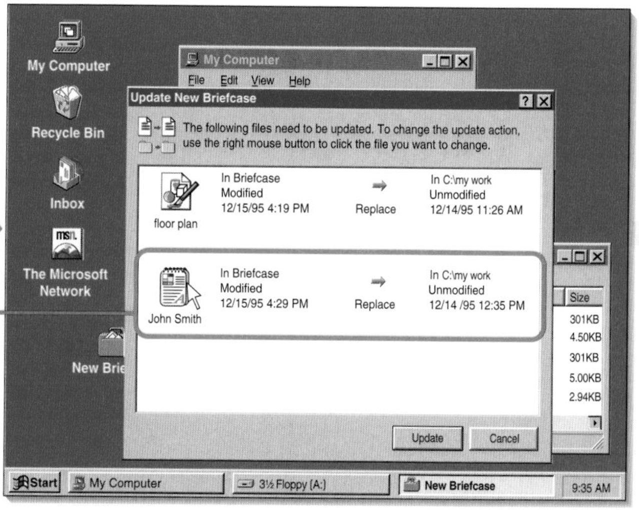

- This area displays the name of each file that needs to be updated.

- This area displays the way Windows will update each file.

- This area displays the status of each file on the office computer.

8 To change the way Windows will update a file, click the file using the **right** button. A menu appears.

TIP

You can create a new briefcase every time you want to work away from the office.

Delete an old briefcase as you would delete any file.

Note: Deleting a briefcase does not remove the original files from your computer.

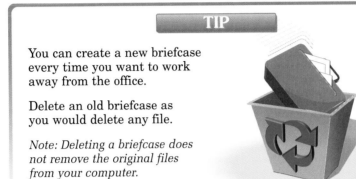

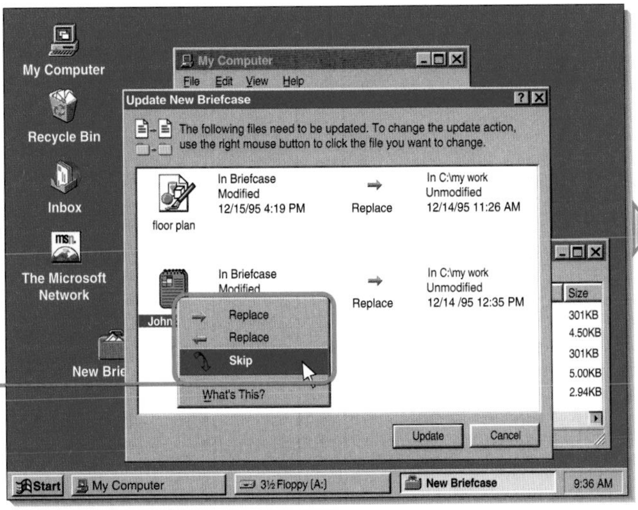

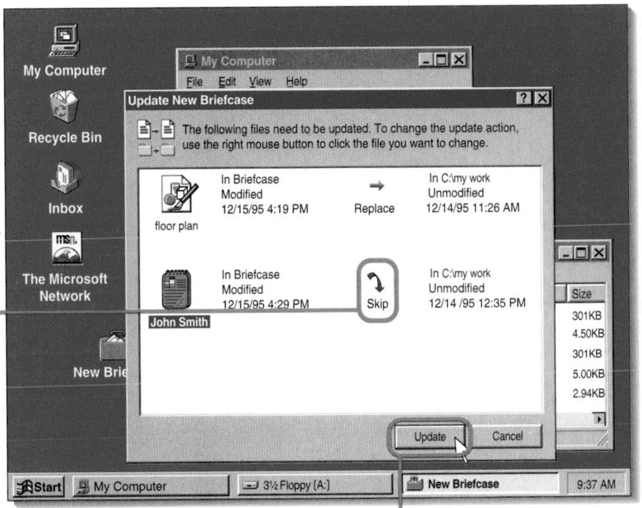

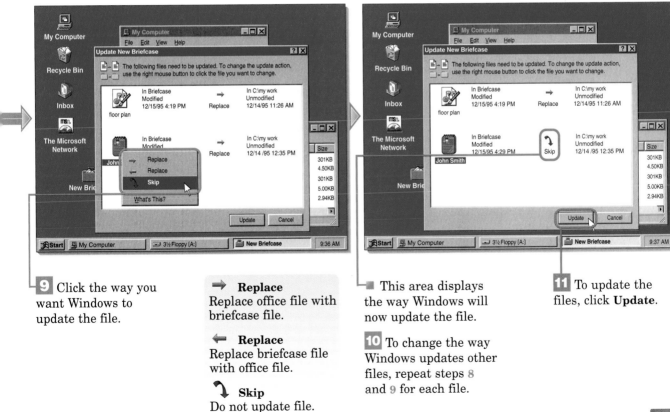

9 Click the way you want Windows to update the file.

→ **Replace**
Replace office file with briefcase file.

← **Replace**
Replace briefcase file with office file.

Skip
Do not update file.

■ This area displays the way Windows will now update the file.

10 To change the way Windows updates other files, repeat steps 8 and 9 for each file.

11 To update the files, click **Update**.

In this chapter you will learn how to use a network to share information and equipment.

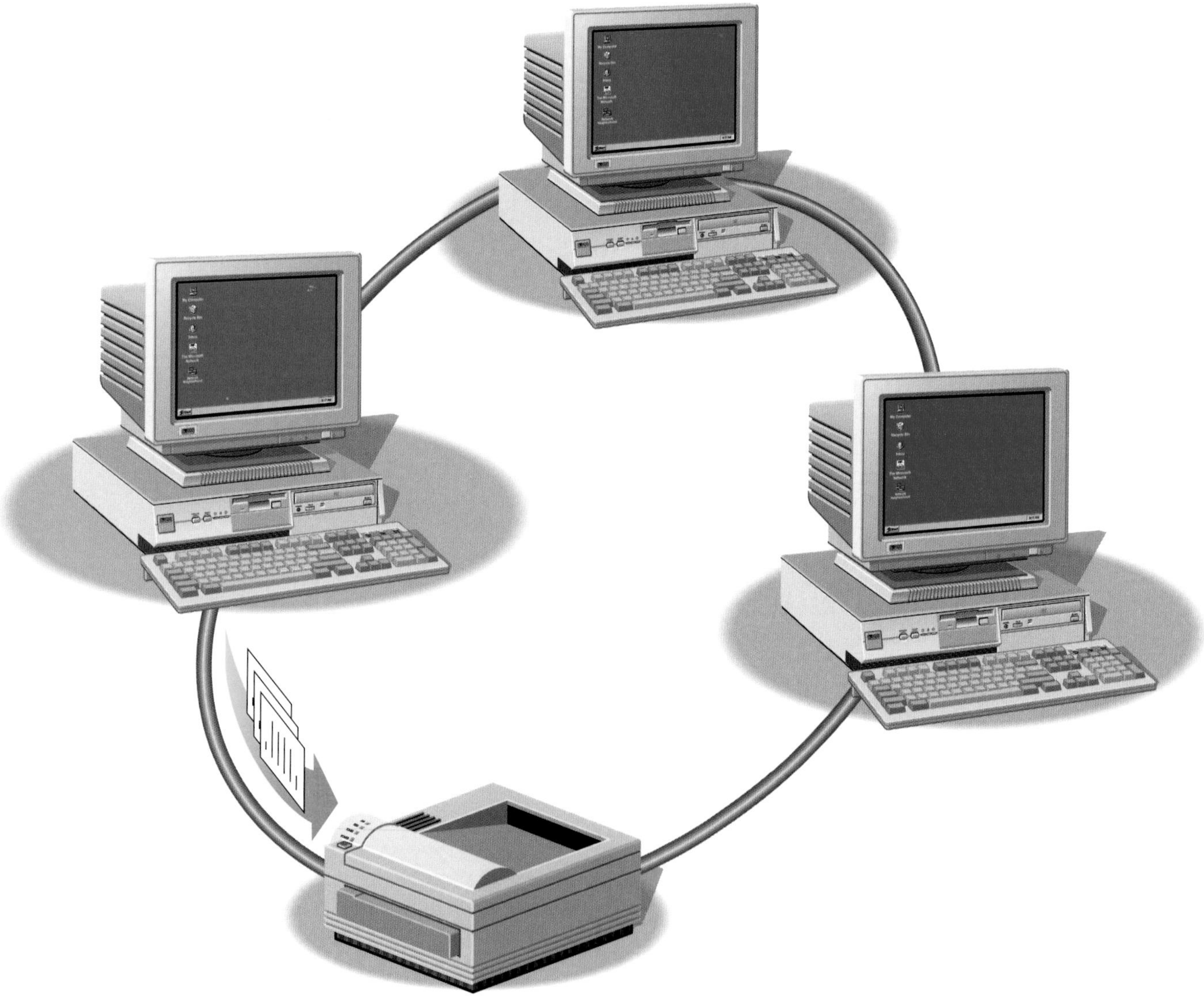

CHAPTER 17: NETWORKS

Introduction to Networks 278

Turn on Sharing 279

Name Your Computer 282

Share Information .284

Share a Printer 288

Set the Default Printer 290

Browse Through a Network 292

Find a Computer 294

INTRODUCTION TO NETWORKS

A network is a group of connected computers that allow people to share information and equipment.

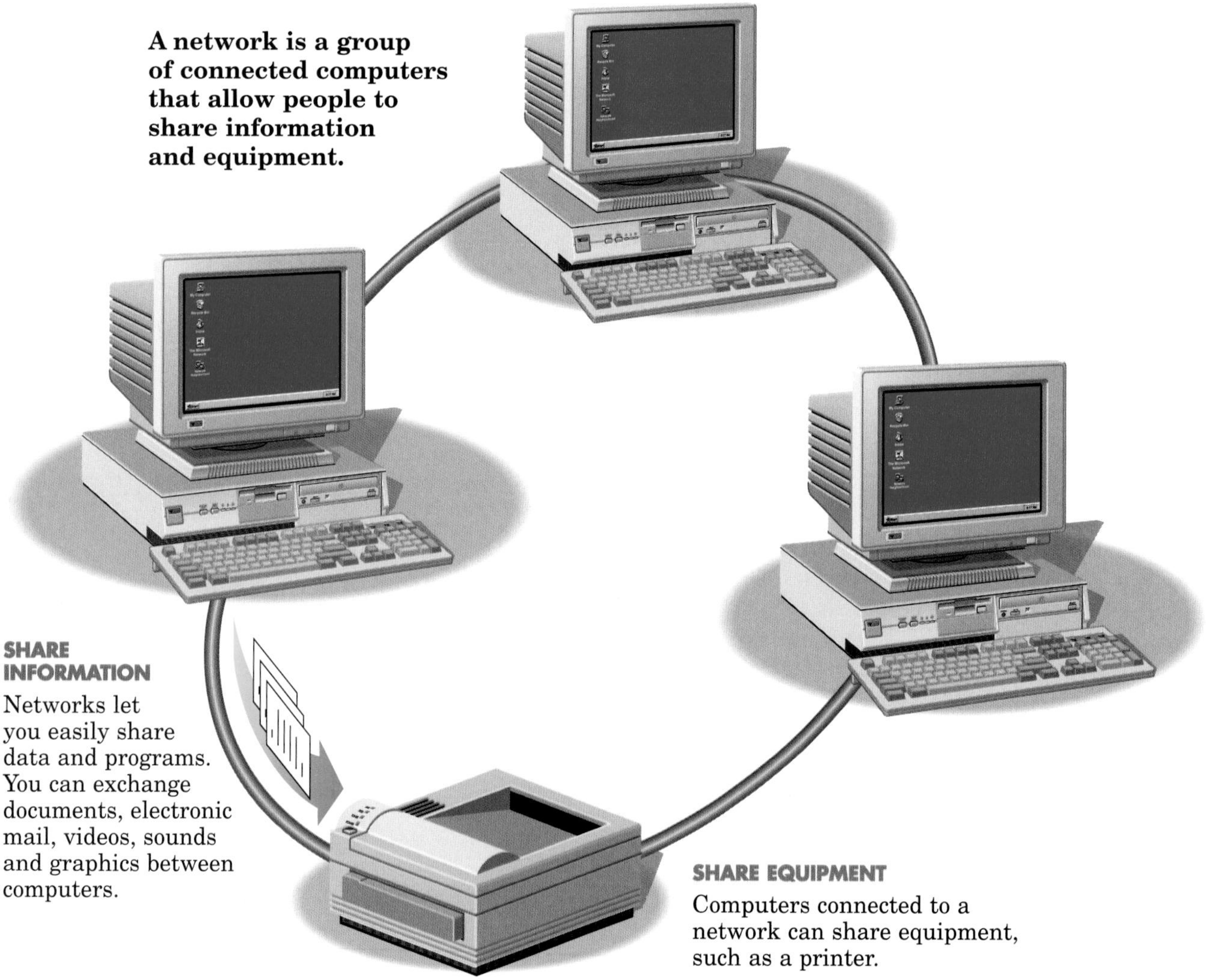

SHARE INFORMATION

Networks let you easily share data and programs. You can exchange documents, electronic mail, videos, sounds and graphics between computers.

SHARE EQUIPMENT

Computers connected to a network can share equipment, such as a printer.

TURN ON SHARING

Before you can share information or a printer with individuals on a network, you must set up your computer to share resources.

TURN ON SHARING

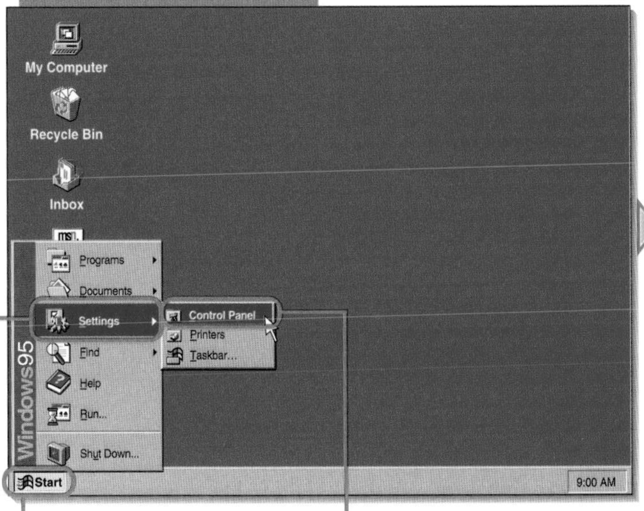

1 Click **Start**.

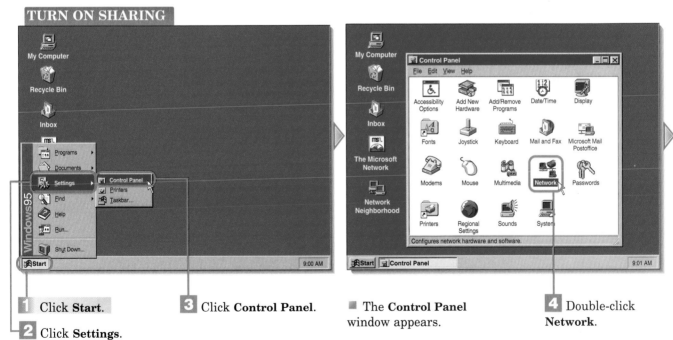

2 Click **Settings**.

3 Click **Control Panel**.

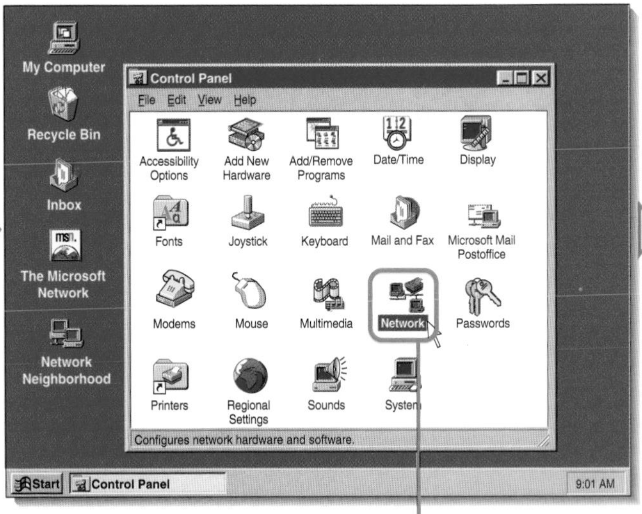

■ The **Control Panel** window appears.

4 Double-click **Network**.

CONTINUED

TURN ON SHARING

You can choose to give individuals on a network access to your files and/or printer.

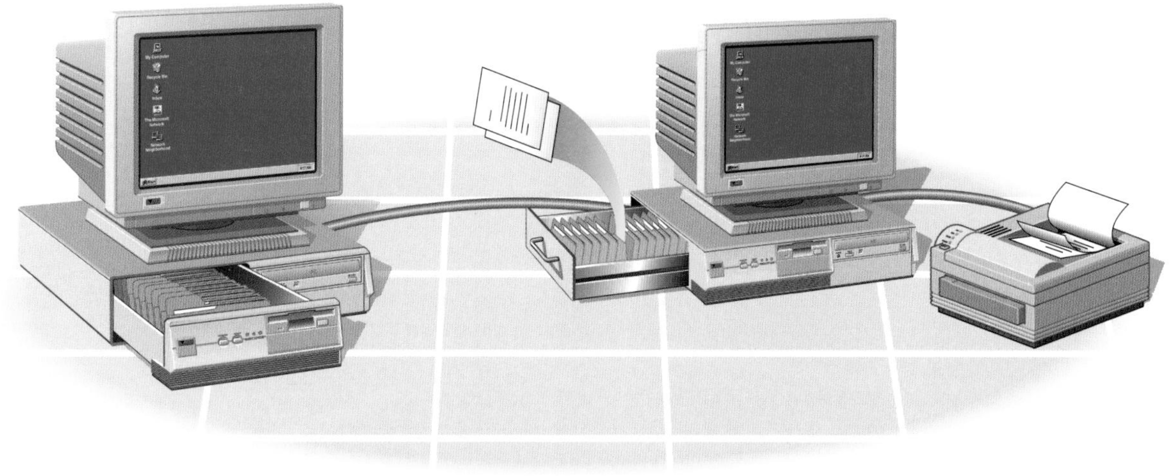

TURN ON SHARING (CONTINUED)

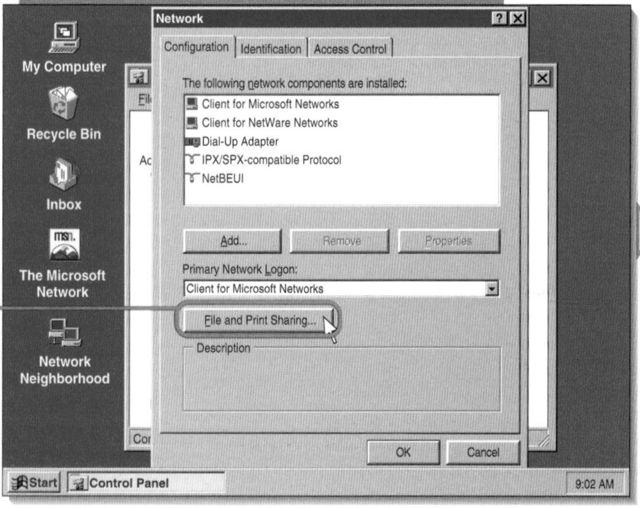

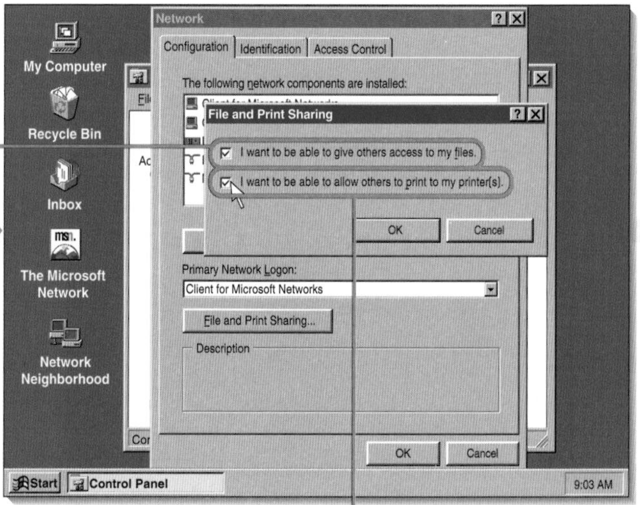

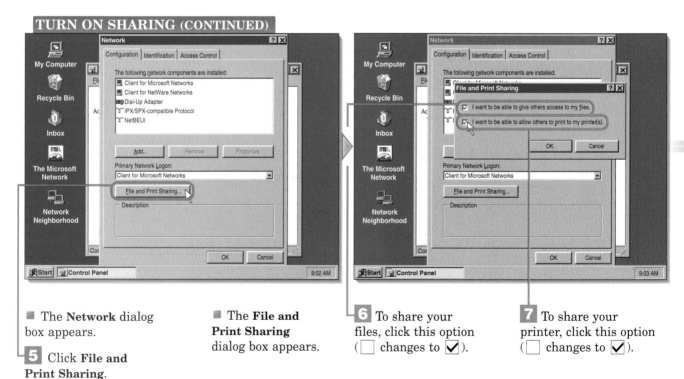

■ The **Network** dialog box appears.

5 Click **File and Print Sharing**.

■ The **File and Print Sharing** dialog box appears.

6 To share your files, click this option (☐ changes to ☑).

7 To share your printer, click this option (☐ changes to ☑).

TIP

Once you set up your computer to share information and/or a printer, you must specify exactly what you want to share.

- To specify the information you want to share, refer to page 284.
- To specify the printer you want to share, refer to page 288.

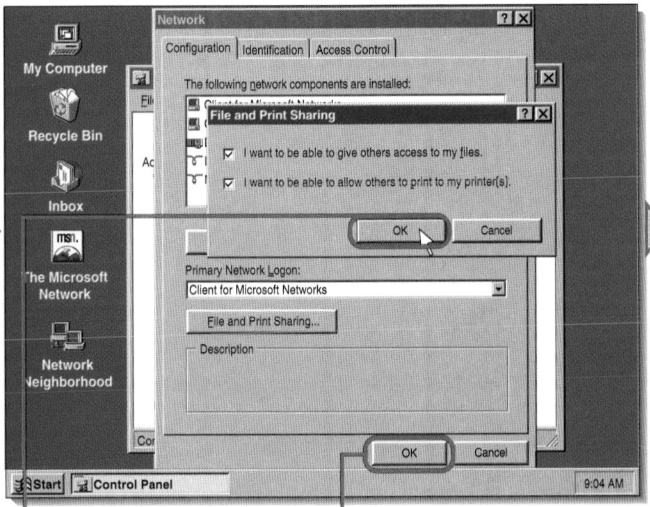

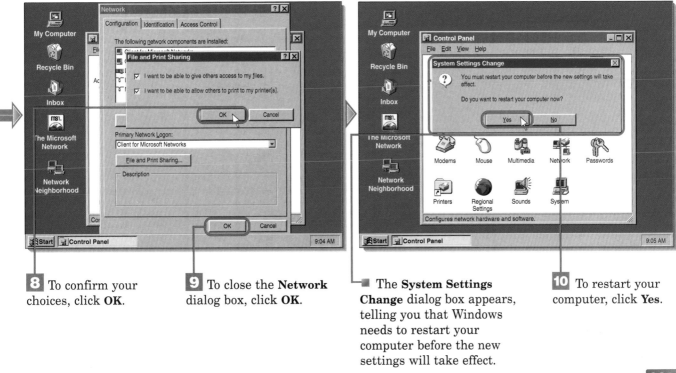

8 To confirm your choices, click **OK**.

9 To close the **Network** dialog box, click **OK**.

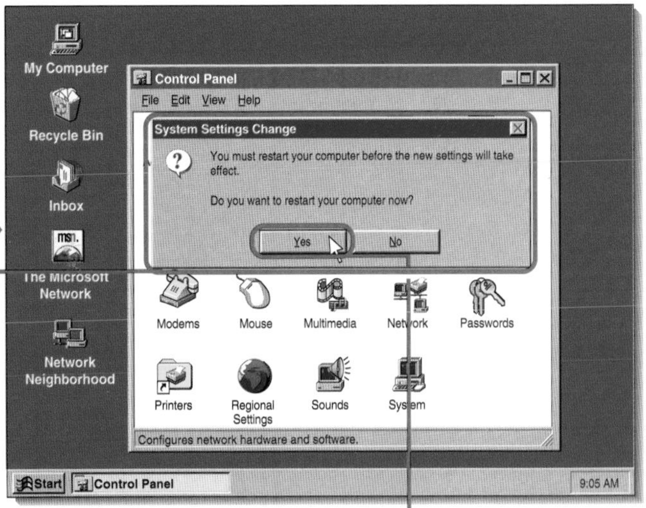

- The **System Settings Change** dialog box appears, telling you that Windows needs to restart your computer before the new settings will take effect.

10 To restart your computer, click **Yes**.

NAME YOUR COMPUTER

You can change the name of your computer on a network.

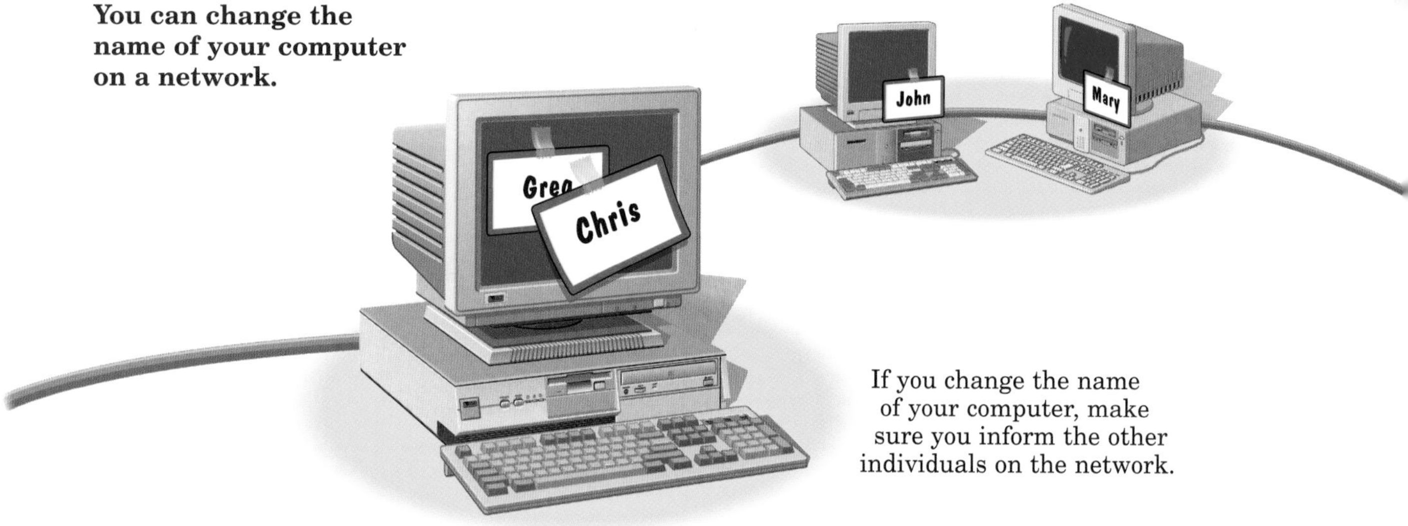

If you change the name of your computer, make sure you inform the other individuals on the network.

NAME YOUR COMPUTER

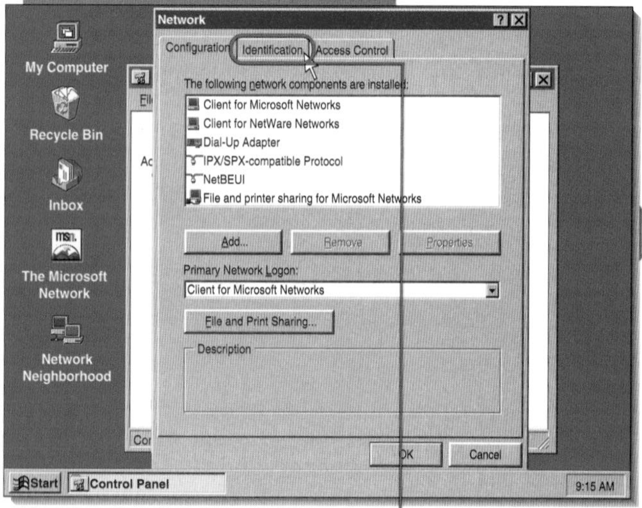

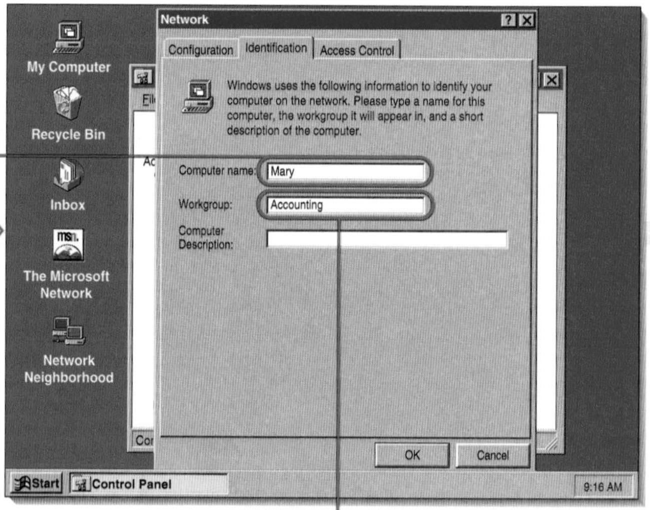

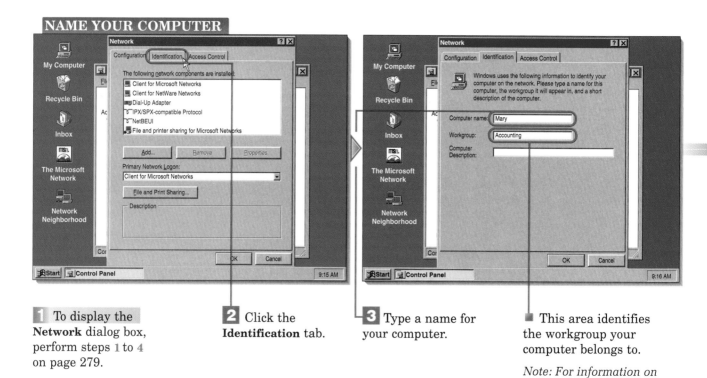

1 To display the **Network** dialog box, perform steps 1 to 4 on page 279.

2 Click the **Identification** tab.

3 Type a name for your computer.

■ This area identifies the workgroup your computer belongs to.

*Note: For information on workgroups, refer to the **Tip** on page 283.*

TIP

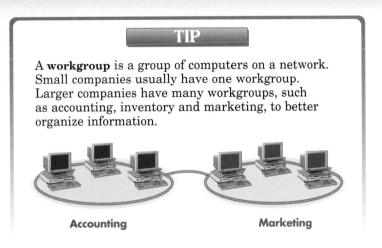

A **workgroup** is a group of computers on a network. Small companies usually have one workgroup. Larger companies have many workgroups, such as accounting, inventory and marketing, to better organize information.

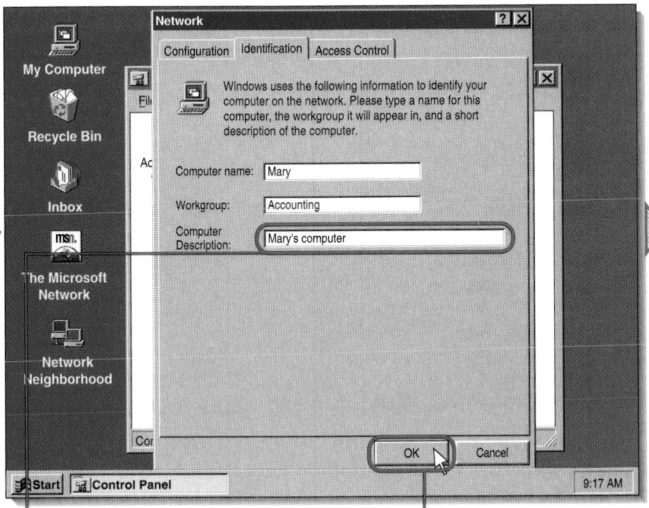

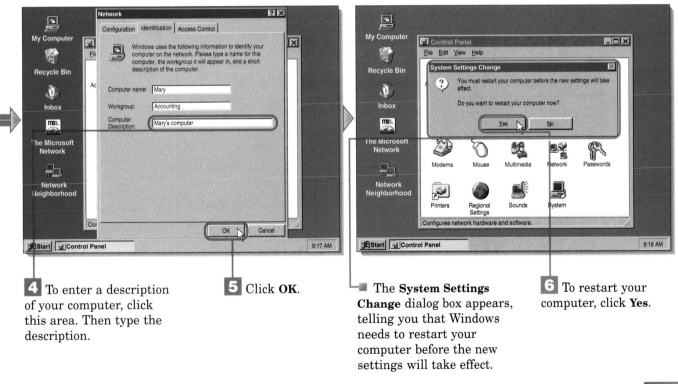

4 To enter a description of your computer, click this area. Then type the description.

5 Click **OK**.

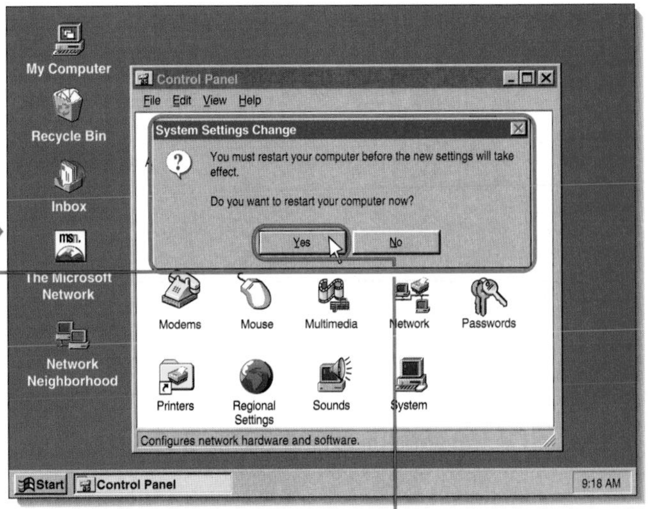

■ The **System Settings Change** dialog box appears, telling you that Windows needs to restart your computer before the new settings will take effect.

6 To restart your computer, click **Yes**.

SHARE INFORMATION

You can specify exactly what information you want to share with individuals on a network.

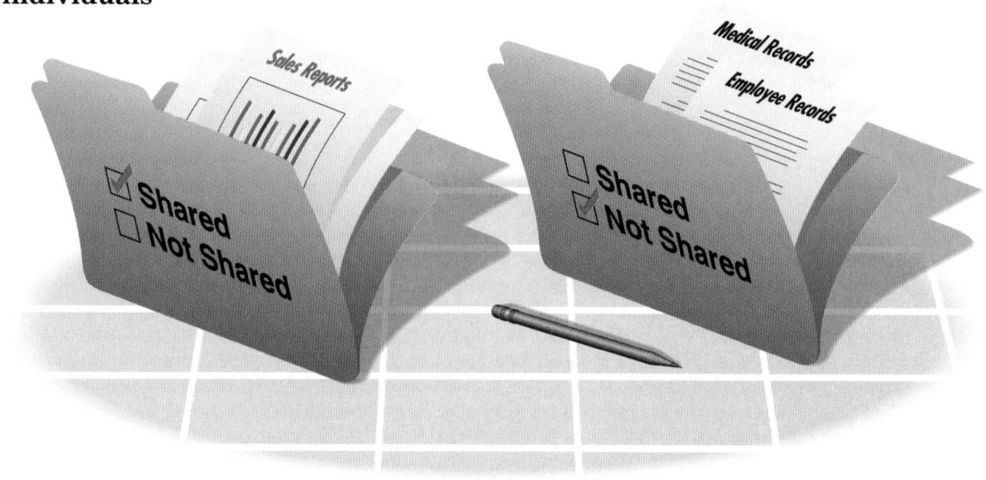

SHARE INFORMATION

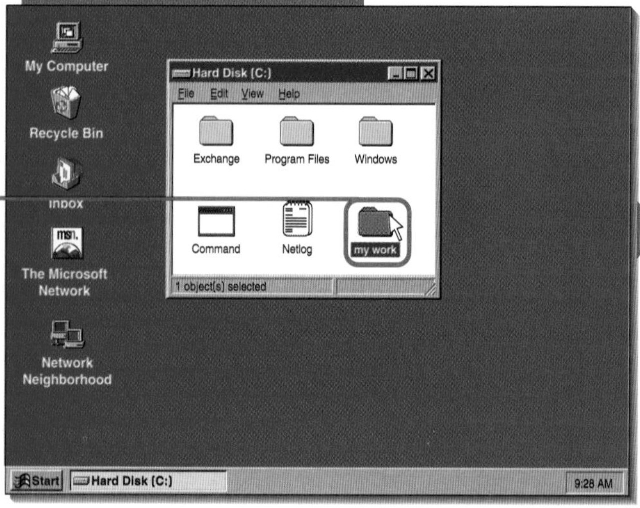

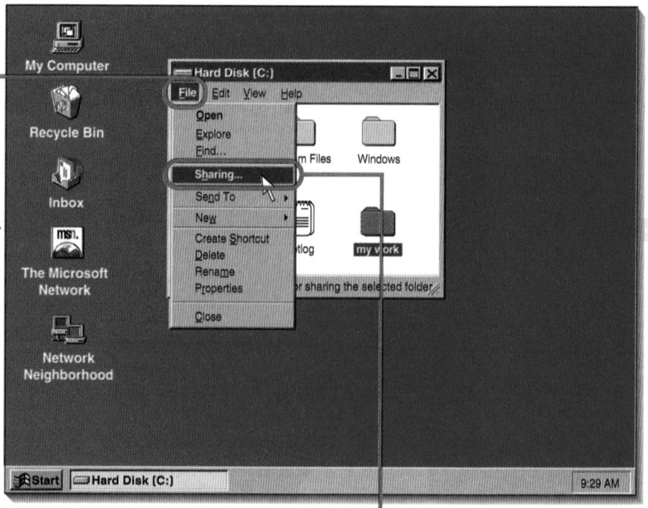

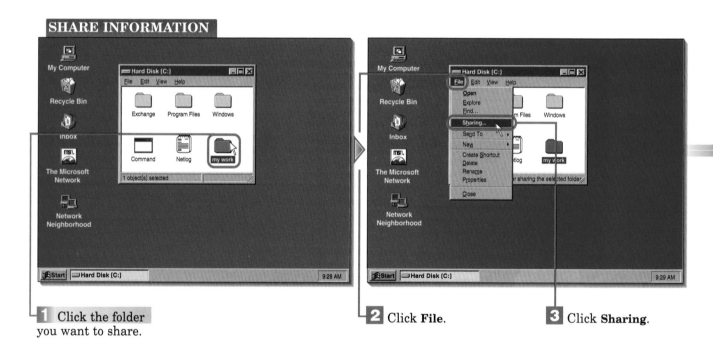

1 Click the folder you want to share.

2 Click **File**.

3 Click **Sharing**.

TIP

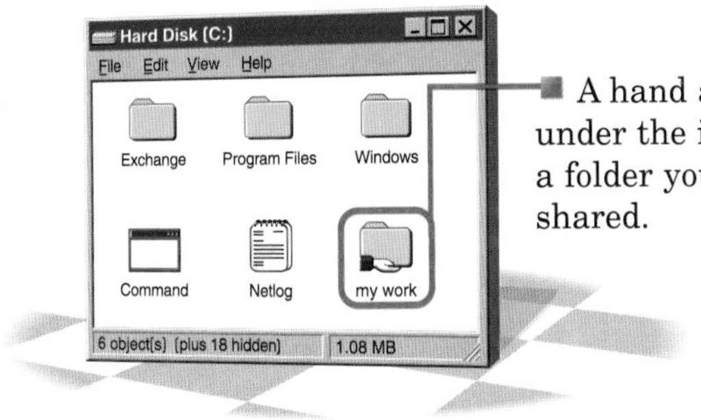

■ A hand appears under the icon for a folder you have shared.

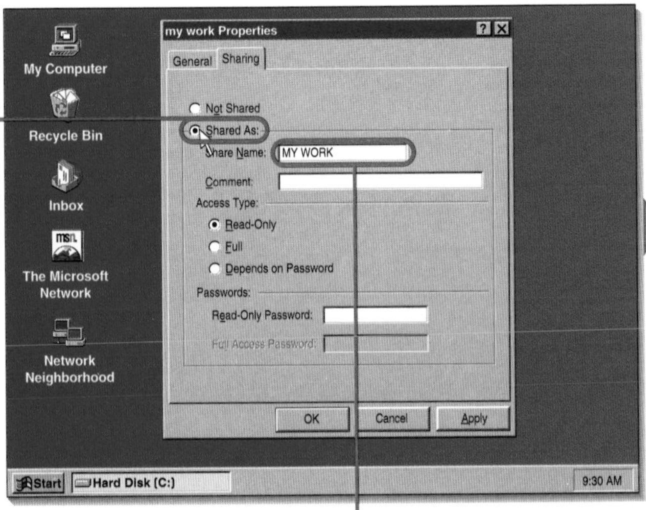

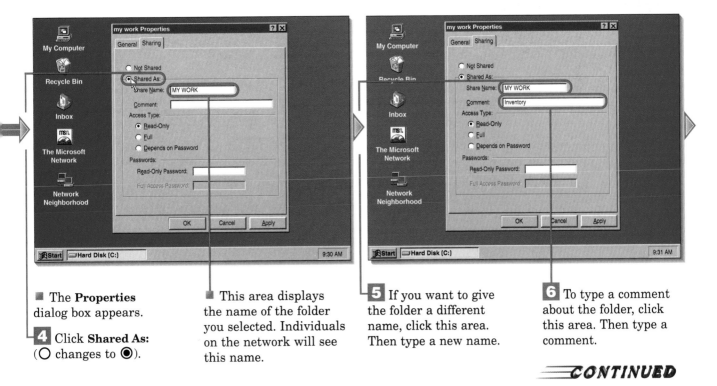

■ The **Properties** dialog box appears.

4 Click **Shared As:** (○ changes to ◉).

■ This area displays the name of the folder you selected. Individuals on the network will see this name.

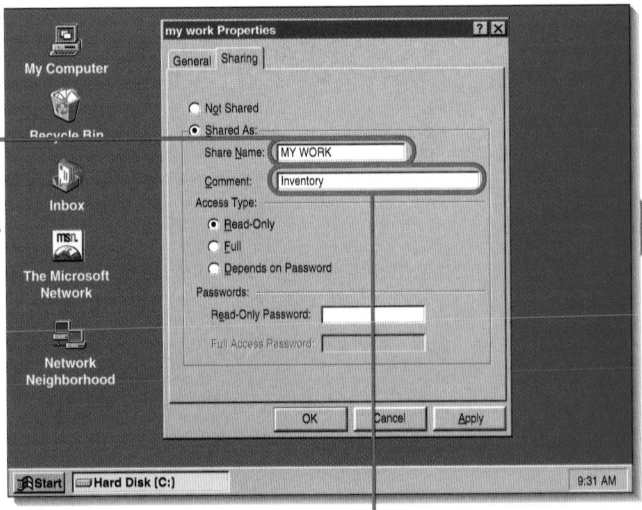

5 If you want to give the folder a different name, click this area. Then type a new name.

6 To type a comment about the folder, click this area. Then type a comment.

CONTINUED

SHARE INFORMATION

You can give individuals on a network one of three types of access to your information.

Read-Only

All individuals on the network can read, but not change or delete, information.

SHARE INFORMATION (CONTINUED)

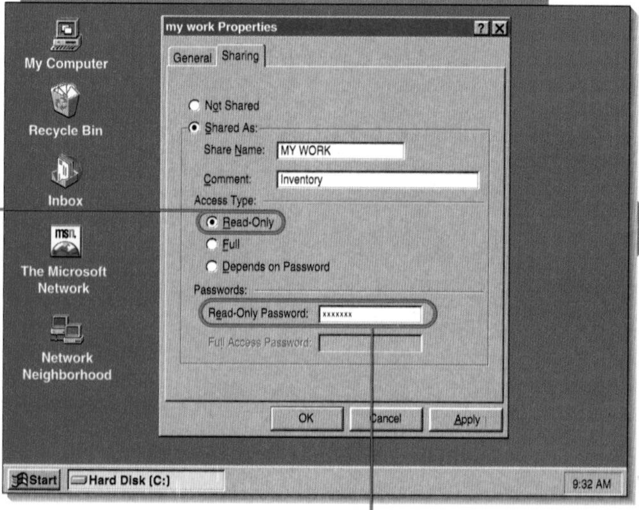

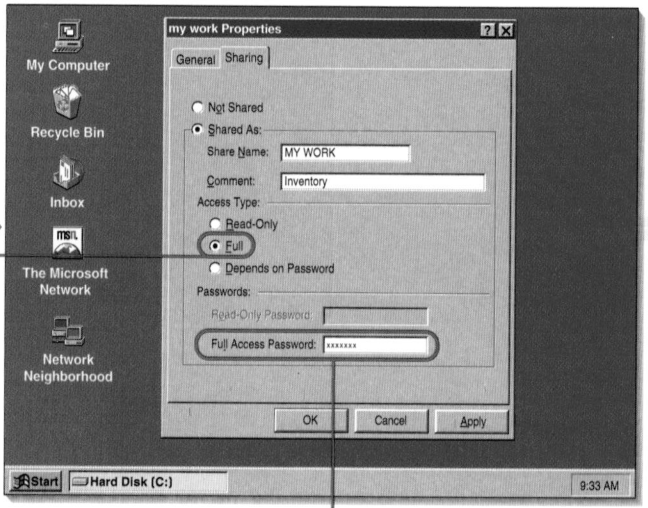

Read-Only

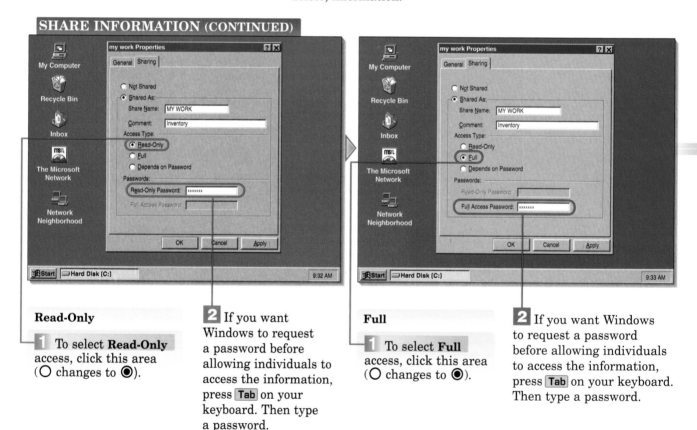

1 To select **Read-Only** access, click this area (○ changes to ◉).

2 If you want Windows to request a password before allowing individuals to access the information, press Tab on your keyboard. Then type a password.

Full

1 To select **Full** access, click this area (○ changes to ◉).

2 If you want Windows to request a password before allowing individuals to access the information, press Tab on your keyboard. Then type a password.

Full

All individuals on the network can read, change and delete information.

Depends on Password

Some individuals on the network get Read-Only access, while others get Full access. The type of access depends on which password they enter.

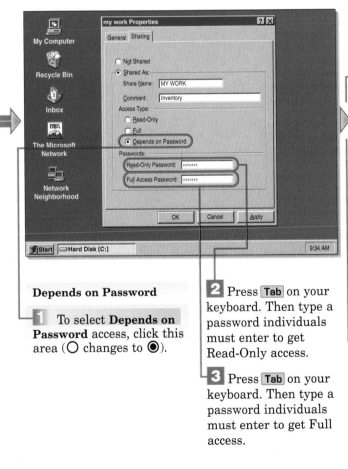

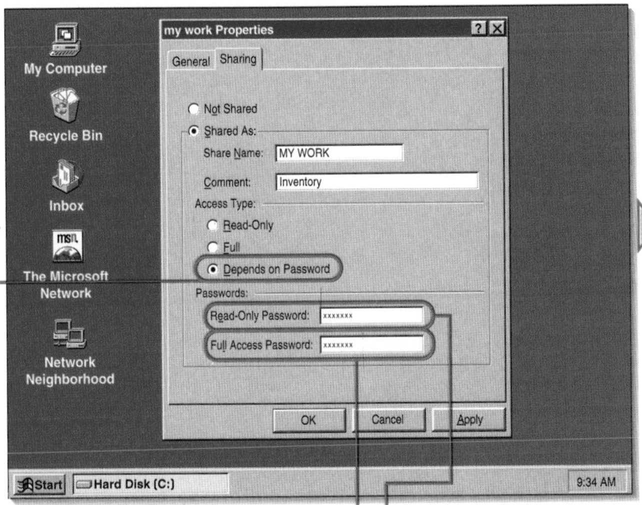

Depends on Password

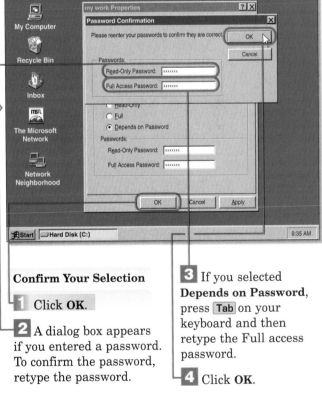

1 To select **Depends on Password** access, click this area (○ changes to ◉).

2 Press Tab on your keyboard. Then type a password individuals must enter to get Read-Only access.

3 Press Tab on your keyboard. Then type a password individuals must enter to get Full access.

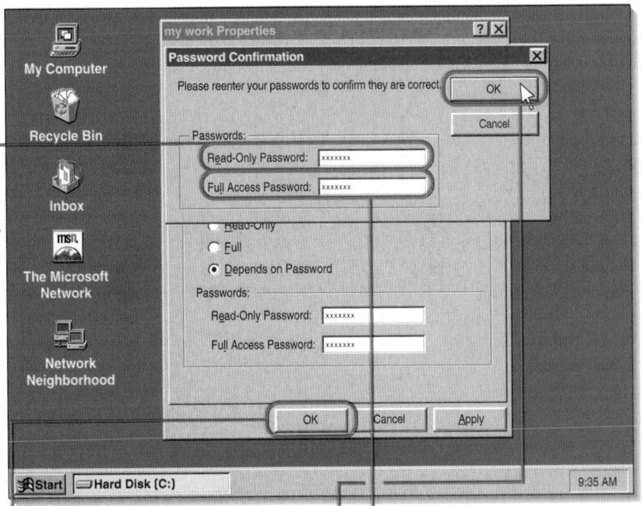

Confirm Your Selection

1 Click **OK**.

2 A dialog box appears if you entered a password. To confirm the password, retype the password.

3 If you selected **Depends on Password**, press Tab on your keyboard and then retype the Full access password.

4 Click **OK**.

SHARE A PRINTER

You can share your printer with other individuals on a network.

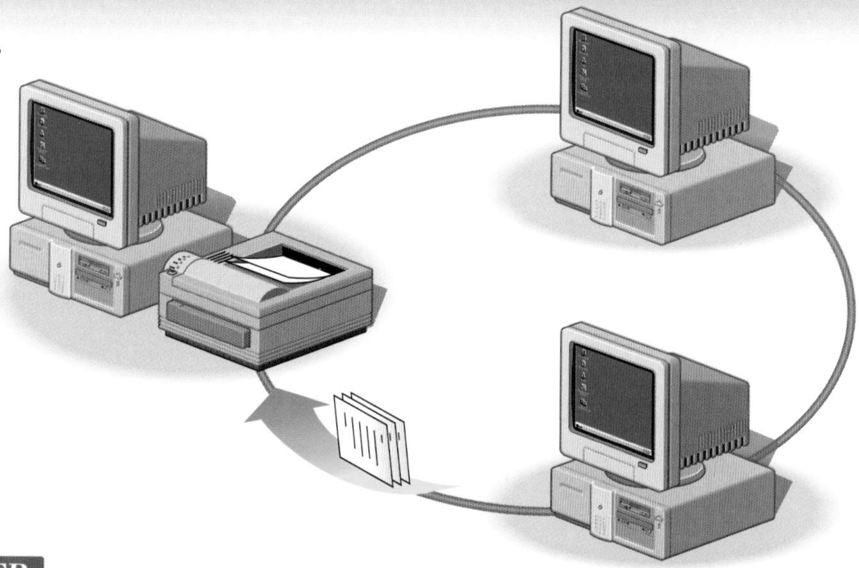

SHARE A PRINTER

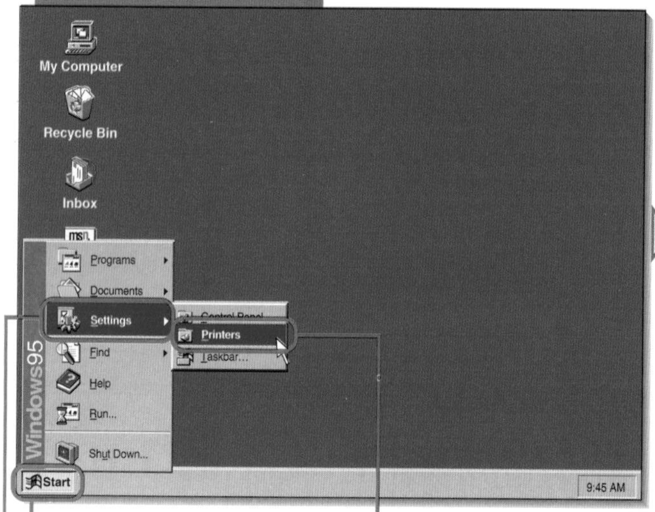

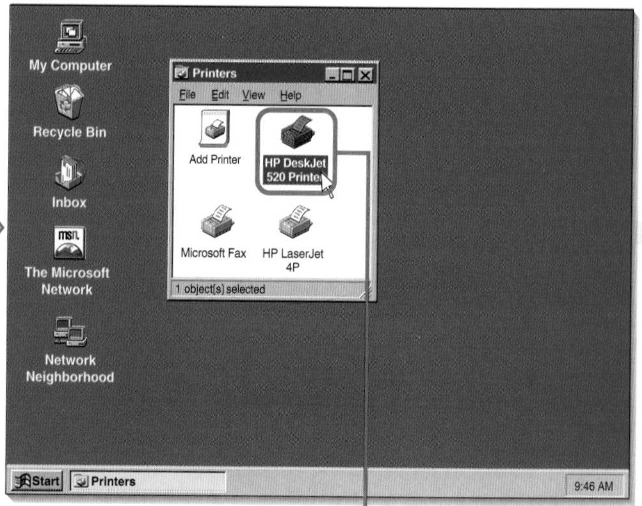

1 Click **Start**.

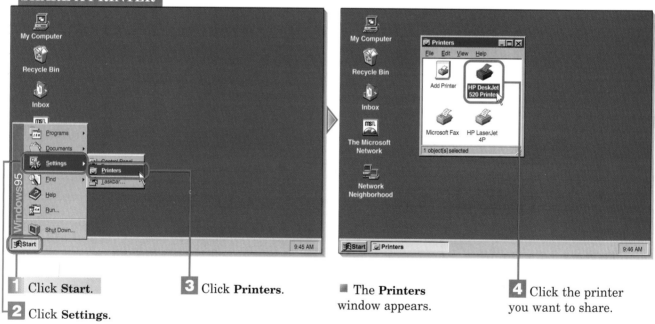

2 Click **Settings**.

3 Click **Printers**.

■ The **Printers** window appears.

4 Click the printer you want to share.

TIP

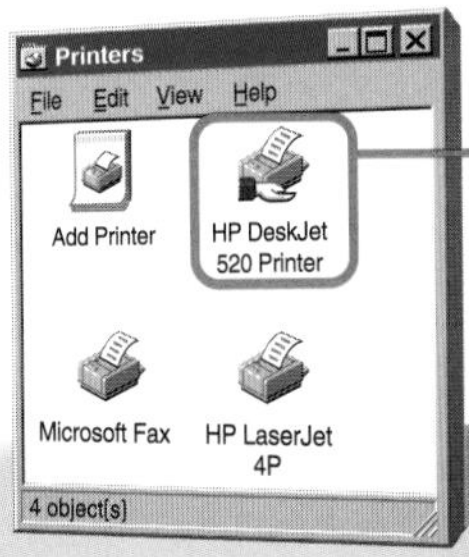

■ A hand appears under the icon for a printer you have shared.

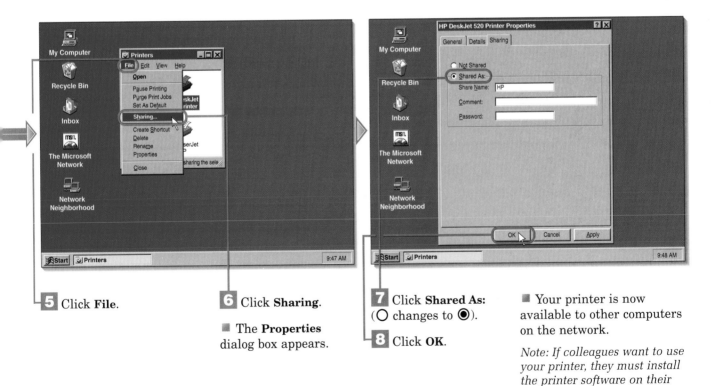

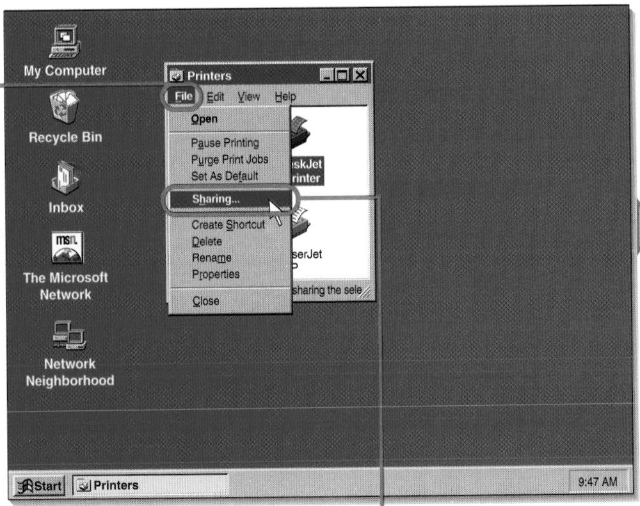

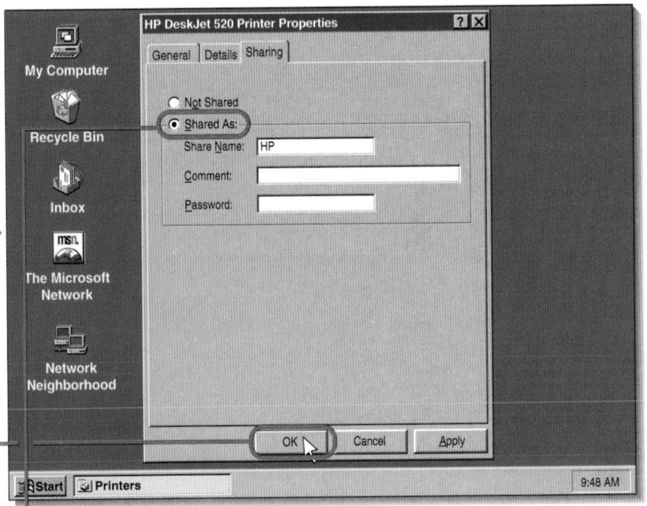

5 Click **File**.

6 Click **Sharing**.

■ The **Properties** dialog box appears.

7 Click **Shared As:** (○ changes to ◉).

8 Click **OK**.

■ Your printer is now available to other computers on the network.

Note: If colleagues want to use your printer, they must install the printer software on their computers. To do so, they must perform the steps starting on page 194.

SET THE DEFAULT PRINTER

If you have access to more than one printer, you can choose one to automatically print your documents.

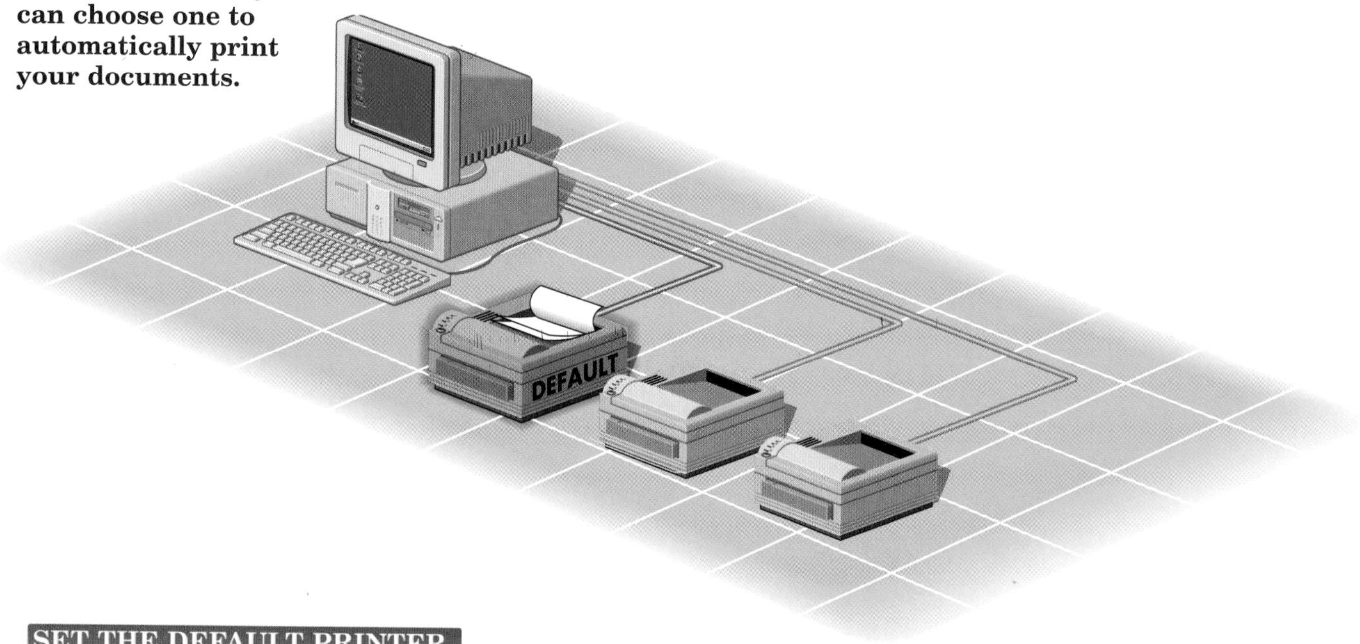

SET THE DEFAULT PRINTER

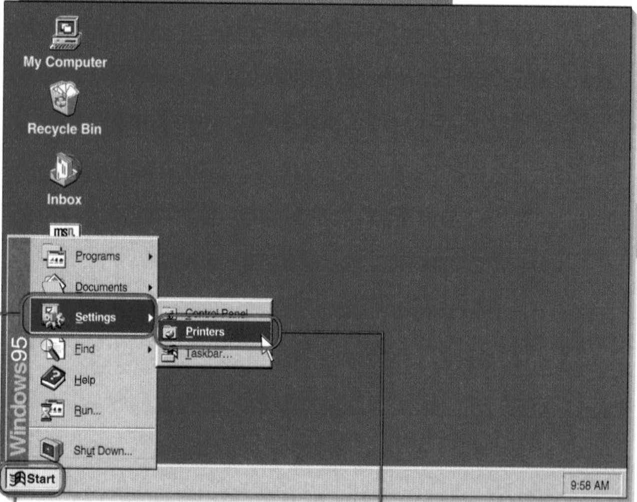

1 Click **Start**.

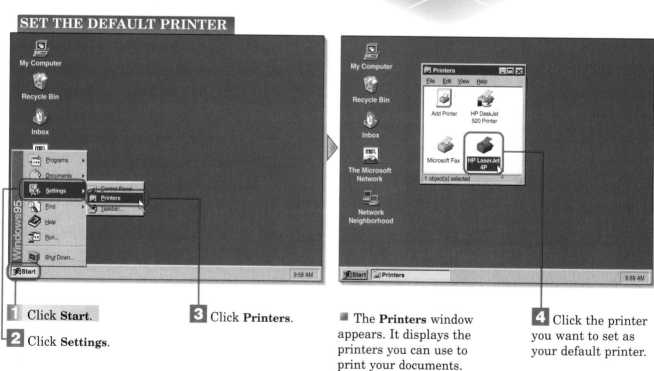

2 Click **Settings**.

3 Click **Printers**.

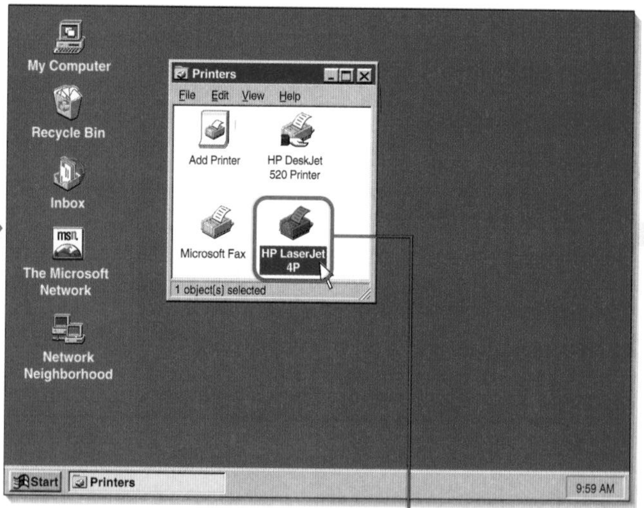

■ The **Printers** window appears. It displays the printers you can use to print your documents.

4 Click the printer you want to set as your default printer.

TIP

When selecting your default printer, choose the printer you use most often. Unless you specify another printer, your computer will automatically use the default printer.

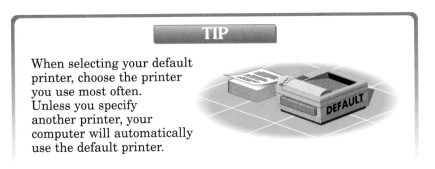

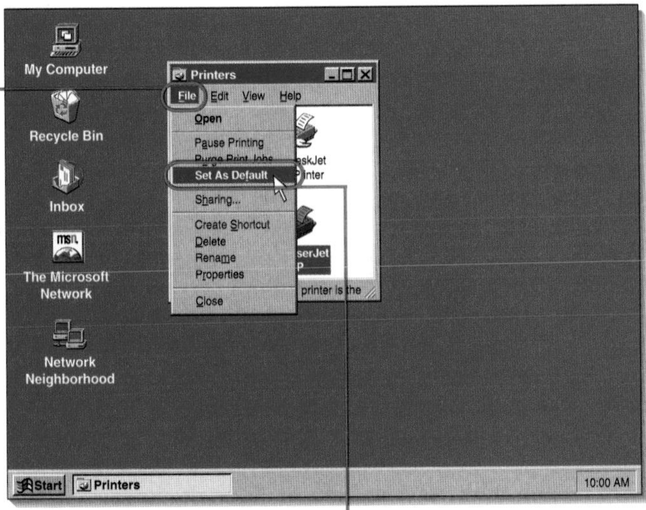

5 Click **File**.

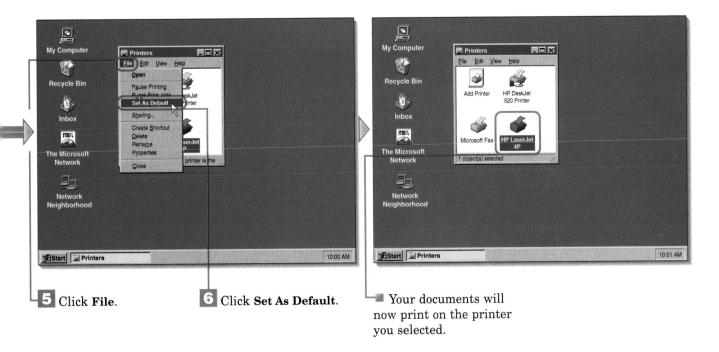

6 Click **Set As Default**.

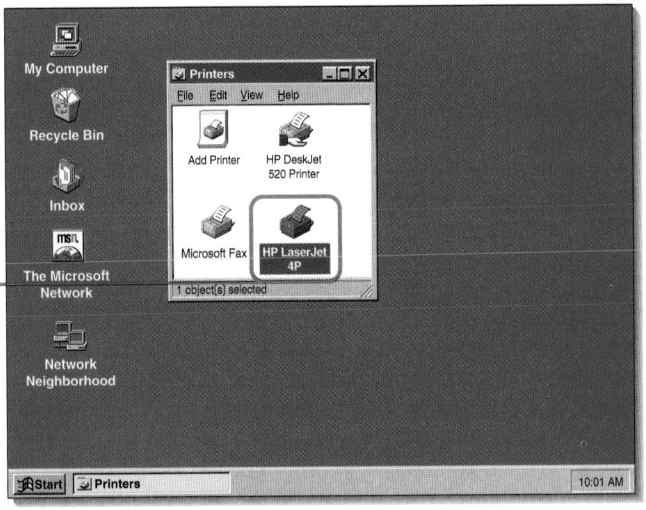

■ Your documents will now print on the printer you selected.

BROWSE THROUGH A NETWORK

You can easily browse through the information available on your network.

BROWSE THROUGH A NETWORK

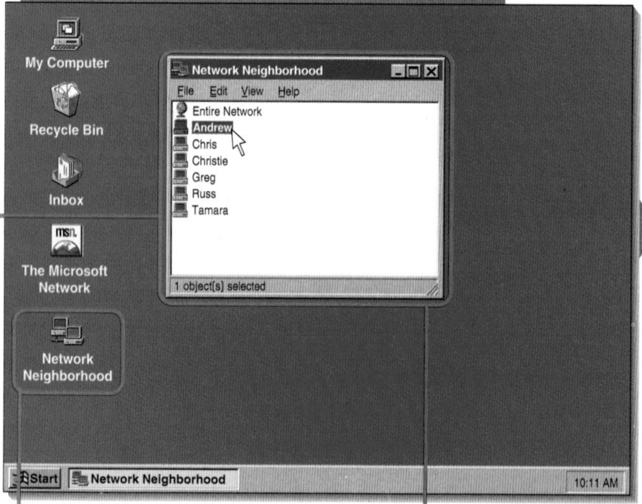

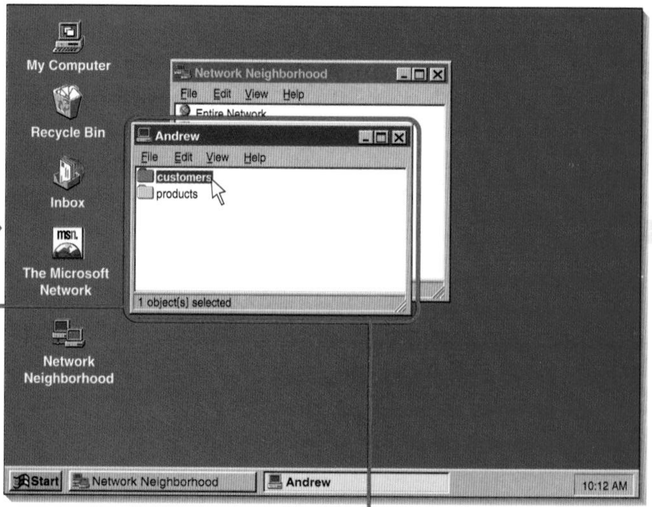

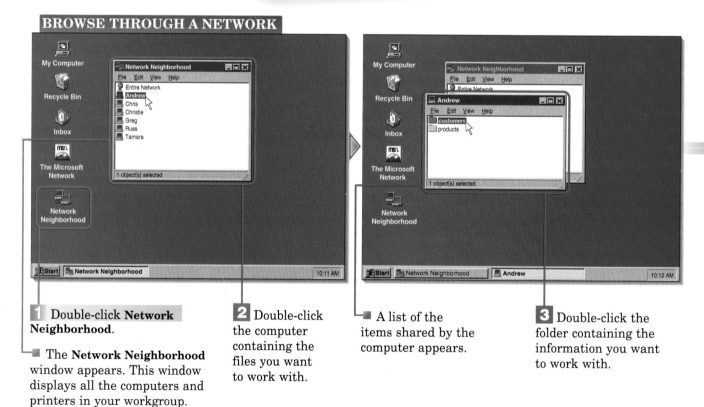

1 Double-click **Network Neighborhood**.

■ The **Network Neighborhood** window appears. This window displays all the computers and printers in your workgroup.

2 Double-click the computer containing the files you want to work with.

■ A list of the items shared by the computer appears.

3 Double-click the folder containing the information you want to work with.

TIP

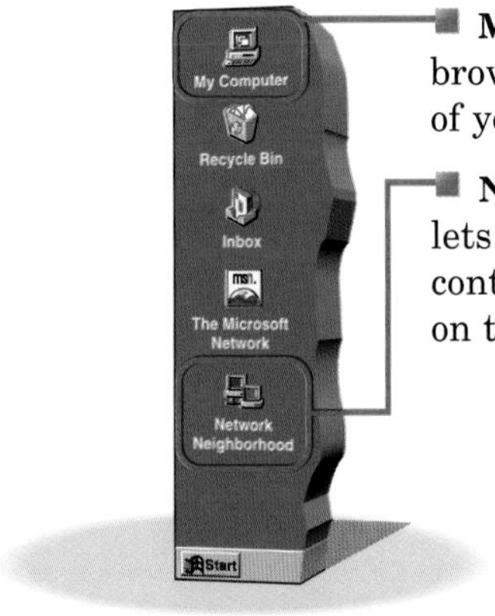

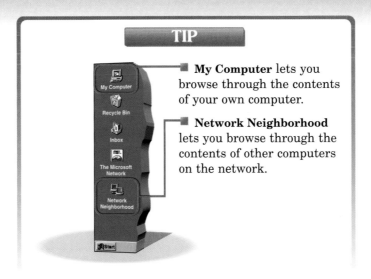

■ **My Computer** lets you browse through the contents of your own computer.

■ **Network Neighborhood** lets you browse through the contents of other computers on the network.

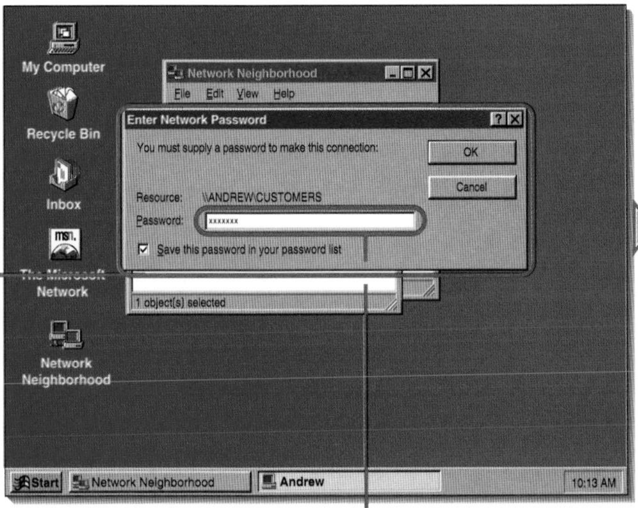

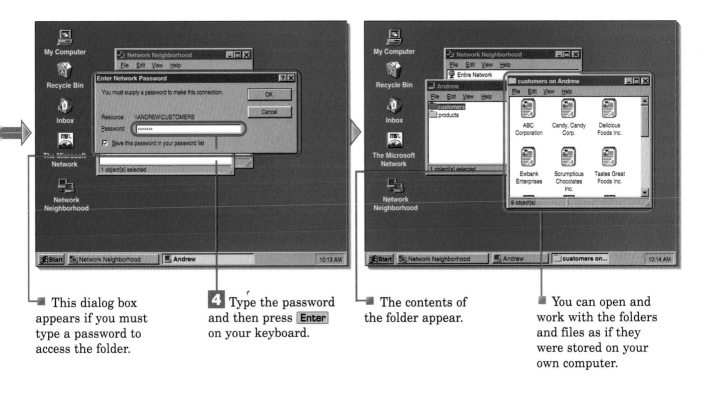

■ This dialog box appears if you must type a password to access the folder.

4 Type the password and then press **Enter** on your keyboard.

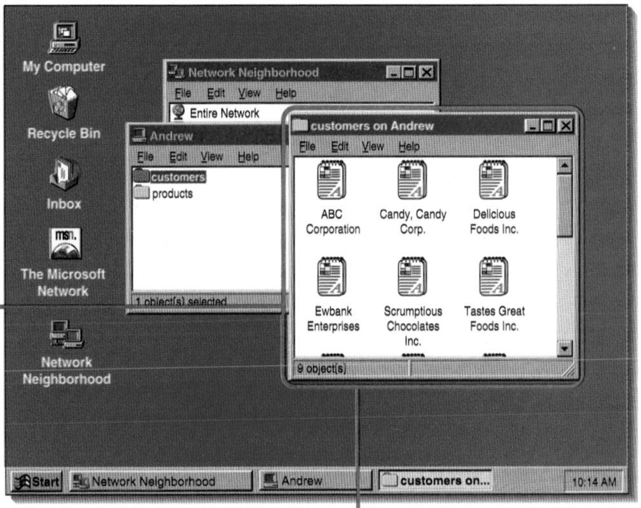

■ The contents of the folder appear.

■ You can open and work with the folders and files as if they were stored on your own computer.

FIND A COMPUTER

You can quickly locate a computer on a network. This is especially useful if your network consists of hundreds of computers.

FIND A COMPUTER

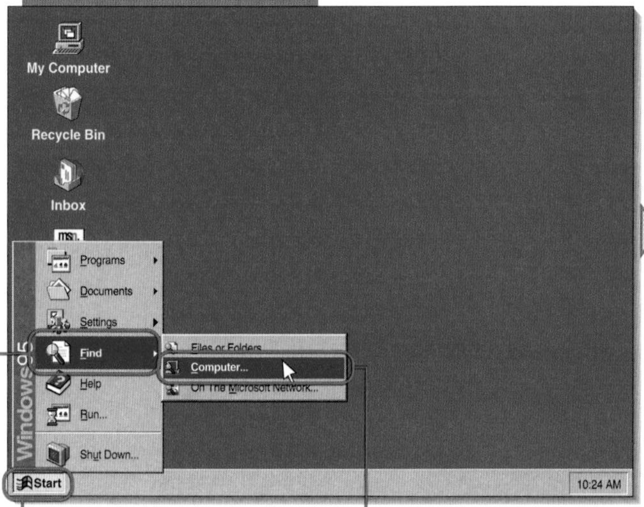

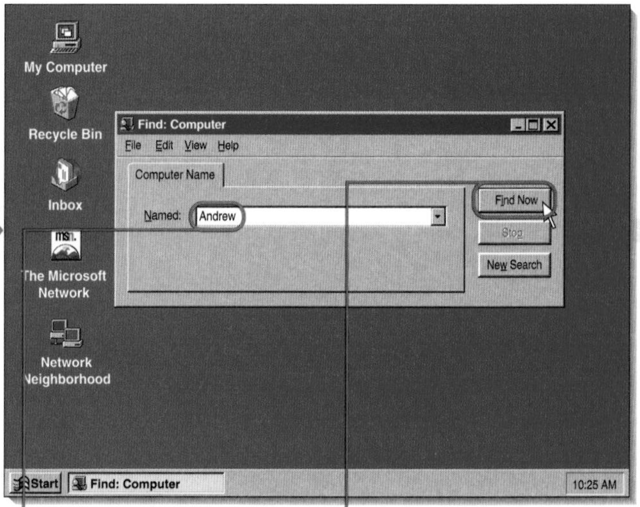

1 Click **Start**.

2 Click **Find**.

3 Click **Computer**.

■ The **Find: Computer** dialog box appears.

4 Type the name of the computer you want to find.

5 To start the search, click **Find Now**.

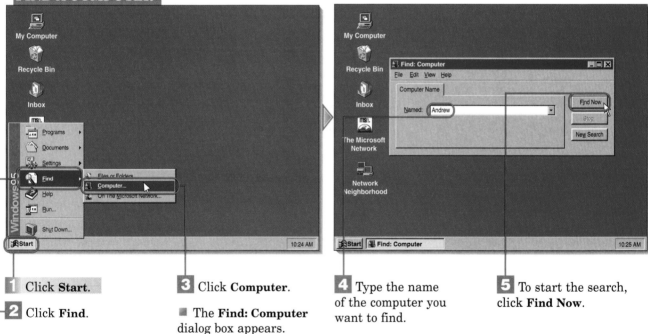

TIP

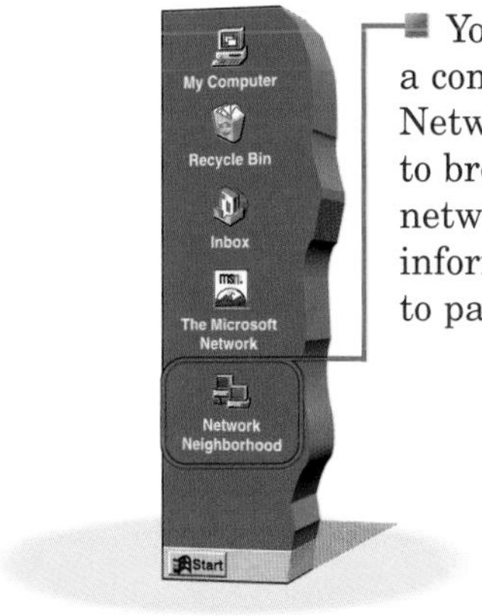

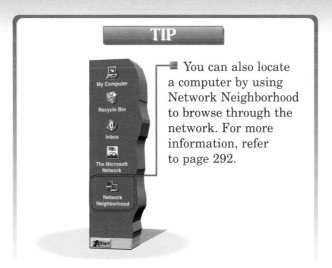

■ You can also locate a computer by using Network Neighborhood to browse through the network. For more information, refer to page 292.

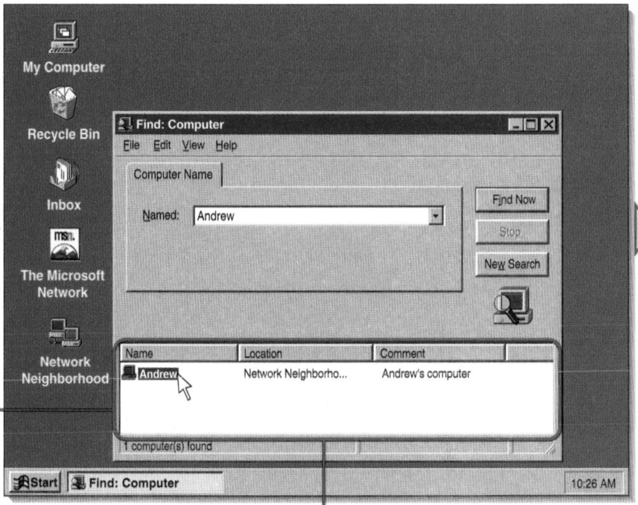

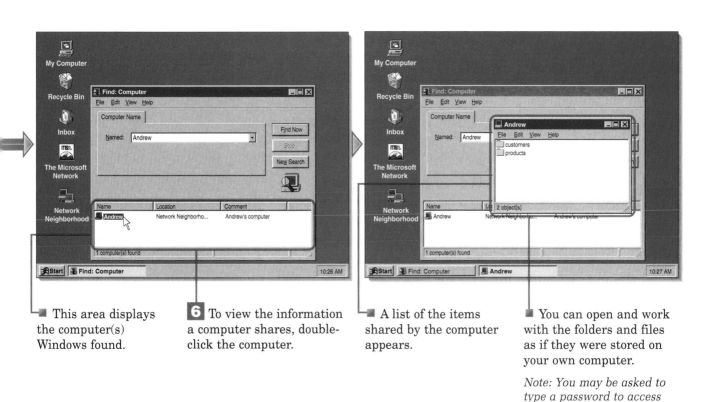

■ This area displays the computer(s) Windows found.

6 To view the information a computer shares, double-click the computer.

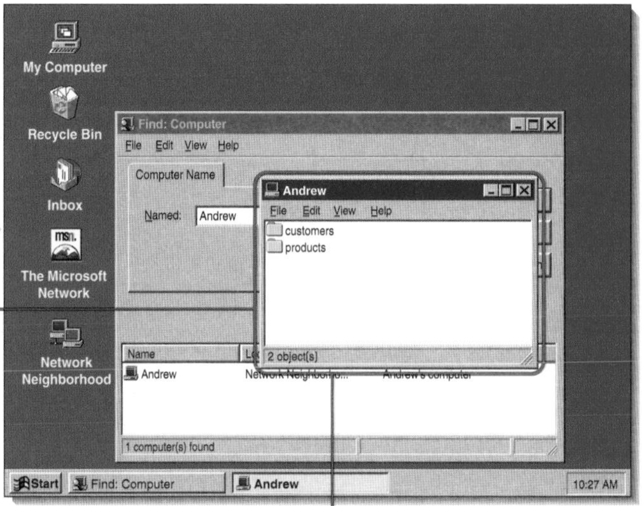

■ A list of the items shared by the computer appears.

■ You can open and work with the folders and files as if they were stored on your own computer.

Note: You may be asked to type a password to access some shared items.

In this chapter you will learn how to access information on a computer at work when you are at home or traveling.

CHAPTER 18: DIAL-UP NETWORKING

Introduction to Dial-Up Networking 298

Set Up Office Computer 299

Set Up Connection to Office Computer . . .302

Dial In to Office Computer 306

INTRODUCTION TO DIAL-UP NETWORKING

INTRODUCTION

When at home or traveling, you can use Dial-Up Networking to access information on a computer at work.

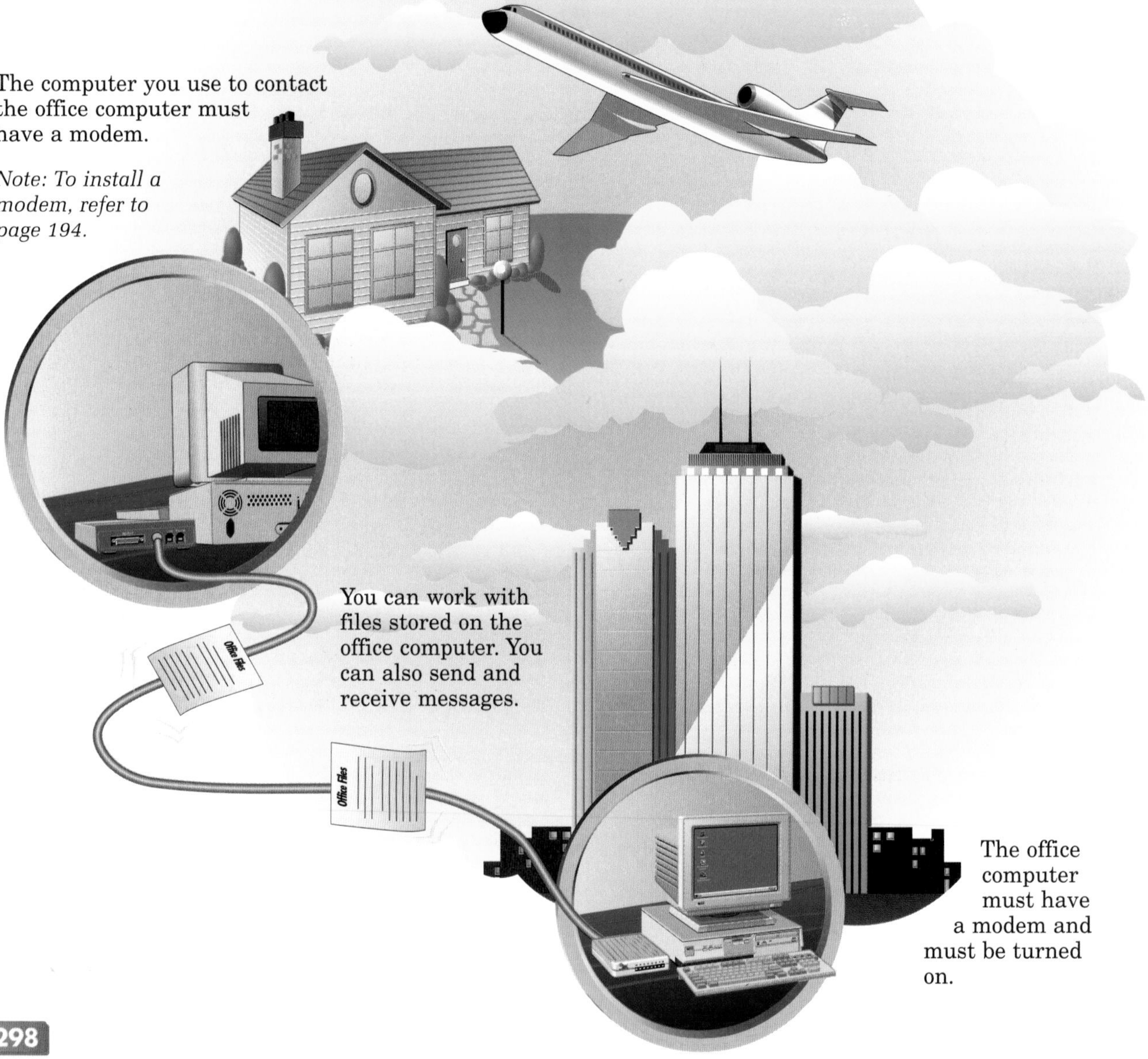

The computer you use to contact the office computer must have a modem.

Note: To install a modem, refer to page 194.

You can work with files stored on the office computer. You can also send and receive messages.

The office computer must have a modem and must be turned on.

SET UP OFFICE COMPUTER

Before you can dial in to an office computer, you must set up the computer.

To set up the office computer, you must buy the Microsoft Plus! package, which is available at computer stores.

SET UP OFFICE COMPUTER

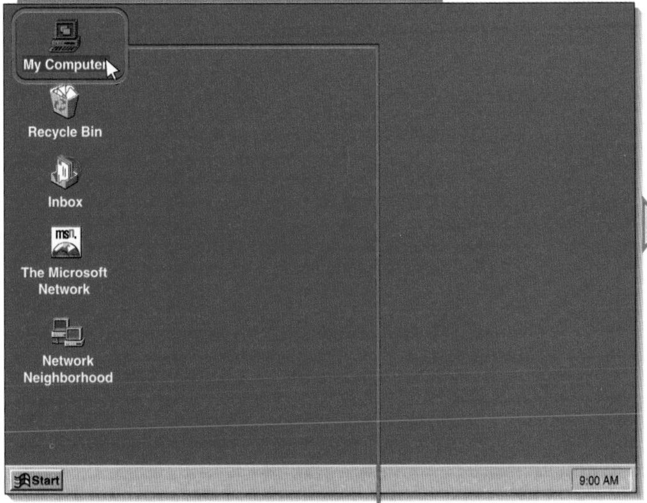

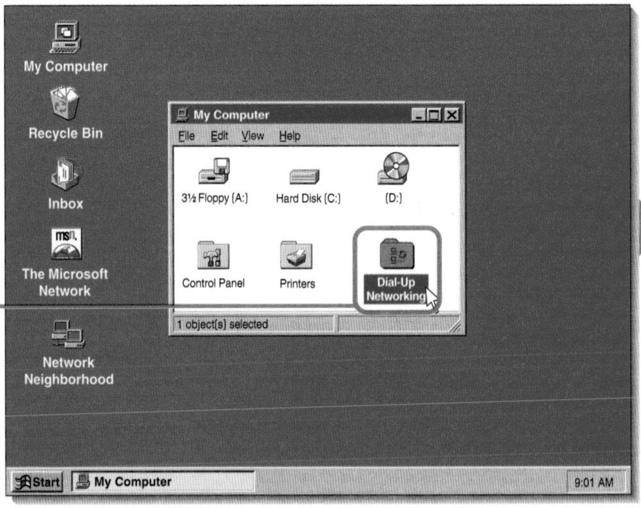

Perform the following steps on the office computer.

1 Double-click **My Computer**.

■ The **My Computer** window appears.

2 Double-click **Dial-Up Networking**.

*Note: If **Dial-Up Networking** is not available, you must add the Windows component, which is found in the Communications category. To do so, refer to page 186.*

*When you add Dial-Up Networking, you may be asked to provide a computer and workgroup name. For information on workgroups, refer to the **Tip** on page 283.*

CONTINUED

SET UP OFFICE COMPUTER

You can assign a password so only those people who know the password can access information stored on the office computer.

SET UP OFFICE COMPUTER (CONTINUED)

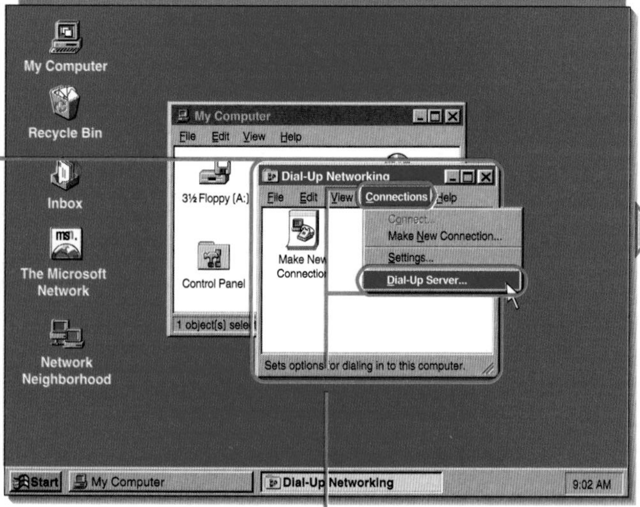

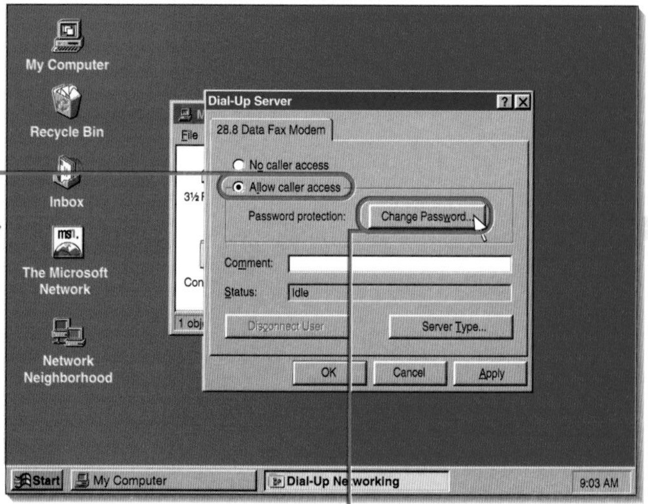

■ The **Dial-Up Networking** window appears.

*Note: If the **Welcome to Dial-Up Networking** or **Make New Connection** dialog box appears, press **Esc** on your keyboard to close the dialog box.*

3 Click **Connections**.

4 Click **Dial-Up Server**.

*Note: If **Dial-Up Server** is not available, you must install the Dial-Up Networking Server component from the Microsoft Plus! package.*

■ The **Dial-Up Server** dialog box appears.

5 Click **Allow caller access** (○ changes to ◉).

6 To assign a password, click **Change Password**.

IMPORTANT

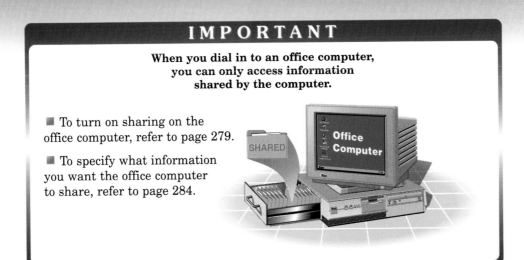

When you dial in to an office computer, you can only access information shared by the computer.

- To turn on sharing on the office computer, refer to page 279.
- To specify what information you want the office computer to share, refer to page 284.

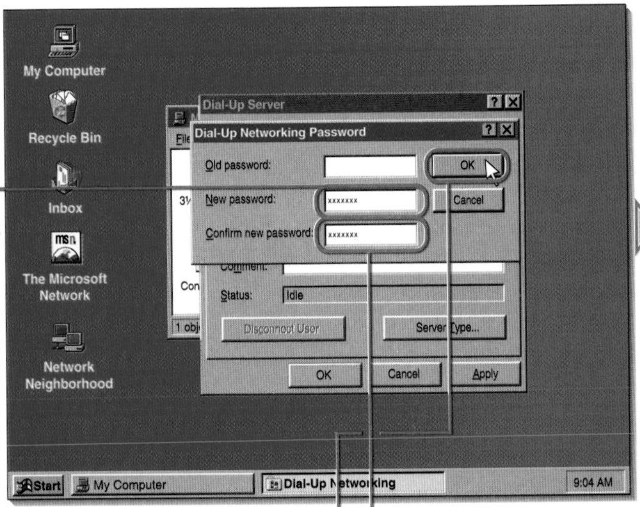

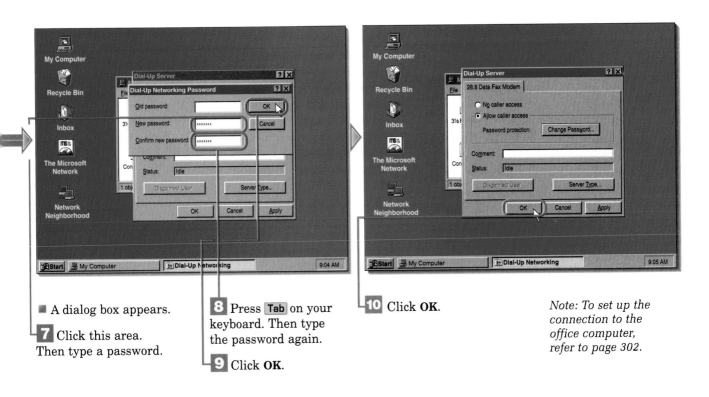

- A dialog box appears.

7 Click this area. Then type a password.

8 Press Tab on your keyboard. Then type the password again.

9 Click **OK**.

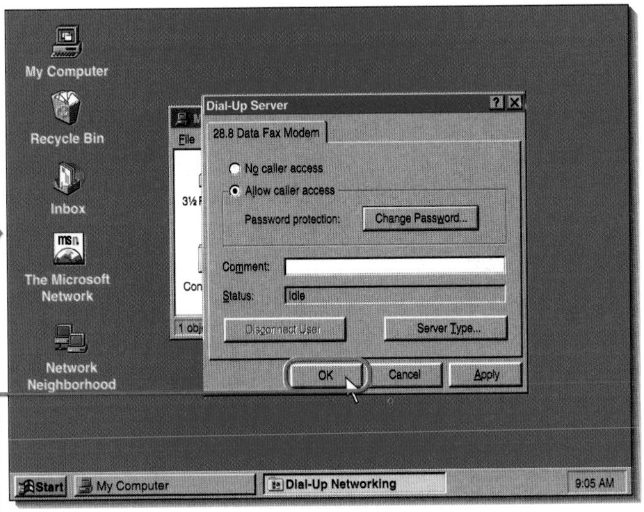

10 Click **OK**.

Note: To set up the connection to the office computer, refer to page 302.

SET UP CONNECTION TO OFFICE COMPUTER

Before connecting to the office computer, you must tell Windows about the computer you want to contact.

SET UP CONNECTION TO OFFICE COMPUTER

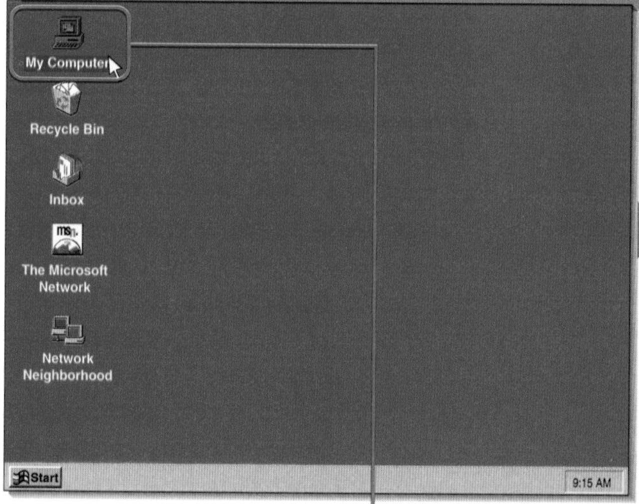

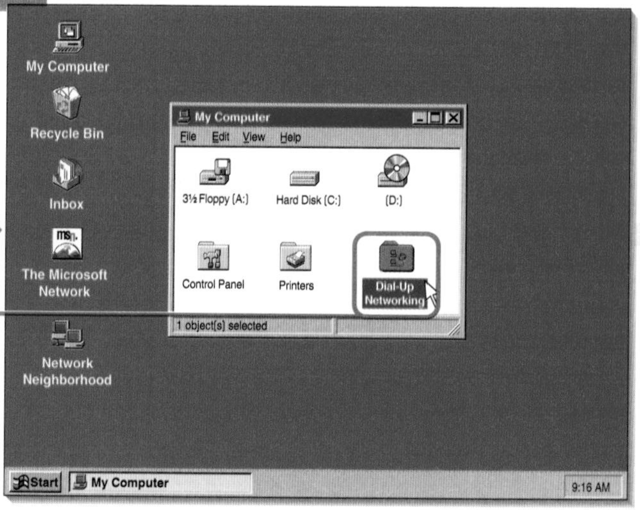

Perform the following steps on your home or portable computer.

1 Double-click **My Computer**.

■ The **My Computer** window appears.

2 Double-click **Dial-Up Networking**.

*Note: If **Dial-Up Networking** is not available, you must add the Windows component, which is found in the Communications category. To do so, refer to page 186.*

*When you add Dial-Up Networking, you may be asked to provide a computer and workgroup name. For information on workgroups, refer to the **Tip** on page 283.*

IMPORTANT

To use Dial-Up Networking, both the office computer and the computer you use when at home or traveling must have a modem. Both computers must also be turned on.

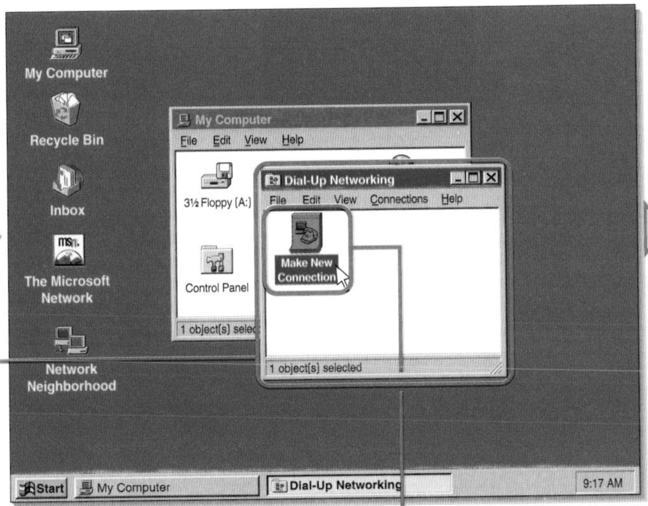

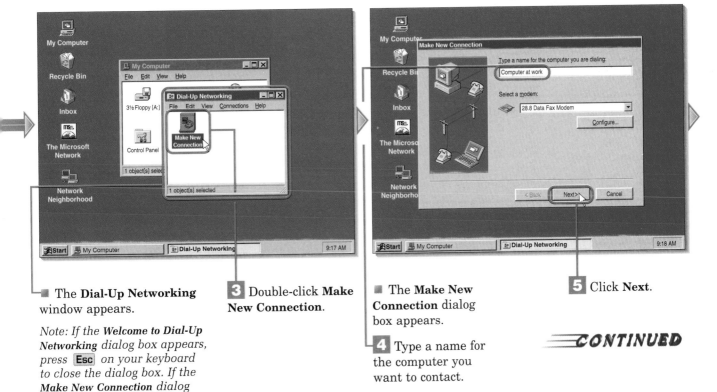

■ The **Dial-Up Networking** window appears.

*Note: If the **Welcome to Dial-Up Networking** dialog box appears, press* **Esc** *on your keyboard to close the dialog box. If the **Make New Connection** dialog box appears, skip to step 4.*

3 Double-click **Make New Connection**.

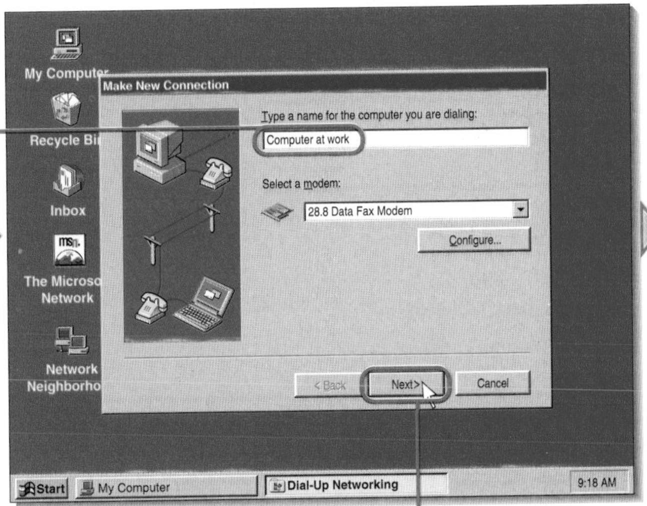

■ The **Make New Connection** dialog box appears.

4 Type a name for the computer you want to contact.

5 Click **Next**.

CONTINUED

SET UP CONNECTION TO OFFICE COMPUTER

Windows will store the information you enter about the office computer. This will help you quickly connect to the computer later on.

SET UP CONNECTION TO OFFICE COMPUTER (CONTINUED)

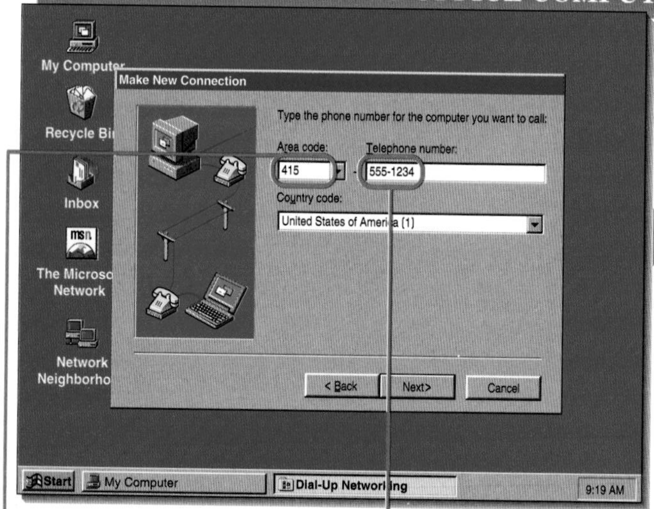

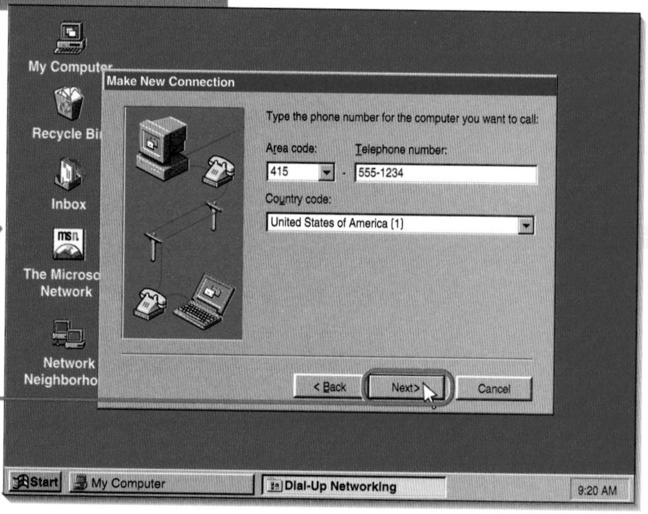

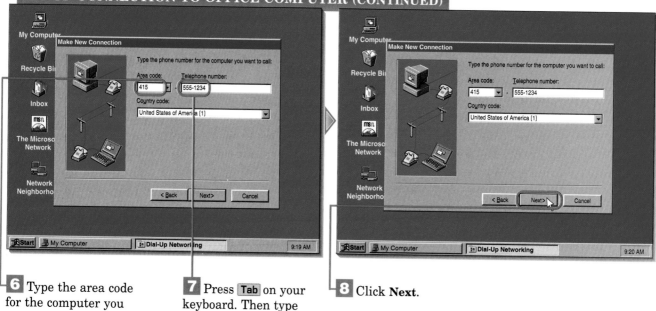

6 Type the area code for the computer you want to contact.

7 Press Tab on your keyboard. Then type the telephone number.

8 Click **Next**.

TIP

You only need to set up a connection to an office computer once. After the connection is set up, you can easily dial in to the computer at any time. To do so, refer to page 306.

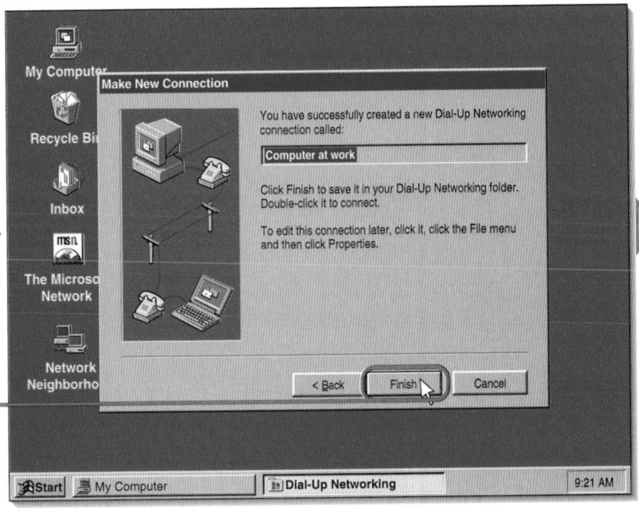

9 Click **Finish**.

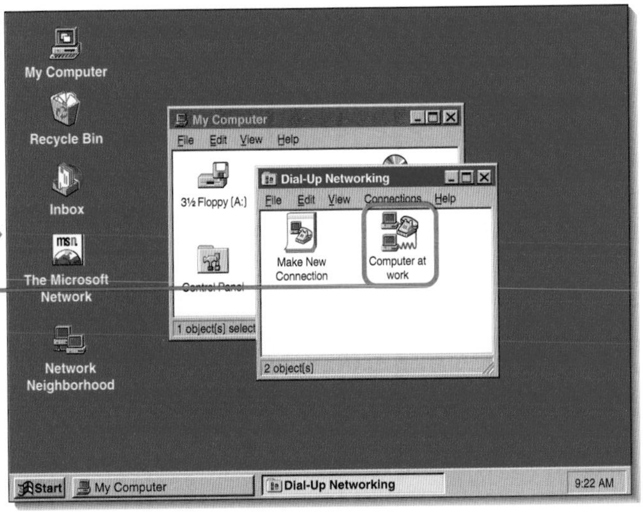

■ An icon appears for the connection you set up.

Note: To use this icon to connect to the office computer, refer to page 306.

DIAL IN TO OFFICE COMPUTER

After you set up a connection to the office computer, you can dial in to the computer to access information.

DIAL IN TO OFFICE COMPUTER

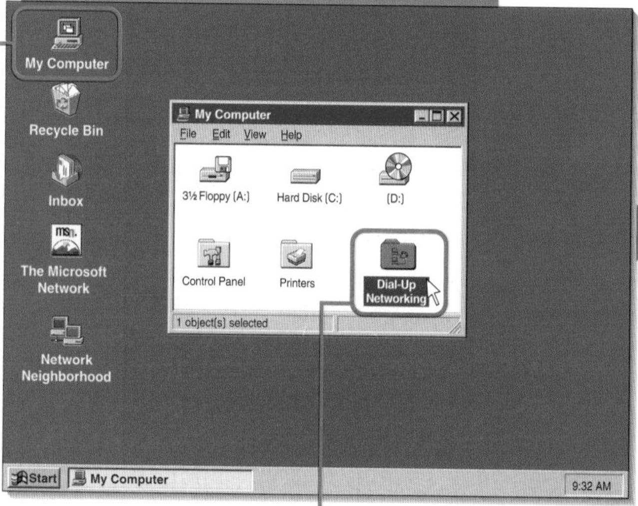

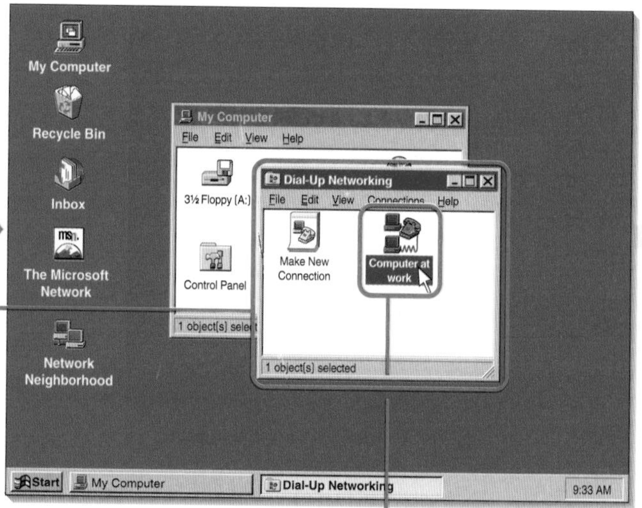

Perform the following steps on your home or portable computer.

1 Double-click **My Computer**.

■ The **My Computer** window appears.

2 Double-click **Dial-Up Networking**.

■ The **Dial-Up Networking** window appears, displaying an icon for each connection you have set up.

Note: To set up a connection, refer to page 302.

3 To connect to a computer, double-click the icon for the computer.

■ The **Connect To** dialog box appears.

TIP

Connecting to an office computer lets you access information you need while away from the office. You can update files, exchange electronic mail, send faxes and access information on a network as if you were directly connected to the office computer.

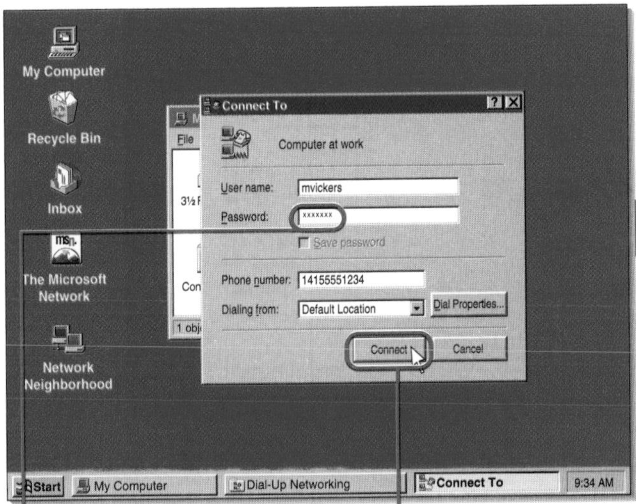

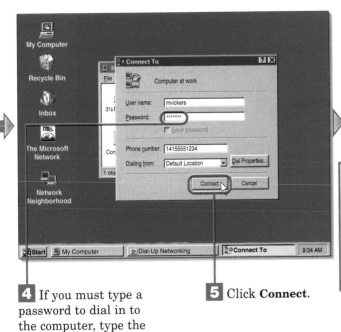

4 If you must type a password to dial in to the computer, type the password.

5 Click **Connect**.

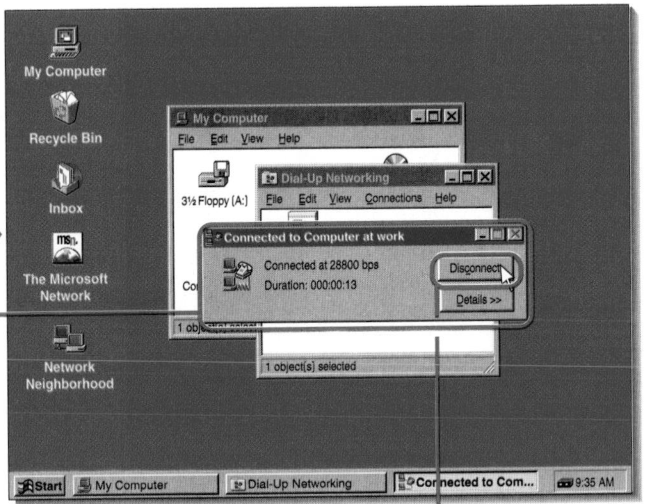

■ This dialog box appears when you are successfully connected to the office computer.

■ You can use the Find feature to display the files shared by the office computer. For more information, refer to page 294.

6 To disconnect, click **Disconnect**.

In this chapter you will learn how to directly connect two computers to share information.

CHAPTER 19: DIRECT CABLE CONNECTION

Set Up Direct Cable Connection 310

Re-Establish Direct Cable Connection 314

SET UP DIRECT CABLE CONNECTION

You can use a special cable to directly connect two computers to share information.

Guest

The guest is a computer that can access information on the host and the network attached to the host.

Cable

Make sure you plug the cable into both computers before performing the steps below. You can buy the required cable at most computer stores.

SET UP DIRECT CABLE CONNECTION

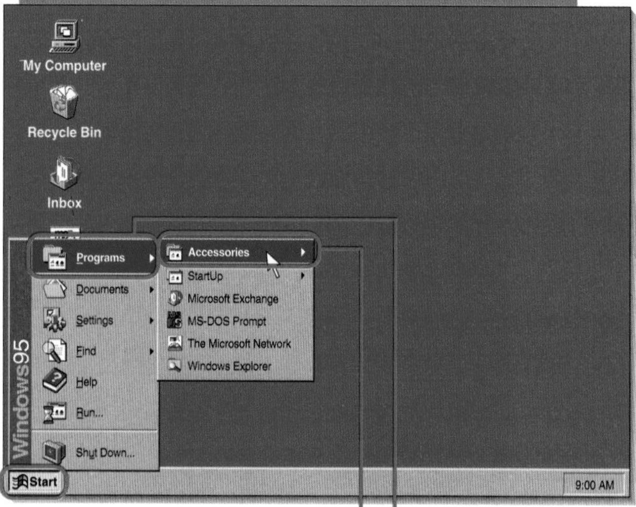

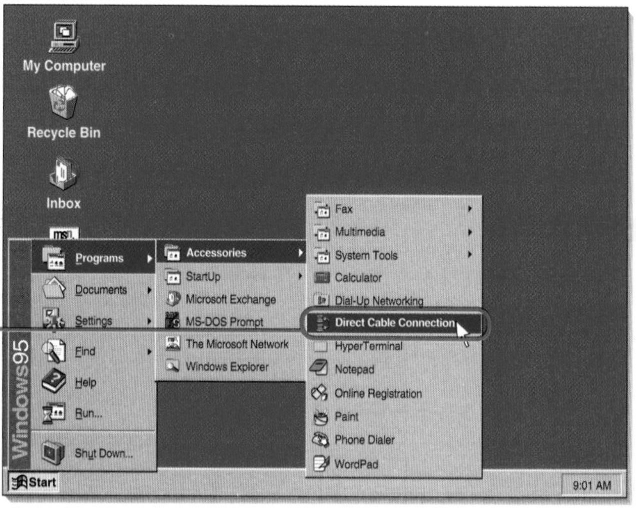

Set Up Host Computer

1. On the host computer, click **Start**.
2. Click **Programs**.
3. Click **Accessories**.
4. Click **Direct Cable Connection**.

*Note: If **Direct Cable Connection** is not available, you must add the Windows component, which is found in the Communications category. To do so, refer to page 186.*

*When you add Direct Cable Connection, you may be asked to provide a computer and workgroup name. For information on workgroups, refer to the **Tip** on page 283.*

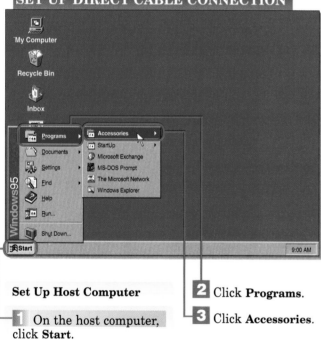

Host

The host is a computer that provides information. Make sure the host is set up to share the information the guest wants to access.

- To turn on sharing on the host computer, refer to page 279.
- To specify what information you want the host computer to share, refer to page 284.

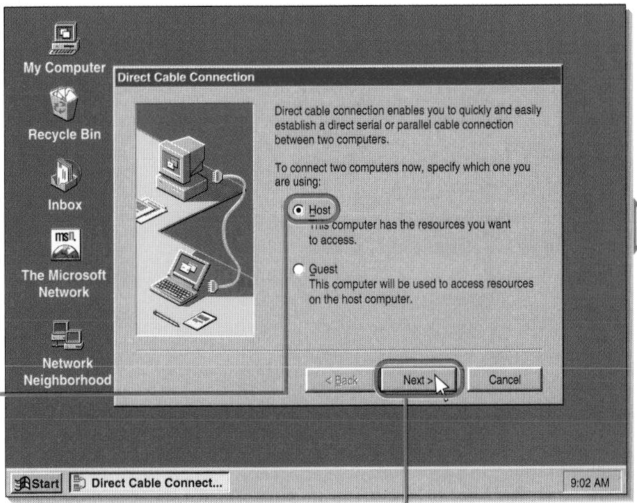

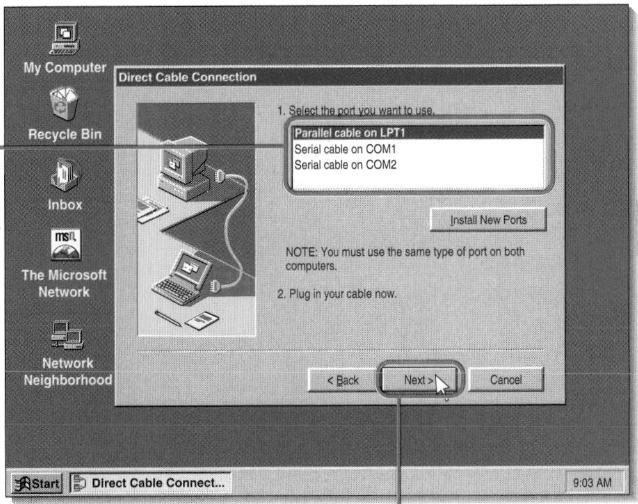

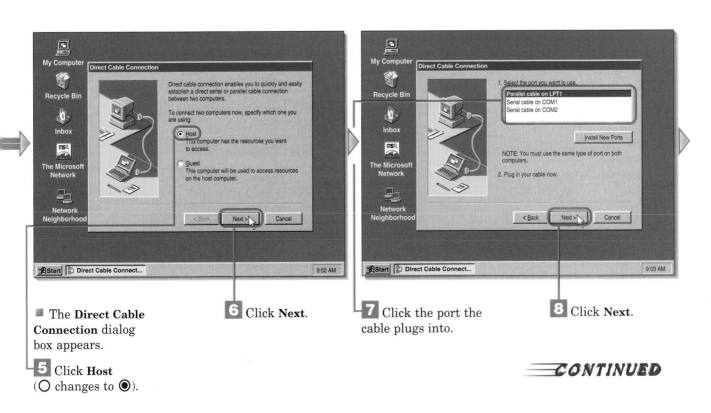

- The **Direct Cable Connection** dialog box appears.

5 Click **Host** (○ changes to ◉).

6 Click **Next**.

7 Click the port the cable plugs into.

8 Click **Next**.

CONTINUED

SET UP DIRECT CABLE CONNECTION

You must set up both the host and guest computers before the computers can exchange information.

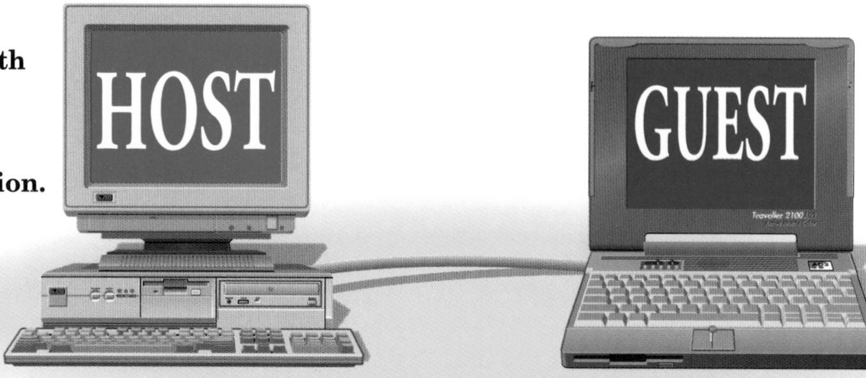

SET UP DIRECT CABLE CONNECTION (CONTINUED)

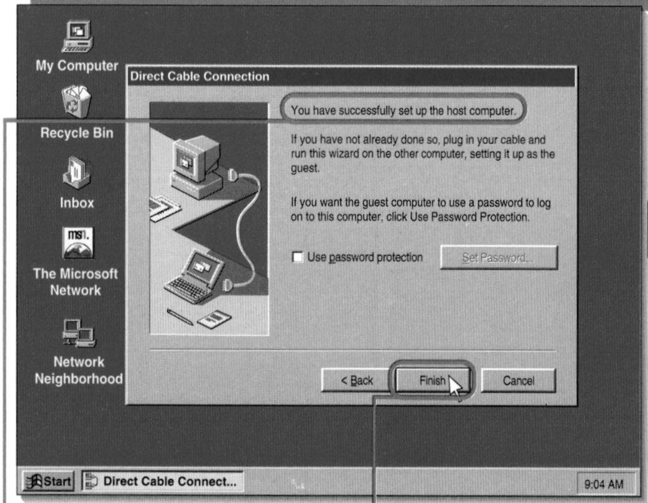

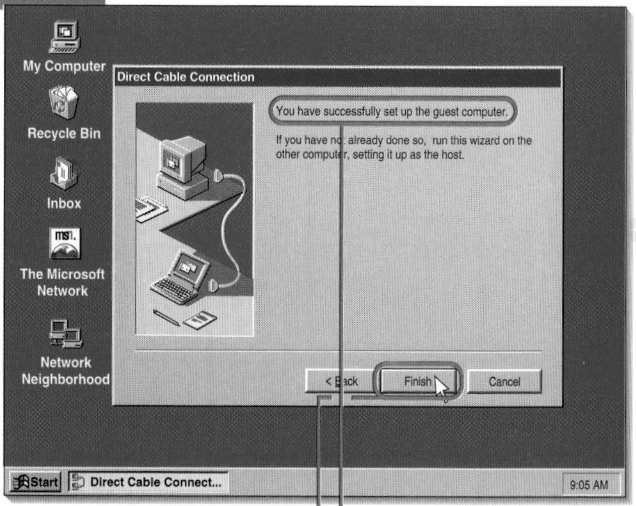

■ This message appears when you finish setting up the host computer.

9 Click **Finish**.

■ A dialog box appears, telling you the status of the connection.

Set Up Guest Computer

1 On the guest computer, perform steps 1 to 8 starting on page 310, selecting **Guest** in step 5.

■ This message appears when you finish setting up the guest computer.

2 To connect the guest and host computers, click **Finish**.

TIP

You only need to set up a direct cable connection between two computers once. After you set up a connection, you can easily reconnect the computers at any time. For more information, refer to page 314.

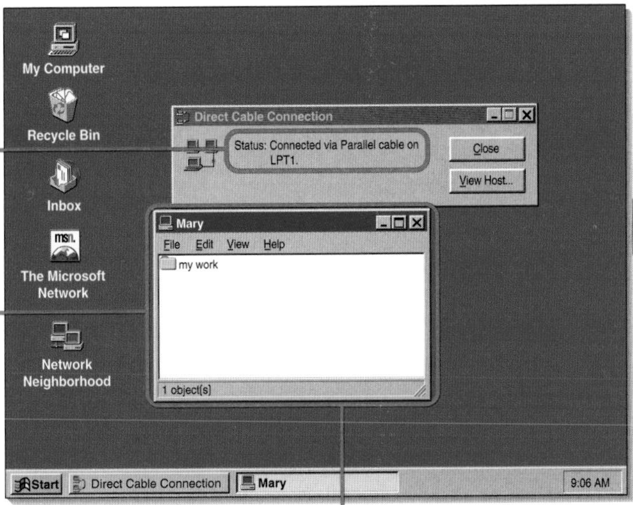

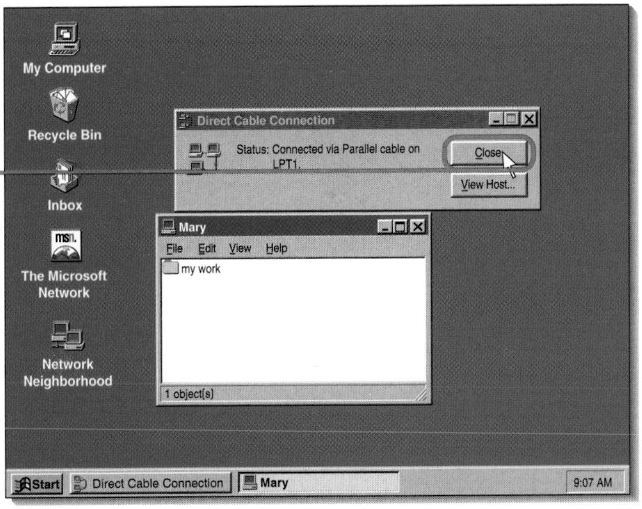

- This message appears when the computers are successfully connected.

- A window also appears, displaying the items shared by the host computer.

- You can open and work with the folders and files in the window as if the information were stored on the guest computer.

Note: You can access information on a network connected to the host. To find a computer on the network, refer to page 294.

Close the Connection

1 Click **Close**.

RE-ESTABLISH DIRECT CABLE CONNECTION

Once you set up a direct cable connection between two computers, you can quickly exchange information at any time.

RE-ESTABLISH DIRECT CABLE CONNECTION

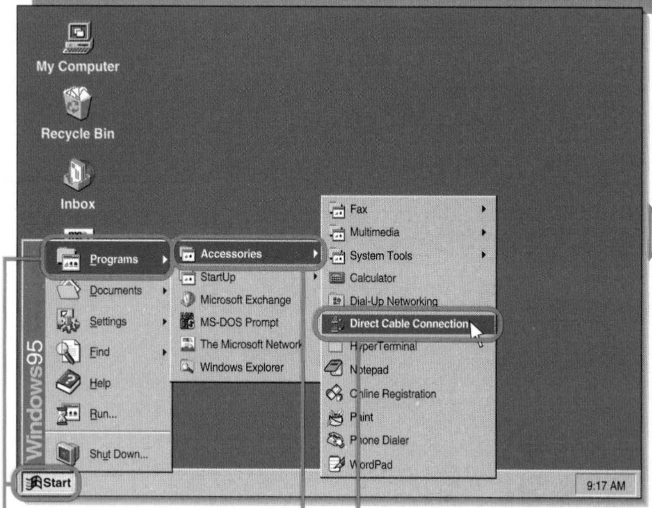

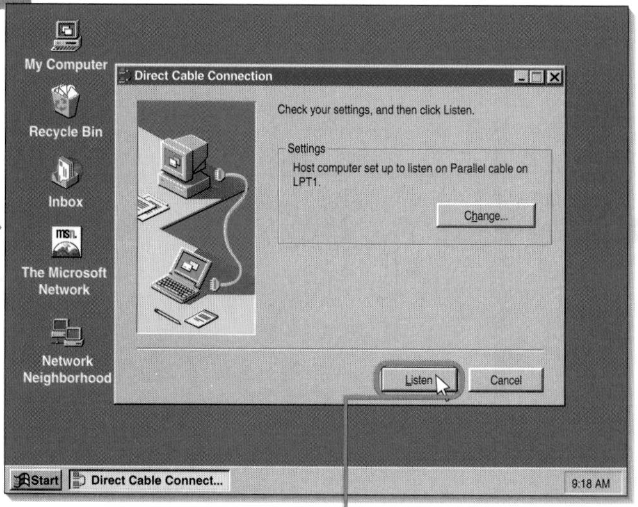

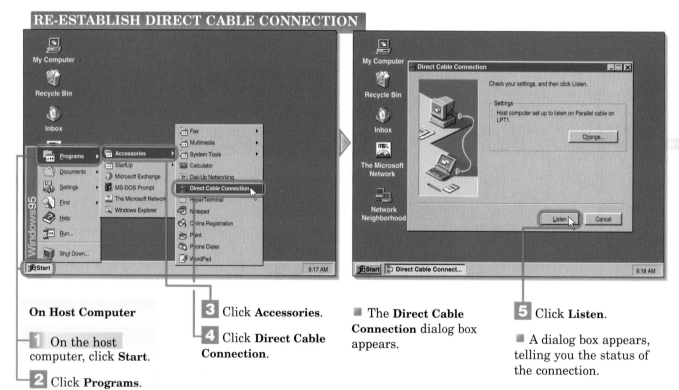

On Host Computer

1 On the host computer, click **Start**.

2 Click **Programs**.

3 Click **Accessories**.

4 Click **Direct Cable Connection**.

■ The **Direct Cable Connection** dialog box appears.

5 Click **Listen**.

■ A dialog box appears, telling you the status of the connection.

TIP

You can use Direct Cable Connection to transfer files from your office computer to a portable computer. This lets you use office files when at home or traveling.

If you want the files to update automatically when you return to the office, use the Briefcase feature.

Note: For information on the Briefcase feature, refer to the Briefcase chapter starting on page 266.

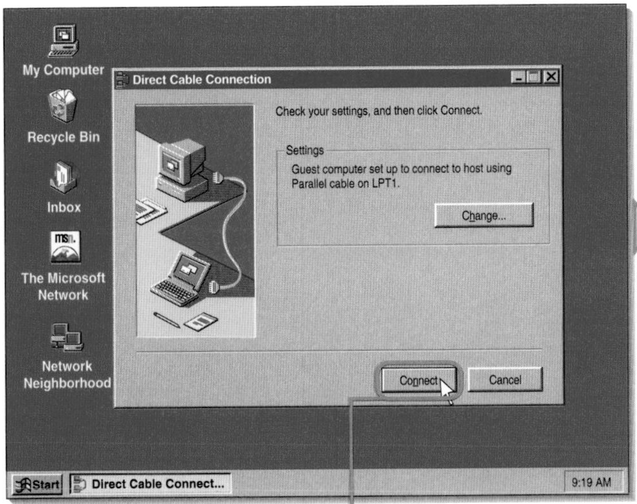

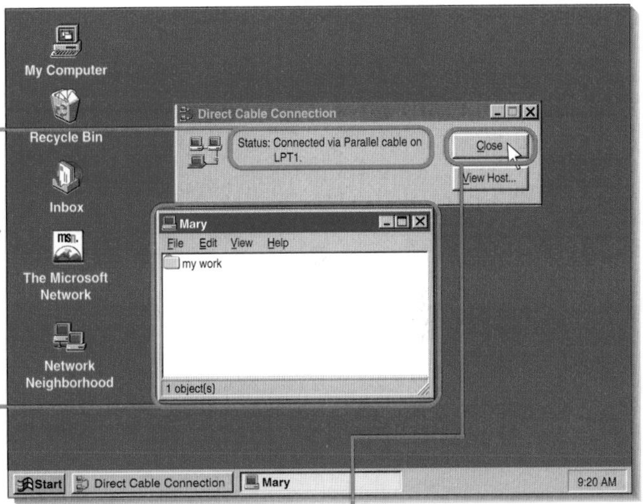

On Guest Computer

1 On the guest computer, perform steps 1 to 4 on page 314.

■ The **Direct Cable Connection** dialog box appears.

2 Click **Connect**.

■ This message appears when the computers are successfully connected.

■ A window also appears, displaying the items shared by the host computer. You can open and work with the folders and files in the window as if the information were stored on the guest computer.

Close the Connection

1 Click **Close**.

INDEX

A

access on networks
  Full, 286, 287
  Depends on Password, 287
  Read-Only, 286
active window, 16
address books, 169
  adding names to, 166-167
animation files, playing, 136-139
applications, finding, 91
arranging
  icons, 52-53
  windows, 18, 19
Auto Arrange feature, using, 52-53

B

back up. *See* Microsoft Backup
  devices and strategies, 228-229
Briefcase, using, 266-275
briefcases
  creating, 266-269
  deleting, 275
  files in
    updating, 272-275
    working with, 270-271
browsing
  through MSN categories, 250-251
  through networks, 292-293
bulletin boards, MSN, 247
  conversations on, 257
  messages
    creating, 260-261
    displaying, 254-255
    reading, 256-257
    replying to, 258-259
bytes, 60, 235

C

canceling printing, 77
cascading windows, 18
categories, MSN, browsing through, 250-251
CD-ROM drives, 47
CDs
  adjusting volume, 127
  playing music, 124-126
changes, undoing in Paint, 37
Chat World, MSN, 253
chatting on MSN, 246, 252-253
clicking with mouse, 3
closing
  MSN, 263
  Paint, 41
  windows, 21
color depth, changing, 120-121
colors, changing on screen, 106-107
components, Windows
  adding, 186-189
  deleting, 189
compressing disks, 220-225
computers
  backing up. *See* Microsoft Backup
  dialing in to office, Dial-Up Networking, 306-307
  finding on networks, 294-295
  naming on networks, 282-283
  setting up, Dial-Up Networking, 299-301
  viewing contents of, 48-49
connecting to MSN, 248-249
connections, setting up, Dial-Up Networking, 302-305
contents of computer, viewing, 48-49
conversations on MSN, 257
copying
  files to floppy disks, 66-67
  files to folders, 65
  floppy disks, 216-219
  folders to floppy disks, 67

D

- databases, 190
- date
  - changing, 102-103
  - displaying on screen, 6
- default printer, setting, 290-291
- defragmenting disks, 212-215
- deleting
  - e-mail messages, 175
  - files, 78-79
  - folders, 79
  - Windows components, 189
- Depends on Password network access, 287
- desktop, 4, 5
  - adding parts of document to, 94-95
  - adding scraps to, 94-95
  - adding shortcuts to, 92-93
- desktop publishing, 190
- detecting disk errors, 208-211
- Dial-Up Networking
  - dialing in to office computers, 306-307
  - introduction to, 298
  - setting up connections to office computers, 302-305
  - setting up office computers, 299-301
- dialing in to office computers, 306-307
- Direct Cable Connection
  - guest computer, 310
  - host computer, 311
  - re-establishing, 314-315
  - setting up, 310-313
- directories, creating, 62-63
- Disk Defragmenter program, using, 212-215
- disks
  - 3.5 inch, 206
  - 5.25 inch, 207
  - compressing, 220-225
  - copying, 216-219
  - defragmenting, 212-215
  - detecting errors, 208-211
  - double-density, 206, 207, 217
  - formatting, 204-207
  - high-density, 206, 207, 217
  - repairing errors, 208-211
- displaying
  - bulletin board messages, 254-255
  - file information, 54-55
  - folders in Windows Explorer, 86
- documents, adding parts to desktop, 94-95
- domain names, 167
- DOS
  - commands and programs, working with in Windows, 26-27
  - prompt, using, 26-27
- double-clicking with mouse, 3
- dragging with mouse, 3
- drawing
  - lines in Paint, 34-35
  - shapes in Paint, 32-33
- drawings. *See* Paint
- drivers, 201
- DriveSpace, using, 220-225

E

- e-mail. *See also* Microsoft Exchange
  - address books, 169
    - names, adding to, 166-167
  - addresses, 167
  - deleting messages, 175
  - domain names, 167
  - Internet addresses, 167
  - messages
    - deleting, 175
    - forwarding, 178-179

    - inserting files in, 172-173
    - reading, 174
    - replying to, 176-177
    - sending, 168-171
  - names, adding to address books, 166-167
  - reading messages, 174
  - replying to messages, 176-177
  - sending messages, 168-171
- electronic mail. *See* e-mail
  - using MSN, 246
- embedded information. *See* object linking and embedding
- emptying Recycle Bin, 82-83
- equipment, sharing on networks, 278
- erasing areas in Paint, 36-37
- errors on disks
  - detecting, 208-211
  - repairing, 208-211
- exiting
  - MSN, 263
  - Paint, 41
  - Windows, 7
- Explorer. *See* Windows Explorer

F

- Favorite Places on MSN, adding items to, 262-263
- faxes. *See also* Microsoft Exchange
  - changing how modems answer, 158-159
  - printing, 163
  - sending, 154-157
  - viewing, 160-162
- files, 49
  - animation, playing, 136-139
  - backing up. *See* Microsoft Backup
  - briefcase
    - updating, 272-275
    - working with, 270-271
  - canceling sent to printer, 77
  - copying
    - to floppy disks, 66-67
    - to folders, 65
  - deleting, 78-79
  - displaying information for, 54-55
  - finding, 90-91
  - inserting in e-mail messages, 172-173
  - MIDI, playing, 136-139
  - moving to folders, 64-65
  - opening, 70, 71
  - pausing sent to printer, 76
  - previewing, 72-73
  - printing, 74
  - renaming, 68-69
  - restoring
    - backed up, 240-243
    - deleted, 80-81
  - selecting, 60-61
  - sorting, 56-57
  - sound, playing, 136-139
  - transferring on MSN, 247
  - video, playing, 136-139
  - viewing sent to printer, 75
- finding
  - applications, 91
  - computers on networks, 294-295
  - files, 90-91
- floppy disks. *See* disks
- floppy drives, 47
- folders, 49
  - copying to floppy disks, 67
  - creating, 62-63
  - deleting, 79
  - displaying in Windows Explorer, 86
  - hiding in Windows Explorer, 87

moving, 65
renaming, 69
selecting, 61
fonts, adding to computer, 182-185
formatting disks, 204-207
forwarding e-mail messages, 178-179
Full network access, 286, 287

G

games, 190
graphics, 190
guest computers, 310
re-establishing Direct Cable Connection, 315
setting up Direct Cable Connection, 312-313

H

hard drives, 46
hardware, 2
setting up, 194-201
Help feature, using, 22-23
hiding
folders in Windows Explorer, 87
taskbar, 116-117
high color, 121
host computers, 311
re-establishing Direct Cable Connection, 314
setting up Direct Cable Connection, 310-312

I

information, 2
exchanging between programs. *See* object linking and embedding
sharing on networks, 278, 284-287
inserting files in e-mail messages, 172-173
installing
hardware, 194-201
programs, 191-193
Windows components, 186-189
Internet
addresses, 167
using MSN, 247
items
adding to Favorite Places, 262-263
arranging in windows, 52-53
changing size of, 50
moving, 51

J

joining MSN chat rooms, 252-253

K

kilobytes, 55, 60, 235

L

lines
drawing, 34-35
erasing, 36-37
linked information. *See* object linking and embedding

M

maximizing windows, 13
Media Player, using, 136-139
messages
bulletin board
creating, 260-261
displaying, 254-255
reading, 256-257
replying to, 258-259
e-mail
deleting, 175
forwarding, 178-179
inserting files in, 172-173

reading, 174
replying to, 176-177
sending, 168-171
Microsoft Backup
backing up
all files, 239
files, 236-237
named files, 238-239
selected files, 232-235
devices, 228
introduction, 228-229
restoring files, 240-243
starting, 230-231
strategies, 229
Microsoft Exchange, 11
starting, 152-153
using to exchange e-mail, 166-179
Microsoft Network, The. *See* MSN
MIDI files, playing, 136-139
minimizing
all windows, 20
windows, 12
modems, changing how they answer faxes, 158-159
mouse
clicking, 3
double-clicking, 3
dragging, 3
pads, 111
settings, changing, 110-113
using, 3
moving
files to folders, 64-65
folders, 65
items in windows, 51
taskbar, 114
windows, 14
MS-DOS prompt, using, 26-27
MSN
bulletin boards, 247
messages
creating, 260-261
displaying, 254-255
reading, 256-257
replying to, 258-259
categories, browsing through, 250-251
chat rooms, joining, 252-253
Chat World, 253
chatting, 246
connecting to, 248-249
conversations, 257
electronic mail, 246, 249. *See also* e-mail
Favorite Places, 249
adding items to, 262-263
files, transferring, 247
Internet, 247
main areas on, 249
Member Assistance, 249
setting up, 249
signing out, 263
Today, 249
music, playing CDs, 124-126
My Computer, 5

N

names, adding to address books, 166-167
naming computers on networks, 282-283
network access
Depends on Password, 287
Full, 286, 287
Read-Only, 286

networks
browsing through, 292-293
finding computers on, 294-295
introduction to, 278
naming computers on, 282-283
sharing
information, 284-287
printers, 288-289

O

object linking and embedding (OLE), 147
editing embedded information, 146-147
editing linked information, 148-149
embedding information, 142-145
embedding vs. linking, 143
linking information, 142-145
opening
drawings in Paint, 42-43
files, 70, 71

P

Paint, 11
adding text to drawings in, 38-39
drawing lines in, 34-35
drawing shapes in, 32-33
erasing areas in, 36-37
exiting, 41
opening saved drawings in, 42-43
saving drawings in, 40-41
starting, 30-31
undoing last change in, 37
pausing printers, 76
playing
animation files, 136-139
MIDI files, 136-139
music CDs, 124-126
sound files, 136-139
video files, 136-139
Plug and Play, 199
ports, 198
previewing files, 72-73
printers
pausing, 76
setting default, 290-291
sharing on networks, 288-289
viewing files sent to, 75
printing
canceling, 77
faxes, 163
files, 74
program events, assigning sounds to, 128-131
programs, 2
adding, 191-193
adding to Start menu, 96-97
examples of, 11
starting, 10-11
starting automatically, 98-99
types, 190

Q

Quick View, using, 72-73

R

re-establishing Direct Cable Connection, 314-315
Read-Only network access, 286
reading messages
bulletin board, 256-257
e-mail, 174
recording sounds, 132-135

- Recycle Bin, 5
  - appearance, 81
  - emptying, 82-83
- renaming
  - files, 68-69
  - folders, 69
- repairing disk errors, 208-211
- replying to messages
  - bulletin board, 258-259
  - e-mail, 176-177
- resolution, screens, changing, 118-119
- restarting computer in MS-DOS mode, 27
- restoring files
  - backed up, 240-243
  - deleted, 80-81

S

- saving drawings in Paint, 40-41
- ScanDisk, 11, 208-211
- scraps, adding to desktop, 94-95
- screens
  - color depth, changing, 120-121
  - colors, changing, 106-107
  - resolution, changing, 118-119
  - savers, setting up, 108-109
- scrolling through windows, 24-25
- selecting
  - files, 60-61
  - folders, 61
- sending
  - e-mail messages, 168-171
  - faxes, 154-157
- setting up
  - connections to office computers, Dial-Up Networking, 302-305
  - Direct Cable Connection, 310-313
  - hardware, 194-201
  - MSN, 249
  - office computers for Dial-Up Networking, 299-301
  - screen savers, 108-109
- settings, changing for mouse, 110-113
- shapes
  - drawing, 32-33
  - erasing, 36-37
- sharing
  - information on networks, 284-287
  - printers on networks, 288-289
  - turning on, 279-281
- shortcuts, 5
  - adding to desktop, 92-93
- shutting down Windows, 7
- signing out of MSN, 263
- size, changing for items, 50
- sizing
  - taskbar, 115
  - windows, 15
- smileys, 261
- sorting items in windows, 56-57
- sound files, playing, 136-139
- sounds
  - assigning to program events, 128-131
  - recording, 132-135
- spreadsheets, 190
- Start button, 5, 117
- Start menu, adding programs to, 96-97
- starting
  - Microsoft Backup, 230-231
  - Microsoft Exchange, 152-153
  - Paint, 30-31
  - programs, 10-11
    - automatically, 98-99
  - Windows, 4

- Windows Explorer, 84-85

storage devices, 46-47
switching between windows, 16-17

T

taskbar, 5
- hiding, 116-117
- moving, 114
- sizing, 115

text, adding to drawings in Paint, 38-39
tiling windows, 19
time, changing, 102-103
title bars, 5
true color, 121
turning on sharing, 279-281

U

Undo feature, using in Paint, 37
updating briefcase files, 272-275

V

video files, playing, 136-139
viewing
- contents of computer, 48-49
- faxes, 160-162
- files sent to printer, 75

volume, adjusting for CDs, 127

W

wallpaper, adding, 104-105
windows, 5
- arranging items automatically in, 52-53
- cascading, 18
- changing size of items in, 50
- closing, 21
- maximizing, 13
- minimizing, 12
- minimizing all, 20
- moving, 14
  - items in, 51
- scrolling through, 24-25
- sizing, 15
- sorting items in, 56-57
- switching between, 16-17
- tiling, 19

Windows 95
- components
  - adding, 186-189
  - deleting, 189
- desktop, 4, 5
- exiting, 7
- introduction, 2, 5
- screen items, 5
- shutting down, 7
- starting, 4

Windows Explorer
- folders, displaying, 86
- folders, hiding, 87
- starting, 84-85

word processors, 190
WordPad, 11
workgroups, 283

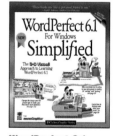

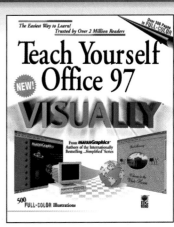

DUMMIES PRESS

The fun & easy way to learn about computers and more!

SUPER STAR

Windows 3.1 For Dummies,™ 2nd Edition
by Andy Rathbone

ISBN: 1-56884-182-5
$16.95 USA/$22.95 Canada

SUPER STAR

MORE Windows For Dummies™
by Andy Rathbone

ISBN: 1-56884-048-9
$19.95 USA/$26.95 Canada

NATIONAL BESTSELLER!

Personal Finance For Dummies™
by Eric Tyson

ISBN: 1-56884-150-7
$16.95 USA/$22.95 Canada

VIII
FINALIST
Eighth Annual Computer Press Awards 1992

PCs For Dummies,™ 2nd Edition
by Dan Gookin & Andy Rathbone

ISBN: 1-56884-078-0
$16.95 USA/$22.95 Canada

FOR MORE INFO OR TO ORDER, PLEASE CALL 800-762-2974

For volume discounts & special orders please call Tony Real, Special Sales, at 415-312-0644

DOS For Dummies,® 2nd Edition
by Dan Gookin

ISBN: 1-878058-75-4
$16.95 USA/$22.95 Canada

FINALIST
Ninth Annual Computer Press Awards 1993

The Internet For Dummies™
by John Levine & Carol Baroudi

ISBN: 1-56884-024-1
$19.95 USA/$26.95 Canada

Macs For Dummies,™ 2nd Edition
by David Pogue

ISBN: 1-56884-051-9
$19.95 USA/$26.95 Canada

FOR MORE INFO OR TO ORDER, PLEASE CALL 800-762-2974

For volume discounts & special orders please call Tony Real, Special Sales, at 415-312-0644

IDG BOOKS®

TRADE & INDIVIDUAL ORDERS

Phone: **(800) 762-2974**
or **(317) 895-5200**
(8 a.m.–6 p.m., CST, weekdays)
FAX : **(317) 895-5298**

EDUCATIONAL ORDERS & DISCOUNTS

Phone: **(800) 434-2086**
(8:30 a.m.–5:00 p.m., CST, weekdays)
FAX : **(817) 251-8174**

CORPORATE ORDERS FOR 3-D VISUAL™ SERIES

Phone: **(800) 469-6616**
(8 a.m.–5 p.m., EST, weekdays)
FAX : **(905) 890-9434**

Qty	ISBN	Title	Price	Total

Shipping & Handling Charges

	Description	First book	Each add'l. book	Total
Domestic	Normal	$4.50	$1.50	$
	Two Day Air	$8.50	$2.50	$
	Overnight	$18.00	$3.00	$
International	Surface	$8.00	$8.00	$
	Airmail	$16.00	$16.00	$
	DHL Air	$17.00	$17.00	$

Subtotal ________________

CA residents add applicable sales tax ________________

IN, MA and MD residents add 5% sales tax ________________

IL residents add 6.25% sales tax ________________

RI residents add 7% sales tax ________________

TX residents add 8.25% sales tax ________________

Shipping ________________

Total ________________

Ship to:

Name ________________________________

Address ________________________________

Company ________________________________

City/State/Zip ________________________________

Daytime Phone ________________________________

Payment: □ Check to IDG Books (US Funds Only)
□ Visa □ Mastercard □ American Express

Card # ________________ Exp. __________ Signature ________________

maranGraphics™